American School of Prehistoric Research

PEABODY MUSEUM · HARVARD UNIVERSITY

BULLETIN NO. 30

D1089373

General View of the Abri Pataud, Les Eyzies (Dordogne). Photograph taken in July 1958 from near the Railway Bridge over the Vézère River.

EXCAVATION OF THE

ABRI PATAUD

LES EYZIES (DORDOGNE)

Hallam L. Movius, Jr.

General Editor and Director of Excavations

CONTRIBUTORS

Hallam L. Movius, Jr.   Joakim J. Donner
Sheldon Judson   Joan F. Wilson
William R. Farrand   William H. Drury
Jean Bouchud   Harvey M. Bricker
S. Peter Dance   Ginette Billy
              Pierre Legoux

PEABODY MUSEUM OF ARCHAEOLOGY AND ETHNOLOGY

HARVARD UNIVERSITY, CAMBRIDGE, MASSACHUSETTS

1975

PREFATORY NOTE

The publication of this first volume in a series of monographs on the excavations at the Abri Pataud has been funded by a grant from the National Science Foundation (GN-40796), and we are deeply grateful to them for their further support of this project, which they have been generous in sponsoring since its inception.

The American School of Prehistoric Research, a department of the Peabody Museum, is delighted to have this volume appear as *Bulletin* Number 30 in its publication series and feels that its long-term support of Professor Movius's research in paleolithic archaeology, through support of his curatorial and research activities, is most appropriate in terms of the life-long commitment to that field of research by the founder of the School, George Grant MacCurdy. The members of the School eagerly await publication of Volume Two of this series which is currently in the editor's hands. We know it will be an important contribution to our knowledge of prehistoric life in France.

Stephen Williams, *Chairman*
American School of Prehistoric Research

Contents

Illustrations

Excavation of the
Abri Pataud

Introduction

The Abri Pataud, a large rock-shelter at Les Eyzies (Dordogne) in the Périgord region of southwestern France, lies at the foot of the west-southwesterly-facing limestone cliff flanking the Vézère Valley on the northern outskirts of the village of Les Eyzies. It was chosen for excavation after extensive reconnaissance in this classic area where a considerable amount of research on the Upper Palaeolithic has been conducted since the Lartet-Christy era of the early 1860s. Notwithstanding the fact that over a hundred Upper Palaeolithic sites (including several type localities) have been investigated in the Dordogne, the stratigraphic sequence in this key region was still very poorly known and little understood as of 1950. An impressive sequence of superimposed occupations was revealed in a test trench excavated in 1953 in the talus slope in front of the Abri Pataud, which produced a wealth of archaeological material. The results (Movius 1954, 1955) were regarded as sufficiently promising to justify the purchase of the property a few years later. This transaction was finally negotiated in 1957, and subsequently the site was officially presented to the French government, which made the Muséum National d'Histoire Naturelle administratively responsible for it. The latter organization in turn placed it under the control of the Musée de l'Homme. Professor Henri V. Vallois was appointed to represent the French interests in the operation, which is actually a joint Franco-American project under the auspices of the Musée de l'Homme on the one hand and the Peabody Museum of Harvard University on the other. By mutual agreement, however, the operational control has been throughout in the hands of the writer, and his parent institution was given exclusive excavation rights to the site until 1978 – i.e., for a 20-year period.

The actual excavation of the Abri Pataud was completed during a total of six field seasons between 1958 and 1964 (no excavating was conducted in 1962). Throughout the project, the major source of financial support was the National Science Foundation, and on behalf of the Peabody Museum of Harvard University, the writer wishes to express his profound thanks to the Foundation for the following grants: G-2085 (1958-1959), G-10,928 (1960-1961), GS-139 (1963-1964), GS-1094 (1966-1967) and GS-2047 (1968-1970), without which the successful accomplishment of this vast undertaking would have been impossible. Additional funds have been generously provided by the Wenner-Gren Foundation for Anthropological Research (1959, 1961, 1965, and 1971), the Wilkie Brothers Foundation (1956, 1959, and 1961, the Milton Fund, and the Peabody Museum, as well as several anonymous donors to each of whom the writer is profoundly grateful. Summaries of the results achieved during each season of the excavation are set forth in a series of Progress Reports submitted annually to the National Science Foundation, covering the periods of the grants listed above.

In addition to the Field Director and his wife, a total of 78 individuals, some of whom were present during more than a single season, participated in the actual excavation of the site and/or the enormous amount of laboratory work associated with the operation. These individuals represented eleven countries, as follows: U.S.A., 53; Canada, 1; England, 8; France, 2; Italy, 3; Belgium, 2; Holland, 1; Germany, 5; Denmark, 1; Algeria, 1; and India, 1. On a season-by-season basis, the names of all staff members, their country of origin (if other than the U.S.A.) and their major assignment are given below:

First Season; 1958 (May 7 to September 14)
  Excavation Foreman: Philip E.L. Smith
  Cataloguer: Elizabeth Baldwin
  Field Assistants: Martha White; Joan T. Bamberger; Cynthia Irwin; Robert J. Rodden; Karl Heider; and Hind Sadek.
Second Season; 1959 (June 4 to September 19)
  Excavation Foreman: James R. Sackett
  Cataloguer: Nancy H. Smith
  Secretary: Margot G. Collett (England)
  Draftsman: Jonathan Gell
  Field Assistants: Frank Hole; Joan T. Bamberger; Kwang-Chih Chang; C. Loring Brace; Nicholas C. David (England); Keith H. Basso; David W. Moody; Sonia Cole (England); Gérard Bailloud (France); and June Fairbank (England).
Third Season; 1960 (June 15 to September 10)
  Excavation Foreman: James R. Sackett
  Assistant Excavation Foreman: Nicholas C. David (England)
  Cataloguer: Margaret Depopolo
  Draftsman: Jonathan Gell
  Field Assistants: Elizabeth A. Morris; Ralph M.

Rowlette; David A. Horr; Eugene Giles; Wolfgang Taute (Germany); Thomas S. Chambers; Sally Schanfield; Glynn L. Isaac (England); Sonia Cole (England); Penelope Rainey; and Philip H. Auerbach.

Fall-Winter-Spring Season; 1960-1961 (September 15 to June 14)

Chief Research Assistant: Nicholas C. David (England)

Draftsman: Jonathan Gell

Laboratory Assistant: Margaret Depopolo

Research Assistant: Elizabeth A. Morris

Fourth Season; 1961 (June 15 to September 13)

Excavation Foreman: Nicholas C. David (England)

Assistant Excavation Foreman: Ralph M. Rowlette

Cataloguer: Margaret Depopolo

Draftsman: Jonathan Gell

Field Assistants: Augustus Sordinas; Robert Whallon, Jr.; Jeremiah F. Epstein; Claude A. Vaucher; Stefano Natonek (Italy); Elsebet S. Jørgensen (Denmark); A. Prakash Khatri (India); Hilke Hennig (Germany); Nadja de Vries (Holland); Elena L. Laguzzi (Italy); Roland Paepe (Belgium); Orville Elliott; Katharine Kirkham; Jean-P. Maître (Algeria); and Frank D. Davis (Germany).

1962 Season; site closed, no excavations conducted.

Fifth Season; 1963 (June 12 to September 7)

Excavation Foreman: Nicholas C. David (England)

Assistant Excavation Foreman: Augustus Sordinas

Cataloguer: Anne Hoover

Draftsman: Jocelyne Laurent (France)

Field Assistants: Harvey M. Bricker; Copley Crosby; Paul Mellars (England); Mary Pohl; Larry Robbins; George V. Shkurkin; William Simmons; Paule Spitaels (Belgium); James B. Stoltman; Morgan Tamplin (Canada); Mariella Taschini (Italy); Peter J. Taylor (England); John E. Terrell; and Aimee M. Wilson.

Fall-Winter-Spring Season; 1963-1964 (September 16 to June 6)

Chief Research Assistant: Nicholas C. David (England)

Draftsman: Aimee M. Wilson (September to February); Adrienne Cohn (March to June)

Laboratory Assistant: Leslie L. Engle

Research Assistant: Harvey M. Bricker

Sixth Season; 1964 (June 8 to September 12)

Excavation Foreman: Harvey M. Bricker

Assistant Excavation Foreman: Augustus Sordinas

Draftsman: Adrienne Cohn

Cataloguer: Leslie L. Engle

Secretary: Sally Sordinas

Field Assistants: David Abrams; Peter Banks; Alan Bilsborough (England); Carter Brown; R. Berle Clay; Joakim Hahn (Germany); Patty Kirkpatrick; Joy Oppenheimer; Roger Rose; Morgan Tamplin (Canada); James V. Taylor; Donna Taylor; and Wighart von Koenigswald (Germany).

With only a limited number of exceptions, the performance of all those listed above was exceedingly satisfactory – in some cases exceptional – and the Field Director is grateful to all of them for their help, cooperation, and interest in the project. A small number of the group have continued to conduct research in Old World Palaeolithic archaeology on a professional basis, in addition to those whose doctoral dissertations have been incorporated into this memoir.

The summer seasons 1965-1971 were devoted to (a) sorting out and storing the collections; (b) transferring the attribute measurements from the original work sheets onto the punch cards, typing and punching the latter; (c) drafting the final versions of the plans, sections, charts, etc.; (d) editing and correcting the final manuscript; and (e) typing the latter. With regard to the successful achievement of these somewhat onerous tasks, the Field Director is grateful to the following:

1965: Jane Britten, Harvey M. Bricker, Paul Mellars, and Carmel Shira.

1966: Jane Britten, Alison S. Brooks, and Harry Scheels.

1967: Jane Britten, Alison S. Brooks, and John Yellen.

1968: Amy Cooper and Paul Ossa.

1968-1969: Harvey M. Bricker spent the winter in the Dordogne assisting the Field Director with the final checking and editing of various contributions to the present memoir. For his expert and invaluable help the Field Director finds it difficult to express his thanks adequately.

1969: John Christiansen (professional draftsman) and his wife, Sylvia Christiansen (typist/secretary), began the final preparation of the plans, sections, and text for publication. Harvey M. Bricker assisted the Field Director with the supervision of this work.

1970 and 1971: Ferdinand T. Abrehart (professional draftsman) and his wife, Stephanie Abrehart (typist/secretary), very competently and successfully took over the work initiated by the Christiansens in 1969. Peter Timms (three months) and David de Gravelle (one month) worked in the Abri Pataud laboratory during the 1970 season, and in 1971 Peter Timms returned for a one-month period. Also in 1971 Harvey M. Bricker spent three weeks at Les Eyzies with the expedition checking and taking care of final editorial problems.

It is virtually impossible for the writer to express the deep admiration and gratitude which he experienced in connection with the expertly rendered drawings of the archaeological materials from the site, by M. Pierre Laurent, who worked long hours in order to complete the assignment. Everything he accomplished was achieved in his spare time during the academic year at the Université de Bordeaux, and during regular periods in the summer season when he came to Les Eyzies and worked under the direct supervision of various members of the expedition staff. The results speak for themselves: his series of drawings of the artifactual materials and art objects from the Abri Pataud, produced over a period of ten years, rank at the top by any standards. It is a great pleasure and personal privilege to take this opportunity of thanking him for his eminently successful accomplishment.

A glance at the outstandingly fine plans, sections, and other drawings that appear in the various volumes of this memoir will in some measure reveal the extremely impressive nature of the results of the efforts of Messrs. Christiansen and Abrehart. The contribution of each of the others whose names appear above is not so readily apparent. Suffice it to say that the compilation of the present memoir could never have been consummated without their help and cooperation. Particularly, Mrs. Christiansen and Mrs. Abrehart merit our profound gratitude for the outstandingly dependable manner in which each of them handled their typing assignments.

With the exception of the two contributions by Mme. Ginette Billy and Dr. Pierre Legoux (vol. I, part 2) dealing with the fossil skeletal materials and teeth discovered at the Abri Pataud, the series of papers presented in this volume are primarily concerned with various aspects of the intricate problems of Pleistocene ecology, or environment. They are of an interdisciplinary nature and embrace the allied fields of geology (or geomorphology), paleontology (both vertebrate and invertebrate), paleobotany (palynology), pedology (soil analysis), climatology and paleoecology — in short those disciplines of the natural sciences that are directly related to Palaeolithic archaeology. Admittedly, the primary data must be provided by specialists in these closely allied fields of the natural sciences concerned with Pleistocene ecology, but in the final analysis the work of evaluating, collating, and synthesizing can be accomplished only by the archaeologist. In a very real sense, new knowledge in this broad field increases more or less in geometric proportion to the cross-disciplinary effort. In other words, the more disciplines and techniques that can be focused on a given problem, the higher becomes the probability of accurate chronological interpretations by multiple complementary results. Nevertheless, until comparatively recently, modern investigations by natural historians had never been consistently integrated with intensive research focused on the culture-historical aspects of Palaeolithic archaeology.

In connection with the Abri Pataud project, every possible effort has been made to bring specialized techniques to bear on the data with a view to understanding and interpreting the complex series of events involving those aspects of *both* the natural and cultural history which took place during the time span under consideration. Since, by virtue of their dependence upon what their environment has to offer, and their technological inability to control that environment to any appreciable extent, primitive hunting and gathering peoples generally manifest cultural patterns which are intelligible only in terms of ecological adaptation. It is this very tendency of primitive societies to exist in close harmony with what their particular environment offers that constitutes the most promising avenue of approach to an understanding of their cultures, with special reference to the nature of their basic subsistence economy. With a view to relating the ultimate results to the cultural succession, detailed studies of the evidence for environmental changes during Last Glacial times in southwestern France have been made; these embrace the following:

Geology. The study of glacial episodes in the Massif Central, depositionary and erosive processes in the periglacial region, and the associated sequence of events involved in terrace formation in the Dordogne and Vézère Valleys have contributed the most basic and fundamental evidence of all the natural sciences bearing on the actual sequence of events that took place in southwestern France during Last Glacial times. In the final analysis, the findings of scientists must be evaluated and synchronized with the geological evidence.

Soil Analysis (*Pedology*). Important evidence bearing on climatic alteration has been provided by the detailed analysis of soils and sedimentary processes. At the Abri Pataud an impressive sequence of changing soils is registered.

Paleontology. Analysis and identification of faunal remains (both vertebrate and invertebrate) associated with the various horizons at this extensive occupation site are of obvious importance. It has been determined, however, that with the exception of the invertebrate remains and those of certain microtine mammals and birds, very little pertinent information of climatic/ecological significance can be based on this line of evidence.

Paleobotany *(Palynology).* A detailed study of the Last Glacial flora remains (pollen) from the site potentially could have added considerably to our knowledge of changing vegetational patterns during Last Glacial times. Of all the natural sciences that contribute data bearing on the changing ecologies of early Upper Palaeolithic times, this area of knowledge is perhaps the most crucial. In order to obtain valid results, however, it is necessary to count a minimum of 1,000/2,000 grains of pollen, and to consider a vast number of samples. It is hoped that an investigation along these lines can be organized in the near future.

Climatology and Ecology. An investigation of the flora currently flourishing near the present tree line on the now extinct volcanoes of the Massif Central has revealed important information bearing on Last Glacial conditions in the Les Eyzies region. On this basis one can state with confidence that there is very little likelihood that tundra/taiga conditions existed there at any time during the 15,000 years or so represented by the various occupations at the Abri Pataud.

It is believed that these data have led to a better understanding of man's use of and degree of dependence on his environment at the early Upper Paleolithic (hunting-gathering) level of his development. Although interpretation of the environment is basic to an understanding of Upper Palaeolithic culture dynamics, up to the present this unfortunately has been neglected in favor of an outmoded typological approach, based solely on an examination and classification of the cultural remains, as an end in itself. Contained in this volume are the reports of the outstandingly able team of natural scientists who have conducted research in connection with the Abri Pataud project in an effort to reclaim the evidence bearing on the successive natural environments (or ecologies) that prevailed during the long span of time under consideration. The Field Director is more than grateful to each and every one of them for their patience, interest, and helpful advice. He only hopes that this volume measures up to their high standards of scholarship.

Hallam L. Movius, Jr.

PART 1. THE NATURAL SCIENCES

I

Summary of the Stratigraphic Sequence

Hallam L. Movius, Jr.

DEPARTMENT OF ANTHROPOLOGY
HARVARD UNIVERSITY

The Abri Pataud, one of a number of caves and rock-shelters formed in the west-southwesterly-facing Upper Cretaceous (Coniacian) limestone cliff which dominates the Vézère River between the villages of Tayac and Les Eyzies, is located within the confines of Les Eyzies approximately midway between the Abri de Cro-Magnon and the Château des Eyzies. It lies beside the departmental road (D.47) which leads from Périgueux to Sarlat, and it has been known to Palaeolithic archaeologists and collectors ever since the 1860s when a small, diagonal lane was cut into the talus deposits in front of the abri leading from route D.47 up to the courtyard in front of the Pataud farm. Since a summary history of the investigations has been presented elsewhere (Movius 1960, 1961), the essential facts will not be repeated here. Suffice it to say that, on the basis of the results of a test trench dug in the talus slope in 1953 (Movius 1954, 1955), the land was purchased, and joint large-scale Franco-American excavations were undertaken in 1958-1964 on behalf of the Musée de l'Homme on the one hand and the Peabody Museum of Harvard University on the other. Throughout, this work was under the direction of the writer, and certain of the preliminary results have been published elsewhere (Movius and Vallois 1960; Movius 1960, 1961, 1965a, 1965b, 1965c, 1966). The site, which is at an elevation of +75.76 meters above sea level, consists of a large, west-southwesterly-facing rock-shelter some 90 meters long at the base of the cliff, together with the talus deposits in front of it. These slope down to rest on the surface of the 6-meter Würm terrace of the Vézère approximately 12 meters below. The archaeological levels continue some meters to the north of the main excavation; to the south they extend at least as far as the courtyard in front of the Pataud farm, where D. Peyrony (1909) reported his discovery of a Solutrean occupation overlying an Upper Aurignacian (= Upper Périgordian) horizon. In the area of the joint Franco-American excavations, the overhang of the shelter, which formerly protruded some 12 meters westward from the cliff face, now scarcely

exists. Furthermore, the talus has lost its original form, having been cut into by the small lane that leads up to the Pataud farm from the departmental road.

The shelter was formed during Early and Middle Würm times by the differential weathering of the less resistant strata of the Upper Cretaceous (Coniacian) limestone cliff. Its continued enlargement resulted from a process of renewal brought under by the retreat of one zone of the cliff face itself under the influence of subaerial erosion, together with chemical and mechanical weathering. As the cliff wall retreated, the existing overhang was continually undermined, and losing its support, large portions of it collapsed in the form of massive blocks and slabs, often of enormous size, that fell into the deposits accumulating through weathering of the shelter roof and walls. Concomitantly, materials disintegrating from the cliff face or falling down from the plateau above the site were either deposited in the mouth of the shelter or slid down the talus. Deposition on the floor of the site was compensated for by the increased space provided by decay of the roof, and the shelter itself, which presumably retained a rather similar form throughout much of the early Upper Palaeolithic range of time (i.e., from ca. 35,000 B.P. to ca. 20,000 B.P.), moved continuously, though at varying rates (controlled by the then prevailing climatic conditions), upward and backward following the cliff.

The excavations of 1958-1964 were concentrated in an area some 12 meters square (on the site of the former Pataud barn and farmyard), and this was reduced to 6 meters by 12 meters in 1959, covering the area of the original shelter and extending out from the face of the cliff on the east as far as the top of the talus slope on the west. These operations were coordinated by the use of a grid system consisting of six 2 m.-wide trenches (I to VI) running west-east, each of which was divided in turn into a series of 2 m.-wide squares (A-G) running north-south. In 1963 this excavated area was extended 4 m. to the north

(Trenches VII and VIII) in order to investigate the two uppermost levels in more detail, and a large pit 2 m. by 4 m., designated Extension 1, was dug down to bedrock in front of the main site. A series of small 1 m.^{2} soundings were also made in the lane between the main excavation and the 1953 Test Trench on the one hand and the Pataud farm on the other. These

"extensions" provided very useful information concerning the aerial extent of the various archaeological horizons, but they did not contribute any new stratigraphic data. The following summary of the stratigraphy is based entirely on the sequence at the main excavation.

GENERAL STRATIGRAPHY

The stratigraphic sequence at the Abri Pataud, and the area immediately adjacent to the site proper, covers an interval of time extending from the Mousterian to the Solutrean. Only the Périgordian I (= Châtelperronian) level, the Périgordian Va (*Front Robert*), the Périgordian Vb (*Éléments tronquées*), and the Aurignacian V are missing from what is otherwise a virtually complete early Upper Palaeolithic succession. Neither the Mousterian nor the Solutrean is represented at the main excavation, but the former is present at the Abri Vignaud, situated immediately adjacent to the Abri Pataud directly below the courtyard in front of the Pataud farmhouse, where two Mousterian levels appear below a series of early Upper Périgordian strata yielding Aurignacian and Upper Périgordian artifacts (Peyrony 1947). The Solutrean was found in the area of the farmhouse courtyard some 10 meters above, and D. Peyrony (1909) also states that it occurred near the main excavation (the site of the old Pataud barn that was demolished prior to the beginning of the 1958 season) and on the talus below the lane in the same general area. During the recent excavations, however, no traces of a Solutrean horizon were detected *in situ* in either of these loci, although a few fragmentary Solutrean pieces were found in secondary position in the 1963 test trench on the talus, and in the 1 m. square pits between the main excavation and the Pataud farmhouse.

The stratigraphy of the main site along the 6 m. east-west section line (i.e., the line separating Trenches III and IV) is summarized below. The figures given for the thickness of the several deposits are average readings in each case.

A. Surface Humus, 10 cm. This deposit contains some organic material and a few modern objects (iron, glass, pottery, etc.).

B. Éboulis above Level 1, 50 cm. A coarse yellow- to buff-colored éboulis containing angular to subangular limestone fragments lying in a gritty, sandy matrix. In it there were some large subparallelogram-shaped

blocks, the last of a series of roof-falls which occurred at intervals throughout the history of the site.

C. Level 1 (? Lower Solutrean), 5 cm. Fine-grained éboulis with some slight reddish ochre staining. A vague scatter of archaeological material, including one typical *pointe à face plane*, was localized in this level which occurred in the extreme northern portion of the excavated site. This horizon had been somewhat cryoturbated.

Radiocarbon Dates. No samples were recovered from this horizon at the Abri Pataud, but what is believed to be a corresponding level (Couche 31) at Laugerie-Haute:Ouest has been dated to 20,890 B.P., or 18,940 B.C. (GrN-1188; Vogel and Waterbolk 1963, p.167), suggesting that the latter occupation is some 1,000 years younger than the underlying Proto-Magdalenian.

D. Éboulis 1-2, 1.20 m. Composed mainly of thermoclastically derived elements, this deposit underlay the exceedingly limited and patchy remnants of Level 1. It contained numerous large fallen blocks. The nature of this deposit serves to emphasize the fact that the final occupations of the site took place during a regime of fairly intense cold, and therefore they should be considered only as moments in this longer climatic episode.

E. Level 2 (Proto-Magdalenian), 35 cm. Dark gray to black, coarse stony éboulis grading at the rear of the site into vertically lying "Back Éboulis" exfoliated from the rear wall of the abri, presumably as the result of frost action. With the exception of an eastward continuation of Level 2 in the northern sector of the site, the main occupation was delimited on the west by a line of large rockfalls extending in a north-south direction more or less parallel to the cliff directly below the line of maximum projection of the overhang of the existing abri. There were two major subdivisions of Level 1, designated Lens 1 (Upper and Lower) and Lens 2; in places these were in contact with each other without any clearly defined sterile layer separating them. Certainly the microstratigraphic evidence of these lenses suggests a series of short occupations, separated from each other by brief intervals when the site was temporarily abandoned. Thickest in the north, Level 2 terminated ca. 2.50 m. from the southern limit of the excavation. Both the paleontological data and the results of Farrand's analysis of the Level 2 sediments indicate that during this interval of time relatively cold and rigorous climatic conditions prevailed in the Les Eyzies region.

Radiocarbon Dates. In terms of the total number of C-14 dates that have been determined, this horizon should be one of the best-dated Upper Palaeolithic levels in Europe. In point of fact, no less than thirteen determinations have been published by the Groningen Laboratory, three of which range from 19,780 B.P. (= 17,830 B.C.) to 19,210 B.P. (= 17,260 B.C.) and may be ignored as too young. The central range, eight of the thirteen figures, varies between 20,240 B.P. (= 18,290 B.C.) and 20,960 B.P. (= 19,010 B.C.) with the average at 20,600 B.P. (=18,650 B.C.). But there are two additional measurements, the highest, to consider. The figures are as follows:

GrN-1862: 21,940 B.P. ± 250 (19,990 B.C.)
GrN-4231: 21,380 B.P. ± 340 (19,430 B.C.)

Both these latter dates have been published by Vogel and Waterbolk (1963, p.167; 1967, p.113). If it is true that no C-14 date which is too old in a given instance can be determined, then the figure for GrN-1862 must be accepted as the age of Level 2. This is an excellent agreement with the measurement of a sample (GrN-1876) from the corresponding Proto-Magdalenian level (Couche 36) at the nearby site of Laugerie-Haute: Ouest, which has been dated to 21,980 B.P. (= 20,030 B.C.) by Vogel and Waterbolk (1963, p. 167).

F. Éboulis 2-3, 75 cm. A virtually sterile deposit, which consisted of a light-colored, loosely textured sediment almost identical with the Éboulis 1-2 formation. The fact that this accumulation was effected during conditions of fairly intense cold is substantiated by the occurrence of a 25 cm. to 30 cm. thick zone of typical *éboulis sec* (i.e., an "open-work") formation in the central portion of the deposit. The lower zone of Éboulis 2-3 (ca. 25 cm. thick) consisted of a deposit of light reddish-brown éboulis at the base of which Level 3 was encountered. According to Farrand, the latter stratum represents a true soil formed during a relatively mild interval of brief duration. The intensity of pedogenetic activity was far less pronounced than in the case of the underlying Éboulis 3-4: Red, however, and in this respect it was apparently intermediate between the Level 5 (Périgordian IV) and the Éboulis 10-11: Wash and Level 11 (Early Aurignacian) episodes, each of which is briefly mentioned below.

G. Level 3 (Périgordian VI), 50 cm. Throughout, the matrix of this horizon consisted of a fine-grained, angular sandy material, the color of which had been modified as the result of occupation. As in the case of the overlying Level 2, this layer was confined to a narrow area (ca. 3 m. wide) between a row of large fallen roof-blocks below the line of maximum projection of the then existing abri and the rear wall of the shelter. The Level 3 deposits consisted of a thin dark, black- to brown-colored, ashy lens which contained artifacts, a quasi-sterile, dark buff-colored to reddish tan éboulis (some 18 cm. to 20 cm. thick) containing numerous small- to medium-sized congelifracts, and the main occupation horizon. The latter, which was of a reddish or reddish brown color, contained a series of basin-shaped hearths (average diameter: ca. 1 m.) and associated areas of ash spread, broken river-stones and numerous locally developed reddish lenses derived from the decomposition of lumps of hematite. This horizon, which rested directly on the uppermost yellow- to buff-colored zone of the Éboulis 3-4, merged with the vertically lying "Back Éboulis" towards the rear wall of the site to the east. In the northern sector of the site there was a lower lens of Level 3 that rested directly on Éboulis 3-4: Red, which is briefly described below. Following the removal of Level 3, the excavation area was reduced to an area 12 m. by 6 m.

Radiocarbon Dates. A total of four dates has been published by Vogel and Waterbolk (1963, p. 166; 1967, p. 114) from three samples from this horizon, one of burned and two of unburned bone. The oldest date, from a sample of unburned bone, is as follows:

GrN-4721: 23,010 B.P. ± 170 (21,060 B.C.)

The following figure is the oldest date obtained for a sample of burned bone:

GrN-1892: 21,540 B.P. ± 160 (19,590 B.C.)

Thus the age of Level 3 (Périgordian VI) is some 1,000 years older than the oldest figure for the overlying Level 2 (Proto-Magdalenian), discussed above. There are no other dates available for the Périgordian VI from any other sites in Western Europe to serve for comparative purposes.

H. Éboulis 3-4, ca. 60 cm. to 75 cm. The deposits separating Level 3 from Level 4 were subdivided into the following units from top to base:

(a) Éboulis 3-4: Yellow
(b) Éboulis 3-4: Red
(c) Level 4a
(d) Éboulis 3-4: Tan (including a "Pebbly-Red" Zone)

The salient features pertaining to each of these subdivisions are set forth below:

(a) *Éboulis 3-4: Yellow.* The distribution of this accumulation was limited to the Rear of the site due to the presence of an enormous fallen block (ca. 2.50 m. thick) in the Front, the flat base of which rested directly on the surface of Éboulis 3-4: Red. It was a loose, uncompacted formation up to 25 cm. thick that contained small- to medium-sized unweathered and angular to subangular blocks lying in a coarse, gritty, yellowish-colored matrix. In all essential respects, this deposit was very similar to both the overlying Éboulis 1-2 and Éboulis 2-3 accumulations.

(b) *Éboulis 3-4: Red.* Throughout, this subdivision of Éboulis 3-4 consisted of fine, rather clayey or silty particles, which resulted from extensive weathering and pedogenetic activity subsequent to deposition. According to Farrand, this formation is the most important single soil horizon at the Abri Pataud. It was accumulated and formed during an extensive interval of relatively mild and humid conditions marked by aeolian activity. It contained numerous medium- to large-sized stones, most of which were more heavily weathered on the upper surface than they were at the base. The huge block mentioned above, which rested on the surface of this stratum, represented the final collapse of the overhang of the shelter; following this event, the site, with the exception of the rearmost portion, ceased to be a large rock-shelter. This weathering interval was also recognized at the nearby Abri du Facteur (Commune de Tursac) by Mme. Leroi-Gourhan (1968, pp. 129-130) and by Laville (1968, pp. 144-145; see also Laville et Thibault 1967). Mme. Leroi-Gourhan has proposed calling it the "Tursac Oscillation."

(c) *Level 4a.* This thin stratum (ca. 3 cm. to 5 cm. thick) represented a single brief Late Noaillian (ex-Périgordian V_c) occupation of the shelter. It consisted of a discontinuous series of thin hearths and dark ashy lenticules that occurred sporadically at the base of Éboulis 3-4: Red and overlying Éboulis 3-4: Tan.

(d) *Éboulis 3-4: Tan* (including the "Pebbly-Red" Zone). Of a tannish-brown color, this formation (ca. 15 cm. to 25 cm. thick) was generally compact with a gritty, somewhat sandy matrix. It contained an abundance of large- to medium-sized limestone blocks. Towards the Front of the site there was a change in facies; the deposit became redder and it contained a great abundance of pebble-sized, subangular limestone inclusions of small size. Both this "Pebbly-Red" deposit and the homotaxial Éboulis 3-4: Tan formation directly overlay the uppermost unit that was assigned to Level 4.

Radiocarbon Dates. One assumes that the Level 4 (Noaillian) occupation terminated some time before, or at the latest by 26,000 B.P. (= 24,050 B.C.), on the basis of the figure given below. Thus the interval of time represented by Éboulis 3-4, a deposit which averages just over 1 m. thick, would cover a span of almost 3,000 years. This is admittedly a long time, but the nature of the Éboulis 3-4: Red unit, the average thickness of which is ca. 25 cm., supports the 3,000-year estimate for the duration of the interval in question. According to Dr. Farrand (see p. 61), the weathering of this stratum took place during an interval of *non-deposition* of éboulis, under relatively temperate and humid climatic conditions. This view is supported by the paleontological evidence as well. The éboulis was first deposited, then weathered; hence the contact between Éboulis 3-4: Red and the overlying Éboulis 3-4: Yellow represents a hiatus, or pause, in the deposition at the abri. This marks the boundary between depositionary Cycles II and III at the Pataud rock-shelter.

I. Level 4 (Noaillian), 50 cm. The surface of Level 4 was transitional with the overlying Éboulis 3-4: Tan/"Pebbly-Red" formation, although it was coarser and became progressively coarser with depth. In general it was a medium-sized stony éboulis with a tightly packed matrix, consisting of fine- to medium-sized particles. The Upper Subdivision was dark brown, the Middle consisted of a series of lighter-colored brown, reddish- or orange-colored lenses, whereas the Lower units were dark reddish brown or black. This level covered all of the Rear area of the site; in the Front (Trenches II to IV, Squares B-C) a large block of Éboulis 4-5 roof-fall occupied the area. Only the Lower Subdivision extended westward to the A Squares in the Front of the site; the Middle and Upper Subdivisions were mainly confined to the Rear area behind the large roof-fall. In spite of fairly numerous attempts at drainage (e.g. a ditch associated with one of the hearths in the Middle Subdivision), it seems that a very marked increase in humidity, resulting in the erosion of natural runoff channels and even the redeposition of certain portions of various layers, was the major reason for the abandonment of the site following the Level 4 occupation. The fauna demonstrates, however, that this deposit was accumulated under conditions that were fairly cold (see pp.

143-144 of Dr. Jean Bouchud's report), which persisted until the time of the weathering of the Éboulis 3-4: Red, briefly described above.

Radiocarbon Dates. Only one radiocarbon date has been determined thus far for this thick and extremely rich horizon. It was collected in the Middle Subdivision of the layer, and it is as follows:

GrN-4280: 27,060 B.P. ± 370 (25,110 B.C.)

This date, published by Vogel and Waterbolk (1967, p. 114), seems too early on a priori grounds, but the possibility of contamination with older materials has been very carefully investigated, and no evidence whatsoever for any sort of stratigraphic or typologic mixture was found. Therefore, one must accept the figure in question for the time being, since there is nothing to support the view that the sample contained enough disturbed material and/or material older than level 4 to falsify seriously the result of the measurement.

It should be added that a somewhat longer interval of time between the uppermost Périgordian IV (Level 5) and the Middle unit of the Noaillian (Level 4) is indicated by the archaeological evidence, particularly the fact that the assemblage from the Lower Subdivision of this latter horizon is so completely different in *all* essential respects in comparison with the Upper portion of the underlying Level 5 (Périgordian IV). When C-14 dates are available for more samples from Level 4, it is hoped that this problem will be less obscure. In the final analysis, 500 years does not provide very much time into which to crowd all the events that transpired during the time-interval in question.

J. Éboulis 4-5, 20 cm. to 25 cm. (average). With the exception of two small, thin, localized lenses containing a few undiagnostic Upper Périgordian pieces, this stratum, which varied in thickness from 10 cm. to 12 cm. in the Rear of the site, up to 30 cm. to 35 cm. in the Front, was virtually sterile from an archaeological point of view. It varied in color from a reddish brown in the Front to a light buff- or yellow-color in the Rear, and it contained a few medium- to large-sized stones lying in a tightly packed, rather fine-grained matrix. Over much of the Front of the site it was represented by the massive block of roof-fall which was up to 1 m. thick. This rock rested directly on Level 5. According to Farrand, the Éboulis 4-5 deposit was accumulated during a brief, cold, and somewhat moist interval.

K. Level 5 (Périgordian IV), Rear: 25 cm.; Front: 70 cm. This very rich occupation layer consisted of two completely distinct and separate units (a) Rear and (b) Front; the salient features of each of which are summarized below.

(a) *Level 5: Rear.* As the result of fairly extensive earth-moving operations in the rear of the site by the Périgordian IV settlers, all traces of the underlying Éboulis 5-6 and Level 6 (Evolved Aurignacian) deposits were removed for the purpose of increasing the available head room. Furthermore, since the archaeological assemblage from Level 5: Rear corresponds to that from the uppermost units of Level 5: Front, these episodes of digging/cleaning operations took place throughout the entire time-span of the occupation in question. The Level 5: Rear deposits consisted of a stony éboulis lying in a sandy matrix. In color the upper units were brownish black; towards the base they became redder (due to hematite staining), and they rested partly on the underlying frost-shattered bedrock and partially on the Éboulis 6-7 deposit. On the section (fig. 1), the truncated surface of Level 6, as well as the overlying Éboulis 5-6, may be clearly seen. The lenses of Level 5: Rear all feather out against the eastward slope of the "ridge" dividing the Front from the Rear sector of this stratum.

(b) *Level 5: Front.* The Level 5 occupation in the Front of the site was effected on the heavily weathered but nonetheless rough and uneven surface of a series of large blocks of the Éboulis 5-6 rockfall. This surface sloped uniformly up from the entrance of the shelter towards the back wall in the east. Its highest point, which formed a sort of north-south "ridge", was always located in the eastern portion of the C squares and this feature constituted a clear physical separation between Level 5 accumulations in the Front and Rear sectors of the site. In color the upper units of the Level 5: Front were dark reddish brown to gray; those of the Middle Subdivision were medium-brown to gray; in the lower portion of the stratum they were black to medium-brown, becoming a light brown or tan at the base, which consists of coarse micaceous sand. Abundant medium- and small-sized congelifracts were present throughout these 70 cm. thick sediments. Aurignacian-type tools occurred in the Lower (N:28) and the Middle (N:6) Subdivisions of the deposits in the Front of the site, demonstrating that the process of cleaning operations in the Rear of the shelter began early in the Périgordian IV occupation. According to Farrand's analysis (see p. 45), the basal sand in and around the extensive Éboulis 5-6 rockfall in the Front of the site is of aeolian origin. Furthermore, his detailed study of Level 5 sediments has clearly shown that the prevailing climatic conditions during the prolonged

Périgordian IV occupation of the site were fairly mild, but nonetheless moist (perhaps a double episode with a short intervening colder interval). Throughout, this pedogenetic period was accompanied by a pronounced aeolian influence.

Radiocarbon Dates. The following date has been determined for the Middle-1 horizon in the Front of the site:

GrN-4631:   21,780 B.P.   ± 215   (19,830 B.C.)

This figure can certainly be ignored as too young, but there are three additional dates, for two samples from the same 10 cm. thick Lens (K-1) in the Lower Subdivision of Level 5: Rear of the site. They are as follows:

GrN-4477:   26,600 B.P.   ± 260   (24,650 B.C.)
GrN-4662:   27,660 B.P.   ± 260   (25,710 B.C.)
GrN-4634:   28,150 B.P.   ± 225   (26,200 B.C.)

These dates purport to establish the age of the beginning of the latest stage of the Périgordian IV occupation at the Abri Pataud. The average figure for the two samples of burned bone – ca. 27,900 B.P. (= 25,950 B.C.) – falls within the limits of the statistical error and can perhaps be accepted as fixing the date of the beginning of the uppermost Périgordian IV occupation at the site. But this figure provides no information whatsoever bearing on the time-span covered by this occupation, during which a total of ca. 70 cm. of deposit accumulated in the Front of the site. Accordingly, an estimated figure of ca. 29,000 B.P. (= 27,050 B.C.) has been taken as providing a provisional date for the Lower-2 unit of Level 5: Front of the site, on the basis of a probable time-span of 1,000 years for the duration of the occupation in question, but perhaps this latter figure is too high. For it must be emphasized once again that the suggested starting date for this horizon is *not* based upon radiocarbon evidence.

L. Éboulis 5-6, 60 cm. As stated above, both the Éboulis 5-6 and Level 6 (Evolved Aurignacian) deposits were absent in the Rear of the site, having been removed by the Périgordian IV digging/cleaning operations. In the Front sector Éboulis 5-6 was virtually sterile, and in part it graded into the lowest deposits of Level 5, which consisted of a stratum of oxidized brown micaceous sand containing a very few small stones. The major portion of this unit, however, consisted of two layers of large rectangular blocks up to 60 cm. thick and 1.20 cm. in length. The upper surface of the upper series of this roof-fall was heavily weathered. Between these rocks the matrix was of a pale yellow color, well sorted and sandy.

Radiocarbon Dates. Although no samples from Level 6 have ever been measured, it is very reasonable to assume that the latest Aurignacian occupation at the Abri Pataud was over by 32,000 B.P. (= 30,050 B.C.), or at the latest by 31,500 B.P. (= 29,550 B.C.). This would leave an interval of approximately 2,500 to 3,000 or so years before the estimated beginning of the Level 5 (Périgordian IV) occupation. This figure is supported by Dr. Farrand's geological evidence, indicated by the fact that the upper surface of the enormous limestone rockfall, the uppermost unit of Éboulis 5-6, is very considerably weathered, as witnessed by its rounded and smoothed surface. Furthermore, there is a considerable amount of windblown sand in and around these big blocks, as well as the deposits constituting the basal subdivision of Level 5, and the greatest part, if not all, of this sand comes from the floodplain of the nearby Vézère River. This has been definitely demonstrated by an analysis of the heavy minerals. Therefore, this accumulation of aeolian sand, together with the weathering of the surface of the Éboulis 5-6 rockfall, took place during an interval of time when little or no éboulis was being accumulated in the site, an interval which marks the boundary between depositionary Cycles I and II in terms of the Abri Pataud sequence. On the basis of the radiocarbon evidence, this interval corresponds almost exactly with the dates for the Denekamp Oscillation in the Low Countries (Vogel and van der Hammen 1967; van der Hammen, et al. 1967).

M. Level 6 (Evolved Aurignacian), 10 cm. This horizon marked a change in depositionary processes and, to some extent, in kind of occupation at the Abri Pataud. Instead of well-defined occupation horizons, as found in the cases of Levels 2-5, for example, traces of settlement were now distributed in and between blocks of limestone, and they seemed to have occurred during intervals of fairly constant rockfall. These discontinuous traces of occupation were often localized and frequently lacking in matrix, hence materials from them may descend as much as 30 cm. from their original level, thus bringing horizons into contact with each other that may have been separated by appreciable intervals of time. As a result of this new type of depositionary process (insofar as the Abri Pataud is concerned), the lens system of designating subdivisions of a given level, employed in the case of the exceedingly rich overlying horizons, ceased to represent adequately the archaeological situation, and therefore it became necessary to introduce a new system of subdivision designation. Accordingly, the terms "Upper, Middle, and Lower" were adopted for those normally dark ashy units of a given horizon distinguished on a color, consistency, or grain-size basis, and "Zone" for those strata homotaxial with the major units into which derived cultural materials have been infiltrated. In certain instances the zone deposits were faintly discolored, but normally this was not the case, especially near the Front of the site, where in a sense the cultural sequence was completely dominated by the pedological changes believed to have been accentuated by the proximity of this area to the mouth of the abri.

The Level 6 (Evolved Aurignacian) horizon consisted of a fairly fine-grained, buff-colored matrix with thin strata of *éboulis sec*, which contained an abundance of small- to medium-sized subangular limestone congelifracts. There was some limited discoloration, due to ash scatter and staining of the deposits that were locally separable into two relatively dark subdivisions. Both the fauna and the characteristics of the sediments indicate that the climate was somewhat colder and more rigorous at this time than it had been during the interval represented by the overlying Périgordian IV and Noaillian of Levels 5 and 4.

Radiocarbon Dates. No samples have been measured from this level, which is in the uppermost unit of the Cycle I deposits at the Abri Pataud. All the Cycle I sediments were apparently accumulated rapidly under the conditions of a fairly rigorous climate. On the basis of the C-14 dates for the underlying horizons, however, it is very unlikely that the Level 6 occupation can be younger than ca. 31,500 B.P., or 29,550 B.C.

N. Éboulis 6-7, 50 cm. As explained above, Level 5 rested directly on this formation in the Rear of the shelter. Éboulis 6-7 consisted of a coarse, gritty, yellow- to buff-colored matrix containing some large-sized blocks, fallen from the roof, and numerous small- to medium-sized, subangular congelifracts.

O. Level 7 (Intermediate Aurignacian-b), Upper: 8 cm. to 10 cm.; Lower: ca. 20 cm. to 30 cm. The actual occupation area, or main deposits, of Level 7 (D. Peyrony's Aurignacian II with flattened, lozenge-shaped uncleft bone points) was limited to the D and E Squares in the Rear portion of the site. Towards the west, Zone material from Level 7 could be traced into Square A to a point ca. 1.70 m. east of the 0-line where it became lost in the talus. Two subdivisions were distinguished in the D and E Squares, the upper one being a medium- to light-colored reddish brown deposit, and the lower one a dark brown to black stony stratum with a greasy and somewhat gritty

texture. The latter filled a large, oval, basin-shaped depression that was limited in front by the Éboulis 7-8 rockfall, and in the Rear by the back éboulis, a formation of more or less vertically lying limestone slabs indicating the position of the rear wall of the shelter at the time of this occupation. In the northern portion of the depression an interesting hearth complex, designated W, X, and Y, came to light.

Radiocarbon Dates. Two series of dates have been determined for this horizon, and the contradictory evidence which they present has been fully discussed elsewhere (Movius 1963, pp. 134-135). The final corrected figures as published by Vogel and Waterbolk (1967, pp. 114-115) are given below. All three of them are from the same sample, a lump of fine homogeneous charcoal.

GrN-3105: 29,300 B.P. ± 450 (27,350 B.C.)
GrN-3117: 32,800 B.P. ± 450 (30,850 B.C.)
GrN-3116: 32,900 B.P. ± 700 (30,950 B.C.)

Vogel and Waterbolk emphatically state that GrN-3105 is obviously too young and need not be considered further. This means that the age of Level 7 on the basis of the C-14 measurements is ca. 32,800 B.P., or 30,850 B.C.

P. Éboulis 7-8, 50 cm. to 60 cm. The upper portion of this formation consisted of a series of large blocks fallen from the roof. Elsewhere the deposit, like Éboulis 6-7, was a coarse, gritty, yellow- to buff-colored éboulis mixed with subangular congelifracts of all sizes.

Q. Level 8 (Intermediate Aurignacian-a), ca. 50 cm. During the process of excavating the large basin-shaped depression in Level 7, briefly described above, the prehistoric occupants of the Abri Pataud removed the major portion of the Level 8 deposits in the D and E Squares down to the Lower Subdivision of this horizon. Thus the Upper and Middle Subdivisions in this sector were only represented by Zone material extending out to the Front of the site. Whereas the various subdivisions of Level 8 were dark and contained a high component of ash, especially in the vicinity of the two hearths in the Middle (Hearth A) and Lower (Hearth Z) Subdivisions, the Zone deposits were virtually identical with the containing éboulis and could be detected only on the basis of the occurrence in them of cultural materials. Often the latter were considerably abraided, especially as one approached the A Squares in the Front of the site. Between the Middle and Lower Subdivisions and associated Zone Complexes of Level 8, an interesting formation of éboulis occurred. This deposit was of a yellowish to reddish yellow color; it was also more compact and more heavily weathered than the stratum separating the Upper and Middle Subdivisions of this horizon. Furthermore, it contained rounder and smaller inclusions than did the latter, and the matrix was finer with a higher component of sand-sized grains. In other words, this accumulation apparently marked a minor depositionary break in the Level 8 sequence of strata.

Radiocarbon Dates. Only one of a series of excellent samples of ash collected in Hearth A in the Middle Subdivision of Level 8 has thus far been measured. It gave the following result:

GrN-6163:   31,800 B.P.   ± 280   (29,850 B.C.)

This figure was announced in a letter from Dr. W.G. Mook dated Groningen, 12 March 1971. In view of the fact that the dates for the overlying Level 7 (see above) average ca. 1,000 years older, this figure is obviously too young and cannot be accepted.

R. Éboulis 8-9, 10 cm. to 15 cm. No large fallen roof-blocks occurred in this stratum which separated Level 8: Lower/Lower Zone from Level 9, and which was identical with Éboulis 7-8 in all essential respects.

S. Level 9 (? Intermediate Aurignacian), 10 cm. to 12 cm. This stratum consisted of a discontinuous series of red- and black-stained éboulis that were at first taken to represent part of Level 8. Although it yielded a total of only 32 artifacts, Level 9 represented a definite Aurignacian occupation, albeit a very minor one.

Radiocarbon Dates. No dates are available for this horizon.

T. Éboulis 9-10, 30 cm. to 35 cm. Virtually sterile, this layer of typical yellow- to buff-colored éboulis separated Level 9 from the underlying Level 10 horizon.

U. Level 10 (? Intermediate Aurignacian), 5 cm. to 7 cm. Very similar to Level 9, the Level 10 horizon likewise consisted of a thin minor occupation, which yielded a total of 50 catalogued pieces. It was very thin in Trench II and only became significant in Trench V, suggesting that the main concentration lies to the north of the excavated area of the site.

Radiocarbon Dates. No dates are available for this horizon.

V. Éboulis 10-11, 35 cm. Yellow- to buff-colored éboulis which consisted of an upper (buff) facies and a lower one that had been washed down from above. This deposit appeared to inaugurate the depositionary cycle that includes the overlying Level 10 and Éboulis

9-10. Farrand's very competent sediment analysis study, has shown that the basal stratum, designated Éboulis 10-11: Wash by the excavators, was accumulated during a brief, moist, and relatively mild interval of incipient pedogenesis and increased aeolian activity.

W. Level 11 (Early Aurignacian-b), 45 cm. to 75 cm. On the basis of the occurrence of a small series of cleft-base bone points, this occupation should be assigned to the Aurignacian I as defined by Denis Peyrony.

After the removal of Éboulis 10-11, the reddish brown surface of a very sandy deposit was encountered that extended over the entire area of the excavation. It contrasted markedly with the overlying, predominantly yellow- to buff-colored deposits and marked the surface of Level 11. The following four major subdivisions were noted:

(a) Éboulis-a
(b) Upper Deposits (2 minor subdivisions)
(c) Stony Facies
(d) Dark Stratum (main occupation horizon)

The Lower Subdivision, in which seven small, basin-shaped hearths and two shallow pits occurred, extended over the entire area of the excavation, and it constituted the main occupation horizon of Level 11. In the Front it was subdivided into two strata. Level 11: Rear directly overlay the exfoliated and frost-cracked bedrock; in the Front it was underlain by Éboulis 11-12, except at those points where it rested unconformably on Level 12 as the result of the fact that the prehistoric occupants had artificially leveled the area. The so-called Stony Facies consisted of derived Back Éboulis that apparently had washed down the slope from above; it did not extend to the Front of the shelter. Throughout, the matrix of the Level 11 deposit was reddish brown (Subdivisions A, B, and C) or brownish black (due to a high increment of ash, especially in Subdivision D), and it consisted of a medium- to fine-grained, somewhat micaceous, gritty sand. Apparently, together with the Éboulis 10-11: Wash deposit, this marks a minor climatic amelioration when moist and relatively mild conditions prevailed, during which incipient pedogenetic activity and increased aeolian influence took place. Therefore, according to Farrand, there is evidence here for a minor weathering episode in the earlier portion of the Middle Würm sequence. It is tentatively suggested that this brief interval of mild climate should be correlated with the so-called Interstade d'Arcy, as defined by Mme. Leroi-Gourhan (1964, p. 14). Although he refrained from proposing a name for it, this climatic oscillation had already been described by Bouchud (1952) some twenty years ago at the Abri Castenet (Commune de Sergeac), Dordogne.

Radiocarbon Dates. For this level only one of a number of samples of burned bone has been measured, and it gave the following dates for both fractions, the extract and the residue:

GrN-4326: 32,000 B.P. ± 800 (30,050 B.C.)
GrN-4309: 32,600 B.P. ± 550 (30,650 B.C.)

Although Vogel and Waterbolk (1967, p. 146) accept a central date of ca. 33,000 B.P. (= 31,050 B.C.) for both Levels 12 and 11, it is apparent on the basis of the stratigraphic evidence that Level 12 must be slightly older than 33,000 and Level 11 must be slightly younger. The major conclusion, therefore, is that the two occupations were very close to one another in time, and that C-14 was unable to separate them successfully.

X. Éboulis 11-12, 15 cm. to 20 cm. The Éboulis 11-12 stratum consisted of two facies: one yellowish in the east and south of the area, the other reddish yellow situated in the western and northern sectors of the excavation. This deposit, 15 cm. to 20 cm. thick on the average, attained a maximum thickness of 30 cm. in places, but it thinned out markedly towards the north and east. Several of the hearths, as well as the two pits, of Level 11, were dug into this stratum at the time the occupation was effected.

Y. Level 12 (Early Aurignacian-a), 10 cm. The original extent of Level 12 towards the Rear of the site could not be determined, since it was removed in that sector when the Level 11 settlers cleared and leveled the area prior to occupation. This horizon varied in thickness from 15 cm. on the east to 5 cm. on the west. Its color was generally reddish or yellowish brown, and it contained numerous medium- to small-sized subangular congelifracts in marked contrast to the overlying Level 11 deposit. At several points Level 11 actually rested unconformably on Level 12; in fact along the eastern edge of Level 12 both of the Level 11 pits, as well as the basin of one of the hearths, were dug into the surface of the Level 12 deposit. In the southern portion of the excavated area a total of four hearths were found in association with Level 12.

Radiocarbon Dates. There are three dates for this horizon from two samples, one of burned and one of unburned bone. One of them — GrN-4310: 31,000 B.P. ±500 (= 29,050 B.C.) — is obviously too young and need not be considered further. This leaves the following two figures:

GrN-4327: 33,000 B.P. ± 500 (31,050 B.C.)
GrN-4719: 33,260 B.P. ± 425 (31,310 B.C.)

These dates are in very satisfactory agreement with each other and may be considered reliable. The former sample consisted of burned bone and the latter of unburned bone.

Z. Éboulis 12-13, 20 cm. This unit consisted of a typical light yellow limestone éboulis with an average thickness of 20 cm. In places it was up to 30 cm. thick, however, whereas elsewhere it became very thin (ca. 3 cm.). The congelifracts were all of medium to small size and only very slightly weathered.

A'. Level 13 (Basal Aurignacian-b), 10 cm. to 15 cm. This occupation layer, which yielded a total of only 57 catalogued pieces, consisted of a doubly truncated remnant of a formerly more extensive deposit. Along its eastern margin it abutted against the exfoliated plaques of the bedrock near the rear wall of the shelter, and a portion of it was truncated at the time of the leveling of the floor of the site prior to the Level 11 occupation. Of a reddish yellow color, this horizon averaged 10 cm. to 15 cm. thick. Its western limit was apparently artificial, and it was either formed by erosion or, more likely, by human activities during the time of the Level 12 occupation. It extended farther toward the west than did either the underlying Éboulis 13-14 or Level 14; in fact it lay on a surface obliquely truncating the latter units, presumably resulting from cleaning operations in antiquity. No hearths came to light in Level 13 in the area of the main excavation.

Radiocarbon Dates. No dates are available for Level 13.

B'. Éboulis 13-14, ca. 25 cm. A typical reddish yellow- to buff-colored éboulis containing numerous small- to medium-sized subangular congelifracts, Éboulis 13-14 averaged ca. 25 cm. thick but the deposit was less than 7 cm. thick in some places. Its eastern limit either abutted against the exfoliated rear wall of the then-existing shallow shelter, or was truncated by the Level 11 occupation surface. The western edge of this deposit was likewise truncated, sometimes obliquely and sometimes vertically, by the overlying Level 13.

C'. Level 14 (Basal Aurignacian-a), ca. 20 cm. Level 14, the earliest occupation layer represented at the Abri Pataud, increased markedly in thickness in the direction of the main hearth area in the southern sector of the excavation. Here Level 14 was ca. 25

cm. thick, whereas towards the north it was only 12 cm. or less in thickness. In and immediately adjacent to the hearth area a large, irregular, shallow pit was found. In length (N-S) this feature measured ca. 2.00 m., its width (W-E) being ca. 75 cm., and it was believed by the excavators to have been in part artificial and in part due to the occupants having taken advantage of a natural depression. This pit had been dug into the Basal Éboulis to a total depth of some 25 cm. Only in the area of this pit was it possible to subdivide Level 14 during excavation: the Upper unit varied in color from yellowish red to reddish brown, and it was composed of close-set, predominantly small limestone fragments in a loose matrix of fine sand containing some mica; in it several localized patches of black ashy material were noted. The Lower unit, which varied in color from reddish yellow to reddish brown, was a moderately loose sediment composed of close-set medium- to small-sized limestone congelifracts lying in a matrix of fine sand, also containing some particles of mica. At its base, this sediment exhibited a dark red color that appeared to be due to intense hematite staining. Two localized patches of a sticky, plastic, light reddish yellow clay were found in the basal unit of Level 14, and this material is believed to have been imported into the site by man. Four major hearths and a minor one occurred in Level 14.

Radiocarbon Dates. There are three dates from two samples collected in the Level 14 stratum. One of them consisted of burned bone, the other of unburned bone. The results are as follows:

GrN-4610:   33,300 B.P.   ± 760   (31,350 B.C.)
GrN-4507:   34,250 B.P.   ± 675   (32,300 B.C.)
GrN-4720:   33,330 B.P.   ± 410   (31,380 B.C.)

Certainly these dates are very close, in fact they are all within the limits of the statistical error. Vogel and Waterbolk (1967, p. 116) accept a central value of 34,000 B.P. (= 32,050 B.C.) as the approximate age of this, the earliest, level at the Abri Pataud.

D′. Basal Éboulis (Below Level 14), 1.80 m. Below Level 14, where the latter horizon was present, and below Levels 12 and 13 in the westernmost sector of the site, there was a thick sequence of virtually sterile éboulis, which was subdivided into four major units. In the C Squares on the east this deposit abutted against the exfoliated Back Éboulis, but elsewhere it rested on the westward sloping bedrock. Beyond the limits of the main excavation the Basal Éboulis merged with the talus deposits in front of the site.

The uppermost subdivision of this deposit varied in color from yellow to very pale brown. In the A Squares, directly below Level 12, the upper several centimeters exhibited a slight pink staining. Throughout, it was moderately compact, and the predominantly large- to medium-sized limestone congelifracts were angular to subangular. They lay in a matrix of sand, the grain size of which was fine to medium.

Below came a loose, uniformly reddish yellow stratum that contained subangular to subrounded, large- and medium-sized limestone fragments that rested in a matrix of fine to medium sand which contained numerous particles of mica. The underlying subdivision varied in color from a very pale yellow (or light buff) to a very light brown, and in it local patches of limonite staining were noted. It was composed of large- to medium-sized limestone fragments that lay in a very loose matrix of fine and medium sand. The lowermost subdivision was of a pale yellow to buff color. It was a very loose deposit (almost an *éboulis sec*), and the angular to subangular limestone fragments, which were of all sizes but predominantly of large to very large size, were lying in a matrix of medium-sized to coarser sand in which local areas of limonite staining were noted. On approaching the water table at the base, this deposit became very wet and some minor calcite incrustations occurred.

E′. Cemented Limestone Fragments, over 20 cm. Strictly speaking this formation is not a separate stratigraphic unit of deposition; rather it is composed of the basal portion of the Basal Éboulis: Pale Yellow Subdivision that had been subjected to secondary modification — i.e., the limestone fragments had been encrusted with redeposited calcite formerly dissolved in groundwater to such an extent that the incrustations had coalesced. With increasing depth in the deposit, the interstices between the limestone fragments were found to be more and more filled with calcite, the net result being a solid mass of limestone fragments completely "frozen" in calcite, thus forming an extremely hard stalagmitic crust. Over an area ca. 30 cm. square this formation was penetrated to a depth of ca. 20 cm. with points and cold chisels, but the bedrock base of the formation was not reached.

F′. Bedrock, Coniacian (Upper Cretaceous) Limestone. The Coniacian limestone was drilled to a depth of 1.70 m. at three separate points, and on this basis it was concluded that it was indeed the bedrock and *not* an enormous block of roof-fall.

CONCLUSIONS

From the series of dates set forth above, a far more satisfactory absolute chronology for the early Upper Palaeolithic in France can be established than was hitherto available. Two interesting facts stand out: (a) the Aurignacian apparently ran the full course of its development during a time-span of only 4,000 years or so, and (b) the Upper Périgordian development took place during an interval of approximately equal duration – i.e., 4,450 years. The Proto-Magdalenian, which overlies the Périgordian VI, appeared some 22,000 years ago and was replaced by the Early Solutrean a thousand or so years later. This time-scale provides a date not only for the human remains from Level 2 (Proto-Magdalenian) at the Abri Pataud, but also for those from the classic Abri de Cro-Magnon situated some 200 meters due north of the locality under consideration (Movius 1971). Thus it seems likely that the various skulls and other human material from the Upper Zone of the deposits at the Cro-Magnon rock-shelter are younger than approximately 31,500 B.P. (ca. 29,550 B.C.) on the basis of the estimated date for the Level 6 occupation at the Abri Pataud.

REFERENCES

Bouchud, Jean
  1952. "Etude des Rongeurs et des Oiseaux de l'Abri Castanet," *Bull. Soc. Préh. Fr.*, vol. 49, no. 5-6, pp. 267-271.

Hammen, T.C. van der, G.C. Maarleveld, J.C. Vogel, and W.H. Zagwijn
  1967. "Stratigraphy, Climatic Succession and Radiocarbon Dating of the Last Glacial in the Netherlands," *Geologie en Mijnbouw*, vol. 46, pp. 79-95.

Laville, Henri
  1968. "L'Abri du Facteur à Tursac (Dordogne). IV – Etude sédimentologique du remplissage," *Gallia-Préhistoire*, vol. 11, no. 1, pp. 133-145.

Laville, Henri, et Claude Thibault
  1967. "L'oscillation climatique contemporaine du Périgordien supérieur à burins de Noailles dans le sud-ouest de la France," *C.R. Acad. Sci. Paris*, vol. 264, pp. 2364-2366.

Leroi-Gourhan, A. (Mme.)
  1968. "L'Abri du Facteur à Tursac (Dordogne). III – Analyse pollinique," *Gallia-Préhistoire*, vol. 11, no. 1, pp. 123-132.

Leroi-Gourhan, Arlette et André
  1964. "Chronologie des grottes d'Arcy-sur-Cure (Yonne). I – Climats du quaternaire récent," *Gallia-Préhistoire*, vol. 7, pp. 1-35.

Movius, H.L., Jr.
  1954. "Les Eyzies: A Test Excavation," *Archaeology*, vol. 7, no. 2, pp. 82-90.
  1955. "Une fouille préliminaire à l'Abri Pataud, Les Eyzies (Dordogne)," *Bull. Soc. Etudes et Recherches Préh.*, Les Eyzies, no 5, pp. 33-40.
  1960. "Bas-Relief Carving of a Female Figure Recently Discovered in the Final Perigordian Horizon at the Abri Pataud, Les Eyzies (Dordogne). *Festschrift für Lothar Zotz*: Steinzeitfragen der Alten und Neuen Welt, pp. 377-387 and 5 pls. L. Röhrscheid, Bonn.

  1961. "The Proto-Magdalenian of the Abri Pataud, Les Eyzies (Dordogne)," *Bericht über den V. Internationalen Kongress für Vor- und Frühgeschichte*, Hamburg, 1958, pp. 561-566.
  1963. "L'âge du Périgordien, de l'Aurignacien et du Proto-Magdalénien en France sur la base des datations au carbone 14," *Bull. Soc. Mér. Spél. Préh.* (Aurignac et l'Aurignacien: Centenaire des Fouilles d'Edouard Lartet), t. 6-9 (1956-59), pp. 130-142.
  1965a. "Upper Perigordian and Aurignacian Hearths at the Abri Pataud, Les Eyzies (Dordogne)," *Miscelánea en Homenaje al Abate Henri Breuil*, vol. 2, pp. 181-196.
  1965b. "Aurignacian Hearths at the Abri Pataud, Les Eyzies (Dordogne)," *Symposium in Honor of Dr. Li Chi on his Seventieth Birthday*, pt. 1, pp. 1-14. Published by the Institute of History and Philology, Academia Sinica, Taipei, Taiwan.
  1965c. "Preliminary Results of the Abri Pataud Excavations, Les Eyzies (Dordogne) 1958-1961," *Atti del VI Congresso Internazionale delle Scienze Preistoriche e Protostoriche*, Rome, 1962, vol. 2, pp. 151-157.
  1966. "The Hearths of the Upper Perigordian and Aurignacian Horizons at the Abri Pataud, Les Eyzies (Dordogne), and their Possible Significance," *Amer. Anth.*, vol. 68, no. 2, pt. 2, pp. 296-325 and 14 pls.
  1971. "The Abri de Cro-Magnon, Les Eyzies (Dordogne), and the Probable Age of the Contained Burials on the Basis of the Evidence of the Nearby Abri Pataud," *Anuario de Estudios Atlánticos*, no. 15 (1969), pp. 323-344. Madrid, Las Palmas.

Movius, H.L., Jr., and Henri V. Vallois
  1960. "Crâne proto-magdalénien et Vénus du Périgordien final trouvés dans l'Abri Pataud, Les Eyzies (Dordogne)," *L'Anthropologie*, vol. 63, no. 3-4, pp. 213-232.

Peyrony, Denis
    1909. "Sur la stratigraphie du gisement Pataud, dit Morson, aux Eyzies (Dordogne)," *C.R. Assoc. Fr. Avance. Sci*, 38ᵉ Session, Lille, p. 139 (3ᵉ partie).
    1947. "Le remplissage des vallées de la Vézère et de la Beaune, et ses rapports avec les industries préhistoriques," *Gallia,* vol. 5, pp. 180-184.

Vogel, J.C., and T.C. van der Hammen
    1967. "The Denekamp and Paudorf Interstadials," *Geologie en Mijnbouw,* vol. 46, pp. 188-194.

Vogel, J.C., and H.T. Waterbolk
    1963. "Groningen Radiocarbon Dates IV," *Radiocarbon* (published by Amer. J. Sci.), vol. 5, pp. 163-202.
    1967. "Groningen Radiocarbon Dates VII," *Radiocarbon* (published by Amer. J. Sci.), vol. 9, pp. 107-155.

II

Geological and Geographical Setting

Sheldon Judson

DEPARTMENT OF GEOLOGICAL AND GEOPHYSICAL SCIENCES
PRINCETON UNIVERSITY

The Abri Pataud is located in the northeastern part of the Aquitanian Basin. It lies on the left[1] side of the Vézère River in the village of Les Eyzies-de-Tayac. The purpose of this chapter is ʿto present the geological and geographical setting of the site, both regional and local; to record some of the Late Pleistocene events of the area; and to discuss how they may or may not be related to the Upper Palaeolithic occupation levels of the site.

Fieldwork for this study was begun in the summer of 1957 before the archaeological excavations were opened and continued during the summer of 1958.

The writer was assisted during a two-month season in 1957 by the late Professor Vinton Gwinn and by Professor John C. Stewart. In 1958 Benjamin Morgan worked with the writer during another two-month season. The writer visited the site for four days in 1968.

In addition to the above individuals, the writer is indebted to Professor Hallam L. Movius, Jr., Director of the Expedition, for assistance and many courtesies. Financial assistance was provided by NSF Grant No. G-3483 and the Department of Geological and Geophysical Sciences, Princeton University.

PHYSICAL SETTING

REGIONAL GEOLOGY AND GEOGRAPHY

Geologically the Abri Pataud lies in the northeastern portion of the Aquitanian Basin, a feature which embraces most of southwestern France. The basin is similar to the larger Paris Basin to the north and the smaller Rhodanian Basin to the east. Structurally it has the shape of a broad saucer open toward the Atlantic on the west. To the north lie the older deformed rocks of Brittany, to the northeast and east is the Massif Central of crystalline rocks of Paleozoic and Precambrian age, topped in places by volcanics of Pleistocene age. The southeastern margin is ill-defined; here the Aquitanian Basin merges with the Rhodanian Basin. The Pyrenees clearly demark the basin on the south.

Older rocks of Jurassic and Cretaceous age rim the basin on the north, east and south, and younger units of Tertiary and Pleistocene age lie toward the center of the basin and the Atlantic shore. The Abri Pataud is located in a section underlain by massive beds of marine limestone, Upper Cretaceous (Coniacian) in

age. On the broad, rolling interfleuves of the region is the so-called Siderolithic, deeply weathered fluvial deposits of Eocene age. It is in the Cretaceous limestone that the Abri Pataud was formed as were several other rock-shelters along the Vézère River Valley such as Laugerie-Haute, La Madeleine, and Le Moustier.

The geographic subdivisions reflect the bedrock and are shown in figure 1. The drainage pattern of the basin is fairly complex. But about two-thirds of the area drains into the estuary of the Gironde River via the Garonne which gathers water from the south and east. The smaller northeastern part of the basin drains into the Gironde via the Dordogne River.

It is the Dordogne River which receives the Vézère and along the latter the Abri Pataud is located. The Dordogne not only flows west to the marine limit, but also it rises in a once-glaciated country to the east in the Massif Central. As this study began it was hoped that a tie could be made between the marine and glacial sequences, and that these in turn could be carried up the Vézère to the Abri Pataud. We will have more to say of this in later sections.

In the Köppen-Geiger climatic classification the Aquitanian Basin lies in the Cxb zone, a warm temperate zone. The mean temperature of the coldest

---

[1] The terms left and right bank or side are commonly used in French geological and geographical literature. The usage thus agrees with that found in American engineering and geographic publications.

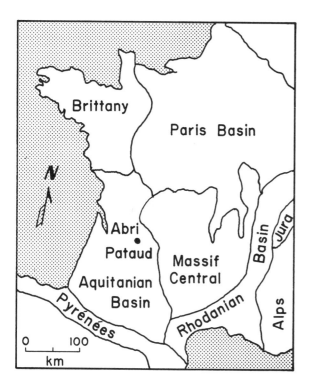

Figure 1. Major Physiographic Divisions of France Showing the Location of the Abri Pataud.

although a small extent of Jurassic limestone is also exposed in the left wall of the Vézère Valley near St. Cirq, about 5 km. downstream from Les Eyzies. Here faulting of the axis of a low, northwesterly trending anticline brings the older rocks to the surface. The limestone beds, magnificently exposed in the precipitous valley walls, are only slightly deformed. At Les Eyzies they dip very gently toward the northeast. It is in these cliffs that the Abri Pataud was formed. The limestone ranges from very fine-grained, almost lithographic, to clayey, silty, and sandy rock. Locally it contains flint nodules as does the Jurassic limestone upstream.

On the interfleuves discontinuous deposits of Eocene age, the Siderolithic, unconformably overlie the Cretaceous beds. This is a terrestrial deposit, presumably stream laid, and now deeply weathered. The texture varies widely and the deposit includes sand, clay, and siliceous gravel.

In the valley bottom are gravels, sands, and silts which form the floodplain and terraces of the Vézère River, and the low alluvial cones of the small gullies tributary to the Vézère. Deposits of travertine have formed in recent geological time in the lower course of the Beaune River where it enters the Vézère at Les Eyzies. Many of the slopes below the limestone cliffs are underlain by fragments pried from the cliffs and similar to the éboulis found in the Abri Pataud.

The Vézère, where it has cut into the limestone beds, has developed a valley floor which in many places is encased in broad, meandering loops; the relief is high, a hundred or more meters. The valley floor narrows from over one kilometer wide at the junction of the Vézère with the Dordogne to 500 m. at Les Eyzies.

The climatic environments vary from the plateau-like interfleuves to the valley bottom and from one valley wall to the other. At Les Eyzies the Vézère Valley is oriented northeast-southwest. Hence the Abri Pataud opens onto the valley bottom to the south-southwest. The micro-climate varies between this wall and the abri to the opposite, northeast-facing wall. This is reflected in the vegetation, which on the northeast-facing wall is heavier and more continuous. On the abri side of the valley, temperatures are higher, evaporation greater, and effective precipitation for plant growth less than on the opposite valley wall.

We have no recorded weather observation at Les Eyzies. Probably the data from Périgueux (table 1 and fig. 2A) represent an average picture of the climate at Les Eyzies. On the south-facing walls one would expect higher temperature, greater water deficit, a longer period of soil moisture recharge in the fall and winter, as well as a fewer number of months

month is 18°C to -3°C but close to the higher value. The mean temperature of the warmest month is less than 22°C, and at least four months have means over 10°C. Rain is lowest during the summer months with two highs, one in the fall and the other in late spring. The coincidence of temperature maximum and rainfall minimum helps to create a water deficit in the soil during the summer and early fall as suggested in figure 2A; based on data from Périgueux about 45 km. northwest of Les Eyzies. Additional characteristics of the climatic stations in the Aquitanian Basin are listed in table 1.

In the Massif Central the climate is, as to be expected, cooler and moister. Not only is total precipitation greater but so is the effective precipitation (figs. 2B and 2C). At Puy-de-Dôme the climate is rigorous, which accounts for the tundralike vegetation of the high massif described by Wilson in this volume.

LOCAL GEOLOGY AND GEOGRAPHY

The Vézère joins the Dordogne from the northeast and for a map distance of 35 km. upstream the sedimentary Cretaceous rocks dominate the valley walls. At this point the older Jurassic strata appear,

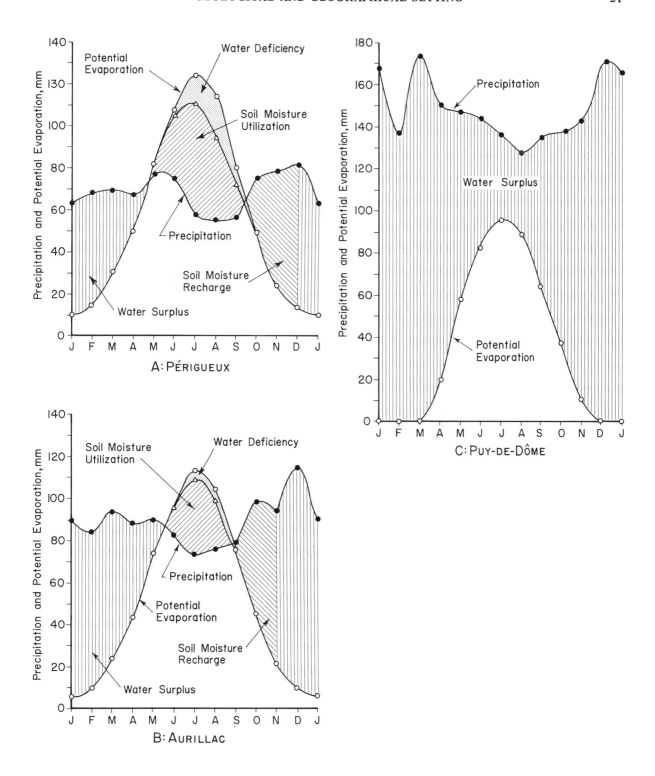

Figure 2. Water Balance Diagrams. A. Périgueux, B. Aurillac, C. Puy-de-Dôme. Data from C.W. Thornthwaite Associates "Average Climatic Water Balance Data for the Continents, Pt. V, Europe" vol. 17, no. 1; Centerton, N.J. 1964. Forty years of record for each station.

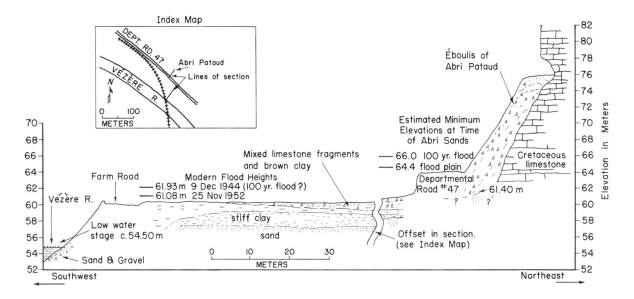

Figure 3. Cross Section Showing Relation of Sediments of the Abri Pataud to Those of the Vézère Valley Floor at Les Eyzies.

during which the absolute minimum is below 0°C. Conversely, one would expect variations in the other direction on the facing valley wall.

Climatic variations between valley wall and between valley and upland must have existed during the occupation at Abri Pataud, a subject returned to later in this chapter.

THE SITE AND THE VÉZÈRE VALLEY

Farrand gives a detailed discussion of the sediment analysis of the Abri Pataud deposits in the following chapter. Here we wish to examine the site in relation to the Vézère River and its history. Specifically, what stratigraphic relation exists between the river deposits and terraces on the one hand and the deposits in the abri on the other?

Farrand describes the éboulis deposits of the abri and reports that culture-containing beds of éboulis overlie culturally sterile éboulis. These in turn overlie river sand and gravel. The éboulis are derived by mechanical weathering of the roof and back wall of the abri, and the underlying sands represent some past stage of the Vézère River.

The relationships of the abri and its deposits to the Vézère and its deposits are shown in figure 3. The

éboulis of the shelter overlie river-laid sands at an elevation of about 61.40 m. A boring made by us on the opposite side of Departmental Road No. 47 from the site encountered river sand at about 58.40 m. This grades upwards into silt and clay and is overlain by a mixture of clay and limestone fragments (éboulis). The section in figure 3 is offset ca. 60 m. downstream and continues from near the road to the Vézère. This portion of the section, based on a series of hand-augered holes, shows that clay gives way to river sand at about 2.50 m. below the surface. The section taken as a whole demonstrates that there is no direct correlation between the culture-bearing beds in the abri with river deposits of the Vézère River.

We can now turn to the relation of the river sands in the abri to river deposits in the Vézère Valley adjacent to the site. The modern river has flooded this area at least six times since 1904. The highest flood on record (9 December 1944) reached an elevation of 61.93 m.[2] (fig. 3). The flood of 1843 is estimated to have been of about the same magnitude, although no local records are available. It appears that the surface shown in figure 3 is the floodplain of the 10-year flood, and that the 1944 and 1843 floods

[2] The record level attained by the "Great Flood" of October 1962, which was artificially controlled by the opening of the floodgates at the Donzère Dam, is not considered here.

represent the 100-year floods which reached higher than the river sands exposed in the excavation of the abri.

The cultural deposits in the abri are contained in the éboulis deposits derived by gravity fall. They overlie sands previously deposited by the Vézère. From figure 3 we can see that the fine materials expected in the modern floodplain are missing in the abri. Assuming that they were once present, then, by extrapolating from the sedimentary sequence in the floodplain, the level of the ancient floodplain, prior to the formation of the éboulis in the abri, was a minimum of 3 m. higher than the sand and a minimum of 4 m. above the present floodplain. The 100-year flood level, again extrapolating from the present, would have been at least 5.50 m. above the present floodplain (see fig. 3).

We have no evidence which indicates when the river reached its present level. It may have dropped to its present level at any time subsequent to the deposition of the sands in the abri.

As Farrand points out, the filling of the abri with éboulis began an estimated 35,000 years B.P. Elsewhere in the valley of the Vézère, shelters and their cultural levels are within reach of the modern floods. These include Laugerie-Haute (Upper Périgordian - Early Magdalenian), La Madeleine (Magdalenian), and Le Moustier (Mousterian). Thus the stream does not seem to have been much different in level during the last 50,000 years, and the presumption is in favor of a Vézère that was at essentially its present level when the Abri Pataud was occupied.

Are there terrace levels or deposits in the Vézère with which the river sands below the abri can be correlated?

We have mapped the terrace levels and, where exposed, have examined their sediments in the Vézère Valley from 7 km. upstream from Les Eyzies to the confluence of the Vézère with the Dordogne at Limeuil. Approximately 60 percent of the valley floor is occupied by the modern floodplain. This is subdivided into a low, narrow segment hugging the river edge. It stands on average about 3 m. above low-water level and has a maximum width of about 30 m. It is flooded every 2 or 3 years. Above this is the main valley floor at about 5 m. above low-water

stage. This is the floodplain level shown in figure 3. It is flooded by the 10-year flood and is 300 to 400 m. wide in some places. Exposures and hand-augering show that it is underlain by sediments similar to those at Les Eyzies (see fig. 3). In places along the valley wall and presently protected from erosion by the Vézère River are higher levels whose sediments record higher levels of flow than that of the present. These terraces are underlain immediately beneath the surface by stream gravels of quartz, chert, and crystalline rock. No deposits of clay or silt typical of the upper portion of a floodplain are preserved. The remnants of gravels show no consistent levels from which former stream levels can be constructed. If the floodplain level estimated to be related to the river sands in the Abri Pataud is projected along the Vézère, however, all deposits older than the modern floodplain lie above the projected gradient. Accordingly, we conclude that there is no terrace level or any riverine deposits in the Vézère Valley which we can suggest as equivalent to the river sands in the Abri Pataud.

In closing this section we may summarize as follows:

1. The archaeological stratigraphy in the Abri Pataud cannot be physically correlated with the history of the Vézère River.

2. The archaeological stratigraphy is younger than some river-laid sands forming the lowest sedimentary units in the abri. These sands represent a river which had a gradient at least 4 m. above the modern Vézère.

3. The river sands in the abri have no demonstrable stratigraphic equivalent in the terraces or sediments of the Vézère Valley.

4. We cannot say with certainty whether the Vézère established its present grade before, during, or after the occupation of the Abri Pataud. In view of this uncertainty, there is the possibility that flood waters could have introduced a sand fraction into the abri from the Vézère during the interval of éboulis accumulation, assuming that the river had a flood flow 5.50 m. above the present high-water mark. This would have brought flood levels up to an elevation of about 66 m. As we will see later, Farrand attributes the emplacement of a small volume of Vézère sand in the éboulis to wind action.

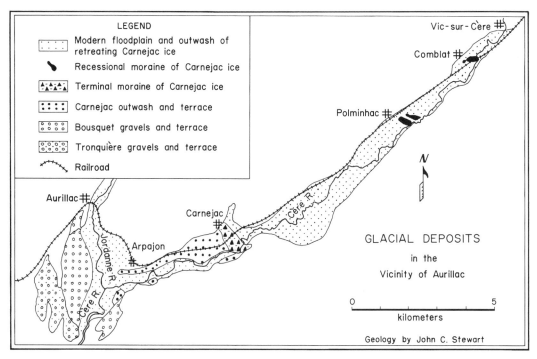

LEGEND
Modern floodplain and outwash of retreating Carnejac ice
Recessional moraine of Carnejac ice
Terminal moraine of Carnejac ice
Carnejac outwash and terrace
Bousquet gravels and terrace
Tronquière gravels and terrace
Railroad

GLACIAL DEPOSITS
in the
Vicinity of Aurillac

0   kilometers   5

Geology by John C. Stewart

Figure 4. Glacial Deposits in the Cère Valley, Near Aurillac. Mapping by John C. Stewart.

FURTHER OBSERVATIONS

We have demonstrated that we cannot relate the events in the Abri Pataud directly to events in the Vézère Valley, nor can we establish a geologic chronology in the Vézère Valley which is in whole or in part synchronous with the events in the Abri Pataud. We can make some further observations, however, and in the following pages we report briefly on Late Pleistocene Glaciation in the Massif Central, on the relation of this ice to the Dordogne Valley, and on the conditions in the Lower Dordogne Valley.

GLACIATION IN THE MASSIF CENTRAL

The details are not established, but it has long been clear that the Massif Central was glaciated several times during the Pleistocene. We examined one area in some detail in an attempt to establish a glacial sequence that could be applicable to the Dordogne Valley. We chose to study the Cère River Valley.[3] The Cère enters the Dordogne near the town of Bretenoux, and the Jordanne enters the Cère just south of Aurillac.

[3] The bulk of these investigations were conducted by Professor John C. Stewart, Brooklyn College.

The Pleistocene deposits in the Upper Cère Valley are shown in figure 4. The oldest deposits are those of the Tronquière terrace (named for a small locality 3 km. south of Aurillac) and of the Bousquet terrace (named for a small village 4 km. south of Aurillac). The Tronquière terrace stands about 42 m. above the grade of the Jordanne River and the Bousquet terrace stands about 23 m. above the present grade. Their deposits have similar lithologies. Gravels up to boulder size are deeply weathered basalts and andesites. Other crystallines have been decomposed beyond recognition. It is impossible on the basis of internal structure or field relations to assign these deposits to glaciofluvial, glacial, or fluvial origin. Their precise age is not known but they most certainly predate the Würm.

Glacial deposits of Würm age are represented by both till and outwash. The most significant feature is the cross-valley moraine at the town of Carnejac and the outwash terrace related to it. The low moraine stands 12 m. above the Cère River, is steep on its upstream face, and downstream grades gently into an outwash terrace that can be traced 4 km. downstream to near Arpajon. Andesite and basalt dominate the lithology of the deposits, but other rock types are present. Thus at Arpajon outwash gravels show the following pebble lithology: andesite, 53 percent; basalt, 24 percent; quartz, 10 percent; schist, 7 percent; chert, 4 percent; and limestone, 2 percent. Chemical decomposition is noticeable on both the schists and limestone to a depth of ca. one meter. Limestone is absent to a depth of about 35 cm. below the surface.

Two additional constructional moraines partially block the valley upstream from the Carnejac moraine. One is at Polminhac, the other at Comblat (see fig. 4).

Essentially no valley train is associated with the Polminhac moraine, and in the case of the moraine at Comblat the remaining remnant of the outwash plain merges with the modern floodplain about 300 m. downstream from the moraine.

The well-preserved constructional forms indicate that the deposits of till and outwash represent Würm ice. We cannot say more except that it is almost certain that glacial ice stood in this and other valleys of the Massif Central during the time of the Upper Palaeolithic occupation of the Abri Pataud at Les Eyzies.

OUTWASH OF WÜRM AGE NEAR BRETENOUX

On its way to the Dordogne the Cère flows in a precipitously walled valley which drops 400 m. in 40 km. The glacial deposits described above existed upstream from this steep valley section. In the Bretenoux area there are water-laid gravels thought to be outwash from the Würm ice, which halted at Carnejac ca. 80 km. upstream.

The gravels, which underlie a terrace here called the Biars terrace for the village of the same name, have the form of a low cone whose apex points upstream toward the Cère canyon. Lithologically it is similar to the outwash of the Carnejac ice except for the addition of granite and gneiss, which are exposed along the Gorge of the Cère. Weathering is similar to that on the outwash of the Carnejac moraine. The deposits are younger than those of the higher terrace of the Bretenoux area mapped on the French geologic maps as *alluvions anciennes*. There is no direct tie

between the Biars terrace upstream to the outwash terrace of the Carnejac ice, and only modern river deposits can be found in the Gorge of the Cère. But it is entirely reasonable to assign the Biars terrace to an advance of the Würm ice, and probably to more than a single stage.

Downstream from the junction of the Cère with the Dordogne it is increasingly difficult to identify deposits contemporary with the Biars terrace deposits. By the time one has proceeded downstream as far as Floriac, 15 km. along the Dordogne to the west, there exists no low terrace correlative with the Biars terrace. Either it has been destroyed by erosion or the Biars terrace originally graded to the modern valley floor. We are of the strong opinion that the latter is the case, and that the Biars terrace and its terrace cone are only a local development near the junction of the Cère with the Dordogne.

Assuming that the Biars terrace is of Würm age, it is still impossible to extend this time line down the Dordogne farther than 15 km. There is no chance of directly correlating the Würm deposits with either the Vézère River Valley or with the Abri Pataud.

THE LOWER DORDOGNE VALLEY

We spent some time examining the Dordogne near its junction with the Gironde estuary. None of our data are applicable to an understanding of the Abri Pataud, except perhaps to note the nature of the river during the Pleistocene. Thus, during the Upper Palaeolithic occupation of the Abri Pataud, the sea level was lower and the estuary of the Gironde did not exist; a through-flowing river emptied into the Atlantic at some point beyond the present estuary. Borings along the Dordogne and the Gironde reveal a bedrock floor beginning about at Pessac, the upstream limit of present tidal influence, and continuing at least to Pointe de Grave at the estuary mouth. Here the bedrock floor is 50 m. below sea level, and presumably it declines still more farther west. The shore line of Würm time is estimated to have been ca. 120 km., more or less, west of the present shore.

CONCLUSIONS

This study has proved disappointing from the standpoint of developing a regional chronology of Late Pleistocene events into which the sequence and the Abri Pataud could be fitted. We have found (1) that the stratigraphy of the site cannot be stratigraphically tied to the deposits of the Vézère River; (2) that the Late Pleistocene chronology of the Vézère is not understandably recorded in the river deposits and other features of the valley; (3) that a detailed Last Glacial chronology from the region is not available; and (4) what glacial sequence can be demonstrated is not amenable to strict stratigraphic correlation with the Abri Pataud.

In a more positive way we can say that at some time before the accumulation of the éboulis in the Abri Pataud, the Vézère River flowed at least 4 m. above its present level. It then dropped to its present level probably by the time the occupation of the site began. During this occupation, valley glaciers existed in the Massif Central to the east and extended down valleys to within approximately 600 m. above sea level. The outwash from some of these glaciers reached the Dordogne River, but they did not appreciably change its grade except locally. To the west, sea level dropped and the shoreline stood over 100 km. farther west than today, and the estuary of the Gironde, if it existed, was displaced westward as well.

Glaciation was accompanied by a displacement of climate and vegetation belts. The warm temperate climate, such as that of today or of the Interglacial Periods, was replaced by more rigorous conditions perhaps similar to those now found in the higher portions of the Massif Central. Locally, the climate and vegetation was affected by the details of the topography of the Vézère Valley, which served to ameliorate the climate at least on the southwestward-facing valley wall in which the Abri Pataud is located. The details of this climate are recorded and discussed in the subsequent chapters by Farrand, Donner, Wilson, and Drury.

TABLE 1

Station	Elevation Meters	Mean Annual T°C	Mean Annual Ppt. mm.	Mean daily Min. of coldest month	Absolute min.	No. months mean min. of month 0°C	No. months absolute min. of month 0°	Yrs. of Record
Arcachon	10	13.8	874	3.4	-9.6	0	6	40
Cazaux	20	12.7	881	2.0	nd	nd	nd	40
Bordeaux	47	12.9	833	1.8	-13.0	0	8	40
Bergerac	33	12.8	730	0.6	-10.6	0	7	40
Périgueux	87	12.2	821	0.0	-17.8	0	8	40
Brive	112	12.4	1011	-0.1	-20.5	1	7	40
Tulle	250	11.5	1204	-0.5	−15.5	2	7	40
St. Cère	152	12.4	948	0.4	nd	nd	nd	40
Aurillac	685	9.5	1065	-1.8	-1065	3	6	40
Le Puy	715	9.6	649	-2.4	-27.0	3	6	40
La Courtine	765	8.4	1375	-2.3	nd	5	nd	40
Puy-de-Dôme	1467	4.2	1770	-4.4	-21.0	6	4	40

Table 1. Climatic Data for Selected Stations in the Aquitanian Basin and the Massif Central. From **Heinrich Walter and Helmut Leith**, Klima-diagramm – Welt Atlas, Gustav Fischer Verlag, Jena, 1960.

III

Analysis of the Abri Pataud Sediments

William R. Farrand

DEPARTMENT OF GEOLOGY & MINERALOGY
THE UNIVERSITY OF MICHIGAN

The writer is most grateful to H.L. Movius, Jr., who strongly encouraged him to undertake this kind of sedimentological study, and who made available all the resources, material, and information of the Abri Pataud Excavations. His experience and insight were invaluable in evaluating the nature and stratigraphy of those sediments that had been entirely removed before the writer was introduced to the Abri Pataud (in 1964). I wish also to express my gratitude to Mrs. John P. Miller who made available the notebooks of her late husband who had begun the sedimentological study of the Abri Pataud in 1958.

Numerous French colleagues have been especially helpful in giving good counsel and in helping with certain analyses of the sediments. Eugène Bonifay introduced the writer to his particular methods of cave sediment analysis, and has been a constant consultant. Messrs. H. de Lumley and H. Laville have also discussed the Abri Pataud sediments with the writer and have guided him on visits to numerous other cave sites in southwestern France. Madame Mireille Ters very kindly provided the heavy mineral analyses that were so useful in determining the different sources of sediments. Professor Georges Millot opened his laboratory in Strasbourg to the writer during the first two critical years of this study; and two members of Millot's team, Mlle. Hélène Paquet and M. Güröl Ataman, kindly provided the clay mineral and chemical analyses, respectively.

Finally, and most important, the entire study would certainly not have been done without the support in the form of a postdoctoral fellowship to the writer, provided by the Air Force Office of Scientific Research and the National Academy of Sciences during the academic year 1963-1964.

INTRODUCTION

GEOLOGICAL FRAMEWORK

The Abri Pataud was, during the time it was occupied by prehistoric man, a rock-shelter or *abri-sous-roche,* that is, an undercut reentrant along the base of a bedrock limestone cliff in which man or beast could find shelter from the elements by virtue of the overhanging bedrock roof. The maximum depth of the abri from the drip line of the brow to the contemporary back wall was probably never greater than 10 to 12 meters. Thus, the abri was naturally illuminated by daylight throughout its existence, although direct sunlight, except for the late afternoon sun, undoubtedly did not enter far into the shelter.

By the time of the Proto-Magdalenian occupation (Level 2), however, the overhang had been reduced to only 6 meters by a series of collapses of the brow. About 20,000 years ago the abri was entirely filled by sediments, natural and artificial. Many similar rock-shelters still exist along the limestone cliffs bordering the Vézère River, and many collapsed and filled shelters have been brought to light in archaeological excavations, e.g., Laugerie-Haute. Thus, the abri at the Pataud site is by no means a unique occurrence in this valley.

The lateral extent of the abri cannot be determined on the basis of the excavation reported here. Our excavation extends 16 meters along the base of the rock cliff, but there is no reason to think that the rock-shelter may not have had a lateral extent two or three times as great as that of the area excavated.

The height of the abri, that is, from floor to ceiling, is difficult to reconstruct; however, for the time of the occupations of Levels 4 and 5 a reasonable estimate of the height of the abri would be about 4 meters.

Both the height and the depth of the abri, and perhaps also its lateral extent, changed through time. The change is best documented by the progressive shift of the inner wall of the abri, which stood about

3 to 4 meters east of the O m. N-S grid line during the occupations of Levels 14 through 12, then shifted to a position about 7 m. east during Level 11 time, and finally retreated to a line about 12 m. east during Level 4 time, since which time the inner wall has been stable (fig. 1). This amounts to a retreat of 8 or 9 m. over some 7,000 to 9,000 years. We shall discuss the details of this evolution of the configuration of the abri in a later section.

The Abri Pataud faces slightly south of west, and the uppermost deposits preserved therein lie about 14 m. above the Vézère floodplain surface, or about 76 m. above sea level (see p. 8). The lowest known occurrence of bedrock within the excavated area lies at about the same altitude as the present floodplain surface, thus about 62 m. above sea level, and alluvial sand was encountered at that same altitude in the 1953 test trench (fig. 1). It is not known whether the Vézère deposits extend all the way to the bedrock valley wall at this altitude, although this is very likely since the occurrence of Vézère sand in the 1953 Test Trench is separated only 9 or 10 m. horizontally from the lowest known occurrence of bedrock.

It is very interesting that the occurrence of Vézère sand in the 1953 Test Trench lies at the same altitude as the present floodplain surface just a few tens of meters to the west, and this floodplain is flooded at

the present time whenever the Vézère spreads out of its banks, as it did, for example, several times during the years of the excavation (1958-1964). Therefore, one can conclude that the Vézère was flowing and flooding at essentially the same level some 30,000 years ago as it is today. It seems most likely that the river has remained constantly at this same level during the last 35,000 years or so, although one cannot rule out, in the absence of suitable data, the possibility of a lower river stage at some time during these 35,000 years. On the other hand, there is certainly no evidence in the Abri Pataud that the Vézère was ever significantly higher during the past 35,000 years than it is today. None of the Abri Pataud deposits that lie at an altitude higher than that of the present floodplain show any characteristics of fluvial deposition, nor is there any evidence of an erosional interval that could be attributed to scouring by the waters of the Vézère.

ORIGIN OF THE ABRI PATAUD

The overhanging rock ledge that formed the Abri Pataud during Upper Palaeolithic times apparently developed in a manner similar to the numerous rock-shelters that presently exist along the Vézère

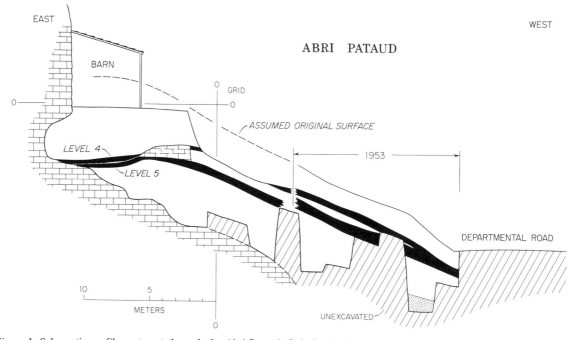

Figure 1. Schematic profile east-west through the Abri Pataud. Only Levels 4 and 5 are shown; note that they dip both inward and outward from the area of large roof falls. Vézère sand is exposed in the bottom of the 1953 trench at the same altitude as the surface of the modern Vézère floodplain, which is not shown but abuts the departmental road immediately to the west of this section. Note also that the bedrock floor of the abri rises in step fashion towards the inner wall, each step representing a period of retreat of the rear wall.

Valley. Like the Abri Pataud the great majority of the modern rock-shelters lie well above the level of the river, and they cannot be attributed to fluvial erosion or undercutting. Moreover, the observation that many of the smaller niches that line the bedrock walls of the valley seem to follow the stratification of the limestone suggests that such niches are localized by differential weathering of the bedrock. More specifically, some limestone strata are more soluble, more permeable, or more susceptible to frost weathering than are other limestone strata. The more susceptible layers begin to form niches, and certain of these niches may become enlarged into rock-shelters.

Once formed, a rock-shelter will begin to accumulate a sedimentary fill that under a climate similar to that of southwestern France during Last Glacial times will consist of limestone debris (éboulis) resulting from solution and frost weathering of the ceiling and walls, as well as of sediments brought in from outside the shelter by running water, the wind, or human beings. It is this sedimentary fill and its variations that are of most interest to the geologist studying the paleoenvironment of prehistoric habitations, and this will be the primary concern of this chapter.

On the other hand, the question of origin of the Abri Pataud is of some interest. It is only of geologic interest, however, since the lowermost deposits in the abri are archaeologically sterile. Moreover, we know at one limit that the abri was in existence in Basal Aurignacian times. The sterile éboulis below Level 14 averages 1.65 m. thick, thus representing about 1,000 years of accumulation according to our extrapolation of the rate of sedimentation determined for Levels 7 through 14 (fig. 10). On this basis, the earliest deposits would date from about 35,000 B.P. It is certainly possible, however, that the abri was in existence long before that date and that whatever sediment had accumulated was evacuated by the Vézère, or that the slope of the floor of the abri was too steep to retain the debris. Any further estimation of the date of origin of the abri would be pure speculation.

In summary, it can be said that the Abri Pataud originated some 35,000 or more years ago by processes of differential weathering of the limestone bedrock walls of the valley. Frost action and solution of the limestone produced an overhanging rock ledge that increased in size until some 27,000 years ago. After that time the abri became progressively smaller owing to instability and successive collapses of the bedrock roof, and it was completely filled with sedimentary debris and no longer functioning as a rock-shelter after about 20,000 years ago.

THE SEDIMENTARY FILL OF THE ABRI PATAUD

Geologically the filling of the Abri Pataud is relatively simple. With the exception of the Éboulis 3/4: Red, the fill consists of limestone éboulis with greater or lesser additions of windblown (eolian) sand and of human occupational debris. The eolian component is volumetrically always a minor element, except in the base of Level 5, in Éboulis 10/11, and perhaps in the Éboulis 3/4:Red. Similarly, human occupational debris does not play an important role in determining the character of the sediments except in the cases of Levels 2, 3, 4, and 5. In the other occupational horizons human debris is volumetrically a very minor component. Such a characterization, or simplification, of the sedimentary fill is in no way a denial of the presence of very real and important variations in the composition of the éboulis, as we shall see.

The Éboulis 3/4:Red differs markedly from the underlying and overlying sediments in the near total absence of any material larger than 1 mm. in diameter, its strong brown color, and its high percentage of clay-size sediment. These and other characteristics mark the Red Éboulis as a weathered horizon, if not in fact a true soil. It thus constitutes a sedimentary unit significantly different from the rest of the

fill, and at the same time its surface is a stratigraphic break of some importance.

ARCHAEOLOGICAL STRATIGRAPHY

Although given in detail elsewhere in this volume, the stratigraphic succession determined by the archaeologists at the Abri Pataud is repeated below for convenience. Each archaeologically rich horizon has been designated a level and numbered serially from top to bottom in the section. The intervening relatively sterile units have been called "éboulis" and have been numbered with respect to the levels that they separate.

Éboulis 0/1	Post-Early Solutrean
Level 1	Early Solutrean (?)
Éboulis 1/2	
Level 2	Proto-Magdalenian
Éboulis 2/3	
Level 3	Périgordian VI
Éboulis 3/4: Yellow	
Éboulis 3/4: Red	
Level 4	Noaillian
Éboulis 4/5	

Level 5	Périgordian IV
Éboulis 5/6	
Level 6	Evolved Aurignacian
Éboulis 6/7	
Level 7	Intermediate Aurignacian (b)
Éboulis 7/8	
Level 8	Intermediate Aurignacian (a)
Éboulis 8/9	
Level 9	Intermediate Aurignacian (?)
Éboulis 9/10	
Level 10	Intermediate Aurignacian (?)
Éboulis 10/11	
Level 11	Early Aurignacian (b)
Éboulis 11/12	
Level 12	Early Aurignacian (a)
Éboulis 12/13	
Level 13	Basal Aurignacian (b)
Éboulis 13/14	
Level 14	Basal Aurignacian (a)
Basal Éboulis	

GEOLOGICAL UNITS

The sedimentary fill of the Abri Pataud has been subdivided into six major geological units (a through f), each comprising one or more of the archaeological stratigraphic units. This subdivision is based on the general homogeneity of the sediments and the presence of distinct interruptions or changes in type of sedimentation. The subdivisions are as follows:

a. Limestone éboulis, pale brown (10 YR 7/4) to pale yellow (10 YR 7/6), relatively fine-grained (in general 40 to 60% of the sediment is smaller than 2 mm. in grain size), highly angular limestone fragments; this unit includes several large blocks of the collapsed roof of the shelter, the largest of which measures 5.5 m. east-west and 2 m. high; includes archaeological Levels 1, 2, and 3; average thickness is 2.73 m. from the top of Level 1 to the base of Éboulis 3/4:Yellow.

b. Sandy loam (top) to loamy sand (base), reddish yellow (7.5 YR 6/6) to strong brown (7.5 YR 5/7); rare limestone fragments are somewhat rounded; average thickness 36 cm.; archaeologically nearly sterile (= Éboulis 3/4:Red).

c. Limestone éboulis, dark reddish brown (5 YR 3/4), moderately fine-grained (50 to 60% finer than 2 mm.), limestone fragments somewhat rounded;

archaeologically rich (Level 4, Noaillian); averages 26.8 cm. thick.

d. Limestone éboulis, strong brown (7.5 YR 5/6), somewhat coarser than units c and e (about 40% finer than 2 mm.), rather angular limestone fragments; includes very large block resulting from roof collapse (ca. 5 m. east-west, 1 m. thick, and more than 6 m. north-south); archaeologically nearly sterile; averages 37 cm. thick and constitutes the entirety of Éboulis 4/5.

e. Limestone éboulis with abundant occupational debris, thinly bedded, varying in color from dark brown (7.5 YR 3/2 to 4/4), dark reddish brown (5 YR 3/3), brown (10 YR 4/3) to strong brown (7.5 YR 5/6) from bed to bed; moderately well-rounded limestone fragments; basal layers rich in micaceous sand; archaeologically very rich (Level 5, Périgordian IV); averages 27.3 cm. thick within the area of the site, but thickening down the talus slope in front of the abri, where it averages 62.5 cm. thick in Extensions 1 and 2.

f. Limestone éboulis, pale yellow (2.5 Y 8/4 or 10 YR 8/6) to very pale brown (10 YR 7/4), rather coarse-grained (in general only 20 to 40% finer than 2 mm.); the matrix is distinctly sandy; limestone fragments rather angular except in the lowest 50 cm. where they are moderately well rounded to well rounded; includes numerous limestone blocks in the size range of 20-30 cm. to 1 m., but lacking in giant blocks such as those in units a and d. One conspicuous exception to this general characterization is Éboulis 10/11: Wash, a strong brown sandy lens at the inner limit of Éboulis 10/11. The name "Wash" was given to this stratum because of its wedge-shaped configuration against the bedrock wall of the abri. On the whole, archaeological remains are rather scarce, although local concentrations (Levels 6 through 14, all Aurignacian) are present; the occupational layers can, in some cases, be traced by their color (black charcoal or red ochre), but the percentage of cultural debris relative to limestone éboulis is in all cases quite small; average thickness 4.78 m., of which the lowermost 1.65 m. ("Basal Éboulis") is sterile.

The total average thickness of the fill is 8.79 m. (see appendix 1).

METHODS OF STUDY

BACKGROUND AND PREVIOUS WORK

Geological study and more particularly sedimentological study played a very small role or none at all in the interpretation of prehistoric cave sites prior to 1940. Since that time several European geologist-prehistorians, inspired by the work of Lais (1941) have developed techniques for the systematic study of cave and rock-shelter sediments and have applied these techniques in different areas: in France (Bonifay 1956, de Lumley 1969, Laville 1964, 1969); in Switzerland (Schmid 1958); in Germany (Brunnacker and Streit 1967); and in Hungary (Vértes 1959). The general goal of such studies is an interpretation of the paleoenvironment, and specifically the paleoclimate, under which the cave or rock-shelter deposits accumulated. It is desirable to have an independent source of information on paleoclimate because of complications in interpretations based on fossil floras and faunas. In caves inhabited by man the macroflora and macrofauna incorporated in the strata may have been strongly influenced by the habits and particularly the diet of the inhabitants; micro-flora (pollen) is lacking in many cases because of poor preservation; and the job of washing and screening for a large sample of microfauna may be rather time consuming. On the other hand, the sedimentary framework in which the artifacts are found is always present and has been found to be quite amenable to paleoclimatological interpretation in certain areas. If pollen and microfauna are also present, then there is the possibility of independent checks on the interpretation.

Paleoclimatic interpretation of the sediments is based on two groups of variables: (a) those concerning the character of the sediment as it originally accumulated, and (b) those concerning the changes, mainly weathering, undergone by the sediment since it was deposited. In extreme cases, the latter may completely mask the former, although in the usual case some aspects of the original sediment can be observed in spite of changes imposed by weathering.

In this study the parameters in category (a) are granulometry, degree of sorting, abundance of travertine concretions, heavy mineral suite, and the degree of human influence. In category (b) they are the abundance of clay-size fraction, variations in clay mineralogy (in part), rounding and porosity of the stone fraction, abundance of soil concretions, calcimetry and pH of the fine fraction.

SAMPLING

Ideally geological sampling of the sediments should be done simultaneously with the archaeological excavation and should be done by the geologist. In practice this is often not possible, and samples must be taken from sections remaining after the conclusion of the excavation, as was the case for the majority of samples studied here. Only the lowermost deposits in the site (Sample Series AP 6) and the talus sediments in Extension 1 (Sample Series AP 11) were sampled at the same time as they were being exposed by the archaeologists. However, sampling after the termination of excavation at the Abri Pataud does not seem to have introduced any complications into our study. It is, nevertheless, conceivable that sampling from old sections could introduce a bias, especially if the site in question had been nearly completely emptied by archaeologists, as was commonly the practice in the past, so that only marginal sections of the deposits remain, for example, against the back and side walls of a rock-shelter. Such sections may not be at all typical.

Another complication in dealing with rock-shelter and cave sediments that formed under frost climates is the coarseness of these sediments. All sizes of rock debris from clay particles to rock fragments measuring several meters on a side may be included in a given stratum. This is generally the case in southwestern France. Commonly, granulometric studies are limited to the size fraction less than 2 mm. in diameter. Such a restriction, however, would mean ignoring more than half of the volume of sediments in many rock-shelter strata. In addition, it has been shown (e.g., Bonifay 1956) that the coarse rock fraction of the sediment can be extremely informative in the interpretation of paleoclimates, not only as far as the granulometry is concerned, but also in the morphology and porosity of the rock fragments. Thus, it is deemed very important to study the coarse fraction as well as the fine fraction of such sediments.

Nevertheless, there is a practical limit to the size of rock fragments that can be taken to the laboratory. Bonifay (1956) chose a longest dimension of 10 cm. as the upper limit of materials submitted to laboratory tests, and this arbitrary limit has been adopted by Laville (1964) and by us for this study. However, even this relatively small size limit imposes the necessity of taking relatively large samples, commonly 10 to 20 kg., in order to assure an adequate statistical sample of the larger fragments.

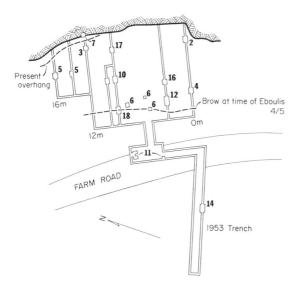

Figure 2. Map view of the locations of sediment sampling columns at the Abri Pataud.

In general practice, one samples a vertical column of sediments from the top to the bottom of the stratigraphic succession within a rock-shelter or cave. The sampling column is chosen so as to pass through as typical a section of sediments as possible. If the geologist has not been able to follow the excavation in detail, he must rely on the archaeologist's opinion of what is most typical.

At the Abri Pataud we have been able to expand our sedimentological study to include several sampling columns scattered throughout the site, both under the former abri and outside on the talus (figs. 2 and 3). The goal of such a sampling program was to verify the assumption that a single sampling column is really representative of the entire site, and we believe that this is the first time anyone has attempted such verification. In anticipation of the presentation of our results it can be said that the various sampling columns showed excellent agreement with one another, and at the same time the differences in amplitude of certain parameters, especially between samples from under the abri and those on the talus, were helpful in pointing out lateral variations in the processes affecting the sediments.

At the Abri Pataud we collected 18 different series of samples, numbered AP 1 through AP 18. Thirteen of these series are the sampling columns from the site

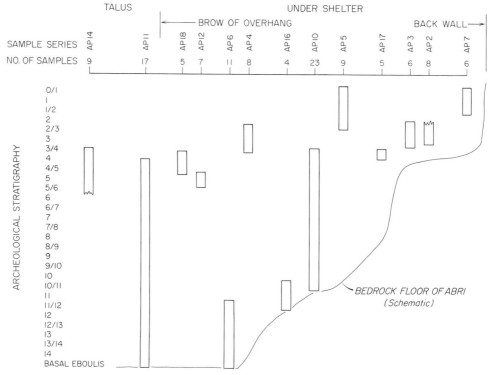

Figure 3. Schematic profile east-west through the Abri Pataud showing the relation of sampling columns to stratigraphy and to position inside or outside the shelter.

itself (including the talus) and are shown in figures 2 and 3. The other five are miscellaneous samples taken for specialized studies, such as bedrock (AP 9), modern éboulis (AP 8), sandy layers (AP 13), and Vézère floodplain sand (AP 15). Individual samples within each series are numbered consecutively from top to bottom of the sampling column, e.g., AP 5-1, AP 5-2, etc. The exact stratigraphic position of the various samples can best be seen in plate I.

Typical sampling columns, such as those shown in plate II, are about 25 cm. wide, 15 to 20 cm. deep, and the individual samples were about 5 to 15 cm. thick. The thickness of an individual sample and the vertical interval between samples in a given column were dictated by the degree of vertical variation in the sediments. Even in relatively thick beds in which there was no obvious variation, samples were taken every 20 to 25 cm. apart. The sediment was loosened with a small pick and a brush, and care was taken not to break up the rock fragments in the process. Rock fragments that were apparently shattered by frost after being incorporated in the sediment (*cailloux gélivés* of Bonifay 1956) were noted and bagged separately. All rock fragments within the sample area that were larger than 10 cm. were noted, measured, and discarded.

FIELD ANALYSIS

Preliminary treatment of the samples was effected in the field and consisted of the following steps:

1. The total sample ($\leqslant$ 100 mm. particle size) was spread out on a canvas or plastic sheet and allowed to dry to a constant weight in the sun; any particularly fragile bone fragments or flints were separated at this time; then the sample (including the fragile materials) was weighed.

2. The entire sample was then sieved dry through two nested 18-inch-diameter sieves, one with a 10 mm. screen and the other with a 2 mm. screen; after collecting a 1- or 2-kg. sample of the fraction finer than 2 mm., we washed the material retained on the two sieves in order to remove any fine sediments, especially clay, that adhered to the larger rock fragments; the material on the sieves was again dried and weighed; the result of this operation was to divide the total sample into three fractions:

Fraction A, comprising sediment between 100 mm. and 10 mm.;
Fraction B, the sediment between 10 and 2 mm.; and
Fraction C, the sediment finer than 2 mm.

3. At this point all the cultural debris (flint, bones, exotic stones, etc.) was separated from the A frac-

tion, weighed and called Fraction D. The weight of Fraction D was not included in the sum A+B+C.

Thus, in the field one can immediately obtain an analysis of the overall granulometry of the rock-shelter sediments; this is shown in the far left (A, B, and C fractions) and far right (D fraction) columns of plate I. One can, therefore, immediately evaluate the overall coarseness of the sediment and the amount of matrix (C fraction), as well as the intensity of human habitation (D fraction) from layer to layer throughout the abri fill. The only equipment required at this stage is a pair of sieves, a balance capable of weighing 20 or 25 kg., running water, and either a sunny climate or a large oven. There is no theoretical basis for separating the A from the B fraction at 10 mm.; this is done simply for convenience. One should think of the total sediment as being composed of two principal components by size, the rock fragments (A + B fractions) and the fine (C) fraction, which is composed primarily of individual mineral grains, sand size and smaller.

LABORATORY ANALYSIS

In the laboratory a number of studies were conducted on both the A fraction (rock fragments) and the C fraction (fines). The B fraction, which consists primarily of small limestone fragments between 10 and 2 mm., was not studied in detail because the small size of the fragments makes them difficult to manipulate. The B fraction enters into the granulometric analysis only.

The A fraction was first divided into nine size classes of 10 mm. each on the basis of the longest dimension of each fragment, according to the Bonifay (1956) method. However, in order to be consistent with the phi units[1] used to describe the granulometry of the fine fraction, the size distribution of the A and B fraction were later regrouped into phi units. Thus:

2-4 mm.	=	-1 to -2 phi
4-8 mm.	=	-2 to -3
8-16 mm.	=	-3 to -4
16-32 mm.	=	-4 to -5
32-64 mm.	=	-5 to -6
64-96 mm.	=	-6 to -6.5

These units are, therefore, the basis for the histograms of granulometry shown in plate IV, where each bar is one phi unit wide except the bar at the far left which is only 0.5 phi in width.

[1] Phi units are a convenient logarithmic transformation of the Wentworth grade scale based on the relation log d = -Φ (log 2), where d is the grain diameter.

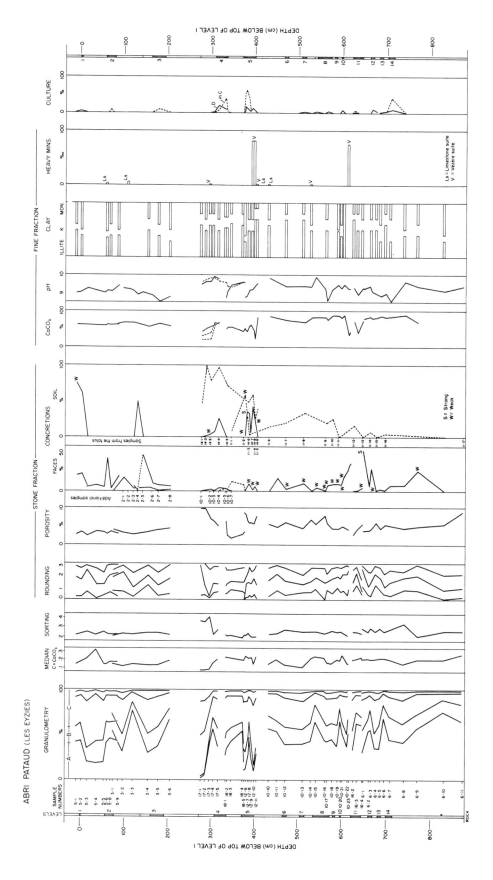

Plate I. Sedimentological analysis of the Abri Pataud.

Plate II. Typical sampling columns at the Abri Pataud: A. Column AP 2; B. Column AP 3; C. Column AP 5. For locations refer to figures 2 and 3.

Next, the stones in each size class of each sample were evaluated for roundness. Roundness in general terms refers to the degree of blunting of originally angular edges of a rock fragment and is independent of the overall shape of the fragment. The scale of roundness goes from very angular to very well rounded. Roundness has been rigorously defined and quantified by different workers in different ways, e.g., as the radius of curvature of the most angular corner of a fragment, or the ratio of that radius to the longest axis of the fragment. However, when dealing with rock fragments that are, on the whole, quite angular or have recently been fractured so that there are freshly broken surfaces it is difficult to draw significant conclusions from the results of such roundness indices. For example, some rock fragments in a sample may have been moderately well rounded and then broken (perhaps by freeze-thaw) before being incorporated into the sediment. Thus, they will probably have some very angular corners and some well-rounded corners. Another frost-derived fragment of the same size may be bounded by angular corners all around. If one applies the criteria given above to these two fragments, the numerical result will be essentially the same, since it is based only on *the* most angular corner and the overall dimensions of the fragment.

Because of such ambiguity it was decided to divide the rock fragments simply into four roundness classes by visual inspection (see pl. III) in a manner similar to the Power's roundness scale (see Folk 1968, p. 11). First, the end members of the roundness spectrum were isolated, namely, those fragments with only angular corners (Class 0) and those fragments with only rounded corners (Class 3). The remaining fragments were separated into intermediate categories, those fragments with more angular corners than rounded corners (Class 1) and those fragments with more rounded corners than angular ones (Class 2). Reproducibility of roundness determinations under this system was evaluated by repeated determinations on the same sample by the same person and by different persons, and it was found to be satisfactory. The class number assigned to each category was intended to be used in the calculation of a roundness index, as done by Bonifay (1956), but it was found that a single numerical value masked some of the information that could be shown in graphical form, as in plate I.

The porosity of rock fragments in each sample was also measured, once again using a method of Bonifay (1956) which consists of immersing dry rock fragments in water until saturated (usually two hours), weighing them while saturated and then weighing them once again after drying at $105°$C to constant weight. Porosity was measured systematically on all fragments between 30 and 50 mm. diameter in all samples. Larger and smaller fragments were not measured in order to limit the sample to a manageable size and to a size range abundantly represented in all the samples. Significant variation in porosity throughout the Abri Pataud section was found (plate I), the range of values lying between 1 and 10% by weight.

The rock fragments were also inspected for traces of concretionary coatings. Two kinds of such coatings were found: (a) a travertinelike concretionary layer formed on the limestone fragments before they were completely detached from the bedrock wall and (b) a chalky soil carbonate that formed on the fragments after they had become part of the sedimentary fill on the floor of the abri. The former could be recognized by its smooth or mamillary surface, slightly more pinkish or orange in color than the limestone itself. In most cases this travertine formed only a very thin film (less than a millimeter thick), but in a few cases it was distinctly more prominent (e.g., AP 5-6, AP 10-23, AP 6-1). In all cases where present it was strictly limited to one face of a rock fragment, and on that face it terminated abruptly at the freshly broken edge. Furthermore, on certain fragments one face, weathered and somewhat rounded, could be identified as the former surface of the bedrock wall and the opposite face, bounded by fresh, angular edges, identified as the fracture along which the fragment was detached from the wall by freeze-thaw. Travertine concretions were found exclusively on the freshly fractured face. These observations constitute the major argument for the hypothesis that this type of concretion formed in a crack in the bedrock wall prior to the fragment having been detached completely from the bedrock. Such concretions are equivalent to the *concrétions p* (= *paroi*) of Bonifay (1956).

The soil concretions, the second type mentioned above, consisted of chalky white or dense, dull grayish white carbonate forming a discontinuous coating on one or several faces of a rock fragment. In cases where this kind of concretion was rather heavy, it generally cemented together sand and silt grains from the sedimentary matrix, thus having a granular and dirty appearance. On the other hand, on those rock fragments on which this type of concretion was weakly developed it commonly took the form of chalky dendritic patterns apparently related to plant rootlets. This type of concretion is similar to that called *concrétions s* (= *sol*) by Bonifay (1956), and because of its correlation with other evidence of weathering as well as its similarity to secondary soil carbonate (e.g., in a C_{ca} horizon), it is considered to

Plate III. Example of Roundness categories (*émoussé* = rounded) utilized in the Abri Pataud study.

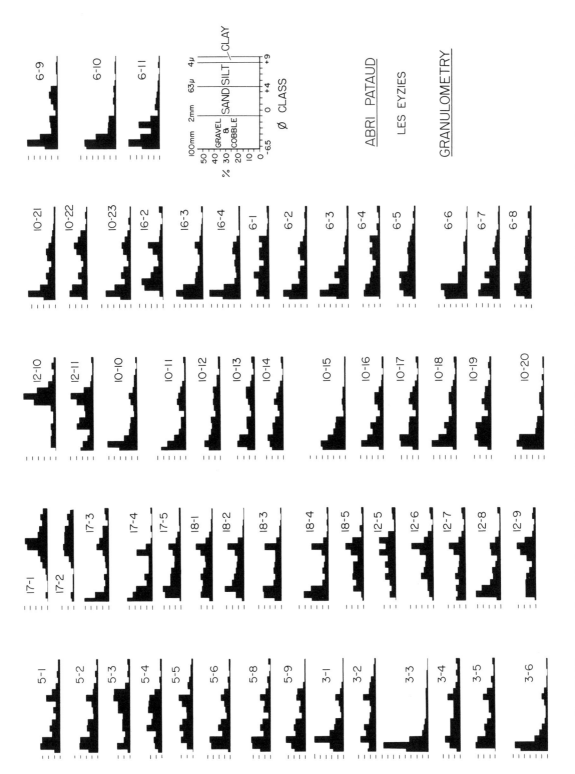

Plate IV. Histograms of particle-size distribution at the Abri Pataud. All bars represent one-phi-interval except the bar at the far left, which is only one-half phi in width. The histograms are arranged in stratigraphic order from AP 5-1 (top left) to AP 6-11 (bottom right).

mark the presence of a pedogenic horizon within the sediments. The intensity of soil carbonate development is one indication of the intensity of the former weathering interval of which it marks the presence. A further clue to the interpretation of such carbonate is its occurrence in the modern soil presently forming on the surface of the limestone éboulis at the Abri Pataud (e.g., samples AP 5-1 and 5-2; see pl. I). The intensity of soil concretions in the modern soil at the northern wall of the excavated area (AP 5 series) is distinctly stronger than at any level lower in the section. This observation appears to indicate that the soil-forming intervals of Upper Palaeolithic times recorded in the Abri Pataud sediments, e.g., Éboulis 3/4 Red, were of shorter duration than the time elapsed since the abri was completely filled (roughly 20,000 years ago).

The C fraction (less than 2 mm. diameter) was also submitted to a number of tests. First, grain-size distribution was determined by sieving for the sand fraction and by means of the Bouyoucos hydrometer for the silt and clay fractions. The results are presented here in various ways. The overall granulometry of the total sample is shown by means of histograms at one-phi intervals (pl. IV). These histograms show very clearly the polymodal nature of the total sample, one peak lying in the range of single-mineral (sand) grains, two others in the rock-fragment (A) fraction. The total granulometry is also shown in plate I (column at the far left) in terms of the A, B, and C fractions, the latter being divided into its sand (2 to 0.063 mm.), silt (0.063 to 0.002 mm.), and clay (less than 0.002 mm.) fractions.[2] For the C fraction alone, the median and the degree of sorting (Trask's coefficient) are given in the second and third columns from the left in plate I.

Chemical analysis of the C fraction consisted of spectrographic analysis of the major elements (appendix 2), determination of the component soluble in hydrochloric acid ("carbonate-equivalent"), and measurement of pH. The results of the latter two determinations are given in plate I.

The principal interest in the major element analysis lies in the determination of SiO_2, Al_2O_3, Fe_2O_3, and CaO, both because they constitute the bulk of each sample (90 to 100%) and because they are the major rock-forming components in the limestone bedrock of the region. At first glance it was noticed that SiO_2, Al_2O_3, and Fe_2O_3 increased several-fold in all beds that seemed, on the basis of independent evidence, to have undergone weathering. Upon closer inspection, however, it seems that the variations in abundance of

[2] Note that different upper limits for the clay-size fraction have been shown in plate I, 0.002 mm., and plate IV, 0.0039 mm.

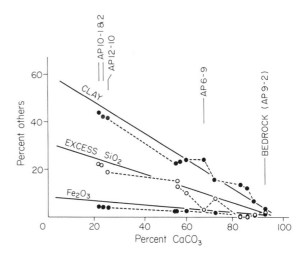

Figure 4. Progressive change in mineralogy of éboulis samples through weathering. Solid straight lines show the calculated change that would be produced by the simple decalcification of bedrock, specifically sample AP 9-2. The points show the actual analyses of éboulis samples from the abri sediments. The scatter of the points is apparently due to minor variations in the composition of the bedrock and to the removal of some of the weathering products by groundwater.

these constituents can be explained simply as the result of greater or lesser decalcification of éboulis that originally had approximately the same chemical composition throughout the section. It is not necessary, and probably not even warranted, to invoke an absolute increase in these constituents in the weathered horizons. This relationship is shown in figure 4, in which these major elements are grouped as "clay mineral" (Al_2O_3 + SiO_2 in the ratio 1/3), "excess SiO_2" (essentially quartz) which is the total SiO_2 in a given sample *less* the SiO_2 used in the calculation of "clay mineral," and "Fe_2O_3". The percentages of these compounds are plotted against the percentage of $CaCO_3$ in each sample. At the extreme right of figure 4 is plotted the analysis of a sample of bedrock (AP 9-2), and the straight, solid lines in the figure show the progressive increase in "clay mineral," excess SiO_2 and Fe_2O_3 that would result from the progressive reduction of $CaCO_3$ below its original value of 94.6%. It can readily be seen that the compositions of the other samples can easily be interpreted to be the results of decalcification of éboulis that originally had a composition close to that of sample AP 9-2. The scatter about the straight lines is apparently a function of slight differences in the bedrock that contributed to different éboulis layers or of a "contamination" of the éboulis by windblown material or human debris. Therefore, the "clay mineral," SiO_2 and Fe_2O_3 increase in the weathered horizons *relative* to the $CaCO_3$-content of these horizons, but there is no absolute increase in these compounds. Indeed, there may have been some removal of them by pedogenic processes, since in general the values for all three fall slightly below the line calculated on the basis of simple decalcification.

The complete chemical analysis discussed above was done on only a dozen samples chosen for their specific interest. On the other hand, the $CaCO_3$-equivalent and pH were measured on the C fraction of all the samples. The $CaCO_3$-equivalent was determined by reacting a representative sample of the C fraction sediment finer than 0.125 mm. diameter with HCl until reaction ceased. Only the finest part of the C fraction was analyzed in the interests of economy of time and materials, since it has been shown for similar deposits that nearly all the variation in calcimetry of the total C fraction is explained by variation in calcimetry of the finer part of that fraction (Laville 1964, p. 44). The values of "$CaCO_3$-equivalent" range from about 90% (in the lower half of the section) to near 20% in the most strongly weathered layers (Éboulis 3/4: Red and Level 5: Base).

The pH of a slurry of the total C fraction in distilled water was determined by means of a pH meter. The pH values, which range between 8.5 and 10, show very little agreement with the $CaCO_3$ values (see plate I and table 3). Tables 1, 2, and 3 were constructed in order to evaluate, if possible, the interrelationship between $CaCO_3$-content and pH and the relationship of each to human habitation and weathering phenomena. Table 1 shows rather clearly that there is no essential difference in $CaCO_3$-content between habitation levels and semi-sterile éboulis. On the other hand, table 2 shows a distinct tendency for occupation levels to show a more acid pH than that found in the semi-sterile éboulis. Seven out of eight samples with pH values lower than 8.9 come from occupation levels. The 25 samples from levels have an average pH of 9.1 whereas the 34 éboulis samples average 9.3. Thus, it seems warranted to suggest that human wastes and garbage tend to produce more acid conditions in the sediments of habitation levels.

On the other hand, table 3 demonstrates rather clearly the relationship of $CaCO_3$-content to weathering phenomena. The totals at the bottom of table 3 are the most revealing. Samples that come from weathered layers or from layers with concretionary soil carbonate exhibit a distinctly lower percentage of

TABLE 1

Calcium carbonate content in C fraction correlated with habitation, weathered, or soil-concretion horizons.

% $CaCO_3$	Level	Éboulis	Total	Weathered Horizon	Soil Concretions
21-25	0	2	2	2	1
26-30	1	0	1	1	0
31-35	0	1	1	1	0
36-40	1	0	1	0	0
41-45	1	3	4	4	2
46-50	2	0	2	2	2
51-55	2	1	3	2	2
56-60	3	5	8	4	4
61-65	4	5	9	2	4
66-70	3	4	7	0	1
71-75	0	1	1	0	0
76-80	2	1	3	0	1
81-85	5	6	11	0	0
86-90	1	5	6	0	0
Totals	25	34	59	18	17

TABLE 2

pH of C fraction as correlated with habitation, weathered, or soil-concretion horizons.

pH	Level	Éboulis	Total	Weathered Horizon	Soil Concretions
8.5	2	1	3	0	0
8.6	0	0	0	0	0
8.7	1	0	1	0	0
8.8	4	0	4	2	2
8.9	2	2	4	1	1
9.0	1	3	4	0	2
9.1	3	2	5	0	0
9.2	4	6	10	5	4
9.3	3	2	5	1	0
9.4	2	4	6	0	1
9.5	0	3	3	1	0
9.6	1	7	8	5	4
9.7	0	0	0	0	0
9.8	1	3	4	2	3
9.9	1	1	2	1	1
Totals	25	34	59	18	18

TABLE 3

pH vs. CaCO$_3$-content in the C fraction at the Abri Pataud.

Per Cent CaCO$_3$

pH	21 to 25	26 to 30	31 to 35	36 to 40	41 to 45	46 to 50	51 to 55	56 to 60	61 to 65	66 to 70	71 to 75	76 to 80	81 to 85	86 to 90	Total	Weathered	Un-Weathered
8.5										1		1	1		3	0	3
8.6															0	0	0
8.7							1								1	0	1
8.8					1	1		1						1	4	2	2
8.9				1				2					1		4	2	2
9.0								1	2				1		4	2	2
9.1									3	1			1		5	0	5
9.2			1		1	1		1	2	1		1	1	1	10	7	3
9.3		1								2	1		1		5	1	4
9.4								1	1	1		1	2		6	1	5
9.5					1									2	3	1	2
9.6	1				1		2	1					2	1	8	5	3
9.7															0	0	0
9.8	2									1				1	4	3	1
9.9									1				1		2	1	1
Total	3	1	1	1	4	2	3	7	9	7	1	3	11	6	59		
Weathered	3	1	1	0	4	2	2	5	5	1	0	1	0	0		25	
Unweathered	0	0	0	1	0	0	1	2	4	6	1	2	11	6			34

(1 = underlined entries are from beds with evidence of weathering.)

$CaCO_3$ than layers that are lacking in indicators of postsedimentary alteration. Samples with indicators of weathering or soil carbonate account for 23 out of 31 samples with less than 65% $CaCO_3$. In contrast, only 2 samples out of 28 with more than 65% $CaCO_3$ show any obvious signs of alteration, and in both cases (Sample AP 17-5 and 6-1) it is a question of soil carbonate that may have simply been translocated from overlying horizons and thus may not reflect weathering of the éboulis in which it is found. The bimodal nature of $CaCO_3$ variation in these sediments is clearly shown by the row of totals at the bottom of table 3 where there are two maxima: one at 61 to 65% and another at 81 to 85%.

Therefore, one can draw the conclusions that (a) human occupational layers tend to have relatively low pH values and (b) weathered layers tend to have low $CaCO_3$ values. Since there is a fairly large overlap in the pH ranges, however, the first generalization cannot be applied indiscriminately; a fairly large number of samples is necessary for its correct application. The second conclusion seems more decisive and easier to apply, although there also is some overlap. Unfortunately these generalizations are not mutually exclusive.

MINERALOGICAL STUDIES

The clay minerals and heavy minerals in the C fraction of the Abri Pataud sediments were identified by two French laboratories specializing in these subjects. The clay minerals were identified by Mlle. Hélène Paquet in the laboratory of Professor Georges Millot at Strasbourg. The three major families of clay minerals in the fraction finer than 2 microns have been identified, and their abundance relative to total clay minerals has been estimated to the nearest 10% (third column from the right in plate I where "Mon" is montmorillonite and "Kc" is kaolinite with perhaps minor quantities of chlorite). Kaolinite is in general the least abundant and the least variable of the three mineral groups. The average abundance and variation in 60 samples of sediment and bedrock is as follows:

TABLE 4

Mineral	Average Abundance	1 Standard Deviation
Kaolinite	18.2%	± 7.4%
Illite	50.3%	± 13.6%
Montmorillonite	31.1%	± 16.5%

In detail, wherever there is an increase in illite, there is a concomitant decrease in montmorillonite, the value of kaolinite being almost constant from sample to sample. Under the humid, temperate climate of Western Europe – both now and during the Last Glaciation – montmorillonite is the clay mineral most susceptible to weathering, and kaolinite is the least susceptible (Millot 1964, pp. 127-128). Therefore, on the basis of clay minerals alone, beds with relatively high values of montmorillonite and low values of illite (less than 40%) can be interpreted as having undergone little or no weathering, and vice versa. The limestone that gave rise to the bulk of these sediments contains 40% montmorillonite, 40 to 60% illite, and 0 to 20% kaolinite.

Another means of evaluating the degree of weathering undergone by a series of similar sediments is the Ratio A of illite (*Rapport A* of Klingebiel and Latouche 1962), where

$$\text{Ratio A} = \frac{\text{intensity of the 001 reflection of illite}}{\text{intensity of the 002 reflection of illite}}$$

On the basis of Ratio A Klingebiel and Latouche recognize aluminous illites (where A is < 2) and ferriferous illites (where A is > 3). The latter, which are also known as "hydrated illites" or "open micas," are related genetically to formations depleted of carbonates and "intensively leached." Thus, as a rule, one can say that the higher the value of Ratio A, the more weathering a given sediment has undergone. At the Abri Pataud, for the illite in the limestone bedrock Ratio A averages about 4 and in the abri sediments Ratio A varies between 2 and 9 (fig. 5). Only three layers have significantly high values (A = 7 to 9): the lower half of Level 4, within Level 5, and in Éboulis 10/11. Moreover, in Levels 4 and 5 the montmorillonite content is low, confirming the presence of weathering; unfortunately the x-ray diagrams from Éboulis 10/11 were very poor, indicating the presence of much amorphous material in the fraction smaller than 2 microns and very little illite was present, so that one can say very little about the clay mineral composition. Surprisingly the Ratio A values from the Éboulis 3/4: Red, which appears to be relatively highly weathered, are not particularly high (3 to 5), although the montmorillonite content in that unit is distinctly low (20%).

The heavy minerals in the Abri Pataud sediments were studied by Madame Mireille Ters in Paris; the fraction between 50 and 500 microns was examined and the results are presented in fig. 6. Sixteen samples were submitted, and they represent typical sediments from the abri as well as of limestone bedrock, fluvial sand from the Vézère floodplain, and the *Sables du Périgord*. (The latter are sands of Eocene age that cover much of the limestone plateaux in the Périgord region.) The samples could be separated into three

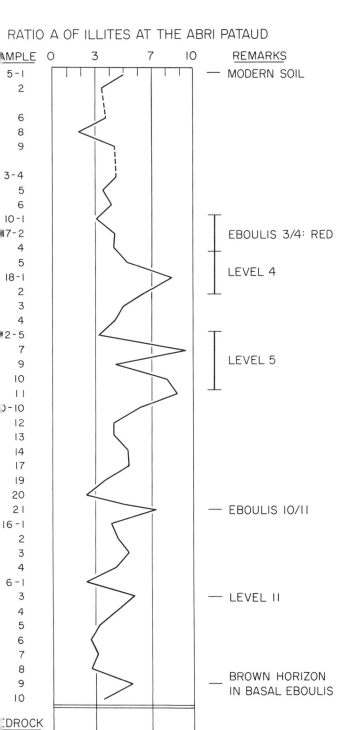

RATIO A OF ILLITES AT THE ABRI PATAUD

Figure 5. Variation of Ratio A (*rapport A* of Klingebiel and Latouche 1962), which is the ratio of the 001 to the 002 peak of illite determined by x-ray diffraction. Higher values indicate greater degrees of weathering.

groups on the basis of their heavy mineral suites. The first group is characterized by relatively high amounts of anatase, zircon, tourmaline, and staurolite; the second group contains abundant hornblende and garnet and very little of the first four mentioned minerals; the third group is intermediate, having a mixture of those minerals characterizing the first two suites.

The essential problem to be attacked by the study of the heavy minerals was not one of paleoclimate, but of the provenience of the sandy matrix of the abri sediment. Certain strata, notably the basal portion of Level 5 and Éboulis 5/6, are conspicuously sandy, the sand being composed predominantly of quartz and mica. The limestone bedrock is also rather sandy, both quartz and mica being quite conspicuous in hand specimens. Therefore, it was first proposed that the sandy matrix between the limestone fragments was simply the product of disintegration by freeze-thaw and by solution of the limestone. This process can be observed in the Abri Pataud today along the rock wall where the former barn of the Pataud farm was situated (fig. 1). The bedrock itself formed the back wall of the barn, and the rock face was cut in order to form a straight wall. This artificial cutting into the bedrock removed the "case-hardened" or annealed surface that characterizes the bedrock face elsewhere along the present-day cliff. The result is that this former barn wall is now the source of a continual rain of fine sand particles that accumulate on ledges along the back wall of the site. Several samples of this sand were collected; it is quite similar to the matrix of the éboulis in its abundance of quartz and mica, and it is pale yellow like the limestone and unlike the strong reddish brown Vézère sand.

Three samples of "barn wall sand" provide the basis for estimating the rate of accumulation of this sand that results from disintegration of the bedrock. The samples are as follows:

AP 9-1, collected 16 June 1964, weight 1410 grams
AP 9-6, collected 1 September 1964, weight 35.3 grams
AP 9-6 *bis*, collected 13 July 1967, weight 226.8 grams

All three samples were collected from a horizontal concrete slab with surface area of 1485 cm.[2] that was installed in May 1958; it is located at the base of the old barn wall at the east end of Trench I. The rates of accumulation thus measured on the whole surface of the concrete slab are:

AP 9-1, July 1958 to June 1964, 1410 g in 6 years, or 235 g/yr, or 0.64 g/day

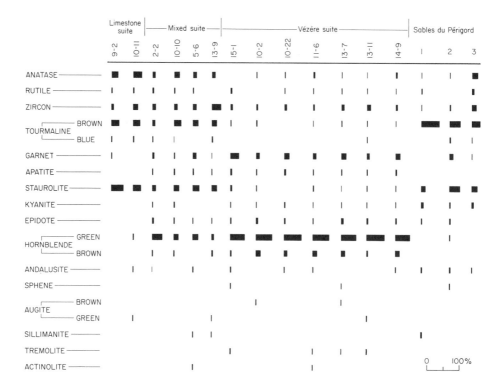

Figure 6. Histograms of heavy mineral distributions in Abri Pataud sediments, Vézère sand, the local bedrock, and the *Sables du Périgord*. The determinations, by Madame M. Ters, Paris, were made on the 50- to 500-micron fraction of the sediments.

AP 9-1 to 9-6, 35.3 g in 78 days, or 0.45 g/day

AP 9-6 to 9-6 bis, 226.8 g in 1046 days, or 0.22 g/day

AP 9-1 to 9-6 bis, 1672 g in 3316 days, or 0.5 g/day or 182.5 g/yr.

The density of this newly accumulated sand is low, about 1.35 g cm^3, so that a daily accumulation of 0.5 gram over the entire surface sampled amounts to a thickness of only 0.00025 cm. and a yearly thickness increment of 0.09 cm. In 1000 years, however, such an accumulation would total 90 cm. and this appears to be a reasonable estimate in comparison with an overall sedimentation rate on the order of 100 cm. per 1000 years for éboulis at the Abri Pataud (see fig. 10). This estimate is certainly exaggerated for such a long-term calculation because compaction would cause a progressive increase in sediment density, but it does show the importance of this contribution to the sedimentary fill.

In spite of this superficial similarity, however, between the sand originating from the disintegration of the bedrock and that found in the éboulis, a preliminary heavy mineral analysis shows a preponderance of hornblende in the basal sands of Level 5, and it is

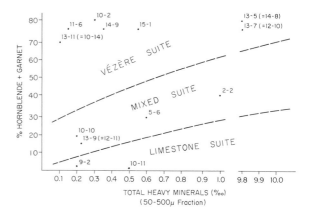

Figure 7. Plot of the abundance of hornblende + garnet vs. total heavy minerals in the Abri Pataud sediments. Hornblende and garnet are abundant in the Vézère sand, but very rare in the local limestone (see fig. 6). This plot clearly distinguishes the three heavy mineral suites discussed in the text.

extremely unlikely that great quantities of hornblende could have been derived from the limestone. The problem of provenience of the sandy matrix of the Abri Pataud sediments was examined, therefore, by considering the heavy mineral suites of the most likely sources − the bedrock, the Vézère floodplain and the *Sables du Périgord*. Two samples of bedrock (AP 9-2 and AP 10-11; see fig. 6) show high anatase, zircon, tourmaline, and staurolite, but practically no hornblende or garnet at all. On the other hand, the Vézère sand (AP 15-1) contains less than 1% anatase and tourmaline, very little zircon and staurolite, but it is rich in hornblende and garnet. The three samples of the *Sables du Périgord* are rather similar to the limestone, although they show a preponderance of tourmaline and less anatase and zircon than the limestone; hornblende is essentially absent, and garnet is not an important component. The similarity of the *Sables du Périgord* to the Cretaceous limestone on which they lie is not surprising, since the former are interpreted as the weathering residual of the latter (Glangeaud 1909). In contrast, the bulk of the floodplain sand has been transported by the Vézère from the crystalline rocks of the Massif Central.

The clear opposition of heavy mineral suites of the bedrock and of the Vézère sand facilitates the interpretation of provenience considerably (fig. 7). The *Vézère suite* is represented by AP 15-1 (floodplain sand) and the six samples nearly identical to it. The sandy matrix of the stratigraphic units represented by those samples (Éboulis 3/4: Red; the base of Level 5, Éboulis 7/8 and Éboulis 10/11) must have been derived in large part from the Vézère floodplain, and apparently by the wind, since there is no evidence of the action of running water in the abri. The *limestone suite* is characterized by the two bedrock samples, AP 9-2, and AP 10-11, and it is approximated by the four sediment samples from Éboulis 1/2, Éboulis 2/3 and Éboulis 5/6. However, these latter four samples appear to be mixtures of the Vézère suite and of the pure limestone suite. They contain the four minerals that dominate the limestone, but also a moderate amount of hornblende and some garnet that could not have come from the limestone, which has essentially no hornblende (fig. 6). Thus, we can speak also of a mixed suite of heavy minerals.

The amount of mixture in the heavy mineral suites can be evaluated semi-quantitatively by considering the percentage of heavy minerals by weight in the total C fraction, i.e., light and heavy minerals taken together. The limestone itself contains predominantly calcite, quartz, and mica with only 0.2 to 0.5 parts per thousand of heavy minerals. In contrast, one sample of Vézère sand contains 0.64 parts per thousand heavy minerals, and some abri samples with the Vézère suite of heavy minerals run as high as 10 parts per thousand. Thus, in a mixture of equal parts of limestone residue and Vézère sand, the Vézère heavy mineral suite would predominate.

Thus, if one considers the percentage of heavy minerals in the C fraction of each of the four samples showing the "mixed suite," one finds that the higher the percentage of total heavy minerals, the higher the percentage of hornblende and garnet (typical of Vézère sediments) in a given sample, as shown in fig. 7. Part of the increase in percentage of heavy minerals in AP 2-2 and 5-6 with respect to AP 10-10 and 13-9 and to limestone samples AP 9-2 and 10-11 is due to decalcification of the matrix. The first pair of samples has only about 65% CaCO$_3$ in comparison to greater than 90% in the others. However, the major part of the increase is undoubtedly due to an addition of Vézère sand, since no amount of decalcification could produce hornblende and garnet in sediments originally lacking those minerals.

Therefore, one can conclude that the sandy sediments represented by samples AP 10-2, AP 10-22, AP 11-6, AP 13-5, AP 13-7 (=12-10), AP 13-11 (=10-14), and AP 14-9 were derived primarily from the Vézère floodplain by wind action. On the other hand, the other four samples represent sandy sediments derived primarily from disintegration of the bedrock but containing a contribution of sand blown from the floodplain. No sample of éboulis matrix that was analyzed shows a heavy mineral suite that could have been derived exclusively from the limestone bedrock. Thus one can conclude that eolian activity was continuously present, but that its intensity varied considerably with time.

DISCUSSION OF THE RESULTS

PRESENTATION OF RESULTS

The results of the analyses discussed above are displayed primarily in the form of a chart (pl. I) on which the variation of each parameter is plotted with respect to its stratigraphic position in the site. In this manner one can readily observe the simultaneous changes in the character of the sediments as a function of time. The main series of samples utilized in the construction of this chart is listed in stratigraphic position along the left margin. Additional samples that supplement the information given by the former are listed next to the columns headed "Concretions." Of particular interest in this connection are the samples from the talus (series AP 11 and AP 14) that give additional information on the presence of soil concretions. Other displays of data are found in plate IV (detailed granulometry) and in tables 1 through 4.

FORMATION OF THE ABRI PATAUD SEDIMENTS

In the absence of any indications of the activity of running water within the Abri Pataud sediments, the sources of the sedimentary fill are threefold:
a) breakup of the surrounding bedrock;
b) windblown debris; and
c) debris introduced by the human inhabitants.
Volumetrically, the first of these is by far the most important; the second is an important contributor to the sandy matrix of certain strata, and perhaps it played at least a minor role in the build-up of all strata; the third type of debris is volumetrically unimportant except in the case of certain rich occupational horizons.

Treating these three sources of sediment in inverse order, it is easy to see that human occupational debris can be readily identified. Its presence is, after all, the reason for the excavation in the first place. Animal bones, flint implements and chipping debris, exotic stones (mainly quartz and quartzite pebbles from the Vézère), and art work (engravings and painting) are obviously the result of habitation of the abri. The remains of bones of large animals may or may not have been brought in by the human inhabitants. However, the fact that they are found nearly exclusively in the occupational levels strongly suggests that the bones were introduced by man. In terms of our sedimentological study the occupational debris in the 100 to 10 mm. fraction of our samples was isolated as the D fraction, and its abundance has been plotted in the extreme right column of plate I. The D fraction, however, is not a very good guide to the intensity of habitation. The living area at any given time in the past was not uniformly distributed over the area that was excavated. Moreover, the sampling columns were chosen so as to avoid the richest parts of the occupational layers, since our emphasis is on the character of the natural sediments. Therefore, it is very unlikely that the D fractions of the various samples represent comparable parts of the living areas of the several habitations.

A more reliable estimate of the intensity of habitation is the abundance of cultural debris in the C fraction of the samples, although we are dealing with the same samples and thus the same limitations mentioned above. Nevertheless, statistically there is a greater likelihood that the quantity of small chips and fragments of bone and flint in the C fraction will be more representative of the intensity of habitation than will be a handful of larger flints and bones in the A fraction, especially for the less rich horizons. For example, the presence or absence of a single large flint fragment can make a great difference in the weight percentage of the D fraction, whereas a few small flakes more or less in the C fraction will have but little influence on the percentage. An estimate of the cultural debris in the C fraction is also included in the column headed "Culture" in plate I.

Both types of estimates show the relatively great intensity of habitation in Levels 4 and 5, as well as in Level 14. Without doubt, the values shown for Levels 2 and 3 are considerably underestimated, because the samples shown here were taken a good distance away from the main concentration of cultural debris in those horizons. The "Culture" column of plate I should be interpreted very conservatively, and perhaps simply in terms of the presence or absence of cultural debris in a given sample.

Sediment blown by the wind from the Vézère floodplain into the Abri Pataud must have been limited to fine sand and silt sizes. These are the sizes most easily transported by the wind, and these are the sizes of sediment found in the floodplain (samples AP 15-1 and 15-2). The problem of separating the eolian and the limestone components of the éboulis matrix cannot be resolved, however, in terms of the grain-size distributions. Although the Vézère sand is somewhat less well sorted than the insoluble residue of the limestone, it does fall into the same size class, mainly between 0.25 and 0.063 mm. (fig. 8). Arguments based on the heavy mineral suites discussed above are more decisive; in certain strata the sandy matrix must have come primarily from the floodplain, e.g., Éboulis 3/4: Red and the base of Level 5. The sandy matrix of other strata shows varying degrees of mixture of the Vézère and the limestone heavy mineral suites. The mixture seems to be about 50-50 in terms of heavy mineral percentages, but this must be interpreted as the result of a considerably greater contribution from the disintegrating limestone than from the floodplain because the limestone had many fewer heavy minerals to contribute, volume for volume, than does the Vézère.

At the present time the Vézère floodplain does not seem to be a source of windblown sand and silt. Although intensively cultivated, the floodplain surface is largely stabilized by a vegetational cover. However, this presumably was not the case during the period of time represented by the Abri Pataud sedimentary accumulation. It is likely that the Vézère was a braided (overloaded) stream during glacial times, although not fed directly by a glacier, and that

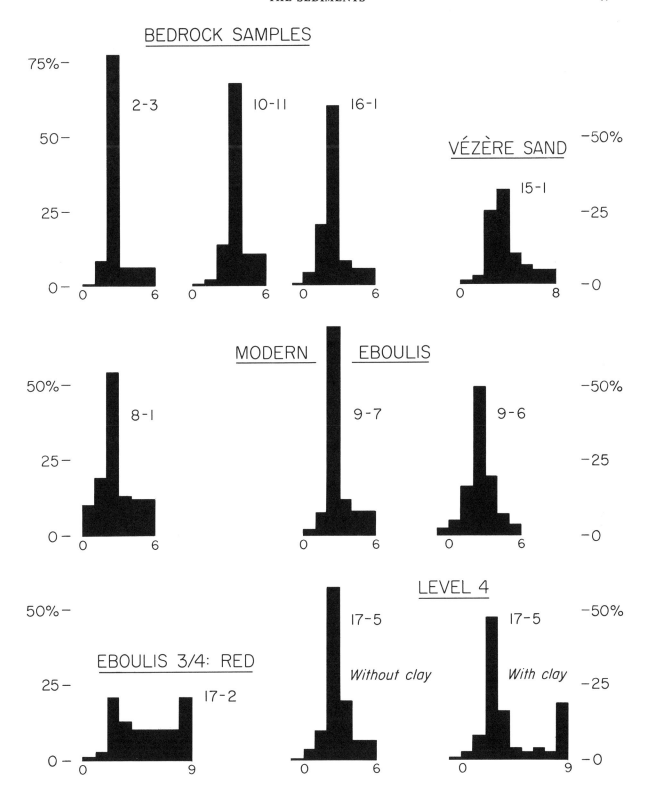

Figure 8. Histograms of the decalcified residues of the local bedrock, Vézère sand, and éboulis samples. The strong similarities show that it would be difficult to separate these sediments by granulometry alone, except for the heavily weathered Éboulis 3/4: Red horizon.

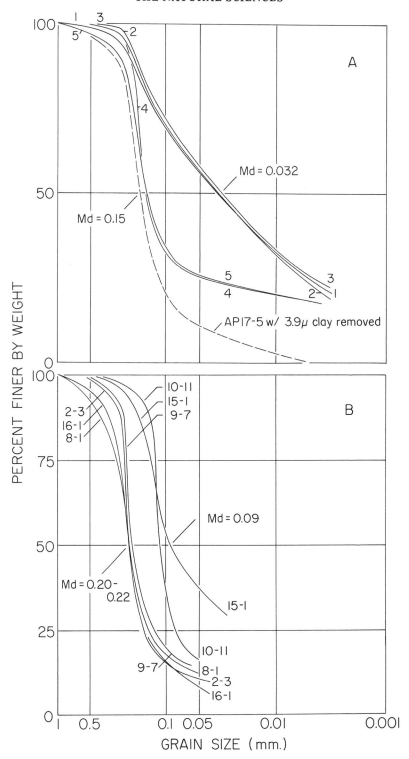

Figure 9. Cumulative granulometric curves of decalcified sediment at the Abri Pataud. A (above): Decalcified sediments from the AP 17 series showing the effects of weathering. Note the poor degree of sorting and especially the increase in the abundance of clay-size particles in samples AP 17-1, 2, and 3 relative to AP 17-4 and 5. Dashed curve shows similarity between these curves and those in 9B. B (below): Decalcified bedrock (samples 2-3, 10-11, and 16-1), modern éboulis (8-1), barn wall sand (9-7) and Vézère sand (15-1). The Vézère sand has a distinctly different granulometry, and bedrock 10-11 is definitely finer than the other rock samples, although just as well sorted.

its floodplain was barren and dry much of the year. Under those conditions deflation by the wind could have been considerable.

The contribution of the limestone bedrock to the Abri Pataud fill is in part extremely obvious and in part a question of interpretation. It is certainly obvious that large sections of the former bedrock roof collapsed and became incorporated into the sediments. Furthermore, all the rock fragments in the éboulis, with the exception of the volumetrically rare river stones brought in by man, are of limestone of the same kind as that composing the roof and walls of the abri. Thus, there can be no question about the source of the rock fragments. The source of the fine sedimentary matrix that fills the spaces between the rocks is another question, and we have already seen that the study of the heavy mineral fraction reveals that there has been a considerable contribution of sand blown from the floodplain in certain strata, and probably at least a minor contribution to all strata.

The C fraction of the Abri Pataud sediments is composed of three parts: calcite, as grains or finely disseminated, from 60 to 90% in relatively unweathered layers; heavy minerals, 1% or less in all layers; and light minerals, mainly quartz and muscovite, making up the balance, thus from 10 to 40% by weight of unweathered layers. Decalcification of several pieces of bedrock show that it is not unreasonable to find from 13 to 32% insoluble residue ("sand") in the local limestone. In contrast, the sand of the Vézère contains only 2 to 6% $CaCO_3$, or, in other words, consists of more than 90% insoluble residue. Therefore, the sandy matrix of the unweathered strata in the abri with as much as 60 to 90% carbonate must have been derived principally from the limestone. Furthermore, the grain-size distribution of the sandy éboulis matrix and of the insoluble residue of the limestone are essentially identical, with a median value always near 0.2 mm. (fig. 9B). The Vézère sand, on the other hand, is in general somewhat finer; the medians of the two samples analyzed are 0.09 mm. (AP 15-1) and 0.04 mm. (AP 15-2). Moreover, wind deflation from the floodplain to the abri should have favored transport of the finer sizes of the Vézère alluvium thus tending to decrease the median grain size of the abri sediments; this is not what we observe. A still further argument against a floodplain origin for the bulk of the sediment in the Abri Pataud is the color of the Vézère sand, a dark reddish brown (5 YR 3/4, moist), in contrast to the very pale yellow (2.5 Y 8/6, moist) of the bulk of the unweathered éboulis in the abri.

It can be concluded, therefore, that the vast majority of the matrix of the Abri Pataud éboulis came from the disintegration of the local bedrock.

Only those strata with an overwhelming Vézère-like heavy mineral suite and a reddish brown color should be considered as sediments strongly influenced by wind-transported Vézère sand. Specifically, Éboulis 3/4: Red, the basal layers of Level 5, and Éboulis 10/11: Wash are examples of the latter case. Éboulis 7/8 is problematical; it consists of light-colored éboulis with only a very small percentage of heavy minerals (1%), but those heavy minerals are distinctly of the Vézère suite (sample AP 13-11 of fig. 6).

From the point of view of paleoclimatology, it is interesting to ask the question whether limestone éboulis, such as that filling the Abri Pataud, is still forming today. The present-day rock-shelters along the Vézère Valley do not seem to be accumulating rock fragments on their floors, but this may be a misleading observation, since it is not known in many cases to what extent these rock-shelters have been cleaned out by the local people during very recent times. On the other hand, in the smaller niches that run more or less horizontally along the limestone cliffs and that have not yet developed into full-sized rock-shelters, one can observe spalling of the rock face and the accumulation of the spalls on the adjacent ledge (pl. V). When this spall debris first forms it is much more tabular than the rock fragments found in the abri sediments, but after exposure for a few years on the ledge, the fragments break down into more and more equidimensional pieces, resembling very closely the smaller rock fragments of the Würm-age éboulis. Moreover, these rock fragments are rather angular. On the other hand, rock fragments fist size or larger are very rare in the modern accumulation.

The mechanism that produces this spalling is not yet clearly demonstrated. Although the rock fragments in the abri are attributed principally to freeze-thaw action, the occurrence of spalling in areas of seeping water and vegetation on the cliff face suggests the possibility of wetting and drying of the limestone face as a mechanism that encourages spalling. Furthermore, freezing temperatures are rather uncommon under the present climate of the Vézère Valley.

Measurement of the rate of accumulation of the presently forming éboulis was begun by the late John P. Miller and is being continued by the present writer, but a definitive study of the processes currently operating on such a cliff face under the present climate remains to be done.

A final point in connection with éboulis accumulation concerns the occurrence of the large blocks of rock several square meters in horizontal dimensions and more than one meter thick that resulted from collapse of the abri roof. In general, the size and

Plate V. Examples of spalling on the present-day cliff. A. Growing niche, or incipient rock-shelter, along the cliff face a few tens of meters south of the Abri Pataud. Note the apparent stratigraphic control of this horizon of weathering, and the grassy vegetation growing within the overhang. B. Recent spalls that have fallen from the back wall of the same niche as shown in photo A. Note the abundance of vegetation and the flatness of the spalls. C. Modern éboulis that has accumulated on the threshold of the same niche shown above. The clean square area with sunglasses marks the location of sample AP 8-3. In the upper right corner of the photo one can see the *route départementale* that passes in front of the Abri Pataud.

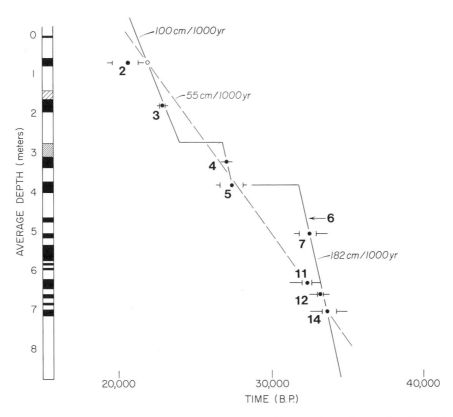

Figure 10. Curve of sedimentation rate of the Abri Pataud sediments. This curve is based on radiocarbon dates for habitation levels (boldface numbers) and the average thicknesses of the units (see appendix 1).

abundance of limestone éboulis is interpreted as a function of frost action, but it seems unreasonable to suggest that these large blocks of the roof were detached directly by the freeze-thaw process. More likely, during the progressive enlargement of a rockshelter by frost action and solution the overhanging brow becomes more and more unstable and finally founders under its own weight. This certainly seems to be a logical explanation of the major roof-falls at the Abri Pataud because they occurred at times when the abri seems to have had the greatest extent of overhang, as nearly as we can tell from our reconstruction of the abri — that is, during and just after the times of Levels 5 and 4.

An alternative explanation for similar large rockfalls in southeastern France is offered by Escalon de Fonton (1971) who attributes them to earthquakes, perhaps related to volcanicity in the Massif Central or elsewhere. His review of the evidence suggests a particularly high incidence of rockfalls in Magdalenian and later times, which are not of concern to us here. However, the mechanism should be taken into consideration.

SEDIMENT THICKNESS AND RATE OF SEDIMENTATION

The average thickness of the sedimentary units in the Abri Pataud was calculated from the thickness of the archaeological units measured on the east-west section drawings available in July, 1965. The thickness was measured at one-meter intervals along each section, wherever the archaeological level or éboulis in question was shown as a distinct unit. The number of observations and the average thicknesses for each unit are given in appendix 1, and they are shown graphically in the columns at the right and left of plate I. The average thickness of the total sediment accumulation below the top of Level 1 is 8.79 m.

The rate of sedimentation in the abri has been calculated on the basis of the average thicknesses discussed in the previous paragraph in combination with the radiocarbon age determination available for the site. The sedimentation rate is shown graphically in figure 10. The mean rate from Level 14 through Level 2 is 55 cm. per 1000 years. The curve is drawn through the oldest date for Level 2, since it is considered that the age range shown by all the dates for Level 2 is too great to be realistic, and the oldest dated sample is least likely to be contaminated by younger carbon (H.M. Bricker, personal communication). Allowance must be made, however, for periods of nondeposition and weathering during which the rate was much less than the average value. Two main periods of weathering are shown in the sedimentation curve by the horizontal portions that imply an absence of sedimentation for two intervals each of some 3000 or 4000 years duration. This is undoubtedly an oversimplification, but adequate for this kind of analysis. The steep portions of the curve indicate that in the major éboulis-forming periods the rate of accumulation was on the order of 100 to 182 cm. per 1000 years.

In greater detail the sedimentation rate must have been even more variable than suggested in figure 10. Certainly the large roof blocks 1 or 2 m. thick did not require 1000 years to fall. They obviously fell instantaneously. On the other hand, fine-grained éboulis such as Éboulis 2/3 probably accumulated somewhat more slowly than suggested in figure 10. Furthermore, in the cases of Levels 2, 4, and 5 which are rich in occupational debris, it would be unwarranted to apply the same sedimentation rate as that for semisterile limestone éboulis.

Moreover, the sedimentation rates suggested here apply only to the Abri Pataud. It would be unwise to suggest that these rates are applicable in detail in any other rock-shelter, even in the same valley. Differences in bedrock and in exposure, as well as in the configuration of the abri and in the intensity of human occupation, must be taken into account. The rates given here can be used only as a general guide in a regional analysis of the rock-shelter sedimentation.

VARIATION WITHIN THE PRIMARY SEDIMENTS

The parameters considered of major importance in characterizing the original, unweathered sediments in the Abri Pataud are (a) the size and abundance of rock fragments, i.e., the A + B fraction, (b) the size and degree of sorting of the fine, or C fraction, (c) the heavy mineral composition of the C fraction, and (d) the presence and abundance of travertine concretions. The original sediments also determine certain other parameters shown on plate I, such as the $CaCO_3$ content and clay mineral composition, but these parameters are best discussed in terms of the postdepositional changes that they have undergone (see next section).

The abundance of rock fragments (A + B fraction) in the éboulis is shown in plate I and their size distribution is shown by the six bars at the left in each histogram in plate IV. In general, the percentage of A + B fraction oscillates around 50 to 60% of the total sample, although there are some marked deviations. For example, some layers of éboulis secs (openwork rubble) are composed of as much as 75% A frac-

tion, which is dominated by quite large fragments; compare samples AP 3-3, 3-6, 10-15, and 6-10 on plates I and IV. In contrast, some strata of fresh, unweathered éboulis have relatively little A + B fraction, as little as 30 to 35% in AP 5-3 through 5-5, and in these cases the rock fraction is composed of relatively small limestone fragments (see plate IV).

It has been generally considered that the size and abundance of rock fragments in the A + B fraction of such rock-shelter sediments are a direct function of the intensity of frost shattering of the bedrock walls of the shelter (Bonifay 1956, 1962). However, recent experiments on frost shattering of limestones have raised some serious doubts about such interpretations (Guillien and Lautridou 1970; Coutard et al. 1970). These experiments expose solid blocks of different kinds of limestones to repeated cycles of freeze and thaw under different conditions, such as, sudden temperature drop, gradual temperature drop; freezing at -5°, -15°, and -30°C; and different moisture conditions. The general conclusions drawn from these studies are:

a. Some limestones break down considerably more quickly than others under the same freeze-thaw conditions,

b. Limestone that is completely dry does not react at all to freezing,

c. Different kinds of limestones require different degrees of saturation before they begin to break down; the differences depend largely on the porosity of the limestone and the size of the pores,

d. For a given limestone, the quantity and the mean size of the fragments are primarily a function of the number of freeze-thaw alternations, i.e., the greater the number of freeze-thaw cycles, the greater the amount of debris detached from the rock and the smaller the mean size of the resulting debris. Moreover, for some limestones, the quantity and the size of the debris may also be a function of the degree of saturation of the pores; however, for calcarenites (sandy limestones), such as that of the Abri Pataud, the amount of moisture available does not seem to be a major determinant, as long as some moisture is present.

e. For a given limestone, different intensities of frost account for second-order differences in the amount of frost debris produced after a given number of cycles and differences in the granulometry of the debris. The breakdown occurs somewhat more rapidly and the median size of the particles is generally smaller with greater cold. This difference is considerably more marked between samples frozen at -5° and -30°C than it is between samples frozen at -15° and -30°C; the difference between samples frozen -15° and -30°C is negligible in most cases. The intensity of freezing, moreover, seems to influence the form of the individual frost-derived fragments — those produced at $-30°C$ tend to be somewhat flatter than those produced at $-5°C$.

In summary, these experiments on frost weathering of limestones show that *smaller fragments* will be produced by:

i. more freeze-thaw cycles;

ii. greater intensity of freezing; and

iii. greater degree of saturation of the rock.

And, a *greater quantity* of debris per freeze-thaw cycle will, in general, be produced either by:

i. greater intensity of frost, or

ii. greater degree of saturation of the rock.

Thus, the size and abundance of frost debris is a complicated function of *time* (number of freeze-thaw cycles), *temperature* (intensity of frost) and *moisture* (degree of saturation), with the overall result that, for any given limestone, the size of the resulting debris is inversely proportional and the quantity of debris directly proportional to each of these factors. Unfortunately, it is impossible to evaluate the effect of each of these factors separately in the absence of independent information about one or more of them.

One limitation in the application of the experimental results of rock-shelter sediments concerns the upper size limit of frost-derived fragments. The experiments were run on solid blocks of limestone about 100 mm. on a side, thus imposing an artificial limit on the largest fragments removed by freezing. On the limestone wall of a rock-shelter, however, the only limit is that imposed by the spacing of cracks and bedding planes, and these cracks may be much more widely spaced than 100 mm. To add to this complication, it must be emphasized that two different kinds of fragments are produced by the freezing and thawing of a natural bedrock outcrop. The first of these may be called "frost spalls"; they are relatively small chips of rock removed from a solid rock surface by the growth of interstitial ice. The experiments cited above deal exclusively with such fragments, and their longest dimension is commonly less than 30 mm. However, water may freeze within any natural crack or system of cracks in the rock, and the entire block of rock bounded by those cracks may thus be detached. We can call these fragments "frost blocks." Frost blocks are not dealt with in the experiments, and the largest size of the blocks that may be detached in this fashion is not really known. They are obviously limited by the natural spacing of the cracks, but it is intuitively questionable whether freezing of water in cracks could detach blocks as large as one meter cube, such as are commonly seen in rock-shelter deposits in the Dordogne. On the other hand, it might be considered reasonable to

suggest that blocks 10, 20, or 30 cm. on a side might be detached by freeze-thaw activity.

One of the most important findings of the experiments on frost shattering of limestones is that the greater the number of freeze-thaw cycles to which a given rock is exposed, not only the greater amount of frost spalls produced, but also the smaller the mean size of those spalls. In other words, the initial frost spalls themselves, in turn, are broken down into smaller fragments by the ensuing freeze-thaw cycles. This process does not continue indefinitely, however; the ultimate particle size distribution tends to stabilize after a certain number of cycles, being controlled by the size of the original components of the limestone, such as sand grains, fossils, ooliths, muddy matrix, etc. This stabilized particle-size distribution is attained relatively rapidly for many limestones that were studied, i.e., after only some 100 to 200 freeze-thaw cycles. If, then, one can assume that the frost blocks and frost spalls detached from the walls and ceiling of the Abri Pataud were exposed to at least 100 cycles, one can reasonably compare the Abri Pataud éboulis with the experimental frost debris.

A crude approximation of freezing conditions in the Abri Pataud is based on the assumption that during Last Glacial times there were about 100 freeze-thaw alternations per year at the ground surface, but only one cycle per year at the depth of greatest penetration of frost into the ground. This depth remains unknown, but it is reasonable to assume that it was equal to or greater than 100 mm. Then, let us assume that the uppermost 100 mm. of the accumulating éboulis in the Abri Pataud underwent on the average 50 freeze-thaw cycles per year. Given a sedimentation rate of 1 to 2 mm. per year (fig. 10), an initial layer of éboulis 100 mm. thick would have been subject to freezing conditions on the average of 50 times per year for some 50 to 100 years, making a total of 2500 to 5000 cycles. The experiments reported by the Caen laboratory (Guillien and Lautridou 1970; Coutard et al. 1970) span only 200 freeze-thaw cycles at the most. Since the Abri Pataud sediments were exposed to from 10 to 25 times as many cycles, it seems reasonable to make comparisons with the experimental results.

The experimental results cannot be applied to the Abri Pataud very rigorously, however, because fine chronological control, i.e., from bed to bed, or from sample horizon to sample horizon, is lacking. Such control would be necessary in order to answer questions about the variation of éboulis production per unit time. On the other hand, the size of the frost fragments may provide some measure of frost activity on the basis that smaller mean fragment size results from a greater number of freeze-thaw cycles or from lower freezing temperatures. In a general way one could conclude that an éboulis horizon with smaller fragments is an indication of a greater intensity of frost activity, although one cannot determine whether there were more freeze-thaw cycles per unit time or a uniform number of freeze-thaw cycles but of variable amplitude.

With these experimental and theoretical considerations in mind, one can examine the particle-size distribution of the Abri Pataud éboulis (pls. I and IV). With the exception of the éboulis secs and the heavily weathered layers, the size distributions of the great majority of the Abri Pataud éboulis match quite well the size distributions of the experimental frost debris, especially that of calcarenites apparently similar to the Abri Pataud bedrock. The histograms in plate IV are the most revealing; they show the size distribution to be polymodal. At least two modes are evident in nearly all the histograms, and in many of them three distinct modes can be seen, for example in Samples AP 5-1, 5-2, 5-6, 5-8, 12-11, 10-16, 10-18, 10-21, 10-22, 10-23, 6-3, 6-7, and 6-11. These modes fall into the following size classes: 64 to 16 mm., 8 to 4 mm., and 0.250 to 0.125 mm. The smallest of these modes is in the C fraction of the samples and corresponds to the principal size of the sandy particles constituting the local bedrock, as well as to the median size of the Vézère River sand (compare fig. 8). The two larger modes both are composed of fragments of the local bedrock, and both fall into the range of particle sizes obtained in the freeze-thaw experiments mentioned above.

Only four out of 59 samples shown in plate IV suggest that the largest mode of rock fragments may occur at or beyond 100 mm. which is the arbitrary upper limit of the Abri Pataud samples. In terms of the histograms in plate IV, this means that the apparent maximum of the coarsest mode for these few samples is in the -6.5 to -6 phi interval; see Samples AP 17-3, 17-4, 12-11, and 10-11. However, five other samples have a high percentage of their total granulometry in the -6.5 to -6 phi class: AP 3-6, 10-15, 10-20, 6-6, and 6-10. Since 100 mm. is also the maximum size of the limestone blocks used in the freeze-thaw experiments, one encounters the problem in the application of the experimental results that was mentioned earlier, namely that rock fragments of the order of 100 mm. were not produced in the freeze-thaw experiments, because those experiments were run on blocks not larger than 100 mm. Thus, the question has not been resolved whether such fragments could be frost spalls or whether they are frost blocks, the size of the latter being a function of the spacing of natural cracks in the bedrock and not necessarily a function of frost intensity. Furthermore, there is another possible interpretation of these larger rock fragments; perhaps they are not the direct products of frost activity at all.

In the Abri Pataud samples, as can be seen in plate IV, those samples with a mode near 100 mm. are all found in beds of éboulis secs (openwork rubble), with the exception of AP 12-11. Moreover, a number of other samples with a prominent mode between 64 and 32 mm. also come from beds of éboulis secs such as AP 3-3, 10-10, 16-3, 6-3 and 6-11. Furthermore, most of these éboulis secs are found in association with prominent rockfalls which are represented by huge blocks of limestone generally one to several meters in length. This is very clearly the case for Sample AP 3-6 from Éboulis 3/4: Yellow, where the éboulis secs are found immediately above and below the east end of the two-meter-thick roof-block that directly overlies Éboulis 3/4: Red. That roof-block obviously must have fallen at least 2 m. or 3 m. vertically and hit the floor with a thundering impact. The weaker portions of the block undoubtedly shattered upon impact, and that shattering — not frost action — produced the coarse éboulis secs. As mentioned earlier, it would be unrealistic to attribute such a coarse layer to frost action, although the successive roof collapses were certainly the result of the progressive undercutting of the rock-shelter overhang during previous frost activity.

Therefore, it appears that the Abri Pataud éboulis can be explained as follows: (i) the coarsest mode, > 16 mm., appears to be primarily the result of shattering of roof-blocks as they collapse, although there probably is some contribution to this mode by freeze-thaw activity; (ii) the two finer modes coincide exactly with the granulometric results of the freeze-thaw experiments cited previously; and (iii) the finest mode, 0.250 to 0.125 mm. is mainly the result of the reduction of the bedrock to its ultimate components by freeze-thaw activity, but it has been augmented to a greater or lesser degree by a windblown contribution from the floodplain, as discussed previously under the heading of "Heavy Minerals." The occurrence of these several modes is given in stratigraphic order in table 5.

An attempt to interpret the detailed evolution of the Abri Pataud éboulis is thwarted, however, by the lack of a precise, bed-to-bed chronologic control, as mentioned earlier. Variation in the mean particle size is not of much help either. In a general way, the median of the total granulometry is smaller in the upper part of the section, i.e., Éboulis 0/1 through Éboulis 3/4: Yellow, than it is below the top of Éboulis 5/6. But the median reflects the combined influence of the three principal modes discussed above, and is thus not amenable to easy interpretation. One could suggest that the smaller median means a greater evolution of the freeze-thaw debris, thus greater cold, from the time of Éboulis 3/4: Yellow onward. It is obvious, however, from the presence of large blocks that there were more frequent roof-falls during Aurignacian times; the debris from those roof-falls would tend to shift the median towards larger sizes even with uniform freeze-thaw conditions. On the other hand, the median value of the 4 to 2 mm. mode alone, which is strongly correlated with frost activity according to the experimental results, is on the whole somewhat finer in the upper part of the section where its value is generally close to 2 mm. In the lower part of the section the median value of this mode lies between 3 and 4 mm. This observation strengthens the interpretation that somewhat colder conditions probably existed during the time represented by the beds Éboulis 0/1 through Éboulis 3/4: Yellow than during the period prior to Level 5.

Table 5 shows clearly that the great majority of the samples (45 of 59) are characterized by the presence of the > 16 mm. mode. Not as many samples (only 33 of 59) show a distinct mode in the 4 to 2 mm. interval, although 7 or 8 other samples contain abundant coarse material in this size range that is not concentrated into a distinct mode. Samples with only the coarsest mode present are from beds of *éboulis secs*; and samples with only the finest mode present come from weathered layers. When these two end members are removed from consideration, the remainder of the samples above AP 3-6 and below AP 10-10 are quite similar; they are in general trimodal. Differences do appear, however, in the middle of the Abri Pataud section where the 4 to 2 mm. mode is lacking in most samples and where there is commonly a greater percentage of fine fraction than coarse fraction, especially in the AP 12 series. The reduced importance of the 4 to 2 mm. mode must mean a reduction in frost activity during the time represented by those beds. The increase in the fine mode appears to be primarily due to an increase in the windblown component, and this is confirmed by heavy mineral studies.

Therefore, one can conclude from the granulometric analysis that the time from the beginning of sediment accumulation in the Abri Pataud until the close of Éboulis 5/6 was an interval of frequent roof collapses and rather vigorous frost action. The abundance of large limestone blocks in the Aurignacian layers, and the occurrence of seven beds of *éboulis secs* constitute the prime evidence for this conclusion. This was followed by a time of lessened frost activity during the accumulation of the sediments of Level 5

through Éboulis 3/4: Red. Several enormous roof-falls occurred during this interval, apparently the result of the extensive undercutting by frost that had taken place during the preceding period. This was also a time of considerable eolian activity and, as we shall see, of two intervals of weathering. Beginning with Éboulis 3/4: Yellow frost action set in once more with vigor, and, according to the analysis presented above, the frost action was somewhat stronger than during the earlier periods represented at the Abri Pataud. Moreover, there were fewer roof-falls, and only three beds of *éboulis secs* were sampled in this interval.

Concerning the primary features of the C fraction, the median grain-size and the degree of sorting show a few interesting variations. The Trask coefficient of sorting (pl. I), with one or two exceptions, remains constant in the range 2.0 to 2.5, i.e., moderately well sorted. The median grain-size also is rather constant at or somewhat less than 0.2 mm. These values are exactly those found for decalcified samples of the local bedrock (fig. 8), and they form one of the arguments for the hypothesis that much of the sedimentary matrix came from the disintegration of the bedrock. Apparent exceptions to this conclusion, Samples AP 10-12 and 10-13, are noticeably finer, but they can be explained by variations in the limestone itself. The insoluble residue from bedrock Sample AP 10-11, which was apparently part of the abri ceiling at the time the sediments represented by AP 10-12 and 10-13 were forming, has a median value distinctly smaller than the other bedrock samples analyzed (fig. 8).

The principal exception to the generalizations given above is the Éboulis 3/4: Red, which is much finer and more poorly sorted. Other characteristics of this stratum that have been mentioned previously are the near total absence of rock fragments (less than 5% A + B fractions) and a Vézère heavy mineral suite. Moreover, Éboulis 3/4: Red has a relatively very high clay content, a low $CaCO_3$ content, a strong brown color, and contains soil concretions. These last four characteristics indicate that we are dealing with a weathered horizon. Specifically, the high clay content alone can explain the deviations in the median and sorting coefficient that are shown on Plate I. This is illustrated in figure 9A in which cumulative curves of decalcified sediment of the AP 17 series show clearly the smaller median and the poorer sorting of the uppermost three weathered samples (AP 17-1, 2, and 3) relative to the lower two relatively unweathered samples. The latter have curves identical to those of decalcified bedrock (fig. 9B), if one subtracts the clay content (the dashed curve in fig. 9A). Thus, it appears that the small median and poor sorting of Éboulis

TABLE 5

Analysis of the rock fraction of the Abri Pataud sediments.

INTERPRETATION

A = Rockfall	E = Weathered horizon
B = Abundant freeze-thaw	! = particularly strong
C = Weak freeze-thaw	? = of questionable importance
D = Abundant eolian material	* = interpreted from other evidence

AP sample #	> 16 mm. mode	4 to 2 mm. mode	Abundant coarse debris, but no distinct mode	Very coarse and fine modes present but no 4 to 2 mm. mode	Fine mode more abundant than coarse	Fine mode only	INTERPRETATION
5-1	X	X					A,B
5-2	X	X					A,B
5-3	X			X	X		A,B!
5-4		X					B!
5-5		X!					B
5-6	X	X					A,B
5-8	X	X					A,B
3-1	X						A,C
5-9	X	X					A,B
3-2	?	X					B
3-3	X						A
3-4			X				B
3-5	X	X					A,B
3-6	X						A,C
17-1						X	E
17-2						X	E
17-3	X			X			A,E,D?
17-4	X	?		X			A,D
17-5	?	?	?				A,B
18-1		?	X				B
18-2	X			X			B
18-3	X			X			A,B
18-4	X			X			A,B
18-5	?	X					B,D?,E
12-5		?		X?	X		B,D,E
12-6		X!			X		B,D,E
12-7		?	X		X		B,D
12-8	X			X			A,B,D
12-9		X			X		B,D
12-10						X	D,E
12-11	X	X!			X		A?,B,D
10-10	X						A,C

AP sample #	> 16 mm. mode	4 to 2 mm. mode	Abundant coarse debris, but no distinct mode	Very coarse and fine modes present but no 4 to 2 mm. mode	Fine mode more abundant than coarse	Fine mode only	INTERPRETATION
10-11	X?			?			A,B
10-12			X				B
10-13	X	X					A,B
10-14			X				B,D?*
10-15	X						A
10-16	X	X					A,B
10-17	X	?					A,B
10-18	X	X					A!,B
10-19			X?				B
10-20	X						A,C
10-21	X	X					A,B
10-22	X	X					A,B,D*
10-23	X	X					A,B
16-2	-X-						B
16-3	X						A,C
16-4	X						A,C
6-1	?	X					B
6-2	X	?					A,B
6-3	X	X!					A,B
6-4	X	?					A,B
6-5	X	X					B
6-6	X						A
6-7	X	X!					A,B
6-8	X	X					A,B
6-9	X	X					A!,B
6-10	X						A
6-11	X	X!					A!,B

3/4: Red are due to weathering and not related to some difference in the primary sedimentation process. Furthermore, the similarity of the decalcified grain-size distribution of AP 17-4 and 17-5 to that of the local bedrock and the dissimilarity of all the curves of the AP 17 series to those of the Vézère sand (fig. 9B) are arguments in favor of the hypothesis that weathering of limestone éboulis produced the sandy matrix of Éboulis 3/4: Red. The hypothesis seems to be contradicted by the Vézère heavy mineral suite, but the small percentage of heavy minerals, only 0.3 parts per thousand in AP 17-3, suggests that the eolian contribution from the Vézère floodplain was not overwhelming. (For comparison, contrast the heavy mineral abundances of 9.8 to 10.0 parts per thousand in the base of Level 5 and in Éboulis 10/11: Wash.)

The final characteristic of the primary sediment to be discussed is the presence of travertine concretion of the faces of certain rock fragments. As shown in plate I, travertine concretion is found in nearly all levels of the site, but its abundance varies considerably. Also its intensity varies from stratum to stratum; this has been noted for cases in which the concretion is particularly strong in the "Faces" column of plate I and those in which the concretion is very thin. In general where the concretion is very abundant, i.e., where it is present on 50% or more of the fragments (by weight), it is also strongly developed. Travertine concretion is particularly abundant in four different levels: (i) the surface of Level 2 (AP 5-6); (ii) in Éboulis 2/3 (AP 2-5); (iii) just above and just below Level 11 (AP 10-23 and 6-1); (iv) and in Basal Éboulis (AP 6-9). Throughout the rest of the section the abundance of travertine concretion remains, in general, below 20%, and in a few layers it is absent altogether. On the whole, travertine concretion seems least abundant in the strata from Éboulis 3/4: Red downward through Level 5 into the upper part of Éboulis 5/6. This part of the section is also characterized, as discussed previously, by the lowest quantities of A fraction and by weathering phenomena.

The paleoclimatic interpretation of travertine concretion in these sediments rests on the assumption that moisture is necessary for the solution and translocation of the $CaCO_3$ from the limestone into superficial cracks where it is precipitated by evaporation. Accordingly, an increase in the abundance of concretions is interpreted as being produced by an increase in available moisture.

It must be noted, however, that the increase in moisture indicated by the travertine did not take place during the period of time represented by the sediments in which the rock fragments with travertine are found. The travertine was deposited in cracks in the bedrock wall *prior* to the breaking away of the rock fragments (see p. 36). Therefore, the period of increased moisture occurred before, however not long before, the period of accumulation of the sediments in which the travertine concretion is found. For example, the abundant and strong travertine concretion found in the top of Level 2 (AP 5-6) apparently formed during the time equivalent to the early part of Level 2 or the upper part of Éboulis 2/3. Thus, for a correct reading of the times of increased moisture, the peaks of concretions in the "Faces" column of plate I should all be displaced somewhat downward, i.e., earlier in time.

MODIFICATION OF THE PRIMARY SEDIMENTS

Some of the original sediments have undergone modification since the time of deposition, and these modifications can be measured in terms of rounding, porosity, and soil concretion in the rock fraction, and calcimetry, pH, and clay minerals in the C fraction.

Rounding and porosity must be considered together. The rock fragments are very angular when first formed by freeze-thaw activity, but they may become more and more rounded as the result of mechanical wear or chemical solution. Rounding due to mechanical wear can be distinguished from that due to solution by means of observations on the porosity of the fragments. High roundness and a low porosity similar to that of the local bedrock indicate that physical abrasion was the cause of the roundness. In contrast high roundness and high porosity occurring together point to chemical weathering that attacked the intergranular cement of the rock at the same time as it attacked the external corners.

In the Abri Pataud no stratum contains a very great number of well-rounded fragments; most samples contain roughly 50% angular and subangular fragments and 50% subrounded to rounded. Two levels are, however, dominated slightly by subrounded and rounded fragments, one is the Basal Éboulis and the other is the Éboulis 3/4: Red – Level 4 – Éboulis 4/5 – Level 5 Complex. The two lowermost samples of the Basal Éboulis (AP 6-10 and 6-11) have about 70% of their fragments more rounded than angular. These fragments, moreover, have a relatively high porosity indicating that they have been subject to considerable solution. This solution apparently resulted from the concentration of ground water flow at and near the bedrock floor of the abri. The lowermost 10 to 20 cm. of the Basal Éboulis are tightly cemented in a thick layer of stalagmitic travertine.

Except for the uppermost level of Éboulis 3/4: Red (which contains very few rock fragments at all) the percentage of rounded and subrounded fragments remains constantly at 50 to 90% throughout the central portion of the section, down to and including the very top of Éboulis 5/6 (AP 12-11). In these same layers are found the highest porosity values, although the porosity is not as consistently high as is the roundness. The porosity is nearly 10% in Éboulis 3/4: Red; it drops to average values in Level 4 and quite low values in Éboulis 4/5; and then rises again to about 9% in the top of Level 5 and 8% in the very top of Éboulis 5/6. Here again, as in the Basal Éboulis, relatively high roundness and high porosity occur together, suggesting that solution of the limestone fragments has been the common cause.

No stratum in the Abri Pataud seems to have undergone mechanical rounding in the absence of chemical solution, although this phenomenon is known from the other Dordogne rockshelters in which well rounded, low porosity éboulis (called *éboulis concassés*) are attributed to grinding during cryoturbation. Very little evidence of cryoturbation was seen in the Abri Pataud, however. Level 1 is somewhat convoluted in the northern part of the site suggesting cryoturbation, and Movius (personal communication) reported cryoturbation in the Upper Subdivision of Level 3 in the central portion of the site.

Concretionary soil carbonate is evident in four horizons in the Abri Pataud. In the two uppermost samples (AP 5-1 and 5-2) this carbonate is certainly related to the modern soil currently developing on the Éboulis 0/1. In these samples 60 to 75% of the fragments (by weight) are coated in part with soil carbonate. This is a greater abundance than in any bed within the abri proper, but it is comparable to the development of soil carbonate in certain layers on the talus slope in front of the abri (AP 14 series, see pl. I).

A problematical peak of soil carbonate occurs in Éboulis 2/3 (AP 2-4). This sample was taken just *above* the stratigraphic position of the paleosol that immediately overlies Level 3 in the southern sector of the site. Its relationship to that paleosol is not clear, although it is not impossible that the secondary carbonate was transported laterally down the slope toward the back wall of the abri (see fig. 1).

A major concentration of soil concretions begins in Éboulis 3/4: Red and builds to a maximum in the underlying Level 4. As we have seen above, Éboulis 3/4: Red is rich in clay, and contains rounded, porous rock fragments that are few in number. With the presence of these indicators of weathering it is not surprising to find a concentration of soil carbonate at the base of this layer as another indication of pedogenesis.

Another strong peak, in reality a double peak, of soil carbonate occurs in Level 5. Once again, other characteristics of weathering, such as the dominance of the fine fraction, relatively high roundness and high porosity, correlate with the soil concretions to indicate that here we are dealing with another weathered horizon. Moreover, all of these parameters show a greater intensity of weathering at the top and at the base of Level 5 and a distinct interruption at the horizon of samples AP 12-7 and 12-8.

The dashed curve in the column headed "Soil" in plate I indicates the intensity of soil carbonate accumulation on the talus slope in front of the abri. (Strata stratigraphically higher than Level 4 were not present on the talus.) The difference between the solid and dashed curves shows the difference in intensity of soil-forming processes under the abri and under the open sky. On the talus, in contrast to the abri, some soil formation was taking place throughout the entire period of deposition of sediments from the Basal Éboulis up to Éboulis 3/4, and probably later. However, the intensity of soil concretions is much greater in Level 5: Talus and Éboulis 3/4: Talus than it is in the underlying beds. Therefore, this observation shows good agreement with the beds within the shelter.

Consideration of soil-carbonate concretions leads up directly to the subject of calcium carbonate content in general. The $CaCO_3$-equivalent has been determined for the C fraction of all the samples, as explained previously, and we find that the C fraction of apparently unweathered éboulis contains from 60 to 90% of material soluble in HCl. The uppermost 3 or 4 m. of the sedimentary fill shows no essential variation; the $CaCO_3$-equivalent remains constant at about 60%. Deeper in the section the $CaCO_3$-equivalent is also nearly constant but at a higher value; from the top of Éboulis 5/6 down to the Basal Éboulis the value remains close to 85 or 90%, except in Éboulis 10/11 and Level 11. In the two major weathered strata, however, one finds marked decreases in $CaCO_3$-content. In Éboulis 3/4: Red the value drops to 20 or 25%. In Level 5 the value is generally less than 50%, and a low of 25% is found at the base of Level 5. The $CaCO_3$-equivalent in the intervening Level 4 and Éboulis 4/5 is only 50 to 60%.

The decreases in $CaCO_3$ content are once more indications of weathering of the éboulis after its formation. $CaCO_3$ is among the first components of the sediment matrix to be removed by groundwater leaching. No further remarks are necessary concerning Éboulis 3/4: Red and Level 5 in which we have already noted numerous other indices of weathering, e.g., reduced A fraction, increased clay content, increased porosity, etc. However, we can note in passing that in both of these cases where one finds a notable decrease in $CaCO_3$ content, one also finds strong indications of soil-carbonate concretions in the immediately subjacent strata. Éboulis 10/11 and Level 11, on the other hand, do not show obvious indications of weathering other than the low $CaCO_3$ values, but they are not altogether lacking in such evidence. In the case of Level 11, Sample AP 16-2 shows only 40% $CaCO_3$-equivalent and the next lower Sample, AP 16-3, contains soil carbonate that, although not heavy, is evidence of the downward movement of the carbonate leached from the upper part of Level 11. In Éboulis 10/11 no soil carbonate was found, but the heavy mineral analysis demonstrates that a considerable amount of the matrix of Éboulis 10/11: Wash came from the Vézère floodplain. In fact, Éboulis 10/11: Wash contains the greatest amount of heavy minerals of all the samples analyzed, 10 parts per thousand, a fact that undoubtedly explains the strong brown color of this stratum. The inference that one can draw from Éboulis 10/11: Wash is that it represents a relatively mild, but brief episode during which sedimentation within the shelter slowed considerably and/or eolian activity on the floodplain increased markedly. The decrease in $CaCO_3$ may be attributed either to leaching of the matrix during this relatively stable period, or to the influx of a great amount of carbonate-poor Vézère sand. The heavy minerals support the latter conclusion. This interval of weathering or stability as seen at the Abri Pataud is not a major one, but we shall see that it may provide some support for regional correlation.

As was mentioned in an earlier section, the pH of the sediment matrix does not have a strong correlation with the carbonate content. The pH, on the other hand, varies primarily with the intensity of human occupation, being apparently a direct function of the accumulation of acid body wastes and refuse.

Clay mineral studies were not particularly useful at the Abri Pataud, but the results can be used as a general guide to postdepositional alteration of the sediments. As mentioned earlier, montmorillonite is the least stable clay mineral species under the present climate of temperate Europe. In the Abri Pataud one finds the percentage of montmorillonite remains relatively high and constant, at about 40 or 50%, both above and below the major weathered complex of Éboulis 3/4: Red through Level 5. In that weathered complex, however, montmorillonite drops to 20 or 30%, furnishing another index of weathering in those strata. Unfortunately, the determination of

abundance of the various clay minerals is semi-quantitative at best, and it would not be wise to interpret the percentages shown on plate I to any greater extent.

Another way of looking at clay minerals is by means of Ratio A to the illites. As explained previously, Ratio A has relatively high values in sediments that have been weathered. Two horizons at the Abri Pataud have conspicuously high values of Ratio A: Levels 4 and 5. This is not surprising in Level 5, since one finds many other indications of weathering there, but the high values of Ratio A in Level 4 are not so readily explained. The clay in Level 4 may be illuviated, i.e., washed down, from the overlying Éboulis 3/4: Red, or the weathering shown by the clay minerals in Level 4 may be in part a result of the rather intense human occupation of the site at that time.

PEDOGENETIC HORIZONS

Evidence of some degree of soil development, or pedogenesis, can be found at four different levels in the Abri Pataud. The uppermost of these is the "brown soil" or brown-stained zone immediately above Level 3; next is the pair of weathered horizons that have been discussed above in some detail — Éboulis 3/4: Red and Level 5; and finally Éboulis 10/11: Wash and Level 11, which show evidence of weak weathering or at least a period of stability.

The soil above Level 3 has not been singled out in the preceding discussion, and it does not stand out conspicuously on plate I. This soil was sampled, however, in three different places; it is a relatively thin horizon, but it is readily obvious at the site. This soil is best seen on the south side of the excavation area, where it developed under the open sky; the overhang had completely disappeared from the southwestern part of the excavated area (Trench I, Squares A, B, and C) by the time of Level 3, and pedogenetic activity was able to operate with full vigor. Sample AP 4-3 was collected in this area, but it is not shown on plate I (see fig. 2 for location). The other two samples of this soil horizon, AP 2-6 and 3-4, were collected in parts of the shelter that are still today under the overhang, and they do not show quite as strong a development, because these localities have always been more or less protected from the elements. Nevertheless, these three samples have a number of characters in common. All have a relatively small A fraction, from 17.4% in AP 4-3 to 30.4 and 31.8% in AP 3-4 and 2-6, respectively, and they all have relatively high amounts of silt and clay, 11.2 and 18.5%. AP 2-6 shows 3.5% of clay alone, which is more than that found in Level 5, but not as much as in Éboulis 3/4: Red. All are darker than the normal éboulis in the site; their Munsell colors at 10 YR 5/6 (yellowish brown) to 10 YR 6/7 (brownish yellow), moist. Clay mineral analysis was made of only one of these three samples (AP 3-4), and it shows a distinctly low abundance of montmorillonite and a relatively high value of Ratio A, both of which are indications of weathering.

The limestone fragments in the A fractions of all three samples, however, are predominantly angular, and there is no marked reduction in the $CaCO_3$ content. These observations argue against a prolonged period of pedogenesis at this time horizon in the Abri Pataud.

On the other hand, Éboulis 3/4: Red presents a striking exception to the generally pale yellow color of the Abri Pataud sediments. Its strong brown or reddish yellow color (7.5 YR 5 - 6/6), its increased clay content (up to 12.4% less than 2 microns), the near-absence of A fraction, the high porosity and relatively well-rounded nature of the limestone fragments, its low carbonate content and the presence of soil-carbonate concretions, and the reduced montmorillonite content among the clay minerals — all these are strong arguments favoring the interpretation of Éboulis 3/4: Red as an important horizon of weathering. It is certainly the most important horizon of weathering, and it is definitely the most important pedogenetic horizon in the Abri Pataud. Furthermore, the trends in these parameters, as shown in plate I, indicate in general a gradual decrease in intensity with depth as one would expect in the case of a soil developing in place. Thus, there can be no possibility that this stratum is a transported or colluvial deposit. Furthermore, Éboulis 3/4: Red is nearly sterile archaeologically, and thus the variations in the parameters listed above cannot be attributed to human activity.

The case is not so clear in Level 5. First of all, human influence was abundant, and it is somewhat an open question how much modification might be attributed to that influence. However, the similarity between the modification of the sediments of Level 5 and those of Éboulis 3/4: Red is so great that one is tempted to discount the possibility of significant human influence. A further complication is the twofold nature of the weathering phenomena in Level 5, as clearly can be seen in plate I. All parameters except pH show a double peak in Level 5. The first peak is located in Lenses Q and R and the second is found in Lenses V and X of Level 5; the middle lenses of Level 5 are distinctly less weathered. The amplitudes of the two peaks are about the same, and in general they have values that indicate a lesser degree

of weathering than in Éboulis 3/4: Red. The A fraction is never reduced to less than 11%, and the clay content is never greater than 30%. Porosity values are similar to those in Éboulis 3/4: Red, but the fragments are not as well rounded. Carbonate content is not as low as in Éboulis 3/4: Red except in one sample, AP 12-10, but soil-carbonate concretions are just as strongly developed. Even the clay minerals reflect the twofold nature of Level 5; montmorillonite is low both at the top and at the bottom of the bed and has higher values in the middle section.

Another difference between Level 5 and Éboulis 3/4: Red is shown by the heavy minerals found in them. The Basal Lenses of Level 5 are conspicuously sandy, and that sand contains a high percentage of heavy minerals, 9.8 parts per thousand; they are of the Vézère suite. This value is surpassed at the Abri Pataud only in Éboulis 10/11: Wash, which has 10 parts per thousand. For comparison, Éboulis 3/4: Red contains only 0.3 parts per thousand heavy minerals, and although these heavy minerals also are dominated by Vézère types, the small abundance must indicate a marked difference in eolian transport from the floodplain between Level 5 and Éboulis 3/4: Red times.

The great abundance of heavy minerals and the strongly reduced A fraction in Level 5 suggest a time of both reduced frost action and increased wind activity. At such a time pedogenetic processes would have an increased effect, and this is best seen in the reduced carbonate content and the reduction of montmorillonite. Another indication, moreover, can be seen in the site. A great part of Level 5 lies directly on the surfaces of a series of large roof-collapse blocks. The upper surfaces of these blocks exhibit a gray, weathered appearance, and the excavators noticed in chiseling through them that the upper parts of the rocks were definitely softer than the rest. This softening, undoubtedly due to solution of part of the intergranular calcite cement, is another indication of a period of reduced sedimentation in the abri and a greater attack by weathering processes on the exposed surfaces.

The evidence for pedogenesis in Éboulis 10/11: Wash and in Level 11 is distinctly weaker than that in the cases just discussed. As was mentioned in an earlier discussion, carbonate analysis gave the first clue to the presence of weathering in these horizons, $CaCO_3$-equivalent drops to 33% in Éboulis 10/11: Wash and 39% in the middle of Level 11. In the case of Level 11 part of the leached carbonate has been redeposited immediately below (Sample AP 6-1). Also in Level 11 the abundance of montmorillonite drops distinctly and the value of Ratio A rises to about 5. There is no evidence of soil carbonate in Éboulis 10/11: Wash; and the clay minerals were not determined. However, heavy minerals of the Vézère type are in great abundance, 10 parts per thousand, indicating a marked increase in eolian activity relative to éboulis deposition within the shelter at the time this deposition was taking place. In view of this eolian contribution, it cannot be stated with certainty that the decreased carbonate content of Éboulis 10/11: Wash is due entirely to pedogenetic leaching. The Vézère sand contains less than 10% $CaCO_3$, and any mixture of this carbonate-poor sand with limestone sand from the abri walls will have a lower carbonate content than the limestone sand alone by virtue of dilution. Some leaching of carbonate must have occurred, however, because the resulting product (Éboulis 10/11: Wash) is much richer in heavy minerals than is either end member.

In summary, some pedogenesis must have occurred at four different times, at least, during the sedimentary history of the Abri Pataud. The earliest and least marked of these soil-forming periods occurred during Early Aurignacian times (Level 11 and Éboulis 10/11: Wash). Leaching of carbonate was the dominant activity, although some degradation of montmorillonite took place. During this time there was an increase in wind transport of floodplain sand into the shelter relative to éboulis production. The next pedogenetic episode occurred during the early phases of the Périgordian IV occupation (Level 5: Lower). In this case there is a demonstrable decrease in éboulis production and an increase in eolian activity as well. The carbonate content decreases strongly and soil-carbonate concretions are abundant. Fine clay is not particularly abundant, however, and the limestone fragments are dominantly angular. Therefore, the weathering in Level 5 does not seem to have been as intense as that in Éboulis 3/4: Red. Furthermore, the

double peak of weathering in Level 5 raises the question of the possibility of two pulses of mild climate separated by a colder episode, or as an alternative hypothesis, the possibility of human activity as an explanation for the "cold" nature of the éboulis in the middle lenses of Level 5. Perhaps the strata sampled (from Trench II, Square A) represent materials derived from other layers and thrown out of the interior of the abri in the process of "housecleaning."

The next younger pedogenetic episode is that represented by Éboulis 3/4: Red, and this is by far the clearest and strongest record of soil development in the Abri Pataud. The near absence of A fraction and the prominence of the fine clay fraction, along with the other indices of weathering that were mentioned previously, point to a fairly extended mild interval conducive to weathering. The 3,000 years allowed for this interval (based on the C-14 dates) on the sedimentation rate curve (fig. 10) gives a rough idea of the time allowed. In addition to parameters indicative of weathering, the regular decrease in intensity of these parameters with depth provides another strong argument that Éboulis 3/4: Red is a soil formed in situ.

The youngest pedogenetic episode recorded at the Abri Pataud is that represented by the soil zone immediately overlying the Périgordian VI occupation (Level 3). The intensity of soil formation in this case seems to be intermediate between that of Level 5 and that in Éboulis 10/11: Wash and Level 11, although it is closer to the latter. There is a distinct reduction in the A fraction and an augmentation in silt and clay, and there is some reduction of montmorillonite. The carbonate content, however, does not reflect an episode of leaching. Without the obvious field evidence of a soillike stratum at this horizon in the site, this pedogenetic horizon might have been overlooked.

PALEOCLIMATOLOGY OF THE ABRI PATAUD SEDIMENTS

CLIMATIC INFERENCE FROM THE SEDIMENTS

In review, we have seen that a number of the sedimentological parameters observed in Abri Pataud sediments can give certain indications of the climate under which they were developing. Variations in the abundance of limestone fragments in the A + B fraction suggests fluctuations in the intensity of freeze-thaw activity. On the other hand, the amount of fine clay (less than 2 microns) must be a function of breakdown during weathering, because such clay is not abundant either in the parent bedrock or in the floodplain sands. Rounding and porosity fluctuate in

parallel fashion at the Abri Pataud; increases in both parameters suggest weathering under relatively moist conditions. The abundance of travertine concretions is also an index of the quantity of moisture available. Decreases in the $CaCO_3$-equivalent and concomitant presence of soil-carbonate concretions indicate solution weathering, and therefore, relatively moist and mild conditions. Variations in clay mineral abundance, especially decrease in montmorillonite, are indicative of chemical weathering requiring relatively mild and moist conditions. Heavy minerals, on the other hand, provide only indirect help in establishing paleoclimate. In the case of the Abri Pataud, more heavy minerals of the Vézère type indicate a greater eolian influence on site sedimentation *relative* to éboulis sedimentation from the bedrock.

By combining these various parameters one can establish a paleoclimatic sequence for the Abri Pataud. The following characterizations are based especially on the parameters listed in parentheses:

A. Éboulis 0/1 through Éboulis 2/3: *Cold, somewhat moist episode.* (Moderately fine to coarse angular éboulis of low porosity; moderately abundant $CaCO_3$; moderate to great amount of travertine; high montmorillonite.)

B. Soil above Level 3: *Brief mild episode with incipient pedogenesis.* (Reduced A fraction and increased silt plus clay; slight decrease in $CaCO_3$; definite decrease in montmorillonite.)

C. Level 3 and Éboulis 3/4: Yellow: *Cold and dry with major roof collapse.* (Abundant coarse, angular A fraction of low porosity; very little travertine; high montmorillonite.)

D. Éboulis 3/4: Red: *Major warm, moist pedogenetic episode.* (Near absence of A fraction; strong increase in fine clay; increased eolian influence; high porosity and roundness; low $CaCO_3$ and low montmorillonite; soil-carbonate concretion abundant.)

E. Level 4 and Éboulis 4/5: *Brief cool, somewhat moist episode, colder in Éboulis 4/5, ameliorating into Level 4; includes a major roof collapse.* (Moderately abundant A fraction, decreasing upward; low to intermediate porosity, increasing upward; moderately well rounded; intermediate $CaCO_3$ values; rather low montmorillonite.)

F. Level 5: *Prolonged warm, moist pedogenetic interval, apparently double, with marked eolian influence.* (Greatly reduced A fraction and some increase in fine clay; moderately to well rounded; high porosity; intermediate to low $CaCO_3$-equivalent and abundant soil-carbonate concretions; intermediate to low montmorillonite, very abundant Vézère heavy minerals.)

G. Éboulis 5/6 through Level 10: *Cold and somewhat moist episode including numerous small roof collapses; period of major increase in the size of the shelter.* (Abundant, rather angular A fraction of intermediate to relatively high porosity; moderate amount of travertine; high $CaCO_3$.)

H. Éboulis 10/11: Wash through Level 11: *Brief moist and relatively mild interval, perhaps double, of incipient pedogenesis and increased eolian activity.* (A fraction abundant and angular; low porosity, increased amount of travertine; low $CaCO_3$-equivalent; soil-carbonate concretions below Level 11; very abundant Vézère heavy minerals in Éboulis 10/11: Wash.)

I. Éboulis 11/12 through Basal Éboulis: *Cold episode with fluctuating humidity.* (Abundant, mostly angular A fraction of intermediate porosity; 2 or 3 peaks of travertine abundance; high $CaCO_3$ values; intermediate to high abundance of montmorillonite.)

The paleoclimatic interpretations are summarized in table 6 which shows the relationships with cultural designations and radiocarbon dates.

COMPARISONS WITH OTHER SITES IN THE DORDOGNE

Other studies of sediments in caves and rock-shelters in this part of France have been summarized recently by Laville (1969), and in particular the study of the nearby sites of Laugerie-Haute (Laville 1964) and of the Abri du Facteur (Laville 1968; Leroi-Gourhan 1968) provides information for direct comparison with the paleoclimatic interpretations of the Abri Pataud sediments.[3] Unfortunately, however, correlation among these sites is still based largely on hypothetical studies in which a number of problems, at least of terminology, remain to be resolved. Radiocarbon dates are too few in number to throw light on some of the apparent chronological discrepancies; and, moreover, not all the dates reported seem to be equally acceptable, for example, those from the Abri du Facteur.

Nevertheless, there is much agreement in paleoclimatic interpretations from sites in this area. Specifically the two major episodes of amelioration at the Abri Pataud are similarly found at the Abri du Facteur, although there are minor differences. For example, the Noaillian Level at the Abri du Facteur, which is equivalent to Level 4 at the Abri Pataud on the basis of typological evidence, shows a somewhat temperate climate (Leroi-Gourhan 1968), followed by a slight halt in sedimentation (Laville 1968), correlative with the pedogenetic interval of Éboulis 3/4: Red at the Abri Pataud. This mild interval has been called the "Tursac Oscillation" by Leroi-Gourhan (1968).

The sediments at the Abri Pataud, however, suggest a much more marked period of temperate climate than that suggested by the Abri du Facteur data. There is a much greater accumulation of colloidal

---

[3] Since the preparation of this manuscript Laville has completed his doctoral dissertation (Univ. de Bordeaux 1973) which is a modified and much more complete statement of his conclusions than the works cited herein. Accordingly, some of Laville's conclusions mentioned above should be reconsidered.

clay and a much stronger decalcification in Éboulis 3/4: Red at the Abri Pataud than in any level at the Abri du Facteur.

There is also a similarity with the climatic sequence interpreted from the site of Les Jambes, near Périgueux (Dordogne), where the occupation yielding Noailles burins is found in the base of a layer of a sandy clay with only 5% A fraction (Laville and Thibault 1967). The sediment was deposited under conditions of increasing humidity and milder temperatures; then it was weathered into a *sol brun calcaire*. According to Laville and Thibault (1967, p. 2365), the humid, mild conditions began during the most intensive Noaillian occupation at Les Jambes; thus those conditions would parallel the climatic change seen at the Abri Pataud. On the other hand, the *sol brun calcaire* at Les Jambes is attributed to the W III/W IV Interstadial by the authors. From their description, however, that soil seems similar in strength to the soil recorded in the Éboulis 3/4: Red at the Abri Pataud. Accordingly, it is suggested here that the *sol brun calcaire* of Level 2 at Les Jambes was formed, or at least began to form, during the "Tursac Oscillation". Perhaps it should be attributed to both the "Tursac Oscillation" and the W III/W IV Interstadial, thus explaining its strong development. In contrast, Laville (1968) states that no true soil formed at the Abri du Facteur at this time.

The Noaillian occupation is dated at 23,180 ± 1500 years ago (Gsy-69) at the Abri du Facteur, but its age is 27,060 ± 370 years (GrN-4280) at the Abri Pataud. For relatively old dates such as these, there is a tendency for the ages to be too young rather than too old because of contamination. Therefore, of the two ages, the Abri Pataud figure seems preferable, but more dates are urgently needed to resolve this apparent conflict. Whatever the exact age of the Noaillian occupation may be, the maximum of the "Tursac Oscillation" must be somewhat younger; this is confirmed stratigraphically both at the Abri Pataud and at the Abri du Facteur.

The warm, moist interval indicated by Level 5 at the Abri Pataud also has its counterpart in the Abri du Facteur. There are greater differences in this case, however, than in the case of those discussed in the preceding paragraph. First of all, there is a discrepancy at Abri du Facteur, where pollen analysis identifies this interval as the most temperate at that site, but sediment analysis indicates a "very cold" climate for the same strata, which was followed (in the next higher stratum) by a mild, humid interval (Laville 1968). This discrepancy is probably to be explained by the open nature of the *éboulis secs* of the "Gravettian" Level at the Abri du Facteur which would have allowed the infiltration of pollen from

higher levels. Nominally, this temperate interval, identified as the "Paudorf Interstade" by Leroi-Gourhan (1968), spans a longer interval in terms of industries at the Abri du Facteur than at the Abri Pataud. At the Abri du Facteur the mild interval based on pollen analysis encompasses the Evolved Aurignacian and Aurignaco-Périgordian, or "Gravettian," occupations, whereas at the Abri Pataud only the Périgordian IV horizon is included in the warm interval marked by Level 5. As explained above, however, the pollen may have filtered from higher levels down into the Aurignacian levels at the Abri du Facteur, giving a false impression of the duration of the warm interval in question. Furthermore, sedimentological analysis indicates that this mild interval at the Abri du Facteur follows the "Gravettian" occupation, whereas at the Abri Pataud warm, moist conditions seem to have begun slightly prior to the Périgordian IV occupation and continued into its early phases. Therefore, sedimentological analysis at the two sites is at odds, if the two Périgordian IV and "Gravettian" occupations were indeed contemporary.

The minor mild interval indicated by pedogenetic features immediately following the Périgordian VI (Level 3) occupation at the Abri Pataud is apparently not known from other sites in this area (Laville 1969), and certainly it was not recorded either at Laugerie-Haute (Laville 1964) or at the Abri du Facteur (Laville 1968). It is nevertheless quite distinct at the Abri Pataud, where it interrupts a long interval of strong thermoclastic activity.

The earlier mild but brief interval at the Abri Pataud, which occurred during the time represented by Éboulis 10/11: Wash and Level 11 (Early Aurignacian), is also difficult to find in other sites of the area. Furthermore, the brief temperate interval known as the "Interstade d'Arcy" and usually found in an Aurignacian II context (Laville 1969) cannot be identified at the Abri Pataud. A weak amelioration in the Aurignacian II level at the Abri du Facteur, however, has been correlated with the "Interstade d'Arcy" by Leroi-Gourhan (1968); it may be incompletely represented there, because of a hiatus in the Abri du Facteur section. In the absence of definitive radiocarbon dating for the various sites involved, one can raise the question of the reliability of temporal correlation on the basis of typological designations. As a working hypothesis one can suggest that the "Interstade d'Arcy", as recognized at the Abri du Facteur, is represented by the mild interval of Level 11 at the Abri Pataud. At both the Abri Pataud and the Abri du Facteur this was only a brief interval of temperate climate. At the Abri Pataud its age is about 32,600 years, but at the Abri du Facteur it is apparently younger than 27,890 years. Leroi-

Gourhan (1968) among others, however, has rejected the latter age. At the type site at Arcy-sur-Cure the Interstade d'Arcy occurred some 30,370 years ago, and thus in closer agreement with the Abri Pataud.

With respect to the relatively cold episodes, there is good agreement between the results from the Abri Pataud and other sites in southwestern France. In general, Basal and Later Aurignacian times were characterized by cold, somewhat humid climate with much thermoclastic activity. Similarly, Final Périgordian, Proto-Magdalenian, and Lower Solutrean times were comparatively cold and rather humid. Laville (1969) calls this period the most rigorous and driest of Würm III times. At the Abri Pataud, however, the presence of travertine concretions and the somewhat reduced carbonate content of the sediments argue for somewhat moister conditions.

TABLE 6

Summary of climatic interpretation of Abri Pataud.

Unit	Culture	Climate	Date (B.P.)
0/1	sterile		
1	Lower Solutrean	Cold,	
1/2	sterile	somewhat	
2	Proto-Magdalenian	moist	22,000
2/3	sterile		
Soil on Level 3		Mild	
3	Périgordian VI		23,000
3/4: Yellow		Cold, dry	
3/4: Red		Warm, moist	
4	Noaillian	Cool,	27,000
4/5	sterile	somewhat moist	
5	Périgordian IV	Warm, moist	28,000
5/6	sterile		
6	Evolved Aurignacian		
6/7	sterile	Cold,	
7	Intermediate Aurignacian b	somewhat	
7/8	sterile	moist	32,800
8	Intermediate Aurignacian a	(not as cold	
8/9	sterile	as above Level 3)	
9	Intermediate Aurignacian (?)		
9/10	sterile		
10	Intermediate Aurignacian (?)		
10/11	sterile	Mild, moist	
11	Early Aurignacian b		32,600
11/12	sterile		
12	Early Aurignacian a	Cold,	33,260
12/13	sterile	with	
13	Basal Aurignacian b	fluctuating	34,000
13/14	sterile	humidity	
14	Basal Aurignacian a		

APPENDIX 1

SEDIMENT THICKNESS IN THE ABRI PATAUD

Unit	N	Average Thickness	Cumulative Thickness Below Top of Level 1
Level 1	4	2.3 cm.	2.3 cm.
Éboulis 1/2	5	55.8	58.1
Level 2	25	19.4	77.5
Éboulis 2/3	13	62.5	140.0
Brown soil above Level 3	7	22.0	162.0
Level 3	14	30.2	192.2
Éboulis 3/4: Yellow	15	81.3	273.5
Éboulis 3/4: Red	5	36.0	309.5
Level 4	33	26.8	336.3
Éboulis 4/5	25	37.0	373.3
Level 5	25	27.3	400.6
Éboulis 5/6	15	66.2	466.8
Level 6	13	7.7	474.5
Éboulis 6/7	19	30.9	505.4
Level 7	18	9.8	515.2
Éboulis 7/8	15	20.3	535.5
Level 8	14	37.6	573.1
Éboulis 8/9	9	7.5	580.6
Level 9	12	4.4	585.0
Éboulis 9/10	6	10.7	595.7
Level 10	8	2.4	598.1
Éboulis 10/11	6	23.5	621.6
Level 11	14	22.2	643.8
Éboulis 11/12	7	16.3	660.1
Level 12	7	9.3	669.4
Éboulis 12/13	5	12.2	681.6
Level 13	5	7.4	689.0
Éboulis 13/14	4	11.2	700.2
Level 14	4	14.0	714.2
Basal Éboulis	4	165.0	879.2

APPENDIX 2

Chemical analysis of Abri Pataud sediments by direct-reading spectrometer under the direction of Güröl Ataman, Institut de Géologie, Strasbourg, France.

Horizon	Sample	Original Analyses (%)**					Reconstructed Compounds*		
		SiO_2	Al_2O_3	CaO	Loss on Ignition	Fe_2O_3	Clay Mineral	Excess SiO_2	$CaCO_3$
Éboulis 3/4: Yellow	3-6	19.4	3.95	41.5	31.9	1.57	15.8	7.5	72.5
Éboulis 3/4: Red	10-1	54.6	10.8	12.4	11.9	4.45	43.2	22.2	22.1
	10-2	53.6	10.5	13.3	12.2	4.17	42.0	22.1	23.7
	10-3	28.4	6.04	33.9	26.3	2.69	24.2	10.3	59.8
Éboulis 4/5	18-2	30.7	5.8	31.5	25.2	2.9	23.2	13.3	56.2
	18-3	32.0	5.6	31.3	25.7	2.41	22.4	15.2	55.9
Level 5	12-10	49.7	10.4	14.6	12.8	3.9	41.6	18.5	26.1
Éboulis 5/6	12-11	9.97	4.9	48.8	36.9	1.26	13.3	0	83.9
	10-10	9.06	3.02	50.03	37.1	1.22	12.08	0	86.6
Basal Éboulis	6-8	5.87	1.57	54.0	39.4	0.79	6.28	1.16	89.6
	6-9	21.1	6.05	37.9	29.7	2.28	24.2	2.9	67.6
Bedrock	9-2	4.22	0.82	54.6	41.6	0.50	3.28	1.76	94.6

*Percentages calculated as follows:

Clay mineral = 1 part Al_2O_3 + 3 parts SiO_2

Excess $SiO_2 = SiO_2$ remaining after calculation of clay mineral

$CaCO_3 = 1.785$ x CaO; CO_2 is presumed to be part of the material lost on ignition.

Loss on Ignition includes primarily H_2O, CO_2, and organic matter.

**All samples except 9-2 (bedrock) include from 0.1 to 9.9% other constituents (reported as MgO, Mn_3O_4, TiO_2, etc.) presumably in the form of heavy minerals.

REFERENCES

Bonifay, E.
1956. "Les sédiments détritiques grossiers dans les remplissages des grottes," *L'Anthropologie*, no. 5-6, pp. 447-461.
1962. *Les terrains quaternaires dans le sud-est de la France*. Delmas, Bordeaux.

Brunnacker, K. and R. Streit
1967. "Neuere Gesichtspunkte zur Untersuchung von Höhlensedimenten," *Jahresheft für Karst- und Höhlenkunde*, vol. 18, part 7, pp. 29-44.

Coutard, J.P., et al.
1970. "Gélifraction expérimentale des calcaires de la campagne de Caen; comparaison avec quelques dépôts périglaciaires de cette région," *Centre de Géomorph., C.N.R.S., Caen, Bull.* no. 6, pp. 7-44.

Escalon de Fonton, M.
1971. "Stratigraphie, effondrements, climatologie des gisements du sud de la France, du Würm III à l'Holocène," *Bull. Assoc. Fr. Etude Quat.*, 8e année, no. 29 (1971-72), pp. 199-207.

Folk, R.L.
1968. *Petrology of Sedimentary Rocks*. Hemphill's, Austin, Texas.

Glangeaud, P.
1909. "Les facies de l'Oligocène aux environs de Bergérac et dans la Dordogne," *Bull. Soc. Géol. Fr.*, ser. 4, vol. 9, pp. 434-441.

Guillien, Y., and J.P. Lautridou
1970. "Recherches de gélifraction expérimentale du Centre de Géomorphologie. I – Calcaires des Charentes," *Centre de Géomorph., C.N.R.S., Caen, Bull.* no. 5, pp. 1-45.

Klingebiel, A., and C. Latouche
1962. "Etude cristallographique des illites, dans les séries éocènes du Bordelais," *C.R. Acad. Sci. Paris*, vol. 262, pp. 142-144.

Lais, R.
1941. "Uber Höhlensedimente," *Quartär*, vol. 3, pp. 56-108.

Laville, H.
1964. "Recherches sédimentologiques sur la paléoclimatologie du Würmien récent en Périgord," *L'Anthropologie*, vol. 68, nos. 1-2 and 3-4, pp. 1-48 and 219-252.
1968. "L'Abri du Facteur à Tursac (Dordogne). IV – Etude sédimentologique du remplissage," *Gallia-Préhistoire*, vol. 11, no. 1, pp. 133-145.
1969. "Le remplissage des grottes et abris du sud-ouest de la France," *Etudes Françaises sur le Quaternaire*, supplement to Bull. Assoc. Fr. Etude Quat., pp. 77-80.

Laville, H., and C. Thibault
1967. "L'oscillation climatique contemporaine du Périgordien supérieur à burins de Noailles dans le sud-ouest de la France," *C.R. Acad. Sci. Paris*, vol. 264, pp. 2364-2366.

Leroi-Gourhan, A. (Mme.)
1968. "L'Abri du Facteur à Tursac (Dordogne). III – Analyse pollinique," *Gallia-Préhistoire*, vol. 11, no. 1, pp. 123-132.

Lumley, H. de
1969. "Le Paléolithique inférieur et moyen du Midi méditerranéen dans son cadre géologique. I – Ligurie-Provence," 5th supplement to *Gallia-Préhistoire*. Editions du C.N.R.S., Paris.

Millot, G.
1962. *Géologie des argiles*. Masson, Paris.

Schmid, E.
1958. *Höhlenforschung und Sedimentanalyse*. Schriften des Instituts für Ur- und Frühgeschichte der Schweiz, no. 13. Basel.

Vértes, L.
1959. *Untersuchungen an Höhlensedimenten-Methoden und Ergebnisse*. Régészeti Füzetek, ser. 2, no. 7. Budapest.

I V

Etude de la Faune de l'Abri Pataud

Jean Bouchud

CENTRE NATIONAL DE LA RECHERCHE SCIENTIFIQUE

1. LE PROBLEME DES OS CASSES ET DE LEUR CONSERVATION

La faune récoltée à l'Abri Pataud est très abondante. Le poids des débris recueillis de 1958 à 1964 est d'environ 1.590 kilogrammes. Avant d'aborder l'étude paléontologique des espèces identifiées, il convient d'examiner le problème posé par les os cassés et celui de leur conservation. Il est banal de dire que la fréquence des restes provenant des divers segments osseux du squelette d'un animal fossile ne correspond jamais aux rapports anatomiques. Cependant, dans un gisement préhistorique, l'intervention humaine ne saurait tout expliquer: déjà A. Gaudry (1876) en étudiant les restes de 1.900 Hipparions découverts dans le Pontien de Pikermi, en Grèce s'étonnait de n'y rencontrer que *trois humerus*.

Depuis cette époque, bien des auteurs se sont penchés sur les problèmes de désarticulation et de conservation des différentes parties du squelette (Mathew 1901, Rivière 1904, Weigelt 1927, Peï 1937, Muller 1950, Sothwell 1953, Flerov et Zablotski 1961, Toots 1964, Van Valen 1964, Guthrie 1967).

De telles connaissances sont en effet indispensables aux paléontologistes at aux paléoécologistes qui se proposent de retrouver la composition des faunes disparues, les rapports qui existent entre les différentes espèces et le nombre exact des individus à partir des débris osseux conservés; enfin les recherches conduites à partir de la faune pour la connaissance des paléoclimats et de leurs vicissitudes ne sauraient se passer de telles données. L'auteur du présent travail a étudié pendant une douzaine d'années (1950-1962) les principales espèces paléolithiques rencontrées dans les gisements du Sud-Ouest de la France.

Le renne *(Rangifer tarandus guettardi)* en est l'espèce dominante depuis le Moustérien jusqu'au Magdalénien terminal. Ses débris faciles à identifier en font un sujet de choix pour l'étude de la conservation des restes osseux. Les recherches conduites à l'Abri Pataud sur un matériel particulièrement abondant (1.590 kg.) récolté dans des conditions stratigraphiques très précises ont confirmé mes résultats antérieurs (Bouchud 1966). En outre, la méthode générale d'étude progressivement élaborée permet de

pénétrer dans la vie quotidienne des chasseurs paléolithiques (Bouchud 1964) et à ce titre elle intéresse le préhistorien.

Pour une espèce déterminée, ici le renne, on doit identifier non seulement les os intacts ou les parties faciles à reconnaître mais aussi les petits éclats de diaphyse. Naturellement, il y a une limite à un tel travail et celle-ci varie avec l'habilité de l'opérateur et la nature du segment osseux considéré. Ainsi le canon postérieur, ou métatarsien, peut être reconnu sur des fragments ayant moins d'un centimètre de long car sa diaphyse présente une section caractéristique. Le canon antérieur, ou métacarpien, demande déjà des fragments plus importants; le fémur en dehors de la ligne âpre, l'humérus en dehors de la crête du deltoïde, et le tibia, excepté dans sa partie supérieure et moyenne, exigent des morceaux ayant plusieurs centimètres de long, car leurs surfaces courbes sont assez semblables.

En pratique, la détermination des fragments se fait en comparant l'éclat d'os considéré avec le segment dont il est supposé provenir; on peut aussi s'aider d'un traité d'ostéologie (Bouchud *in* Lavocat 1966). Cette façon de procéder est assez longue au départ, mais l'opérateur se familiarise très vite avec l'ostéologie du renne, ou des autres espèces, et il peut alors travailler rapidement. Les débris de renne étant toujours très abondants on doit écarter sans hésitation ceux dont la reconnaissance est douteuse.

Les résultats obtenus avec le renne sont exposés dans les tableaux I et II. Le premier fournit le nombre d'éclats identifiés pour chaque segment osseux *(fréquences relatives)* en fonction des principales divisions stratigraphiques tandis que le second renferme les pourcentages correspondants *(fréquences absolues)* ce qui permet d'effectuer toutes les comparaisons nécessaires à partir des données obtenues sur l'animal actuel. Le squelette du renne se compose de 314 os dont le détail est consigné dans la première colonne du tableau I *(fréquences relatives)*. Les pourcentages correspondants *(fréquences absolues)* sont inscrits dans la colonne homologue du tableau II.

TABLEAU I—Distribution en fréquences relatives (nombre de pièces) des différentes parties du squelette de *Rangifer tarandus* en fonction des unités stratigraphiques.

Parties du squelette (Fréquences relatives)		*R. tarandus* actuel	PROTO-MAGDALÉNIEN	PÉRIGORDIEN VI	NOAILLIEN Éboulis 3/4	Supérieur	Moyen	Inférieur
RAMURES		2	126	203	35	95	100	114
OS DU CRANE		43	29	14	9	10	15	9
ROCHER		2	10	3	–	17	12	6
MAXILLAIRE		2	13	24	11	10	21	4
MANDIBULE		1	78	132	62	271	181	99
DENTS LACTEALES S.		8	14	11	7	33	14	20
DENTS LACTEALES I.		14	24	27	9	32	21	41
DENTS PERMANENTES S.		14	178	146	39	297	161	95
DENTS PERMANENTES I.		20	200	168	83	442	210	144
APPAREIL HYOIDIEN		9	–	–	–	–	–	–
SCAPULUM		2	10	17	29	46	18	14
COTES		28	15	224	433	922	344	202
VERTEBRES C.D.L.		26	1	30	24	33	39	20
SACRUM		5	–	–	–	2	–	–
VERTEBRES CAUDALES		11	1	2	–	2	3	–
STERNUM		7	–	2	3	4	1	7
OS INNOMINE		6	2	4	4	14	3	1
	A	–	1	–	2	5	7	2
HUMERUS	B	2	41	41	30	203	97	62
	C	–	2	9	5	23	5	3
	A	–	7	7	3	9	4	3
RADIUS	B	2	59	81	110	501	333	210
	C	–	3	2	4	28	9	3
	A	–	2	12	1	–	5	1
CUBITUS	C	2	4	1	3	–	3	–
	A	–	6	2	1	8	3	1
METACARPIEN	B	2	54	48	72	417	197	143
	C	–	12	38	12	63	22	20
	A	–	4	6	15	29	14	3
FEMUR	B	2	28	101	94	638	192	116
	C	–	2	1	1	16	2	6
	A	–	–	–	–	22	2	1
TIBIA	B	2	90	46	134	1.086	622	282
	C	–	1	6	4	47	43	12
	A	–	35	2	–	145	39	56
METATARSIEN	B	2	140	321	457	2.622	1.348	821
	C	–	8	14	18	98	60	51
PERONE		2	–	4	2	43	16	2
ROTULE		2	2	5	5	26	12	7
STYLETS A. & P.		24	1	53	12	19	19	15
ASTRAGALE		2	3	12	3	20	10	6
CARPE & TARSE		22	13	50	33	78	53	33
PHALANGES I, II, A. & P.		16	12	158	29	99	53	60
SABOTS A. & P.		8	4	27	3	4	1	3
SESAMOIDES		24	–	26	2	5	–	3
Nombre d'éclats osseux		314	1.235	2.080	1.803	8.484	4.314	2.701
Poids total des débris en kg.			32,4	69,2	41,3	310,7	129,6	129,2
Poids des débris identifiés en kg.			10,8	15,9	10,3	60,1	27,6	23,2
Pourcentages correspondants			31,5%	22,5%	25,1%	19,2%	20,0%	18,1%
Poids des os brûlés en kg.			1,860	1,326	0,562	1,471	0,849	2,609
Pourcentages correspondants			5,42%	1,32%	1,34%	0,47%	0,61%	1,97%

PÉRIGORDIEN IV AURIGNACIEN

Éboulis 4/5	Supérieur	Moyen	Inférieur	Extension 2	Couche 11	Couche 12	Couche 13	Éboulis 13/14	Couche 14	Groupement des données
11	237	132	139	70	22	—	1	5	37	1.327
—	37	16	20	6	2	—	—	2	12	181
—	40	12	21	5	1	—	4	1	5	137
—	6	1	15	2	1	—	—	—	—	108
9	166	126	260	51	24	—	15	17	48	1.539
—	30	21	69	10	—	3	—	1	6	239
1	53	38	73	9	1	—	2	2	7	340
2	106	100	210	35	23	3	—	—	12	1.407
13	249	251	574	110	15	—	12	10	50	2.531
—	—	—	1	—	1	—	1	1	—	4
3	20	13	26	11	7	1	1	7	19	242
26	457	381	596	98	171	2	4	9	97	3.981
2	34	31	38	14	6	5	1	13	20	311
—	1	—	—	—	—	—	—	—	—	3
—	1	—	13	1	2	—	—	—	—	25
—	4	1	4	—	2	—	—	—	—	28
2	5	6	15	1	4	2	—	—	2	65
—	20	19	53	9	3	—	—	—	7	128
12	112	99	153	40	14	1	6	16	45	972
—	15	8	41	6	1	—	—	—	5	123
—	3	8	19	7	—	1	—	—	5	76
27	474	241	428	52	25	7	15	38	160	2.761
—	7	8	29	8	1	3	—	—	1	106
2	5	—	3	3	—	3	—	2	12	51
2	13	—	1	—	—	—	—	—	4	31
3	5	8	2	11	4	—	—	5	5	64
28	362	216	334	64	13	4	22	37	133	2.144
1	35	32	48	19	8	1	—	—	8	319
1	21	19	28	5	5	—	1	—	2	153
16	365	225	367	20	27	1	14	1	33	2.238
—	11	26	38	11	5	1	—	—	4	124
—	—	4	12	4	—	—	—	—	5	50
73	1.054	541	735	192	38	11	57	89	271	5.321
—	13	19	31	14	1	10	—	—	2	203
2	6	—	2	41	—	5	—	7	3	343
141	1.924	1.089	1.489	201	109	16	56	91	270	11.095
—	38	48	107	36	4	1	—	—	5	488
—	14	16	30	6	—	—	—	—	1	134
1	36	43	92	6	4	—	—	1	—	240
—	152	144	171	39	6	3	4	12	20	670
1	19	24	41	18	1	10	—	—	1	169
3	238	262	466	125	5	24	—	8	34	1.425
10	412	423	415	202	37	9	3	20	89	2.031
—	35	50	82	28	4	—	2	6	14	263
—	78	78	111	43	2	2	—	9	27	386
392	6.913	4.779	7.402	1.633	599	129	221	410	1.481	44.576
107,8	264,0	112,6	225,9	49,4	70,2	12,5	3,92	6,30	23,50	1588,5
28,7	39,3	23,9	54,9	10,6	16,4	1,5	0,94	1,84	7,50	333,5
26,0%	14,9%	21,2%	23,4%	21,5%	23,4%	12,1%	24,0%	29,3%	30,6%	21%
0,125	6,367	5,518	8,568	1,754	2,734	5,254	0,111	0,337	2,128	41,573
0,11%	2,41%	4,66%	3,65%	3,5%	3,9%	41,9%	2,9%	5,4%	9,3%	2,61%

TABLEAU II—Distribution en fréquences absolues (pourcentages) des différentes parties du squelette de *Rangifer tarandus* en fonction des unités stratigraphiques.

Parties du squelette (Fréquences absolues)		R. tarandus actuel — Parties du squelette	R. tarandus actuel — Pourcentages correspondants	PROTO-MAGDALÉNIEN (1958-1963)	PÉRIGORDIEN VI	Éboulis 3/4	NOAILLIEN Supérieur	NOAILLIEN Moyen	NOAILLIEN Inférieur
RAMURES		2	0,64	10,202	9,760	1,941	1,1198	2,3180	4,221
OS DU CRANE		43	13,15	2,348	0,673	0,499	0,1179	0,3477	0,333
ROCHER		2	0,64	0,810	0,144	–	0,2004	0,2782	0,222
MAXILLAIRE		2	0,64	1,053	1,154	0,610	0,1179	0,4868	0,148
MANDIBULE		1	0,33	6,316	6,346	3,438	3,1943	4,1956	3,665
DENTS LACTEALES S.		8	2,56	1,134	0,529	0,388	0,3890	0,3245	0,741
DENTS LACTEALES I.		14	4,50	1,943	1,298	0,499	0,3772	0,4868	1,518
DENTS PERMANENTES S.		14	4,50	14,413	7,019	2,163	3,5007	3,7320	3,517
DENTS PERMANENTES I.		20	6,42	16,194	8,077	4,603	5,2098	4,8679	5,332
APPAREIL HYOIDIEN		9	2,88	–	–	–	–	–	–
SCAPULUM		2	0,64	0,810	0,817	1,609	0,5422	0,4173	0,518
COTES		28	8,97	1,214	10,769	24,016	10,8675	7,9740	7,479
VERTEBRES C.D.L.		26	8,34	0,081	1,442	1,331	0,3890	0,9040	0,741
SACRUM		5	1,60	–	–	–	0,0236	–	–
VERTEBRES CAUDALES		11	3,53	0,081	0,096	–	0,0236	0,0695	–
STERNUM		7	2,24	–	0,096	0,166	0,0471	0,0232	0,259
OS INNOMINE		6	1,92	0,162	0,192	0,222	0,1650	0,0695	0,037
HUMERUS	A	–	0,21	0,081	–	0,111	0,0589	0,1623	0,074
	B	2	0,21	3,320	1,971	1,664	2,3927	2,2485	2,296
	C	–	0,21	0,162	0,433	0,277	0,2711	0,1159	0,111
RADIUS	A	–	0,21	0,567	0,337	0,166	0,1061	0,0927	0,111
	B	2	0,21	4,777	3,894	6,101	5,9052	7,7191	7,775
	C	–	0,21	0,243	0,096	0,222	0,3300	0,2086	0,111
CUBITUS	A	–	0,33	0,162	0,577	0,056	–	0,1159	0,037
	C	2	0,33	0,324	0,048	0,166	–	0,0695	–
METACARPIEN	A	–	0,21	0,486	0,096	0,056	0,0943	0,0695	0,037
	B	2	0,21	4,372	2,308	3,993	4,9151	4,5665	5,294
	C	–	0,21	0,972	1,827	0,666	0,7426	0,5100	0,740
FEMUR	A	–	0,21	0,324	0,289	0,832	0,3418	0,3245	0,111
	B	2	0,21	2,267	4,856	5,214	7,5200	4,4506	4,295
	C	–	0,21	0,162	0,048	0,056	0,1886	0,0464	0,222
TIBIA	A	–	0,21	–	–	–	0,2593	0,0464	0,037
	B	2	0,21	7,287	2,212	7,432	12,8006	14,4182	10,441
	C	–	0,21	0,081	0,289	0,222	0,5540	0,9968	0,444
METATARSIEN	A	–	0,21	2,834	0,096	–	1,7091	0,9040	2,073
	B	2	0,21	11,336	15,433	25,347	30,9052	31,2471	30,396
	C	–	0,21	0,647	0,673	0,998	1,1551	1,3908	1,888
PERONE		2	0,64	–	0,192	0,111	0,5068	0,3709	0,074
ROTULE		2	0,64	0,162	0,340	0,277	0,3065	0,2782	0,259
STYLETS A. & P.		24	7,70	0,081	2,548	0,666	0,2240	0,4404	0,555
ASTRAGALE		2	0,64	0,243	0,577	0,166	0,2357	0,2318	0,222
CARPE & TARSE		22	7,05	1,053	2,404	1,830	0,9194	1,2286	1,222
PHALANGES I, II, A. & P.		16	5,13	0,972	7,596	1,609	1,1669	1,2286	2,222
SABOTS A. & P.		8	2,56	0,324	1,298	0,166	0,0471	0,0232	0,111
SESAMOIDES		24	7,70	–	1,250	0,111	0,0589	–	0,111
Pourcentages totaux			100,00	100,000	100,000	100,000	100,0000	100,0000	100,000
Nombre d'éclats osseux		314		1.235	2.080	1.803	8.484	4.314	2.701

PÉRIGORDIEN IV   AURIGNACIEN

Éboulis 4/5	Supérieur	Moyen	Inférieur	Extension 2	Couche 11	Couche 12	Couche 13	Éboulis 13/14	Couche 14	Groupement des données (% correspondants)
2,81	3,4283	2,7621	1,8779	4,287	3,673	–	0,45	1,22	2,498	2,9769
–	0,5352	0,3348	0,2702	0,367	0,334	–	–	0,49	0,810	0,4061
–	0,5786	0,2511	0,2837	0,306	0,167	–	1,81	0,24	0,338	0,3073
–	0,0868	0,0209	0,2026	0,122	0,167	–	–	–	–	0,2423
2,30	2,4013	2,6365	3,5126	3,123	4,006	–	6,79	4,15	3,241	3,4525
–	0,4340	0,4394	0,9322	0,612	–	2,33	–	0,24	0,405	0,5362
0,25	0,7667	0,7951	0,9862	0,551	0,167	–	0,91	0,49	0,473	0,7627
0,51	1,5333	2,0925	2,8371	2,143	3,840	2,33	–	–	0,810	3,1564
3,32	3,6019	5,2521	7,7547	6,736	2,504	–	5,43	2,44	3,376	5,6779
–	–	–	0,0135	–	0,167	–	0,45	0,24	–	0,0090
0,76	0,2893	0,2720	0,3513	0,674	1,168	0,77	0,45	1,71	1,283	0,5429
6,63	6,6107	7,9724	8,0519	6,001	28,547	1,55	1,81	2,20	6,550	8,9308
0,51	0,4918	0,6487	0,5134	0,857	1,002	3,88	0,45	3,17	1,350	0,6977
–	0,0145	–	–	–	–	–	–	–	–	0,0067
–	0,0145	–	0,1756	0,061	0,334	–	–	–	–	0,0561
–	0,0579	0,0209	0,0540	–	0,334	–	–	–	–	0,0628
0,51	0,0723	0,1256	0,2026	0,061	0,668	1,55	–	–	0,135	0,1458
–	0,2893	0,3976	0,7160	0,551	0,501	–	–	–	0,473	0,2872
3,06	1,6201	2,0716	2,0670	2,450	2,337	0,77	2,72	3,90	3,038	2,1806
–	0,2170	0,1674	0,5539	0,367	0,167	–	–	–	0,338	0,2759
–	0,0434	0,1674	0,2567	0,429	–	0,77	–	–	0,338	0,1705
6,89	6,8567	5,0429	5,7822	3,184	4,173	5,43	6,79	9,27	10,803	6,1939
–	0,1013	0,1674	0,3918	0,490	0,167	2,33	–	–	0,068	0,2378
0,51	0,0723	–	0,0405	0,184	–	2,33	–	0,49	0,810	0,1144
0,51	0,1881	–	0,0135	–	–	–	–	–	0,270	0,0695
0,76	0,0723	0,1674	0,0270	0,674	0,668	–	–	1,22	0,338	0,1436
7,14	5,2365	4,5198	4,5123	3,919	2,170	3,10	9,95	9,02	8,980	4,8098
0,26	0,5063	0,6696	0,6485	1,164	1,335	0,77	–	–	0,540	0,7156
0,26	0,3038	0,3976	0,3783	0,306	0,835	–	0,45	–	0,135	0,3432
4,08	5,2799	4,7081	4,9581	1,225	4,507	0,77	6,33	0,24	2,228	5,0206
–	0,1591	0,5440	0,5134	0,674	0,835	0,77	–	–	0,270	0,2782
–	–	0,0837	0,1621	0,245	–	–	–	–	0,338	0,1122
18,62	15,2466	11,3204	9,9297	11,758	6,344	8,53	25,79	21,71	18,298	11,9369
–	0,1881	0,3976	0,4188	0,857	0,167	7,75	–	–	0,135	0,4554
0,51	0,0868	–	0,0270	2,511	–	3,88	–	1,71	0,203	0,7695
35,97	27,8316	22,7872	20,1162	12,309	18,197	12,40	25,34	22,19	18,231	24,8901
–	0,5497	1,0044	1,4456	2,205	0,668	0,77	–	–	0,338	1,0948
–	0,2025	0,3348	0,4053	0,367	–	–	–	–	0,068	0,3006
0,26	0,5208	0,8998	1,2429	0,367	0,668	–	–	0,24	–	0,5384
–	2,1987	3,0132	2,3102	2,388	1,002	2,33	1,81	2,93	1,350	1,5031
0,26	0,2748	0,5022	0,5539	1,102	0,167	7,75	–	–	0,068	0,3791
0,76	3,4428	5,4823	0,2956	7,655	0,835	18,61	–	1,95	2,296	3,1968
2,55	5,9598	8,8512	5,6066	12,370	6,177	6,98	1,36	4,88	6,009	4,5563
–	0,5063	1,0462	1,1078	1,715	0,668	–	0,91	1,46	0,945	0,5900
–	1,1283	1,6321	1,4996	2,633	0,334	1,55	–	2,20	1,823	0,8659
100,00	100,0000	100,0000	100,0000	100,000	100,000	100,00	100,00	100,00	100,000	100,0000
392	6.913	4.779	7.402	1.633	599	129	221	410	1.481	44.576

L'expérience conduit à un certain nombre de groupements, de séparations, ou de divisions. Ainsi le rocher à l'intérieur duquel se trouve le mécanisme délicat de l'oreille interne est un os particulièrement robuste qui doit être distingué de l'ensemble des os craniens très fragiles; les vertèbres cervicales, dorsales, et lombaires fort semblables entre elles sont comptées ensemble tandis que la séparation est maintenue entre vertèbres sacrées et vertèbres caudales. Dans le même ordre d'idées, on doit distinguer les sabots d'avec le groupe des phalanges (I) et (II). Le partage des divers os longs en trois parties, la région articulaire proximale (A), la diaphyse (B), et l'extrêmité distale (C), est imposée par le fait que le nombre des éclats diaphysaires est toujours bien supérieur à celui des fragments qui proviennent des extrémités proximales et distales.

Outre le nombre des éclats osseux récoltés, le premier tableau donne aussi la masse totale des débris de renne recueillis, la masse des débris identifiés, le pourcentage correspondant et enfin la masse des os brûlés et cela pour chaque unité stratigraphique.

Pour interpréter plus facilement cette série de faits, il est utile de commencer par l'examen de la répartition stratigraphique des dents et des mandibules.

Le renne possède dans la première année de son existence trois molaires de lait et une molaire définitive par demi-mandibule; au début de la seconde année une deuxième monophysaire apparaît; enfin au cours de la troisième année perce la dernière monophysaire tandis que les dents déciduales sont remplacées par trois prémolaires permanentes. A ce moment la denture définitive du renne est complète.

En résumé, pendant les trois premières années de sa vie, le renne acquit progressivement quatre, cinq, et enfin six dents qu'il conservera jusqu'à la fin de son existence.

Le chercheur suédois F. Skuncke (1953) a calculé le nombre d'animaux des différentes classes d'âge contenues dans une population naturelle intégralement protégée contre les prédateurs. Grâce à ces valeurs et aux remarques exposées ci-dessus, il est possible de déterminer le nombre de dents de différents types rencontrés dans une population naturelle. Le tableau III expose les données suédoises, et le nombre de dents en fonction de l'âge contenues dans une population naturelle comprenant 1.000 rennes. Ainsi que les pourcentages correspondants, les fréquences absolues sont, au départ, très différentes des valeurs calculées par le chercheur suédois, mais cela tient au fait le renne acquiert progressivement sa denture définitive.

Dans une population naturelle comprenant mille rennes le nombre total des dents par demi-mandibule s'élève à 5.354; pour simplifier, les incisives et les canines sont écartées de ce décompte; les dents supérieures ou inférieures se répartissent ainsi:

Molaires de lait 1.677
Prémolaires définitives 1.323
Molaires définitives 2.354
Nombre total de dents 5.354

Les trois rapports suivants:

$$\frac{\text{Maxillaires}}{\text{Mandibules}} = 1,000$$

$$\frac{\text{Molaires de lait inférieures}}{\text{Nombre total de dents inférieures}} = 0,313$$

$$\frac{\text{Prémolaires inférieures}}{\text{Molaires inférieures}} = 0,562$$

permettent d'interpréter la répartition des dents de renne récoltées en fonction des unités stratigraphiques (tableau IV). Ces rapports sont numérotés de (1) à (5) selon qu'ils s'appliquent aux dents supérieures ou aux dents inférieures.

TABLEAU III

Distribution des dents à l'intérieur d'une population naturelle comprenant 1.000 *Rangifer tarandus*

Dents	ANNÉES												Totaux
	0	1	2	3	4	5	6	7	8	9	10	11	
Données de Skuncke (1953) (%)	23,1	18,4	14,4	11,6	9,0	7,0	5,6	4,0	3,4	2,0	0,8	0,7	100%
Population comprenant 1.000 *Rangifer tarandus*	231	184	144	116	90	70	56	40	34	20	8	7	1.000
Nombre de dents correspondant	924	920	864	696	540	420	336	240	204	120	48	42	5.354
Pourcentages correspondants	17,3	17,2	16,1	13,0	10,1	7,8	6,3	4,5	3,8	2,2	0,9	0,8	100%

TABLEAU IV. Distribution des dents de *Rangifer tarandus* en fonction des unités stratigraphiques

Types de dents (Fréquences relatives)	AURIGNACIEN (Couche 14)	PÉRIGORDIEN IV				NOAILLIEN				PÉRIGORDIEN VI	PROTO-MAGDALÉNIEN	Renne actuel (1.000 bêtes)
		Extensions 1 et 2	Inférieur	Moyen	Supérieur	Inférieur	Moyen	Supérieur	Éboulis 3/4			
Maxillaires / Mandibules	1 / 4	2 / 6	10 / 72	2 / 20	6 / 29	4 / 24	15 / 42	6 / 54	9 / 20	15 / 49	8 / 43	1.000 / 1.000
Rapport Maxillaires / Mandibules (1)	0,250	0,333	0,138	0,100	0,206	0,166	0,357	0,111	0,450	0,306	0,186	1,000
Dents lactéales inférieures / Dents définitives inférieures	7 / 50	9 / 110	73 / 574	38 / 251	53 / 249	41 / 144	21 / 212	32 / 442	9 / 83	27 / 168	24 / 200	1.677 / 3.674
Rapport Dents lactéales / Dents définitives (2)	0,122	0,075	0,112	0,131	0,175	0,210	0,089	0,072	0,097	0,138	0,107	0,313
Prémolaires inférieures / Molaires inférieures	18 / 32	53 / 57	221 / 353	112 / 139	106 / 143	60 / 84	100 / 112	212 / 230	35 / 48	75 / 93	96 / 104	1.323 / 2.354
Rapport Prémol. infér. / Molaires inf. (3)	0,562	0,929	0,625	0,805	0,741	0,714	0,892	0,921	0,729	0,806	0,923	0,562
Dents lactéales supérieures / Dents définitives supérieures	6 / 12	10 / 35	69 / 210	21 / 100	30 / 106	20 / 95	14 / 161	33 / 297	7 / 39	11 / 146	14 / 178	1.677 / 3.674
Rapport Dents lact. sup. / Dents déf. sup. (4)	0,500	0,285	0,328	0,210	0,283	0,210	0,086	0,111	0,179	0,075	0,078	0,313
Prémolaires supérieures / Molaires supérieures	2 / 10	13 / 22	91 / 119	48 / 52	53 / 53	45 / 50	86 / 66	168 / 129	24 / 15	72 / 74	83 / 95	1.323 / 2.354
Rapport Prémol. sup. / Molaires sup. (5)	0,200	0,590	0,764	0,923	1,000	0,900	1,303	1,302	1,600	0,972	0,873	0,562

Parmi eux les rapports (1), (2), et (4) sont plus petits que les valeurs théoriques tandis que les rapports (3) et (5) demeurent toujours supérieurs pour les raisons suivantes:

Le dentaire, os robuste qui constitue le mandibule, est parcouru par un canal à parois épaisses; il résiste mieux à l'écrasement que le maxillaire, os fragile, creusé de sinus volumineux aux parois minces.

TABLEAU V. Détail de la distribution des dents de *Rangifer tarandus* en fonction des unités stratigraphiques

Dents inférieures

Catégories dentaires	PROTO-MAGDALÉNIEN	PÉRIGORDIEN VI	Éboulis 3/4	NOAILLIEN Supérieur	Moyen	Inférieur	Éboulis 4/5	PÉRIGORDIEN IV Supérieur	Moyen	Inférieur	Extension 2	AURIGNACIEN Couche 11	Couche 12	Couche 13	Éboulis 13/14	Couche 14	Totaux généraux
d 1	7	4	–	15	4	4	–	9	6	11	3	–	–	–	–	2	65
d 2	11	6	1	11	5	10	1	18	9	22	4	–	–	–	1	2	101
d 3	6	17	8	6	12	27	–	26	23	40	2	1	–	2	1	3	174
P 2	32	24	15	66	32	18	1	33	40	65	17	2	–	2	3	5	355
P 3	27	31	9	75	34	23	–	35	43	85	19	–	–	–	4	7	392
P 4	37	20	11	71	33	19	2	38	29	71	17	1	–	3	–	6	358
M 1	32	26	14	63	29	24	1	36	29	101	13	2	–	2	2	10	384
M 2	39	32	17	71	39	30	2	46	62	132	17	3	–	4	–	13	507
M 3	33	35	17	96	43	30	7	61	48	120	27	7	–	1	1	9	535
Totaux partiels	224	195	92	474	231	185	14	302	289	647	119	16	–	14	12	57	2.871
Mandibules	43	49	20	54	42	24	1	29	20	72	6	4	–	1	1	4	370

Dents supérieures

Catégories dentaires	PROTO-MAGDALÉNIEN	PÉRIGORDIEN VI	Éboulis 3/4	NOAILLIEN Supérieur	Moyen	Inférieur	Éboulis 4/5	PÉRIGORDIEN IV Supérieur	Moyen	Inférieur	Extension 2	AURIGNACIEN Couche 11	Couche 12	Couche 13	Éboulis 13/14	Couche 14	Totaux généraux
D 1	4	1	–	5	4	1	–	9	7	15	1	–	1	–	–	2	50
D 2	2	8	3	16	6	7	–	10	11	32	6	–	1	–	1	3	106
D 3	8	2	4	12	4	12	–	11	3	22	3	–	1	–	–	1	83
PM	83	72	24	168	86	45	1	53	48	91	13	17	3	–	–	2	706
M 1	18	20	6	48	22	14	1	16	19	39	8	2	–	–	–	3	216
M 2	31	21	5	42	23	17	–	22	18	38	10	3	–	–	–	4	234
M 3	46	33	4	39	30	19	–	15	15	42	4	1	–	–	–	3	251
Totaux partiels	192	157	46	330	175	115	2	136	121	279	45	23	6	–	1	18	1.646
Maxillaires	8	15	9	6	15	4	–	6	2	10	2	–	–	–	–	1	78

Les dents lactéales possèdent, contrairement aux monophysaires, une cavité interne importante limitée par des parois médiocres, elles sont donc plus fragiles que les dents définitives, inférieures ou supérieures.

Les prémolaires, à la mandibule, sont plus abondantes, ou ce qui revient au même, les molaires sont moins numbreuses que les rapports théoriques (3) et (5) ne le laisseraient supposer. Inversement, les prémolaires supérieures seraient plus résistantes que les molaires. L'examen des données groupées du tableau V montre que dans le groupe des monophysaires les M1 sont moins fréquentes que les M2, elles mêmes moins répandues que les M3. Le classement s'opère dans le même ordre pour les dents déciduales d1 – d2 et d3.

La distribution des dents fossiles dépend donc de leur résistance mécanique à l'écrasement. C'est un point que j'ai souligné dans un travail récent (Bouchud 1966).

Cette explication est elle encore valable en ce qui concerne les différentes parties du squelette? En ce qui concerne le crâne des animaux, cela fait aucun doute; on ne trouve jamais ni les cornets du nez, ni le vomer, mais on rencontre parfois le rocher. Ainsi dans les 1.588 kg. de débris de renne provenant de l'Abri Pataud, j'ai identifié 131 rochers, une douzaine de condyles occipitaux, de basioccipitaux, et de basisphénoïdes, deux prémaxillaires, et quatre fragments d'appareil hyoïdien. La fragilité mécanique semble bien une cause de destruction pour certains os. Cependent il semble difficile d'expliquer ainsi la grande rareté des humérus et des fémurs par rapport aux os canons.

R.D. Guthrie (1967) a traité récemment ce problème à partir des restes de chevaux (*Equus caballus*) et de bison (*Bison priscus = Bison crassicornis*) découverts dans le Pleistocène récent de l'Alaska.

Pour les membres antérieurs et postérieurs, les os proximaux et distaux sont les plus rares, la fréquence maximum appartenant aux os canons, métacarpiens et métatarsiens.

La construction plus ou moins robuste des os, l'épaisseur des parois dasphysaires, l'importance plus ou moins grande du tissu spongieux rendent compte des pourcentages observés en ce qui concerne les os longs proprement dits (Guthrie 1967). Les carnivores, ainsi que les phénomènes chimiques et bactériens s'attaquent aux segments enveloppés d'une masse charnue importante: fémur et humérus, et facilitent leur disparition. Les os canons, pauvres en chair sont partiellement protégés par la peau contre les actions microbiennes (Flerov et Zablotski 1961). Quant aux phalanges la taille joue un rôle important en facilitant leur découverte par les chercheurs. Par ordre de

fréquences décroissante, elles se rangent ainsi: phalanges (I) – phalanges (II) – sabots.

Les sabots du bison, au point de vue anatomique, sont deux fois plus nombreux que ceux du cheval, mais dans les restes fossiles, le sabot caballin est deux fois plus répandu que le sabot bovin. La grande taille du premier par rapport au second facilite sa découverte (Guthrie 1967).

J'ai développé un point de vue presque identique (Bouchud 1966), dans le cas du *Rangifer tarandus*; le *corps entier* a été apporté à l'Abri Pataud puisque on retrouve, avec une fréquence très variable d'ailleurs, les divers éléments squelettiques. Mais le crâne et tous les os longs furent brisés par les chasseurs qui recherchaient le cerveau et la moelle. La principale cause de destruction est ici l'homme et si les éléments proximaux et distaux des membres sont rares, les causes exposées ci-dessus ne sont pas suffisantes pour expliquer complètement les faits.

La soudure des épiphyses, pour un segment osseux déterminé marque la fin d'une évolution au cours de laquelle il acquiert sa résistance maximum or l'âge auquel cette soudure est achevée varie considérablement d'un élément à l'autre comme on peut le vérifier, grâce au tableau VI.

TABLEAU VI

Ages correspondant à la soudure des épiphyses chez *Rangifer tarandus*

1° – Soudure des os du bassin à la cavité cotyloïde . . . . . fin de la première année

2° – Soudure des épiphyses distales du fémur et de l'humérus . . . . début de la 3ème année

3° – Soudure des épiphyses proximales des phalanges . . . vers 2 ans 1/2

4° – Soudure de l'épiphyse distale des os canons . . . . . début de la 3ème année

5° – Soudure de l'épiphyse distale du radius et du tibia . . début de la 4ème année

6° – Soudure du plateau tibial . . . vers 4 ans 1/2

7° – Soudure de la tête de l'humérus et du fémur . . . . vers 4 ans 1/2 – 5 ans

8° – Soudure des épiphyses vertébrales . . . . début de la 5ème année

Pour interpréter correctement les tableaux I et II, il est nécessaire de partir d'une population naturelle. Dans un troupeau intégralement protégé contre les prédateurs (Skuncke 1953) il y a, pour un millier de rennes:

jusqu'à un an	230 animaux		
de un à deux ans	185 animaux	soit 770	ayant plus d'un an
de deux à trois ans	148 animaux	soit 585	ayant plus de deux ans
de trois à quatre ans	117 animaux	soit 437	ayant plus de trois ans
de quatre à cinq ans	92 animaux	soit 320	ayant plus de quatre ans
de cinq à six ans	69 animaux	soit 228	ayant plus de cinq ans
. . . . .	. . . . .	. . . .	. . . .
de dix à quatorze ans	27 animaux	soit 27	ayant plus de dix ans

Dans ces conditions, les phalanges dont l'épiphyse proximale est soudée proviennent de 500 rennes environ, les canons dont la croissance est achevée appartiennent à 441 bêtes tandis que les humérus ayant terminé leur évolution ne sont plus que 245. A côté de la structure de l'os envisagée au point de vue mécanique, il faut faire une place au nombre d'animaux qui occupent la classe d'âge correspondant à la soudure des épiphyses du segment considéré. En effet c'est le nombre de bêtes au départ qui conditionne le nombre de débris récoltés dans les stations préhistoriques. La résistance aux actions chimiques, bactériennes, ou mécaniques agit ensuite.

La taille intervient certes dans la récolte des débris (Guthrie 1967) mais son rôle demeure restreint car paléontologistes et préhistoriens *tamisent* leurs déblais pour en tirer le maximum de documents.

La discussion précédente peut se résumer ainsi. Dans le cas de l'Abri Pataud, et de tous les gisements du Sud-Ouest de la France la probabilité de découverte des diverses parties du squelette dépend:

1°. Du nombre d'animaux contenus dans la classe d'âge déterminée par l'usure des dents et la soudure des épiphyses. C'est ce que j'appelle la *probabilité de rencontre*, définie par un coefficient inférieur à l'unité, obtenu en divisant par 1.000 le nombre des animaux contenus dans les diverses classes d'âge (tableau III).

2°. De la résistance du matériel à l'écrasement. Ainsi les M3 sont plus abondantes que les M2, elles mêmes plus fréquentes que les M1. L'humérus et le fémur sont moins résistants que les canons. Leurs parois diaphysaires sont plus minces, leurs cavités médullaires plus volumineuses, et le tissu spongieux plus abondant. Dans ces conditions les *probabilités de rencontre*, multipliées[1] par les *probabilités de destruction* plus importantes expliquent le petit nombre des surfaces articulaires distales et la grande rareté des têtes humérales et fémorales.

3°. Le nombre des restes diaphysaires est une fonction caractéristique de la forme de la diaphyse. Ceci explique le pourcentage élevé des restes de canon postérieur, le pourcentage plus faible des débris de canon antérieur, et le petit nombre de fragments d'humérus ou de fémur. La probabilité de rencontre, comme dans le cas précédent, intervient.

4°. Certains os, ceux de la tête en particulier, demeurent fragiles toute la vie de l'animal. Ils restent toujours rares.

5°. Dans une station préhistorique, la répartition des restes osseux n'est jamais aléatoire au sens propre du terme. L'homme dépeçait le gibier à tel endroit, le cuisinait à un autre, et le consommait ailleurs. Il est donc important de fouiller une surface considérable; sans cette précaution, la distribution des débris osseux risque d'être plus ou moins modifiée. Ainsi s'explique en partie les fluctuations observées dans les pourcentages contenus dans le tableau II.

1. La probabilité d'une série d'évènements s'obtient en se multipliant les probabilités des divers évènements qui composent la série.

2. LA FAUNE DU PROTO-MAGDALENIEN

CERVIDAE

Les débris de renne *(Rangifer tarandus)* représentent 80% du nombre total des éclats osseux récoltes. Les autres espèces identifiées sont les suivantes (tableau VII).

TABLEAU VII

Espèces et débris osseux provenant du Proto-Magdalénien

Macrofaune			Rongeurs		
Rangifer tarandus	1235	(85,5%)	*Lepus variabilis*	7	(5,6%)
Cervus elaphus	38	(2,7%)	*Microtus agrestis-arvalis*	43	(34,4%)
Capreolus capreolus	1		*Arvicola scherman*	64	(51,2%)
Bos sp.	28	(1,9%)	*Eliomys quercinus*	11	(8,8%)
Equus caballus	40	(2,8%)			
Elephas primigenius	1				
Capra ibex	36	(5,0%)	Oiseaux		
Rupicapra rupicapra	37				
Canis lupus	23	(2,0%)	*Coracia graculus*	3	
Vulpes vulpes	6		*Turdus viscivorus*	12	
Panthera leo, race *spelaea*	2	(0,1%)	*Larus argentatus*	1	

On retrouve toutes les espèces citées par D. Peyrony (1938) dans le niveau correspondant de Laugerie-Haute à l'exception d'*Aquila chrysaëtus, Haliaëtus albicilla, Lagopus lagopus,* et *Charadrius apricarius.*

Le renne est représenté par les différentes parties de son squelette; les chasseurs apportaient donc les corps entiers de leurs victimes à l'Abri Pataud; cependant tous les os longs, les maxillaires et les mandibules sont invariablement brisés et il est presque impossible de prendre des mesures.

TABLEAU VIII

Liste des bois de *Rangifer tarandus* rencontrés dans le Proto-Magdalénien

(Pmg. — 82). 1 morceau de perche portant la meule mais brisé au-dessus de l'andouiller postérieur. L = 250 mm., A = 26,0 x 18,0 mm.

(Pmg. — 89). 1 débris d'empaumure. L = 150 mm.

(Pmg. — 97). 1 morceau de perche. Partie située au-dessus de l'andouiller postérieur mais s'arrêtant au départ de l'empaumure. L = 170 mm., B = 38,0 x 33,0 mm., C = 30,0 x 33,0 mm.

(Pmg. — 105). 1 bois de chute; meule en partie conservée, perche brisée avant l'andouiller postérieur. Amorce de l'andouiller d'oeil à 15,0 mm. de la meule, départ de l'andouiller de glace à 86,0 mm. de la meule. L = 185 mm., A = 15,0 x 15,0 mm., B = 15,0 x 15,0 mm.

(Pmg. — 116). 1 digitation isolée provenant d'une empaumure. L = 125 mm.

(Pmg. — 124). 1 bois comprenant la partie supérieure de la perche avec l'empaumure. Perche de type *arcticus*, (pl. I, n° 1). L = 300 mm., B = 21,0 x 27,5 mm., C = 30,0 x 19,0 mm.

(Pmg. — 135). 1 morceau de perche sectionné au niveau de la meule et avant l'andouiller postérieur. Andouiller de glace à 42 mm. de la meule. A = 23,0 x 20,0 mm., B = 24,0 x 14,0 mm.

(Pmg. — 1963-36). 1 grand bois de massacre ♂ travaillé (fig. 1). Un trou a été percé au niveau de l'andouiller de glace. La perche pratiquement ronde appartient au type *"arcticus"*; elle est peu courbée par rapport au crâne et elle est dépourvue d'andouiller postérieur. L = 550 mm., A_0 = 52,2 x 50,0 mm., A = 50,0 x 40,0 mm. A_1 = 47,0 x 36,0 mm., B = 40,0 x 36,0 mm., C = 38,0 x 30,0 mm.

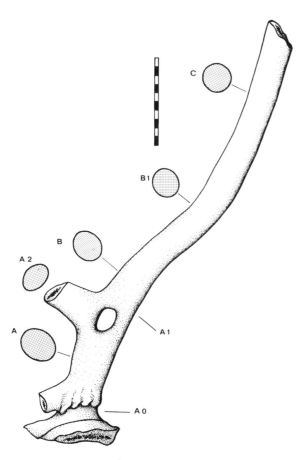

Figure 1. Proto-Magdalénien. Bois de *Rangifer tarandus* travaillé par l'homme. La forte taille de la perche et sa section ronde caractérisent un renne de toundra. - L = 550 mm.; A_0 = 52,0 x 50,0 mm.; A = 50,0 x 40,0 mm.; A_1 = 47,0 x 36,0 mm.; B = 40,0 x 36,0 mm.; C = 38,0 x 30,0 mm.

Un fait intéressant est à signaler: la présence d'os de foetus reconnaissables par leur petite taille et l'absence de canal médullaire. Les épiphyses ont disparu. Voici la longueur des diaphyses conservées:

humérus: 37,0 mm, radius: 40,0 mm, tibia: 43,5 mm.

Ces valeurs correspondent à un foetus de 4 mois (Kelsall 1957). Le rut ayant lieu vers la fin septembre et la mi-octobre, on doit admettre la présence de l'homme et du renne pendant les mois de janvier-février.

Les débris de bois de renne sont peu nombreux: un peu plus d'une vingtaine mais huit piéces seulement méritent d'être décrites.

La longueur totale de la piéce est appelée L. La section A désigne les diamêtres maximum et minimum pris un peu au dessus de la meule; la section B se place peu aprés l'andouiller postérieur; et la section C est située au départ de l'empaumure. Dans quelques pièces bien conservées, A_0 se place entre la meule et le pédicule, tandis que A_1 est mesuré au dessus de l'andouiller de glace.

La répartition des dents et des mandibules en fonction de l'âge et des mois de l'année sera discutée dans le section traitant de l'habitat humain.

Immédiatement aprés *R. tarandus* vient le *Cerf élaphe* (tableau VII, 38 éclats d'os). Il est représenté par quelques dents isolées, des fragments de radius et surtout des débris de tibia, de canon antérieur, et postérieur dont aucun n'est mesurable. L'animal cependant était de grande taille comme le prouve la trouvaille suivante.

En 1958 contre la paroi de l'abri trois crânes apparemment intacts de *C. elaphus* femelle furent découverts. Deux étaient réunis par leurs faces palatines et reposaient verticalement sur les condyles occipitaux. Les rostres étaient assez abimés. Un crâne de jeune, mal conservé, était posé lui aussi sur le trou occipital, il appuyait sa face palatine contre le bloc formé par les deux calvariums précédents. Le dégagement des piéces livra deux crânes de femelles âgées de 2 et 14 ans d'aprés l'attrition dentaire (Baumann 1949); les boîtes crâniennes portaient un enfoncement identique dont le contour rappelle celui que provoque le coup de merlin du boucher. Un fait analogue a été observé sur un crâne fossile de Bovidé découvert par le docteur J. Allain (1952) dans le Magdalénien supérieur de Saint-Marcel (Indre). Les préhistoriques auraient, semble-t-il, abattu par cette technique des animaux vivants pris au piège. Ces piéces très fragiles ont été renforcées en coulant par la blessure du plâtre dans la cavité cranienne. Pour comble de malchance les rostres ont été brisés accidentellement et il fallu consolider les morceaux sans pouvoir reconstituer les crânes.

Les deux biches étaient de trés grande taille: la longueur totale de chaque crâne dépassait 370 mm. La minceur et le modelé de la partie postérieure de la boîte crânienne permettent d'exclure *Cervus megaceros* et d'affirmer la détermination *Cervus elaphus*.

Le tableau IX résume les mesures prises sur les dents au niveau du collet.

Le crâne jeune privé des os nasaux, du frontal, des pariétaux et de la région occipitale, a été emprisonné

TABLEAU IX

Crânes de *Cervus elaphus* du Proto-Magdalénien. Dimensions des dents

Cervus elaphus femelle (14 ans)	Longueur de la série dentaire	p2	p3	Dents supérieures			
				p4	M^1	M^2	M^3
Série dentaire g.	118,0	13,0 x 18,0	15,0 x 16,8	19,0 x 11,8	22,0 x 18,0	23,0 x 25,0	24,5 x 25,7
Série dentaire d.	115,0	12,0 x 16,0	15,0 x 17,0	18,0 x 12,0	22,0 x 19,5	22,8 x 25,0	24,0 x 25,0
Cervus elaphus femelle (2 ans)	L	P2	P3	P4	M^1	M^2	M^3
Série dentaire g.	123,0	18,0 x 17,0	19,0 x 18,0	20,8 x 16,0	23,0 x 20,0	25,0 x 24,0	25,0 x 26,0
Série dentaire d.	123,0	17,0 x 18,0	18,5 x 17,0	21,0 x 16,5	22,0 x 18,5	25,0 x 24,0	26,0 x 29,0

par sa face supérieure dans un bloc de plâtre ce qui a permis de conserver la face palatine. Les dents temporaires sont bien conservées et la M_1 est a demi-sortie de l'alvéole. L'animal était âgé de 6 mois au moment de la mort (Baumann 1949). La série dentaire occupe une longueur de 87 mm. dont 62mm. pour les dents lactéales.

Une partie d'os canon a pu être attribué avec un point de doute à *Capreolus capreolus*.

BOVIDAE et EQUIDAE

Les Equidés et les Bovidés sont représentés par des éclats de diaphyses (fémur, tibia, phalanges, débris de bassin). Certains ont pu être attribués soit au genre *Equus* soit au genre *Bos*, mais un bon nombre d'entre eux, de taille réduite, ont du être rangés sous le vocable: *Bos* ou *Equus*.

Il faut mentionner des débris de mandibule et des dents isolées, le tout en mauvais état.

Equus caballus est représenté par une moitié de symphyse mandibulaire portant trois incisives trés abimées. On peut y a ajouter des débris de molaires inférieure et supérieure. Il faut mentionner néanmoins un morceau d'hémi-mandibule gauche d'*Equus caballus gallicus* où manque seulement la M_3 (pl. I, n°4). Voici les dimensions prises au niveau de l'alvéole:

(Pmg.- 61).- *Equus caballus gallicus.* 1 hémi-mandibule droite.

P_2 = 29,0 x 13,6 mm., P_3 = 29,0 x 16,0 mm., P_4 = 28,9 x 17,4 mm.,

M_1 = 30,0 x 17,9 mm., M_2 = 29,0 x 18,4 mm., M_3 = (?) mm.

Une partie antérieure de scapulum portant la cavité glénoïde appartient à *Bison priscus* si l'on s'en rapporte aux données d'Olsen (1960). La cavité articulaire mesure 67, 0 x 89,0 mm. Deux molaires assez bien conservées ont fourni les mesures suivantes prises au niveau du collet.

M^3 sup. d. : 33,0 x 30,8 mm.

M^1 sup. d. : 32,0 x 30,0 mm.

Il faut noter la présence d'îlots d'émail dans la région interlobaire. Ce caractère, normal chez *Ovibos moschatus*, est rare chez les vrais Bovidés.

CAPRINAE et RUPICAPRINAE

Contrairement aux Bovidés et aux Equidés, rares dans le Proto-Magdalénien, *Capra ibex* et *Rupicapra rupicapra* sont très répandus. Ils sont représentés par des restes d'os longs: canons, tibia, fémur, os du carpe et du tarse, des phalanges et une vingtaine de dents isolées, quelques mandibules et un débris de cheville osseuse pour *Capra ibex*.

Les dimensions des dents, pour ces deux espèces, varient régulièrement depuis le collet jusqu'au niveau de la table dentaire, aussi les mesures sont toujours prises au niveau du collet dans le cas des dents isolées. La longueur des séries dentaires inférieures ou supérieures est estimée au niveau des alvéoles. Quand les dents sont implantées, les mensurations sont obligatoirement prises au niveau de la table; moins caractéristiques que dans le premier cas, elles donnent néanmoins l'ordre de grandeur des espèces étudiées.

Voici une série de mesures dentaires prises avec *Capra ibex* et *Rupicapra rupicapra*. Le diamètre antéro-postérieur est placé le premier et le diamètre transverse vient ensuite.

TABLEAU X

Proto-Magdalénien. Mesures prises sur les restes de *Capra ibex*

(Pmg. – 27).   1 mandibule avec M_1, M_2 et M_3. M_1 = 12,0 x 7,5 mm., M_2 = 15,0 x 8,0 mm., M_3 = 22,0 x 9,5 mm.

(Pmg. – 93).   1 mandibule avec P_2, M_1, M_2 et M_3. P_2 = 8,0 x 5,7 mm., M_1 = 12,0 x 8,0 mm., M_2 = 15,0 x 8,5 mm., M_3 = 27,0 x 8,0 mm.

TABLEAU XI

Proto-Magdalénien. Mesures prises sur les restes de *Rupicapra rupicapra*

(Pmg. – 6).   1 morceau de mandibule, dépourvu de M_3, L = 42,0 mm.

(Pmg. – 15).   1 molaire supérieure gauche 9,5 x 11,0 mm.

(Pmg. – 34).   1 M_1 inférieure droite M_1 = 9,0 x 6,9 mm.

(Pmg. – 93).   1 maxillaire supérieur sans la M_3: P_2 = 5,0 x 5,0 mm., P_3 = 5,0 x 6,0 mm., P_4 = 5,8 x 8,0 mm., M_1 = 9,0 x 10,0 mm., M_2 = 12,0 x 11,8 mm.

    1 morceau de mandibule sans les prémolaires P_3 et P_4: P_2 = 7,5 x 6,0 mm., M_1 = 12,0 x 9,8 mm., M_2 = 9,5 x 8,0 mm., M_3 = 26,0 x 8,5 mm.

(Pmg. – 134).   1 série de dents inférieures isolées: P_3, P_4 et M_1. P_3 droite = 5,8 x 4,0 mm., P_4 droite = 9,0 x 6,0 mm., M_1 droite = 10,0 x 6,5 mm., M_1 gauche = 10,0 x 7,0 mm.

PROBOSCIDAE

Le mammouth (*Elephas primigenius*) est représenté par un morceau de défense travaillée par l'homme.

CANIDAE

Un certain nombre de restes osseux appartiennent à *Canis lupus*. L'apparence extérieure des os, leur état physique, les conditions de leur récolte, enfin

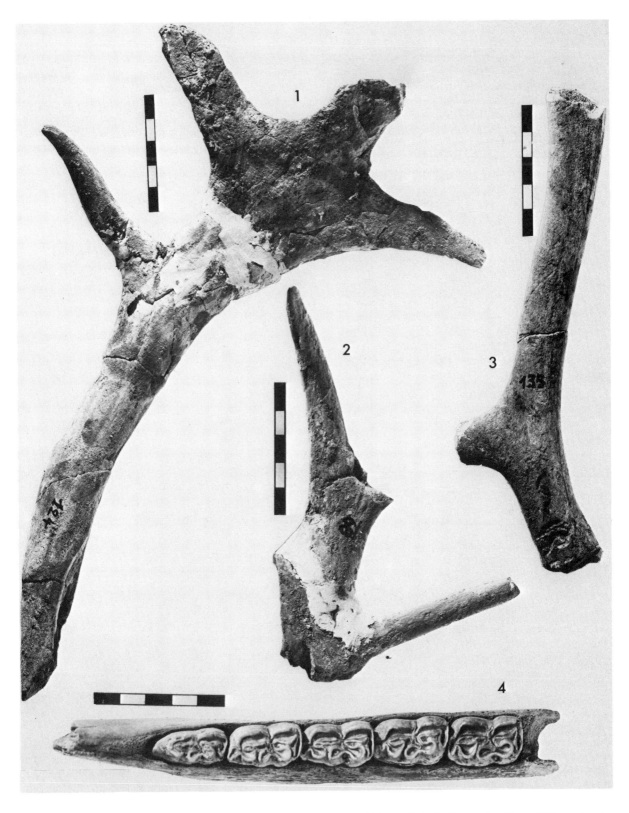

PLANCHE I. Le matériel figuré se rapporte entièrement au Proto-Magdalénien. 1. Bois de *R. tarandus* (Pmg. -124), perche de type *"arcticus"*. 2. *R. tarandus* (Pmg. -89), débris d'empaumure. 3. *R. tarandus* (Pmg. -135), morceau de perche. 4. *Equus caballus gallicus* (Pmg.-61), hémi-mandibule droite.

TABLEAU XII

Proto-Magdalénien. *Canis lupus.* Dimensions des os ayant appartenu au même animal

(Pmg. – 54).   1 radius droit intact. L = 210 mm. Extrémité proximale: 17,5 x 26,6 mm. Extrémité distale: 35,5 x 18,5 mm.

1 humérus brisé. Extrémité distale: 39,0 x (?) mm.

1 tibia droit intact. L = 233 mm. Extrémité proximale: 53,0 x 47,0 mm. Extrémité distale: 22,2 x 31,0 mm.

1 tibia gauche intact. L = 231 mm. Extrémité proximale: (?) x 47,0 mm. Extrémité distale: 23,0 x 31,9 mm.

1 fémur brisé. Extrémité distale = 44,0 x (?) mm.

(Pmg. – 5)   1 calcaneum droit intact. L = 61,0 mm.

1 calcaneum gauche intact. L = 61,0 mm.

(Pmg. – 45)   1 astragale droit. Diamètre antéro-postérieur: 39,0 mm. Diamètre transversal: 24,0 mm.

(Pmg. – 34).   4 métatarsiens droits intacts.

P2. Longueur totale: 85,0 mm.
P3. Longueur totale: 95,5 mm.
P4. Longueur totale: 98,5 mm.
P5. Longueur totale: 88,0 mm.

2 phalanges gauches intactes.

1 phalange (II). Longueur totale: 37,0 mm.
1 phalange (III). Longueur totale: 30,4 mm.

4 métatarsiens gauches dont deux sont intacts.

P2. Longueur totale: 84,8 mm.
P3 et P4. Non mesurables.
P5. Longueur totale: 88,0 mm.

3 phalanges gauches intactes.

1 phalange (II). Longueur totale: 37,0 mm.
1 phalange (III). Longueur totale: 31,9 mm.
1 phalange (V). Longueur totale: 30,9 mm.

2 métacarpiens droits dont un seul est intact.

M1 est brisé. Non mesurable.
M3. Longueur totale: 90,0 mm.

2 phalanges gauches intactes.

1 phalange (II). Longueur totale: 31,0 mm.
1 phalangine (II). Longueur totale: 28,0 mm.

2 métacarpiens gauches dont un seul est intact.

M1. Longueur totale: 85,8 mm.
M2 est brisé. Non mesurable.

les mesures prises attestent leur appartenance au même animal.

Le tableau XII résume les principales mesures prises, le diamètre antéro-postérieur est toujours placé avant le diamètre transversal.

Toutes ces valeurs sont en accord avec les données de M. F. Bonifay (*in* Lavocat 1966).

Vulpes vulpes est représenté par deux prémolaires isolées (Pmg.-58 et Pmg.-108), deux morceaux de mandibules (Pmg.-53 et 54), trois morceaux de bassin (Pmg.-16, 56, et 58), un métacarpien (Pmg.-108) et un métatarsien (Pmg.-78). La distribution de ces restes fait supposer que l'animal était dépecé sur place, la peau étant rapportée à l'abri. Les extrémités des pattes et le crâne demeurés en place, s'échappaient de la peau pendant sa dessication.

Par contre, *Canis lupus* dont le squelette est partiellement conservé aurait été introduit tout entier dans l'abri.

LEPORINAE, MICROTIDAE, et GLIRIDAE

Leurs débris sont très abondants, mais leur état de conservation ne les rend pas tous utilisables. Cependant la présence de *Lepus variabilis*, des genres *Microtus, Arvicola* et de l'espèce *Eliomys quercinus* a été reconnue.

Le liévre variable (*L. variabilis*) est représenté par une incisive supérieure (Pmg.-85) reconnaissable à sa section subcarrée et à la position latérale occupée par le sillon antérieur. Il faut y ajouter quelques débris peu importants tels qu'une extrémité proximale de radius (Pmg.-32) et un calcaneum (Pmg.-109).

Les *Microtinae* sont représentés par diverses parties du squelette, des dents, surtout par des incisives isolées et des mandibules édentées. On rencontre ainsi *Microtus agrestis* et *Microtus arvalis* avec tous les types intermédiaires de la M_1 inférieure.

Les ossements d'*Arvicola* sont très nombreux: os des membres, dents isolées, mandibules édentées. Cependant une série de boîtes crâniennes et de mandibules bien conservées ont permis d'identifier *Arvicola scherman*.

(Pmg.-24). Quatre mandibules.

Deux portions de crâne (région orbitaire).

Cinq incisives inférieures isolées.

Une incisive supérieure isolée.

(Pmg.-34). Un crâne avec les incisives et les molaires. Arcades zygomatiques brisées. Partie postérieure de la boîte crânienne détruite.

Deux mandibules droit et gauche avec les incisives et la M_1.

Deux morceaux de crâne, région palatine et partie antérieure de la boîte crânienne conservées.

Trois morceaux de mandibules. Trois incisives inférieures et une incisive supérieure isolée.

La détermination précise d'*A. scherman* est basée sur la forme de la constriction orbitaire (Miller 1912), la proclivité des incisives supérieures (Heim de Balsac et Guislain 1955) et la taille réduite des pièces étudiées: *Arvicola scherman* est sensiblement plus petit qu'*A. Amphibius*.

Deux mandibules édentées (Pmg.-3 et Pmg.-24) sont attribuées à *Eliomys quercinus*. Elles se reconnaissent à leur petite taille, aux alvéoles destinées à recevoir les racines des molaires ainsi qu'à la perforation de l'apophyse angulaire.

LES OISEAUX

Le genre *Larus* a été reconnu sur un coracoïde (Pmg.-45) dont la partie proximale est légèrement abimée. La taille de la pièce permet d'écarter les mouettes, trop petites, et les goélands: *Larus hyperboreus* et *Larus marinus* qui sont trop grands. Par la taille, *Larus fuscus* et *Larus argentatus* restent seuls en ligne de compte. J'attribue le coracoïde à *Larus argentatus*, espèce moins fréquente dans l'intérieur des terres sauf dans les régions où les eaux gèlent, donnée en accord avec le froid rigoureux du Proto-Magdalénien.

Les *Turdidae*, bien représentés, n'ont pas été chassés semble-t-il. Deux squelettes assez complets (Pmg.-41 et Pmg.-78) ont été découverts dans les niveaux supérieurs du Proto-Magdalénien. Dans les deux cas les os trouvés tous ensemble, sont en général brisés. Quelques uns ont pu être mesurés.

(Pmg.-41) Cubitus — L = 42,0 mm.

Fémur — L = 31,7 mm.

(Pmg.-78) Tibia — L = 51,8 mm.

Tarse — L = 34,0 mm.

Par la taille et le modelé de détail je rapporte ces deux squelettes à *Turdus viscivorus* la Grive draine.

La présence du Chocard des Alpes (*Coracia graculus*) est attestée par trois cubitus (Pmg.-47, 48, et 50) brisés et un morceau de tibia (Pmg.-46).

OSSEMENTS DIVERS

Il faut signaler des restes d'amphibiens: radio-cubitus et tibia-péroné appartenant au genre *Bufo* et une série de vertèbres de poissons.

3. LA FAUNE DU PERIGORDIEN VI

CERVIDAE

Le renne (*Rangifer tarandus*) est en augmentation (93%) par rapport au niveau précédent (80%). On retrouve les mêmes espèces mais dans des proportions différentes qui permettront dans une prochaine section de suivre les vicissitudes du climat.

TABLEAU XIII

Espèces et débris osseux provenant du Périgordien VI

Macrofaune			Rongeurs		
Rangifer tarandus	2.080	(91,2%)	*Lepus variabilis*	14	(25,0%)
Cervus elaphus	19	(0,9%)	*Microtus agrestis*	14	(25,0%)
Capreolus capreolus	1		*Microtus arvalis*	14	(25,0%)
Bos sp.	71	(3,1%)	*Arvicola scherman*	13	(23,8%)
Equus caballus	66	(2,9%)	*Eliomys quercinus*	1	(1,2%)
Capra ibex	24	(1,0%)	Oiseaux		
Rupicapra rupicapra	10				
Sus scrofa	1	(0,1%)	*Gyps fulvus*	1	
Elephas primigenus	1		*Coracia graculus*	1	
Canis lupus	4		*Lagopus mutus*	4	
Vulpes vulpes	14	(0,8%)	*Otus scops*	1	
Ursus spelaeus	1		Poissons		
			Vertèbres de Salmonidés	14	

Toutes les parties du squelette du renne sont représentées. Comme précédemment il n'y a pas d'os intacts et les mesures ne sont guère possibles. Signalons quelques débris de foetus dont un radius sans épiphyses:

(Pg. VI-194). 1 radius − L = 50,0 mm.

L'animal serait âgé de cinq mois (Kelsall 1957). Le rut ayant lieu entre la fin septembre et la mi-octobre, ces données supposent la présence de l'homme et du renne dans la région pendant les mois de février-mars.

Les débris de perche ne sont pas très nombreux, mais il existe un bon nombre de bois de massacre. Les pédicules portent parfois les signes extérieurs de leur mue prochaine, pour les autres la radiographie du pédicule permet d'en connaître l'état de vascularisation et de déterminer le mois de l'année correspondant à la mort de l'animal (Bouchud 1966).

Je reviendrai sur ce sujet à propos de l'habitat humain.

TABLEAU XIV

Liste des bois de *Rangifer tarandus* trouvés dans le Périgordien VI

(Pg. VI-125 A).	1 bois de massacre ♀, 2 ans, signe de mue *(fin mai)*. Longueur totale: 60 mm. Meule peu marquée. A_1 = 19,0 x 18,0 mm. Départ de l'andouiller d'oeil au niveau de la meule.
(Pg. VI-143).	1 bois de massacre ♂, 3 ans *(mois de septembre)*. Longueur totale: 340 mm. Meule peu marquée. Andouiller d'oeil réduit à une minuscule saillie placée au contact de la meule. A 15 mm. au dessus, départ de l'andouiller de glace. Perche à courbure *"arcticus"*, dépourvue d'andouiller postérieur et brisée à la base de l'empaumure. (Pl. II. n° 3). A_1 = 26,0 x 24,0 mm., A = 29,0 x 21,0 mm., B = 23,0 x 18,0 mm., C = 19,0 x 16,0 mm.
(Pg. VI-148).	1 bois de massacre ♀, 2/3 ans, *(mois de mars-avril)*. Longueur totale: 130 mm. Pas d'andouiller. La perche s'aplatit très vite et présente une carène à sa face antérieure. A_1 = 24,0 x 23,0 mm., A = 22,0 x 21,0 mm.

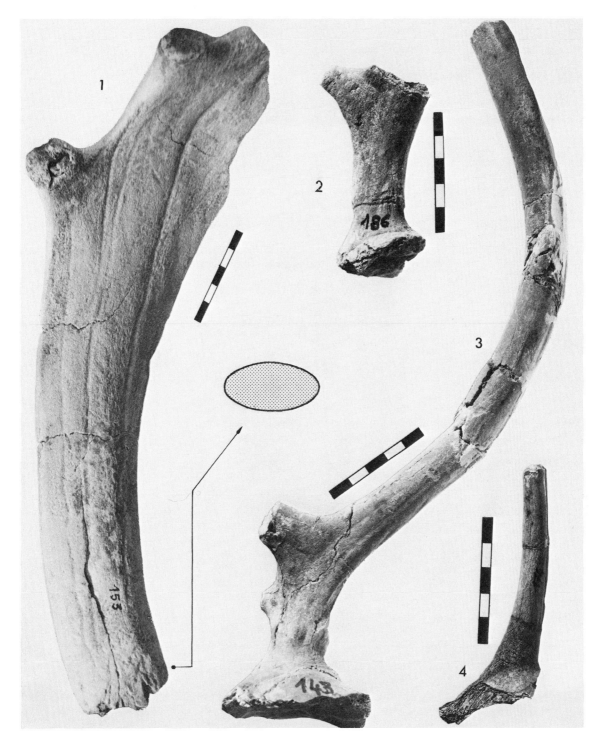

PLANCHE II. Le matériel figuré se rapporte entièrement au Périgordien VI. 1. *Rangifer tarandus caribou* (Pg. VI-153 D). Noter la lourdeur et la section aplatie de cet andouiller de glace. 2. *Rangifer tarandus* (Pg. VI-186 A). Bois de massacre femelle, noter au dessous de la meule le sillon annonciateur de la mue prochaine *(mois de mai)*. 3. *Rangifer tarandus* (Pg. VI-143). Bois de massacre mâle, perche de type "arcticus", *mois d'octobre*? La perche fissurée ne se prête pas à la radiographie. 4. *Rangifer tarandus* (Pg. VI-174). Bois de première année (dague), complètement calcifié, provient d'un jeune abattu entre les mois d'*octobre* et de *mai*.

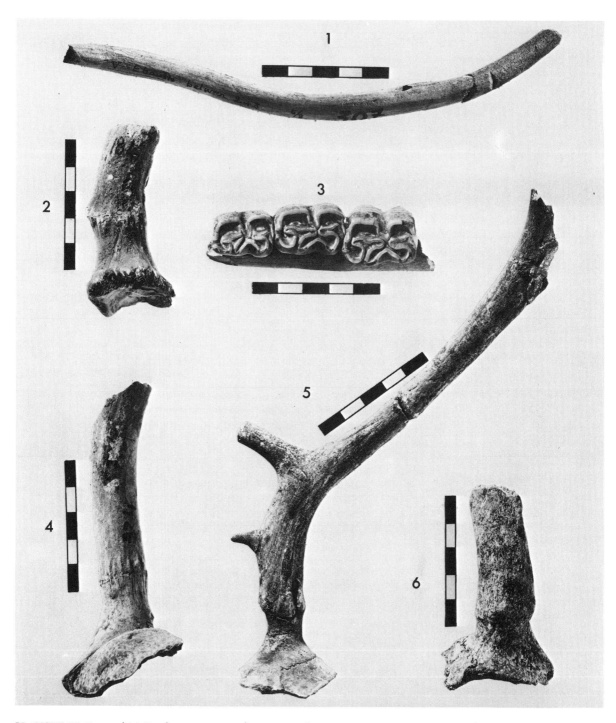

PLANCHE III. Le matériel figuré se rapporte entièrement au Périgordien VI. 1. *Rangifer tarandus* (Pg. VI-307). Débris de perche de seconde année provenant sans doute d'une femelle. La minceur de la corticale témoigne d'une calcification incomplète (*mois d'août?*). La pièce a été travaillée par l'homme à son extrémité gauche. 2. *Rangifer tarandus* (Pg. VI-184). Bois de massacre femelle, au dessous de la meule on aperçoit le signe précurseur de la mue prochaine (*mois de mai*). 3. *Equus caballus* (Pg. VI-326). Morceau de mandibule avec P_4, M_1 et M_2. 4. *Rangifer tarandus* (Pg. VI-324). Bois de massacre femelle, au niveau de la meule, signe de la mue prochaine (*mois de mai*). 5. *Rangifer tarandus* (Pg. VI-360). Bois de massacre femelle, noter le signe de la mue prochaine au niveau de la meule (*mai*). 6. *Rangifer tarandus* (Pg. VI-154). Bois de massacre de femelle. A l'examen radiographique, la calcification s'achève (*octobre*).

TABLEAU XIV *Suite*

(Pg. VI-152 A).	1 bois de massacre ♀, 2/3 ans, (*mois de novembre*). Longueur totale: 116 mm. A 38 mm. de la meule, départ d'un andouiller de glace aplati (pl. VI, n° 2). $A_1 = 19,0$ x 17,0 mm., $\qquad$ A = 23,0 x 16,0 mm.
(Pg. VI-152 B).	1 morceau de perche portant l'andouiller postérieur. Longueur totale: 165 mm., B = 17,0 x 11,0 mm.
(Pg. VI-152 C).	1 morceau de perche anormal. Longueur totale: 125 mm. La perche brisée accidentellement pendant la croissance s'est séparée par la suite (pl. VIII, n° 3).
(Pg. VI-153 A).	1 morceau de perche à courbure "*tarandus*" comprenant la région de l'andouiller postérieur; celui-ci est brisé. Longueur totale: 180 mm., B = 15,7 x 13,0 mm., $\qquad$ C = 19,5 x 11,0 mm.
(Pg. VI-153 B).	1 morceau d'empaumure de grande taille. Longueur totale: 185 mm.
(Pg. VI-153 C).	1 morceau d'empaumure de taille réduite. Longueur totale: 245 mm.
(Pg. VI-153 D).	1 morceau d'andouiller de glace (pl. II, n° 1). Longueur totale: 333 mm. Section à l'extrémité proximale: 47,0 x 25,0 mm. L'aplatissement de la pièce et la lourdeur des digitations caractérisent le renne de forêt, *Rangifer tarandus caribou*.
(Pg. VI-154).	1 bois de massacre ♀ 3/4 ans, (*mois d'octobre*). Longueur totale 70 mm. Meule peu marquée (pl. III, n° 6). $A_1 = 22,0$ x 19,0 mm., $\qquad$ A = 22,0 x 20,0 mm.
(Pg. VI-157 A).	1 bois de massacre ♀, 4/5 ans (*mois de novembre*). Longueur totale: 119 mm. Meule bien marquée. Andouiller d'oeil marqué par un léger renflement placé à quelques millimètres au dessus de la meule. Andouiller de glace brisé au départ situé à 39 mm. au dessus de la meule. Perche brisée un peu au dessus de cet andouiller. A = 23,0 x 21,0 mm., $\qquad$ $A_1 = 21,0$ x 19,0 mm.
(Pg. VI-157 B).	1 morceau d'andouiller provenant d'un jeune animal. Longueur totale: 109 mm. Section: 15,0 x 9,0 mm.
(Pg. VI-157 C).	1 morceau de perche à courbure "*arcticus*". L'andouiller postérieur manque. B = 19,0 x 16,0 mm.
(Pg. VI-157 D).	1 morceau d'empaumure de jeune. Longueur totale: 147 mm.
(Pg. VI-157 E).	1 morceau d'empaumure. La plus grande longueur est de 250 mm. La légèreté des digitations caractérise le renne de toundra (pl. V, n° 1).
(Pg. VI-157 F).	1 bois de massacre ♀, 3/4 ans, signe de mue (*mai*). A 35 mm. de la meule départ d'un andouiller brisé peu après son détachement (pl. V, n° 3).
(Pg. VI-160 A).	1 débris d'andouiller. Animal jeune. Longueur totale: 94,0 mm.
(Pg. VI-160 B).	1 débris d'andouiller. Longueur totale: 104,0 mm.
(Pg. VI-174).	1 dague. Longueur: 105 mm. Calcification complète (*novembre à mai*), (pl. II, n° 4).
(Pg. VI-175).	1 bois de massacre ♀, 6/7 ans. Longueur: 235 mm. A faible distance de la meule départ de l'andouiller d'oeil brisé. A 110 mm. de la meule amorce de l'andouiller de glace. Pas de signe de mue (*septembre à novembre*), (pl. IV, n° 4).
(Pg. VI-176 A).	1 bois de massacre ♀, 2 ans, signe extérieur de la mue (*mai*). Longueur totale: 60 mm. Pas d'andouiller. $A_1 = 14,0$ x 11,0 mm., $\qquad$ A = 15,0 x 10,0 mm.
(Pg. VI-176 B).	1 bois de massacre ♀, adulte de grande taille, 5/6 ans, (*fin septembre*). Longueur totale: 235 mm. Meule assez bien marquée. Andouiller d'oeil brisé à son départ la meule. Andouiller de glace brisé, départ à 110 mm. de la meule. La face postérieure de la meule étant abîmée, certaines mesures ne sont pas possibles, $A_1 = (?)$ x 37,0 mm., $\qquad$ A = (?) x 35,0 mm.
(Pg. VI-176 C).	1 morceau de perche à courbure "*arcticus*" provenant d'un mâle robuste. Longueur totale: 320 mm., région de l'andouiller postérieur réduit à une simple excroissance. B = 24,0 x 17,0 mm.
(Pg. VI-178).	1 morceau de perche brisé au-dessus de l'andouiller postérieur. Longueur totale: 225 mm,; B = 24,0 x 17,0 mm.
(Pg. VI-184).	1 bois de massacre ♀, 3 ans, meule à peine marquée, signe de mue externe (*mai*). $A_1 = 18,0$ x 17,0 mm., $\qquad$ A = 18,0 x 18,0 mm. (pl. III, n° 2).

TABLEAU XIV *Suite*

(Pg. VI-186).	1 débris de perche (ou d'andouiller?). Longueur totale: 125 mm.
(Pg. VI-186 A).	1 bois de massacre ♀, 3/4 ans, signe de mue externe (*mai*). Meule à peine marquée. A = 20,0 x 18,0 mm. (pl. II, n° 2).
(Pg. VI-189).	1 bois de massacre ♀, 3 ans? (*fin octobre*). Pas d'andouiller d'oeil, andouiller de glace brisé au départ, à 35 mm. de la meule. Face postérieure abîmée. A_1 = (?) x 28,0 mm., A = (?) x 17,0 mm., (pl. IV, n° 3).
(Pg. VI-190).	1 morceau de perche provenant d'un mâle robuste, sectionné au dessous de la meule. Longueur totale: 215 mm. Pas d'andouiller d'oeil, andouiller de glace réduit à une carène placée à la partie antérieure de la perche. A = 43,0 x 36,0 mm.
(Pg. VI-264 A).	1 bois de massacre ♀, 3 ans, perche de type "*tarandus*" (*décembre à mai*). Longueur totale 350 mm. Sur la meule, minuscule andouiller d'oeil. A 28 mm. de la meule, premier andouiller de glace brisé peu après son départ. A 65 mm. de la meule second andouiller de glace brisé lui aussi. A_1 = 25,0 x 23,5 mm., A = 26,5 x 14,0 mm. Mesure prise entre le premier et le second andouiller. B = 19,5 x 11,0 mm., C = 17,5 x 10,0 mm. (pl. IV, n° 1).
(Pg. VI-264 B).	1 bois de massacre ♀, 3 ans, perche de type *tarandus*. Longueur totale: 360 mm. Au contact de la meule, petit andouiller de glace brisé, deux autres andouillers se détachent respectivement à 23 et 60 mm. de la meule. Un fragment d'andouiller postérieur est visible sur le coude de la hampe. Les réparations faites au niveau de la meule et des andouillers ont empêché de prendre des mesures. A_1 = 23,4 x 23,0 mm., B = 21,7 x 18,0 mm. (pl. V, n° 2).
(Pg. VI-307).	1 débris de perche, première année. Longueur totale: 200 mm. Croissance non achevée (*mois d'août*). La pièce, peu calcifiée à été raclée par l'homme. La minceur de la zone corticale est attestée par l'impreinte des vaisseaux conservée à certains endroits.
(Pg. VI-324).	1 massacre de ♀ de seconde année. Longueur totale: 120 mm. Signe de mue (*mois de mai*), meule peu marquée. (pl. III, n° 4). A_1 = 19,0 x 18,0 mm., A = 19,0 x 16,0 mm.
(Pg. VI-360).	1 massacre de ♀ de seconde année. Longueur totale: 212 mm. Minuscule andouiller d'oeil à 26 mm. de la meule à 26 mm. de la meule à peine marquée. Andouiller de glace brisé au départ, à 52 mm. de la meule. Perche de type *tarandus* brisé au dessous de l'andouiller postérieur (pl. III, n° 5). A_1 = 15,0 x 14,0 mm., A = 18,0 x 16,0 mm., B = 16,5 x 9,5 mm.

Il faut mentionner quelques restes exceptionnels: un prémaxillaire droit (Pg. VI-143) dont la présence confirme ce qui a été dit à propos de la résistance des os à l'écrasement, et deux ramures particulières. La première (Pg. VI-152 C) provient d'un animal de deux ans environ; elle a été brisée pendant sa croissance mais les vaisseaux du velours ayant assuré l'alimentation sanguine, la partie supérieure qui s'était inclinée vers le crâne a cru d'abord dans cette direction puis elle s'est redressée peu à peu et elle a repris une orientation normale (pl. VIII, n° 3).

Le morceau d'andouiller de glace (Pg. VI-153 D) cité dans le tableau provient d'un renne de forêt. Ces animaux sont surtout caractérisés par la forme particulière de la ramure dont la section fortement aplatie et l'aspect compact sont les traits principaux (pl. II, n° 1). La section très aplatie de la pièce fossile (47,0 x 25,0 mm.) la lourdeur de sa forme caractérisent *Rangifer tarandus caribou*, espèce géo-graphique à laquelle nous rapportons la pièce décrite. C'est le seul bois de renne de forêt du tableau précédent; tous les autres appartiennent au type de la toundra.

Pour terminer, mentionnons une calotte crânienne et une mandibule. La calotte (Pg. VI-144) comprend une partie des os frontaux porteurs des pédicules, des pariétaux, et du supraoccipital. Les perches sont brisées à une faible distance des meules. Les signes extérieurs de la mue sont du type femelle. L'animal âgé de deux ans aurait été abattu vers la fin mai. La mandibule au contraire (Pg. VI-153) provient d'un sujet âgé de 12 à 14 ans. On observe en effet la dislocation de la table dentaire; la M_2 a été expulsée.

Cervus elaphus, est médiocrement représenté par des débris osseux provenant des os canons du radio-cubitus et de l'humérus. Il faut y ajouter des molaires brisées et une mandibule (Pg. VI-285) dont la M_3 a été perdue. L'attribution des dents corres-

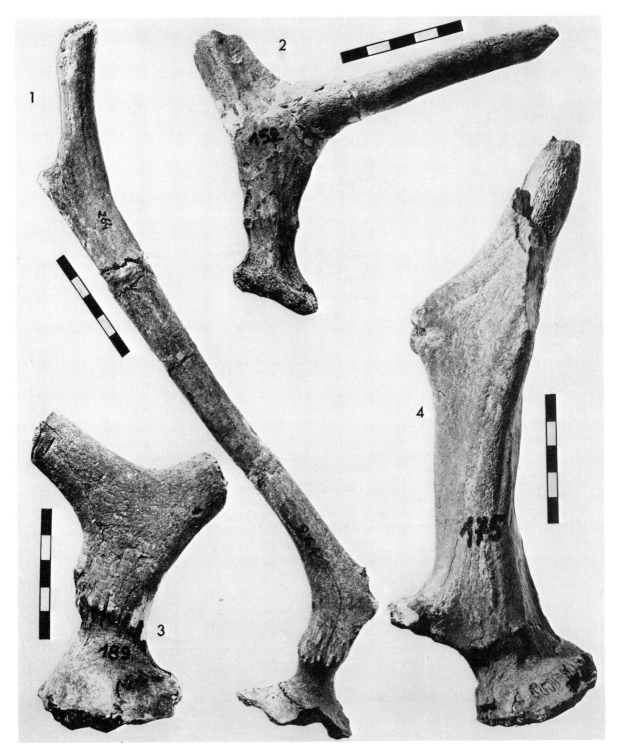

PLANCHE IV. Le matériel figuré se rapporte entièrement au Périgordien VI. 1. *Rangifer tarandus* (Pg. VI-264 A). Bois de massacre de femelle, type "*tarandus*", calcification complète *(décembre à mai)*. 2. *Rangifer tarandus* (Pg. VI-152). Massacre de femelle, calcification presque complète *(mois de novembre)*. 3. *Rangifer tarandus* (Pg. VI-189). Bois de massacre de femelle, calcification presque complète *(octobre?)*. 4. *Rangifer tarandus* (Pg. VI-175). Bois de massacre de mâle, pas de signe de mue *(fin septembre à novembre)*.

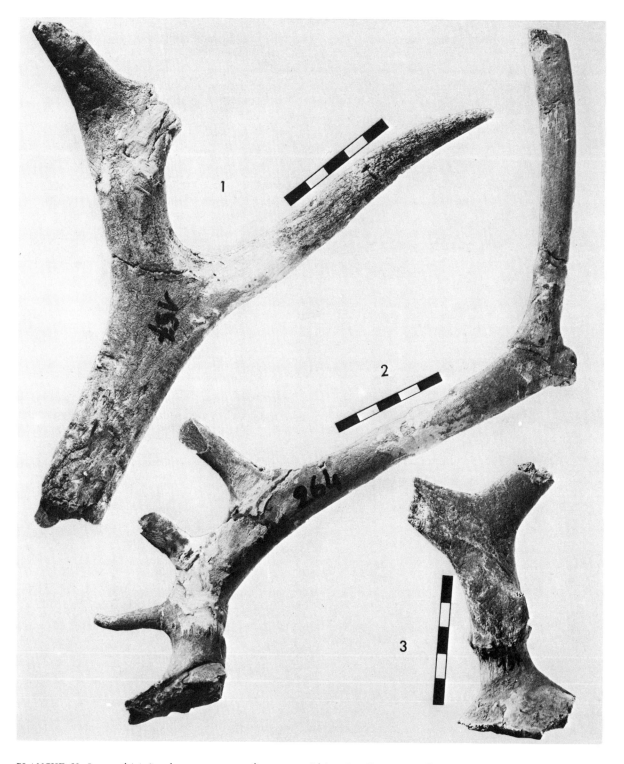

PLANCHE V. Le matériel figuré se rapporte entièrement au Périgordien VI. 1. *Rangifer tarandus* (Pg. VI-157 E). Morceau d'empaumure. La légèreté des digitations caractérise le renne de toundra. 2. *Rangifer tarandus* (Pg. VI-264 B). Bois de massacre femelle, noter l'existence d'un andouiller supplémentaire au dessus de l'andouiller de glace; la perche est de type *«tarandus»*. La partie restaurée du pédicule ne permet pas la radiographie. 3. *Rangifer tarandus* (Pg. VI-157 F). Bois de massacre de femelle, signe de mue prochaine visible au niveau de la meule (*mai*).

pond à un animal âgé de plus de dix ans (Baumann 1949). La série dentaire diminuée de la M_3 occupe un longueur de 140 mm.

Une molaire supérieure M_1 a été attribuée à *Capreolus capreolus* dont nous n'avons pas découvert d'autre reste.

BOVIDAE et EQUIDAE

Dés fragments osseux en nombre assez important proviennent des Bovidés et des chevaux.

Leur répartition reste conforme à ce qui a été écrit dans le premier section de ce travail. Les dents nombreuses sont fréquemment brisées mais une série de mesures a été prise. Leur forte taille permet de les rapporter à *Equus caballus gallicus*, cependant une molaire inférieure M_2 appartient indiscutablement à *Equus hydruntinus Regalia*.

(Pg. VI-204). 1 molaire inférieure M_2 : 23,0 x 15,0 mm.

Les mesures sont prises au point P (Prat 1966); le sillon lingual est étroit et anguleux tandis que le sillon vestibulaire est trés profond.

TABLEAU XV

Périgordien VI. Mesures prises sur les restes d'Equidés et de Bovidés

Equidés

(Pg. VI-192). 1 hémi-mandibule d'*Equus caballus gallicus* dépourvue de M_3. Longueur de la série dentaire incomplète, au niveau des lavéoles: 159 mm. Dimensions des dents au niveau des alvéoles: P_2 = 36,5 x 18,0 mm., P_3 = 31,0 x 20,0 mm., P_4 = 31,0 x 20,0 mm., M_1 = 30,0 x 19,0 mm., M_2 = 30,0 x 18,0 mm.

(Pg. VI-326). 1 morceau de mandibule d'*Equus caballus gallicus* avec P_4, M_1 et M_2. (pl. III, n° 3). Au niveau de la mandibule, P_4 = 29,0 mm., M_1 = 28,0 mm., M_2 = 25,5 mm.

Dents isolées d'*Equus caballus gallicus*

(Pg. VI-286). 1 M^1 = 32,0 x 30,0 mm.

(Pg. VI-297). 1 P^4 = 27,0 x 27,8 mm. et M^1 = 27,0 x 28,4 mm.

(Pg. VI-299). 1 M^2 = 32,0 x 30,0 mm. et M^3 = 29,5 x 25,0 mm.

(Pg. VI-297). 1 M_1 = 30,0 x 21,2 mm.

(Pg. VI-441). 1 M_2 = 27,8 x 21,0 mm.

Bovidés

(Pg. VI-150). 1 sabot bien conservé, 1 = 107 mm. Dimensions de la surface articulaire: 56,0 x 42,0 mm. Hauteur du sabot: 59,0 mm. Par sa forme et son modelé, il proviendrait d'un *Bison priscus* (Olsen 1960).

(Pg. VI-181). 1 phalange (I) bien conservée, appartient à *Bison priscus* (Olsen 1960). Hauteur: 87,0 mm. Articulation proximale: 47,0 x 48,0 mm. Articulation distale: 34,0 x 48,0 mm.

(Pg. VI-190). 1 extrémité distale de canon antérieur: 99,5 x 53,0 mm.

(Pg. VI-190). 1 cubo-naviculaire: 76,0 x 87,5 mm.

(Pg. VI-190). 1 extrémité distale de tibia: 69,5 x 86,0 mm.

(Pg. VI-190). 1 hémi-mandibule droite, mal conservée. P_2 et P_3 sont perdues, M_1 est brisée et M_3 présente une attrition anormale des cuspides 2 et 3. Mesures prises au niveau des alvéoles: L = 180,00 mm. Série des prémolaires: 1 = 60,0 mm. Série des molaires: 1 = 120,0 mm., P_4 = 23,0 x 16,0 mm., et M_2 = 34,0 x 18,5 mm.

(Pg. VI-429). 1 série de débris appartenant au même animal.

1 extrémité proximale de canon antérieur droit: 47,5 x 89,5 mm.

1 magnum droit, dimensions maximum: 51,5 x 57,0 mm.

1 onciforme droit, dimensions maximum: 49,8 x 41,8 mm.

1 tête de côte et quelques morceaux de diaphyses.

En valeur absolue et en valeur relative la quantité d'Equidés et de Bovidés s'est accrue considérablement:

Proto-Magdalénien

Périgordien VI

Bovidés: (28) soit 15,5%   (71) soit 33,5%
Equidés: (40) soit 22,1%   (66) soit 31,1%

Rien ne permet de décider si l'on a affaire à *Bos primigenius*, ou à *Bison priscus*, mais l'ensemble de la faune présentant un caractère steppique marqué on peut admettre la présence d'un fort pourcentage de *Bison priscus*.

CAPRINAE et RUPICAPRINAE

Ces deux groupes accusent une forte diminution par rapport au niveau précédent.

	Proto-Magdalénien	*Périgordien VI*
Capra ibex	(36) soit 19,9%	(24) soit 11,3%
Rupicapra rupicapra	(37) soit 20,4%	(10) soit 4,7%

Les dents nombreuses sont souvent abîmées; les débris osseux proviennent surtout des phalanges, des sabots et des os canons. Quelques mesures ont été prises.

TABLEAU XVI

Périgordien VI. Mesures prises sur les dents de *Capra ibex*

(Pg. VI-166).   1 morceau de mandibule portant M_2 (14,0 x 7,8 mm.) et M_3 (19,0 x 7,0 mm.). Les mesures sont prises au niveau des alvéoles.

SUIDAE

Sus scrofa: une incisive inférieure isolée (Pg. VI-159).

PROBOSCIDAE

Elephas primigenius. Le mammouth est représenté par un fémur brisé comprenant la tête, le col et l'extrémité proximale de la diaphyse.

CANIDAE et URSIDAE

Leurs restes sont moins répandus que dans le niveau précédent.

	Proto-Magdalénien	*Périgordien VI*
Canis lupus	23	4
Vulpes vulpes	6	9

Ces différences s'expliquent par le fait que *Canis lupus* n'était pas chassé systématiquement. Dans le Proto-Magdalénien, les débris provenaient de deux animaux dont le corps entier avait été apporté dans l'abri; il en a été de même pour les débris d'os longs (cubitus, fémur) de côtes et les métatarsiens découverts dans le niveau sous-jacent (Pg. VI-205 A).

Les restes de *Vulpes vulpes* proviennent de sujets différents comme le prouvent les différences de taille observées. Ces débris, non mesurables comprennent des phalanges, des métacarpiens, des métatarsiens, une dent isolée, et un astragale (Pg. VI-159, 165, 174, 176, 228, et 460). Les animaux chassés étaient préparés sur le terrain et les hommes rapportaient les peaux qui renfermaient encore les extrémités des pattes (métacarpiens et métatarsiens).

LEPORIDAE, MICROTIDAE, et GLIRIDAE

Une mandibule gauche (Pg. VI-165) dont la branche montante est brisée porte une incisive dont la section sub-carrée et l'épaisseur de l'émail caractérisent *Lepus timidus*. La série dentaire mesure 19,9 mm. A la même espèce ont été attribués des morceaux d'humérus et de cubitus (Pg. VI-149, 272, et 428) cinq métacarpiens et métatarsiens brisés (Pg. VI-148, 186, 262, et 428), un fémur brisé au niveau du troisième trochanter (Pg. VI-323) dont le condyle articulaire mesure 20,9 mm. et enfin un tibia intact (Pg. VI-323 A) dont voici les dimensions.

Longueur totale: 138,5 mm.
Extrémité proximale. 21,9 x 20,2 mm.
Extrémité distale: 10,0 x 16,0 mm.

Les restes d'*Arvicola*, moins répandus que dans le Proto-Magdalénien (13 au lieu de 64) comprennent des os longs (humérus, cubitus, fémur mais surtout tibia), des dents isolées, des mandibules et des morceaux de crâne dont certains, assez bien conservés (Pg. VI-149 et 160), permettent de les attribuer à *Arvicola scherman* (Heim de Balsac et Guislain 1955).

Deux mandibules abîmées mais porteuses de la M_1 ont appartenu à *Microtus arvalis* (Pg. VI-158 et 189); enfin une mandibule édentée mais reconnaissable aux alvéoles des dents radiculées et à la perforation de l'apophyse angulaire atteste la présence d'*Eliomys quercinus.*

LES OISEAUX

Tous les os sont brisés mais leur état de conservation est néanmoins suffisant pour permettre une détermination précise. Voici les espèces reconnues.

Lagopus mutus, (Lagopède muet). Un humérus (Pg. VI-l46), deux coracoïdes (Pg. VI-l47), un fémur (Pg. VI-l60).

Coracia graculus, (Chocard des Alpes). Un humérus (Pg. VI-125).

Otus scops, (Hibou petit-duc). Un métatarse (Pg. VI-274).

Gypaëtus barbatus, (Gypaète barbu). Un fémur de grande taille (Pg. VI-l6l) reconnaissable aux orifices pneumatiques de la fosse poplitée et à la forme de la gorge péronière.

4. LA FAUNE du NOAILLIEN

CERVIDAE

Les espèces rencontrées dans ce niveau sont pratiquement les mêmes que celles de la couche précédente, mais leurs nombres varient considérablement (tableau XVII).

TABLEAU XVII

Espèces et débris osseux du Noaillien

Macrofaune			Rongeurs		
Rangifer tarandus	17.302	(95,4%)	*Lepus variabilis*	16	(34,0%)
Cervus elaphus	268	(1,6%)	*Lepus sp.*	22	(46,8%)
Capreolus capreolus	47		*Microtus sp.*	4	(8,6%)
Bos sp.	326	(1,8%)	*Arvicola scherman*	5	(10,6%)
Equus caballus	135	(0,7%)			
Equus hydruntinus	2		Oiseaux		
Capra ibex	34	(0,4%)			
Rupricapra rupicapra	44		*Corvus corax*	2	
Sus scrofa	1		*Coracia graculus*	2	
Canis lupus	2	(0,1%)			
Vulpes vulpes	13		Poissons		
Ursus spelaeus	3				
Felis spelaeus	3		*Vertèbres de Salmonidés*		

Rangifer tarandus demeure toujours l'éspèce dominante. Dès les éboulis 3/4 elle devient plus nombreuse que dans le Périgordien VI. Les pourcentages oscillent entre 87,3 et 95,7%. Toutes les parties du squelette sont représentées et l'on note l'abondance des cartilages costaux calcifiés et des débris de ramures mais sur les 135 pièces énumérées dans la liste ci-dessous, une dizaine seulement méritent d'être figurées et décrites.

TABLEAU XVIII

Rangifer tarandus. Liste des bois rencontrés dans le Noaillien

Éboulis 3/4

(Noail.-499).	1 dague brisée (*novembre à juin*).
(Noail.-635).	4 débris de perche et un bois de massacre de ♀ âgée.
(Noail.-620).	1 massacre de ♀, 2/3 ans, signe de mue (*mai-juin*).

Niveau supérieur

(Noail.-365).	1 bois de massacre ♀, 4/5 ans, signe de mue (*mai*). Longueur totale: 320 mm., A = 20,0 x 22,0 mm. (pl. VI, n° 3).
(Noail.-366).	1 morceau de perche ♂, 4/5 ans. Longueur totale: 200 mm. section aplatie: B = 25,0 x 40,0 mm.
(Noail.-367).	1 morceau de perche, partie supérieure brisée sous l'empaumure.
(Noail.-401).	2 morceaux de perche.
(Noail.-405).	1 bois de massacre, ♀, 3/4 ans, signe de mue (*mai-juin*).
(Noail.-407).	3 fragments de perche.
(Noail.-469).	1 bois de massacre, ♀, 3/4 ans, signe de mue (*mai-juin*).
(Noail.-477).	1 morceau de bois de velours (*août-septembre*).
(Noail.-478).	1 pédicule de ♀, 4/5 ans, signe de mue (*mai*), (pl. VI, n° 5).
(Noail.-480).	2 morceaux de perche et un cornillon.
(Noail.-503).	1 dague, 100 mm. (*novembre à juin*).
(Noail.-537).	1 morceau de dague (*novembre à juin*), (pl. VII, n° 4).
(Noail.-538).	1 morceau de dague (*novembre à juin*).
(Noail.-540).	1 morceau de perche, ♂, type *arcticus*, A = 20,0 x 21,0 mm.
(Noail.-640).	1 bois de massacre ♀, 3/4 ans, signe de mue (*mai-juin*).
(Noail.-644).	1 morceau de perche ♂, bois rond, (*octobre-novembre*).
(Noail.-649).	Quelques fragments de perche. Un bois de chute, ♀ 2/3 ans, (*mai-juin*).
(Noail.-675 A).	1 massacre de ♀, 5/6 ans (*octobre à mai*) et un morceau d'empaumure.
(Noail.-681 A).	1 morceau d'empaumure et une perche brisée au dessous de l'andouiller postérieur.
(Noail.-683 A).	3 morceaux d'andouiller.
(Noail.-864).	1 bois de massacre ♀, 4/5 ans, pas d'andouiller d'oeil, andouiller de glace à 105 mm. de la meule, signe de mue externe (*mai*). Longueur totale: 205 mm., A = 23,0 x 20,0 mm., (pl. VII, n° 1).
(Noail.-782).	3 morceaux de perche.
(Noail.-951).	4 débris de perche.

Niveau moyen

(Noail.-410).	1 bois de massacre ♀, 4/5 ans, A = 19,0 x 21,0 mm., (*fin septembre*).
(Noail.-454).	1 bois de massacre ♀, 4/5 ans, A = 21,0 x 21,0 mm., signe de mue (*mai-juin*).
(Noail.-483 A).	1 bois de massacre ♂, A = 14,0 x 20,0 mm.
(Noail.-483 B).	1 bois de massacre ♀, 4/5 ans, signe de mue (*mai*), (pl. VI, n° 2).
(Noail.-483 C).	3 morceaux de perche travaillés par l'homme.
(Noail.-483 D).	4 morceaux de perche non travaillés et un cornillon.
(Noail.-507).	1 dague brisée (*novembre à juin*), (pl. VII, n° 2).
(Noail.-508).	1 bois de massacre ♀, 2 ans, A = 17,0 x 21,0 mm. (*juillet-août*); 1 bois de chute ♂ A = 40,0 x 42,0 mm.
(Noail.-556).	1 bois de massacre ♀, 2 ans, signe de mue (*mai-juin*).
(Noail.-572).	1 bois de massacre ♀, 2/3 ans, (*octobre*); 3 débris de perche.
(Noail.-599).	1 bois de massacre ♀, 2/3 ans, (*octobre*).

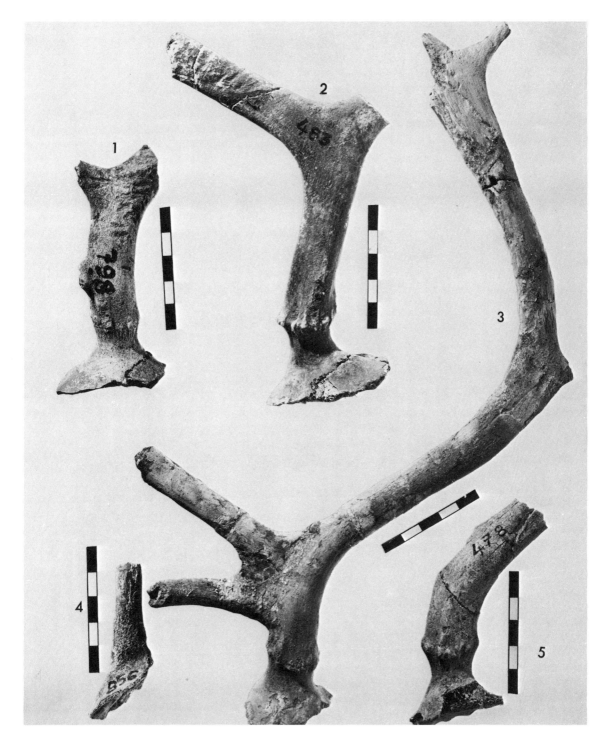

PLANCHE VI. Le matériel figuré se rapporte entièrement au Noaillien. 1. *Rangifer tarandus* (Noail.-798). Bois de massacre femelle, au niveau de la meule, signe de mue (*mai-juin*). (Niveau moyen). 2. *Rangifer tarandus* (Noail.-483 B). Bois de massacre femelle, signe de la mue prochaine (*mai*). (Niveau moyen). 3. *Rangifer tarandus* (Noail.-365). Bois de massacre femelle, signe de mue prochaine (*mai*). (Niveau supérieur). 4. *Rangifer tarandus* (Noail.-856). Bois de massacre de première année (dague), calcification complète (*octobre à juin*). (Niveau moyen). 5. *Rangifer tarandus* (Noail.-478). Bois de massacre femelle, signe de mue prochaine (*mai*). (Niveau supérieur).

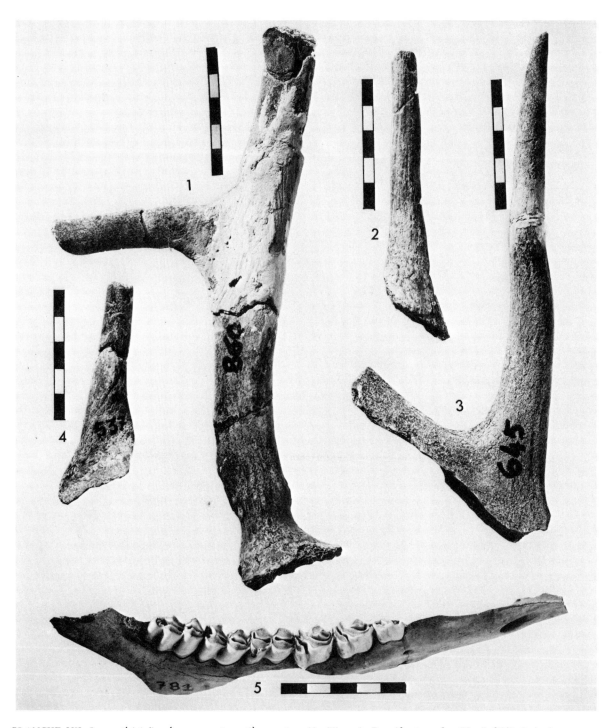

PLANCHE VII. Le matériel figuré se rapporte entièrement au Noaillien. 1. *Rangifer tarandus* (Noail.-864). Bois de massacre femelle, signe de mue prochaine (*mai*). (Niveau moyen). 2. *Rangifer tarandus* (Noail.-507). Bois de première année (dague), calcification achevée (*novembre à juin*). (Niveau moyen). 3. *Rangifer tarandus* (Noail.-645). Morceau d'empaumure de renne de toundra. (Niveau inférieur). 4. *Rangifer tarandus* (Noail.-537). Bois de première année (dague), calcification complète (*novembre à juin*). (Niveau supérieur). 5. *Rangifer tarandus* (Noail.-781). Mandibule portant une denture complète, l'animal était âgé de 4 à 5 ans. La série dentaire mesure 108 mm. (Niveau supérieur).

TABLEAU XVIII *Suite*

(Noail.-798).	9 débris de perche; un bois de massacre ♀, un bois de massacre ♀ 2/3 ans, signe de mue *(mai-juin)*, (pl. VI, no. 1).
(Noail.-835).	1 bois de massacre ♀, 5/6 ans, signe de mue *(mai)*, (pl. VIII, n° 2).
(Noail.-856).	1 dague brisée *(octobre à juin)*, (pl. VI, n° 4).
(Noail.-858).	1 morceau de perche.
(Noail.-860).	1 bois de massacre ♀, 3 ans, signe de mue *(mai-juin)*.
(Noail.-863).	1 morceau de perche.
(Noail.-890).	1 débris de perche.
(Noail.-893).	1 bois de massacre ♂, 2/3 ans, signe de mue *(décembre)*.
Niveau inférieur	
(Noail.-376).	1 bois de massacre ♀, 3/4 ans, signe de mue *(mai-juin)*.
(Noail.-416).	3 morceaux de perche.
(Noail.-450).	1 bois de chute travaillé par l'homme, l = 200 mm. environ, A = 37,0 x 30,5 mm.
(Noail.-489).	1 débris de perche.
(Noail.-546).	1 morceau de dague.
(Noail.-547).	1 bois de massacre ♀, 3 ans, courbure anormale, (pl. VIII, n°4).
(Noail.-573).	3 débris de perche dont l'un est travaillé.
(Noail.-589).	1 débris de perche travaillé.
(Noail.-598).	1 bois de massacre ♀, 3 ans, signe de mue *(mai-juin)*.
(Noail.-645).	1 digitation d'empaumure, l = 165 mm. environ, (pl. VII, n° 3).
(Noail.-839).	1 débris de perche.
(Noail.-853).	8 morceaux de perche.
(Noail.-855).	2 morceaux de perche.
(Noail.-869).	4 morceaux de perche et 1 morceau d'empaumure.
(Noail.-870).	1 bois de massacre ♀, 3 ans *(octobre à mai)*.
(Noail.-871).	1 morceau de perche.
(Noail.-879).	2 morceaux de perche.
(Noail.-895).	2 morceaux de perche.

Le niveau moyen a livré cinq bois intéressants dont quatre appartiennent à des femelles et le dernier à un jeune mâle.

La ramure Noail.-365, (Pl. VI, n° 3) est un bois de renne de toundra femelle dont la longueur totale estimée sur la courbure postérieure atteint 355 mm. En A la section est de 20,0 x 22,0 mm. L'andouiller d'oeil et l'andouiller de glace forment un bloc unique qui se détache de la hampe à 12 mm. environ de la meule. Sur le cercle de pierrures un sillon très net indique une mue prochaine *(mai-juin)*. L'andouiller postérieur, brisé dès son départ, se détache au point de rebroussement de la hampe; la section mesurée immédiatement au dessous est: B = 25,0 x 18,0 mm.

Noail.-478 est un bois de massacre provenant d'une femelle âgée de 4/5 ans (pl. VI, n° 5), la mue prochaine est indiquée par un léger sillon placé au dessous et contre la meule. On n'aperçoit aucune trace de l'andouiller d'oeil.

Le massacre le plus âgé porte le numéro Noail.-483 B, il provient d'une femelle de 5/6 ans; une amorce d'andouiller d'oeil est visible au niveau de la meule tandis que l'andouiller de glace, brisé peu après son origine, en est distant de 50 mm. environ. Le cercle de pierrures est interrompu en son milieu par le sillon annonciateur de la séquestration prochaine *(mai-juin)*.

L'unique bois de mâle (Noail.-483 A) provient d'un très jeune animal, 2/3 ans environ. Ses dimensions sont faibles: A = 14,0 x 21,0 mm. L'andouiller d'oeil manque et l'andouiller de glace se sépare de la perche à 70 mm. du cercle de pierrures.

Les pièces Noail.-798 (pl. VI, n° 1), Noail.-835 (pl. VIII, n° 2) et Noail.-860, sont des massacres de femelles âgées respectivement de 2/3 ans, 5/6 ans, et 3 ans porteurs des signes d'une mue prochaine, (*mai-juin*). Le bois Noail.-547, récolté dans le niveau inférieur, est un massacre fortement courbé en S (pl. VIII, n° 4) et brisé au-dessous de l'andouiller postérieur. Il appartenait très probablement à une femelle dans sa seconde année.

Les rennes de première année sont représentés par trois dagues: Noail.-856 (pl. VI, n° 4), Noail.-537 (pl. VII, n° 4), et Noail.-507 (pl. VII, n° 2) dont la croissance est achevée. Les porteurs furent tués entre le mois d'octobre et le mois de juin de l'année suivante.

Citons encore trois pièces intéressantes. La première (Noail.-781) est une mandibule dont la série dentaire est complète, la longueur de la série dentaire est de 108 mm. (pl. VII, n° 5). L'animal était âgé de 4/5 ans. La seconde est une prémolaire supérieure anormale (Noail.-856), la muraille jugale, très haute est conique tandis que le croissant lingual se réduit à un petit bourrelet situé au-dessus du cingulum (pl. X, n° 4). La troisième est une portion de crâne de *R. tarandus* réduit à sa région otique (Noail.-858).

Voici maintenant une série de mesures prises sur les os longs.

TABLEAU XIX

Taille moyenne et limites extrêmes de variations des principaux segments osseux de *Rangifer tarandus* récoltés dans tous les niveaux du Noaillien

Humérus. Diamètre transversal du condyle articulaire

n = 9   M = 44,2 mm.   W = 41,2   50,0 mm.

Radius. Extrémité proximale. Diam. antéro-post. x diam. transv.

n = 25   M = 25,5 x 43,9 mm.   W = 25,2 x 39,0   27,8 x 49,0 mm.

Radius. Extrémité distale. Diamètre antéro-post. x diam. trans.

n = 20   M = 27,7 x 42,2 mm.   W = 24,0 x 39,0   32,0 x 47,0 mm.

Canon antérieur. Extrémité proximale. Diam. antéro-post. x diam. transv.

n = 4   M = 22,8 x 32,7 mm.   W = 22,4 x 32,0   22,9 x 34,0 mm.

Canon antérieur. Extrémité distale. Diam. antéro-post. x diam. transv.

n = 100   M = 21,9 x 41,1 mm.   W = 20,5 x 38,0   24,0 x 46,0 mm.

Tibia. Extrémité distale. Diam. antéro-post. x diam. transv.

n = 65   M = 31,9 x 37,6 mm.   W = 32,0 x 37,7   34,8 x 41,0 mm.

Cubo-naviculaire. Diam. antéro-post. x diam. transv.

n = 18   M = 29,2 x 33,5 mm.   W = 24,0 x 29,8   32,2 x 38,5 mm.

Astragale. Hauteur maximum x largeur maximum

n = 25   M = 44,3 x 28,3 mm.   W = 38,3 x 25,7   49,2 x 31,1 mm.

Calcaneum. Longueur maximum

n = 1   L = 85,8 mm.

Canon postérieur. Extrémité distale. Diam. antéro-post. x diam. transv.

n = 135   M = 23,1 x 40,3 mm.   W = 23,0 x 37,0   24,2 x 48,0 mm.

N.B. Dans le tableau ci-dessus, n désigne le nombre de pièces, M désigne les valeurs moyennes et W exprime l'amplitude de la variation.

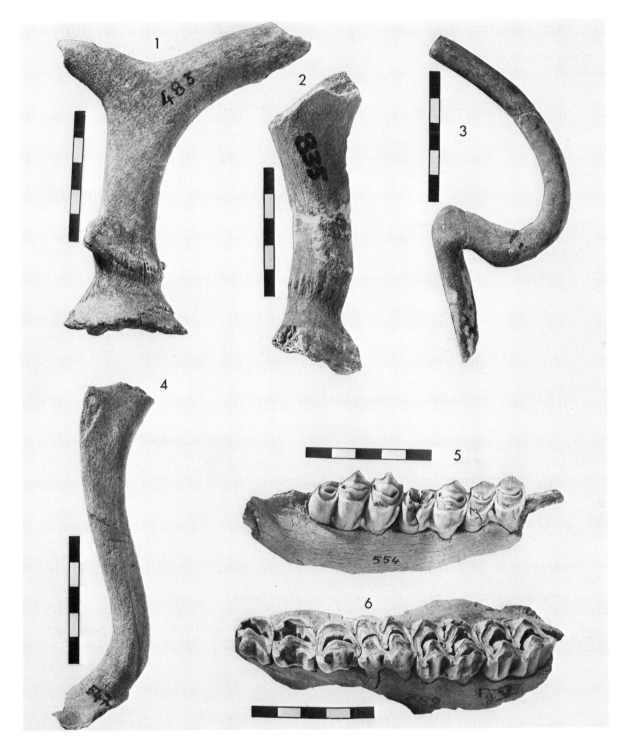

PLANCHE VIII. Le matériel figuré, à l'exception de la fig. 3, appartient au Noaillien. 1. *Rangifer tarandus* (Noail.-483 B). Bois de massacre femelle, signe de mue prochaine (*mai*). (Niveau moyen). 2. *Rangifer tarandus* (Noail.-835). Bois de massacre femelle, signe de mue prochaine (*mai*). (Niveau moyen). 3. *Rangifer tarandus* (Pg. VI-152 C). Morceau de perche anormale. La pièce brisée pendant la croissance s'est réparée par la suite. 4. *Rangifer tarandus* (Noail.-547). Bois de massacre à courbure anormale. (Niveau inférieur). 5. *Cervus elaphus* (Noail.-554). Mandibule brisée, de forte taille portant les trois molaires M_1, M_2 et M_3. (Niveau moyen). 6. *Cervus elaphus* (Noail.-782). Maxillaire supérieur droit portant une denture complète. (Niveau moyen).

Le cerf élaphe (*Cervus elaphus*) est médiocrement représenté. Ses débris sont environ 60 fois moins nombreux que ceux de *Rangifer tarandus*. Ils comprennent essentiellement des éclats de diaphyses mais toutes les parties du squelette sont présentes. Voici une série de mesures prises.

TABLEAU XX

Noaillien. Mesures prises sur les restes de *Cervus elaphus*

(Noail.-459). 1 maxillaire supérieur gauche portant une denture complète (pl. IX, n° 7). $P^2 = 13,9$ mm., $P^3 = 13,9$ mm., $P^4 = 13,8$ mm., $M^1 = 19,0$ mm., $M^2 = 22,3$ mm., $M^3 = 22,0$ mm.

(Noail.-547). 1 mandibule brisée (pl. IX, 2). $P^3 = 16,6$ mm., $P^4 = 18,8$ mm., $M^1 = 20,8$ mm.

(Noail.-554). 1 mandibule brisée (pl. VIII, 5). $M_1 = 22,0$ mm., $M_2 = 24,5$ mm., $M_3 = 34,3$ mm.

(Noail.-782). 1 maxillaire supérieur droit portant une denture complète (pl. VIII, 6). $P^2 = 13,0$ mm., $P^3 = 14,0$ mm., $P^4 = 13,8$ mm., $M^1 = 18,3$ mm., $M^2 = 19,0$ mm., $M^3 = 22.0$ mm.

(Noail.-591). 1 extrémité proximale de canon postérieur: 40,2 x 39,1 mm.

(Noail.-600). 1 extrémité distale d'humérus droit: 61,2 x 58,2 mm.

1 extrémité proximale de radius droit: 33,8 x 58,8 mm.

1 extrémité distale de radius gauche: 41,8 x 59,9 mm.

1 extrémité proximale de cubitus, diamètre de la cavité glénoïde: 31,0 mm.

1 extrémite distale de canon antérieur: 32,0 x 49,0 mm.

1 os innominé gauche, diamètres de la cavité cotyloïde: 46,8 x 48,0 mm.

1 extrémité distale de tibia: 44,0 x 54,4 mm.

1 cubo-naviculaire gauche: 43,0 x 47,5 mm.

1 astragale gauche: 60,0 x 40,0 mm.

1 calcaneum gauche, longueur totale: 125,0 mm.

Les débris d'os longs: (Noail.-591 et Noail.-600) proviennent du même animal comme le prouve l'engrènement des surfaces articulaires de l'humérus avec le cubitus, du calcaneum avec l'astragale, le cubo-naviculaire et le tibia. Il faut ajouter à la liste précédente, toujours sous l'indicatif (Noail.-600) un magnum, un semi-lunaire et une malléole externe.

Capreolus capreolus, le Chevreuil, signale sa présence par un très petit nombre d'éclats de diaphyse et une phalange (I) brisée (Noail.-895 C); aucun os long n'est intact et il n'existe point de pièce mesurable. Quelques rares dents isolées sont fragmentaires.

BOVIDAE et EQUIDAE

Les débris de Bovidés (140) et d'Equidés (135) sont nettement plus nombreux que les restes de Cervidés mais il s'agit presque toujours de débris osseux et d'éclats de diaphyses non mesurables; enfin un lot important de fragments d'os (226) reconnaissable à l'épaisseur de la diaphyse ne peuvent être attribués, du fait de leur taille réduite, soit au genre *Bos* soit au genre *Equus* et de ce fait ils sont rangés dans le tableau XIII sous la rubrique *Bos* ou *Equus*.

Les Éboulis 3/4 le niveau supérieur et les «Test pits» B, N, Q, et U ont fourni des morceaux de mandibule et des dents inférieures isolées dont les dimensions sont consignées dans le tableau suivant:

TABLEAU XXI

Noaillien. Mesures prises sur les restes de Bovidés

Éboulis 3/4

(Noail.-618). 1 morceau de mandibule (pl. IX, n° 4). $P_2 = 9,5$ mm., $P_3 = 17,0$ mm., $P_4 = 22,0$ mm. $M_1 = 25,5$ mm.

(Noail.-666). 1 morceau de mandibule portant les molaires M_1 et M_2. $M_1 = 24,0$ mm., $M_2 = 26,0$ mm.

(Noail.-709). 1 scaphoïde. Diamètre antéro-postérieur: 65,5 mm. Diamètre transversal: 41,0 mm. Hauteur maximum: 39,9 mm.

TABLEAU XXI *Suite*

Niveau supérieur

(Noail.-656). 1 morceau de mandibule portant les molaires M_2 et M_3. M_2 = 29,0 mm., M_3 = 41,5 mm., mesures prises au niveau des alvéoles dentaires.

(Noail.-410). 1 morceau de mandibule possédant la denture de lait. m_3 est brisée, M_1 = 36,5 mm. au niveau de l'alvéole, M_2 perce tout juste l'alvéole.

Tests pits

(Test pit B). 1 molaire inférieure M_1 brisée. Au niveau de la table: 35,0 x 13,0 mm.

1 molaire inférieure M_2 usée au tiers de la hauteur. Au collet: 29,8 x 20,5 mm.

1 molaire inférieure M_3 usée au tiers de la hauteur. Au collet: 46,0 x 19,0 mm.

(Test pit N). 1 molaire inférieure M_1 usée au tiers de la hauteur. Au collet: 28,0 x 21,0 mm.

1 molaire inférieure M_3 usée au tiers de la hauteur. Au collet: 51,5 x 21,0 mm.

(Test pit Q). 1 molaire inférieure M_1 usée à mi-hauteur. Au collet: 26,0 x 19,0 mm.

1 molaire inférieure M_1 peu usée. Au collet: 26,0 x 18,0 mm.

1 molaire inférieure M_2 peu usée. Au collet: 29,5 x 21,0 mm.

1 molaire inférieure M_2 usée à mi-hauteur. Au collet: 30,5 x 21,0 mm.

1 molaire inférieure M_3 brisée à mi-hauteur. Au niveau de la table: 43,0 x 14,8 mm.

1 molaire inférieure M_3 usée au tiers de la hauteur. Au collet: 49,0 x 17,0 mm.

(Test pit U). 1 molaire inférieure M_3 brisée. Au niveau de la table: 46,0 x 17,0 mm.

Les dents ne permettent en aucun cas une attribution précise, soit à *Bos primigenius*, soit à *Bison priscus*. Toujours dans les Éboulis 3/4 une phalangine (Noail.-871) pourrait appartenir à *Bos primigenius* d'après les données d'Olsen (1960). Pour les mêmes motifs une extrémité distale de tibia (Noail.-544) proviendrait de la même espèce. Cependant l'examen d'une série relativement importante de termes de comparaison ne m'a pas convaincu absolument du bien-fondé des critères invoqués par l'auteur. Les dimensions maximum de la région articulaire sont les suivantes:

(Noail.-544). 1 extrémité distale de tibia: 65,5 x 41,3 mm.

Les belles pièces sont rares chez les Equidés. Comme dans le cas précédent on a surtout affaire à des éclats de diaphyse dont certains sont difficilement identifiables. Des maxillaires, des mandibules et des dents isolées ont permis de réaliser le tableau XXII.

TABLEAU XXII

Noaillien. Mesures prises sur les restes d'Equidés

Éboulis 3/4

(Noail.-667). 1 prémolaire supérieure P^2 brisée, mesures prises au dessous de la table dentaire: 42,0 x 28,0 mm.

Niveau supérieur

(Noail.-458/459). 1 extrémité distale de canon antérieur: 52,0 x 39,0 mm.

(Noail.-377). 1 molaire inférieure M_2, mesures prises au dessous de la table dentaire: 30,0 x 19,0 mm. le fût étant brisé.

Niveau moyen

(Noail.-562). 1 extrémité distale de canon antérieur: 52,0 x 37,0 mm.

(Noail.-837). 1 prémolaire supérieure P^4: 27,2 x 26,8 mm., mesures prises au dessous de la table dentaire.

(Noail.-863). 1 prémolaire supérieure P^3: 26,5 x 27,0 mm., mesures prises au dessous de la table dentaire.

1 prémolaire supérieure P^4: 30,5 x 27,5 mm., mesures prises au dessous de la table dentaire.

TABLEAU XXII *Suite*

(Noail.-892).	1 maxillaire supérieur gauche portant une denture complète d'*Equus caballus gallicus*. Longueur de la série dentaire: 172,0 mm. P^2 = 39,0 x 26,0 mm., P^3 = 30,5 x 29,0 mm., P^4 = 27,0 x 30,0 mm., M^1 = 24,0 x 28,8 mm., M^2 = 25,0 x 27,2 mm., M^3 = 28,6 x 25,0 mm. Les mesures sont prises au niveau de la table dentaire mais la série dentaire est estimée au niveau des alvéoles (pl. IX, n° 1).

Niveau inférieur

Toutes les mesures sont prises au niveau de la table dentaire.

(Noail.-415).	1 morceau de mandibule d'*Equus caballus gallicus* portant les trois prémolaires (pl. IX, n° 3). P_2 = 36,0 mm., P_3 = 31,8 mm., P_4 = 30,9 mm.
(Noail.-451).	1 molaire supérieure M^1: 31,2 x 30,0 mm.
(Noail.-464).	1 molaire inférieure M_2: 26,8 x 17,5 mm.
(Noail.-897 C).	1 molaire inférieure M_2: 26,1 x 15,9 mm.
(Noail.-902 A).	1 molaire supérieure M^3 sortant de l'alvéole: 37,6 x 26,7 mm.

Test pit U

(Test pit U).	1 molaire inférieure M_3: 33,0 x 15,0 mm.

Normalement les mesures sont prises au point P de F. Prat (1966) dans le cas des dents isolées, au niveau de la table dentaire quand les dents sont incluses dans le maxillaire ou la mandibule et au-dessous de la partie renflée de la table dentaire si le fût de la dent isolée est brisé au-dessus du point P. Les dents d'Equidés du Noaillien sont de deux types. Les premières, de forte taille pourraient appartenir à l'*Equus caballus germanicus Nehring* tandis que les secondes, nettement plus petites caractériseraient le cheval de Solutré. En l'absence d'os longs intacts et particulièrement des canons et des phalanges la distinction spécifique demeure difficile car les limites extrêmes de variation des dents se chevauchent (Gromova 1949).

Deux molaires inférieures brisées présentent des traits asiniens, par exemple, la médiocrité des dimensions. Les mesures sont prises au point P (Prat 1966).

(Noail.-782).	1 molaire inférieure M_2 : 22,8 x 13,2 mm.
	1 molaire inférieure M_3 : inférieur à 29,0 mm., la dent est abîmée.
	Ces dents sont rapportées à *Equus hydruntinus Regalia*.

CAPRINAE et RUPICAPRINAE

Leur nombre fluctue d'un niveau au suivant; minimum dans les Éboulis 3/4 (7,4%) il oscille entre 11,3% et 15,4% dans les couches du Noaillien. Il y a lieu de penser que le corps des animaux était apporté tout entier à l'Abri Pataud, mais leur nombre étant minime à côté des restes de *Rangifer tarandus* on ne rencontre pas toutes les parties du squelette. On trouve surtout des éclats de diaphyse d'os longs, des morceaux de maxillaires, de mandibules, des dents isolées et des chevilles osseuses.

Voici la liste des trouvailles utilisables.

TABLEAU XXIII

Noaillien. Mesures prises sur les restes de *Capra ibex* et de *Rupicapra rupicapra*

Éboulis 3/4

(Noail.-322).	*Rupicapra rupicapra*. 1 fragment de molaire.
(Noail.-616).	*Capra ibex*. Les mesures sont prises au collet de la dent. P_4 = 10,8 x 7,1 mm., M_2 = 16,0 x 10,8 mm.

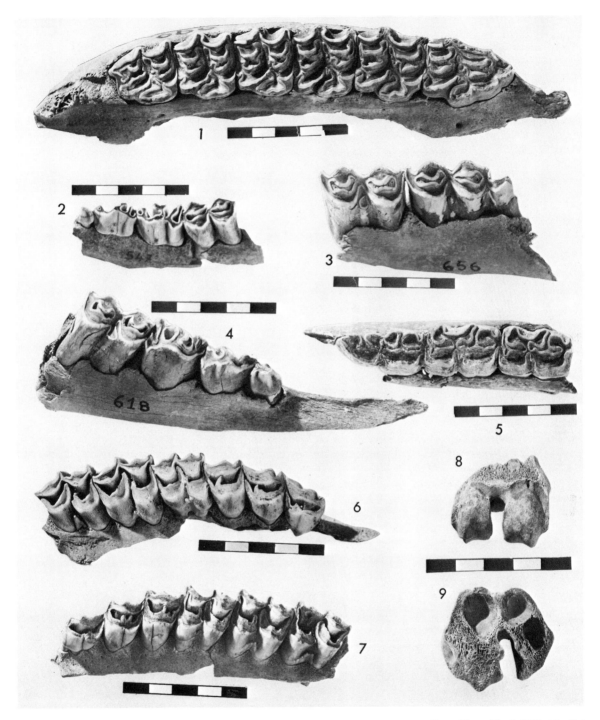

PLANCHE IX. Le matériel figuré provient du Noaillien et du Périgordien IV. 1. *Equus caballus gallicus* (Noail.-892). Maxillaire supérieur gauche portant une denture complète. (Niveau moyen). 2. *Cervus elaphus* (Noail.-547). Mandibule brisée portant les prémolaires P_3, P_4 et la molaire M_1. (Niveau inférieur). 3. *Bos sp.*, (Noail.-656). Morceau de mandibule portant la M_2 et la M_3. (Niveau supérieur). 4. *Bos sp.*, (Noail.-618). Morceau de mandibule portant les trois prémolaires et la M_1. 5. *Equus caballus (gallicus)*, (Noail.-415). Morceau de mandibule portant les trois prémolaires. (Niveau inférieur). 6. *Cervus elaphus* (Éboulis 4/5-902). Maxillaire supérieur portant une denture complète. 7. *Cervus elaphus* (Noail.-459). Maxillaire supérieur portant une denture complète. (Niveau supérieur). 8 et 9. *Rangifer tarandus* (Pg. IV-955). Deux extrémités distales d'os canons ont été râclées et transformées en outils par l'homme, (Niveau supérieur).

TABLEAU XXIII *Suite*

Niveau supérieur

(Noail.-446).	*Capra ibex.* 1 extrémité proximale de canon antérieur: 45,0 x 24,5 mm.
(Noail.-446).	*Capra ibex.* 1 extrémité proximale de radio-cubitus: 43,0 x 23,0 mm.
(Noail.-503).	*Capra ibex.* 2 incisives brisées.
(Noail.-401).	*Rupicapra rupicapra.* 1 molaire inférieure M_3 brisée.
(Noail.-471).	*Rupicapra rupicapra.* 1 molaire inférieure M_3 brisée.
(Noail.-532).	*Rupicapra rupicapra.* 1 mandibule droite. Longueur de la série dentaire: 67,2 mm. au niveau alvéolaire. P_2 = 5,0 mm., P_3 = 6,0 mm., P_4 = 7.0 mm., M_1 = 10,0 mm., M_2 = 11,0 mm., M_3 = 18,0 mm. Les mesures sont prises au bord alvéolaire.
(Noail.-532).	*Rupicapra rupicapra.* 1 mandibule portant les dents de lait et la M_1. m_2 = 7,0 mm., m_3 = 13,0 mm., M_1 = 10,6 x 7,0 mm.
(Noail.-968).	*Rupicapra rupicapra.* 1 morceau de mandibule avec P_3, P_4 et M_1; P_3 = 6,0 mm., P_4 = 9,0 mm., M_1 = 10,5 mm.

Niveau moyen

(Noail.-876).	*Capra ibex.* 1 prémolaire inférieure P_4 et 1 sabot brisés.
(Noail.-448).	*Rupicapra rupicapra.* 1 molaire supérieure M^3: 14,0 x 11,0 mm. au collet.
(Noail.-561).	*Rupicapra rupicapra.* 1 molaire supérieure M^1: 12,2 x 7,8 mm. au collet.
(Noail.-684 A).	*Rupicapra rupicapra.* 1 cheville osseuse gauche. Longueur totale: 92,0 mm., diamètres à la base: 18,5 x 18,0 mm.
(Noail.-686 A).	*Rupicapra rupicapra.* 1 extrémité distale de canon antérieur: 17,2 x 28,0 mm.
(Noail.-876).	*Rupicapra rupicapra.* 1 molaire inférieure M_1: 9,8 x 6,8 mm. au collet.

Niveau inférieur

(Noail.-415).	*Rupicapra rupicapra.* 1 prémolaire supérieure P^2: 6,0 x 6,0 mm. au collet.
(Noail.-415).	*Rupicapra rupicapra.* 1 prémolaire supérieure P^3: 5,9 x 8,0 mm.
(Noail.-546).	*Rupicapra rupicapra.* 1 cubo-naviculaire: 24,9 x 29,9 mm.
(Noail.-896 A).	*Rupicapra rupicapra.* 1 molaire inférieure M_1: 12,0 x 8,0 mm. au collet.
(Noail.-896 C).	*Rupicapra rupicapra.* 1 molaire supérieure M^2: 11,0 x 14,0 mm. au collet.
(Noail.-896C).	*Rupicapra rupicapra.* 1 molaire supérieure M^3: 12,0 x 10,6 mm.

Tests pits

Test pit Q.	*Rupicapra rupicapra.* 1 molaire inférieure M_2 peu usée. Au collet: 12,0 x 6,7 mm.
Test pit U.	*Rupicapra rupicapra.* 1 molaire inférieure M_3. Au collet: 18,0 x 7,0 mm.
Test pit U.	*Rupicapra rupicapra.* 1 molaire inférieure M_3. Au collet: 20,0 x 7,0 mm.

SUIDAE

Dans le niveau supérieur du Périgordien V la présence de *Sus scrofa*, le sanglier, est marquée par la découverte d'un sabot (Noail.-677 A) et une prémolaire inférieure PM_2 provient du test pit Q.

CANIDAE, URSIDAE, et FELIDAE

Les restes de *Canis lupus* et de *Vulpes vulpes* sont rares dans le Noaillien; on ne rencontre plus de belles pièces comme dans le Proto-Magdalénien.

En ce qui concerne le renard, il s'agit de *Vulpes vulpes* et non d'*Alopex lagopus* dont rien ne permet de soupçonner la présence. Les Éboulis 3/4 ont livré quelques éclats d'os longs et une canine fragmentaire tandis que le niveau supérieur renferme un os innominé brisé (Noail.-386), deux morceaux de canines (Noail.-361 et Noail.-631), un métacarpien V (Noail.-407), et un éclat de tibia (Noail.-643). Absent du niveau moyen, on le retrouve dans l'horizon inférieur grâce à un métatarsien brisé (Noail.-488).

Deux canines fragmentaires (Noail.-644 et Noail.-837) et une incisive supérieure droite (Noail.-782) découvertes dans les niveaux supérieur et moyen sont attribuables à *Canis lupus*.

Une canine d'*Ursus spelaeus* (Noail.-291) provient des Éboulis 3/4; quelques débris dentaires sans intérêt se rencontrent dans les couches supérieure et inférieure.

Le lion des cavernes (*Panthera leo*, race *spelaea*) est présent dans la couche supérieure. Nous lui avons attribué quatre canines supérieures brisées (Noail.-372; Noail.-388; Noail.-355; et Noail.-647). Leur reconnaissance est basée sur l'aplatissement de la face linguale et sur la présence d'un double sillon visible tant sur la face linguale que sur le côté jugal.

LEPORIDAE et MICROTIDAE

Dès les Éboulis 3/4 le genre *Lepus* est abondant (20 débris); il est représenté par des restes de métacarpiens (Noail.-352), de métatarsiens (Noail.-617), deux extrémités distales d'humérus (Noail.-617 et Noail.-795), deux morceaux d'extrémité distale de tibia (Noail.-663 et Noail.-677 A), et une épiphyse isolée (Noail.-870 A). Deux incisives supérieures ont permis d'identifier *Lepus variabilis* (E. Koby 1959 et 1960). Notons aussi la présence d'incisives supérieures n'offrant pas les traits caractéristiques du lièvre variable (Noail.-334 et Noail.-895 D); leur médiocre état de conservation rend vaine tout essai de reconnaissance précise.

Le niveau supérieur renferme un volume de restes osseux légèrement inférieur au précédent mais il appartient à tout le squelette: extrémité proximale de radius (Noail.-401 et Noail.-601), diaphyse tibiale (Noail.-528 et Noail.-677), molaires isolées (Noail.-630), mandibule brisée (Noail.-778), cavité glénoïde d'omoplate (Noail.-637), phalangine (Noail.-687), et morceau de cubitus (Noail.-780).

Les strates moyenne et inférieure demeurent pauvres: deux cavités glénoïdes de scapulum

(Noail.-563 et Noail.-688), deux extrémités distales de tibia (Noail.-549 et Noail.-888), deux morceaux de tibia, (Noail.-849 et Noail.-854), deux cubitus (Noail.-833 et Noail.-789), et un radius brisé (Noail.-789).

Le genre *Arvicola* est présent grâce à des mandibules dans les Éboulis 3/4 (Noail.-672 A et Noail.-674) qui semblent appartenir à *Arvicola terrestris*. En l'absence de crânes il n'est pas possible de savoir s'il s'agit, comme dans les niveaux précédents, d'*Arvicola scherman* (Heim de Balsac et Guislain 1955). Le niveau moyen ne contenait qu'un fémur (Noail.-600).

Deux mandibules (Noail.-390 et Noail.-600) et un fémur (Noail.-474) appartiennent à *Microtus agrestis*; ces restes proviennent des Éboulis 3/4, des horizons moyen et inférieur.

CORVIDAE

Les Éboulis 3/4 et la couche moyenne contenaient quelques restes de *Corvidae: Coracia graculus*, le chocard des Alpes et *Corvus corax*, le grand corbeau.

Éboulis 3/4

(Noail.-351).	*Coracia graculus*. 1 cubitus brisé.
(Noail.-625).	*Corvus corax*. 1 coracoïde.

Couche moyenne

(Noail.-876).	*Coracia graculus*. 1 sacrum brisé.

DIVERS

Un petit nombre de vertèbres de poissons découvertes dans le niveau moyen appartiennent probablement à des Salmonidés.

5. LA FAUNE du PÉRIGORDIEN IV

Le Périgordien IV a livré une très grosse quantité de matériel (760 kg.) dont une bonne partie (21% environ) est identifiable jusqu'au niveau de l'espèce. Aux espèces déjà rencontrées dans les couches précédentes viennent s'ajouter: *Elephas primigenius*, le mammouth, *Ovibus moschatus*, le boeuf musqué et *Lynx lynx*, le lynx boréal; on doit noter la disparition d'*Equus hydruntinus*.

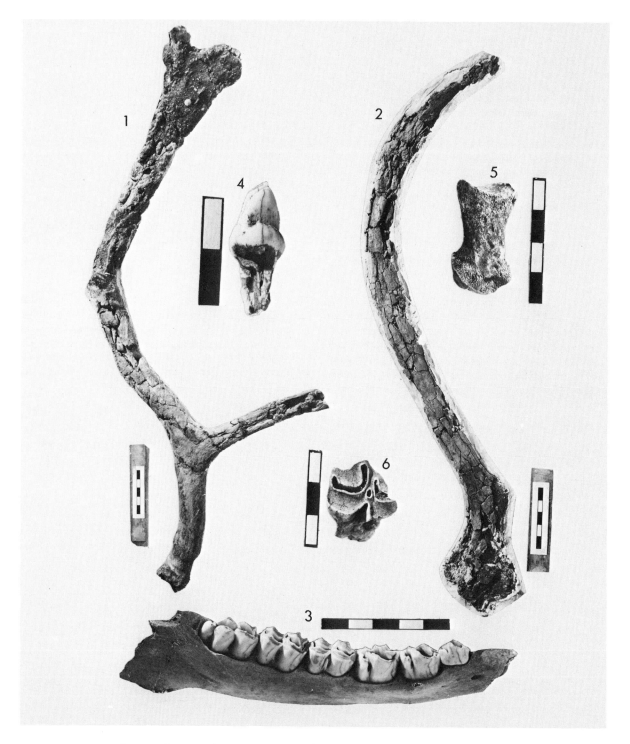

PLANCHE X. Le matériel figuré provient à l'exception d'une pièce du Périgordien IV. 1. *Rangifer tarandus* (Pg. IV-1192). Bois de massacre femelle, perche de type "*tarandus*". (Niveau inférieur). 2. *Rangifer tarandus* (Pg. IV-1194). Bois de massacre, probablement mâle, perche du type "*arcticus*". (Niveau inférieur). 3. *Rangifer tarandus* (Pg. IV-767). Mandibule de renne âgé de 3 à 4 ans. Longueur de la denture: 105 mm. (Niveau inférieur). 4. *Rangifer tarandus* (Noail.-856). Prémolaire supérieure anormale. (Niveau moyen). 5. *Rangifer tarandus* (Pg. IV-1156). Phalange mordue par l'homme. (Niveau moyen). 6. *Ovibos moschatus* (Ext. 2, Pg. IV-1254). Molaire supérieure brisée.

TABLEAU XXIV

Espèces et débris osseux du Périgordien IV

Macrofaune			Rongeurs		
Rangifer tarandus	21.119	(97,4%)	*Lepus variabilis*	135	(95,8%)
Cervus elaphus	172		*Microtus agrestis*	1	(2,5%)
Capreolus capreolus	10	(1,1%)	*Microtus sp.*	4	
Bos sp.	48		*Arvicola sp.*	1	(0,7%)
Equus caballus	44	(0,2%)			
Capra ibex	26		Oiseaux		
Rupicapra rupicapra	20	(0,2%)	*Corvus corax*	36	(73,5%)
Elephas primigenius	5		*Coracia graculus*	7	(14,3%)
Ovibos moschatus (Ext. II)	1		*Columba oenas*	3	(6,1%)
Canis lupus	39		*Perdix perdix*	3	(6,1%)
Vulpes vulpes	161				
Lynx lynx	4	(1,1%)	Amphibiens et Poissons		
Ursus spelaeus	6				
Crocuta crocuta spelaea	3		*Bufo* et *Rana sp.* abondants		
Mustela sp.	1		Pas de vertèbres de poisson		

CERVIDAE

Rangifer tarandus demeure toujours l'espèce dominante dans les couches principales et le pourcentage de ses débris osseux ne descend jamais au-dessous de 97%. Les ramures sont nombreuses et toutes les parties du squelette son représentées; leur bon état de conservation a permis de prendre des séries de mesures. Cependant les Éboulis 4/5 n'ont livré que 392 pièces dont quelques unes seulement sont mesurables.

Voici la description des ramures récoltées; seules les pièces intéressantes sont figurées.

TABLEAU XXV

Liste des bois de *Rangifer tarandus* provenant du Périgordien IV

Niveau supérieur

(Pg. IV-603).   4 morceaux de dague *(mois d'août).*

(Pg. IV-608).   2 morceaux de perche.

(Pg. IV-801).   5 morceaux de perche et une dague brisée *(octobre à juin).*

(Pg. IV-956).   10 morceaux de perche.

(Pg. IV-958).   2 morceaux de perche.

(Pg. IV-960).   1 morceau de perche.

(Pg. IV-985).   2 morceaux de perche.

(Pg. IV-1000).   1 morceau de perche.

(Pg. IV-1040).   1 morceau de perche.

(Pg. IV-1043).   1 dague, longueur totale: 180 mm., diam. à la base: 13,0 x 10,0 mm.

(Pg. IV-1048).   1 morceau de perche.

(Pg. IV-1065).   1 bois de chute ♂, 3/4 ans *(décembre).*

(Pg. IV-1071).   1 bois de perche ♀, 3/4 ans. (pl. XI, n°2): longueur totale: 240 mm.

(Pg. IV-1072).   5 morceaux de perche.

(Pg. IV-1099).   5 morceaux de perche.

(Pg. IV-1101).   3 morceaux de perche et 1 dague en voie de croissance.

(Pg. IV-1106).   1 morceau de perche avec le départ de l'empaumure.

(Pg. IV-1108).   1 morceau de perche.

TABLEAU XXV *Suite*

(Pg. IV-1119).	4 morceaux de perche.
(Pg. IV-1120).	1 morceau de perche.
(Pg. IV-1128).	1 morceau de perche.
(Pg. IV-1131).	1 morceau de perche.
(Pg. IV-1137).	14 morceaux de perche.
(Pg. IV-1139).	8 morceaux de perche.

Niveau moyen

(Pg. IV-410).	1 morceau de perche.
(Pg. IV-454).	1 massacre bois de ♀, 2/3 ans, croissance achevée *(novembre à mai)*.
(Pg. IV-483).	1 bois de massacre ♂, 2/3 ans, 14,0 x 20,0 mm. à 3 cm. de la meule. 1 bois de massacre ♀ brisé au dessus de la meule, 4/5 ans, signe extérieur de la mue *(mai)*.
(Pg. IV-508A)	4 morceaux de perche. 1 bois de chute ♂: 40,0 x 42,0 mm. au dessus de la meule. 1 bois de massacre de ♀: 17,0 x 21,0 mm. au dessus de la meule *(juillet-août)*.
(Pg. IV-549).	4 morceaux de perche dont 2 sont travaillés par l'homme.
(Pg. IV-553).	1 bois de chute ♂: 36,0 x 26,0 mm. au dessus de la meule *(novembre)*. 1 bois de massacre ♀ brisé *(août?)*.
(Pg. IV-554).	6 morceaux de perche.
(Pg. IV-556).	1 morceau de perche travaillé par l'homme.
(Pg. IV-557).	2 morceaux de perche.
(Pg. IV-560).	1 digitation d'empaumure.
(Pg. IV-572).	3 morceaux de perche. 1 bois de massacre de ♀, 2/3 ans *(octobre à mai?)*.
(Pg. IV-788).	10 morceaux de perche. 1 bois de massacre de ♀: 18,0 x 16,2 mm., signe de mue *(mai-juin)*. 1 bois de massacre de ♀, 2 ans, 18,0 x 18,4 mm. au dessus de la meule, mue prochaine *(mai-juin)*.
(Pg. IV-788).	1 bois de massacre de ♂; 19,8 x 21,0 mm. au dessus de la meule. 1 dague brisée *(octobre à mai)*.
(Pg. IV-832).	1 morceau de perche.
(Pg. IV-835).	1 bois de massacre ♀, 5/6 ans, mue prochaine *(mai)*.
(Pg. IV-837).	1 bois de chute ♂: 35,0 x 33,0 mm. au dessus de la meule, 4/5 ans, *(novembre-décembre)*.
(Pg. IV-856).	6 morceaux de perche. 1 dague *(septembre-octobre)*.
(Pg. IV-860).	1 morceau de perche. 1 bois de massacre de ♀: 18,0 x 21,0 mm., 2/3 ans, mue prochaine *(juin)*. 1 bois de massacre de ♀: 21,7 x 22,0 mm., 2/3 ans, amorce de l'andouiller d'oeil à 13 mm. de la meule, départ de l'andouiller de glace à 110 mm. de la meule *(septembre?)*.
(Pg. IV-863).	1 morceau de perche et 1 morceau d'andouiller.
(Pg. IV-868).	3 morceaux de perche.
(Pg. IV-875).	1 dague brisée.
(Pg. IV-892).	2 morceaux de perche.
(Pg. IV-893).	1 bois de massacre de ♂ brisé.

Niveau inférieur

(Pg. IV-729).	1 dague travaillée par l'homme. Signe de mue?
(Pg. IV-763).	1 morceau de perche: 280 mm., bois de chute de ♀.
(Pg. IV-824).	1 morceau de dague.
(Pg. IV-769).	1 morceau de perche.
(Pg. IV-948).	8 morceaux de perche.
(Pg. IV-1177).	2 morceaux de perche.
(Pg. IV-1178).	6 morceaux de perche.
(Pg. IV-1180).	2 morceaux de perche.

(Pg. IV-1181).	3 morceaux de perche. 1 bois de massacre brisé.
(Pg. IV-1185).	4 morceaux de perche.
(Pg. IV-1188).	3 morceaux de perche et une digitation d'empaumure.
(Pg. IV-1191).	6 morceaux de perche. 1 bois de massacre de mâle (pl. XI, n°4), 6/7 ans, mue prochaine *(novembre)*.
(Pg. IV-1192).	1 bois de massacre de ♀, 3/4 ans (pl. X, n° 1), type *tarandus*.
(Pg. IV-1194).	1 bois de massacre: probablement ♂, type *arcticus*. (pl. X, n° 2). 1 morceau d'empaumure, longueur 330 mm.
(Pg. IV-1199).	3 morceaux de perche.
(Pg. IV-1203).	3 morceaux d'empaumure.
(Pg. IV-1205).	2 morceaux de perche.
(Pg. IV-1217).	4 morceaux de dague.

Le bois de massacre Pg. IV-1071 (pl. XI, n° 2) provenant du niveau supérieur appartenait à une femelle. La longueur maximum de la pièce est de 240 mm. Les diamètres du pédicule sont de 24,0 x 20,0 mm. L'andouiller d'oeil, brisé à son départ, arrive au contact de la meule tandis que l'andouiller de glace en est distant de 42,0 mm. environ; les diamètres de la perche en A atteignent 20,0 x 19,0 mm., mais à son point de rupture situé au-dessous de l'andouiller postérieur ils sont encore de 20,0 x 13,0 mm.

Trois autres pièces dignes d'intérêt proviennent du niveau inférieur. Pg. IV-1191 est un bois de massacre (pl.XI, n° 4) ayant appartenu à un mâle particulièrement vigoureux; écrasé sous des blocs rocheux il a dû être consolidé sur sa face interne par un revêtement de plâtre aussi les diamètres antéro-postérieurs restent seuls valables. Celui du pédicule atteint 49/50 mm. Le détachement de l'andouiller d'oeil s'opère au contact d'une meule à peine visible, la partie conservée, longue de 130 mm., mesure 30 mm. de large en son milieu; orienté obliquement vers le haut, l'andouiller de glace long de 140 mm. quitte la perche au contact du premier (diamètre médian: 30/31 mm). La perche mal conservée, aurait eu un diamètre d'environ 60 mm. Il est impossible de savoir si ce massacre était proche de la mue *(novembre)*, mais l'extrême réduction de la partie spongieuse donne à penser qu'elle devait avoir lieu incessamment.

Pg.IV-1192 était un bois de massacre de femelle, (pl.X, n° 1) pratiquement complet; lui aussi était écrasé sous des blocs rocheux et seul un enrobage dans une résine vinylique a permis de le recueillir; pour le conserver, il a fallu l'inclure dans une couche de plâtre. La longueur de la perche estimée le long de l'arc postérieur est de 455 mm. Sa courbure appartient au type *tarandus*. L'andouiller d'oeil manque totalement tandis que l'andouiller de glace (longueur 195 mm., diamètre: 20/21 mm.) se dirige obliquement vers le haut; il quitte le merrain à 75 mm. de la meule à peine visible. L'andouiller d'oeil est à peine marqué enfin la perche s'achève par un aplatissement très net porteur de deux chevillures brisées qui n'ont pas été retrouvées. L'animal était âgé d'environ 3 à 4 ans.

La ramure (Pg. IV-1194), écrasée sous des quartiers de roc, a été conservée de la même façon. Le bloc de plâtre où elle est incluse se voit partiellement sur la photo (pl. X, n°2). Longue de 700 mm. sur sa courbure postérieure de type *arcticus,* elle appartient à un renne de toundra mâle; elle ne présente pas de trace d'andouiller postérieur et ceux de la base ont été détruits.

Le morceau d'empaumure (Pg. IV-1195) n'a pas été figuré. Par ses dimensions il pourrait appartenir au gros bois de mâle (Pg. IV-1191). Il se compose d'un morceau de perche de 180 mm. terminé par deux digitations longues de 240 mm.; le diamètre de la perche était de 50/52 mm. Ecrasé par les blocs tombés de la voûte de l'abri, la pièce a été enrobée d'abord de résine puis renforcée par un corselet de plâtre.

Les Éboulis 4/5 et les «extensions» I et II n'ont pas livré de ramures.

Les divers segments osseux du squelette de *Rangifer tarandus* récoltés dans les niveaux du Périgordien IV ont permis d'effectuer plus de 600 mesures dont le détail ne saurait être reproduit ici. Dans le tableau ci-dessous figurent le nombre des pièces mesurées, les dimensions moyennes, et les valeurs extrêmes. On notera la fréquence des phalanges (I) et (II), des os canons et la rareté des mesures relatives à l'humérus et au fémur. Le matériel récolté dans les «extensions I et II est compris dans le décompte. Plus de 70% des phalanges appartiennent à ce secteur.

TABLEAU XXVI

Taille moyenne et limites extrêmes de variation des principaux
segments osseux de *Rangifer tarandus* récoltés dans tous les niveaux
du Périgordien IV

Humérus. Diamètre transversal de l'articulation distale.
n = 27   M = 43,5 mm.   W = 39,8   47,0 mm.

Radio-cubitus. Extrémité proximale. Diam. ant.-post. x diam. transv.
n = 33   M = 25,2 x 34,8 mm.   W = 23,5 x 38,5   27,1 x 47,1

                      Extrémité distale. Diam. ant.-post. x diam. transv.
n = 16   M = 29,5 x 41,8 mm.   W = 24,6 x 36,0   34,0 x 46,8 mm.

Canon antérieur. Extrémité proximale. Diam. ant.-post. x diam. transv.
n = 9   M = 24,1 x 33,1 mm.   W = 22,4 x 30,9   28,8 x 38,8 mm.

Canon antérieur. Extrémité distale. Diam. ant.-post. x diam. transv.
n = 69   M = 22,1 x 41,9 mm.   W = 21,0 x 40,0   23,9 x 46,1 mm.

Tibia. Extrémité distale. Diam. ant.-post. x diam. transv.
n = 46   M = 31,5 x 36,5 mm.   W = 30,1 x 34.0   34,3 x 41,6 mm.

Astragale. Hauteur maximum x largeur maximum.
n = 88   M = 45,0 x 28,4 mm.   W = 41,6 x 26,8   50,0 x 31,1 mm.

Cubo-naviculaire. Diam. ant.-post. x diam. transv.
n = 81   M = 30,5 x 33,7 mm.   W = 28,4 x 32,4   37,2 x 42,9

Calcaneum. Longueur maximum.
n = 18   M = 92,3 mm.   W = 85,0   101,0 mm.

Canon postérieur. Extrémité proximale. Diam. ant.-post. x diam. transv.
n = 3   M = 30,4 x 34,8 mm.   W = 29,0 x 32,0   33,2 x 40,8 mm.

Canon postérieur. Extrémité distale. Diam. ant.-post. x diam. transv.
n = 77   M = 23,8 x 42,5 mm.   W = 21,3 x 39,0   25,7 x 45,0 mm.

Phalanges (I). Hauteur maximum estimée le long de la face antérieure.
n = 117   M = 46,6 mm.   W = 41,0   53,2 mm.

Phalanges (II). Hauteur maximum estimée le long de la face antérieure.
n = 117   M = 34,1 mm.   W = 28,3   39,6 mm.

N.B. Dans le tableau ci-dessus n désigne le nombre de pièces, M désigne
la moyenne et W exprime l'amplitude de la variation.

Le nombre de maxillaires et de mandibules provenant des niveaux périgordiens est assez important: 127 mandibules et 20 maxillaires, mais ce sont surtout des pièces brisées et la longueur de la série dentaire n'est fournie que par un très petit nombre de pièces complètes.

(Pg. IV-799). Couche supérieure. Une mandibule de 3 ans. Longueur de la série dentaire: 1 = 103 mm.

(Pg. IV-603). Couche supérieure. Une mandible de 4 à 5 ans environ. (pl. XI, n° 5). Longueur de la série dentaire: 1 = 105 mm.

(Pg.IV-767). Couche inférieure. Une mandibule de 3 ans (pl.X, n°3). Longueur de la série dentaire: 1 = 105 mm.

Il s'agit là de données intéressantes car c'est entre trois et quatre ans que la série dentaire atteint sa longueur maximum, ensuite elle se raccourcit par suite de la formation de facettes de contact entre les dents et principalement la Ml et la M2; vers la neuvième année le raccourcissement peut atteindre 10 mm.

Cervus elaphus est peu représenté en comparaison de *Rangifer tarandus:* à peine 172 pièces pour tout le Périgordien IV. On rencontre des débris appartenant à tout le squelette de l'animal mais le nombre de restes intéressants est très petit. Les cerfs sont toujours de très forte taille. Les Éboulis 4/5 ont fourni quatre pièces intéressantes.

Les restes de *Capreolus capreolus* sont encore moins répandus que ceux du cerf élaphe: à peine deux douzaines de pièces pour tout le Périgordien IV. Ils proviennent d'animaux nettement plus robustes que leurs congénères actuels. La majeure partie du

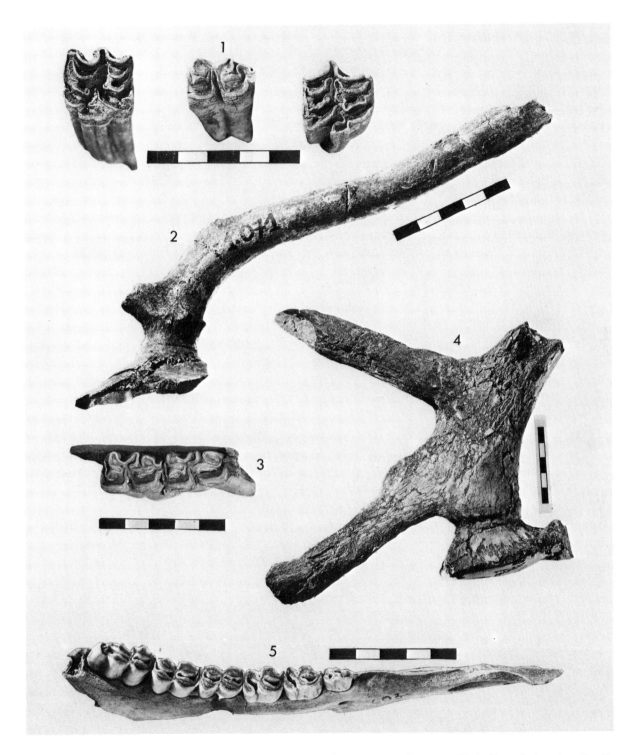

PLANCHE XI. A l'exception d'une seule pièce, le matériel figuré provient du Périgordien IV. 1. *Equus hydruntinus Regalia* (Extension I, Level H). 2 molaires supérieures et une molaire inférieure. 2. *Rangifer tarandus* (Pg. IV-1071). Bois de massacre femelle, calcification complète (*novembre à mai*). (Niveau supérieur). 3. *Equus caballus* (Noail.-782). Morceau de mandibule portant les molaires M_1 et M_2. (Niveau supérieur). 4. *Rangifer tarandus* (Pg. IV-1191). Bois de massacre mâle, signe de mue prochaine (*novembre*). (Niveau inférieur). 5. *Rangifer tarandus*, (Pg. IV-603). Mandibule de 4 à 5 ans, longueur de la série dentaire: 105 mm. (Niveau supérieur).

squelette est représentée mais les phalanges, les sabots et les éclats de métapodes sont les plus nombreux. Peu de pièces ont fourni des mesures.

Le chevreuil n'est pas représenté dans les Éboulis 4/5, ses restes apparaissent dans le niveau supérieur avec trois molaires brisées. La couche moyenne a fourni des restes de phalanges et un morceau de molaire inférieure M_3. Voici l'essentiel des mesures prises.

TABLEAU XXVII

Périgordien IV. Mesures prises sur les restes de *Cervus elaphus* et de *Capreolus capreolus*

(Eb. 4/5-899).	*Cervus elaphus*. 1 extrémité distale de canon postérieur: 49,0 x 31,6 mm.
(Eb. 4/5-899).	*Cervus elaphus*. 1 molaire inférieure M_3: 34,0 x 16,0 mm. au collet.
(Eb. 4/5-901).	*Cervus elaphus*. 1 morceau de mandibule avec les dents de lait m_2, m_3 et la molaire M_1 qui perce l'alvéole (cinquième mois, *octobre-novembre*, Baumann 1949).
(Eb. 4/5-902).	*Cervus elaphus*. 1 maxillaire supérieur droit (pl. IX, n° 6). Série dentaire complète, $l = 117$ mm., série des prémolaires: 49,0 mm., série des molaires: 67,4 mm. $P^2 = 18,9$ mm., $P^3 = 17,4$ mm., $P^4 = 17,4$ mm., $M^1 = 19,0$ mm., $M^2 = 23,0$ mm., $M^3 = 23,0$ mm.
(Pg. IV-736).	*Capreolus capreolus*. 1 phalange (I) brisée. $l = ?$, dimensions de l'articulation proximale: 15,5 x 14,1 mm.
(Pg. IV-1169).	*Capreolus capreolus*. 1 phalange (II) intacte, $l = 30,0$ mm.
(Pg. IV-1208).	*Capreolus capreolus*. 1 cubo-naviculaire: 20,9 x 24,0 mm.
(Pg. IV-1208).	*Capreolus capreolus*. 1 extrémité distale d'humérus, diamètre transversal: 29,5 mm.

Les niveaux dits «Extensions I et II» à l'exception de *Rangifer tarandus* n'ont point livré de restes de Cervidés.

BOVIDAE et EQUIDAE

Les restes de ces deux familles représentent à peine la moitié de ceux des Cervidés. On a surtout affaire à des éclats de diaphyses provenant surtout des métapodes et à des dents brisées.

Dans le groupe des Bovidés on notera deux molaires provenant des Éboulis 4/5, une molaire de lait a été découverte dans la couche moyenne et le niveau inférieur a fourni une molaire inférieure M_3.

Le Périgordien IV de l' «Extension 2» renfermait une molaire supérieure M^1 d' *Ovibos moschatus*. Etant donné l'intérêt climatologique de cette espèce actuellement circumpolaire nous l'avons reproduite (pl. X, n° 6). Le sondage de 1953 avait livré un débris de molaire d'*Ovibos moschatus* malheureusement cette pièce a été égarée.

En ce qui concerne les Equidés, nous noterons l'absence d' *Equus hydruntinus* rencontré à plusieurs reprises dans le Périgordien V; elle s'explique sans doute par la note de froid vif apportée par le boeuf musqué et le mammouth. Quelques dents isolées sont bien conservées. Le tableau ci-dessous résume les informations obtenues.

TABLEAU XXVIII

Périgordien IV. Mesures prises sur les restes de Bovidés et d'Equidés

Éboulis 4/5

(Eb. 4/5-449).	*Bos sp.* 1 molaire supérieure M^3: 38,0 x 26,0 mm. au dessous de la table dentaire, le fût est brisé à mi-hauteur.
(Eb. 4/5-899).	*Bos sp.* 1 molaire inférieure M_3: 35,0 x 14,2 mm. au dessous de la table dentaire, le fût est brisé à mi-hauteur.

Niveau supérieur

(Pg. IV-945).	*Bos sp.* 1 molaire de lait inférieure *M_3* très usée, $l = 35,0$ mm. au niveau du collet.
(Pg. IV-1053).	*Equus caballus*. 1 molaire inférieure droite M_3: 31,0 x 13,0 mm. au niveau de la table dentaire.

Niveau inférieur

(Pg. IV-683).   *Bos sp.* 1 molaire inférieure M_3: 46,0 mm. au milieu du fût.

(Pg. IV-1177).   *Equus caballus gallicus,* 1 molaire supérieure M^2: 26,9 x 27,5 mm. au point P; protocône: 16,0 16,0 mm. soit 59,0%.

(Pg. IV-723).   *Equus caballus gallicus,* 1 prémolaire supérieure P^4: 25,8 x 25,8 mm. sous la table dentaire; protocône: 15,0 mm. soit 58,0%.

Extension 2

(Pg. IV-1964).   *Ovibus moschatus.* 1 molaire supérieure M^1 brisée.

Les dents d'Equidés présentent les caractères *Equus caballus germanicus Nehring* malheureusement aucun métapode intact n'est là pour confirmer cette détermination (Gromova 1949).

CAPRINAE et RUPICAPRINAE

Capra ibex et *Rupicapra rupicapra* sont représentés par des éclats de diaphyse peu utilisables mais aussi par des débris dentaires souvent bien conservés et de ce fait porteurs d'information numérique.

Le bouquetin (26) est un peu plus abondant que le chamois (20). Voici la distribution du matériel en fonction des divisions stratigraphiques.

La distinction entre les dents de *R. rupicapra* et de *Capra ibex* est parfois pénible; dans le cas des dents de lait elle est presque impossible car les limites de variation de la série dentaire se chevauchent (Koby 1964). La remarque demeure valable pour les os du carpe et du tarse. Ici, nous avons utilisé les différences de taille qui sont considérables. Les dents définitives du bouquetin sont beaucoup plus fortes que celle du chamois. La cheville osseuse brisée (Pg. IV-823) et son homologue (Pg. V-684 A) du Noaillien s'apparentent étroitement par la silhouette et par la taille à *Rupicapra rupicapra pyrenaïca.* Les mesures sont pratiquement celles qui ont été obtenues par Koby (1964) sur les chamois de la grotte de la vache

TABLEAU XXIX

Périgordien IV. Mesures prises sur les restes de *Capra ibex* et de *Rupicapra rupicapra*

Éboulis 4/5

(Eb. 4/5-544).   *Rupicapra rupicapra.* 1 molaire supérieure gauche M^1: 10,0 x 11,6 mm. au collet.

(Eb. 4/5-544).   *Rupicapra rupicapra.* 1 molaire supérieure M^2 gauche, au collet: 11,0 x 12,0 mm.

Niveau supérieur

(Pg. IV-799).   *Capra ibex.* 1 maxillaire supérieur brisé portant la M^2 et la M^3, au collet: M^2 = 11,0 x 14,0 mm. et M^3 = 18,0 x 13,0 mm.; hauteur des fûts: environ 42 à 43 mm.

(Pg. IV-975).   *Rupicapra rupicapra.* 1 condyle huméral: diamètres: 28,5 x 32,0 mm.

(Pg. IV-1047).   *Rupicapra rupicapra.* 1 molaire inférieure M_3: 16,5 x 6,0 mm. au collet.

(Pg. IV-1062).   *Rupicapra rupicapra.* 1 condyle huméral, diamètre transversal: 30,0 mm.

Niveau moyen

(Pg. IV-645).   *Capra ibex.* 1 molaire inférieure M_1: 11,0 x 6,6 mm. au collet.

(Pg. IV-719).   *Capra ibex.* 1 prémolaire inférieure P_3: 9,5 x 5,5 mm. au collet.

(Pg. IV-736).   *Capra ibex.* 1 sabot antérieur; l = 36,0 mm., diamètres maximum de l'articulation: 10,7 x 10,2 mm.

(Pg. IV-1176).   *Capra ibex.* 1 molaire supérieure M^2: 15,0 x 19,0 mm. au collet.

(Pg. IV-1143).   *Rupicapra rupicapra.* 1 molaire inférieure M_1, au collet: 9,4 x 7,0 mm.

Niveau inférieur

(Pg. IV-753).   *Capra ibex.* 1 prémolaire supérieure P^2: 7,0 x 11,2 mm. au collet.

(Pg. IV-735).   *Capra ibex.* 1 cubo-naviculaire; diamètre antéro-postérieur: 22,0 mm., diamètre transversal: 24,8 mm.

(Pg. IV-823).   *Rupicapra rupicapra.* 1 phalange (I) et une cheville osseuse brisées.

(Pg. IV-1207).   *Rupicapra rupicapra.* 1 mandibule brisée portant les prémolaires. P_2 = 5,0 mm., P_3 = 6,0 mm., P_4 = 8,0 mm.

(Ariège). L'isard vivait donc en Dordogne pendant les périodes froides du Paléolithique supérieur.

En ce qui concerne le bouquetin, nous ne disposons d'aucun élément permettant de choisir entre la forme pyrénéenne, *Capra ibex pyrenaïca* et le type alpin *Capra ibex ibex.*

PROBOSCIDAE

Cinq lamelles d'ivoire et un débris de défense ont été retirés des différents niveaux du Périgordien IV. La présence d'*Ovibos moschatus,* espéce arctique par excellence, permet d'attribuer logiquement ces restes à *Elephas primigenius.*

CANIDAE, URSIDAE, FELIDAE et HYENIDAE

Rares dans le Proto-Magdalénien, le Périgordien VI et le Noaillien, les restes de *Vulpes vulpes* deviennent aussi abondants que ceux du cerf élaphe dans le Périgordien IV. Les niveaux précités renferment surtout des métacarpiens, des métatarsiens, et quelques débris de maxillaires et de mandibules; le renard était dépouillé sur place par l'homme qui abandonnait sa chair. Ici au contraire, *Vulpes vulpes* devient l'objet d'une chasse systématique et le chasseur rapporte le corps entier comme en témoigne l'abondance des os longs et des diverses parties du squelette. L'animal était-il mangé? On ne saurait l'affirmer mais il convient d'envisager cette hypothèse; en effet, la putréfaction d'une masse de viande importante aurait incommodé les habitants de l'abri.

Les canines percées par l'homme sont assez fréquentes mais les prémolaires et les molaires, plus robustes, sont mieux conservées et fournissent un certain nombre de mesures. La grande taille des carnassières et des molaires caractérisent indiscutablement le renard commun *Vulpes vulpes* (Koby 1959); rien ne permet d'affirmer la présence d'*Alopex lagopus* qui ne serait nullement déplacée à côté d'*Ovibos moschatus.* Les mesures suivantes confirment les données de Koby (1959) et de Martin (1968).

Canis lupus est peu représenté en comparaison de *Vulpes vulpes.* Ses restes se réduisent à une vingtaine de débris de crânes, de mandibules et de dents isolées. Les os du squelette se limitent à un unique morceau

TABLEAU XXX

Périgordien IV. Mesures prises sur les restes de *Vulpes vulpes* et de *Canis lupus*

Niveau supérieur

(Pg. IV-1044).   *Vulpes vulpes.* 1 extrémité distale d'humérus; diamètre transversal: 19,0 mm.

(Pg. IV-1100).   *Vulpes vulpes.* 1 calcaneum; longueur totale: 28,2 mm.

Niveau moyen

(Pg. IV-761).   *Canis lupus.* 1 prémolaire inférieure P_3: 14,0 mm. au collet.

(Pg. IV-944).   *Vulpes vulpes.* 1 calcaneum; longueur totale: 34,0 mm.

(Pg. IV-976).   *Vulpes vulpes.* 1 extrémité distale d'humérus: diamètre transversal: 20,0 mm.

(Pg. IV-827).   *Vulpes vulpes.* 1 morceau de mandibule gauche portant M_1, M_2 et M_3. M_1 = 15,0 mm., M_2 + M_3 = 10,0 mm.

(Pg. IV-827).   1 morceau de mandibule droite portant M_1, M_2 et M_3. M_1 = 16,0 mm., M_2 + M_3 = 11,0 mm.

(Pg. IV-1149).   *Vulpes vulpes.* 1 mandibule droite où manquent P_1 et P_2: longueur de la série des prémolaires: 35,0 mm.; longueur de la carnassière: 15,0 mm.: longueur M_2 + M_3 = 10,0 mm.

Niveau inférieur

(Pg. IV-723).   *Vulpes vulpes.* 1 extrémité distale d'humérus; diamètre transversal: 20,0 mm.

(Pg. IV – Test pit Q).   *Vulpes vulpes.* 1 extrémité distale d'humérus; diamètre transversal: 21,0 mm.

(Pg. IV-929).   *Canis lupus.* 1 prémolaire inférieure P_2: 12,0 mm. au collet.

(Pg. IV-1198).   *Canis lupus.* 1 maxillaire supérieur brisé portant la P^1 et la P^2; diamètre antéro-postérieur au niveau du collet: P^1 = 8,0 mm., P^2 = 15,0 mm.

(Pg. IV-1900).   *Canis lupus.* 1 prémolaire inférieure P_3: 15,7 mm. au collet.

(Pg. IV-1203).   *Canis lupus.* 2 prémolaires inférieures P_3 et P_4; au collet: P_3 = 12,8 mm., P_4 = 15,0 mm.

d'extrémité distale d'humérus. Le loup, semble-t-il, n'a pas été chassé systématiquement comme le renard. A côté de plusieurs canines percées, une petite série de dents bien conservées a permis de prendre diverses mesures. Les résultats sont consignés dans le tableau XXX.

Le genre *Ursus* est présent dans le niveau supérieur par un calcaneum droit dont les dimensions sont les suivantes:

(Pg. IV-920). *Ursus spelaeus*. 1 calcaneum droit, diamètre antéro-postérieur: 55,5 mm., diamètre transversal: 67,0 mm.; articulation avec le naviculaire: 30,0 x 42,0 mm.

Ces fortes dimensions correspondent à l'espèce *Ursus spelaeus*. Voici les valeurs obtenues à partir d'un calcaneum d'Ours des cavernes provenant de la Grotte de Montgaudier en Charente (Coll. Inst. Pal. Humaine).

Montgaudier. U. spelaeus, 1 calcaneum droit. Diam. antéro-post.: 60,0 mm., diam. transv.: 78,0 mm.; articulation avec le naviculaire: 30,5 x 49,0 mm.

Un *Ursus arctos* découvert dans la Grotte Bernard, près de Foix, en Ariège, donne des valeurs beaucoup plus petites.

Grotte Bernard. 1 calcaneum droit. Diam. antéro-post.: 44,0 mm.; diam. transv.: 54,0 mm.; artic. naviculaire: 27,0 x 36,5 mm.

Le niveau moyen a fourni quelques débris de molaires inférieures caractéristiques du genre *Ursus* mais insuffisants pour aboutir à la détermination spécifique (Pg. IV-1162).

Plus intéressante est la présence de *Lynx lynx* dont une phalange (II) brisée, un morceau de radius et une dent été découvertes dans le niveau moyen. Il s'agit d'une canine supérieure brisée un peu au-dessous du collet; cette pièce porte sur ses faces labiale et linguale le double sillon propre aux *Felidae*. Voici les dimensions de cette dent:

(Pg. IV-1166). *Lynx lynx*. 1 phalange (II) brisée. 1 morceau de radius. 1 canine supérieure gauche. Longueur de la partie émaillée sur la face labiale: 1 = 20,0 mm.; au collet, diam. ant.-post.: 8,8 mm.; diam. transv.: 7,0 mm.

Le niveau inférieur renferme deux restes de *Crocuta spelaea*: une incisive et une carnassière de lait.

(Pg. IV-821). *Crocuta spelaea*. 1 carnassière de lait portant des traces d'attrition. Au collet, diamètre antéro-postérieur, 1 = 26,8 mm.

(Pg. IV-980). *Crocuta spelaea*. 1 incisive supérieure gauche I^3 portant des traces d'attrition.

Dans ce niveau, il convient de signaler la découverte de deux vertèbres appartenant au genre *Mustela*. Les dimensions médiocres des pièces conviendraient à *Mustela erminea* (Pg. IV-1197).

LEPORIDAE et MICROTIDAE

Les restes provenant du genre *Lepus*, presque aussi nombreux que ceux du renard commun (161) se placent en troisième position derrière *C. elaphus* (172). Ils sont près de neuf fois plus abondants que dans le Noaillien. Deux incisives supérieures (Pg. IV-603 et Pg. IV-1120) offrent tous les traits de *Lepus variabilis*: la section sub-carrée, l'épaisseur de l'émail, et le sillon labial proche du bord interne (E. Koby 1959 et 1960); au contraire l'incisive inférieure (Pg. IV-1120) est attribuable à *Lepus europaeus*. Etant donné l'existence d'éléments froids dans la faune *(Elephas primigenius* et *Ovibos moschatus)* j'attribue tous ces restes à l'espèce *Lepus variabilis;* les particularités dentaires utilisées pour distinguer les deux espèces comportent parfois des exceptions.

Les diverses parties du squelette sont représentées mais tous les os longs sont brisés et les pièces utilisables demeurent rares. Voici quelques mesures:

Niveau supérieur
(Pg. IV-1100). *Lepus variabilis*. 1 calcaneum abîmé; 1 = 34,0 mm. environ.

Niveau moyen
(Pg. IV-1159). *Lepus variabilis*. 1 calcaneum; 1 = 37,0 mm. 1 astragale droit; diam. ant.-post.: 17,0 mm., diam. transv.: 9,5 mm. 1 astragale gauche, diam. ant.-post.: 16,5 mm., diam. transv.: 8,0 mm.

Niveau inférieur
(Pg. IV-764). *Lepus variabilis*. 1 calcaneum; 1 = 35,0 mm.

Dans le niveau supérieur, un fémur brisé a été attribué à *Arvicola sp*. (Pg. IV-1054). Le niveau moyen a livré une mandibule droite de *Microtus agrestis* (Pg. IV-1147), une incisive et des molaires isolées.

PHASIANIDAE, COLUMBIDAE, et CORVIDAE

Le Périgordien IV, à l'exception du niveau supérieur, a livré une importante quantité de restes d'oiseaux mais quatre espèces seulement ont été reconnues.

Dans les Éboulis 5/6, j'ai identifié quelques débris de *Perdix perdix*: un humérus brisé (Pg. IV-1235), une extrémité proximale du fémur et une extrémité distale de métatarsien (Pg. IV-1244). Actuellement, la Perdrix grise est largement répandue dans le centre et l'ouest de l'Europe cependant elle pénètre pas dans l'extrême nord.

Trois espèces rupicoles sont représentées dans les niveaux moyen et inférieur: *Corvus corax* (36), *Coracia graculus* (7) et *Columba oenas* (3) mais la première reste de loin la plus répandue.

Le grand corbeau vit actuellement en Europe depuis le cercle polaire jusqu'à la Méditerranée mais avec une densité de peuplement très faible. Ami des rochers inaccessibles, il est cependant très répandu dans les stations de plaine du Pléistocène supérieur. Le Chocard des Alpes, hôte normal des Alpes, des Pyrénées, et des montagnes du sud de l'Europe est de loin l'espèce la plus abondante, et cela dès le Quaternaire moyen, des stations françaises de plaine. C'est une espèce des plus banales pendant le Paléolithique supérieur.

La distinction des os longs des trois espèces: *Columba livia, Columba oenas* et *Columba palumbus* reste délicate car en dehors des critères de taille le modelé anatomique est pratiquement le même. Pour les séparer, il convient de tenir compte des conditions locales et de l'ensemble de la faune. Le pigeon biset (*C. livia*) qui vit en petit nombre dans les falaises rocheuses au bord de la mer et accidentellement dans les fissures de rochers à l'intérieur des terres est à écarter. Les deux autres pigeons, partiellement migrateurs, sont très répandus en Europe mais la palombe (*C. palumbus*) préfère les paysages boisés tandis que *Columba oenas* (Pigeon colombin) recherche plutôt les boisements de «parc» très ouverts et les rochers. Ce type de paysage étant certainement le plus

TABLEAU XXXI

Périgordien IV. Liste des Oiseaux identifiés

Niveau moyen. Columba oenas (Pigeon colombin).

(Pg. IV-1209).	1 extrémité distale de tibia.
(Pg. IV-1213).	1 cubitus brisé.
(Pg. IV-1247).	1 tarse et 1 phalange abîmés.

Niveau moyen. Corvus corax (Grand corbeau).

(Pg. IV-821).	1 coracoïde brisé.
(Pg. IV-1147).	1 phalange et 1 tarse brisés.
(Pg. IV-1174).	1 tarse brisé.
(Pg. IV-1175).	1 morceau de tarse, des phalanges et des griffes.

Niveau inférieur. Corvus corax.

(Pg. IV-733).	1 morceau de cubitus.
(Pg. IV-829).	1 cubitus et 1 métacarpien brisés.
(Pg. IV-1185).	1 coracoïde et 1 métacarpien brisés.
(Pg. IV-1187).	1 coracoïde brisé.
(Pg. IV-1191).	1 extrémité distale de cubitus.
(Pg. IV-1195).	1 tibia et 1 cubitus brisés.
(Pg. IV-1196).	1 extrémité proximale de cubitus.
(Pg. IV-1197).	1 métacarpien brisé.
(Pg. IV-1198).	1 métatarse brisé.
(Pg. IV-1200).	1 coracoïde et 1 extrémité distale de cubitus.
(Pg. IV-1203).	1 tibia et 1 métacarpien brisés.

Niveau inférieur. Coracia graculus (Chocard des Alpes).

(Pg. IV-765).	1 fémur brisé (extrémité distale).
(Pg. IV-768).	1 extrémité proximale.
(Pg. IV-1191).	1 morceau de coracoïde.
(Pg. IV-1198).	1 morceau de coracoïde.
(Pg. IV-1199).	1 morceau de coracoïde.
(Pg. IV-1201).	1 fémur et 1 cubitus brisés.

répandu durant le Périgordien IV, je rapporterai tous les restes de pigeon à l'espèce *Columba oenas*.

L'abondance des restes d'oiseaux dans le Périgordien IV et leur rareté dans les couches supérieures posent le problème de leur chasse éventuelle par l'homme (Bouchud 1968 a). La présence en force de *Corvus corax* et de *Coracia graculus* paraît exclure celle de l'homme mais leurs restes étant contenus dans des niveaux où la densité de l'occupation humaine est considérable, c'est l'hypothèse de la chasse qui doit être retenue.

6. LA FAUNE DES COUCHES AURIGNACIENNES

Le terme de «Couches aurignaciennes» désigne ici celles qui portent les numéros allant de 6 à 14. Ces mots, pris dans un sens très large, ne préjugent pas de la nature exacte des industries lithiques qu'elles renferment.

Des tableaux donnant les fréquences relatives et absolues des diverses parties du squelette de *Rangifer tarandus* ont été établis comme pour les couches proto-magdaléniennes, périgordiennes et noailliennes (voir les tab. I, II, IV, et V). Ils conduisent aux mêmes résultats et aux mêmes conclusions en ce qui concerne le bris des os par l'homme et leur conservation ultérieure dans les niveaux archéologiques, aussi nous ne les publierons pas dans le but d'alléger notre texte. Il est cependant nécessaire de connaître le décompte global des débris osseux pour donner une interprétation climatique des diverses espèces identifiées et c'est ce qui est réalisé dans les tableaux XXXII et XXXIII.

Si pour les divers niveaux aurignaciens nous donnons le nombre global des débris fossiles attribués à chaque espèce, nous ne détaillerons que les matériaux dignes d'intérêt, toujours dans un souci d'allègement du texte.

En ce qui concerne les mesures prises sur les divers segments osseux, il s'agit toujours des mesures classiques ou des dimensions maximales des pièces; le diamètre antéropostérieur (ou longitudinal) est toujours inscrit avant le diamètre transversal et les mesures de l'extrémité proximale précèdent toujours les dimensions de l'extrémité distale. Les mensurations dentaires sont faites au collet pour les Cervidés, les Bovidés, les Capridés, et les Carnivores; pour les Equidés nous utilisons le point P défini par F. Prat (1968) mais quant le fût est brisé les dimensions sont estimées soit au-dessous de la table dentaire, soit au niveau de l'alvéole osseux; nous opérons de la même manière pour la longueur totale d'une série dentaire.

ÉBOULIS 5/6 et COUCHE 6

Les Éboulis 5/6 ont livré des restes de *Rangifer tarandus*, dont un pédicule provenant d'un bois de massacre, un canon postérieur brisé de *Cervus elaphus* et un coracoïde de *Coracia graculus*.

La Couche 6 renferme, en petit nombre, des Bovidés, des Equidés, des rongeurs, et des oiseaux (tableau XXXIV).

ÉBOULIS 6/7 et COUCHE 7

Les Éboulis 6/7 sont très pauvres; ils ont livré très peu de débris de renne, de Cerf élaphe, de Bovidés, et d'Equidés. En revanche, la Couche 7 est assez riche en espèces et en matériel comme le montre le tableau XXXV.

CERVIDAE

Rangifer tarandus demeure l'espèce dominante de la Couche 7 avec 395 débris osseux non mesurables provenant de toutes les parties du squelette; citons aussi deux morceaux de perche (Au.-31). *Cervus elaphus* vient ensuite avec 6 dents et 74 morceaux de diaphyse.

Cervus elaphus L. (Au.-29), 1 molaire inf. M3, usée aux 2/3. (Au.-30), 1 sésamoïde et 1 débris de molaire supérieure. (Au.-31), 1 molaire inf. M2, sortie incomplète de l'alvéole, au collet: 23, 2 x 15,5 mm., 11/12 mois (*avril-mai*); 1 molaire inférieure M1, au collet: 20,0 x 14,0 mm., usure de toutes les cuspides; 1 prémolaire sup., très usée, au collet: 15,9 x 18,2 mm.; 1 incisive usée.

Capreolus capreolus L. (Au.-26), 2 incisives usées; 1 prémolaire inf. P4 à peine sortie de l'alvéole; 2 extrémités distales de canon antérieur brisées; 2 morceaux d'extrémités distales d'humérus.

Le chevreuil (*Capreolus capreolus*) est peu représenté. On ne le rencontrera plus dans les autres couches aurignaciennes; cette absence correspond à une péjoration climatique.

BOVIDES et EQUIDAE

Les restes des Bovidés ne permettent pas d'atteindre le niveau de la détermination spécifique.

Bos sp. (Au.-27), 1 molaire brisée et 1 éclat de tibia. (Au.-29), 2 éclats de tibia. (Au.-31), 1 molaire sup. brisée. (Au.-70), 1 molaire inf. M1, au collet: 24,8 x 16 mm. (Au.-327), 2 morceaux de molaire supérieure.

Equus caballus est six fois plus abondant que le genre *Bos*; pour une dizaine de dents mesurables, il y a une cinquantaine d'éclats osseux reconnus.

On a affaire au cheval de Solutré, (*Equus caballus gallicus*). La forme du protocône et l'importance de

TABLEAU XXXII. – Répartition globale des débris osseux propres aux diverses espèces pour les couches proto-magdaléniennes, noailliennes et périgordiennes.

Industries humaines	Pourcentage de *R. tarandus* dans la faune étudiée	Nombre d'éclats d'os de *R. tarandus* identifiés	Toundra, steppe froide, ou steppe tempérée froide							Steppe-forêt		Montagne	
			Bos sp.	*Bos ou Equus sp.*	*Equus caballus*	*Equus hydruntinus*	*Elephas primigenius*	*Ovibos moschatus*	*Sus scrofa*	*Cervus elaphus*	*Capreolus capreolus*	*Capra ibex*	*Rupicapra rupicapra*
PROTO-MAGDALÉNIEN	81,9	1.235	28	94	40	–	1	–	–	38	1	36	37
PÉRIGORDIEN VI	85,7	2.080	71	155	66	–	–	–	1	19	1	24	10
ÉBOULIS 3/4	92,8	1.803	26	45	25	1	–	–	–	31	5	7	–
NOAILLIEN Supérieur	87,3	8.484	35	97	26	1	–	–	1	140	32	18	12
NOAILLIEN Moyen	95,7	4.314	25	70	30	–	–	–	–	52	4	2	10
NOAILLIEN Inférieur	89,9	2.701	54	114	54	–	–	–	–	45	6	7	.22
ÉBOULIS 4/5	84,8	392	6	3	2	–	–	–	–	50	–	2	7
PÉRIGORDIEN IV Supérieur	97,9	6.913	18	46	8	–	1	–	–	54	4	7	6
PÉRIGORDIEN IV Moyen	98,1	4.779	6	29	14	–	2	–	–	34	–	4	2
PÉRIGORDIEN IV Inférieur	97,9	7.402	3	48	14	–	1	–	–	34	6	12	3
PÉRIGORDIEN IV Extension 2	98,0	1.633	15	2	6	–	1	7	–	–	–	1	2

| | | | | | Espèces carnivores | | | | | | | | Microfaune et divers | | | | |
Panthera leo, race spelaea	Lynx lynx	Crocuta crocuta, race spelaea	Ursus spelaeus	Canis lupus	Vulpes vulpes	Mustela sp.	Lepus variabilis	Lepus sp.	Microtus sp.	Microtus anglicus	Lemmus lemmus	Arvicola scherman	Eliomys quercinus	Bufo ou Rana sp.	Pisces	Aves
2	–	–	–	23	6	4	2	5	46	3	–	62	11	10	5	8
–	–	–	1	4	9	–	–	14	14	–	–	13	1	–	15	7
–	–	–	1	–	6	–	16	–	1	–	–	3	–	–	1	2
3	–	–	1	1	6	–	–	16	2	–	–	1	–	–	3	1
–	–	–	–	1	–	–	–	4	1	–	–	1	–	–	–	1
–	–	–	1	–	1	–	–	2	–	–	–	–	–	–	–	–
–	–	–	–	–	–	–	–	–	–	–	–	–	–	–	–	–
–	–	–	–	2	5	–	1	16	–	–	–	–	–	–	–	3
–	4	–	1	6	51	–	–	49	5	–	–	–	–	–	–	6
–	–	3	1	28	86	1	–	49	1	–	–	–	–	–	–	36
–	–	–	4	3	19	–	–	20	–	–	–	–	–	–	–	2

TABLEAU XXXIII. – Répartition globale des débris osseux propres aux diverses espèces pour les couches aurignaciennes

| Couches Aurignaciennes | Pourcentage de *R. tarandus* | Nombre d'éclats d'os de *R. tarandus* | Toundra, steppe froide, ou steppe tempérée froide | | | | | | Steppe-forêt | |
			Bos sp.	*Bos ou Equus sp.*	*Equus caballus*	*Equus hydruntinus*	*Elephas primigenius*	*Sus scrofa*	*Cervus elaphus*	*Capreolus capreolus*
Éboulis 5/6	–	6	–	1	–	–	–	–	1	–
Couche 6	–	–	5	–	7	–	–	–	–	–
Éboulis 6/7	–	5	4	–	7	–	–	–	6	–
Couche 7	70%	395	10	–	60	6	2	3	80	7
Éboulis 7/8	–	10	–	4	–	–	–	–	2	–
Couche 8	–	3	5	–	5	–	–	3	3	–
Éboulis 8/9	–	–	–	–	–	–	–	–	1	–
Couche 9	–	–	–	–	1	–	–	–	–	–
Éboulis 9/10	–	–	–	–	–	–	–	–	–	–
Couche 10	–	–	1	–	–	–	–	–	–	–
Éboulis 10/11	–	30	3	–	–	–	–	–	–	–
Couche 11	62%	599	4	–	359	–	1	1	2	–
Éboulis 11/12	–	–	–	–	1	–	–	–	–	–
Couche 12	73%	129	7	3	37	–	–	–	–	–
Éboulis 12/13	–	–	–	–	1	–	–	–	–	–
Couche 13	98,6%	221	–	–	–	–	–	–	3	–
Éboulis 13/14	100%	410	–	–	–	–	–	–	–	–
Couche 14	99%	1.481	2	–	1	–	–	–	10	–

Montagne		Espèces carnivores				Rongeurs, Oiseaux, Amphibiens, et Poissons												
Capra ibex	*Rupicapra rupicapra*	*Ursus spelaeus*	*Canis lupus*	*Vulpes vulpes*	*Lepus sp.*	*M. arvalis-agrestis*	*Microtus nivalis*	*Microtus sp.*	*Pitymys subterraneus*	*Arvicola scherman*	*Arvicola terrestris*	*Arvicola sp.*	*Eliomys quercinus*	*Apodemus sylvaticus*	*Aves*	*Bufo ou Rana sp.*	*Discoglossus sp.*	*Pisces*
—	—	—	—	—	—	—	—	—	—	—	—	—	—	—	1	—	—	—
—	—	—	—	1	—	—	—	—	—	—	—	7	—	—	1	—	—	—
—	—	—	—	—	—	—	—	—	—	—	—	—	—	—	—	—	—	—
—	4	—	1	—	—	—	—	4	—	—	—	33	2	—	7	106	—	—
—	—	—	—	—	—	—	—	—	—	40	—	—	—	—	1	31	—	—
—	1	—	—	—	—	50	26	—	1	—	4	—	12	4	23	500*	1	4
—	—	—	—	—	—	—	—	—	—	—	—	—	—	—	—	—	—	—
—	—	—	—	—	—	—	—	—	—	—	—	—	—	—	3	—	—	—
3	—	—	—	—	—	—	—	—	—	—	—	—	—	—	—	—	—	—
2	—	—	—	—	—	—	—	—	—	—	—	—	1	—	1	—	—	—
—	—	1	7	62	3	2	—	—	—	—	—	—	—	—	1	—	—	—
—	—	—	1	—	—	—	—	—	—	—	—	—	—	—	3	—	—	—
1	—	—	4	2	—	—	—	—	—	—	—	—	—	—	—	—	—	—
—	—	—	—	—	—	—	—	—	—	—	—	—	—	—	—	—	—	—
—	—	—	—	—	—	—	—	1	—	—	—	1	—	—	—	—	—	—
—	—	—	—	1	—	—	—	—	—	—	—	—	—	—	—	—	—	—
1	—	—	4	1	—	—	—	—	—	—	—	—	—	—	—	—	—	—

500 est un nombre approximatif, mais certainement inférieur au nombre réel, des restes d'Amphibiens récoltés.

TABLEAU XXXIV

Éboulis 5/6 et Couche 6. Espèces identifiées et débris osseux correspondants

Éboulis 5/6

Rangifer tarandus L.	(Au.-65), 1 pédicule abîmé provenant d'un bois de massacre.
Cervus elaphus L.	(Au.-119), 1 canon postérieur brisé.
Coracia graculus L.	(Au.-41), 1 coracoïde brisé.

Couche 6

Bos sp.	(Au.-56), 3 molaires de lait brisées. (Au.-56), 1 sésamoïde. (Au.-70), molaire infér. M1 usée au niveau du mésostyle; au collet: 23,0 x 18,5 mm.
Equus caballus L.	(Au.-11), une molaire sup. de lait brisée et un morceau d'incisive. (Au.-59), 2 éclats de diaphyse de tibia et un morceau de canon ant.
Vulpes vulpes L.	1 mandibule de renard commun. Série dentaire: 62,0 mm.; carnassière: 16,0 mm.; M1 + M2 = 10,2 mm.
Arvicola sp.	(Au.-3, Au.-6, Au.-10 et Au.-62), 1 mandibule et 3 morceaux de mandibule. (Au.-5), 2 cubitus et un tibia.
Coracia graculus L.	(Au.-3 et Au.-58), 2 cubitus brisés. (Au.-3), 1 métacarpien.

TABLEAU XXXV

Couche 7. Espèces identifiées et débris osseux correspondants

Macrofaune			Rongeurs	
Rangifer tarandus L.	395	(69,6%)	*Microtus sp.*	4
Cervus elaphus L.	80		*Arvicola sp.*	33
Capreolus capreolus L.	7	(15,3%)	*Eliomys quercinus L.*	2
Bos sp.	10	(1,8%)	Oiseaux	
Equus caballus L.	60		*Aegypius monachus L.*	1
Equus hydruntinus Reg.	6	(11,6%)	*Anthus spinoletta L.*	1
Sus scrofa L.	3	(0,5%)	*Motacilla sp.*	2
Rupicapra rupicapra L.	4	(0,8%)	*Perdix perdix L.*	3
Elephas primigenius Bl.	2	(0,4%)	Amphibiens	
Canis lupus L.	1		*Bufo sp.*	102
			Rana sp.	4

l'indice correspondant plaident en faveur de cette interprétation qui sera confirmée par l'étude du matériel dentaire provenant de la Couche 8(tableau XXXVI).

TABLEAU XXXVI

Mesures prises sur l'Equidé de la Couche 7 aurignacienne

Equus caballus gallicus

(Au.-23).	1 molaire inf. M3 incomplètement sortie de l'alvéole, en P: 35,0 x 14,0 mm.
	1 prémolaire sup. P2 très usée, au dessous de la table: 37,0 x 24,0 mm., protocône: 11,0 mm., soit 29,4%
(Au.-28).	2 prémolaires inf. P4, en P: 29,1 x 15,9 mm. et 29,0 x 17,5 mm., pli ptychyostylide marqué.
	1 molaire inf. M1, en P: 27,8 x 15,0 mm.
	1 molaire inf. M2, en P: 27,5 x 15,0 mm.
(Au.-31).	1 molaire sup. M3 brisée.
(Au.-83).	1 molaire sup. M2, en P: 24,0 x 27,0 mm., protocône: 13,2 mm. soit 48,8%, pas de pli caballin.

Deux incisives inférieures brisés et des éclats de diaphyse de petite taille ont appartenu très probablement à *Equus hydruntinus Reg.*

SUIDAE

Le sanglier (*Sus scrofa*) est représenté par des dents.

Sus scrofa L. (Au.-31), 1 prémolaire inf. P2, au collet: 10,2 x 9,0 mm. (Au.-49), 1 molaire sup. M2, au collet: 36,0 x 17,0 mm. (Au.-82), 1 incisive inf. brisée.

RUPICAPRINAE

Un petit nombre de restes dentaires ont appartenu au chamois.

Rupicapra rupicapra L. (Au.-31). 1 molaire supér. M1, au collet: 9,0 x 10,2 mm. 1 molaire supér. M2, au collet: 12,0 (?) x 11,0 (?) mm., pièce abîmée. 2 débris de molaires supérieures.

PROBOSCIDAE

La Couche 7 a fourni deux lames dentaires (Au.-25), d'*Elephas primigenius* Blum., interprétation basée sur la position stratigraphique du matériel.

RONGEURS

Leurs débris ne sont pas très nombreux. Le genre *Arvicola* est le plus représenté, suivi par le genre *Microtus*. L'absence de crânes ne permet pas d'atteindre l'espèce. Une mandibule édentée et un fémur caractéristiques appartiennent à *Eliomys quercinus* (Lérot).

Arvicola sp. (Au.-92), 1 morceau de crâne; 9 incisives sup.; 7 incisives inf.; 7 molaires inf. M1 et M2; 1 radius, 1 cubitus, 3 fémurs et 3 tibias.

Microtus sp. (Au.-83), 1 mandibule édentée; 3 tibias brisés.

Eliomys quercinus L. (Au.-28), 1 mandibule édentée et 1 fémur sans épiphyse.

OISEAUX

Aegypius monachus L. (Au.-62), 1 phalange.

Perdix perdix L. (Au.-31), 1 tête d'humérus et 1 coracoïde. (Au.-49). 1 humérus brisé.

Anthus spinoletta L. (Au.-83), 1 cubitus intact, 1 = 27,0 mm.

Motacilla sp. (Au.-30), 1 extr. distale d'humérus, (Au.-92), 1 cubitus intact, 1 = 21,0 mm.

Les restes de perdix (*P. perdix*) sont assez bien conservés pour permettre la séparation d'avec le genre *Lagopus*. Les difficultés commencent avec les Motacillidés. Il est cependant possible de distinguer le genre *Anthus* d'avec le genre *Motacilla*.

L'humérus du genre *Anthus* présente une tubérosité sus-épicondylienne qui s'achève par une double apophyse où s'attache le long extenseur de la main. Dans le genre *Motacilla* une dépression très marquée isole cette double apophyse de la gouttière du triceps brachial et la rejette en arrière du plan de celle-ci. Chez *Anthus*, au contraire, l'absence de cette fossette place la double apophyse et la gouttière du triceps dans le même plan. Ces remarques permettent d'isoler les genres quant à l'humérus, mais il n'est pas possible d'atteindre le niveau spécifique.

Le cubitus est plus long et plus robuste chez *Anthus*, cependant des traits anatomiques rendent possible l'isolement d'avec son homologue chez *Motacilla*. La dépression brachiale où s'insère le muscle correspondant est plus creusée sous la surface glénoïdale chez le premier. Pour *Anthus*, contre et sous le rebord de la surface glénoïdale interne, s'ouvre une petite cavité circulaire très profonde où s'insère l'extenseur externe de la main. Chez *Motacilla*, cette fossette, à peine marquée est limitée par un contour ovale allongé transversalement.

AMPHIBIENS

Ils sont uniquement représentés par des Anoures. Nous n'avons pas rencontré de restes de reptiles. Leurs débris sont peu nombreux en comparaison du matériel récolté dans les couches inférieures. Tous sont très fragmentaires; les vertèbres manquent et les urostyles sont peu nombreux. Ils appartiennent à des animaux de petite taille ou à des jeunes du genre *Bufo*. Les restes de *Rana* sont très rares.

Bufo sp. (Au.-92), 22 humérus; 8 radius-ulna; 24 ilions; 7 urostyles; 25 fémurs; 16 tibia-fibula. Les épiphyses manquent.

Rana sp. (Au.-92), 3 ilions; 1 tibia-fibula.

ÉBOULIS 7/8 et COUCHE 8

Les Éboulis 7/8 ont livré des restes de *Rangifer tarandus* et des éclats de grosses diaphyses appartenant à des Bovidés ou des Equidés. Il faut noter la présence de *Cervus elaphus*. La petite faune est assez abondante. *Arvicola scherman* a été identifié sur une partie de crâne possédant le rostre et les incisives (Heim de Balsac et Guislain 1955).

Dans la Couche 8, la grosse faune est médiocrement représentée en comparaison des rongeurs, des oiseaux et des amphibiens. Elle serait en quelque sorte l'équivalent des «Couches à Rongeurs» propres à certains niveaux aurignaciens.

TABLEAU XXXVII

Éboulis 7/8 et Couche 8. Espèces identifiées et débris osseux correspondants

Faune des Éboulis 7/8:

Macrofaune		Rongeurs	
Rangifer tarandus L.	10	*Arvicola scherman* S.	40
Cervus elaphus L.	2		
Amphibiens		Oiseaux	
Bufo sp.	31	*Perdix perdix* L.	1

Faune de la Couche 8:

Macrofaune		Rongeurs	
Rangifer tarandus L.	3	*Eliomys quercinus* L.	12
Cervus elaphus L.	3	*Microtus arvalis-agrestis*	50
Bos sp.	5	*Microtus nivalis* M.	26
Equus caballus L.	5	*Pitymys subterraneus* de S.L.	1
Sus scrofa	3	*Arvicola scherman* S.	4
Rupicapra rupicapra L.	1	*Apodemus sylvaticus* L.	4
Amphibiens		Oiseaux	
Bufo sp.	>500	*Perdix perdix* L.	9
Discoglossus sp.	1	*Coleus monedula*	3
		Coracia graculus L.	3
Poissons		*Otis tetrax* L.	1
Salmo sp.	3	*Anthus spinoletta* L.	3
		Motacilla sp.	4

Voici maintenant les détails essentiels concernant la macrofaune. En dehors des Equidés, ils ne retiendront guère notre attention.

Rangifer tarandus L. (Au.-174), 1 débris de perche et 2 éclats de diaphyse.

Cervus elaphus L. (Au.-145), 1 sabot. (Au.-174), 1 molaire de lait sup. D3. (Au.-175), 1 éclat de diaphyse.

Bos sp. (Au.-174), 1 molaire inf. M3 sortant de l'alvéole, fût brisé à 1 cm. de la table dentaire: 43,0 x 16,9 mm. (Au.-83), 1 molaire inf. M3, peu usée, au collet: 43,5 mm. (Au.-152), 1 incisive très usée.

Equus caballus L. (Au.-174), 1 hémi-mandibule portant toute les dents. (Au.-112, Au.-151, Au.-171), 3 éclats de tibia.

Equus hydruntinus Reg. (Ext. I, niv. H). 1 prémolaire sup. P2, fût brisé. 1 prémolaire inf. P2, fût brisé. 2 molaires inf. M2 fût brisé.

Sus scrofa L. (Au.-110), 1 morceau de maxillaire sup. avec I3 d. (Au.-142), 1 morceau de canine sup. (Au.-148), 1 morceau de canine inf.

Rupicapra rupicapra L. (Au.-114), 1 morceau de mandibule g. portant P3, P4 et M3.

L'hémi-mandibule de cheval possède une série dentaire complète dont la longueur totale estimée au niveau des alvéoles atteint 186 mm. Les fûts brisés au dessus du collet ont été mesurés séparémment au niveau des alvéoles.

La longueur considérable de la série dentaire rejoint

les limites inférieures de la variation de la série dentaire chez *Equus caballus germanicus;* cependant les dimensions des dents et les caractères morphologiques demeurent les mêmes que ceux de l' *Equus caballus gallicus.* Comme chez cette espèce, les prémolaires occupent un espace inférieur (88,9 mm.) à celui des molaires (91,0 mm.); l'émail assez mince, peu plissé, le métaconide arrondi relié au métastylide sub-triangulaire par un sillon lingual concave, largement ouvert, viennent confirmer cette interprétation.

La mandibule provient sans doute d'un mâle robuste. Les dimensions des dents sont contenues dans le tableau XXXVIII.

Le niveau H de «l'extension I», équivalent stratigraphique de la Couche 8 a livré une dent supérieure et trois dents inférieures d'*Equus hydruntinus* reconnaissables à leur petite taille, à la réduction du protocône et à l'étroitesse du sillon lingual (pl. XI, n° 1). Le fût de ces pièces étant brisé, les mesures ont été prises un peu au-dessous de la face occlusale.

TABLEAU XXXVIII

Mesures prises sur les Equidés de la Couche 8 aurignacienne

Equus caballus gallicus. 1 hémi-mandibule (Au.-174), 1 = 186,0 mm.
P2 = 33,0 x 16,1 mm., P3 = 26,0 x 16,4 mm.,
P4 = 29,9 x 18,4 mm., M1 = 31,0 x 17,6 mm.,
M2 = 28,0 x 16,0 mm., M3 = 32,0 x 14,6 mm.

Equus hydruntinus. Extension I, Level H, (pl. XI, n° 1)
P2 sup.: 24,9 x 23,5 mm., protocône: 7,0 mm.
soit 28,1%, P2 inf./ 31,0 x 14,5 mm., M2 inf.:
26,2 x 17,2 mm., M2 inf.: 23,0 x 16,9 mm.

RONGEURS

Leurs restes, fort nombreux, proviennent des pelotes de réjection des rapaces. Ceux-ci ne cohabitant pas avec l'homme témoignent donc de l'habitat temporaire pendant la formation de la Couche 8.

TABLEAU XXXIX

Rongeurs. Liste du matériel récolté dans la Couche 8 aurignacienne

Eliomys quercinus L.

(Au.-110), 1 mandibule g. et 1 fémur. (Au.-112), 1 mandibule g. (Au.-136), 1 mandibule d. (Au.-142), 1 fémur d. intact, 1 = 26,8 mm. (Au.-145), 2 mandibules g., 3 fémurs, 2 d. et 1 g. (Au.-174), 1 mandibule d. et 1 os innominé.

Microtus arvalis-agrestis Pal.

(Au.-114), 1 mandibule d. (Au.-143), 4 mandibules d. et 2 g.; 2 molaires inf. M1, d. et g.(Au.-145), 3 mandibules d. (Au.-146), 1 mandibule d. et 2 tibias. (Au.-151), 3 mandibules d. et 5 g.; 1 molaire M1 d. (Au.-168), 4 mandibules d. et 1 g.; 2 molaires inf. M1 d. et 3 g. (Au.-174), 5 mandibules d. et 7 g.; 1 maxillaire sup. et 3 molaires inf. M1 g.

Microtus nivalis Mar.

(Au.-105), 1 mandibule g. (Au.-142), 1 partie antérieure de crâne avec le rostre; 1 mandibule d. et 1 fémur g. intact, 1 = 17,1 mm. (Au.-145), 1 molaire inf. d. M1. (Au.-152), 1 partie antérieure de crâne avec le rostre et 1 fémur. (Au.-168), 4 parties antérieures de crâne avec le rostre, 2 mandibules et 1 fémur. (Au.-174), 3 rostres, 1 maxillaire sup., 2 mandibules d. et 4 g.; 1 molaire inf. M1 et 1 os innominé.

Pitymys subterraneus de Sélys-Long.

(Au.-145), 1 mandibule d.

Microtus sp.

(Au.-103), 3 humérus et 1 radius. (Au.-108), 1 humérus brisé. (Au.-114), 1 humérus, 3 fémurs, et 1 tibia brisés. (Au.-137), 1 fémur brisé. (Au.-142), 1 morceau de rostre. (Au.-165), 1 fémur brisé.

Arvicola scherman Shaw.

(Au.-168), 2 parties antérieures de crâne avec le rostre, 1 mandibule d. et 1 fémur.

TABLEAU XXXIX *Suite*

Arvicola sp.

(Au.-103), 1 humérus, 2 tibias, et 1 os innominé brisés. (Au.-106), 1 radius et 1 fémur brisés. (Au.-108), 1 incisive inf. (Au.-113), 1 mandibule g. et 1 fémur. (Au.-114), 1 humérus, 1 fémur, 1 tibia, et 1 os innominé. (Au.-127), 2 mandibules d., 1 fémur, et 1 tibia. (Au.-136), 1 molaire inf. M1 et 2 incisives. (Au.-142), 1 morceau de crâne. (Au.-143), 3 mandibules d. et 6 g., 3 humérus, 7 fémurs, 2 tibias, et 1 morceau de crâne. (Au.-145), 1 mandibule brisée, 2 molaires inf. M1 et 1 molaire sup. M2 et 1 cubitus. (Au.-152), 1 fémur intact, 1 = 27,0 mm. (Au.-174), 1 molaire inf. M1 et 2 molaires sup. M2.

Apodemus sylvaticus Lin.

(Au.-145), 1 mandibule g. et 1 fémur. (Au.-168), 1 fémur sans épiphyse. (Au.-171), 1 mandibule d.

Le petit nombre d'espèces reconnues à partir des crânes, des mandibules et des dents isolées permet de déterminer avec une bonne sécurité la majeure partie des os longs. Grâce au matériel abondant ainsi obtenu, il devient alors possible de donner une interprétation climatique de la microfaune. En effet, toutes les espèces rencontrées dans la Couche 8 — à l'exception de *Microtus nivalis Mar.* — vivent actuellement en Dordogne. Leur classement, compte tenu de leurs exigences écologiques et biologiques conduit aux résultats suivants:

1°)   *Formes de forêt:*
        Apodemus sylvaticus et
        Eliomys quercinus 16,5%
2°)   *Formes d'espaces découverts:*
        M. arvalis-agrestis, Pitymys,
        Arvicola scherman, Arvicola sp. 56,7%
3°)   *Formes de montagne:*
        Microtus nivalis 26,8%

Dans ces trois groupes, certaines espèces recherchent les sols humides (*Arvicola, M. arvalis, M.nivalis, Pitymys*); d'autres préfèrent les milieux secs (*E. quercinus*).

Pendant le dépôt de la Couche 8, le climat reste froid; la forêt est clairsemée et les espaces découverts qui prédominent, parfois secs (steppe) sont en général humides (prairies fraîches, bords de rivière). L'hiver long est précédé ou suivi par des saisons intermédiaires courtes comme en témoigne la présence de *M. nivalis* dans la plaine; l'été reste tiède et la température moyenne de juillet dépasse largement + 15° centigrades comme le montre l'abondance d'*Eliomys quercinus.*

OISEAUX

On retrouve une série d'espèces bien connues dans les stations de Paléolithique supérieur français.

TABLEAU XL

Oiseaux. Liste du matériel recueilli dans la Couche 8 aurignacienne

Perdix perdix L.

(Au.-01), 1 extrémité dist. de tibia. (Au.-105), 1 coracoïde, 1 = 37,0 mm., actuel: 35,0 mm. (Au.-114), 1 coracoïde abîmé. (Au.-145), 1 humérus brisé et 1 tarso-métatarse. (Au.-142), 1 humérus et 1 cubitus brisés. (Au.-174), 1 cubitus et 1 tibia brisés.

Coleus monedula L.

(Au.-114), 1 extrémité distale d'humérus, 1 cubitus g. et 1 tarso-métatarse brisés.

Coracia graculus L.

(Au.-152), 1 fémur intact, 1 = 39,0 mm.; 1 fragment de tarso-métatarse; 1 tarso-métatarse intact, 1 = 45,0 mm.

Otis tetrax L.

(Au.-154), 1 humérus brisé.

Anthus spinoletta L.

(Au.-106), 1 cubitus intact, 1 = 27,0 mm. (Au.-145), 1 humérus et 1 cubitus brisés.

Motacilla sp.

(Au.-151), 1 humérus intact, 1 = 14,0 mm., 1 cubitus intact, 1 = 22,0 mm., 1 fémur intact, 1 = 19,0 mm., 1 fragment de tarso-métatarse.

A l'exception d'*Anthus spinoletta* (pipit spioncelle) et de *Coracia graculus* (Chocard des Alpes), formes essentiellement montagnardes, les autres espèces vivent ou pourraient vivre en Dordogne actuellement. La présence du Pipit spioncelle et du Chocard des Alpes dans une station de plaine justifie le caractère froid du climat déjà mis en évidence par la rencontre du campagnol des neiges (*M. nivalis*). Notons cependant l'existence de la canepetière (*Otis tetrax*) rarement citée dans les stations françaises.

AMPHIBIENS et POISSONS

Il faut citer l'extrême abondance des restes d'amphibiens dans le Niveau 8. Le poids total de leurs débris, très fragmentaires dépasse 150 grs. Les vertèbres sont rares et les os du crâne manquent complètement. On découvre surtout des os des membres: humérus, radius-ulna, fémur, tibia-fibula; l'ilion, l'urostyle, et le sacrum, nécessaires à la détermination générique demeurent peu abondants.

Dans leur grande majorité, ces restes divers appartiennent au genre *Bufo, Rana* demeure rare. Le nombre des débris osseux dépasse largement 500; au cours du tri j'ai découvert un humérus de *Discoglossus sp.* en bon état. Aucun reste de lézard ou de serpent n'a été reconnu.

Les poissons sont représentés par quelques vertèbres du genre *Salmo*.

Bufo sp. Environ 150 gr. de débris osseux. Absence d'os craniens; vertèbres rares, os des membres abondants, os des ceintures peu représentés.

Rana sp. (Au.-103), 1 ilion. (Au.-106), 1 ilion. (Au.-114), 1 tibia.

Discoglossus sp. (Au.-107), 1 humérus en bon état.

Salmo sp. (Au.-105), 2 vertèbres de petite taille. (Au.-139), 2 vertèbres de petite taille.

COUCHES 9 — 10 et EBOULIS CORRESPONDANTS

Ces couches et éboulis sont pauvres en matériel et nous n'insisterons pas.

Éboulis 8/9
  Rongeurs. (Au.-167), quelques débris sans intérêt.
  Cervus elaphus L. (Au.-181), 1 molaire brisée.
Couche 9
  Equus caballus L. (Au.-190 A), 1 molaire inf. brisée.
Éboulis 9/10
  Motacilla sp. (Au.-195), 1 cubitus brisé. (Au.-197), 1 cubitus intact, 1 = 27,0 mm. et 1 coracoïde.
Couche 10
  Capra ibex L. (Au.-201), 1 P3 inf., au collet: 12,0 x 7,8 mm. (Au.-203), 1 incisive.
  Bos sp. (Au.-203), 1 molaire inf. M3 brisée.

EBOULIS 10/11 et COUCHE 11

Le matériel provenant des Éboulis 10/11 est pauvre, mais la faune récoltée dans la Couche 11 sous-jacente est très abondante.

Éboulis 10/11.
Bos sp. (Au.-207). 2 morceaux de molaire inf. (Au.-216). 1 fragment de molaire.
Capra ibex L. (Au.-206). 1 molaire sup. M3. (Au.-207). 1 molaire, inf. M1.
Arvicola sp. (Au.-208). 1 mandibule g.
Motacilla sp. (Au.-208). 1 cubitus intact.

CERVIDAE et BOVIDAE

Nous abordons maintenant la description du matériel de la Couche 11. *Rangifer tarandus* est l'espèce la plus représentée quant au nombre des débris. Les

TABLEAU XLI

Couche 11. Espèces identifiées et débris osseux correspondants

Macrofaune			Rongeurs	
Rangifer tarandus L.	599	(62,0%)	*Microtus arvalis agrestis Pal.*	2
Cervus elaphus L.	2		*Lepus sp.*	3
Bos sp.	4			
Equus caballus L.	359	(37,1%)	Oiseaux	
Sus scrofa L.	1		*Coracia graculus L.*	1
Elephas primigenius Blum.	1			
Canis lupus L.	7			
Vulpes vulpes L.	62			
Ursus spelaeus Rosen.	1			

dents, très rares sont brisées, et le reste du matériel se réduit à des phalanges et à des débris d'os longs. Les morceaux de perche sont pratiquement tous travaillés par l'homme.

Rangifer tarandus L. Une série de morceaux de perche travaillée par l'homme: (Au.-228, 231, 235, 238, 242, 246, 249, 251, 252, 253, 256, 262, 263, 264). (Au.-226), 1 extr. dist. d'humérus, d.t.: 42,0 mm. (Au.-233, 249, 255, 264), 4 extr. dist. canon antér.: 40,8 x 20,5 mm.; 40,5 x 20,5 mm.; 39,0 x 20,1 mm., épiphyse non soudée; 39,5 x 20,2 mm.). (Au.-235, 246), 2 phalanges (I), h = 50,0 mm., extr. prox.: 20,8 x 22,4 mm., extr. dist.: abîmée; h = ? , extr. prox.: 20,0 x 20,0 mm., extr. dist.: 12,0 x 16,8 mm. (Au.-262), 1 côte travaillée. (Au.-231), 1 tête de fémur percée et 1 phalange de stylet travaillée. (Au.-331), 1 molaire inf. M3: 24,8 mm.

Cervus elaphus L. (Au.-225), 1 prémolaire inf. P2 et 1 incisive.
Bos sp. (Au.-238), 1 incisive usée. (Au.-263), 1 morceau de cheville osseuse. (Au.-330), 1 morceau de prémolaire sup.

Les restes de Cerf élaphe n'ont guère d'intérêt et ceux des Bovidés ne permettent pas d'atteindre le niveau de l'espèce.

EQUIDAE

Si les restes de *Rangifer tarandus* (599 soit 62,0%)

TABLEAU XLII

Mesures prises sur les Equidés de la Couche 11 aurignacienne *(Equus caballus gallicus)*

Dents inférieures isolées.

(Au.-246).	2 incisives inf. très usées I2 d.
(Au.-250).	2 molaires de lait inf. brisées.
(Au.-330).	2 incisives inf. brisées.
(Au.-221).	P2 g., fût brisé: 34,1 x 16,1 mm.
(Au.-255).	P3 d., dent neuve sortant de l'alvéole.
(Au.-234).	M1 d., fût brisé: 27,5 x 16,4 mm.
(Au.-225).	M1 d., fût brisé: 29,5 x 15,7 mm.
(Au.-250).	M1 g., mesure en P: 28,0 x 17,0 mm.
(Au.-261).	M1 d., fût brisé: 27,0 x 15,5 mm.
(Au.-261).	M1 d., mesure en P: 26,0 x 15,5 mm.
(Au.-225).	M2 g., fût brisé: 27,5 x 16,5 mm.
(Au.-331).	M2 d., mesure en P: 25,7 x 15,9 mm.
(Au.-333).	M2 d., mesure en P: 25,0 x 15,4 mm.
(Au.-261).	M3 d., fût brisé: 37,0 x 13,4 mm.
(Au.-250).	M3 d., mesure en P: 34,3 x 14,0 mm.
(Au.-333).	M3 d., mesure en P: 31,4 x 14,8 mm.
(Au.-250).	D2 lait., fût brisé: 30,0 x 14,0 mm.
(Au.-250).	D3 lait., fût brisé: 31,2 x 14,2 mm.

Dents supérieures isolées

(Au.-246).	P2 d., mesure en P: 35,5 x 25,5 mm., pr.: 8,7 mm. (24,5%).
(Au.-249).	P2 d., mesure en P: 32,5 x 23,7 mm.: pr.: 9,0 mm. (27,6%).
(Au.-249).	P2 g., non mesurable.
(Au.-261).	P2 d., mesure en P: 36,7 x 25,5 mm., pr.: 9,9 mm. (24,5%).
(Au.-261).	P3 g., fût abîmé: 26,1 x 29,2 mm.: pr.: 13,8 mm. (52,8%).
(Au.-331).	P3 d., non mesurable.
(Au.-230).	P4 d., mesure en P: 25,5 x 26,5 mm., pr.: 14,0 mm. (54,9%).
(Au.-246).	P4 d., fût brisé: 27,5 x 28,9 mm., pr.: 13,0 mm. (47,2%).
(Au.-230).	M1 g., fût brisé: 26,1 x 28,2 mm., pr.: 14,1 mm. (54,0%).
(Au.-262).	M1 d., mesure en P: 24,8 x 26,4 mm., pr.: 13,6 mm. (54,8%).
(Au.-262).	M2 d., mesure en P: 24,2 x 25,2 mm., pr.: 12,3 mm. (50,8%).
(Au.-262).	M2 d., fût court: 27,8 x 25,0 mm., pr.: 14,7 mm. (52,8%).
(Au.-250).	M3 d., mesure en P: 28,0 x 25,0 mm. pr.: 16,6 mm. (59,3%).
(Au.-262).	M3 d., mesure en P: 28,5 x 24,2 mm., pr.: 14,7 mm. (51,5%).
(Au.-330).	M3 g., mesure en P: 30,0 x 24,5 mm., pr.: 15,4 mm. (51,3%).

Phalanges

(Au.-331).	1 phalange post. (I), h = 84,5 mm., extr. prox.: 37,0 x 58,0 mm., articulation: 30,5 x 48,0 mm., milieu de la diaphyse: 26,5 x 35,0 mm., extr. dist.: abîmée, non mesurable.
(Au.-234).	1 phalange post. (II), h = 50,7 mm., extr. prox.: 37,8 x 59,0 mm., articulation: 29,0 x 52,5 mm., milieu de la diaphyse non mesurable, extr. dist.: non mesurable.
(Au.-249).	1 phalange post. (II), h = 50,5 mm., extr. prox.: 34,5 x 53,8 mm., articulation: 25,5 x 45,8 mm., milieu de la diaphyse: 25,0 x 43,0 mm., extr. dist.: 28,0 x 48,3 mm.
(Au.-255).	1 phalange post. (II), h = 51,6 mm., extr. prox.: 36,0 x 55,8 mm., articulation: 27,0 x 47,0 mm., milieu de la diaphyse: 25,0 x 45,4 mm., extr. dist.: 29,0 x 50,6 mm.
(Au.-266).	1 phalange antér. (I), h = 84,0 mm., extr. prox.: 25,5 x 52,0 mm., articulation: 28,0 x 47,0 mm., milieu de la diaphyse et extr. dist. non mesurables.
(Au.-221).	1 phalange ant. (II), h = 48,5 mm., extr. prox.: 32,7 x 57,0 mm., articulation: 25,0 x 47,8 mm., milieu de la diaphyse: 23,0 x 47,8 mm., extr. dist.: 27,9 x 50,2 mm.
(Au.-253).	1 phalange antér. (II), l'épiphyse prox. est incomplètement soudée, h = 48,4 mm., extr. prox.: non mesurable, milieu de la diaphyse: 22,0 x 44,0 mm., extr. dist.: 25,8 x 48,0 mm.
(Au.-333).	1 phalange antér. (II), h = 50,0 mm., extr. prox.: 32,5 x 56,0 mm., articulation: 25,0 x 47,0 mm., milieu de la diaphyse: 23,0 x 48,0 mm., extr. dist.: 27,0 x 51,0 mm.

Divers

(Au.-246 et 262).	2 sabots brisés.
(Au.-238 et 249).	2 sésamoïdes.
(Au.-246).	1 scaphoïde.
(Au.-238).	1 magnum.
(Au.-249 et 256).	2 cunéiformes.
(Au.-255).	1 pisiforme.
(Au.-333).	1 morceau d'os canon.
(Au.-255).	1 calcaneum, l = 110,0 mm., *tuber calcis*: 50,0 x 36,0 mm.

sont les plus abondants, les débris d'Equidés dominent par leur masse totale et leur état de conservation (359, soit 37,1%).

Leurs dents, de dimensions assez fortes possèdent un émail peu épais, modéremment plissé. A la mandibule, le sillon lingual concave s'ouvre largement, il réunit un métaconide dilaté et un métastylide presque triangulaire; le pli ptychyostylide reste toujours bien marqué. Au maxillaire supérieur, le protocône allongé présente un sillon médian assez net sur les prémolaires et la M1; l'indice protoconique assez élevé accompagne un pli caballin presque toujours simple. Ce sont là des traits propres au cheval de Solutré, *Equus caballus gallicus n. va.* Les dents, par leur taille considérable mordent sur le domaine de l'*Equus caballus germanicus*. Quant aux extrémités distales des métapodes et aux phalanges leurs dimensions les situent dans la région intermédiaire entre les deux variétés. Par contre les mesures prises sur les autres parties du squelette, les os du carpe, du tarse, et plus particulièrement sur le calcaneum (Au.-255) correspondent curieusement avec les valeurs moyennes des parties correspondante de l'*Equus caballus gallicus*. Il semble donc logique d'attribuer tous ces restes à cette dernière variété. Deux faits sont à noter; par la taille, l'Equidé de la Couche 11 semble se rapprocher des formes solutréennes et magdal-

éniennes plus grande que le cheval de Solutré d'âge périgordien. Certes, les restes que nous avons étudiés sont trop peu nombreux pour permettre une telle affirmation et l'on a peut être affaire à des mâles robustes. La seconde remarque porte sur la place stratigraphique de la Couche 11 qui devrait correspondre à l'Aurignacien I classique dont elle ne renferme aucun des éléments arctiques de cette période très froide. A cette époque on rencontre encore l'*Equus caballus germanicus*; on le trouve par exemple dans le Périgordien II du gisement des Cottés (Bouchud 1961) aujourd'hui attribué à un Aurignacien ancien.

SUIDAE et PROBOSCIDAE

Le sanglier (*Sus scrofa*) prouve sa présence par une extrémité distale de tibia très caractéristique, (d. = 28,7 x 34,3 mm.). Un morceau d'ivoire provenant d'une défense de Proboscidien est attribué à *Elephas primigenius* (mammouth) d'après le caractère froid de l'ensemble de la faune.

Sus scrofa L. (Au.-253). 1 extr. dist. de tibia: 28,7 x 34,3 mm.
Elephas primigenius Blum. 1 morceau de défense.

CANIDAE et URSIDAE

Canis lupus (loup) est peu représenté: quatre morceaux de canine, deux incisives, et une mandibule brisée. Par contre les restes du renard commun (*Vulpes vulpes*) sont nombreux: Ils appartiennent à tout le squelette en proviennent d'au moins trois animaux.

Canis lupus L. (Au.-225), 1 canine et 1 incisive brisées. (Au.-238), 1 mandibule et 1 canine brisée.

TABLEAU XLIII

Couche 11. Mesures prises sur *Vulpes vulpes*

Vulpes vulpes L.

Humérus

(Au.-227), 1 extr. dist., dt. = 15,0 mm. (Au.-231), 1 extr. dist., dt. = 17,8 mm. (Au.-246), 1 morceau de tête. (Au.-249), 1 ext. dist., dt. = 20,0 mm. (Au.-333), 1 ext. dist. dt. = 20,5 mm.

Radius

(Au.-231, 261, et 331), 3 morceaux de diaphyse.

Cubitus

(Au.-251), 1 morceau de diaphyse.

Métacarpien

(Au.-138), 1 morc. (Au.-231), 2 morc. (Au.-233), 1 morc. (Au.-246), 3 morc. (Au.-251), 3 morc. (Au.-252). 1 morc. (Au.-261), 4 morc. (Au.-331), 2 morc. (Au.-332), 1 métacarpien (I), 1 = 38,3 mm.

Phalange (I)

(Au.-246), 1 phalange (I) brisée.

Phalange (II)

(Au.-226, 240, 246, 251), 4 phalanges brisées.

Scapulum

(Au.-246), 1 morceau. (Au.-262), 1 cavité glénoïde.

Os innominé

(Au.-242, 253, 256), 3 morceaux.

Tibia

(Au.-238), 1 extr. dist.: 11,1 x 16,5 mm. (Au.-333), 1 extr. dist.: 11,0 x 15,5 mm. (Au.-253, 264, 331), 3 morceaux de diaphyse.

Astragale

(Au.-261), 1 astragale: 19,1 x 12,4 mm.

Calcaneum

(Au.-251), 1 calcaneum, 1 = 32,0 mm.

Métatarsien

(Au.-253), 1 morc. (Au.-261), 4 morc. (Au.-262), 1 morceau.

Vertèbre

(Au.-261), 1 axis brisé.

Maxillaires et dents isolées

(Au.-261), 1 maxil. sup. brisé. (Au.-333), 1 carnassière sup. g.: 14,0 x 6,0 mm. au collet. (Au.-333), 1 molaire sup. d. M1: 6,5 x 10,5 mm. (Au.-246 and 251), 2 morc. de mandibule édentés. (Au.-251), 1 morc. de mandibule avec la carnassière: 16,5 x 5,0 mm. au collet, et la M1: 7,3 x 4,1 mm. (Au.-252), 1 morc. de mandibule avec la M1: 7,0 x 3,0 mm. (Au.-333), 3 morc. de mandibule dont deux portent la carnassière: 14,4 x 4,0 mm. et 13,7 x 5,1 mm.

(Au.-246), 1 canine sup. g., au collet: 15,0 x 11,4 mm.

L'ours des cavernes est représenté par une canine percée et travaillée.

Ursus spelaeus Rosenm. (Au.-238), une canine inférieure percée dans sa partie radiculaire.

RONGEURS et OISEAUX

Microtus arvalis-agrestis Pal. (Au.-138), 1 mandibule g. (Au.-227), 1 mandibule g.
Lepus sp. (Au.-226), 1 phalange (II). (Au.-238), 1 phalange (II). (Au.-248), 1 vertèbre lombaire brisée.
Coracia graculus L. (Au.-138), 1 cubitus brisé.

Le petite faune, très pauvre, ne renferme pas d'éléments remarquables.

EBOULIS 11/12 et COUCHE 12

La quantité de matériel provenant des Éboulis 11/12 demeure assez faible et ne présente pas un intérêt particulier.

Rangifer tarandus L. Quelques débris osseux sans valeur (Au.-269). 1 morceau de perche.
Equus caballus L. (Au.-265), 1 incisive sup. I1.
Vulpes vulpes L. (Au.-265), 1 tibia complet, l=117,5 mm., extr prox.: 21,0 x 16,0 mm., au milieu de la diaphyse, dt. = 7,0 mm., extr dist.: 9,0 x 13,6 mm.
Rongeurs. (Au.-265 et 268), restes indéterminables.

Oiseaux. (Au.-158 A), 1 fémur et 1 tibia très roulés, indéterminables. (Au.-267), 1 carpo-métacarpe brisé, provenant d'un Fringillidé, indéterminable.

Le matériel de la Couche 12 est plus abondant. Il comprend essentiellement des débris de *Rangifer tarandus* et d'*Equus caballus*. Pour le premier, le nombre des éclats est trois fois plus grand que pour le second mais quant à la masse, le rapport se réduit à deux environ. Les restes d'Equidés ayant fourni un bon nombre de mesures, ce sont eux qui retiendront notre attention.

TABLEAU XLIV

Couche 12. Espèces identifiées et débris osseux correspondants

Rangifer tarandus L.	129	*Capra ibex L.*	1
Bos sp.	7	*Canis lupus L.*	4
Equus caballus L.	37	*Vulpes vulpes L.*	2

On notera dans la Couche 12 l'absence de la microfaune, des oiseaux et des amphibiens.
Voici maintenant le détail des restes intéressants.

Rangifer tarandus L., Eclats de diaphyse et dents brisées.
Bos sp. (Au.-271), 1 éclat de tibia, 2 morc. d'astragale, 1 calcaneum brisé, 1 débris de canon post., 1 scaphoïde brisé. (Au.-279), 1 molaire inf. brisée.

TABLEAU XLV

Mensurations prises sur les Equidés de la Couche 12 aurignacienne *(Equus caballus gallicus)*

Equus caballus gallicus

(Au.-183 C).	1 molaire sup. brisée.
(Au.-271).	6 morceaux de molaire.
(Au.-277).	1 morceau de molaire.
(Au.-278).	1 morceau de molaire inf.
(Au.-282).	1 molaire sup. brisée.
(Au.-273).	1 éclat de tibia.
(Au.-277).	1 éclat de tibia et 2 morceaux de rotule.
(Au.-280).	1 éclat de tibia.
(Au.-212).	1 morc. de mandibule portant la P3: 29,0 x 18,0 mm. et la P4: 30,0 x 19,0 mm., mesures prises au niveau de l'alvéole.
(Au.-337).	1 prémolaire inf. P4, fût brisé: 30,0 x 18,0 mm.
(Au.-279).	1 molaire inf. M3 d., fût brisé: 33,8 x 14,0 mm.
(Au.-271).	1 prémolaire sup. P4, fût: 87,0 mm., mesure en P: 27,6 x 25,0 mm., protocône: 13,5 mm., soit 48,9%.
(Au.-283).	1 prémolaire sup. P4 d., fût: 38,0 mm., mesure en P: 28,7 x 24,0 mm., protocône: 14,7 mm., soit 51,2%.
(Au.-337).	1 prémolaire sup. P4 g., fût brisé: 30,0 x 29,0 mm., protocône: 14,0 mm., soit 46,7%
(Au.-283).	1 molaire sup. M1 g., fût: 36,0 mm., mesure en P: 26,0 x 26,5 mm., protocône: 14,0 mm., soit 53,8%.
(Au.-271).	1 molaire sup. M3 d., fût brisé: 26,0 x 22,0 mm., protocône: 12,0 mm., soit 46,1%.
(Au.-337).	1 incisive sup. I2 d. peu usée.

Les dimensions assez fortes des dents, leur émail peu plissé, la forme du protocône et la faiblesse de son indice, les caractères du métaconide et du métastylide réunis par un sillon lingual très ouvert caractérisent une fois de plus *Equus caballus gallicus n. va.*

Le bouquetin *(Capra ibex)* est représenté par une mandibule brisée portant les prémolaires. Quelques débris de dents et de phalanges appartiennent au loup *(Canis lupus)* et au renard commun *(Vulpes vulpes).*

Capra ibex L. (Au.-277), 1 morceau de mandibule portant les prémolaires, les mesures sont prises au collet. P2 = 5,0 x 4,0 mm., P3 = 7,0 x 5,0 mm., P4 = 9,0 x 6,0 mm.
Canis lupus L. (Au.-275), 2 morc. de phalange (II). (Au.-277), 2 morceau de phalange (II).
Vulpes vulpes L. (Au.-154), 1 morc. de mandibule édenté. (Au.-272), 1 canine brisée.

EBOULIS 12/13 et COUCHE 13

Les Éboulis 12/13 renferment un seul éclat de diaphyse d'*Equus caballus.* La liste ci-dessous se rapporte à la Couche 13.

Le renne *(Rangifer tarandus)* y domine largement (221 éclats de diaphyse et débris dentaires); les autres espèces sont très rares: *Cervus elaphus*: 3, *Arvicola sp.*: 1, et *Microtus sp.*: 1. Voici les pièces ayant quelque valeur.
Rangifer tarandus L. (Au.-290), 1 bois de massacre. Long. totale: 193 mm., pédicule brisé au-dessous de la meule, pas d'andouiller. Au-dessus de la meule: 19,0 x 16,8 mm.(Au.-291), 1 rocher, 1 phalange (I) de stylet post.
Cervus elaphus L. (Au.-289), 3 éclats de diaphyse.
Arvicola sp. (Au.-299), 1 incisive sup.
Microtus sp. (Au.-299), 1 cubitus brisé.

EBOULIS 13/14 et COUCHE 14

Les Éboulis 13/14 livré une certaine quantité de restes de *Rangifer tarandus* (410) dont quelques pièces seulement méritent une description; il faut y ajouter des traces provenant du genre *Lepus.*

Rangifer tarandus L. (Au.-294), 1 mandibule de 4/5 ans, longeur de la série dentaire; 105 mm.: M3 = 21,0 mm. (Au.-306), 1 morceau de mandibule portant les trois molaires; âge supérieur à 13 ans, dislocation de la table dentaire.
Lepus sp. (Au.-292), 1 phalange (I).

Dans la Couche 14, *Rangifer tarandus* demeure

l'élément dominant (1.481) mais un petit nombre de pièces seulement sont mesurables; le Cert élaphe vient ensuite, Bovidés et Chevaux restent à l'état de traces.

TABLEAU XLVI

Couche 14. Espèces identifiées et débris osseux correspondants

Rangifer tarandus.	1.481	*Capra ibex L.*	1
Cervus elaphus L.	10	*Vulpes vulpes L.*	4
Bos sp.	2		
Equus caballus L.	1	*Lepus sp.*	1

TABLEAU XLVII

Couche 14. Mensurations prises sur *Rangifer tarandus*

Rangifer tarandus L.

(Au.-301).	1 molaire inf. M3: 23,0 mm.
(Au.-318).	1 molaire inf. M3: 24,8 mm.
(Au.-317).	1 molaire inf. M3: 23,7 mm.
(Au.-316).	1 morceau de perche.
(Au.-318).	3 morc. de perche.
(Au.-310).	1 extr. dist. canon ant.: 39,9 x 21,6 mm.
(Au.-302).	1 extr. dist. canon post.: 40 x 23,0 mm.
(Au.-309).	1 phalange (I), h = 45,0 mm., extr. prox: 21,0 x 21,0 mm., extr dist: 12,0 x 17,0 mm.
(Au.-317)	1 phalange (I), h = 41,0 mm., extr. prox.: 19,0 x 20,0 mm., extr dist.: ? x 17,4 mm.
(Au.-309)	1 phalange (II), h = 32,0 mm., extr. prox.: 17,0 x 18,0 mm., extr. dist.: 15,8 x 17,0 mm.

Cervus elaphus est représenté par un morceau de mandibule de détermination facile, mais pour les Bovidés les dents isolées ne permettent pas de définir l'espèce correspondante. Depuis la Couche 9, rongeurs, oiseaux, et amphibiens ont pratiquement disparu.

Cervus elaphus L. (Au.-300), 2 éclats de diaphyse. (Au.-302), 3 éclats de diaphyse et 1 morc. de mandibule édentée. (Au.-314), 1 incisive et 1 éclat de diaphyse. (Au.-316), 2 éclats de canon.
Bos sp. (Au.-315), 1 molaire sup. M2 d., hauteur du fût: 44,0 mm. au collet: 28,0 x 29,5 mm. (Au.-315), 1 molaire sup. M2 g., hauteur du fût: 45,0 mm., au collet: 31,0 x 30,0 mm.
Equus caballus L. (Au.-309), 1 éclat de tibia.
Capra ibex L. (Au.-312), 1 morc. de mandibule portant P3, P4 et M1, les dents très usées ne sont pas mesurables.
Vulpes vulpes L. (Au.-302), 1 prémolaire, 2 métacarpiens (II) et (III) brisés et 1 phalange (II).
Lepus sp. (Au.-315), 1 morc. de radius.

CONCLUSIONS GENERALES

Dans cette dernière section, nous distinguerons deux parties. La première examinera les résultats obtenus dans l'étude paléontologique de la faune, dans la seconde j'essaierai de retracer les vicissitudes du climat depuis l'Aurignacien ancien jusqu'au Proto-Magdalénien à partir des changements survenus dans la composition du milieu animal environnant.

La conservation des débris osseux retiendra notre attention tout d'abord. Le matériel surabondant de l'Abri Pataud a permis de dégager un certain nombre de faits très généraux relatifs à la préservation des restes de Cervidés, mais aussi des débris appartenant à des espèces de structure anatomique assez voisine comme *Capra ibex* ou le genre *Gazella*. En effet, l'observation courante montre que les principaux éléments squelettiques se retrouvent toujours dans l'ordre suivant: métapodes, tibia, radio-cubitus, fémur, et enfin humérus. Ceci laisse supposer l'intervention d'une cause purement naturelle puisque les restes du genre *Gazella* possèdent une répartition analogue dans les gisements du Proche-Orient.

Quand on dispose d'un matériel considérable, il devient possible d'attribuer à chaque segment osseux un coefficient, inférieur à l'unité, variable dans des limites assez étroites, qui exprime la *probabilité de découverte* de cet élément. C'est ce qui a été fait pour *Rangifer tarandus* (tab. II, pp. 72-73). Les données de ce tableau conduisent aux conclusions suivantes:

1°) La *probabilité de découverte* des diverses parties d'un squelette dépend:

    (a) du nombre d'animaux contenus dans la classe d'âge déterminée par l'attrition dentaire et la soudure des épiphyses (*probabilité de rencontre*)

    (b) de la résistance du matériel à l'écrasement sous le poids du terrain qui l'emprisonne. Ainsi le fémur et l'humérus dont les parois diaphysaires sont plus minces que celles des os canons sont beaucoup plus rares. La *probabilité de rencontre* multipliée par la *probabilité de destruction* mécanique détermine la *probabilité de découverte* d'un reste osseux déterminé.

2°) Le nombre des restes diaphysaires reconnaissables est une fonction de la forme de la diaphyse. Ceci explique le pourcentage élevé des restes de canon postérieur, le pourcen-tage plus faible des canons antérieurs et le petit nombre des restes de fémur ou d'humérus.

Ces résultats confirmés par l'étude du matériel de l'Abri Pataud ont été élaborés progressivement au cours de mes recherches sur les faunes du Sud-Ouest de la France (Bouchud 1966), du Proche-Orient (El Kebara, Djebel Qafzeh, et d'Afrique.[2]

A l'appui des conclusions précédentes, je donnerai deux exemples tirés de mes travaux antérieurs. Le premier est apporté par la station solutréenne de Badegoule (Cheynier 1949); elle a fourni 2.445 dents inférieures et 205 bois de massacre de *Rangifer tarandus* (Bouchud 1966, pp. 95-95). Il est intéressant de comparer la répartition des dents de ce gisement avec celle d'une population naturelle de 1.000 rennes (Skuncke 1953). Le tri des dents n'offre aucune difficulté et les différences observées dans le tableau ci-dessous sont significatives.

Les valeurs théoriques sont calculées à partir d'une «population intégralement protégée contre les prédateurs» (Skuncke 1953). On pourrait expliquer les écarts constatés entre les pourcentages des dents déciduales appartenant à chaque catégorie en disant que la mortalité pendant les deux premières années de la vie du renne est beaucoup plus élevée que pour le reste de la population. Sous les hautes latitudes, les faons en particulier, mais aussi les jeunes de un à deux ans, sont des proies faciles pour les loups et les grands rapaces (Degerbøl 1957). Tout ceci est parfaitement exact, mais l'explication demeure incomplète. Considérons maintenant la répartition des 205 bois de massacre qui accompagnent les dents. Voici leur distribution:

Faons: 85; mâles: 18; femelles: 102.

---

2. A la demande du Professeur J. Devisse, de la Faculté des Lettres et des Sciences Humaines de Lille, j'ai accepté la détermination de la faune de Tegdaoust (Mauritanie). Ce matériel d'âge pré-islamique et islamique est très mal conservé, mais ici encore les métapodes, les phalanges, et les dents dominent (résultats en cours de publication).

Les fouilles pratiquées sur le site de Qûmran (Jordanie) ont livré une grande quantité de métapodes de mouton *(Ovis aries)*; la possibilité d'un «rite religieux» a été un moment envisagée. Il s'agit d'un phénomène naturel de conservation différentielle (Bouchud, *in* Laperrousaz 1960 et 1961).

TABLEAUX XLVIII

Répartition des dents inférieures dans une population
naturelle de *Rangifer tarandus* provenant du Solutréen IV de
Badegoule (Bordogne)

Dents inférieures	Population naturelle (1.000 Rennes)		Badegoule (Bordogne) (Solutréen)	
Molaires de lait	1.677	(31,3%)	176	(7,2%)
Prémolaires définitives	1.323	(24,7%)	883	(36,1%)
Molaires permanentes	2.354	(44,0%)	1.386	(56,7%)

L'âge des 205 ramures[3] étant connu (Bouchud 1966, pp. 94-95), il est aisé de déterminer le nombre de dents correspondant. On trouve ainsi:

Dents déciduales: 360; prémolaires: 258; molaires: 312.

Il n'est pas possible de convertir ces données en pourcentages pour les comparer avec les résultats du tableau précédent car les chasseurs abattaient des mâles dépourvus de bois pendant les mois d'hiver, et durant les mois de printemps les autres mâles portaient des bois en voie de croissance qui ne se conservent pas; ceci explique d'ailleurs la faiblesse de la *sex-ratio* (1/6) déterminée à partir des ramures. Le point intéressant réside dans le fait que le nombre de dents de lait correspondant aux rennes abattus devrait être de 360 alors que le nombre de dents lactéales récoltées est seulement de 176. Pour expliquer une telle différence on ne saurait invoquer la destruction des jeunes par les prédateurs puisque leurs restes se trouvent dans l'abri. Un ramassage incomplet ne saurait être envisagé car les fouilles ont été conduites avec beaucoup de soin. Il faut donc admettre l'explication mécanique, à savoir la résistance plus ou moins grande des pièces à l'écrasement sous le poids du terrain, dont une preuve directe est fournie par l'examen des restes de *Dama cf. clactoniana* découverts à Fontéchevade, en Charente (Vallois et al. 1958). Des tibias et des canons postérieurs provenant des couches (E_2 soit - 6,50 m.) offrent de curieuses déformations et des traits de fractures particuliers qui ne sont point le fait des chasseurs[4]. On les observe sur des éléments squelettiques que l'homme n'a pas brisés et qui possédaient au moment de l'enfouissement le plateau tibial ou l'articulation distale dans le cas des os canons; grâce à cette disposition, ces pièces

maintenues sur le chant se sont comportées comme des poutres à section rectangulaire soumises à une surcharge appliquée sur leur côté le plus étroit. Tibias et canons postérieurs présentent tous une courbure anormale et les seconds portent sur leurs faces latérales des traits de fracture parallèles (fig. 2). La formule classique de Poncelet: $Q = K \, dh^2/2$ permet de calculer la pression subie par les diaphyses osseuses; K est égal à l'unité puisque la poussée est ici verticale, d exprime la densité moyenne du terrain (1.600 kg. par m³) et h sa profondeur en mètres. La pression croît très vite car la profondeur intervient par son carré. A un mètre au dessous de la surface du sol, elle est de 80 gr/cm² mais entre - 5 m. et - 6,50 m., ce qui est le cas pour les pièces examinées, elle varie de 2 kg à 3,38 kg/cm.² Cette pression exercée tout le long de la diaphyse explique les faits constatés. Après l'enfouissement, l'os perd progressivement sa matrice organique; sous l'action conjointe de l'humidité et du poids du terrain, les pièces maintenues sur le chant, soit par le plateau tibial, soit par la poulie articulaire distale se sont incurvées peu à peu. Dans le même temps, l'altération de la trame de collagène accroissait la fragilité de la diaphyse qui finalement se rompait dans le sens *longitudinal*, exactement comme une poutre trop chargée. Ces traits de fracture sont complètement différents de ceux que le Dr. Henri-Martin (1907-1910) obtenait dans ses expériences de bris des os par percussion[5]. Plus tard, des destructions secondaires ont atteint le plateau tibial et la poulie articulaire distale, sans cela les pièces se seraient couchées sur leurs faces latér-

---

3. A Badegoule, on trouve les bois de massacre à tous les stades de leur développement. Cette remarque rejoint une observation identique faite il y a bien longtemps dans les gisements du Périgord (Lartet et Christy 1875). Elle prouve que l'homme et le renne étaient présents toute l'année dans la région, ou tout au moins qu'ils ne s'en écartaient guère.

4. Je tiens à remercier ici Mademoiselle G. Henri-Martin pour son accueil ainsi que pour les facilités de travail qu'elle a bien voulu m'accorder dans son laboratoire de La Quina, en Charente (1963).

5. Au laboratoire de La Quina (Charente) on peut voir des os de bovidés et de chevaux brisés par percussion; les morceaux ont été recollés. A partir du point d'impact, on observe des traits de fracture en étoile, de plus les angles qui limitent les fragments osseux gardent une valeur à peu près constante mais on ne voit jamais de traits de fracture parallèles.

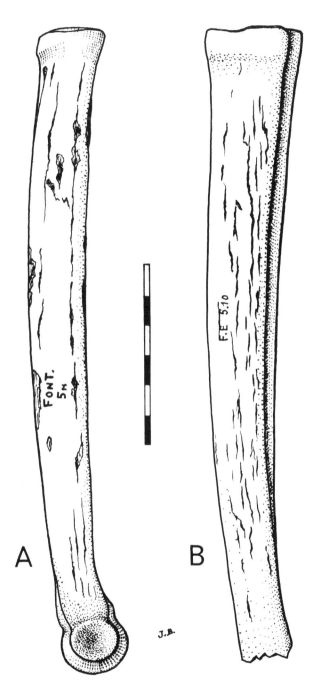

ales et les traits de fracture se situeraient sur les faces antérieures et postérieures.

En résumé, l'étude des restes fauniques provenant de l'Abri Pataud, non seulement confirme nos recherches sur la conservation différentielle des os, mais elle en précise aussi les modalités. Désormais, il est possible d'attribuer à chaque segment osseux de *Rangifer tarandus* une probabilité de découverte définie par les coefficients du tableau II, pages 72-73.

La détermination spécifique exacte du renne fossile demeure toujours un problème délicat. *Rangifer tarandus* reste toujours l'espèce dominante dans toutes les couches de l'Abri Pataud mais aucun segment osseux n'est intact, ce qui rend très difficile la recherche des limites de variation de l'espèce. Quant aux crânes indispensables pour une détermination spécifique précise (Banfield 1961), ils ne se rencontrent jamais dans les habitats paléolithiques car les chasseurs brisaient systématiquement les têtes et les os longs pour consommer le cerveau et la moelle dont ils étaient friands. Il faut donc utiliser les ramures, souvent incomplètes. Cette méthode a été très critiquée par I.I. Sokolov (1937) et A.W. Banfield insiste sur la variabilité considérable des bois. Cependant c'est le seul matériel dont dispose le paléontologiste qui est contraint d'en tenir compte (Arambourg, *in* Vallois et al. 1958, Kalkhe 1960).

Le renne fossile a été découvert pour la première fois par J.E. Guettard (1776), en France, qui a récolté dans le «diluvium» d'Étampes (Seine-et-Marne) une série de ramures brisées.[6] G. Cuvier (1823) confirma cette détermination tandis que A.G. Desmarest (1822) appelait *Cervus guettardi* le renne fossile. Un squelette complet et des morceaux de crâne ont été retirés des tourbes danoises datées de l'oscillation d'Allerød (Degerbøl et Krog 1959), un crâne intact de même âge provient des tourbes d'Irlande (Carte 1863), enfin un dernier crâne d'âge «solutréen» découvert près d'Irkoust, en Sibérie, fut décrit par C.C. Flerov (1934); cette pièce fut détruite pendant la seconde guerre mondiale. Depuis quelques années, la France revient au premier plan pour les découvertes de renne fossile. Un crâne presque intact et un squelette complet proviennent d'une grotte voisine de Foix, en Ariège, où l'homme n'a point vécu (Bouchud 1964 et 1967). Ces pièces, légèrement postérieures à l'oscillation d'Allerød, sont d'âge azilien.[7] Aujourd'hui, on considère le renne comme une espèce polytypique; pour A.W. Banfield (1961)

Figure 2. Fontéchevade (Charente). Niveaux tayaciens. Métapodes de *Dama cf. clactoniana* déformés et fracturés par la pression des terrains sus-jacents. A: canon antérieur, vue latérale; le bord antérieur rigoureusement rectiligne à l'état normal a été déformé par la pression, d'où les fractures longitudinales, la pièce était maintenue sur le chant par la poulie articulaire distale. B: canon postérieur, vue latérale; le bord antérieur est rigoureusement rectiligne à l'état normal, la poulie distale qui le maintenait sur le chant manque. Profondeur d'enfouissement: 5 m. environ.

6. Ces restes sont conservés au Laboratoire de Paléontologie du Museum National d'Histoire Naturelle, à Paris.

7. Les côtes et les morceaux d'os longs qui accompagnaient le crâne isolé ont été datés par le radio-carbone: 9. 150 B.P. ± 1.000 ans (Mme. Delibrias, GIF, 1967, n° 395).

les diverses «espèces» actuelles créées par les auteurs sont en réalité des dèmes que leur isolement transformera, dans les 20,000 années à venir, en véritables sous-espèces géographiques; cet auteur tient le renne du Spitzberg (*Rangifer tarandus platyrhynchus Vrolik)* pour une sous-espèce géographique qui se transformera en véritable espèce pendant la même période.

Dans cette perspective, les rennes découverts au Danemark, en Irlande et à Foix sont les descendants directs, par dérive génétique, des populations qui hantaient la France et les contrées européennes lors de la dernière glaciation. Si l'on passe en revue les ramures, ou les parties de ramures, décrites dans les sections précédentes ou dans nos travaux antérieurs (Bouchud et Wernert 1961; Bouchud 1966) on note la constance d'une série de caractères:

    (a) Section sub-cylindrique ou même cylindrique de la perche

    (b) Andouillers et empaumures à longues digitations

    (c) Courbure de la perche de type «*tarandus*» ou «*arcticus*» (Gripp *in* A. Rust 1943)

Ce sont là les traits que l'on attribue aux «rennes de toundra» actuels, sans revenir pour autant aux conceptions trop rigides de A. Jacobi (1931). On doit noter cependant la présence du «renne de forêt» représenté par un andouiller de glace typique provenant du Périgordien VI. Ces caractères se retrouvent tous sur les ramures récoltées jadis par J.B. Guettard (1776) et sur les bois bien conservés provenant des diverses régions françaises (Bouchud et Wernert 1961). Si l'on envisage maintenant la morphologie du crâne et la taille des os longs, les rennes de la région de Foix offrent tous les caractères que A.W. Banfield (1961) attribue aux formes de toundra actuelles mais ils s'en distinguent pourtant par une hauteur nettement plus faible de la voûte crânienne. Cette différence structurale étant mineure et probablement individuelle, il semble logique de les rapporter tous au stade *Rangifer tarandus guettardi Desmarest 1822*. A dessein, j'ai employé le mot stade. En effet, les rennes sauvages actuels vivent en troupeaux comprenant des dizaines de milliers de bêtes; dans une population nombreuse les mutations individuelles ont peu de chance de se répandre, la sélection naturelle agit lentement (L'Héritier 1954), enfin la durée de la dernière glaciation est trop courte (Ericson, Ewing et Wollin 1964 lui attribuent une durée de 120.000 ans) pour que l'on puisse voir dans le renne würmien une espèce «éteinte» distincte de l'espèce actuelle. On ne saurait écarter cette possibilité *a priori*, mais dans

l'état actuel de nos connaissances, rien ne vient étayer une telle hypothèse. Le renne würmien serait au stade *Rangifer guettardi Desmarest* tandis que les fossiles mésolithiques français et européens représenteraient le stade *Rangifer tarandus guettardi Desmarest*. Le cas du renne est à rapprocher de celui du Cerf élaphe fossile, *Cervus elaphus*, Le Riss terminal des «Abîmes de la Fage», en Corrèze, a livré des ramures de *Cervus acoronatus Beninde* (Guérin 1966, Bouchud 1968b), espèce connue en Allemagne dès le Pléistocène moyen. Par la morphologie osseuse, par la taille et par la denture, ce Cervidé est absolument identique au *Cervus elaphus* du Würm et de l'Holocène dont il s'écarte uniquement par la forme des bois: la «couronne» d'andouillers qui termine le merrain du Cerf élaphe est remplacée par deux andouillers formant entre eux une sorte de pince, même chez les sujets âgés. Pour H.D. Kalkhe (1960), *Cervus acoronatus* n'est pas une espèce distincte de *C. elaphus* mais un stade phylogénétique atteint par une population dont les membres présentent parfois des variations individuelles marquées mais qui conduisent toutes de la forme fossile au Cerf élaphe actuel.[8] Nous adopterons la même attitude à l'égard du renne pléistocène. *Rangifer guettardi* pour le Würm et *Rangifer tarandus guettardi* pour le Mésolithique sont des stades phylogénétiques progressifs atteints par des populations qui conduisent des formes fossiles aux dèmes actuels par isolement géographique d'abord et par dérive génétique ensuite. A l'intérieur de ces deux stades, on distingue des variations individuelles ou régionales parfois importantes qui portent sur la taille du squelette ou la forme de la ramure (Bouchud 1966 et 1967, Bouchud et Wernert 1961). Nous rappelerons simplement que la courbure «*arcticus*» de la perche apparaît dès le Mindel et la courbure «*tarandus*» avec le Riss (Bouchud 1967). Les rennes de l'Abri Pataud et des autres gisements würmiens du Sud-Ouest français seront rapportés à *Rangifer guettardi Desmarest*.

Les autres Cervidés, trop peu nombreux, retiendrons moins notre attention. *Cervus elaphus*, toujours de très grande taille, ferait figure de géant dans les hardes actuelles. Les trois crânes découverts dans le Proto-Magdalénien (Couche 2) possèdent des molaires presque aussi fortes que celles de *Cervus megaceros* (tab. IX, p. 81), cependant dans les couches péri-

---

8. «... Wir geben also nicht dem oder jenem Individuum den Namen, sondern der Population, die in ihrem phylogenetischen Stadium (Mosbach) noch nicht die «Grenze» *acoronatus-elaphus* überschritten hat, obwohl dem Charackter solcher Entwicklungen entsprechend einige Individuen das progressive Merkmal bereits ausbilden.» (Kalkhe 1960, p. 52).

gordiennes, les restes d'os longs permettent d' écarter la présence du grand cerf des toubières. On ne connaît pas de morceaux de ramure. *Capreolus capreolus*, toujours rare, est représenté par des dents et des débris d'os longs plus robustes que ceux de l'espèce moderne.

En ce qui concerne les Bovidés, nous ne disposons d'aucune pièce (chevilles osseuses, métopodes) permettant de choisir entre *Bos primigenius* et *Bison priscus*. Les critères proposés par Stanley J. Olsen (1960) ont essentiellement une valeur statistique; leur emploi plaide en faveur d'une majorité de *Bison priscus*, résultat en accord avec les données de l'ensemble de la faune. Dans le Périgordien IV (Couche 5: Talus), des débris de molaires supérieures attestent la présence du boeuf musqué (*Ovibos moschatus*).

Les restes d'Equidés, peu abondants, ne renferment pas de métapodes intacts; leur identification spécifique repose sur des phalanges, dont un petit nombre seulement est intact, sur des dents isolées et quelques maxillaires supérieurs et inférieurs dont deux ou trois pièces possèdent une série dentaire complète. Depuis le Proto-Magdalénien jusqu'au Périgordien IV, la petite taille des dents et leur morphologie caractérisent le cheval de Solutré (*Equus caballus gallicus n. va.*) Dans cette dernière couche et dans les niveaux aurignaciens sous-jacents 8, 11, et 12 on rencontre quelques dents dont la taille plus considérable rappelle celle des formes solutréennes et magdaléniennes des gisements du Sud-Ouest. Il s'agit de mâles plus robustes sans doute car l'ensemble des dents, des débris osseux et plus particulièrement des os du carpe et du tarse demeure très homogène. Les mesures prises sur les deux dernières catégories se rapprochent étonnamment des valeurs moyennes citées dans la littérature (Prat 1968). Pour être complet, il faut rappeler que dans les niveaux aurignaciens les plus profonds (Aurignacien I et II) la présence d'*Equus caballus germanicus* ne serait pas impossible, mais l'homogénéité du matériel étudié rend cette hypothèse peu probable.

Equus hydruntinus Regalia est présent dans les Couches 3, 4, et 5: dans le Périgordien VI, dans la partie supérieure du Noaillien et du Périgordien IV; on le retrouve aussi dans les niveaux aurignaciens 7 et 8; il disparaît ensuite. Dans tous les cas, on n'a récolté que des dents isolées, sans débris osseux. On admet généralement que *Equus hydruntinus* est une espèce caractéristique des climats tempérés. A la lumière des associations fauniques étudiées, il est préférable de dire qu'il évite les climats extrêmes, trop froids ou trop secs.

L'importance des espèces montagnardes *Capra ibex* et *Rupicapra rupicapra* varie considérablement d'un niveau à l'autre; le maximum est atteint avec 5% dans le Proto-Magdalénien, c'est un point sur lequel nous reviendrons en examinant le problème des vicissitudes climatiques. Les segments osseux sont assez rares, ils comprennent surtout des phalanges brisées, quelques sabots, deux cubo-naviculaires des débris d'humérus, beaucoup de dents isolées et des morceaux de maxillaires et de mandibules. La distinction entre les dents du bouquetin (*C. ibex*) et du chamois (*R. rupicapra*) est assez souvent difficile et même pratiquement impossible dans le cas des dents déciduales (F. Koby 1964). Ce n'est pas le cas pour l'Abri Pataud car le bouquetin est toujours de forte taille. Si les dents isolées sont abondantes, nous n'avons pas cependant de maxillaire ou de mandibule portant la série dentaire complète. Une extrémité distale de canon antérieur (Noail.-446) mesure 45,0 x 24,5 mm.; elle correspond aux plus forte pièces trouvées dans la grotte de l'Observatoire, à Monaco (Boule et de Villeneuve 1929). Les séries dentaires inférieures et supérieures de *Rupicapra rupicapra* sont comparables aux données obtenues par F. Koby (1964) à partir des chamois de la grotte de la Vache en Ariège. Une cheville osseuse (Pg. IV-823) rappelle curieusement celle de *R. rupicapra pyrenaïca* (isard) par sa morphologie et par ses dimensions. L'isard vivait donc en Dordogne pendant les périodes froides du Paléolithique supérieur. Il existe bien des morceaux de chevilles osseuses de *C. ibex* mais ils ne sont pas suffisants pour atteindre le niveau sub-spécifique *alpinus* ou *pyrenaïca*.

Le mammouth (*Elephas primigenius*) se rencontre dans le Proto-Magdalénien (Level 2) où il est représenté par une extrémité distale de défense travaillée par l'homme, dans le Périgordien VI (Level 3) où l'on a découvert une moitié proximale de fémur, enfin dans le Périgordien IV qui a fourni cinq lamelles d'ivoire. La pointe de défense travaillée a pu être apportée de fort loin, mais on imagine mal le transport d'une moitié de fémur sur une distance considérable. On admettra donc la présence du mammouth dans la région.

Un très petit nombre de débris appartiennent au sanglier (*Sus scrofa*), ce sont: une incisive supérieure (Pg. VI-159), un sabot (Noail.-667 A), et une prémolaire inférieure P2.

Les Félidés sont représentés par le lion des cavernes (*Panthera leo, race spelaea*) et le lynx boréal (*Lynx lynx*). Cinq canines sont attribuables au premier: PM-59, Noail.-355, Noail.-372, Noail.-388, et Noail.-647. Toutes sont brisées et ne se prêtent à aucune mesure, mais elles sont identifiables en toute certitude par l'aplatissement de leur face linguale et la présence du double sillon sur leur face externe. Dans le Périgordien IV, une seconde phalange reconnaissable à sa longueur et à sa courbure, un morceau de radius et une canine supérieure (Pg. IV-1166) porteuse du double sillon sur sa face externe ont été attribués au lynx boréal (*Lynx lynx*). Il convient de mentionner la présence de *Crocuta crocuta spelaea* dont une carnassière de lait (Pg. IV-821) et une incisive supérieure gauche I^3 proviennent du Périgordien IV. Le même niveau renferme deux petites vertèbres appartenant au genre *Mustela (Mustela erminea?)*.

L'ours des cavernes (*Ursus spelaeus*) est médiocrement représenté par deux canines brisées, quelques restes osseux et un calcaneum.

Les Canidés ont été parfois systématiquement chassés par l'homme et leurs restes sont plus abondants que ceux des espèces précédentes. *Canis lupus* est moins répandu que *Vulpes vulpes*. Le premier représentait un danger pour l'homme qui le prenait au piège très certainement. Ses ossements sont rares dans les stations préhistoriques. Dans le Proto-Magdalénien de l'Abri Pataud, un corps entier a été rapporté par les chasseurs. La plupart des os longs sont intacts ainsi que les métacarpiens, les métatarsiens, et les phalanges; le crâne, les dents, les côtes, et les vertèbres manquent complètement. Les mesures prises (tab. XII, p. 84) confirment les données de C. Suire (1969): le loup du Würm III était très robuste. Un certain nombre de dents isolées, de métacarpiens, et de métatarsiens provenant des niveaux aurignaciens et périgordiens fournissent des mensurations en accord avec les résultats précédents. Exception faite pour le Proto-Magdalénien, les chasseurs dépouillaient les bêtes sur place. Au cours de cette opération, ils sectionnaient le corps au niveau du cou, les membres aux articulations des pieds et des mains, et abandonnaient tout le reste. Ainsi s'explique la présence de morceaux de crâne, de dents isolées, de mandibules, de métacarpiens, de métatarsiens, et de phalanges dans les gisements. Ces observations demeurent valables pour le renard (*Vulpes vulpes*) dont les segments osseux sont très rares, sauf dans le Périgordien IV. On les trouve en telle quantité dans cette couche qu'il faut bien admettre l'apport d'animaux entiers dans l'abri. Etaient-ils mangés par les chasseurs? Il est difficile de répondre. Les os longs ne sont jamais brûlés, mais ils sont souvent brisés. Leur résistance mécanique à l'écrasement est évidemment plus faible que celle des os du loup ou du renne, cependant la putréfaction d'une masse de chair importante aurait incommodé les habitants de l'abri et attiré une multitude d'insectes et de rongeurs indésirables.

Les mesures prises sur les segments osseux intacts s'accordent bien avec les résultats obtenus par F.

Koby (1959) sur les renards magdaléniens de la grotte de la Vache en Ariège. L'étude des dents isolées, des maxillaires, et des mandibules montre qu'il s'agit toujours de *Vulpes vulpes*. Rien, jusqu'à présent, ne permet de soupçonner la présence de *Vulpes lagopus* (renard bleu ou renard polaire) dans les couches aurignaciennes et périgordiennes, présence qui serait logique à côté d'*Elephas primigenius* et d'*Ovibos moschatus*.

La microfaune retiendra davantage notre attention car elle permettra de suivre les vicissitudes du climat pendant le dépôt des couches aurignaciennes pauvres en grosse faune. Pour faciliter le rappel des résultats déjà obtenus, les différents nombres de débris osseux ont été regroupés dans le tableau XLIX; les éboulis ont été réunis avec les niveaux archéologiques correspondants.

Lepus variabilis, le lièvre variable, a été identifié sur les incisives supérieures découvertes dans les différents niveaux. Les ossements qui les accompagnaient, tous de grande taille, ont été rapportés à cette espèce (F. Ed. Koby 1959a, 1960).

Dans le groupe des campagnols, j'ai reconnu la présence de *Microtus anglicus, Microtus nivalis, Pitymys subterraneus,* et de *Microtus arvalis-agrestis.* Le Proto-Magdalénien a livré trois mandibules bien conservées de la première espèce; la seconde, très abondante dans la Couche 8 (Aurignacien), est représentée par quatre parties antérieures de crâne munies de leur rostre, des mandibules et une série d'os longs, enfin une mandibule droite dont la M_1 montre des triangles T4 et T5 qui confluent largement est attribuée à *Pitymys subterraneus.* Les campagnols des champs, très abondants, renferment *Microtus arvalis* et *Microtus agrestis;* bon nombre de M_1 sont de type intermédiaire aussi avons nous groupé tout ce matériel sous le nom *M. arvalis-agrestis*; quant aux pièces édentées ou mal conservées, elles sont rangées sous le terme de *Microtus sp.* Etant donné la large répartition de ces campagnols leur signification climatique est douteuse.

Une série de partie antérieures de crânes d'Arvicolidés, munies du rostre et des incisives supérieures, a permis d'étudier la constriction orbitaire et la proclivité des incisives. Ces données ont permis d'identifier *Arvicola scherman Shaw.* Les mandibules et les débris d'os longs sont groupés sous le terme d'*Arvicola sp.* La petite taille des pièces permet de les rapprocher de la sous-espèce *Arvicola scherman exitus Miller,* dont l'habitat exclusivement terrestre, s'accomode des altitude modérées et d'un climat relativement humide.

La présence d'*Eliomys quercinus,* facile à reconnaître à partir des mandibules complètes ou édentées et des os longs, surprend toujours un peu dans un contexte faunique froid comme celui du Proto-Magdalénien ou de l'Aurignacien (Couches 7 et 8). Nous verrons ce que l'on doit en penser en étudiant les vicissitudes du climat.

Apodemus sylvaticus (Mulot) est représenté seulement dans la Couche 8 (Aurignacien intermédiaire). Cette espèce recherche les milieux humides; elle remonte vers le nord jusqu'en Suède centrale. Les restes récoltées à l'Abri Pataud ne permettent pas de choisir entre *A. sylvaticus* et *A. flavicollis,* le second étant plus «forestier» que le premier.

Les rongeurs se rencontrent essentiellement depuis le Proto-Magdalénien jusqu'à la Couche 8 comprise (Aurignacien intermédiaire); les Couches 9 à 14 n'en renferment pratiquement pas (tab. XLIX). On ne trouve nulle part d'espèces caractéristiques de biotypes extrêmement froids ou très secs.

Nous avons identifié quatorze espèces d'oiseaux, (tab. XLIX); leur répartition suit à peu près celles des rongeurs. La rareté des rapaces correspond au fait que l'habitat humain était pratiquement continu. Le vautour (*Gyps fulvus*), oiseau relativement sociable, se trouve en compagnie du petit-duc (*Otus scops*) dans le Périgordien VI tandis que le vautour moine

(*Aegypius monachus*) et le gypaète barbu *(Gypaëtus barbatus),* amis de la montagne, demeurent dans la Couche 7 (Aurignacien intermédiaire). Le Proto-Magdalénien a livré un coracoïde de goéland argenté (*Larus argentatus*), hôte des eaux marines et fluviales qui pénètre très loin dans l'intérieur des terres.

Il est intéressant de signaler la présence de la canepetière (*Otis tetrax*), rarement citée dans les stations préhistoriques (Couche 8, Aurignacien intermédiaire). Cet oiseau s'égare parfois jusqu'en Scandinavie. La perdrix grise (*Perdix perdix*) relativement abondante (13,6% de l'ensemble de l'avifaune) se rencontre dans plusieurs couches: Périgordien IV, Couches 7 et 8 (Aurignacien intermédiaire). Le Périgordien VI a livré des restes de lagopède muet (*Lagopus mutus*), espèce de haute montagne qui vit de nos jours dans les régions dénudées de la zone nivale. Le pigeon colombin *(Columba oenas),* ami des parcs ouverts, est représenté dans le Périgordien IV.

La famille des Passériformes aves 75% du nombre total de débris récoltés demeure la plus importante. Un squelette de grive draine (*Turdus viscivorus*) provient du Proto-Magdalénien. Les Couches 7 et 8 (Aurignacien intermédiaire) renferment le pipit

TABLEAU XLIX

Liste des rongeurs, des oiseaux, des amphibiens et des poissons identifiés dan les couches archéologiques proto-magdaléniennes, noailliennes, périgordiennes, et aurignaciennes de l'Abri Pataud (Dordogne).

Espèces identifiées	Proto-Magdalénien	Périgordien VI	Noaillien	Périgordien IV	Eb. 5/6 – C. 6	Eb. 6/7 – C. 7	Eb. 7/8 – C. 8	Eb. 8/9 – C. 9	Eb. 9/10 – C. 10	Eb. 10/11 – C. 11	Eb. 11/12 – C. 12	Eb. 12/13 – C. 13	Eb. 13/14 – C. 14
Rongeurs													
Lepus variabilis	7	14	38	135	—	—	—	—	—	3	—	—	2
Eliomys quercinus	11	1	—	—	—	2	12	—	—	—	—	—	—
Microtus arvalis-agrestis	—	—	—	—	—	—	50	2	—	—	—	—	—
Microtus sp.	46	14	4	6	—	4	—	—	—	—	—	1	—
Microtus anglicus	3	—	—	—	—	—	—	—	—	—	—	—	—
Microtus nivalis	—	—	—	—	—	—	26	—	—	—	—	—	—
Pitymys subterraneus	—	—	—	—	—	—	1	—	—	—	—	—	—
Arvicola scherman exitus	62	13	5	—	—	—	4	—	—	—	—	—	—
Arvicola sp.	—	—	—	1	7	33	36	—	—	—	—	1	—
Apodemus sylvaticus	—	—	—	—	—	—	4	—	—	—	—	—	—

TABLEAU XLIX *Suite*

Espèces identifiées	Proto-Magdalénien	Périgordien VI	Noaillien	Périgordien IV	Eb. 5/6 – C. 6	Eb. 6/7 – C. 7	Eb. 7/8 – C. 8	Eb. 8/9 – C. 9	Eb. 9/10 – C. 10	Eb. 10/11 – C. 11	Eb. 11/12 – C. 12	Eb. 12/13 – C. 13	Eb. 13/14 – C. 14
Oiseaux													
Larus argentatus	1	–	–	–	–	–	–	–	–	–	–	–	–
Otis tetrax	–	–	–	–	–	–	–	1	–	–	–	–	–
Gyps fulvus	–	1	–	–	–	–	–	–	–	–	–	–	–
Aegypius monachus	–	–	–	–	–	1	–	–	–	–	–	–	–
Gypaëtus barbatus	–	1	–	–	–	–	–	–	–	–	–	–	–
Otus scops	–	1	–	–	–	–	–	–	–	–	–	–	–
Lagopus mutus	–	4	–	–	–	–	–	–	–	–	–	–	–
Perdix perdix	–	–	–	3	–	3	9	–	–	–	–	–	–
Columba oenas	–	–	–	3	–	–	–	–	–	–	–	–	–
Turdus viscivorus	12	–	–	–	–	–	–	–	–	–	–	–	–
Anthus spinoletta	–	–	–	–	–	1	3	–	–	–	–	–	–
Motacilla sp.	–	–	–	–	–	2	4	–	–	3	–	–	–
Corvus corax	–	–	2	36	–	–	–	–	–	–	–	–	–
Coleus monedula	–	–	–	–	–	–	3	–	–	–	–	–	–
Coracia graculus	3	1	2	7	4	–	3	–	–	1	–	–	–
Amphibiens													
Bufo sp. et *Rana sp.*	10	–	–	–	–	106	)500	–	–	–	–	–	–
Discoglossus sp.	–	–	–	–	–	–	1	–	–	–	–	–	–
Poissons													
Salmo sp.	5	15	4	–	–	–	4	–	–	–	–	–	–

N.B. Les éboulis et les couches 6 à 14 constituent les couches aurignaciennes *largo sensu*.

spioncelle (*Anthus spinoletta*) et la bergeronnette (*Motacilla sp.*). Le premier vit en haute montagne au dessus de 2.500 m. parmi les rochers et les gazons alpins tandis que la seconde dont le domaine s'étend pratiquement à l'Europe accepte des biotypes assez variés. On retrouve la bergeronnette dans l'Aurignacien ancien (Couche 11).

Les Corvidés méritent une mention particulière. Le grand corbeau (*Corvus corax*) reste l'espèce dominante (33% de l'avifaune). Rare dans le Noaillien, il se cantonne dans les niveaux moyens et inférieurs du Périgordien IV. La Couche 8 (Aurignacien intermédiaire) renferme une petite quantité de choucas (*Coleus monedula*). Enfin le Chocard des Alpes (*Coracia graculus*) arrive en seconde position, (18%), derrière le grand corbeau; il est présent dans presque toutes les couches depuis le Proto-Magdalénien jusqu'à l'Aurignacien ancien (Couche 11). C'est un oiseau de haute montagne. Sa présence dans un gisement de plaine, en compagnie de *Lagopus mutus* et d'*Anthus spinoletta* témoigne du refroidissement du climat.

La proximité de la Vézère explique l'abondance des amphibiens, surtout dans les Couches 7 et 8 (Aurignacien intermédiaire). On a affaire à des crapauds (*Bufo sp.*) et des grenouilles (*Rana sp.*). Le matériel recueilli se compose presque exclusivement d'os longs dépourvus d'épiphyses la plupart du temps, d'os iliaques, de quelques vertèbres et d'un très petit nombre d'urostyles. Les trois derniers éléments permettent de séparer les genres *Bufo* et *Rana*, mais il n'a pas été possible d'atteindre le niveau spécifique. Il convient de signaler la présence du discoglosse ou grenouille peinte (*Discoglossus sp.*) identifié à partir d'un humérus bien conservé.

Des vertèbres de poisson de dimensions variées, (*Salmo sp.*) ont été découvertes dans le Proto-Magdalénien, le Périgordien VI, le Noaillien et l'Aurignacien intermédiaire (Couche 8). D'après D. Peyrony (1932), les saumons remontaient encore la Vézère vers 1930.

Les changements de composition de la faune régionale étudiés en liaison avec la stratigraphie vont nous permettre de retracer les vicissitudes du climat durant le Proto-Magdalénien, le Noaillien, et le Périgordien VI et IV; mais un certain nombre de précautions sont nécessaires. En effet, les faunes liées aux habitats humains sont des faunes triées par les chasseurs, elles ne constituent jamais un échantillon – au sens statistique du terme – du milieu animal environnant. Ainsi l'abondance du renne dans les gisements du Sud-Ouest français a valu au Paléolithique supérieur le nom «d'Age du Renne.» Pendant la même période, à Solutré, le renne était fort abondant mais les chasseurs vécurent aux dépens du cheval qui finit par être la seule espèce représentée dans les couches du Périgordien supérieur (Combier 1956). A Predmost, en Moravie, le mammouth (*Elephas primigenius*) formait la base de l'alimentation humaine tandis que *Bos primigenius* jouait le même rôle dans le Kouban. Certes, l'abondance ou la rareté de tel ou tel animal favorise ou restreint le choix des chasseurs, mais à l'intérieur de ces limites les goûts de l'homme suffisent à fausser considérablement la représentativité des espèces rencontrées dans les stations préhistoriques.

Il est donc préférable d'écarter l'animal dominant quand on tente de déterminer les vicissitudes du climat à partir des changements de composition de la faune recueillie dans les gisements archéologiques.[9] Cela suppose bien sûr un matériel abondant et par

9. Il s'agit d'une simple mesure de prudence; elle ne suppose pas la connaissance précise des conditions matérielles ou des motifs psychologiques qui poussèrent l'homme fossile à vivre aux dépens de telle espèce plutôt que de telle autre.

suite des fouilles d'une certaine ampleur. C'est pourquoi il est souvent difficile d'utiliser des restes d'osseux provenant de fouilles anciennes. L'espèce dominante étant décartée, la petite faune (rongeurs et insectivores), les oiseaux, les amphibiens, les poissons, les mollusques terrestres apportent de précieux renseignements, surtout les deux premières et la dernière catégories car l'homme n'intervenait pas – en général – dans leur introduction dans l'abri.

Dans la description du climat actuel, il faut tenir compte non seulement de la structure spécifique de la faune, mais aussi de l'altitude, de la distance à la mer et des conditions locales. Au cours du Pléistocene, les faits sont beaucoup plus compliqués. L'énorme inlandsis qui recouvrait l'Europe du nord jusqu'à la plaine allemande a joué un rôle primordial. Il a refoulé vers le sud les zônes climatiques provoquant ainsi le déplacement des populations animales. D'une part, bon nombre d'espèces séparées les unes des autres par les distances considérables furent contraintes à vivre ensemble sur des territoires parfois restreints, d'autre part, l'abaissement de la limite des neiges éternelles agit d'une manière analogue en rejetant dans la plaine des espèces strictement montagnardes, Enfin, la brève durée – au sens géologique du terme – de la période quaternaire et le cloisonnement régional créé par les massifs montagneux englacés empêchèrent l'équilibre faune-climat de s'établir complètement. Ainsi s'expliquent des associations étonnantes: coexistence de *Rangifer tarandus* et d'*Eliomys quercinus*, de *Capra ibex*, de *Rupicapra rupicapra* avec les Equidés, l'abondance de *Coracia graculus* dans les gisements de plaine, etc.

L'intervention de l'homme et le déplacement saisonnier des espèces migratrices compliquèrent encore les données précédentes. Ils provoquèrent un mélange supplémentaire d'animaux qui vivaient dans des biotypes très divers et cela d'autant plus facilement que les biotypes étaient plus petits et plus proches, ce qui est le cas dans les pays faiblement accidentés.

Pour faciliter l'interprétation climatique de la faune, on peut répartir les diverses espèces en trois catégories selon le biotype dans lequel elles vivent:

1°) Espèces vivant dans la toundra, la steppe froide ou la steppe tempérée froide:

Rangifer tarandus (de toundra) - *Elephas primigenius* - *Coelodonta antiquitatis* - *Ovibos moschatus*.

2°) Espèces vivant dans la taïga, la steppe-forêt et parfois en montagne:

Rangifer tarandus (de forêt) - *Alces alces* - *Cervus elaphus* - *Capreolus capreolus* - *Sus scrofa - Bison priscus - Bos primigenius - Equus caballus - Equus hydruntinus.*

3°) Espèces exclusivement montagnardes:

Rupicapra rupicapra - Capra ibex.

Les carnivores, rares dans les gisements préhistoriques et souvent ubiquistes, ont été écartés. Pour l'Abri Pataud, j'ai éliminé le renne pour les raisons déjà indiquées et pour chaque couche archéologique à partir du nombre total de débris osseux recueillis, j'ai calculé les pourcentages correspondant à chaque espèce. Les résultats sont consignés dans le tableau L qui constitue un résumé commode du tableau général XXXIII. Une représentation graphique en est donnée par le figure 3, dont la lecture est facilitée par les conventions suivantes:

a) Le contour A, en gros trait plein correspond à *Equus caballus, sensu lato*.

b) Les Bovinés, *Bison priscus* et *Bos primigenius* réunis ensemble, sont représentés par le tracé B.

c) Les Cervidés, *Cervus elaphus* et *Capreolus capreolus* réunis ensemble, sont figurés par le trait tireté C.

d) Le tracé D point-tiret groupe les espèces exclusivement montagnardes: *Capra ibex* et *Rupicapra rupicapra*.

e) Les espèces à répartition discontinue: *Elephas primigenius, Ovibos moschatus, Equus hydruntinus* et *Sus scrofa* ne possèdent pas de représentation linéaire mais leur présence locale est marquée par un carré plein, une circonférence, un triangle plein et un cercle.

L'examen graphique (fig. 3) met trois faits en évidence:

1°) Les tracés relatifs aux Equidés (A) et aux Bovinés (B) restent parallèles.

2°) La representation linéaire des Cervidés (C) varie exactement en sens contraire des tracés A et B.

3°) Le pourcentage des espèces montagnardes (tracé D) décroît rapidement depuis Proto-Magdalénien jusqu'à la partie supérieure du Noaillien; il subit ensuite des oscillations mineures, enfin on note un relèvement sensible à la fin du Périgordien IV.

A partir des données précédentes, on peut interpréter les résultats obtenus. La découverte d'espèces strictement montagnardes dans les stations de plaine

correspond à un refroidissement général du climat et par suite à un abaissement de la limite des neiges éternelles. Les Bovinés, *Bison priscus* et *Bos primigenius*, soulignent l'humidité du climat et l'extension de la forêt et de la steppe où ils vivent. Les Cervidés, plus particulièrement le chevreuil, marquent la progression de la steppe mais ils habitent aussi dans la forêt. Les Equidés sont des formes de la steppe à caractère continental. *Elephas primigenius, Coelodonta antiquitatis, Ovibos moschatus* appartiennent à la toundra-parc.

Dans ces perspectives, le Proto-Magdalénien de l'Abri Pataud apparaît comme une période froide et peu humide où les espèces de la montagne sont abondantes: 40,2%. Avec le Périgordien VI le climat s'adoucit et l'humidité augmente comme le suggère l'accroissement des Bovinés: 37,0%. L'adoucissement du climat se poursuit pendant le dépôt des Éboulis 3/4; bouquetin et chamois ne représentent plus que 12,6% de l'ensemble. Le froid, moins marqué que durant le Proto-Magdalénien, réapparait avec le Noaillien; l'humidité, médiocre dans la partie supérieure de la couche, augmente considérablement dans la partie moyenne et inférieure. Les Éboulis 4/5 se formèrent sous un climat aussi froid que celui du Noaillien, mais nettement plus sec. Dans sa partie supérieure, le Périgordien IV un peu moins tempéré que les Éboulis 3/4, est aussi moins humide; il se refroidit et devient plus sec dans sa partie inférieure.

L'utilisation de la microfaune, des espèces épisodiques et l'emploi des données climatiques de Z. Hokr (1951) complètera les résultats précités. On trouve *Equus hydruntinus* dans les Éboulis 3/4 et la partie supérieure du Noaillien, c'est à dire pendant des épisodes modérés; cette espèce que l'on dit «chaude,» à tort, évite en réalité les climats rigoreux. *Sus scrofa*, hôte du Périgordien VI et de la partie supérieure du Noaillien, accepte des froids très durs mais il refuse les sols gelés en permanence. Le mammouth est présent dans le Proto-Magdalénien, le Périgordien VI, et le Périgordien IV. Ses restes: morceaux de défenses, débris dentaires, moitié de fémur, peu abondants font supposer qu'il ne vivait pas à proximité de l'abri. Les plateaux surplombant la vallée et balayés par le vent ont dû lui servir de refuge pendant l'hiver, mais à la belle saison il émigrait avec le renne et le boeuf musqué[10] sur les pentes du Massif Central, distantes de soixante-dix kilomètres environ, où régnait un

10. Une molaire supérieure d'*Ovibos moschatus* a été découverte dans le Périgordien IV lors du sondage de 1953. Une autre molaire supérieure brisée a été trouvée dans l'Extension 2 en 1963. Elle provient probablement du «talus» du Périgordien IV. Sa place exacte étant imprécise, elle ne figure pas dans le tableau L, page 145.

TABLEAU L. — Pourcentage des espèces autres que *Rangifer tarandus* en fonction des unités stratigraphiques et des variations du climat. Seuls les nombres de débris osseux supérieurs à 50 ont été retenus.

Niveaux archéologiques	Nombre de débris osseux récoltés	Toundra, steppe froide, et steppe tempérée froide		Steppe-forêt, taïga; montagne parfois			Montagne exclusivement				
		Bos sp.	Equus caballus	Equus hydruntinus	Elephas primigenius	Ovibos moschatus	Sus scrofa	Cervus elaphus	Capreolus capreolus	Capra ibex	Rupicapra rupicapra
PROTO-MAGDALÉNIEN	181	15,5	22,1	–	0,6	–	–	21,0	0,6	19,8	20,4
PÉRIGORDIEN VI	192	37,0	34,3	–	0,5	–	0,5	9,8	0,5	12,3	5,1
ÉBOULIS 3/4	95	27,4	26,3	1,1	–	–	–	32,6	5,3	7,3	–
NOAILLIEN Supérieur	265	13,2	9,8	0,4	–	–	0,4	52,8	12,1	6,8	4,5
NOAILLIEN Moyen	123	20,3	24,4	–	–	–	–	42,3	3,3	1,6	8,1
NOAILLIEN Inférieur	188	28,7	28,7	–	–	–	–	24,0	3,2	3,7	11,7
ÉBOULIS 4/5	67	8,9	3,0	–	–	–	–	74,6	–	3,0	10,5
PÉRIGORDIEN IV Supérieur	98	18,4	8,2	–	1,0	–	–	55,1	4,1	7,1	6,1
PÉRIGORDIEN IV Moyen	62	9,7	22,6	–	3,2	–	–	54,8	–	6,5	3,2
PÉRIGORDIEN IV Inférieur	73	4,1	19,2	–	1,4	–	–	46,6	8,2	16,4	4,1
PÉRIGORDIEN IV Couche 7	172	5,8	34,9	3,5	1,2	–	1,7	46,5	4,1	–	2,3
AURIGNACIEN Couche 11	367	1,1	97,8	–	0,3	–	0,3	0,5	–	–	–
AURIGNACIEN Couche 12	45	15,6	82,2	–	–	–	–	–	–	2,2	–

N.B. — L'*Ovibos moschatus* découvert dans le Périgordien IV (sondage de 1953) et dans l'Extension 2 (Talus) ne figure pas dans le tableau ci-dessus.

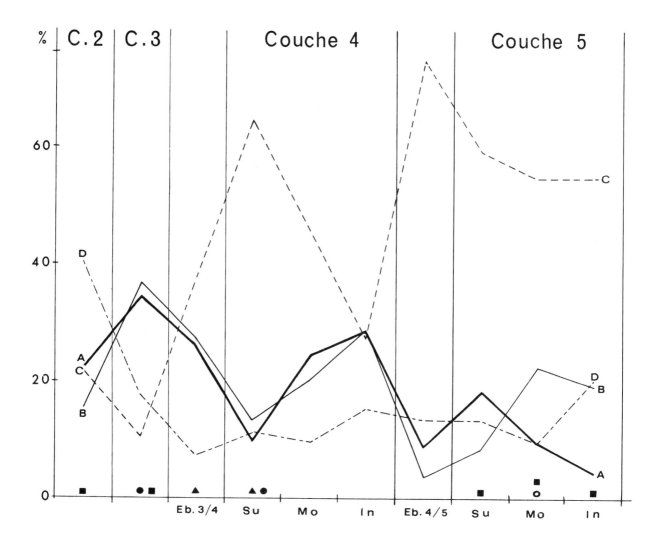

Figure 3. Etude de la faune de l'Abri Pataud. Les changements observés dans la composition de la faune en fonction de la stratigraphie. En gros trait, A: les Equidés au sens large du terme; en trait fin, B: les Bovinés, *Bos primigenius* et *Bison priscus*; en trait tireté, C: les Cervidés *Cervus elaphus* et *Capreolus capreolus*; en trait point-tiret, D: les espèces de montagne, *Capra ibex* et *Rupicapra rupicapra. Elaphus primigenius* est représenté par un carré plein, *Ovibos moschatus* par une circonférence, *Equus hydruntinus* par un triangle plein, et *Sus scrofa* par un cercle plein.

Les pourcentages correspondants figurent en ordonnée et les divisions stratigraphiques sont portées en abscisse.

climat plus frais. *Lepus variabilis* et *Microtus anglicus* hantaient les plateaux froids; le lièvre variable était un gibier de choix, si l'on en juge par l'importance de ses restes, principalement dans le Périgordien IV. Les rongeurs banaux: *Microtus arvalis-agrestis* et *Arvicola scherman*, largement répandus en Europe (Miller 1912, Heim de Balsac et Guislain 1955) gardent une signification climatique limitée. L'abondance d'*Eliomys quercinus* dans le Proto-Magdalénien est intéressante: elle suppose une température moyenne de juillet supérieure à + 15° C (Hokr 1951). Il vivait dans les bosquets abrités du bord de la Vézère ou se

chauffait au soleil dans les anfractuosités des parois rocheuses voisines de l'abri, car il ne craint pas le présence de l'homme. La limite orientale de la distribution du lérot s'étend beaucoup plus loin que le pensait Miller (1912). D'après les auteurs soviétiques (Ognev 1963), elle atteint le 62° de latitude nord en Karélie finlandaise; en U.R.S.S. elle traverse les hauteurs du Valdaï, la partie nord du territoire du Gorki et la province de Kazan sur la rive gauche de la Volga. Selon Formosov (*in* Ognev 1963) cette limite coïncide avec celle du chêne (*Quercus*), de l'érable (*Acer*) et du tilleul *(Tilia).* De moeurs crépusculaires et nocturnes, il ne redoute pas le voisinage de l'homme et hiverne dans les greniers. Essentiellement frugivore, il ne dédaigne point les insectes et les débris carnés. Son association avec le renne se comprend mieux à la lumière des faits précédents.

Les débris fauniques sont peu nombreux dans les couches aurignaciennes, aussi leur interprétation climatique toujours délicate comporte des risques d'erreur non négligeables. Nous tiendrons compte seulement des couches dont le matériel est assez abondant: 100 pièces au minimum qui renferment des restes vraiment significatifs.

La Couche 7 a livré 395 débris osseux de renne et 172 pièces appartenant à diverses espèces. *Rangifer tarandus* domine toujours (69,6%) mais dans le groupe des animaux secondaires le classement s'opère ainsi:

Bos sp.	5,8%
Equus caballus	34,9%
Equus hydruntinus	3,5%
Elephas primigenius	1,2%
Sus scrofa	1,7%
Cervus elaphus	46,5%
Capreolus capreolus	4,1%
Rupicapra rupicapra	2,3%

La petite quantité d'espèces qui vit dans la toundra ou dans la montagne (*E. primigenius, R. rupicapra*), l'importance des Equidés (34,9%) et des Cervidés (50,6%), la présence de formes «tièdes» comme *E. hydruntinus* et *S. scrofa* évoque la steppe tempérée froide. On remarquera la présence du lérot et la disparition du lièvre variable: peut-être le choix humain a-t-il joué pour ce rongeur. Les Arvicolidés et les amphibiens (35 et 106 pièces) forment un contingent appréciable. Dans l'ensemble, le froid modéré reste assez humide.

Le renne manque presque complètement dans les Éboulis 7/8 et la Couche 8 où un petit nombre de débris osseux appartient à de gros Mammifères. Les effectifs de la microfaune sont importants pour ces deux niveaux:

M. arvalis-agrestis	40 pièces
Microtus nivalis	26 piéces
Bufo sp. et *Rana sp.*	500 pièces
Arvicola scherman	40 pièces
Arvicola terrestris	4 pièces
Discoglossus sp.	1 pièce

Le froid n'a pas varié mais l'humidité paraît augmenter. L'étude sédimentologique ne confirme pas cet accroissement; les rapaces font début et les autres espèces aviennes: l'outarde (*Otis tetrax*), la perdrix grise (*Perdix perdix*), le grive draine (*Turdus viscivorus*) et les Corvidés (*Coracia graculus; Coleus monedula*) sont comestibles. On peut se demander si, à l'exemple des oiseaux précédents, les amphibiens n'auraient pas servi de nourriture à l'homme.

Depuis les Éboulis 8/9 jusqu'aux Éboulis 10/11, la faune demeure très pauvre: moins de 30 pièces au total.

De la Couche 11 à la Couche 14, les gros Mammifères reviennent en force; rongeurs et oiseaux se raréfient tandis qu'amphibiens et poissons disparaissent complètement.

Rangifer tarandus, très répandu dans la Couche 11 (599 pièces), est suivi par *Equus caballus* (359 pièces). Ces deux espèces qui représentent respectivement 62,0% et 37,1% de l'ensemble de la faune sont accompagnées par quelques restes de Bovinés, de sanglier et de cerf élaphe; notons enfin le retour du lièvre variable.

Des éboulis pratiquement stériles séparent ce niveau archéologique d'avec la Couche 12. Dans celle-ci le renne (129 pièces), moins abondant en valeur absolue, représente néanmoins 74,0% de l'ensemble; le cheval arrive ensuite (21,2%), le complément étant apporté par les Bovinés et un débris de bouquetin. Au-dessous de cette strate de nouveaux éboulis stériles surmontent la Couche 13. Sur les 224 pièces qu'elle contient, 221 appartiennent au renne (98,7%) et le reste au cerf élaphe.

La Couche 14 est surmontée par des éboulis d'où l'on a extrait, uniquement, une grosse quantité d'ossements de *Rangifer tarandus* (410 pièces; 100%). Le renne est encore en tête dans la Couche 14 où il représente 99,0% des 2.000 éclats osseux recueillis, cerf élaphe, chevaux et Bovinés s'y trouvent en quantités négligeables.

On ne saurait rien dire des niveaux archéologiques pauvres en fossiles (Éboulis 8/9 à 10/11); par contre les Couches 11 à 14 posent un délicat problème: le matériel riche quant au nombre demeure pauvre en espèces. *R. tarandus* et *E. caballus* forment à eux seuls 99% de la faune de la Couche 11 où le renne domine largement (62%). Une répartition aussi anormale est certainement due au choix de l'homme, aussi est-il préférable de ne pas conclure. Dans les niveaux inférieurs, les Equidés se raréfient puis disparaissent au profit du renne dont le pourcentage passe de 62 à 100%. Cette répartition serait-elle le fait des chasseurs où des conditions locales? L'extrême pauvreté des rongeurs et des oiseaux ne permet pas de résoudre ce problème dont la solution relève de la sédimentologie et de la palynologie. Dans l'interprétation du climat, à dessein, j'ai laissé de côté les oiseaux trouvés dans les couches aurignaciennes (tab. XL). Chaque espèce est représentée sauf exception, par un trop petit nombre d'exemplaires pour un niveau archéologique déterminé, enfin peu d'entre elles sont véritablement significatives. La présence de la perdix (*Perdix perdix*) et l'outarde barbue (*Otis tetrax*) dans les Couches 7 et 8 s'accorde bien avec le caractère de steppe tempérée froide, assez humide, de ces niveaux. La présence d'oiseaux de haute montagne, le Chocard des Alpes et le pipit spioncelle (*Coracia graculus* et *Anthus spinoletta*), dans un gisement de plaine apporte une note rude.

Pour en finir avec l'interprétation climatique, il reste à placer les résultats précédents dans la séquence würmienne mais une telle enterprise demande beaucoup de prudence. Pour des raisons purement méthodologiques, les données du géologue ne recoupent pas toujours celles du paléontologiste. Ainsi, d'après l'étude des sédiments, la partie supérieure jaune des Éboulis 3/4 correspond à un épisode froid et sec tandis que leur partie inférieure rouge se serait déposée pendant une période humide et chaude. Après le retrait des débris de *Rangifer tarandus* pour les motifs déjà indiqués, la faune des Eboulis 3/4 ne contient plus que 95 pièces comprenant 6 espèces qu'il est impossible de répartir entre les deux niveaux du sédiment: les échantillons ainsi réalisés ne seraient plus réprésentatifs – au sens statistique du terme – et leur interprétation perdrait toute sa valeur. Pour le paléontologiste qui ne *peut* pas scinder sa faune en deux, il reste un «adoucissement marqué du climat» au lieu des deux épisodes, l'un froid et sec, l'autre humide et chaud, mis en évidence par le géologue. Inversement, les Couches aurignaciennes 11, 13, et 14, très riches en débris osseux, appartenant à une ou deux espèces, ne peuvent fournir aucune interprétation climatique.

Quand on dispose d'un matériel osseux abondant par la quantité et le nombre des espèces – c'est le cas du Noaillien et du Périgordien IV – on peut établir dans chaque couche archéologique trois divisions – supérieure, moyenne, et inférieure – qui permettent de suivre les vicissitudes du climat. Elimination de l'espèce dominante choisie par l'homme dans une faune suffisamment variée au plan spécifique, établissement de groupes représentatifs, répartition des espèces par biotype, utilisation de la microfaune et des oiseaux, ainsi se trouvent définies la méthode, les possibilités, et les limites de l'interprétation climatique de la faune.

Nous savons qu'au Proto-Magdalénien froid et peu humide succède l'adoucissement du Périgordien VI qui s'accentue nettement pendant le dépôt des Éboulis 3/4. Cette période «tempérée» se retrouve dans les gisements proches de l'Abri Pataud. Laugerie-Haute, aux Eyzies, Les Jambes, près de Périgueux (Laville 1964b; Laville et Thibault 1967), Abri du Facteur à Tursac (Bouchud, Laville, Leroi-Gourhan, *in* Delporte 1968). Les divergences mineures, explicables par des phénomènes de contamination organique, portent essentiellement sur les dates fournies par le C-14 pour les Abris Pataud et du Facteur; en outre l'amélioration constatée dans l'étude sédimentologique est plus forte pour le premier abri que pour le second. La concordance reste très bonne et l'on peut tenir pour valable le terme «d'oscillation de Tursac» proposée pour cet adoucissement du climat. En ce qui concerne le Périgordien IV, l'interprétation proposée par Bouchud (1966). «froid atténué, un peu humide» reste confirmée par notre travail actuel; l'accord rest bon avec la sédimentologie, mais pour (H. Laville 1964a) le Périgordien IV s'est formé sous un climat «froid et sec.»

Quant aux Couches aurignaciennes, nos conclusions recoupent celle du sédimentologue, mais ce dernier place un second épisode «doux et humide» vers 32,600 B.P. (Éboulis 10/11 et Couche 11). A titre d'hypothèse de travail, il le tient pour l'équivalent de «l'interstade d'Arcy» (Leroi-Gourhan, *in* Delporte 1968). Le paléontologiste n'a rien à dire sur ce point pour des motifs purement méthodologiques: l'abondante faune de la Couche 11 (911 pièces, carnivores ubiquistes exclus) qui renferme 62,1% de renne et 37,1% d'Equidés ne permet pas de se prononcer en l'absence d'autres espèces.

Si j'ai insisté sur les divers points de désaccord, ce n'est point pour critiquer les recherches de nos collègues mais pour souligner qu'il reste encore beaucoup à faire dans toutes les disciplines si l'on veut aboutir à des résultats cohérents dans l'étude des paléoclimats.

REMERCIEMENTS

La faune de l'Abri Pataud a été déterminée et étudiée par l'auteur de ce travail, avec l'aide de Mme P. Bouchud (†). Les photographies sont dues à M. R. Simon. Les calculs nécessaires à l'établissement des tableaux de fréquences de distribution, de moyennes, de limites de variation ont été faits par Mme Mannu qui a réalisé en outre les divers graphiques. La figure n°1 est due à Mme P. Bouchud (†) et la figure n°2 à Mme Delamare.

RESUME

Les couches proto-magdaléniennes, aurignaco-périgordiennes, et noailliennes de l'Abri Pataud ont livré une importante quantité de débris osseux dans laquelle *Rangifer tarandus* représente 80 à 98% de la masse totale, selon le niveau archéologique considéré. Le reste se compose de: *Cervus elaphus, Capreolus capreolus, Bos primigenius, Bison priscus (?), Capra ibex, Rupicapra rupicapra, Sus scrofa, Equus germanicus, Equus gallicus, Equus hydruntinus et Elephas primigenius*; les rongeurs, les oiseaux et les amphibiens, présents dans diverses couches périgordiennes, sont très répandus dans les niveaux aurignaciens 7 et 8.

L'abondance des restes de *Rangifer tarandus* a permis d'étudier la conservation différentielle des divers éléments du squelette et de calculer un coefficient de probabilité de découverte d'un segment osseux déterminé. En outre, on a montré que l'espèce dominante, au moins pendant le Paléolithique supérieure, correspondait à un choix humain et ne traduisait nullement des conditions climatiques particulières.

Les vicissitudes du climat sont mises en évidence par les changements observés dans la composition de la faune régionale dont on a écarté l'espèce dominante. La multiplication des Cervidés autres que le renne, cerf élaphe et chevreuil, se produit pendant les périodes plus douces et humides, tandis que leur remplacement par les espèces de montagne, bouquetin et chamois s'observe lors du retour à des conditions rigoureuses. Grâce à ces remarques, une oscillation climatique tempérée (Éboulis 3/4) a été mise en évidence à l'Abri Pataud; c'est «l'oscillation de Tursac». Une seconde période tempérée, «l'interstade d'Arcy», révélée par l'étude sédimentologique, ne se retrouve pas au niveau de la faune trop appauvrie au point de vue specifique.

SUMMARY

Levels yielding proto-Magdalenian, Aurignaco-Périgordian, and Noaillian materials at the Abri Pataud have provided a very large quantity of bone remains. *Rangifer tarandus* represents 80% to 90% of the total number in the strata studied. The other species are: *Cervus elaphus, Capreolus capreolus, Bos primigenius, Bison priscus (?), Capra ibex, Rupicapra rupicapra, Sus scrofa, Equus germanicus, Equus gallicus, Equus hydruntinus,* and *Elephas primigenius.* Rodents, birds, and amphibia are present in all Upper Périgordian horizons but they are more numerous in the Aurignacian 7 and 8 levels.

Owing to the plentiful reindeer remains, it was possible to study the differential preservation of the various skeletal parts and to calculate a coefficient of probability of recovery of a specific bony segment. In addition, we have pointed out the fact that the most numerous species, at least during the Upper Palaeolithic, was chosen by man and was not the result of particular climatic conditions.

The vicissitudes of the climate come to light when changes are observed in the regional fauna other than the predominant species. Aside from reindeer, the increase of the Cervidae, red deer and roe deer, occurs during the moister and milder periods, whereas their replacement by the mountain species, ibex and chamois, is noticeable when rigorous climatic conditions return. Thanks to these observations, evidence of a moderate climatic oscillation, called the «Tursac Oscillation,» was brought to light at the Abri Pataud, (Eboulis 3/4). A second relatively temperate period, the «Interstade d'Arcy,» mentioned in the chapter on the sediments was not confirmed because the corresponding level did not yield a sufficient number of species of fauna.

LA FAUNE DE L'ABRI PATAUD

Scientific Name	*Common English Name*	*Scientific Name*	*Common English Name*

MAMMALS

Cervus elaphus	Red deer	
Capreolus capreolus	Roe deer	
Rangifer tarandus	Reindeer	
Bos primigenius	Extinct species; aurochs, wild ox	
Bison priscus	Extinct species, bison	
Ovibos moschatus	Musk-ox	
Capra ibex	Ibex, bouquetin	
Rupicapra rupicapra	Chamois	
Sus scrofa	Wild boar	
Equus germanicus	Extinct species; horse	
Equus gallicus	Extinct species; horse	
Equus hydruntinus	Extinct species; wild ass	
Elephas primigenius	Extinct species; mammoth	

BIRDS

Larus argentatus	Herring gull
Otis tetrax	Great bustard
Gyps fulvus	Griffon vulture
Aegypius monachus	Black vulture
Gypaëtus barbatus	Bearded vulture
Otus scops	Scops owl
Lagopus lagopus	Willow grouse
Lagopus mutus	Ptarmigan
Perdix perdix	Partridge
Columba oenas	Stock dove
Turdus viscivorus	Mistle thrush
Anthus spinoletta	Water pipit
Motacilla sp.	Wagtail
Corvus corax	Raven
Coleus monedula	Jackdaw
Coracia graculus	Alpine chough
Aquila chrysaëthus	Golden eagle
Haliaetus albicilla	White-tailed eagle
Charadrius apricarius	Golden plover

RODENTS

Lepus variabilis	Variable hare; snow hare
Microtus arvalis	Common vole
Microtus agrestis	Field vole
Microtus nivalis	Snow vole
Microtus sp.	Vole (?)
Microtus anglicus	No common name; extinct species
Pitimys subterraneus	Pine vole
Arvicola scherman	Vole rat
Arvicola sp.	Rat (?)
Eliomys quercinus	Garden dormouse
Apodemus sylvaticus	Long-tailed fieldmouse
Microtus nivalis	Snow vole

AMPHIBIANS AND FISH

Bufo sp.	Toad
Rana sp.	Frog
Discoglossus sp.	Painted frog
Salmo sp.	Salmon

BIBLIOGRAPHIE

Allain, J.
1952. «Un coup de merlin préhistorique,» *Bull. Soc. Préh., Fr.,* t. 49, no. 1-2, pp. 26-29.

Banfield, A.W.
1961. *A Revision of The Reindeer and Caribou, genus Rangifer.* Nat. Mus. Canada, Biol. Serv. no. 66, Bull. no. 177, 137 pp. Ottawa.

Baumann, F.
1949. *Die freilebenden Säugetiere der Schweiz.* 1 vol., 485 pp. Bern.

Bouchud, J.
1961. «Etude de la faune du gisement des Cottés (Haute-Vienne),» *L'Anthropologie,* t. 65, pp. 258-270.

1964. «Découverte d'un crâne de Renne fossile dans la grotte Bernard (commune de Saint-Martin-de-Caralp) près de Foix (Ariège),» *C.R. Acad. Sci. Paris,* t. 258, pp. 4305-4307. 1 pl., bib., 7 réf.

1966. *Essai sur le Renne et la climatologie du Paléolithique moyen et supérieur.* 1 vol., 300 pp., 71 tab., 55 fig., 13 pl., bib. 12 pp. Imp. Magne, Périgueux.

1967. « Etude d'un crâne de Renne fossile *(Rangifer guettardi Desmarest)* découvert dans le sud de la France,» *Problèmes actuels de Paléontologie (Evolution des Vertébrés),* no. 163, pp. 557-566, 3 tab., 2 pl., 40 réf., rés. angl. Coll. Inter. C.N.R.S.

1968a. «L'Abri du Facteur à Tursac (Dordogne). II - La faune et sa signification climatique,» *Gallia-Préhistoire,* t. 9, fasc. 6, pp. 113-121, 5 tab. 6 réf.

1968b. «Les Cervidés et les Equidés du gisement quaternaire des Abîmes de la Fage (Corrèze),» *C.R. Somm. Soc. Géol. Fr.,* fasc. 6, pp. 191-192, 7 réf.

Bouchud, J., et P. Wernert
1961. «Remarques sur les formes de bois de Renne recueillis dans les loess d'Achenheim près de Strasbourg et dans les stations paléolithiques du sud-ouest de la France,» *C.R. Acad. Sci. Paris,* t. 252, pp. 378-381, 5 réf.

Boule, M., et L. de Villeneuve
1927. *La Grotte de l'Observatoire à Monaco.* Archives Inst. Pal. Hum., Mém. 1, 105 pp. 13 fig., 26 pl.

Carte, A.
1863. «On the Remains of Reindeer Which Have Been Found Fossil in Ireland,» *J. Geol. Soc. Dublin,* vol. 10, pp. 103-107, 7 tab.

Cheynier, André
1949. *Badegoule, station solutréenne et proto-magdalénienne.* Archives Inst. Pal. Hum., Mém. 23, 230 pp., 114 fig. Masson, Paris.

Combier, J.
1956. *Solutré. Les fouilles de 1907 à 1925.* 1 vol., 222 pp., 32 fig., réf. 7 pp. J. Patissier, Mâcon.

Cuvier, G.
1823. *Recherches sur les ossements fossiles . . .* t. 4, pp. 89-94; voir aussi l'édition de 1835. Paris.

Degerbøl, M.
1957. «The Extinct Reindeer of East-Greenland *(Rangifer tarandus groenlandicus subsp. nov.)* Compared with Reindeer from Other Arctic Regions,» *Acta Arctica,* fasc. 10. København.

Degerbøl, M., and H. Krog
1959. «The Reindeer *(Rangifer tarandus L.)* in Denmark. Zoological and Geological Investigations of the Discoveries in the Danish Pleistocene Deposits,» *Biol. Skr. Dan. Vid. Selsk.,* Bd. 10, nr. 4, 165 pp., rés.

Delporte, H.
1968. «L'Abri du Facteur à Tursac (Dordogne). I - Etude général,» *Gallia-Préhistoire,* t. 9, fasc. 1, pp. 1-112, 63 fig., 92 réf.

Desmarest, A. G.
1822. Tableau encyclopédique méthodique. *Mammalogie,* 2° part., pp. 447, Paris.

Dupont, M.E.
1872. *L'homme pendant les âges de la pierre dans les environs de Dinant-sur-Meuse.* 1 vol. J. Baillières, Paris.

Ericson, D.B., M. Ewing and G. Wollin
1964. «The Pleistocene Epoch in Deep-Sea Sediments,» *Science,* vol. 164, no. 3465, pp. 723-732.

Flerov, C.C.
1933. Review of «The Palearctic Reindeer or Caribou,» *J.Mammalogy,* vol. 14, no. 3, pp. 433-458.

1934. «A New Paleolithic Reindeer from Siberia,» *J. Mammalogy,* vol. 15, no. 3, pp. 239-240.

1952. «Faune de l'U.R.S.S: Mammifères,» *Moschidae et Cervidae.* vol. 1, no. 2, 247 pp. Pub. Acad. Sci. U.R.S.S., trad. angl.

Flerov, C.C., and M. Zablotski
1961. «On the Causative Factors Responsible for the Change in the Bison Range,» *Bull. Moscow Soc. Nat.,* vol. 66, pp. 99-109.

Gripp, K.
1943. «Geologie des Fundpunktes Stellmoor,» *in* A. Rust, «Die alt- und mittelsteinzeitlichen Funde von Stellmoor,» Archäol. Inst. Deutsch. Reich., 1 vol, 242 pp., 107 pl., 34 fig. Neumünster.

Gromova, V.
1949. «Histoire des chevaux (genre *Equus*) de l'ancien monde,» *Trav. Inst. Pal. Acad. Sc. U.R.S.S.,* t. 18, trad. franc. Pietresson de Saint-Aubin, B.R.G.M. Orléans-La Source.

Guérin, C.
1966. «Les Ruminants du gisement quaternaire des Abîmes de la Fage à Noailles (Corrèze),» *C.R. Somm. Soc. Géol. Fr.,* fasc. 11, pp. 340-341.

Guettard, J.E.
1768- *Mémoires sur les différentes parties des sciences et*
1783. *des arts,* t.1, pp. 29-80, pl. V et VI.

Guthrie, R.D.
1967. «Differential Preservation and Recovery of Pleistocene Large Mammals Remains in Alaska,» *J. Paleontology,* vol. 41, pp. 243-246, 5 fig.

Heim de Balsac, H., et R. Guislain
1955. «Evolution et spécialisation des Campagnols du
genre *Arvicola* en territoire français,» *Mammalia,* t.
191, no. 3, pp. 367-390, 6 fig.

Henri-Martin, Dr. B.
1907-   *Recherches sur l'évolution du Moustérien dans le*
1910.   *gisement de La Quina; l'industrie osseuse.* 1 vol.,
315 pp., 67 pl. Schleicher, Paris.

Hokr, Z.
1951. «A Method of the Quantitative Determination of
the Climate in the Quaternary Period by Means of
Mammals Association,» Sbornik of the Geol. Surv.
of Czechoslovakia, vol. 18, *Paleontology,* 19 pp., 2
plates.

Jacobi, A.
1931. *Das Rentier.* Zool. Anz. Erg., Bd. 96, 247 pp.

Kalkhe, H.D.
1960. «Die Cervidenreste aus den Altpleistozäne Sanden
von Mosbach (Biebrich-Wiesbaden),» *Abh. Deutsch.
Akad. Wissen. Berlin,* nr. 7, pp. 44-72, 12 tab.

Kelsall, J.P.
1957. *Continued   Barren-Ground   Caribou   Studies.*
Canadian Wildlife Service, Wildlife Manag. Bull., ser.
I, no. 12, 146 pp. Ottawa.

Koby, F. Ed.
1959a. «Contribution au diagnostic ostéologique différentiel de *Lepus timidus* Linné et de *Lepus europaeus*
Pallas,» *Verhdlg. naturf. Gesellsch. Basel,* t.70
n° 1, pp. 19-44, 5 fig.

1959b. «Les Renards magdaléniens de la grotte de la Vache
avec remarques sur le diagnostic dentaire différentiel
des genres *Vulpes* et *Leucocyon,» Bull. Soc. Préh.
Ariège,* t. 14, pp. 26-34.

1960. «Contribution à la connaissance des Lièvres fossiles
principalement de ceux de la dernière glaciation,»
Verhlg. naturf. Gesellsch. Basel, t.71, n° 1, pp. 149-
173, 6 fig.

1964. «Ostéologie de *Rupicapra pyrenaïca* d'après les
restes de la caverne de la Vache,» *Préh. Spél.
Ariégeoises,* t. 19, pp. 15-31, 10 fig.

Laperrousaz, E.M.
1960. «Les problèmes de l'origine des manuscrits
découverts près de la Mer Morte, à propos d'un livre
récent,» *Numen,* vol. 7, fasc. 1, pp. 26-76, 143 réf.

1961. «Remarques sur l'origine des dépôts d'ossements
d'animaux trouvés à Qumrân,» *Rev. Hist. Relig.,*
no. 3, 9 pp.

Lartet, L., and H. Christy
1875. *Reliquiae Aquitanicae.* 1 vol., 204 pp., 34 fig., 1
atlas with 83 pl. London.

Laville, H.
1964a. «Recherches sédimentologiques sur la paléoclimatologie du Würmien récent en Périgord,» *L'Anthropologie,* t. 68, no. 1-2, pp. 1-48 et no. 3-4, pp.
219-252, 26 fig., 59 réf.

1964b. «Etude géologique du gisement de La Chèvre,» *in*
R. Arambourou et P.E. Jude, *Le gisement de La
Chèvre à Bourdeilles (Dordogne).* 1 vol. 132 pp.,
Imp. Magne, Périgueux.

Laville, H., et C. Thibault
1967. «L'oscillation climatique contemporaine du Périgordien supérieur à burins de Noailles dans le
sud-ouest de la France,» *C.R. Acad. Sci. Paris,* t.
264, pp. 2364-2366.

Lavocat, R.
1966. *Faunes et flores préhistoriques de l'Europe occidentale.* Ouvr. Coll., 1 vol., 478 pp., 137 pl., N.
Boubée, Paris.

Leroi-Gourhan, A. (Mme.)
1968. «L'Abri du Facteur à Tursac (Dordogne). III -
Analyse pollinique,» *Gallia-Préhistoire,* t. 9, fasc. 1,
pp. 123-132. 1 dép., 21 réf.

L'Heritier, Ph.
1954. *Traité de génétique.* t. 1, 345 pp., 58 fig., 115 réf.
P.U.F., Paris.

Martin, Dr. R.
1968.   *Les mammifères fossiles du gisement quaternaire de
Villereversure (Ain). Carnivores, Canidés et Equidés.* Trav. Lab. Géol. Fac. Sc. Lyon, 153 pp., 41
texte-fig., 36 tab., bib. par chapitre.

Mathew, W.D.
1901. *Fossil Mammals of the Tertiary of Northern Col-
orado.* Amer. Mus. Nat. Hist. Mem., vol. 1, pp.
355-457.

Miller, G.S.
1912. *Catalogue of the Mammals of Western Europe.* 1
vol., 1000 pp., 213 fig.

Muller, A.H.
1951. «Grundlagen der Biostratonomie,» *Abh. Deutsch.
Akad. Wissen. Berlin,* Kl. Math. u. allg. Naturw.,
Jahr. g., nr. 3, p. 40.

Ognev, S.I.
1963. Mammals of U.S.S.R. and Adjacent Countries, vol.
5: Rodents; transl. S. Monson, Jerusalem.

Olsen, S.J.
1960. *Post-cranial and Skeletal Characters of Bison and
Bos.* Papers of the Peabody Museum, Harvard
University, vol. 35, no. 4, 12 pp., 24 fig.

Peï, W.C.
1937. «Le rôle des animaux et des causes naturelles dans
la cassure des os,» *Pal. Sinica.* (Ce travail n'a pas pu
être consulté.)

Peyrony, Denis
1932. «Les abris Lartet et du Poisson à Gorge d'Enfer
(Dordogne),» *L'Anthropologie,* t. 42, pp. 241-258,
11 fig.

Peyrony, Denis, et E. Peyrony
1938.   *Laugerie-Haute.* Arch. Inst. Pal. Humaine, n° 19,
81 pp., 56 fig., 7 pl. h. t.

Prat, F.
1968.   *Recherches sur les Equidés pléistocènes en France.*
Thèse de Doctorat ès Sc. Nat., ronéo., 669 pp., 126
tab., 149 fig., bib. 26 pp.

Rivière, R.

1904. «Conservation des ossements humains et des ossements d'animaux dans les gisements préhistoriques.» *Bull. Soc. Préh. Fr.*, t. 1, pp. 154-157.

Skuncke, F.

1953. *Om möjligheterna att förbättra metoderna Renskötseln.* 1 vol., 18 pp. Danderyd, Stockholm.

Sokolov, I.I. (en russe)

1937. «Variations du crâne en fonction de l'âge, du sexe et de la race chez le renne sauvage et le renne domestique,» *L'Industrie soviétique du renne,* vol. 9, pp. 1-100.

Sothwell, J.A.

1953. «An Approach to the Paleoecology of Mammals,» *Ecology*, vol. 36, pp. 327-337.

Suire, C.

1969. *Contribution à l'étude du genre* Canis *d'après des vestiges recueillis dans quelques gisements pléistocènes du sud-ouest de la France.* Thèse de Doctorat

Géol. approf.; (option Pal.), 162 pp., 213 tab., 68 fig., 2 dp.

Toots, H.

1964. «Sequence of Disarticulation in Mammalian Skeletons,» *Contributions to Geology,* vol. 3, no. 2, pp. 37-39, 3 fig., 3 réf.

1965. «Random Orientation of Fossils and its Significance,» *Contributions to Geology,* vol. 4, pp. 59-62.

Vallois, H.V., H. Alimen, C. Arambourg, A. Schreuder, G. Henri-Martin, J. Berlioz, et J. Bouchud

1958. *La grotte de Fontéchevade.* Archives Inst. Pal. Hum., Mém. 29, 262 pp. 16 pl.

Van Valen, L.

1964. «Relative Abundance of Species in Some Fossil Mammals Faunas,» *American Naturalist*, vol. 98, pp. 109-116.

Weigelt, J.

1927. *Rezente Wibertierlichen und ihre Paläogiologische Bedeutung.* 1 vol., 227 pp. Max Weg, Leipzig.

V

The Molluscan Fauna

S. Peter Dance

ZOOLOGY DEPARTMENT
NATIONAL MUSEUM OF WALES
CARDIFF, UNITED KINGDOM

At the invitation of Professor H. L. Movius, Jr., I spent a week during September 1969 studying the large collection of molluscan shells excavated at the Abri Pataud. Most of the material was identified on the spot but some was borrowed for illustrative purposes and for further study. Studied in isolation from the site such material can be misinterpreted, especially by someone with no archaeological background. The ancillary information acquired on the site, as well as the non-marine molluscan material collected in the immediate vicinity, helped me to reach conclusions on the provenance of the excavated material which I believe are relevant and possibly significant. I am most grateful to Professor Movius for inviting me to study the molluscan material at the site, as well as for his advice and encouragement during and after my visit. For granting me leave of absence from my official duties I am likewise most grateful to the Director and Council of the National Museum of Wales.

The material from the Abri Pataud is grouped for convenience into three categories: (1) non-marine shells of contemporary or later ages; (2) fossil shells; and (3) recent marine shells. The remains of non-marine shells provide a limited amount of ecological and climatic information; the fossils, though few in number and kind, are significant archaeologically as they include specimens pierced for suspension; the marine molluscan shells, comprising the bulk of the material, are of paramount importance archaeologically, since many of them are pierced, and all must have been transported considerable distances.

RECENT NON-MARINE SHELLS

Remains of non-marine molluscs were found at several levels and comprised shells of 11 identifiable species and numerous unidentifiable fragments. In table I the number of specimens found in each level is given; species prefixed by * were also found living close to the site in September 1969.

The five species not found living close to the site are widespread in France and probably do live in the vicinity. With the exception of *Helix aspersa* it is unlikely that any of the species listed were once eaten by primitive humans.[1] The conspicuously striped shell of *Theodoxus fluviatilis* is the only one which is likely to have been utilized by prehistoric man for personal adornment. Some of the specimens could be adventitious introductions. *Cecilioides acicula* is a blind, subterranean snail found all over Europe. It requires a moist but adequately drained situation where soil is washed out to leave chinks and tunnels between the stones; the tiny snail insinuates itself into these narrow spaces and in the tracks of decayed roots and worm burrows (Quick 1935). Exceptionally, it may travel long distances underground. While working the Lower Loam of Milton Street Pit, Swanscombe (Kent, England), A. S. Kennard found a single specimen living at a depth of 18 feet from the surface; it had reached that depth by traveling down the hole left by a decayed tree root (Kennard 1944, p. 158). It is not suggested that all the land snails reached their respective levels in this way, since their empty shells could have been washed into subterranean cavities by rain action; this could account for the presence of all the shells in Level 5: Upper.

The presence of *Theodoxus fluviatilis, Pomatias elegans,* and *Chilostoma cornea* at various levels cannot be accounted for so easily. *Theodoxus fluviatilis* is a calcicole species found in clean rivers and

[1] The single shell of *Helix aspersa* from Éboulis 4-5 looks very fresh and is probably adventitious. Two similar shells of the same species were picked up on the site by workmen during my stay.

TABLE I
NON-MARINE SHELLS

Species	Éboulis 1-2	Level 2	Level 3	Level 4: Upper	Level 4: Middle	Level 4: Lower	Éboulis 4-5	Level 5: Upper	Éboulis 6-7	Level 7	Level 8
Theodoxus fluviatilis (L.)	–	–	–	–	1	–	–	–	–	–	–
Pomatias elegans (Müller)	–	–	1	1	–	1	–	–	–	–	–
Anisus leucostomus (Millet)	–	–	–	–	–	–	–	–	–	1	–
Pupilla muscorum (L.)	–	–	–	–	–	–	–	1	–	–	–
Oxychilus cellarius (Müller)	–	1	–	–	–	1	–	–	–	–	–
Oxychilus draparnaudi (Beck)	1	–	–	–	–	–	–	18	–	–	–
Cecilioides acicula (Müller)	–	–	–	–	–	–	–	30	–	–	–
Clausilia bidentata Ström	–	–	–	–	–	–	–	3	–	–	–
Hygromia hispida (L.)	–	1	–	–	–	–	–	–	–	2	–
Chilostoma cornea (Draparnaud)	3	1	–	–	–	–	1	–	1	1	2
Helix aspersa Müller	–	–	–	–	–	–	1	–	–	–	–

TABLE II
FOSSIL SHELLS

Species	Level 2	Level 3	Level 4: Middle	Level 5: Upper	Level 5: Middle	Level 8	Level 12
Ptychopotamides papaveraceus (Basterot)	2P	–	–	–	–	–	–
Tympanotonos margaritaceus (Brocchi)	–	5P+1	–	–	–	–	–
Pirenella plicata (Bruguière)	–	4P	–	–	–	–	–
Lissoceratoides sp.	–	–	7P	–	–	–	–
Hippuritacea	–	–	–	–	–	–	fr
Cyclothyris difformis (Valenciennes in Lamarck)	–	2	2	3+fr	1+fr	fr	–
Echinoid (diademoid)	1P	–	–	–	–	–	–

P = pierced specimen; fr = fragment

streams; it could have been picked up in the nearby Vézère River.[2] *Pomatias elegans* is one of the commonest land snails in the Les Eyzies vicinity. Its shell is about as large as a small *Littorina* with subdued but attractive markings, and one would expect it to have been utilized for ornamental purposes; apparently it was not so utilized. If the irregular hole in the single specimen from Level 4: Lower is not fortuitous it would be reasonable to expect more than one pierced shell to have turned up. As this species lives at present on the very edge of the site it is possible that shells could have fallen into the

excavations while digging was in process. *Chilostoma cornea* is a common land snail around Les Eyzies today and also lives on the edge of the site. It is not large enough to be worth gathering for food and no pierced shells have been found. The two shells from Level 8, however, have the appearance of great antiquity and are almost certainly contemporaneous. *Anisus leucostomus* is a freshwater snail which prefers places liable to dry out completely for short periods. It could have been derived from a temporary puddle or ditch and is not likely to have lived in the Vézère.

FOSSIL SHELLS

Fossil shells of three gastropod species, an unidentifiable ammonite species, and an unidentifiable hippurite fragment were found at several levels (table II). Remains of a fossil brachiopod species and an echinoid were also found and are recorded here for completeness.

The gastropods are of Lower Miocene age and are found in the Aquitanian and Burdigalian deposits of the Bordeaux region. Some are pierced, presumably for suspension (fig. 1, nos. 6-8). The diademoid echinoid from Level 2 has been pierced for suspension in the same way as that from La Ferrassie (Aurignacian III) figured by Oakley (1965). The *Lissoceratoides* have holes in their centers (fig. 1, no. 12), but ammonites of this type may lose their early whorls without human intervention. Similar specimens from the Forneau du Diable, Bordeilles (Solu-

trean III) are in the museum at Les Eyzies and have been illustrated by Oakley (1965). The brachiopods, all referable to the variable *Cyclothyris difformis*, are Cretaceous in origin. Too hard and brittle for piercing, they could have been utilized in some way other than for suspension as ornaments. Rhynchonellid brachiopods "were among the ornamental fossils used by the Upper Palaeolithic cave-dwellers of Grimaldi" (Oakley 1965). It is possible that one or two of the shells discussed under the next heading are really fossils of Pleistocene or Pliocene age (e.g., *Phalium saburon* and *Neverita josephinia*). The material is too scanty and too poorly preserved to decide the question; and, as the majority of the shells discussed are apparently not fossils, these few doubtful ones do not affect the general conclusions drawn from the assemblage as a whole.

RECENT MARINE SHELLS

Most of the marine shells are broken and many samples consist mainly of fragments. With few exceptions, however, it has been possible to identify every species represented (table III). Because of the fragmentary nature of much of the material, it is often impossible to determine how many once-complete

[2] A pierced shell of this species has been recorded from the Magdalenian deposits at La Madeleine, a few kilometers to the north of the Abri Pataud (Fischer 1932). According to Cordier (1955, p. 44) it was probably washed into the site by the flood waters of the Vézère. This seems unlikely as the shell was pierced (and it would have been thick and strong when fresh). Five shells of the similar *Theodoxus jordani* (Sowerby), all pierced, have also been recorded from Palaeolithic deposits at the rock-shelter of Ksâr 'Akil, Lebanon (Altena 1962). To the primitive occupants of these rock-shelters the shells of *Theodoxus* may have seemed just as attractive as some marine shells; and they were much easier to obtain.

specimens are contained in a sample. Consequently the exact number of specimens recovered from each level is usually impossible to assess. Most of the species are common today along the west coast of France but some are unknown there. *Cypraea pyrum* (fig. 1, no. 14) and *Cypraea lurida* (fig. 1, no. 13) are well known inhabitants of the Mediterranean and range southwards far down the coast of West Africa; fragments of *Homalopoma sanguinea* have been dredged off the Atlantic coast of France, but the species is common in shallow water in the Mediterranean; and *Neverita josephinia* (fig. 1, no. 11) is exclusively a Mediterranean species. There is nothing novel about the presence of Mediterranean species at the Abri Pataud site; comparable material has been recorded from other archaeological localities in the Dordogne.

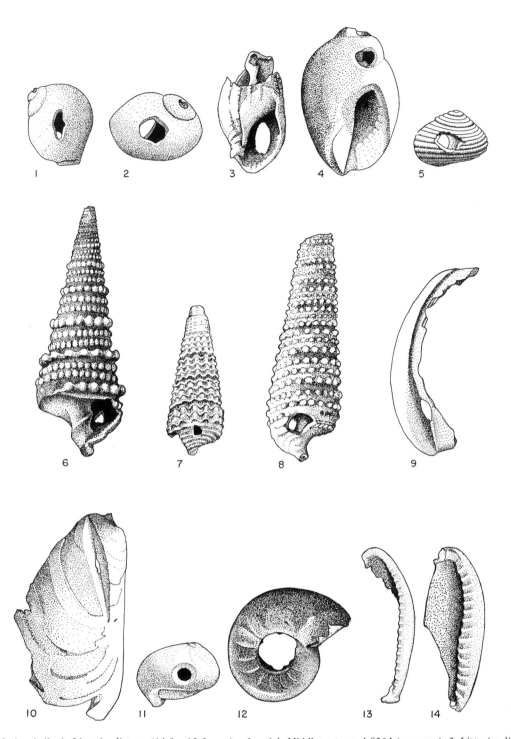

Figure 1. Marine shells. 1. *Littorina littorea* (14.0 x 12.5 mm.) – Level 4: Middle; cat. no. 4-8364 (common). 2. *Littorina littoralis* (13.0 x 12.0 mm.) – Level 4: Middle; cat. no. 4153 (very common). 3. *Nassarius reticulatus* (20.0 x 11.5 mm.) – Level 4: Upper; cat. no. 11,811. 4. *Nucella lapillus* (24.0 x 16.0 mm.) – Éboulis 4-5; cat. no. 11,065. 5. *Homalopoma sanguinea* (4.5 x 6.0 mm.) – Level 3; cat. no. 1362-B. 6. *Tympanotonos margaritaceus* (41.0 x 16.5 mm.) – Level 3; cat. no. 11,797. 7. *Pirenella plicata* (24.5 x 9.0 mm.) – Level 3; cat. no. 697. 8. *Ptychopotamides papaveraceus* (37.0 x 11.5 mm.) – Level 2; cat. no. 2770. 9. *Phalium saburon* – lip fragment (31.5 mm.) – Level 4; Upper; cat. no. 4-5773. 10. *Callista chione* – fragment (34.0 mm.) – Level 4: Upper; cat. no. 6488. 11. *Neverita josephinia* (14.5 x 11.0 mm.) – Level 5: Upper; cat. no. 3363. 12. *Lissoceratoides* sp., (3.0 x 10.0 mm.) – Level 4: Middle; cat. no. 9622. 13. *Cypraea lurida* – fragment (26.0 mm.) – Level 4: Upper; cat. no. 3533. 14. *Cypraea pyrum* – fragment (26.5 mm.) – Level 4: Upper; cat. no. 4-3793.

Fossil shells: nos. 6-8 and 12. *Mediterranean forms:* nos. 5, 11 (hole–natural), 13, and 14. *Pierced for suspension:* a. With rough irregular hole: nos. 1-8; b. With smooth hole: nos. 9 and 10–elongated.

TABLE III

RECENT SHELLS

Species	Level 14	Éboulis 13-14	Level 7	Level 5: Lower	Level 5: Upper	Éboulis 4-5	Level 4: Lower	Level 4: Middle	Level 4: Upper	Éboulis 3-4	Level 3
Patella vulgata L.	—	—	—	—	—	—	—	—	—	—	frs
Gibbula sp.	—	—	—	—	—	—	—	frs	—	—	—
Homalopoma sanguinea (L.)	—	—	—	—	—	—	—	—	—	3P	1P
Littorina littoralis (L.)	1P + frs	2	1	1P + frs	frs	—	2	14P + frs	20P + frs	—	—
Littorina littorea (L.)	—	—	—	—	—	—	2	1P + frs	2P + frs	—	—
Turritella communis Risso	—	—	—	—	—	—	frs	—	—	—	—
Neverita josephinia (Risso)	—	—	—	—	—	—	—	—	1P	—	—
Naticina poliana (Chiaje)	—	—	—	—	—	—	—	—	13 + frs	—	—
Natica sp.	—	—	—	—	—	—	—	—	frs	—	—
Cypraea pyrum Gmelin	—	—	—	—	—	—	—	—	fr	—	—
Cypraea lurida L.	—	—	—	—	—	—	—	—	fr	—	—
Phalium saburon (Bruguière)	—	—	—	—	—	—	—	—	fr P	—	—
Nucella lapillus (L.)	—	—	—	—	—	1P	—	1P + frs	2P	—	—
Nassarius reticulatus (L.)	—	—	—	—	—	—	—	—	1P + 1	—	—
Antalis vulgare (da Costa)	—	—	—	—	—	—	—	—	frs	—	—
Antalis entalis (L.)	frs	—	—	frs	frs	—	—	fr	fr	—	—
Pecten maximus (L.)	—	—	—	—	—	fr	fr	frs	frs	—	—
Chlamys sp.	—	—	—	—	—	—	frs	frs	—	—	—
Laevicardium crassum (Gmelin)	—	—	—	—	—	—	—	frs	—	—	—
Callista chione (L.)	—	—	—	—	—	—	—	—	2P	—	—
Venerupis rhomboides (Pennant)	—	—	—	—	—	—	—	—	1	—	—
Macoma balthica (L.)	—	—	—	—	—	—	—	—	—	—	1

SHELLS PIERCED BY HUMANS

Ten species are represented by shells pierced by human agency. The holes in them are of two types; a. smooth and elongate (*Phalium saburon, Callista chione*) (fig. 1, nos. 9 and 10); b. rough and irregular (*Homalopoma sanguinea, Littorina littoralis, Littorina littorea, Nucella lapillus, Nassarius reticulatus, Ptychopotamides papaveraceus, Tympanotonos mar-* garitaceus, Pirenella plicata) (fig. 1, nos. 1-8). Type a is evidently the result of a filing action; type b was probably produced by a pointed percussion instrument.[3] Collectively this is not a colorful group of shells, and they may have attracted attention less for their colors than for their shapes.

THE ORIGINS OF THE SHELLS

All the non-marine shells belong to species which are common and widespread in Central France today. The fossil gastropod shells could have been brought from the Bordeaux region, and the ammonites and brachiopods could be locally derived. The relatively large numbers of *Littorina littoralis, Littorina littorea*, and *Nucella lapillus* indicate that most of the shells came from the Atlantic coast of France, these three species being unknown in the Mediterranean. Those species which occur in the Mediterranean and are absent from the Atlantic coast are each represented by a single shell or fragment. This suggests that the Upper Palaeolithic inhabitants of the Abri Pataud were prepared to travel to the Atlantic coast for shells but depended on contacts with other tribes for shells from the Mediterranean.

THE SHELLS AS INDICATORS OF CLIMATE

The composition of the non-marine molluscan fauna seems to have remained basically the same for a very long time. *Chilostoma cornea*, which has a southern distribution and is the only species represented which is not living today in the British Isles and Scandinavia, occurred in several levels from Level 8 upwards, and is still living in the Abri Pataud vicinity. This suggests that the climate ca. 20,000 to 34,000 years ago was much the same as it is today. Assuming that most of the marine shells came from the Atlantic coast of France, there is again no indication that the then-prevailing climate was any more rigorous then than it is at present.

[3] The hole in the single *Pomatias elegans* from Level 4: Lower is probably fortuitous, the shell being relatively thin and brittle. That in the single *Neverita josephinia* from Level 4: Upper is smooth, circular, and bevelled (fig. 1, no. 11) and is obviously the work of a boring, predatory mollusc, possibly one of its own kind. Of course this shell would have been admirably suitable for stringing and was probably utilized for that purpose.

REFERENCES

Altena, C.O. van Regteren
  1962. "Molluscs and Echinoderms from Palaeolithic Deposits in the Rock-Shelter of Ksâr 'Akil, Lebanon," *Zool. Meded.*, Leiden, vol. 38, no. 5, pp. 87-99.

Cordier, Gérard
  1956. "Les mollusques des faluns de Touraine: ont-elles été colportées en Dordogne à l'âge du Renne?" *Bull. Soc. Etudes et Recherches Préh.*, Inst. Pratique Préhist., Les Eyzies, no. 6, pp. 39-55. 2 tables.

Fischer, P.-H.
  1932. "Coquilles récoltées par M. Peyrony dans les gisements préhistoriques de la région des Eyzies (Dordogne)," *J. Conchyliol.*, vol. 76, no. 3, pp. 258-261.

Kennard, A.S.
  1944. "The Crayford Brickhearths," *Proc. Geol. Assoc.*, vol. 55, pt. 3, pp. 121-169.

Oakley, Kenneth P.
  1965. "Folklore of Fossils," *Antiquity*, vol. 39, no. 153, pp. 9-16 and no. 154, pp. 117-125.

Quick, H.E.
  1935. "On the Occurrence of *Caecilioides acicula* Müller, in the Gower Peninsula," *Proc. Swansea Sci. Field Nat. Soc.*, vol. 1, pt. 9, pp. 286-289.

VI

Pollen Composition of the Abri Pataud Sediments

The Last Glacial Compared with the Postglacial Pollen Stratigraphy of the Beune Valley

Joakim J. Donner

DEPARTMENT OF GEOLOGY AND PALAEONTOLOGY
UNIVERSITY OF HELSINKI, FINLAND

In connection with the archaeological excavations of the Abri Pataud sediments, samples were collected in 1965 and 1967 for pollen analysis, since it had earlier been shown elsewhere that similar cave sediments can be used for palynological studies of vegetational history. If the studied cave or rock-shelter was occupied when the sediments were formed, as at the Abri Pataud, then the results can be linked with the cultural development based on artifacts. Thus, a direct correlation between archaeology and vegetational history can be established. An interpretation of the Last Glacial pollen composition of the Abri Pataud sediments is, however, possible only if the Postglacial pollen stratigraphy is known in the area. Without such a comparison with the more recent vegetational history conclusions about the meaning of the pollen composition in Last Glacial sediments are hazardous. Since no Postglacial pollen diagrams were available from the neighborhood of Les Eyzies, suitable sediments from sites as near as possible to the Abri Pataud were studied. These sites, sampled in 1961, 1962, and 1963, are in the Beune Valley and the valley of the Petite Beune, a tributary to the Beune. The pollen stratigraphy of the three sites studied was described elsewhere (Donner 1969); only the longest and most complete Postglacial pollen diagram will be included and discussed here, before the results from the Abri Pataud sediments are considered.

POSTGLACIAL POLLEN STRATIGRAPHY OF THE BEUNE VALLEY

The site included here, Beune Valley II (figs. 2 and 3), is immediately south of the stream, about 3 km. east of Les Eyzies and about 0.5 km. east of the road junction where the road to Sarlat forks off the road which follows the Beune Valley. The valley bottom is here flatter than farther downstream near Les Eyzies, and it has a fen vegetation typical for limestone areas. The present vegetation is strongly influenced by human disturbance; raised stream banks and disturbed soil profiles, and various fen types are found. Peat formation has ceased almost entirely, except in some of the *Phragmites* fens flooded in winter. The original fen vegetation probably had in the main a vegetation with *Phragmites, Frangula, Salix, Molinia*, with some *Carex* and *Juncus*[1] (Wilson and Smith

1964). The slopes on each side of the valley have woods with *Quercus pubescens*, mixed with some *Q. ilex*, and in other places with *Q. robur* and *Carpinus*.

The samples were taken in 1963 with a modified Hiller sampler, in which an aluminum groove was inserted in the 50 cm.-long chamber. Thus, 50 cm.-long cores could be taken each time. On top of the gravel reached at 15.6 m. depth there was first some stony sand, silt, and silty sand up to about 14.2 m., then followed mud interrupted by layers of silty and sandy mud, and a layer of sand underneath a dark peat covered with the 1.50 m. thick topmost hard silt, difficult to penetrate. In the preparation of the samples for pollen analysis the acetolysis method was used for all samples, whereas mineral matter was removed with HF and, if they contained coarse particles, by decanting. The samples were stained

[1] See Appendix on p. 172 for list of common names.

with safranin and mounted in glycerol jelly. The total amount of pollen counted in each sample was usually 200 to 300, in some parts of the diagram even less than 100, excluding pollen of aquatics and spores. The sediments were poor in pollen throughout the diagram.

Two diagrams were drawn on the basis of the pollen counts. In the first (fig. 2) the curves for the trees and shrubs were given as well as a total diagram, in which the relationship between trees and shrubs, *Cyperaceae* and the nontree pollen, NAP, excluding *Cyperaceae*, is shown. The percentages in this diagram, as well as in the other one, were based on the total pollen sum, excluding the pollen of the aquatics and the spores, which are shown in the second diagram, together with the identified NAP types (fig. 3). In order to exclude the strong influence of the local vegetation on the diagram at the sampling site in the valley, and thus get an idea of the general vegetational history, particularly of the forest, the percentages for the trees and shrubs in figure 2 were also based on the tree pollen sum, excluding *Corylus* and other shrubs. The curves based on these percentages were drawn with lines. As the tree pollen sum was often very low in the counted samples, these percentages are, in many parts of the diagram, averages based on counts from several samples, from as many as five samples in two cases. The curves are therefore smoother than those in black, which are based on the total pollen sum of trees, shrubs, and non-tree pollen.

The vegetational history of the Beune Valley area is, on the basis of the Beune Valley II diagram, similar in its main outlines to that found in areas in France bordering the Atlantic coast, from southwestern France up to central and northern France, and also to that in Britain, as noted in the more detailed description of the pollen stratigraphy (Donner 1969). The similarity of the vegetational history within the area mentioned above led to the use in France of the zoning introduced for Britain by Godwin (1956, 1960; Godwin, Walker, and Willis 1957), and it was also used for the Beune Valley II diagram. The vegetational history differs, on the other hand, from that in the central parts of the Massif Central, to the east of the area studied in Dordogne, where the division of the diagrams was done on the basis of the zoning for Germany by Firbas (1949) in the investigations by Lemée (1953a, 1953b, 1956) and Lang and Trautmann (1961). The Beune Valley II diagram starts with the first Postglacial Zones IV and V, not separated here, which have a *Pinus* dominance in contrast to the *Betula* dominance in Central Europe, also found in some parts of the Massif Central. The beginning of Zone IV is marked by the steep rise of the *Corylus* curve, here coinciding with a rise of

the *Quercus* curve, the beginning of the *Ulmus* curve and a decline of the *Pinus* curve. The radiocarbon dating of the zone boundary V/VI from a 50 m.-long sample, GrN-4492, gave an age of 9040 ± 60 B.P. (fig. 2). In the middle of Zone VI the *Tilia* curve rises and the amount of *Corylus* decreases. The rise of the *Alnus* curve marks the beginning of Zone VIIa, which ends with the decline of the *Tilia* curve. In those diagrams in which *Ulmus* is insignificant this decline has been used as marking the zone boundary VIIa/VIIb (Paquereau 1964), and has been found to coincide with the *Ulmus* decline where it occurs, as farther north in the Somme Valley (Nilsson 1960). The zone boundary VIIb/VIII was placed at the level where the *Carpinus* curve starts, but the upper part of the Beune Valley II diagram, from the zone boundary VIIa/VIIb upwards, fits better into the pattern of vegetational history in Lévenzon in the southern part of the Massif Central, described by Lemée (1953a). A slight rise in the NAP curve (excluding *Cyperaceae*) shows the first signs of deforestation. A maximum of the *Fagus* curve is followed by a maximum of *Alnus* and the subsequent marked rise of the NAP curve, within Zone VIIb, shows intensified deforestation at the beginning of the Iron Age at ca. 600 B.C., whereas the zone boundary VIIa/VIIb corresponds to the beginning of the Neolithic (Lemée 1953a). The increase of *Pinus* near the top of the diagram is similar to that found in the Cantal, where it is dated to the last century (Lemée 1956). The deposition of silt in the Beune Valley on top of organic sediments is probably caused by the intense deforestation, which allowed running water to transport freshly exposed top layers of the soil into the river and down the valley. Frequent winter floods furthered the spread of silts over the valley floor on each side of the stream.

On the basis of the Beune Valley II diagram it can be assumed that the area had forests already at the time when the oldest Postglacial deposits in the valley were formed, and that *Quercus* and *Corylus* were already present at the time of the *Pinus*-dominated forests of Zones IV and V. The spread of mixed-oak forests was, however, in the beginning of Zone VI, here as elsewhere in Western Europe, initiated by a short period of a strong expansion of *Corylus*, before the spread of *Tilia* and somewhat later of *Alnus*. The sediments and the relatively high proportion of NAP, of which *Cyperaceae* formed an important part, show that there was a fen vegetation in the Beune Valley throughout Postglacial time, even if all the slopes and hills in the surroundings were covered with forest. The deforestation, which became intense in the middle of Zone VIIb, had a drastic influence on the pollen composition by decreasing the relative amount of pollen of trees and shrubs to almost 10 percent in some samples. The low percentages for trees and shrubs is surprising when it is taken into account that large areas still are, and probably have been during the last hundred years, wooded. On the other hand, a large part of the NAP in the upper part of the diagram consists of *Cyperaceae* pollen, produced by the fen vegetation surrounding the site studied, whereas there is only a slight increase in other NAP types towards the top of the diagram. The local influence of the vegetation on the pollen composition at the site studied does not affect those curves of trees and shrubs where the percentages were based on the total tree pollen sum. Therefore, these curves reach higher percentages than the curves based on the total pollen sum, especially in the uppermost part of the diagram, and they reflect the general regional changes in forest composition on higher ground surrounding the valley.

LAST GLACIAL POLLEN COMPOSITION OF THE ABRI PATAUD SEDIMENTS

Most of the samples for pollen analysis were collected from the open trench at the Abri Pataud excavations in September 1965 by Dr. H. Bricker, and only a few additional samples were taken by Dr. Bricker and the author from the same trench in July 1967. Every precaution was taken to obtain as clean samples as possible. The samples were taken from the cleaned wall of the trench, then sieved and placed in airtight glass jars of 7.5 decilitres. The samples collected consisted of only sand and finer material. The laboratory treatment of the samples, which mainly consist of material derived from the Cretaceous limestone into which the rock-shelter was formed, began with the removal of $CaCO_3$. A sample of 2-2.5 decilitres was treated with cold 10 percent HCl. Then the remaining coarse particles were removed by decanting and the sample was left standing in cold HF for 2 to 3 days. Then followed the HF method in which the sample is boiled with HF. The removal of colloidal SiO_2 by heating with HCl was often repeated several times. After the mineral matter had been removed, the acetolysis method was used and the sample was then stained and mounted in glycerol jelly. The amount which remained of the original sample of 2-2.5 decilitres was usually enough for about five slides.

The samples were extremely poor in pollen and, in spite of several slides being counted for each sample, the total amount of pollen counted remained low. It was as low as 33 in several samples and only in one

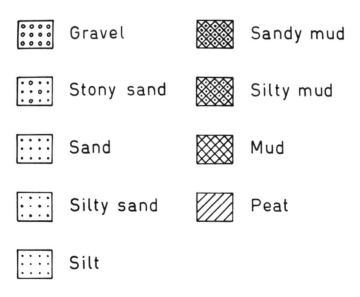

Figure 1. Symbols used in pollen diagrams from the Beune Valley.

BEUNE VALLEY II (DORDOGNE), 1963

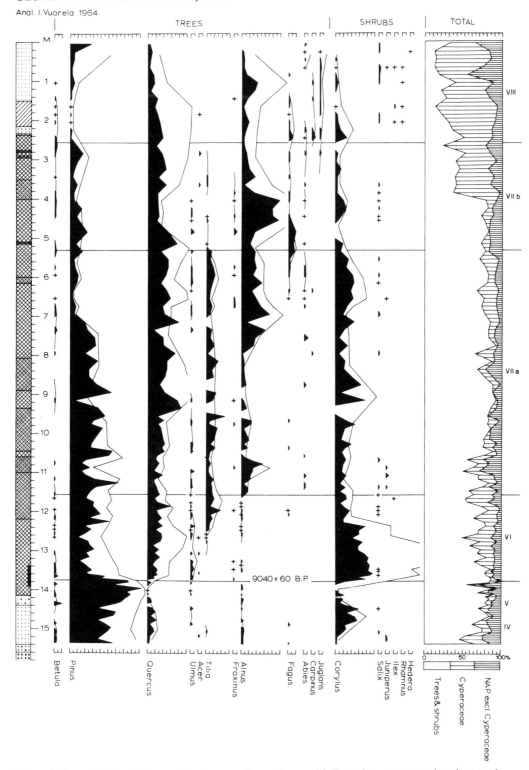

Figure 2. Beune Valley II: tree pollen diagram. Curves drawn with lines give percentages based on total tree pollen (excluding *Corylus*). Radiocarbon date for zone boundary V/VI is for sample GrN-4492.

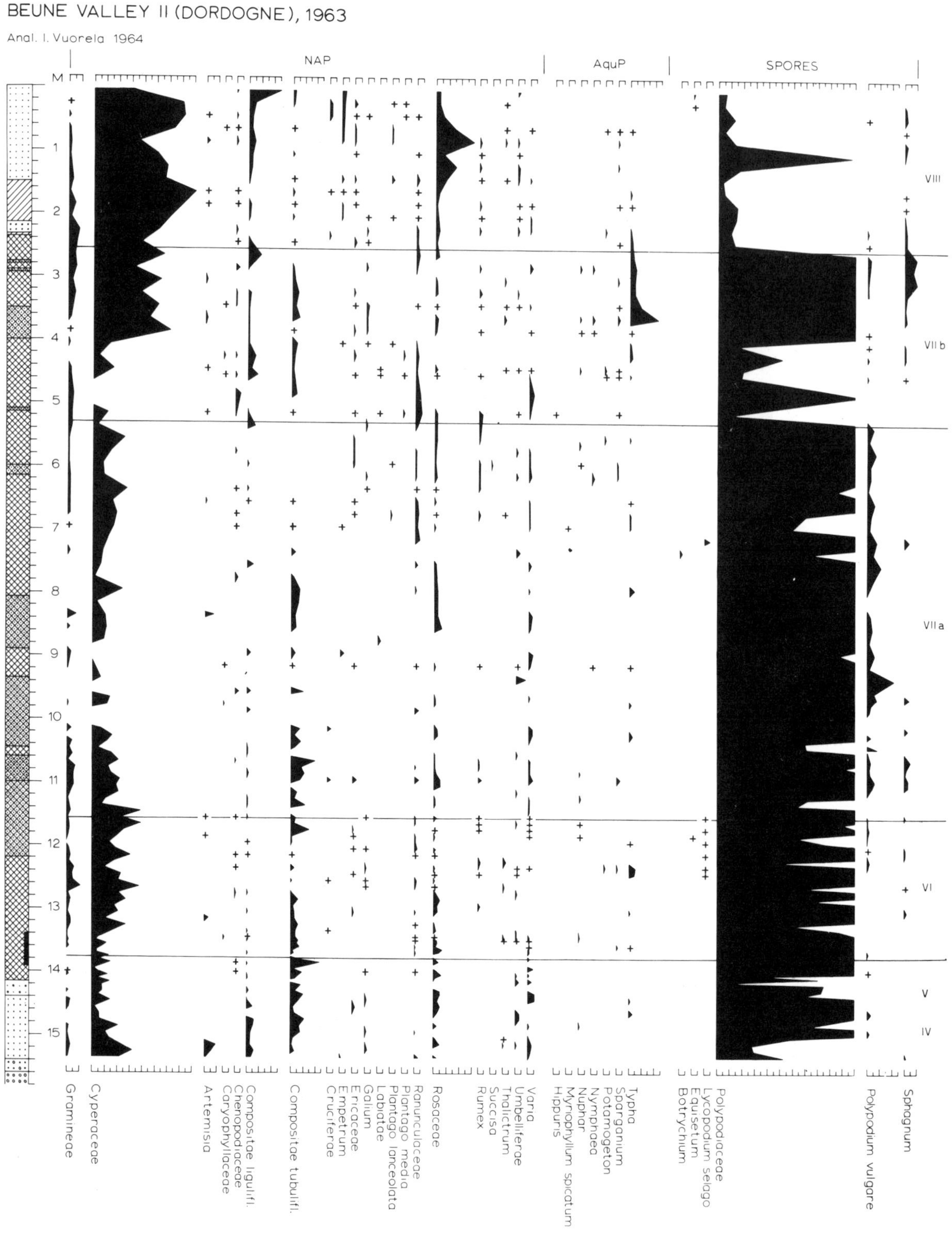

BEUNE VALLEY II (DORDOGNE), 1963

Anal. I. Vuorela 1964

Figure 3. Beune Valley II: non-tree pollen diagram.

were as many as 150 counted. Because of the low number of pollen grains counted in each sample a pollen diagram with all pollen types included was not drawn for the Abri Pataud. The number of pollen types found in the samples was largely dependent on how many pollen grains were counted. An increase in the total amount of pollen also means an increase in pollen types found, and thus many fluctuations, especially in some of the less frequent pollen types in the profile, are without significance in an interpretation of the vegetational history. The results of the pollen counts are given in table 1, in which the analyzed samples are listed in stratigraphic order. The percentages for pollen of trees and shrubs and for non-tree pollen, NAP, as well as for spores, were based on the total amount of pollen, also given in the table. Slides were also made for other samples, but since they did not contain enough pollen for counting they were not included in the table. In addition to the table, a simplified pollen diagram was also drawn (fig. 4). On the left the Upper Palaeolithic levels are given for the occupation layers in the stratigraphic column. The average thicknesses for the horizons are given according to the calculations made by Farrand (personal communication). In the diagram, curves were drawn for only the two most common tree pollen types, *Pinus* and *Quercus*. In addition to these two, a total diagram shows the relationship between trees and shrubs on the one hand and non-tree pollen on the other. Of the nontree pollen the curve for *Compositae* was included in the diagram, in which the percentages of *Artemisia* are marked separately. After the numbers giving the total pollen sum for each sample, the radiocarbon dates for some of the horizons are listed as estimated by Vogel and Waterbolk (1967, p. 116, see also Movius 1963, 1966) on the basis of a series of samples dated from the Abri Pataud. The dates show, if correct, that the average rate of sedimentation in the rock-shelter varied through time.

The dry cave sediments studied in the Abri Pataud, into which the pollen grains became embedded, form a very different matrix from the Postglacial peats and muds of the Beune Valley. A poor preservation of the pollen grains in the sediments of the Abri Pataud could be expected as the sediments were deposited slowly on a dry or damp surface of the rock-shelter and exposed to the air. Some of the pollen grains are, in fact, corroded and badly preserved and difficult to identify, but most are well preserved. When the number of pollen types identified in the rock-shelter sediments are compared with those found in the Beune Valley, it does not seem as if there had been a poorer preservation in the Abri Pataud sediments than in the Postglacial sediments. Twelve tree pollen

types were found in both places, and at the Abri Pataud sediments 23 non-tree pollen types against 20 in the Beune Valley. Thus, there is no marked difference in the number of pollen types found, which indicates that the pollen composition of the rock-shelter sediments of the Abri Pataud is as representative of the Last Glacial vegetation as is the pollen composition of the sediments in the Beune Valley of the Postglacial vegetation. The exposure to the pollen rain was, however, different at the two sites. The site studied in the Beune Valley fen was strongly influenced by the local pollen production of the plants growing at the site, representing through most of the Postglacial Period the fen vegetation in the valley. Pollen of water plants growing in the stream is also present. On the other hand, at the Abri Pataud the pollen composition represents the vegetation of the area outside the south-southwest-facing rock-shelter in which no plants can have been growing, except for some herbs and shrubs near the entrance. The Abri Pataud thus formed a trap open to the pollen from the surrounding vegetation, and since the rock-shelter is slightly raised above the level of the valley floor, it was less affected by the vegetation of plant communities near the stream in the valley. There is, naturally, a total absence of pollen of water plants in the Abri Pataud sediments.

In the interpretation of the Last Glacial pollen composition of the Abri Pataud sediments a comparison with the Postglacial diagram from the Beune Valley shows great differences. In the Abri Pataud diagram the relative amount of trees and shrubs is in most samples below 50 percent, in some parts about 20 to 30 percent, in contrast to the Beune Valley diagram in which the amount of trees and shrubs clearly exceeds 50 percent, except in the uppermost part with human influence. But even here, the main portion of the pollen consists of *Cyperaceae* pollen from the fen vegetation in the valley. Thus, already from the proportions of the main constituents of the pollen, i.e., pollen of trees and shrubs and non-tree pollen, it can be concluded that pollen of open plant communities played a more important role in the Last Glacial diagram. As the number of pollen grains counted per sample was low, not too much importance can be given to the fluctuations found in the percentages, but it is probable that the high percentages of non-tree pollen, mainly caused by *Compositae*, together with a corresponding decrease of tree pollen, in the middle of the diagram were caused by a change in the vegetation. Judging from the ratio of the pollen of trees and shrubs and non-tree pollen, and assuming it to be dependent on the same factors as in diagrams from organic deposits, it is likely that at least part of the tree pollen is from the vegetation surrounding the

ABRI PATAUD, LES EYZIES
Anal. 1966-67

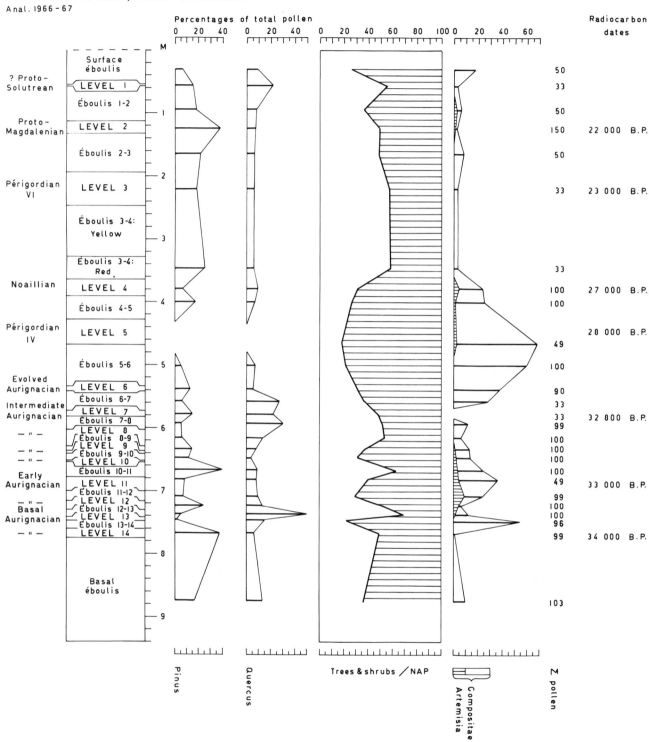

Figure 4. Pollen diagram for the Abri Pataud giving the Upper Palaeolithic levels, average thicknesses of stratigraphic horizons, curves for *Pinus* and *Quercus*, a total diagram of the AP+shrubs/NAP ratio and a curve for *Compositae* with *Artemisia* marked separately. On the right, the total pollen sum for each sample and dates estimated on the basis of a series of radiocarbon determinations from the site (Vogel and Waterbolk 1967).

site. It therefore seems probable that the trees most strongly represented grew in the area, that is *Betula*, *Pinus*, and *Quercus*, whereas all the others occur more sporadically, although some of these, such as *Alnus*, may also have grown in the area. That oak was rather strongly represented, as compared with pine and birch, may be largely due to the calcareous soil. Pine is clearly more strongly represented in areas with acid soils (Bordes, Laville, and Paquereau 1966). The occasional pollen grains of *Carpinus* and *Juglans* hardly represent the Last Glacial vegetation, but pollen of the former has, however, been found in Last Glacial deposits elsewhere in France (Leroi-Gourhan 1965). It may be assumed that throughout most of the time covered by the Abri Pataud sediments, birch, pine (*Pinus silvestris*), and oak, perhaps representing more than one species, grew in the area and that of the shrubs *Juniperus* and *Salix* were also present, and possibly hazel. The deforestation demonstrated in the upper parts of the Beune Valley diagram was caused by widespread forest clearance, but the valley bottom was probably mostly affected by cropping and grazing. During the Postglacial deforestation, the pollen production from the fen vegetation of the valley dominated over the pollen production from the surrounding deforested slopes and hills on the pollen composition at the site studied. In Last Glacial time the situation was different. The streams in the valleys were bordered by gravels and, as seen from the Beune Valley borings, the fens only developed later, during Postglacial time. The Last Glacial parklike forests most likely persisted in sheltered places in the valleys, often protected by steep cliffs, whereas the higher parts between the valleys probably had an open vegetation. The pollen composition of the Abri Pataud sediments thus suggests that the Vézère Valley in front of the site, as well as the lower part of the Beune Valley, formed one of the refugia in which the above-mentioned trees persisted during the Last Glacial Period, a conclusion in agreement with those made earlier about the areas bordering the Massif Central, particularly about the Dordogne (Van Campo and Aymonin 1962; Paquereau 1964; Bordes, Laville, and Paquereau 1966; Planchais 1966). The relatively large amount of non-tree pollen throughout the Abri Pataud diagram suggests that most of the vegetation near the site consisted of open plant communities, perhaps with cold and dry conditions during the period when *Compositae*, including *Artemisia*, was strongly represented, and cool and humid conditions during the periods with more *Gramineae* and *Cyperaceae*. The other pollen types recorded, even if only in small numbers, support this conclusion, as for instance *Alnus* and *Salix*, which were common during periods of greater humidity. Noticeable is the almost total absence of both *Empetrum* and *Ericaceae*.

Of the pollen types often found in steppe samples representing the Last Glacial and also occurring in this profile, may be mentioned *Chenopodiaceae*, *Cruciferae*, *Ephedra*, *Plantago*, *Roseceae*, here mostly *Filipendula*, and *Rumex*, *Thalictrum* and *Urtica*. Of the spores found, those of *Equisetum* are more common in the upper part of the diagram than in the lower. At present *Equisetum palustre* grows in the fens of the Beune Valley. *Polypodiaceae* is, on the other hand, more common in the lower part. In addition, *Sphagnum* spores were found in a number of samples.

The low number of pollen grains counted per sample and the irregular fluctuations in the percentages of the pollen types found make it difficult to trace any changes in the vegetational history. The only possible change seems to be in the middle of the diagram in figure 4, where, during the period beginning with Level 6 and ending with Level 5, a period perhaps indicating a cold climate, during which *Compositae* was dominant and the trees were suppressed, separates two periods during which some trees grew in the area and the climate probably was less rigorous. The upper of these two periods, from Level 4 upwards, was perhaps more humid than the lower, ending at about the time of Level 7. A short climatic fluctuation may have been missed, since the intervals between the analyzed samples in some parts of the diagram represent rather long periods of time, in some instances several thousand years.

As seen from the above discussion, three stages can perhaps be separated in the vegetational history on the basis of the pollen composition in the Abri Pataud sediments. The results are schematically summarized in table 2, in which the radiocarbon dates, the occupation layers, and the Upper Palaeolithic levels are compared with the vegetational history.

TABLE 1 Pollen composition, given as percentages of the total pollen sum, of the Abri Pataud sediments; analyzed 1965-1967.

	Sample number	Betula	Pinus	Quercus	Ulmus	Acer	Tilia	Fraxinus	Alnus	Fagus	Abies	Carpinus	Juglans	Corylus	Salix	Juniperus	Total pollen of trees and shrubs	Cyperaceae	Gramineae	Empetrum
				Tree pollen										Pollen of Shrubs						
Surface éboulis	1	2	6	8	–	2	–	–	6	–	–	–	–	2	–	–	26	14	4	4
Level 1	2	12	15	22	–	–	–	–	–	–	–	–	–	3	–	3	55	18	–	–
Eboulis 1-2	4	2	18	8	–	–	–	–	–	–	2	–	–	2	–	4	36	6	4	–
Level 2	48	–	37	7	–	–	1	–	–	–	–	–	–	1	2	1	49	2	1	–
Eboulis 2-3	7	2	22	6	4	–	–	–	–	2	–	–	–	6	2	4	48	14	8	–
Level 3	8	3	18	6	–	–	–	–	3	–	–	–	–	3	–	24	57	21	15	–
Red éboulis 3-4	10	3	25	6	3	–	3	–	6	–	–	–	–	6	–	6	58	9	–	–
Level 4	B-67	1	7	9	–	–	–	2	1	1	–	–	1	1	1	7	31	3	6	–
Eboulis 4-5	16	–	18	7	–	–	–	–	–	–	–	–	–	–	–	1	26	16	5	2
Level 5	20	4	–	–	–	–	–	–	2	–	–	–	–	4	–	8	18	4	4	–
Eboulis 5-6	21	2	5	7	1	1	–	–	–	–	–	–	1	3	1	–	21	3	2	–
Level 6	22	3	13	5	–	2	–	1	–	–	–	–	–	2	–	5	31	6	–	–
Eboulis 6-7	23	–	6	27	–	3	–	–	–	–	–	–	–	–	–	–	36	9	9	–
Level 7	24	3	15	22	3	–	–	–	–	–	–	3	–	–	–	3	49	9	3	–
Eboulis 7-8	25	1	5	30	–	8	–	–	4	–	1	–	1	1	–	–	51	1	–	–
Level 8	26	19	6	13	1	–	–	–	4	1	–	1	–	6	1	1	53	2	1	–
Eboulis 8-9	23	4	15	8	–	3	1	–	2	–	–	–	–	2	–	2	37	6	3	–
Eboulis 9-10	30	11	12	4	–	–	1	–	1	–	–	–	–	2	–	–	31	–	1	–
Eboulis 10-11	33	5	40	9	–	–	–	–	3	1	–	–	–	1	4	–	63	–	–	–
Level 11	34	4	8	8	–	–	–	2	4	–	–	–	–	–	–	12	38	2	8	–
Eboulis 11-12	37	7	7	9	1	1	–	–	2	–	–	–	–	–	1	1	29	5	7	–
Level 12	38	5	25	13	1	3	–	–	1	–	2	–	–	1	–	1	52	1	7	–
Eboulis 12-13	39	–	5	50	–	12	–	–	–	–	–	–	–	1	–	2	70	–	3	–
Level 13	40	–	1	15	–	–	1	–	1	–	–	–	–	2	1	1	22	–	–	–
Level 14	42	1	39	6	–	1	1	–	–	1	–	–	1	–	1	–	50	–	–	–
Basal éboulis	51	1	16	13	2	1	–	–	–	1	–	–	–	1	–	1	36	5	9	–

Non-tree pollen																					Spores			
Ericaceae	Artemisia	Armeria	Caryophyllaceae	Chenopodiaceae	Compositae	Cruciferae	Dipsacaceae	Ephedra	Galium	Hypericum	Labiatae	Plantago	Polygonum	Ranunculaceae	Rosaceae	Rumex	Thalictrum	Umbelliferae	Urtica	Varia	Equisetum	Polypodiaceae	Sphagnum	Σ pollen
8	–	–	–	4	18	–	–	–	–	–	–	2	–	–	12	–	–	–	–	8	4	–	–	50
–	–	–	–	6	3	–	–	3	–	–	–	–	–	3	3	–	–	–	–	9	36	–	–	33
–	2	–	–	–	4	–	–	–	4	–	–	–	–	–	40	2	–	2	–	–	1	–	–	50
–	1	–	2	2	1	–	–	–	–	–	–	–	–	5	31	3	–	–	–	3	–	1	–	150
–	–	–	–	2	8	2	–	–	–	–	–	4	–	2	2	–	–	–	–	10	18	–	2	50
–	–	–	–	–	3	–	–	–	–	–	–	–	–	–	–	–	–	–	–	3	18	–	–	33
–	–	6	–	3	3	–	–	–	–	–	–	3	–	–	9	3	–	–	–	6	12	–	–	33
–	4	–	–	1	20	16	–	–	7	–	–	1	–	2	2	2	–	2	–	3	–	–	–	100
–	1	–	2	4	24	3	–	–	–	1	–	–	–	1	9	–	–	2	–	4	8	4	1	100
–	2	–	–	–	66	–	–	–	–	–	–	–	–	–	6	–	–	–	–	–	–	–	–	49
–	–	–	1	2	59	1	–	–	–	–	–	–	–	2	1	1	–	2	–	4	9	4	–	100
1	–	–	–	3	38	1	–	–	–	1	1	–	2	3	5	1	–	7	–	–	–	3	–	90
–	–	–	–	3	28	3	3	–	–	–	–	–	–	–	3	–	–	6	–	–	9	33	3	33
–	–	–	–	9	–	–	–	–	–	–	–	–	–	3	12	6	–	–	–	9	3	33	3	33
–	–	–	–	1	12	–	–	–	3	1	–	1	–	7	14	1	–	8	–	1	3	11	–	99
–	–	–	–	4	6	–	–	–	1	–	–	2	–	5	17	6	–	1	–	2	–	7	–	100
–	1	–	–	6	12	–	–	–	–	–	–	3	–	5	19	3	–	–	1	4	–	5	–	100
–	2	–	–	2	12	–	–	–	–	–	–	1	–	6	36	3	–	3	–	3	2	7	1	100
3	3	–	–	1	21	–	3	–	–	–	–	3	–	–	–	–	–	1	–	2	–	2	–	100
–	4	–	–	4	32	–	2	–	–	–	–	–	–	–	4	–	–	–	–	6	–	2	2	49
2	9	1	–	5	15	1	–	–	–	–	–	2	–	4	7	2	–	1	–	10	1	6	1	99
–	4	–	–	3	2	1	–	–	–	–	–	1	–	1	4	–	–	10	–	14	–	1	–	100
–	1	–	–	–	11	–	1	–	–	–	–	–	–	–	2	2	–	–	–	10	–	3	–	100
1	–	2	4	4	57	–	–	–	–	2	–	–	–	–	2	–	–	–	–	6	–	1	–	96
–	–	–	–	–	1	–	–	–	–	–	–	–	–	1	33	3	1	–	–	11	–	1	1	99
–	–	–	–	–	10	–	–	–	–	–	–	5	–	–	20	10	–	–	–	5	–	1	–	103

TABLE 2

Summary of vegetational development in the area surrounding the Abri Pataud.

	Level 1	? Proto-Solutrean	Forest steppe with *Betula,*
22,000 B.P.	Level 2	Proto-Magdalenian	*Pinus*, and *Quercus* mainly
23,000 B.P.	Level 3	Périgordian VI	in sheltered parts of the
27,000 B.P.	Level 4	Noaillian	valleys
28,000 B.P.	Level 5	Périgordian IV	Open plant communities
	Level 6	Evolved Aurignacian	with *Compositae* (cold)
32,800 B.P.	Level 7		
	Level 8		
	Level 9	Intermediate	
	Level 10	Aurignacian	Forest steppe with *Betula,*
33,000 B.P.	Level 11		*Pinus*, and *Quercus* mainly
	Level 12	Early Aurignacian	in sheltered parts of the
	Level 13		valleys
34,000 B.P.	Level 14	Basal Aurignacian	

COMPARISONS WITH LAST GLACIAL VEGETATION IN OTHER AREAS

The sediments at the Abri Pataud represent, according to the radiocarbon determinations, a time of the Middle Weichselian as defined in Britain, where there are several fossiliferous sites in the West Midlands which represent different short interstadials. Together these form the Upton Warren Interstadial Complex, dated to about 50,000 - 23,000 B.P. (West 1968). This complex was preceded and followed by cold periods with glacial advances. The Abri Pataud sediments dating from 34,000 - 22,000 B.P., would thus fall in the younger part of the complex, in which the curve drawn of the climatic change shows a colder period at about 29,000 B.P. separating two interstadials represented by the sites Tame Valley and Brandon (see West 1968, fig. 12.12). On the basis of this comparison, it can be concluded that the Abri Pataud sediments between the Basal Éboulis and the Surface Éboulis were not from the times of extreme cold at the beginning or end of the Middle Weichselian (see fig. 4). In the Netherlands the middle part of the Weichselian (Würm) glaciation, the Pleniglacial, was interrupted by two interstadials, both dated by a number of radiocarbon determinations (van der Hammen, et al. 1967). The first interstadial, Hengelo, began about 39,000 B.P. and ended about 37,000 B.P.; and the second, Denekamp, lasted from about

32,000 B.P. to 29,000 B.P. The cold Pleniglacial vegetational types were either tundra or polar desert, whereas the vegetation during the interstadials was a shrub tundra with birch. A pollen diagram of the cave sediments at the Grotte du Renne, one of the sites in the Arcy-sur-Cure complex in Yonne, at the foot of Morvan, 200 km. southeast of Paris, shows that the Last Glacial vegetation there was open and may be described as steppe (Leroi-Gourhan 1965). Even there a short interstadial, called Arcy, was found, and it has a radiocarbon age of 30,370 B.P. During this interval there was a slight increase of tree pollen, foremost of *Pinus*. Whereas this interstadial corresponds in time with the Denekamp Interstadial in the Netherlands, a subsequent short interstadial found in the diagram and called Paudorf, cannot be correlated with any of the interstadials in the Netherlands. In a pollen diagram of sediments at Combe-Grenal, near Domme, in the Dordogne, representing Würm I and Würm II, in addition to Riss II (Bordes, Laville, and Paquereau 1966), the Last Glacial pollen spectra have low values, 10-20 percent, of tree pollen, mainly *Pinus*, interrupted by intervals during which there was an increase in the tree pollen amount, and deciduous trees were present in addition to *Pinus*. Of the non-tree pollen, *Compositae* was particularly strongly represented during cold periods and *Gramineae* during cool humid periods.

Viewed in the light of the results from the areas discussed above, it becomes clear that the pollen composition found in the Abri Pataud sediments was from a vegetation reflecting comparatively favorable conditions. At the same time that there was a tundra or polar desert in the Netherlands and a steppelike open vegetation in Yonne, there was, at least during interstadials, in some areas around Les Eyzies a forest steppe with mainly birch, pine, and even oak. A comparison with the other areas, however, also shows that the vegetational changes reflected in the Abri Pataud diagram could not with certainty be correlated with any of the interstadials of the Middle Weichselian (Pleniglacial) described above. The period of dry steppe with *Compositae* in the Abri Pataud diagram is, however, likely to represent a cold period between two interstadials. Thus, most of the Abri Pataud diagram would represent interstadial conditions and not the extreme cold climate of the Weichselian. Therefore, in a comparison of the Abri Pataud pollen diagram with Weichselian pollen diagrams from elsewhere this must be taken into account. The difference between the Last Glacial vegetation in the Les Eyzies area and other areas is perhaps overemphasized, since the extremely cold parts of the Middle Weichselian are missing in the Abri Pataud diagram. The fact remains, however, that during this time thermophilous trees, such as oak and possibly alder and hazel, were present in the area and more strongly represented than generally is the case at this time in Western Europe. The Abri Pataud is yet another site which supports the earlier evidence about the existence of Last Glacial refugia in the protected valleys of the areas surrounding the Massif Central, especially in the Dordogne area. The local climatic conditions in the valleys were probably greatly different from those in the more exposed parts of France. The topographical complexity of areas like the Dordogne, however, makes it difficult to determine all the factors influencing vegetational changes, as pointed out by Van Campo and Aymonin (1962) with respect to the Cévennes.

The Last Glacial vegetational history in the Dordogne, as seen from the Abri Pataud diagram and also indicated in the diagram from Combe-Grenal representing Würm I and Würm II, is not only different from that in areas farther north, but also differs from that found in pollen diagrams from the Mediterranean region. In a pollen diagram from lake deposits at Poueyferré in the French Pyrénées, beginning with deposits about 16,000 years old, the pollen composition consisted of about 10 percent trees, mainly pine, and in some samples of the non-tree pollen there was up to 25 percent *Artemisia* (De Vries, Florschütz, and Menéndez Amor 1960). A dry Last Glacial steppe vegetation, in which *Artemisia* was an important element, was also found to have been general during the colder periods of Mindel, Riss, and Würm in Andalusia in southern Spain (Menéndez Amor and Florschütz 1962a; 1964). Interstadial periods during the Würm are shown by the increase of tree pollen, almost totally representing pine. Pollen diagrams from central Italy show that even here there was a cold steppe with *Artemisia* dominating at the end of the Würm, from 25,000 to 15,000 B.P. (Bonatti 1966). Farther east, in Macedonia, Greece, there was also a Last Glacial steppe with *Artemisia*, as seen in a pollen diagram of Würm marl and peat of the Tenagi Philippon (van der Hammen, Wijmstra, and van der Molen 1965).

When the results from the Mediterranean are taken into account in the interpretation of the results from the areas surrounding the Massif Central in southern France, particularly from the Abri Pataud in the Dordogne, the special conditions in the latter area become even more apparent. Similar refugia for thermophilous trees very likely existed in other areas as well, but the valleys of the Dordogne formed one such area during Last Glacial time. It is not probable that the regional differences found in the Last Glacial vegetation are due to differences in the sediments studied, i.e., that cave sediments were studied in southwestern France, whereas organic lake sediments were studied elsewhere. It has been shown, for instance, in northern Spain (Menéndez Amor and Florschütz 1962b, 1963), that pollen analytical results from cave sediments give a picture of the vegetational history comparable with that obtained from organic deposits. To be able to demonstrate possible local, more favorable climatic conditions, as the Last Glacial conditions in the narrow valleys of the Dordogne, the only means, however, is often the pollen analytical study of cave sediments, since lake sediments or peats are lacking. In tracing the areas which formed such sheltered refugia, studies must therefore be directed towards similar areas, in addition to studies of pollen analytically more favorable organic sediments in open country, in which the general regional Last Glacial vegetational history can be studied.

SUMMARY

The pollen composition of the Last Glacial sediments of the Abri Pataud, as compared with the Postglacial pollen diagram from the Beune Valley and with earlier results dealing with the Last Glacial vegetation in the Netherlands, other parts of France and the northern Mediterranean, demonstrates that in addition to a steppe vegetation, probably mainly on the hills, the valley in front of the Abri Pataud also had woodlands. *Betula*, *Pinus*, and *Quercus* grew in the area, and probably also some *Alnus* and *Corylus*. The results confirm the view that some of the valleys in the areas bordering the Massif Central, particularly in the Dordogne, formed refugia in which many trees, including some thermophilous species, persisted during the Last Glacial Period.

ACKNOWLEDGMENTS

The author wishes to thank Professor Hallam L. Movius, Jr., for help and advice throughout the investigation, Dr. Harvey M. Bricker for help in collecting the samples, and Mrs. Irmeli Vuorela for analyzing most of the samples.

APPENDIX

Common Names of Trees, Shrubs, Plants, and Spores Referred to in the Text

Trees

Abies	Fir
Acer	Maple
Betula	Birch
Carpinus	Hornbeam
Fagus	Beech
Fraxinus	Ash
Juglans	Walnut
Pinus	Pine
Quercus	Oak
Tilia	Lime
Ulmus	Elm

Shrubs

Alnus	Alder
Corylus	Hazel
Hedera	Ivy
Ilex	Holly
Juniperus	Juniper
Rhamnus	Buckthorn
Salix	Willow

Non-Arboreal Plants

Armeria	Thrift or Sea Pink
Artemisia	Wormwood, Mugwort, etc.
Carex	Common Sedge
Caryophyllaceae	Chickweed Family
Chenopodiaceae	Goosefoot Family
Compositae	Compositae Family (1)
Cruciferae	Cress Family
Cyperaceae	Sedge Family
Dipsacaceae	Teasel Family
Empetrum	Crowberry
Ephedra	Switch Plant
Ericaceae	Heather Family
Filipendula	Wild Spiraea

Non-Arboreal Plants (Continued)

Frangula	Alder Buckthorn
Galium	Bedstraw
Gramineae	Grass Family
Hypericum	St. John's-Wort
Juncus	Rush
Labiatae	Mint Family
Molina	Purple Moor Grass
Phragmites	Reed Grass
Plantago	Plantain
Polygonum	Knotweed
Ranunculaceae	Buttercup Family
Rosaceae	Rose Family
Rumex	Dock or Sorrel
Succisa	Scabious
Thalictrum	Meadow Rue
Umbelliferae	Wild Carrot Family
Urtica	Nettle

Aquatic Plants (Beune Valley only)

Hippuris	Mare's-Tail
Myriophyllum	Water Milfoil
Nuphar	Pond Lily
Nymphaea	Water Lily Family
Potamogeton	Pond Weed & Other Species (2)
Sparganium	Bur-Reed
Typha	Cat-Tail

Spores

Botrychium	Moonwort
Equisetum	Horsetail
Lycopodium	Club Moss
Polypodiacae	Polybody Fern Family
Polypodium vulgaris	Common Fern
Sphagnum	Bog Moss

(1) This Family constitutes a very large and heterogeneous group of genera with the common characteristic of flowers of the Daisy or Hawkweed type. Since it is virtually impossible to separate the pollen of the various genera, they are generally lumped together in the diagrams under a single heading.

(2) There is no distinctive common name for this genus.

REFERENCES

Bonatti, Enrico
1966. "North Mediterranean Climate During the Last Würm Glaciation," *Nature*, March 5, vol. 209, pp. 984-985.

Bordes, F., H. Laville, and M.-M. Paquereau
1966. "Observations sur le Pléistocène supérieur du gisement de Combe-Grenal (Dordogne)," *Actes. Soc. Linn. Bordeaux*, t. 103. sér. B, no. 10, 19 pp.

De Vries, H.L., F. Florschütz, and Josefa Menéndez Amor
1960. "Un diagramme pollinique simplifié d'une couche de 'gyttja,' située à Poueyferré près de Lourdes (Pyrénées Françaises Centrales), daté par la méthode du radio-carbone," *Proc. Koninkl. Nederl. Akad. Wetensch.*, ser. B, 63, no. 4.

Donner, J.J.
1969. "Holocene Pollen Diagrams from the Beune Valley, Dordogne," *Pollen et Spores*, vol. 11, no. 1, pp. 97-116.

Firbas, Franz
1949. *Spät- und nacheiszeitliche Waldgeschichte Mitteleuropas nördlich der Alpen*. Bd. I, 480 pp. Fischer, Jena.

Godwin, H.
1956. *The History of the British Flora*. 480 pp. Cambridge.
1960. "Radiocarbon Dating and Quaternary History in Britain," *Proc. Royal Society*, ser. B., vol. 153, pp. 287-320.

Godwin, H., D. Walker, and E.H. Willis
1957. "Radiocarbon Dating and Post-Glacial Vegetational History: Scaleby Moss," *Proc. Royal Society*, ser. B, vol. 147, pp. 352-366.

Hammen, T. van der, G.C. Maarleveld, J.C. Vogel, and W.H. Zagwijn
1967. "Stratigraphy, Climatic Succession and Radiocarbon Dating of the Last Glacial in the Netherlands," *Geologie en Mijnbouw*, vol. 46, pp. 79-95.

Hammen, T. van der, T.A. Wijmstra, and W.H. van der Molen
1965. "Palynological Study of a Very Thick Peat Section in Greece, and the Würm-Glacial Vegetation in the Mediterranean Region," *Geologie en Mijnbouw*, vol. 44, pp. 37-49.

Lang, Gerhard, and Werner Trautmann
1961. "Zur spät- und nacheiszeitlichen Vegetationsgeschichte der Auvergne (Französisches Zentralmassiv)," *Flora*, Bd. 150, H. 1, pp. 11-42.

Lemée, Georges
1953a. "Sur la végétation postglaciaire du Lévezon d'après l'analyse pollinique," *Bull. Soc. Bot. Fr.*, t. 100 (Session), pp. 26-29.
1953b. "Observations sur la végétation actuelle et son évolution postglaciaire dans le Massif du Mézenc," *Bull. Soc. Bot. Fr.*, t. 100 (Session), pp. 67-77.
1956. "Sur l'évolution de la végétation dans le Massif du Cantal au tardiglaciaire et au postglaciaire," *Bull. Soc. Bot. Fr.*, t. 103 (Session), pp. 83-94.

Leroi-Gourhan, Arlette and André
1964. "Chronologie des grottes d'Arcy-sur-Cure (Yonne)," *Gallia-Préhistoire*, t. 7, pp. 1-64.

Menéndez Amor, Josefa and F. Florschütz
1962a. "Un aspect de la végétation Espagne Méridionale durant la dernière glaciation et l'Holocène," *Geologie en Mijnbouw*, vol. 41, pp. 131-134.
1962b. "Analisis polínico de sedimentos tardiglaciaires en la Cueva del Tol (Moyá Barcelona)," *Estudios Geologicos*, vol. 18, pp. 93-95.
1963. "Sur les éléments steppiques dans la végétation quaternaire de l'Espagne," *Bol. R. Soc. Española Hist. Nat.* (G), 61, pp. 121-133.
1964. "Results of the Preliminary Palynological Investigation of Samples from a 50 m. Boring in Southern Spain," *Bol. R. Soc. Española Hist. Nat.* (G), 62, pp. 251-255.

Movius, H. L. Jr.
1963. "L'âge du Périgordien, de l'Aurignacien et du Proto-Magdalénien en France sur la base des datations au carbone 14," *Bull. Soc. Mér. Spél. Preh.* (Aurignac et l'Aurignacien: Centenaire des Fouilles d'Edouard Lartet), t. 6-9, pp. 131-142.
1966. "The Hearths of the Upper Perigordian and Aurignacian Horizons at the Abri Pataud, Les Eyzies (Dordogne), and their Possible Significance," *Amer. Anth.*, vol. 68, no. 2, pp. 296-325.

Nilsson, Tage
1960. "Recherches pollenanalytiques dans la Vallée de la Somme," *Pollen et Spores*, vol. 2, pp. 235-262.

Paquereau, Marie-Madeleine
1964. "Flores et climats post-glaciaires en Gironde," *Actes Soc. Linn. de Bordeaux*, t. 101, no. 1, 156 pp.

Planchais, Nadine
1966. "Analyses polliniques en forêt de Prémery (Nièvre)," *Bull. Assoc. Fr. Etude Quat.*, no. 8, pp. 180-190.

Van Campo, M., and G. Aymonin
1962. "Le problème de l'histoire de la flore et de la végétation dans les Cévennes méridionales, vu sous l'angle de l'analyse pollinique," *Flora*, Bd. 152, pp. 679-688.

Vogel, J.C., and H.T. Waterbolk
1967. "Groningen Radiocarbon Dates VII," *Radiocarbon*, vol. 9, pp. 107-155.

West, R.G.
1968. *Pleistocene Geology and Biology with Especial Reference to the British Isles*. 377 pp. Longmans, London.

Wilson, Joan F. and I.M. Smith
1964. A Preliminary Survey of the Vegetation Patterns of the Beune Valley and their Significance. Typewritten report.

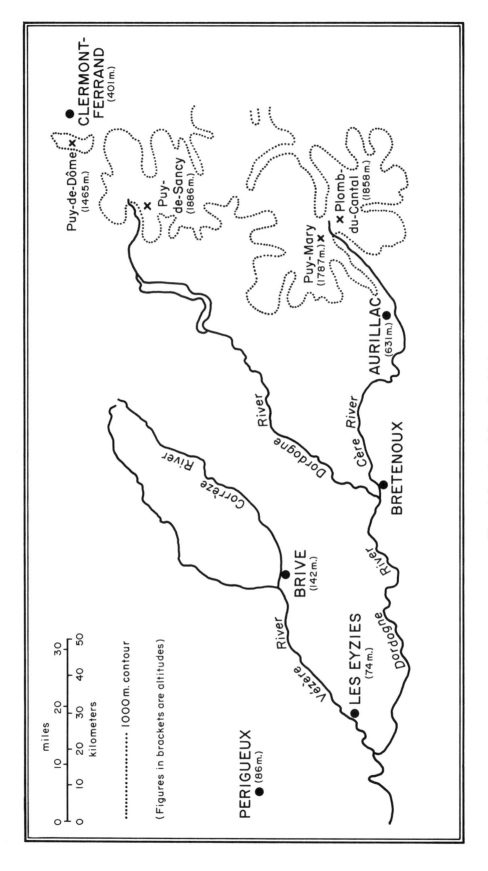

Figure 1. Location of sites referred to in report.

VII

The Last Glacial Environment at the Abri Pataud

A Possible Comparison

Joan F. Wilson

DEPARTMENT OF BIOLOGICAL SCIENCES
UNIVERSITY OF LANCASTER, ENGLAND

The results of the pollen analyses from the occupation levels at Abri Pataud discussed in chapter VI open up the possibility of describing the vegetation types and associated climatic conditions existing in southwestern France during Upper Palaeolithic times. Such investigations are frequently rather inconclusive, and often little more than the broad climatic trends can be determined, especially when the total pollen content of the deposit is small. In this paper, the pollen data are compared with the present-day vegetation at nearby sites where the climate is possibly similar to that at the Abri Pataud during the occupation period. From considerations outlined below, it seems reasonable to suppose that the vegetation types present at the Abri Pataud at that time may be represented today in the Massif Central, and, by identifying the corresponding zones, much more detailed information regarding the vegetation types and climatic conditions can be obtained than would be possible from the pollen alone.

Where can such an area be found? Geological evidence discussed in chapter II indicates that, during the Würm Glaciation, glaciers fed by the ice fields in the Massif Central moved outwards along river valleys such as that of the Dordogne. The valley ice does not, however, appear to have approached within 115 km.

(72 miles) of the Abri Pataud, with the result that the vegetation would never have been subjected to the full rigors of a glacial environment. Moreover, the relatively southern latitude of the area, with consequent high insolation during at least part of the year, would ensure that, at least on south-facing slopes, the periglacial conditions would not have been as continuously severe as at sites in northern Europe.

In order to find an area at a similar latitude where the conditions might be comparable today, it is necessary to ascend to a considerable altitude. The nearest possible site to the Abri Pataud is the upland region of the western Massif Central (fig. 1). Although much more geologically complex than the region around the Abri Pataud, this area has at least one major point in its favor for a comparative study. It is reasonable to suppose that, as the ice moved outwards, the vegetation zones also moved outwards down the valleys in advance of the ice, this trend being reversed as the ice retreated. There is, therefore, a real possibility that at least some of the vegetation assemblages represented at the Abri Pataud for the Last Glacial Period correspond to similar ones in the Massif today at altitudes where the climate may be presumed to be similar.

THE GEOLOGY AND TOPOGRAPHY OF THE MASSIF CENTRAL

Geologically the Massif Central is an extremely complex area, the original granites and limestone strata having been deformed and fractured by Tertiary volcanic activity. In a paper of this type it is obviously impossible to discuss the system in detail, but a few general points are relevant. In the west of the region, with which we are principally concerned,

there is a chain of volcanic peaks and associated phenomena extending from Aurillac in the south to Clermont-Ferrand in the north (fig. 1). These consist of a variety of Tertiary igneous rocks, while the bedrock of the lower areas between the peaks is principally granitic or calcareous.

With such a variety of rock types, the soils developed in the area are highly diverse. These range from relatively infertile acid soils to highly basic soils at greater altitudes.

In addition, the topography of the area is highly variable, as a result of volcanic activity. The steep peaks of the exposed volcanic intrusions contrast sharply with undulating open moorland and grassland at slightly lower altitudes and with the rocky, often steep-sided valleys of the upland area. Thus, in addition to a wide range of soil types, one finds an extremely wide range of slope, aspect, and degree of exposure, and almost any combination of conditions appears to be possible. Within this varied system there is considerable variety in the dominant vegetation type, but it is possible to draw certain general conclusions.

This complex system should be contrasted with the relatively simple system around the Abri Pataud. There the bedrock is almost exclusively horizontally bedded Cretaceous limestone, deeply dissected by steep-sided river valleys, although there are traces of overlying Tertiary deposits of sandstone in some of the plateau areas. The soils developed are, therefore, relatively uniform and the main variation is in slope and aspect. In consequence, the natural vegetation, at least at the present day, tends to be comparatively uniform. It is possible, however, that such differences as do exist were accentuated during the Last Glacial Period.

CLIMATE

The climate of the upland area of the Massif is characterized particularly by the wide fluctuation of temperatures which may be experienced both on a daily and on an annual basis. The winters are long and generally severe, snow remaining on sheltered north-facing slopes until late July at altitudes above 1,700 m. (5,525 ft.). On south-facing slopes, however, the snow usually disappears by the end of May. In the autumn, fresh snow may well be lying by September, especially in sheltered areas. Thus, even in favorable years, the active growing season is likely to be short. During the summer period, the weather above 1,000 m. (3,250 ft.) usually varies between cool, wet periods, with temperatures between 7 and 15°C (45 and 59°F), and shorter hot, dry periods when daytime temperatures, particularly on south-facing slopes, may reach 25 to 30°C (77 to 86°F). It is characteristic of this summer period that, especially on clear days, wide diurnal temperature fluctuations occur, often as great as 25°C (45°F), and relatively few nights pass without ground frost. Such climatic variation, particularly with regard to temperature, will impose severe restrictions on the plant life which will survive in this area, and would be expected to increase the variation between the sites with different topography and soil type.

It may be predicted that similar temperature variations between sites with different orientations would have occurred in the Les Eyzies region during the Last Glacial times. In this context, it is probably worth noting that it is the extremes of temperature experienced at a site, particularly the extremes of low temperature, which will be one of the critical factors in determining which species survive at that locality.

Whether the pattern and magnitude of the precipitation was similar is a different matter. The absence of high land in the immediate vicinity of the Abri Pataud might be expected to reduce the overall precipitation, as is the case today. The presence of ice relatively close, but causing cool air to flow outwards from the Massif and hence cooling any Atlantic airflow, might be expected to increase precipitation towards the values found in the uplands today. Evidence is presented elsewhere in chapter III for the major climatic changes over the period represented by the archaeological remains, but this cannot provide details of the annual pattern of temperature flux and precipitation.

THE UPLAND VEGETATION OF THE MASSIF CENTRAL

The upland vegetation can be broadly divided into two types, the woodlands and the open grasslands and heaths; within these two main types, however, many subdivisions exist.

Woodlands exist up to 1,700 m. (5,525 ft.) in some areas, and it is likely that the present-day tree line in most sectors is an artificial one. To what extent the present forests are representative of the natural vegetation is questionable, since the majority appear to be managed to some extent. The dominant tree species over considerable areas is *Fagus sylvatica*, which is probably native in this area and appears to regenerate freely. Other important types are a variety of conifers: *Pinus* spp., *Picea*, *Abies*, and *Larix* (plate 1). While some of these are native to the area, their present distribution would appear to be mainly the

Plate 1. Dense conifer forest, Plomb du Cantal at approximately 1500 m.

result of forest management. Many other temperate deciduous species are also represented to a lesser extent, notably *Fraxinus excelsior, Acer pseudoplatanus, Acer campestre, Quercus robur, Betula* sp., and *Ulmus* sp.[1] The most frequent shrub species in this forest system are *Corylus avellana, Alnus glutinosa, Cornus mas, Crataegus monogyna, Ilex aquifolium, Rosa* spp., and *Sambucus* sp.

The ground flora within these forests is extremely variable. Where the tree canopy is largely coniferous, the ground flora tends to be sparse, with isolated patches of species such as *Deschampsia flexuosa, Oxalis acetosella,* and *Rubus* spp., and, along road edges and on disturbed ground, a dense growth of ferns of the family *Polypodiaceae.* In areas dominated by deciduous species or mixed conifer-deciduous woodland, the ground flora tends to be much richer, although in dense *Fagus* woodland it is again characteristically sparse. The *Polypodiaceae* are again well represented together with most of the common temperate woodland species typical of deep, moist, relatively eutrophic soils. Along the edges of roads and tracks this flora is enriched by more ruderal species such as *Lotus corniculatus, Scabiosa* spp., *Digitalis purpurea,* and *Silene dioica.*

[1] See Appendix (p. 186) for common names of plant species referred to in the text of this report.

Above the present tree line there is, at most localities, a zone of more open vegetation with scattered conifers and shrub species (plate 2). The most characteristic species of this zone are *Juniperus communis, Sarothamnus scoparius,* and *Genista* sp. There is a generally rich meadow flora including such species as *Viola* spp., *Hieracium* spp., *Festuca rubra, Anthoxanthum odoratum, Scabiosa columbaria, Lotus corniculatus, Dianthus* spp., and *Gentiana lutea,* which persists to the top of all but the steepest peaks.

It is above this level that the greatest diversity of vegetation type occurs, in the absence of the moderating effect of the tree canopy on the environment at ground level. In spite of this diversity of vegetation types in specialized habitats, it is possible to distinguish certain broad trends relevant to the area as a whole. The obvious primary division is that between vegetation on soils over granitic rocks and vegetation on soils derived from more basic volcanic rocks.

In general, the topography of the granite areas is undulating, with moderate slopes, and there is considerable evidence of impeded drainage in many parts. Over considerable areas, which are subjected to grazing by both sheep and cattle, the dominant vegetation is a coarse, relatively species-poor grassland containing *Deschampsia caespitosa, Nardus stricta,* and *Gentiana lutea* (plate 3). In less heavily grazed,

Plate 2. Scrub vegetation above an artificial tree line, Plomb du Cantal at approximately 1700 m.

comparatively well-drained areas, a dry acid heath frequently develops. This is well illustrated in the area to the northeast of the Puy de Sancy. In these heaths, the dominant vegetation consists of *Calluna vulgaris* and *Erica* spp. with some grass species typical of such habitats, such as *Agrostis tenuis* and *Festuca* spp. and a rich bryophyte and lichen flora.

On north-facing slopes and where drainage is impeded, a wetter acid moorland develops. It is characteristic of these areas that peat formation is taking place above the mineral soil. In such places the vegetation is dominated by species of *Vaccinium*, notably *Vaccinium myrtillus*, *V. vitis-idaea*, and *V. uliginosum* with some *Calluna* and *Erica* spp. (plate 4). In disturbed areas, *Juncus* spp. may be locally dominant. This type of vegetation is well illustrated in the area to the east of the Plomb du Cantal.

In rocky stream valleys in the granite areas, which are relatively sheltered, the *Vaccinium* moor vegetation is frequently supplemented by a lush growth of species such as *Genista tinctoria* with *Genistella sagittalis* along road edges.

In areas of extreme waterlogging, small peat bogs may develop. At one site, just below the peak of the Puy de Sancy, there is a small, but well-developed, *Sphagnum* bog with *Eriophorum vaginatum* and *Salix repens* abundant (plates 5 and 6).

On the generally basic soils in the highest, volcanic areas, a rich alpine-type flora develops where grazing and human interference are not severe (plates 7 and 8). The effects of intensive human activity are well illustrated on the Puy de Dôme, where the species composition is considerably reduced as compared with similar areas elsewhere. Typical species occurring at these sites are: *Narcissus pseudonarcissus, Anemone sulphurea, Anemone pulsatilla, Trifolium alpinum, Anthyllis vulneraria, Trollius europaeus, Caltha palustris, Geranium robertianum, Geranium sanguineum, Geranium pyrenaicum, Centaurea montana, Thalictrum* sp., *Hieracium* spp., *Dianthus* spp., *Saxifraga* spp., *Ranunculus* spp., *Galium* spp., *Alchemilla* spp., *Myosotis* spp., and many small ephemerals on those areas only exposed very late in the season by receding snow patches.

It is typical of the flora on these volcanic peaks that, although each has a rich vegetation, each equally has a distinct flora with a few unique species. In part this may be a consequence of the differing composition of the volcanic rocks and hence the soil, but it may also be a reflection of the situation in the area during the Last Glaciation. Although valley glaciers formed in the area and there were extensive snowfields, it is likely that the steep peaks, subjected during the summer to high insolation, provided isolated refugia for the most hardy of the alpine species.

Plate 3. Wet, heavily grazed upland grassland, Plomb du Cantal at 1775 m.

Plate 4. *Vaccinium uliginosum* (Bog Whortleberry) on areas of peat formation, Plomb du Cantal at 1800 m.

Plate 5. *Sphagnum* (Bog Moss) and *Eriophorum vaginatum* (Cotton Grass) bog, Puy de Sancy at 1800 m. Active *Sphagnum* growth is taking place in the foreground.

Plate 6. *Salix repens* (Creeping Willow) in *Sphagnum* bog, Puy de Sancy at 1800 m.

Plate 7. Upland area of alpine vegetation, Puy de Sancy at 1850 m. Note the extensive snow patches persisting in sheltered hollows. The photograph was taken in late July.

Plate 8. Alpine-type meadow vegetation, Puy de Sancy at 1850 m. Note the abundance of dicotyledonous herbaceous species, in contrast with the dominance of grass species on grazed areas at lower altitudes (compare pl. 3).

DISCUSSION

At the maximum of the glacial advance the valley ice was around 115 km. (72 miles) from the Abri Pataud, although parts of the higher land were not covered by permanent snow and ice. It is reasonable to suppose that, as the ice and snow advanced, there was a progressive withdrawal of both plants and animals from the Massif to more favorable areas. This would be most evident in those species whose habitats had been rendered totally uninhabitable, but, to a lesser extent, there would also be some withdrawal of species from the more lowland areas less severely affected.

We would, therefore, expect an aggregation of species to occur in the area to the west of the ice front with a greater diversity of species than is today regarded as usual. This would include species of the lowland woodlands retreating slowly in response to the worsening conditions, and species typical of the upland forests, moors and heaths of the Massif forced out of their former habitats by the physical presence of permanent ice and snow in these areas.

How do the pollen records discussed in chapter VI compare with the vegetation existing in these areas today? In terms of the species composition there

would appear to be considerable similarity. Certain notable exceptions do, however, occur in both the tree and herb pollen types and these will be discussed subsequently. With regard to the tree and shrub pollen, where the remains can generally be identified to the level of the genus at least, this similarity may well be meaningful. Much of the herb pollen, however, can be identified only to the family level, and many of the families involved are large and diverse; so any similarity might well be accidental. In the case of the herb pollen it is only really valid to consider pollen types which belong to small families, to families whose European distribution is characteristic of specific habitats or which have been identified to genus level. Where this is possible the similarity is again marked and possibly meaningful.

When one comes to consider the relative representation of the different pollen types, however, large discrepancies begin to appear. As discussed by Dr. Donner, the Abri Pataud site acted as a pollen trap for pollen from all the surrounding area and no particular group appears to be over-represented, although overall numbers of pollen grains are small in the samples obtained from the site. It is, therefore, likely that large variations in the proportional representation of different types give some measure of the importance of the species producing these types, once account has been taken of the variation in pollen production of the different species and the extent to which this is actually liberated into the atmosphere.

In the tree and shrub pollen there are three major discrepancies. In the first place, there is the relatively high representation of *Quercus* at the Abri Pataud site. At present, *Quercus* is relatively sparsely represented in the western parts of the Massif, but this may well be a reflection of the forest management policy rather than a significant ecological difference.

Secondly, there is the consistently low representation of *Fagus* at the Abri Pataud. Again, it is possible that the dominance of *Fagus* in the forests of the western Massif at present is in part due to forest management. It would appear, however, that *Fagus* is a natural and important component of the forest vegetation in these areas. There is no obvious reason why *Fagus* should not have been well represented in the Les Eyzies area during the Last Glacial Period, since it performs well on similar soils under climatic conditions which are probably very similar in other areas today. This anomalous behavior is equally apparent in the area at the present time, with less than ten individuals recorded within a 15 km. (9.4 miles) radius, although *Fagus* might be expected to grow well on the deeper, moister soils of the north-facing slopes.

A third significant difference is the occurrence of pollen of several more thermophilous genera such as *Juglans*, *Tilia*, and *Carpinus* in the deposits at the Abri Pataud. These are not typically present in periglacial deposits and are not normal components of the forest flora in the Massif today. It is also suggested by Dr. Donner that the *Quercus* pollen in the Abri Pataud deposits may well be from more than one species, and it is possible that here again a more thermophilous element may be represented. This evidence strongly supports the view that the Les Eyzies region provided a refuge for a variety of more temperate and Mediterranean species during the period represented by the deposits, since the valleys, and more particularly the south-facing slopes, were not subjected to the full rigors of the periglacial environment.

In this context, it is worth noting that the Les Eyzies area exhibits similar vegetational "anomalies" at the present day. These are clearly shown on the recently published vegetation map of the area produced by the Centre National de la Recherche Scientifique at Toulouse. Although the bulk of the vegetation can be broadly classified as temperate-European, there is a well-marked Atlantic element which ceases just to the east of Les Eyzies and a strong Mediterranean element, thriving on south-facing slopes with high insolation, which reaches its northernmost limit in this area.

There is little evidence that the Atlantic influence was much reduced during the Last Glacial Period, and the coastal vegetation in the Bordeaux region was probably fairly similar to the natural vegetation at the present day. In this situation, the increasing cold in the uplands and the advance of the ice down the valleys would result in a shortening and steepening of climatic gradients. Thus, species at the coastal end of the spectrum would remain relatively static, while species in the uplands would have to migrate down from the valley heads if they were to survive. In consequence, vegetation types which are normally regarded as distinct today would become telescoped together, producing the type of pollen assemblages which we find.

This is not to say that a random mixture of species resulted. It would appear likely, for example, in the Les Eyzies area that the deciduous woodland, dominated by *Quercus*, occupied the more eutrophic sites in the sheltered valleys, while the more acid soils of the surrounding plateau were occupied by species such as *Pinus* and *Betula*, also strongly represented in the pollen record and more tolerant of harsher conditions and less fertile soils. In this situation, the survival of thermophilous species in sheltered south-facing sites with high insolation is not unlikely. The solar altitude and consequently the incoming radiation load would be similar to that today and would balance the generally lower temperatures to a great extent.

It would, therefore, appear that, although there is a general similarity between the Abri Pataud deposits and the forest flora of the western Massif, the balance between the species both in terms of numbers and their spatial relationship to one another, was somewhat different. It must, however, be borne in mind that the forests of the Massif have been modified to some extent by management, and the natural forest vegetation may well have exhibited a rather different balance of species. A further important consideration is that the herbivore population at the Abri Pataud during the Last Glacial Period was vastly different from that in the Massif today. Selective cropping by herbivores can be an important factor in determining vegetational composition.

With regard to the herbaceous pollen, any detailed analysis is impossible for the reasons mentioned previously. In general, the pollen spectra obtained could possibly fit with the vegetation composition of the Massif areas above the tree line. Too little is known at present about the pollen rain from existing vegetation under various conditions to say more.

Two anomalies do stand out. First is the record for *Ephedra*, which is certainly not a component of the Massif flora today. This genus, however, appears in many periglacial deposits of similar date, although generally absent from such sites today. The second case is that of *Artemisia*, which also appears in many deposits from the Last Glacial Period but does not occur generally in European periglacial regions today. Again, *Artemisia* does not occur widely in the uplands of the Massif, although several rather rare alpine species do occur in other parts of Western Europe. Two comparatively common species, *Artemisia vulgaris* and *A. absinthum*, do occur, however, at lower altitudes in the Massif, normally on disturbed ground. Both these species are able to survive under comparatively extreme climatic conditions. It is, therefore, possible that pollen of this genus can be referred to these more common species typical of disturbed ground which were forced into the periglacial areas as habitats became more restricted in the Last Glacial Period, but today occur more generally in slightly less extreme habitats. Dr. Drury further comments that the incidence of *Artemisia* spp., in parts of western America is greatly increased by grazing pressure, a condition which certainly pertained during the occupation period at the Abri Pataud.

The rather high proportion of herb pollen throughout the period represented by the Abri Pataud deposits suggests, as discussed by Dr. Donner in his report (chapter VI), that there must have been considerable areas of open meadow or parklike vegetation. Presumably these would have been located principally in the plateau areas if, as discussed earlier, the woodland communities were occupying the more sheltered valleys. The general pollen composition, together with the generally low representation of Ericaceous pollen, is possibly an indication that acid heaths did not form as important a part of the vegetation as they do in the Massif today. It must be borne in mind, however, that most members of the *Ericaceae* are self-pollinated or insect pollinated rather than anemophilous, and one would not expect to recover large quantities of pollen except in the immediate vicinity of heath vegetation.

The general indications are, therefore, that the open vegetation was possibly similar to that developed on the more basic soils in the Massif uplands today. As in the case of the tree species, there is the possibility that some more thermophilous herb species survived the Last Glacial Period in the Les Eyzies area, most probably woodland species growing in the sheltered

valleys. With present techniques, however, these are not specifically detectable. It is likely that some areas of heath and acid bog existed, as indicated by the small amounts of Ericaceous pollen and *Sphagnum* spores, though these areas were probably limited in extent.

The evidence is certainly not consistent with the classical concept of a northern taïga forest or tundra system, such as is indicated for north European sites during the Last Glacial Period. Apart from the species composition indicated by the pollen from the Abri Pataud, one would expect to find widespread evidence of frost action, for example cryoturbation effects in the soils, and these do not occur.

Dr. Drury suggests that the evidence is consistent with a similar type of vegetation to that occurring in northwestern Canada today. Here, on floodplains, sand plains, and above the tree line, one has a herb-rich grassland which includes some tundra species, such as *Dryas*, *Vaccinium*, *Betula*, and *Salix*. In such areas, grazing animals such as horses readily survive the winter period.

One final, though very relevant, point is the question of whether a vegetation system of this type would support the fauna known to have existed at this period on the basis of the archaeological evidence. More specifically the problem is whether large herds of reindeer could flourish under these conditions.

At the present day, the European reindeer populations are typically animals of open tundra or arctic heath, although a forest race does exist. Even these animals, however, normally pass at least the summer months in the open arctic heath areas to the north of the northern European forests where they pass the remainder of the year. In all European reindeer there appears to be an essential dietary requirement for certain species of lichen, notably species of *Cladonia*, which occur only in the heath and tundra vegetation.

Experimental introductions of the forest race of reindeer into the Cairngorm area of Scotland have shown that reindeer will survive in this area. Even though the introduced animals have established themselves with a certain degree of success, however, there are some doubts as to whether a truly viable independent population will ever exist. One of the limiting factors in this case would appear to be the shortage of the essential lichens in the natural flora. In the light of this experiment, it would seem unlikely that European reindeer would be able to survive and establish themselves in the Massif area at the present day. Even though open heathlands do exist, they do not appear, on the basis of a rather rapid inspection, to support the essential lichen flora, although many other species of lichen are present.

It is pointed out by Dr. Drury, however, that in North America bison, reindeer (caribou), wild horses, and wild cattle share a habitat of grassy tundra parkland, the reindeer migrating south at some times of the year at least as far as the 49th parallel. Red deer also thrive in adjacent areas. Thus we have, in these areas, a herbivore population resembling that at the Abri Pataud during the Last Glacial Period in a habitat which is very different from that in which European reindeer survive today.

This leaves us in a dilemma. Either the whole interpretation of the pollen data is wildly incorrect, which does not seem likely, or the reindeer of the Dordogne region during the Last Glaciation differed in some way from those found in northern Europe at the present time. It could be, of course, that the dietary habits of the reindeer have changed over the course of several thousand years, or possibly that we are here dealing with a slightly different race of reindeer. There is limited evidence from British remains that at least one additional race of reindeer existed which was intermediate in morphology between the two types which have survived to the present day. As this type now appears to be extinct, it is impossible to determine what its behavior and feeding habits were. It is possible that the reindeer surviving in Europe today represent one extreme of a range of races of which the more southern types have been rendered extinct by human predation. If our interpretation of the vegetation records is in any degree correct, it would appear that the major habitat requirements of at least the forest race of reindeer as it exists at present, a combination of woodland and open upland vegetation, were present at the Abri Pataud during the Last Glacial Period, but this is obviously not the whole answer to the question.

In summary, it would appear that the vegetation and climatic conditions at the Abri Pataud during the period of the Upper Palaeolithic occupation were broadly similar to those in the uplands of the Massif Central today. This would give a mean summer temperature of about 12-15°C (54-59°F) and a mean winter temperature around 0°C (32°F). It must, however, be realized that there would be considerable local variation. On north-facing slopes temperatures would be somewhat lower, especially in the summer, and it is likely that snow would lie on these slopes for considerable periods of the summer months. The landform suggests that the average cloud cover would probably be less than in the Massif at present. The consequent high insolation would result in day temperatures, especially on the south-facing slopes in summer, being high as in the Massif at present — with summer values of 25-30°C (77-86°F) being frequent. The low cloud cover, however, would mean that diurnal fluctuations would be large and extreme radiation losses at night would result in frequent night frosts throughout the year regardless of aspect.

In general, these speculative figures accord well with the evidence from the pollen remains. It is clear, however, that there must have been some sheltered south-facing sites where frosts were much less severe, especially in summer, if species such as *Juglans* and *Tilia* could survive and produce measurable quantities of pollen. The small anomalies which do occur in the vegetation records largely appear to be a reflection of the unique character of the area and are still represented in the present-day vegetation.

Although this comparison may be useful in deducing the environment in which man existed during the Last Glacial Period, it also emphasizes certain problems, particularly with regard to the reindeer populations existing simultaneously in the area. There is no simple answer to these.

ACKNOWLEDGMENTS

This paper is the result of two brief excursions to the western Massif Central, the first in 1967, with Dr. W. Drury of Lincoln, Massachusetts, and the second in 1969. It does not attempt to survey the whole of the highly complex flora of this area; its only purpose is to outline the main features which are relevant to the problem under discussion. I am greatly indebted to Dr. W. H. Drury for enabling the comparisons drawn to include information from a wider field than would otherwise be possible. I am also indebted to Dr. J. J. Donner for allowing free access to his data, discussed in detail in chapter VI, and to Professor Hallam L. Movius, Jr., for his continued interest and support. I am grateful to Dr. Drury for permission to use his photographs for Plates 1, 3, 5, 7, and 8, and to Mr. G. R. Abram for preparing the plates from color transparencies.

APPENDIX

Common Names of Plant Species Referred to in the Text

The common names listed here for the benefit of nonspecialists are the most frequent British names, where one exists. Taxonomy throughout this paper follows that of the "Flora of the British Isles" by Clapham, Tutin, and Warburg, 2nd Edition, Cambridge, 1962, except for a few species not represented in the British flora where the conventions of "Les quatre flores de la France" by P. Fournier, Paris, 1961, are followed.

Trees

Abies spp.	Fir
Acer campestre	Field maple
Acer pseudoplatanus	Sycamore
Betula spp.	Birch
Carpinus betulus	Hornbeam
Fagus sylvatica	Beech
Fraxinus excelsior	Ash
Juglans regia	Walnut
Larix spp.	Larch
Picea spp.	Spruce
Pinus spp.	Pine
Quercus robur *Quercus* spp.	Oak
Tilia spp.	Lime
Ulmus spp.	Elm

Shrubs

Alnus glutinosa	Alder
Cornus mas	Dogwood
Corylus avellana	Hazel
Crataegus monogyna	Hawthorn
Ilex aquifolium	Holly
Juniperus communis	Juniper
Rosa spp.	Rose
Sambucus spp.	Elder
Sarothamnus scoparius	Broom

Ground Flora Species

Agrostis tenuis	Common bent-grass
Alchemilla spp.	Ladies mantle
Anemone pulsatilla	Pasque flower
A. sulphurea	Yellow anemone
Anthoxanthum odoratum	Sweet vernal grass
Anthyllis vulneraria	Kidney vetch
Artemisia absinthum	Wormwood
A. vulgaris	Mugwort
Calluna vulgaris	Heather
Caltha palustris	Marsh marigold
Centaurea montana	Perennial cornflower
Cladonia spp.	Reindeer Moss

Ground Flora Species (continued)

Deschampsia caespitosa	Tufted hair-grass
D. flexuosa	Wavy hair-grass
Dianthus spp.	Pink
Digitalis purpurea	Foxglove
Dryas sp.	Mountain avens
Ephedra spp.	Switch plant
Erica spp.	Heath
Eriophorum vaginatum	Cotton grass
Festuca rubra	Red fescue
Festuca spp.	Fescue
Galium spp.	Bedstraw
Genista tinctoria	Dyers greenweed
Genistella sagittalis	—————
Gentiana lutea	Yellow gentian
Geranium pyrenaiacum	Mountain Cranesbill
G. robertianum	Herb Robert
G. sanguineum	Bloody Cranesbill
Hieracium spp.	Hawkweed
Juncus spp.	Rush
Lotus corniculatus	Birds-foot trefoil
Myosotis spp.	Forget-me-not
Narcissus pseudonarcissus	Daffodil
Nardus stricta	Mat grass
Oxalis acetosella	Wood sorrel
Polypodiaceae	Polypody ferns
Ranunculus spp.	Buttercups
Rubus spp.	Brambles
Salix repens	Creeping Willow
Saxifraga spp.	Saxifrage
Scabiosa columbaria	Small scabious
Scabiosa spp.	Scabious
Silene dioica	Red campion
Sphagnum spp.	Bog moss
Thalictrum spp.	Meadow rue
Trifolium alpinum	Alpine clover
Trollius europaeus	Globe flower
Vaccinium myrtillus	Bilberry
V. uliginosum	Bog whortleberry
V. vitis-idaea	Cowberry
Viola spp.	Violet

VIII

The Ecology of the Human Occupation at the Abri Pataud

William H. Drury*

HATHEWAY SCHOOL OF CONSERVATION EDUCATION
LINCOLN, MASSACHUSETTS

ABSTRACT

Analysis of soils, remains of pollen and mammalian herbivores suggest climatic changes of relatively minor biological effect during the 15,000 years or so of accretion of deposits at the Abri Pataud. Pollen spectra indicating a proportion of tree to nontree pollen comparable to that of today, and the simultaneous hunting of reindeer, red deer, chamois, and wild cattle or bison suggest a mixed vegetation whose species members are at present tolerant of wide climatic variations. A similarly varied vegetation is to be found today near tree line in the Massif Central, and it supports a rich herbivore population. Furthermore, a sustained population of successful hunters during the occupation of the rock-shelters at Les Eyzies likewise suggests a dependable herbivore resource.

The abundance of reindeer remains does not necessarily indicate a tundra habitat of Upper Palaeolithic man similar to that of northern Scandinavia today; nor should wild cattle or bison be regarded as "indicator species" of rigid ecological implications. The application of such typological concepts of habitat have contributed confusion, not help, in understanding the environment of Upper Palaeolithic man.

In essentially all the disciplines involved in deciphering man's Late Pleistocene prehistory, there have been rapid changes in intellectual framework during the last decades. My contribution to the present publication is to explain how contemporary ecological attitudes toward communities can help to reconstruct the Last Glacial environment of the Abri Pataud. We are immediately faced with a dichotomy of interpretation. The classical picture of the Ice Age is one of bitter cold, bleak northern landscape. It raises the question of how man could survive in this place, and why he chose to live in such an unpleasant region. I will try to show that biological evidence in fact suggests a habitat not fundamentally different from that of the resort areas at the heads of the valleys of the Massif Central today. Hence, the area may have been rich in resources and pleasant of aspect during the various Upper Palaeolithic occupations of the Abri Pataud.

In most natural history areas, the developmental or deterministic models formulated in the early twentieth century have now been rejected, but the simplistic structures are so logically attractive that they are still taught in elementary courses. Then, because scholars in one field are hesitant to reject what they have been led to believe is generally accepted by specialists in another field, these models persist and limit the types of conclusions that can be drawn.

Thus, although few geomorphologists now deal seriously with Davis' (1899) theory of cycles of erosion, many botanists and zoologists will use terms and assumptions which originated with Davis. Similarly, nearly all beginning students of biology are taught Clements' (1916, 1936) deterministic models of succession and climax in vegetation. He said that natural systems following disturbance pass through preliminary stages to a stable, self-perpetuating, optimally adjusted equilibrium condition. In order that biotic processes may develop these mature systems, it is necessary that the landscape be stable during long periods of development of the vegetation. The Davis system of cycles of erosion ascribes stability to those surfaces which are removed from the activities of the present cycle of erosion.

The attractive idea of a consistent community which retains its identity through time led men to believe that such environmental complexes moved together in units and the presence of the whole unit ought to be predictable from the clues offered by "important" elements. One or a few "indicator species" could be used to reconstruct an entire environment. Out of this it would be reasoned, for example, that reindeer meant a characteristic wet

*Contribution No. 45 from the Hatheway School of Conservation Education, Massachusetts Audubon Society, Lincoln, Massachusetts.

tundra, mossy climate, reminiscent of contemporary Scandinavia, and the suggestion of coexistence of reindeer and wild cattle or bison must reflect either mistakes in interpretation or a rare exception.

I have recently reviewed a case (Drury 1969) in which special events in the past have been used to explain the coexistence at the mouth of the Gulf of St. Lawrence of some arctic plants with some from the Atlantic coastal plain and some of the Rocky Mountains. Fernald in his early papers explained the unusually rich flora of this region in terms of variety of soil, moisture, climate, and other local details, but later he proposed the nunatak hypothesis and thereby attracted international recognition (Fernald 1925). In his nunatak explanation, Cretaceous peneplain surfaces and persistence of plants on islands in the ice through the Glacial Periods were called upon to explain the persistence of a rich flora, but now nearly every bit of geological and botanical evidence used to support this explanation has been contradicted. It is interesting that in an analysis of the beetles of Newfoundland, Lindroth (1963) has drawn conclusions similar to Fernald's: that a residue of species cannot be explained with reference to contemporary factors, as has Dahl (1964) for the plants.

The question is put in this case whether one considers the evidence provided by the large majority of organisms (90 percent) or a minority (10 percent). How do we weigh the ecological "importance" of one or several species? One should look in the Gulf of St. Lawrence area for topographic variety, bedrock types and soil variety, distribution of forested and treeless regions and of wet and dry sites, and movement of oceanic currents rather than assign causes to remote events in history. An alternate explanation is complex, but it deals only with observable events in operation at present.

Cold currents from Labrador and Baffin Bay make summers on Newfoundland's eastern coastal lowlands cold enough for arctic plants limited by summer heat to grow far south. The same oceanic circumstances (a relatively warm ocean) make mild winters which allow northern outposts of southern plants whose northern distribution is set by cold winters (Damman 1965). Furthermore, the Gulf of St. Lawrence is at the end of an avenue down which continental storm systems pass out of North America almost without regard for where they originate. Thus in the western areas of Newfoundland there are strong continental weather influence (Damman 1965). Between the uplands of the west and the lowlands of the east, large differences in climatic conditions exist close together such that cold summers exist not far from hot summers and cold winters not far from mild ones. In addition, local outcrops of limestone and serpen-

tine occur in the generally acidic bedrock, and topographic extremes are such that in Maritime Canada, ash, oak, elm, and maple grow within a few miles of high arctic willows and matted alpines.

If one considers mature vegetation units to be closed, it is difficult to explain mixtures of arctic, coastal plain, and mountain species "associations", but if each species is considered on its own merits, an area rich in topography, rock types, and climate should support a rich flora. This is the sort of enrichment of the environment's diversity and truncation of climatic gradients which I will come back to in discussing the Late Pleistocene climate of the Dordogne, and the vegetation we might expect to occur near the ice margin. So now let me present some general attitudes by which I would replace the classical attitude that in their natural community, species occupy fixed places in a well-integrated system.

First, there is one aspect of traditional ecological thinking which applies directly to man as a hunter/food-gatherer. It has been remarked as amazing that most plants and animals of which man makes use for food belong to the early stages of vegetation development (Odum 1959). This remark is based on the implicit assumption that early successional stages are of brief duration and of local extent, and that a species has better evolutionary strategies if it adopts the climax (widespread, consistent, and reliable) as its habitat. Within a deterministic system, this would be true, but it has little meaning if vegetation is made up of a number of equally mature, equally viable, and well-adjusted communities of plants and animals, all of which reflect local habitats. For example, we should expect that coarse soils in dry sites exposed to sun and wind will support different vegetation than does a pond or a sheltered, moist site on fine soils without recourse to development (Hack and Goodlett 1960). If vegetation types have similar degrees of permanence, those herbivores will flourish which choose plants which produce a lot of food, i.e., seeds and fruits, or rapidly growing shoots and leaves. Because of developmental preconceptions about vegetation, many contemporary writers apparently regard plants whose strategies involve heavy production of seeds, rapid growth, and short lives to be members of impermanent communities (impermanent on moist, fine soils in sheltered sites, yes, but perennial on exposed sites). These "impermanent" sites (lakes, rock outcrops, coarse soils), although widespread in Davis' youthful topography, should be eliminated in mature topography or on the peneplain. If, however, these "early successional stages" are as successful in their own habitat as any "climax stage," their value as an animal's habitat is measured in their production of food. I presume that because these "successional" species are abundant today and used for food by so many animals, they must be as fit in the passage of time as are the so-called climax species.

Second, another aspect of traditional ecological thinking I want to discard is the idea that mutual adjustments between members of a community select for maximum community efficiency: for example, Slobodkin's (1961) concept that the "prudent predator" adjusts its population so as to keep its prey at maximum production. Natural selection acting on individuals suggests, as Darwin said, that we should see a predator as evolutionarily piggish and lacking in foresight.

A predator crops prey as much as it can and produces as many young as it can nourish to independence (Lack 1954). A large, edible, accessible prey is liable to extermination unless it can escape to sanctuaries (the Pleistocene history of man is associated with the disappearance of large, edible herbivores). The predator that overcrops its prey must, once that prey is destroyed, look for alternative prey, which is presumably less desirable because it is difficult of access, hard to catch, or unsatisfactory in food value or volume. The predator is regulated when it has reduced its habitat to prey species such that the predator's best efforts are necessary for subsistence. At this stage the balance admired by ecological theorists has its momentary existence. The balance is quickly upset as a predator repeatedly turns to alternate prey when local habitat changes (including the predator's presence) lead to changes in availability and numbers of the preferred prey.

Third, a region varied in habitat and supporting a number of croppable prey species is a better environment for continuous occupation than one which produces a high density of a single resource. This is the economic principle of the diversified economy or the financier's diversified portfolio. This means that successful human settlements occur where resources overlap from what the geographer might call several regions; river valleys leading from uplands down to ocean sounds, confluence of rivers, the borders between mountains and plains. My own observations on the location of traditional population centers of Eskimos and Indians indicate that these are associated with varied habitat and mixed resources.

The continuous and apparently intense occupation of the river valleys in southwestern France indicates to me a reliable and hence varied resource, rather than a region whose climate and habitat were uniquely attractive to one or a few herbivores. The variety of faunal remains — reindeer, red deer, roe deer, horse, wild cattle or bison, ibex, and chamois — suggest that the relatively minor changes of climate

which led to a decrease in one resource led to an increase in another.

Fourth, when we examine the climate of the Ice Ages we are first concerned with why ice began to collect in perennial snowfields and then expand outward from mountain centers. We are introduced to the concept that a snowfield tends to make its own weather by cooling air and encouraging precipitation, thus making the weather that much more favorable for the expansion of the ice field. But shortly after that, we are involved in the evidence that in each successive glacial advance the ice stopped at about the same place.

Why didn't the ice continue indefinitely into low latitude? Something must have stopped it, and the obvious suggestions are lack of rain or excess of heat. We suggest glacial climates are cold and wet. Cooler than now or wetter than now, yes, but if we say that it was glacially cold in the Dordogne, we must also say it was dry or give some other reason why the ice did not expand farther to fill the valleys. Somewhere along its advance the snowballing effects of an ice field must have met increasingly stiff resistance in temperature or lack of rainfall, or the ice would have gone all the way to the coast. This steepening of gradients or shortening of the distance between climatically diverse regions brought together organisms of what are different climate regions today, and thereby enriched the fauna and flora of unglaciated regions.

If temperature and rainfall conditions were prevalent such that ice fields expanded out of the Massif Central, colder effects certainly extended into the lowlands, but we do not know what the effects of the sun's high altitude would have been upon conditions during the growing season. Did rain come in the growing season or did it fall as snow only in winter? We can be sure the climate and rainfall distribution was different from what it is now, but we don't know in what details it was different or what effects it had on the changes in the length of the growing season, the depth of frost in winter, and the kinds of plants and animals which grew together.

In France during the Ice Age (as happens today in Newfoundland) one should expect to find plants associated with each other whose distributions today are wholly unassociated. In parts of Canada now, plants of the prairies or steppes grow mixed with alpine plants; in pollen from New England bogs, temperate hot meadow shrubs are found growing with tundra heaths (Davis 1958). We should not say that because we find a certain tundra plant the climate was a cold tundra climate, or that because we find certain animal remains the climate became warmer and more humid, until we know what controls the southern distribution of that particular plant and the northern distribution of the animal. Furthermore, we can only guess at the climate we would produce when we combine the indications provided by all the plants which occur together. We should expect that what they forecast is nothing with which we are familiar today.

Fifth, I think I can best illustrate my concept of Late Pleistocene man's occupation of an environment in terms of what little I know and have read about Canadian Eskimos. I understand that there have consistently been Eskimo groups in the Anderson River-Cambridge Bay area, at Iglulik, Southampton Island, the Belcher Islands, at Frobisher Bay, Pangnirtung, Pond Inlet, Thule, and in southern Greenland's fjords. Certain places have a perennial population where people even in most famine years can survive. Some of these places have thick ice where seals can be hunted all winter, others have open water in winter, while some have a reliable source of caribou.

But some Eskimos, like any group of people, prefer independence and have their pioneering spirits. Certain groups which could not be leaders in the crowded settlements, move out onto other sounds to be their own men. As they move out along the shore they settle on places which attract them, but many of these temporary settlements are vulnerable to heavy snowfalls, or thin winter ice, or failure of the spring thaw, or caribou don't pass by, and in the lean years the outlying population is snuffed out. The numbers of Eskimos and the number of occupied sounds depends on how many years or decades natality and immigration have exceeded mortality and emigration. One regional disaster can return the population to a low level, and survivors then are found in the more secure places (either because they survived there or because they returned to preferred places now less crowded).

The continuity of the archaeological records suggests that the Dordogne was a dependable place for men to make a living during the later Ice Age. What can we learn from the deposits available that will be consistent with the ecological framework I have just reviewed? I expect most groups of Upper Palaeolithic man would have spent most of their time where there was the most favorable combination of attractive forces available. If there were flints, caves, water, sunny sheltered slopes, and consistent varied game within a few days travel, the area would be so much the more attractive.

Let me now turn to the evidence from the excavation at the Abri Pataud and from the present habitat of the Massif Central. Are the lines of evidence from landscape, vegetation, and vertebrates consistent with each other or contradictory? At this stage my knowledge of requirements of individual plant and animal species is not adequate for me to abandon preconceived notions of habitat and environment and look dispassionately at the evidence. So I do not claim to slight deduced models, rather to suggest an alternative model so that archaeologists can confront this one with the alternate, widely accepted, and largely contradictory model so as to see which fits the evidence better. I suggest that we begin with those events for which there is clearest evidence as a point of departure (Levels 4 and 5, Noaillian and Périgordian IV).

THE EVIDENCE

Soils. The column of the excavation is apparently divisible into three main sections; Levels 4 and 5 are in the middle section. Accumulation of debris was apparently much more rapid both above and below this middle section.

Size of particles and relative thickness of éboulis deposits suggest that there was a relatively mild and dry period at the bottom of the middle section and that at the top there was another — a fairly mild and humid oscillation.

There appear to be several minor, colder oscillations between these and a colder interval in Level 3 and above. There appears to have been a long colder episode below Level 5. Warm oscillations of the middle section are suggested to be associated with the transition from the early to the late phase of the Middle Würm and the beds above are suggested to represent late phase of Middle Würm time.

Vegetation. One of the most important observations is that during the Last Glacial and Early Postglacial Period, starting about 34,000 years ago, pollen has consistently indicated that forests were more widespread than they are today. The most conspicuous tree species are birch, pine, and oak; shrubs are hazel, juniper, and willow. Nontree pollen includes sedges, grasses, composites, and the rose family. In the Early Postglacial Period the forest was primarily pine, and later (especially Postglacial Optimum and after) primarily oak. The pollen diagram suggests a rather open forest with denser parklands in some places, and undershrubs in others. When there is a decrease in trees there is a correlated increase in composites, especially *Artemisia*.

It is important to clarify the bottom of the pollen diagrams (Levels 11-14) as to whether they are stages of the early phase of the Main Würm. As it is, the diagram suggests that Levels 5 and 4 are transitional between the early and the late phases of the Middle Würm, and that the beds of age 34,000 years B.P. at the very bottom do indeed belong to the early phase of the Main Würm. The two transitions, at this site, rather closely resemble each other in relative pollen frequencies (from composites through pine to oak maxima). In standard categories, however, the transition from the early to the late phase of the Middle Würm should be a conspicuous amelioration — much more marked than was the transition from the Middle to the Late Würm.

Mammals. Reindeer constitute 80-90 percent of the mammal remains throughout. A good sample of remains suggests that the kill is randomly taken from a wild population; that is, that man was able to kill animals of all ages equally well. Most predators depend disproportionately on young, injured, and old animals and where man is able to select his prey he usually chooses young adults disproportionately. Apparently Upper Palaeolithic man did neither.

From Périgordian IV through Noaillian times there is a steady and marked increase in the occurrence of red deer. In the Noaillian there was also increased use of roe deer, wild cattle, or bison and horse. Chamois shows an increase from the top of the Périgordian IV to the top of the Noaillian and again later in the Proto-Magdalenian. Ibex is more numerous in early Périgordian IV and also during the Proto-Magdalenian.

Excursion into Contemporary Vegetation in the Massif Central. As one travels up the valleys from Les Eyzies to the Massif Central, one passes through areas of vineyards on south-facing slopes. Between the vineyards are sparse grasslands with pines and junipers.

On the valley bottoms at the heads of the valley and covering much of the uplands above Les Eyzies are dry fields with woodlots of mixed oak, chestnut, hazel, and some little beech.

a. On north slopes, and widespread on the uplands (finding its best expression from 300 meters below tree line to 100 meters above tree line) is an area rich in species and lush in aspect. The upland pastures have a thick mat of grass with clumps of pines, scattered junipers, willow, broom, and many wildflowers.

b. A slight shift in aspect or land use is associated with a heavy forest of beech and fir with alder understory and heavy lichen growth on the branches. Common plants of secondary conspicuousness include rose, maple, elderberry, and very conspicuous presence of ferns. In addition, there are many flowers — umbellifers, the rose family, and composites.

c. Above tree line are meadows of grasses (*Agrostis* and *Festuca*, *Danthonia*, *Deschampsia*, and *Anthoxanthum*) with patches of heather, blueberry, wild-

flowers such as hawkweed, anemone, bedstraw, ladies mantle, cinquefoil, saxifrage, geranium, chickweed and *Umbelliferae*, buttercups, legumes such as clover and *Lotus*. In other places there are conspicuous patches of sedges.

d. Near late-snow patches occur rich flower patches of anemone, forget-me-nots, buttercups, cinquefoil, pussytoes, *Veratrum*, hawkweeds, *Trollius*, clover, and daffodils.

e. *Artemisia* (*A. vulgaris* and *A. absinthium*) was found at lower altitudes on artificial talus or gravel piles. Thus it may be that presence of *Artemisia* in deposits near Les Eyzies reflects human activities which made the rock slides more conspicuous near the caves, as much as climatic change. In large parts of western America, increase of *Artemisia* is an indication of grazing by cattle, sheep, and horses.

INTERPRETATION

Soils and Pollen Remains. The classical scheme suggests northern taïga forest and tundra for the environment of man during Middle Würm times. Contemporary Scandinavian forest-tundra suggests bog shrubs, moss blanket, and patches of perennially frozen ground. But if the climate in the Dordogne produced such "typical tundra," we would expect to find widespread manifestations of frost action phenomena such as cryoturbation. We don't, with the exception of local patches of frost features. That sort of climate should also encourage more widespread occurrence of spruce and fir, and, at least in some places, blanket peat bog deposits. There are none.

Lack of confirming evidence (cryoturbation, blanket bogs) argues against a wet brush tundra, but it is consistent with a landscape with widespread areas of dry lichen-grass-sedge vegetation. On ridges and sand plains in Labrador, I have seen open, parklike stands of lichen-carpeted forest, and I understand that the Siberian taïga is like that. In fact, in northwest Canada (Yukon Territory) on river floodplains, on sand plains and again above the tree line on the gracefully sweeping surfaces are grasslands where prairie flowers grow and free-roaming horses readily survive the winter. The grasslands are mixed with mat plants, avens (*Dryas*) and dwarf shrubs (*Vaccinium*, *Betula*, and *Salix*) which are generally accepted as tundra plants.

Mammal Remains. Man chooses his prey but only from what is available, and a good hunter does not go very far for his game. Hunters move camp consistently rather than carry heavy game long distances.

Furthermore, humans have fads and traditions so the minor shifts in secondary prey in the presence of a consistent emphasis on reindeer may be of slight ecological meaning.

The pollen diagrams and the constant heavy predation on reindeer with periodic increase in use of red deer, wild cattle or bison, horse, ibex, and chamois in this context suggest small fluctuations resulting only in local changes in the less common species. This is a common observation of ecologists, but one which is seldom emphasized adequately or appreciated by nonecologists.

Within the classical concept of a tundra environment, we should expect to find more European elk, or moose (*Alces*). The argument that there are no remains because these people either did not hunt elk or because the elk were too ferocious is trivial for a variety of reasons, including the fact that present-day elk, or moose, are not ferocious.

Soils, pollen, and mammal remains indicate an amelioration during Late Noaillian to Éboulis 3-4: Red times, but not as marked a one as traditional concepts of climatic change would expect for an interstadial. If we were not trying to correlate the plant and animal remains with preconceptions of an Ice Age, we would conclude that the changes were not impressive.

Present Vegetation. A clear illustration of the sort of heterogeneity which we should expect in vegetation is offered by the almost unlimited combinations of species growing together above tree line on the Puy de Dôme, Puy de Sancy, Puy Mary, and Plomb de Cantal.

Many classical plant sociologists argue that in original or undisturbed vegetation, groupings are uniform and consistent, but I reject this idea. In Late Glacial and Early Postglacial time, we can expect that there was all manner of disturbance everywhere, including differential cropping by herbivores.

I imagine a vegetation on the uplands above the caves during the ice advances which closely resembled that which now occurs within 300 meters of tree line. I suspect that reindeer would survive well on today's upland meadows of the Massif Central if they were reestablished. In Wood Buffalo Park in Canada and at Big Delta in Alaska, American bison thrive in a parkland of open pine and spruce trees growing in a grassy tundra. There is thus in Canada today evidence that reindeer, wild cattle, horses, and bison can share the same habitat. Red deer (American elk) furthermore, thrive not far away.

I assume that the Périgordian IV and Noaillian Periods cover an interval during which climatic changes resulting in snowfields in the mountains were relatively ineffective in the lowlands. These climate shifts moved species now abundant at the higher levels a few hundred vertical feet toward the outer apron of the Massif, and beech-oak forests occupied some lower plateau areas, while patches of oak grasslands covered the lowlands and the region toward Gironde, the Landes, and Spain. Such a landscape and vegetation has broad tolerance to fluctuations of climate and would allow the species involved to survive in southwestern France throughout the ice advances down to today.

In the rich topography and truncated climatic gradients of the Late Pleistocene, local topographic differences made species of plants grow together (pines, oaks, grasses, spruce, birch, and arctic heaths) which we would now consider to have major climatic significance. My overall conclusion is that habitat variety and favorable climate conditions made ideal circumstances for support of a varied herbivore supply upon which Upper Palaeolithic man thrived.

REFERENCES

Clements, F.E.
  1916. *Plant Succession: An Analysis of the Development of Vegetation.* Publication 242, Carnegie Institution, Washington, D.C. xiii plus 512 pp.
  1936. "The Nature and Structure of the Climax," *J. Ecology*, vol. 24, pp. 252-284.

Dahl, E.
  1964. "Present Day Distribution of Plants and Past Climates," in *The Reconstruction of Past Environments.* Hester and Schoenwetter, no. 3. Fort Burgwin Research Center.

Damman, A.W.H.
  1965. "The Distribution Patterns of Northern and Southern Elements in the Flora of Newfoundland," *Rhodora*, vol. 67, pp. 363-392.

Davis, M.B.
  1958. "Three Pollen Diagrams from Central Massachusetts," *Amer. J. Sci.*, vol. 256, pp. 540-570.

Davis, W.M.
  1899. "The Geographic Cycle," *Geographical Journal*, vol. 14, pp. 481-504.

Drury, W.H.
  1969. "Plant Persistence in the Gulf of St. Lawrence," in *Essays in Plant Geography*, Papers presented at the Symposium in Terrestrial Plant Ecology held at Francis Xavier University, Antigonish, Nova Scotia, October 1966. K. N. H. Greenidge, Ed·, ix plus 184 pp. The Nova Scotia Museum, Halifax, N.S.

Fernald, M.L.
  1925. "Persistence of Plants in Unglaciated Areas of Boreal America," *Mem. Amer. Acad. Arts and Sciences*, 15, no. 3. (*Mem. Gray Herb.*, no. 2, pp. 239-342.)

Hack, J.T., and J.C. Goodlett
  1960. *Geomorphology and Forest Ecology of a Mountain Region in the Central Appalachians.* U.S. Geol. Surv. Prof. Papers, no. 347, 64 pp.

Lack, D.
  1954. *The Natural Regulation of Animal Numbers.* viii plus 343 pp. Clarendon Press, Oxford.

Lindroth, C.H.
  1963. "The Fauna History of Newfoundland, Illustrated by *Carabid* Beetles," *Ent. Sallsk., Opusc. Ent. Suppl.*, vol. 23, 112 pp.

Odum, E.P.
  1959. *Fundamentals of Ecology.* 2nd ed. 546 pp. W.B. Saunders Co., Philadelphia and London.

Slobodkin, L.B.
  1961. *Growth and Regulation of Animal Populations.* 184 pp. Holt, Rinehart and Winston, New York.

IX

Provenience of Flint Used for the Manufacture of Tools at the Abri Pataud

Harvey M. Bricker

TULANE UNIVERSITY
NEW ORLEANS, LOUISIANA

Raw material used for the manufacture of flint tools found in the several assemblages at the Abri Pataud comes from nodules occurring in limestone belonging to three different stages of the Upper Cretaceous. The relative placement of these stages — the Coniacian, the Campanian, and the Maestrichtian — within the Upper Cretaceous is shown below (Gignoux 1950, p. 243):

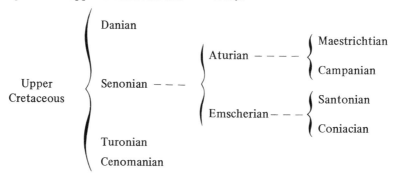

There are no Lower Cretaceous sediments in the Périgord region. The sea was prevented from extending southward because the *Détroit du Poitou* was not yet submerged; one result of this barrier was that certain molluscs found in the Paris Basin could not migrate to Aquitania (Abrard 1944, p. 846). The *Détroit du Poitou* was broached during the Cenomanian transgression, and in the Périgord region Upper Cretaceous sediments were deposited directly upon those of Jurassic age. The former generally represent littoral facies; the shallow-water environment is explained by the proximity of the Périgord to the Massif Central (Delpey 1939, pp. 250, 262-263).

The occurrence of Coniacian, Campanian, and Maestrichtian rocks in the Les Eyzies vicinity and areas to the north, south and west is indicated schematically in figure 1. Two subdivisions of the Coniacian are recognized: (1) a lower unit composed of gray or rusty marls, and (2) an upper unit composed of nodular yellowish limestone. The Campanian rocks are described as very uniform, composed principally of marly limestone and *marno-calcaires*

gélifs containing nodules of flint. The flint nodules are most common in an upper whitish-gray horizon. Maestrichtian sediments are divided into three subdivisions:

(1) the Upper Subdivision, a yellow glauconitic limestone occurring in plaquette form, outcrops only in the immediate vicinity of Bergerac;

(2) the Middle Subdivision, a yellow to whitish-yellow, sometimes sandy, sometimes dolomitic limestone, contains flint nodules at various horizons; toward the northwestern limit of its zone of occurrence (see fig. 1), the nodules are particularly large; and

(3) the Lower Subdivision of the Maestrichtian, a limestone with zones of glauconitic sand; it also contains flint nodules (*Carte Géologique Détaillée de France, Feuille* 182, Bergerac, 1920).

The first investigations of the provenience of flint found at the Abri Pataud were conducted by M. Lionel Valensi (1960) on samples from Level 2 (Proto-Magdalenian). Basing himself on microscopic characteristics, invertebrate fossils, and crystalline structure, Valensi suggested that the flints occurring in the latter assemblage are of three general varieties: (a) Coniacian flint of the Les Eyzies vicinity, sometimes black or dark gray and sometimes blond or honey-colored; (b) Maestrichtian flint from the Caudeau Valley northeast of Bergerac, which is generally light-colored and pseudo-oolithic; and (c) Maestrichtian flint of the Mussidan vicinity, generally light-colored and containing distinctive crystalline structures in the form of either "bundles of needles" or rhombohedrons.

The investigations were widened in 1967 as part of the study of Level 5 (Périgordian IV), when a large series of samples was examined macroscopically by M. Paul Fitte. The results of the Level 5 study were then applied to the other levels at the Abri Pataud, and further samples were examined by Fitte between 1967 and 1969. Fitte's findings (personal communications to the present author and to H.L. Movius, Jr.) permit the recognition of two major series of flints that were used during the various occupations of the Abri Pataud.

Series A. This flint comes from formations of Coniacian and/or Campanian age. This is, for the most part, dark flint, black or dark gray. The black flint from Level 2 was identified by Valensi as Coniacian, but Fitte thinks that some of it is Campanian. The two formations are very similar, and both contain dark flint of very similar nature. Both formations share to a large extent a common suite of microfossils (mainly sponges), and only a comparatively few forms are diagnostic of one or the other formation. In the absence of a microscopic study for all levels such as Valensi did for Level 2, it is impossible to be certain whether a given sample of dark flint is Campanian or Coniacian. As discussed below, this lack of precision is of no great importance in designating possible source areas. The dark flints of Series A are found throughout the Abri Pataud occupations.

Another variety of flint assigned to Series A appears in an unpatinated state as a blond or honey-colored flint. This patinates to either a mottled ("salt-and-pepper") or dull white state. The unpatinated state is found almost exclusively in Level 2, and samples from there were identified by Valensi as being of Coniacian age. The patinated state, occurring throughout the Abri Pataud occupations, was also identified as Coniacian by Fitte.

All the Series A flints can be considered to be "local" raw materials from point of view of the inhabitants of the Abri Pataud. Coniacian rocks outcrop in the immediate vicinity of Les Eyzies, and, although the precise exposures exploited by the prehistoric artisans are unknown, much Coniacian flint must have been contributed to the valley slope talus of the Vézère drainage. Campanian formations are more widespread, but Fitte suggests that the following talus deposits rich in flint nodules are likely to have been those exploited by the Abri Pataud inhabitants:

(a) the talus deposits flanking the right bank of the Vézère River both upstream and downstream from Le Bugue:

(b) deposits on the left bank of the Vézère immediately upstream from its confluence with the Dordogne River;

(c) extensive accumulations in the region of Badefols on the left bank of the Dordogne upstream from Lalande; and

(d) talus formations in the Couze Valley between Saint-Avit-Sénieur and Bayac.

To the extent to which this surmise is correct, all the Series A flints could have been obtained within a small local area extending no more than 12 to 15 km. from the Abri Pataud. The uncertainty about the provenience of the dark Series A flint involves only a slight shift up or down the drainage system. It is, of course, possible that Coniacian and Campanian flints were obtained from the Vézère drainage upstream from the Les Eyzies vicinity. Large nodules of Campanian flint occur, for example, in the walls of the Cro-de-Granville, near Rouffignac, to the northwest of Les Eyzies (as they do at the Grotte de Bara-Bahau, near Le Bugue, in the postulated downstream source area).

Series B. These flints are of Maestrichtian age. The most distinctive variety is a banded flint (*silex rubané*) usually having a buff background with red, white, purple, or brown bands. The basic background color may, however, be dark gray or black. We are unable to identify specific outcrops utilized by the prehistoric artisans, but there is one very prolific source area for this kind of flint in the drainage of the Caudeau River in the area north and east of Bergerac. One distinctive kind of Series B flint is not banded but is rather a solid dark yellow or gold color. According to Fitte, this is known as the "Gavaudun type" of Maestrichtian flint, and it outcrops in the region to the south and west of the area covered in Figure 1. The Gavaudun type, so named because of its frequent occurrence in the Roc de Gavaudun (Lot-et-Garonne) assemblage, is present but rare at the Abri Pataud.

A third kind of flint belonging to Series B is the variety containing "bundles of needles" or rhombohedrons (a six-sided prism whose faces are parallelograms) identified by Valensi from Level 2 (Proto-

Magdalenian). Similar flint can be found today in a quarry exposure northeast of Mussidan in the Isle Valley. Unfortunately, because the identification of this variety depends upon detailed microscopic study, we have no systematic information on its occurrence except in Level 2.

Although rocks of Maestrichtian age occur on the plateau some 10 km. from Les Eyzies, no outcrops of Series B flints are known from there. In the light of present knowledge, the Series B flints must be considered as "exotic" raw materials, contrasting with the local materials of Series A. The Couze Valley, the source of at least some of the Abri Pataud raw material, is 20 to 25 km. from Les Eyzies, and the area north of Bergerac is 35 to 40 km. distant. If the quarry near Mussidan is indeed close to the source of the distinctive flint of Level 2, this is the most distant connection between the Abri Pataud and a flint source — some 50 km. The extent to which the flint nodules of Series B were imported directly to the Abri Pataud and there worked into finished tools varies between occupations; this is discussed separately for the several assemblages in the various archaeological reports.

One flint variety occurring at the Abri Pataud cannot be firmly assigned to either Series A or B. The distinctive characteristic of this flint is its white, lustrous, porcelainlike patination. Some pieces of this flint when broken exhibit a core of blond or gray flint belonging to Series A, but others cannot be identified. This variety occurs almost exclusively in Level 4 (Noaillian, *ex* Périgordian V_c) and it is further discussed in the archaeological report on the assemblages from that level.

Finally, a nonflint siliceous rock called "jasper" (*jaspe*) was used occasionally for the manufacture of tools at the Abri Pataud. This raw material, either a solid gold color or gold with black spots or bands, has been identified by Fitte as of Maestrichtian age. Outcrops of similar material are known today in the Couze Valley in the vicinity of Saint-Avit-Sénieur.

In general, then, the flint used by the prehistoric inhabitants of the Abri Pataud for tool manufacture can be divided into local and exotic categories. With the possible exception of the Mussidan variety of Series B, all the inhabitants regardless of cultural affiliation drew upon a common resource pool. The relative proportions of local to exotic flint vary, however, among the different assemblages. These proportions and possible associations between tool categories and raw material type are considered separately for individual assemblages in the archaeological reports.

ACKNOWLEDGMENT

I am very grateful to Monsieur Paul Fitte for his help and professional advice over a period of years. It is evident that the research reported in this chapter could not have been accomplished without his extensive cooperation.

REFERENCES

Abrard, René
    1944. "Sur la pénétration des formes tempérées dans le nord du Bassin Aquitanien pendant le Crétacé supérieur," *C.R. Acad. Sci. Paris*, t. 218, no. 21, pp. 844-846.

Carte Géologique Détaillée de France, Feuille 182, Bergerac.
    1920. Bergerac.

Delpey, Geneviève
    1939. "Paléogéographie du sud-ouest de la France au Crétacé supérieur," *Bull. Soc. Hist. Nat. Toulouse*, t. 73, pp. 250-265.

Gignoux, Maurice
    1950. *Géologie stratigraphique.* 4e éd. 735 pp. Masson, Paris.

Valensi, Lionel
    1960. "De l'origine des silex Protomagdaléniens de l'Abri Pataud, Les Eyzies," *Bull. Soc. Préh. Fr.*, t. 57, pp. 80-84.

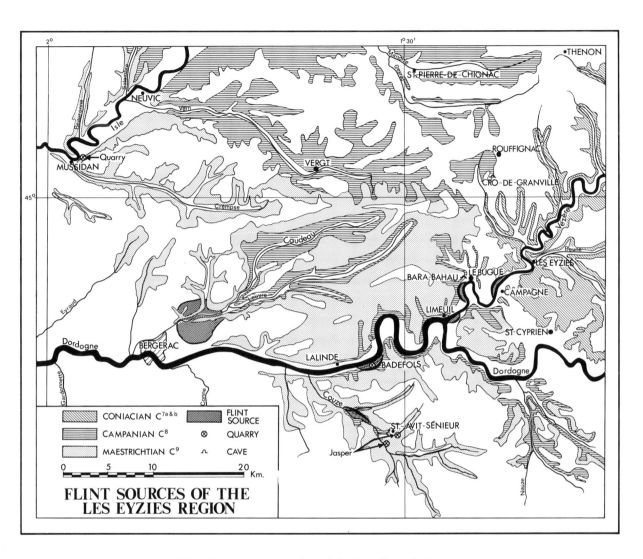

FLINT SOURCES OF THE LES EYZIES REGION

Legend:
- CONIACIAN C$^{7a\&b}$
- CAMPANIAN C^{8}
- MAESTRICHTIAN C^{9}
- FLINT SOURCE
- ⊗ QUARRY
- ∩ CAVE

0   5   10   20 Km.

Map labels: THENON, ST-PIERRE-DE-CHIGNAC, NEUVIC, MUSSIDAN, Quarry, Isle, Vern, VERGT, ROUFFIGNAC, CRO-DE-GRANVILLE, Crempse, Caudeau, Vézère, Beune, LES EYZIES, BARA-BAHAU, LE BUGUE, CAMPAGNE, LIMEUIL, Louyre, ST-CYPRIEN, Eyraud, Dordogne, BERGERAC, LALINDE, BADEFOLS, Dordogne, Gardonnette, Conne, Couze, ST-AVIT-SÉNIEUR, Jasper, Nauze

The schematic representations of the three Upper Cretaceous limestone formations are based upon the Carte Géologique Détaillée de France, Feuille 182 (Bergerac), 1920, and Feuille 193 (Villeréal), 1920.

PART 2. THE HUMAN REMAINS

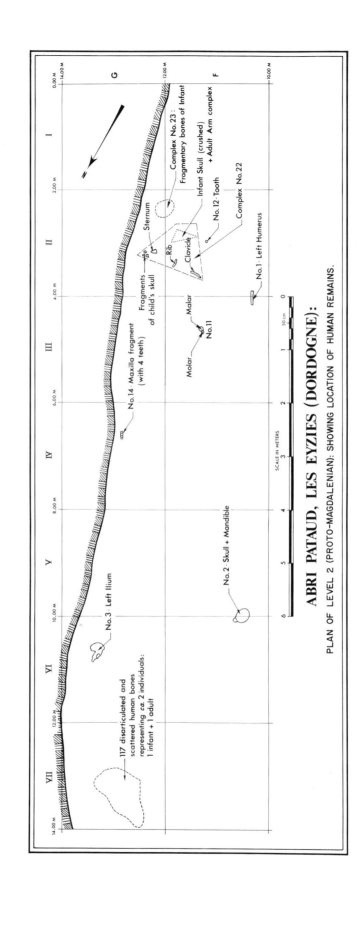

ABRI PATAUD, LES EYZIES (DORDOGNE):

PLAN OF LEVEL 2 (PROTO-MAGDALENIAN): SHOWING LOCATION OF HUMAN REMAINS.

X

Etude Anthropologique des Restes Humains de L'Abri Pataud

Ginette Billy

CENTRE NATIONAL DE LA RECHERCHE SCIENTIFIQUE
LIMOGES, FRANCE

Les restes humains découverts dans la couche proto-magdalénienne de l'Abri Pataud se trouvaient dispersés sur une aire assez vaste s'étendant sur 14 m² environ. Les circonstances de la découverte et la localisation exacte des divers ossements ayant été précisées par ailleurs, nous rappellerons seulement ici l'emplacement et la désignation des pièces qui font l'objet de la présente étude.

Limite des Trenches I et II[1]
    un fragment de vertèbre.
Trench II
    n°7: un radius et un ulna brisés, recueillis dans les éboulis de la zone A.
    n°8: une côte et un péroné brisés (Lens 3).
    Complexe n°22 (Lens 3), comprenant une côte, deux clavicules dont une incomplète, un sternum, deux humérus, un ulna, un radius, une main presque complète, une omoplate incomplète, un crâne écrasé et une mandibule d'enfant.
    Complexe n°23 (Lens 3), comprenant de nombreux fragments d'os d'enfant.
Trench III
    n°6: portion pétreuse de temporal.
    n°11: un fragment de malaire (Lens 2).
Trench IV
    n°13: une phalange (Lens 1).
    n°14: un fragment de maxillaire d'enfant, avec 4 dents (Lens 3).
Trench V
    n°16: un fragment de péroné trouvé dans les éboulis de la zone A.

Limite des Trenches V et VI
    n°2: un crâne complet et une mandibule, dans les éboulis de la zone A.
Trench VI
    n°3: os iliaque incomplet (Éboulis de la zone A).
    n°17: une phalange (Lens 2).
    n°18: un péroné fragmenté (Lens 1).
    n°19: une phalange, près du crâne (Éboulis de la zone A).
    n°20: deux phalanges (Éboulis de la zone A).
Trench VII
    117 os humains, tous numérotés, dont le détail serait évidemment trop long. Ils comportent principalement des vertèbres, des côtes, une clavicule, quatre dents appartenant à la tête n°2, deux rotules, des os de mains et de pieds, ainsi que des os d'enfant. Tous ces os, intimement mélangés, se trouvaient localisés dans un espace réduit en forme d'ellipsoïde de dimensions maximales: 80 cm x 50 cm x 30 cm (épaisseur).

Rappelons que les Trenches I à VI furent fouillées lors de la première campagne en 1958, tandis que les restes osseux de la Trench VII proviennent de la campagne de fouilles de 1963. C'est donc uniquement sur le matériel humain recueilli dans les Trenches I à VI que porte l'étude préliminaire de H.V. Vallois parue dès 1959.

Outre les restes proto-magdaléniens, il convient encore de signaler l'existence à l'Abri Pataud d'un fragment distal de fémur recueilli dans un niveau Noaillien moyen, appelé antérieurement Périgordien Vc (Trench III, Square D, Lens 5). Un tel horizon archéologique, séparé du Proto-Magdalénien par un Périgordien VI, est évidemment très antérieur, comme le montre la datation au Carbone 14 qui lui attribue environ 27.000 ans B.P. C'est le seul reste humain connu jusqu'ici dans une telle couche archéologique.

Bien que gardant à l'esprit la situation de chacune des pièces au moment de sa découverte, nous présen-

---

[1] Nous reprenons la terminologie anglo-saxonne utilisée dans cet ouvrage. Elle concerne les mots suivants:
□Trench(es): Tranchée(s), numérotée(s) de I à VII.
□Square(s): Subdivision(s) des tranchées, designée(s) par les lettres A à G.
□Lens: Subdivision dans chaque couche archéologique.

terons les résultats de notre étude en nous plaçant sur le plan anatomique. Seule, en effet, l'analyse de chaque type d'ossements peut fournir une argumentation nécessaire, susceptible d'aboutir au dénombrement exact des sujets, et, surtout, de préciser, malgré leur dispersion, la répartition des squelettes. En l'absence de vestiges osseux provenant d'un même niveau archéologique, l'étude comparative des restes proto-magdaléniens sera envisagée par ailleurs selon un double point de vue. D'une part, nous les rapprocherons de leurs prédécesseurs aurignaciens, en l'occurrence ceux de Cro-Magnon, leurs voisins, et ceux de Předmost qui, malgré l'éloignement, ont le privilège d'avoir livré un squelette féminin complet. D'autre part, nous orienterons nos comparaisons vers les sujets féminins magdaléniens, soit du Périgord, notamment de Cap-Blanc (von Bonin 1935a), de Saint-Germain-la-Rivière (documents inédits du Professeur Vallois), ou de Laugerie-Basse (de Quatrefages et Hamy 1882), soit de certaines régions plus distantes comme au Mas d'Azil, dans l'Ariège (H.V. Vallois 1961), à l'Abri Lafaye (Tarn-et-Garonne) étudié par E. Genet-Varcin et M. Miquel (1967), ou à Duruthy dans les Landes (E. Genet-Varcin 1965).

1. LA TETE OSSEUSE

En excellent état de conservation, la tête osseuse découverte à la limite des Trenches V et VI (Pièce n° 2) est complète (cf. fig. 1); elle présente seulement quelques pertes de substance localisées à la partie antérieure du pariétal gauche, en avant du bregma, à la mastoïde gauche, ainsi qu'à la base de l'occipital. Le crâne fut entièrement reconstitué dès 1958 mais une restauration permit depuis lors de remonter entièrement l'arcade zygomatique gauche et de remplacer par du ciment les parties manquantes de la voûte. La pièce ne présente par ailleurs aucune déformation; au niveau du massif facial, on relève seulement une cassure de l'extrémité des os nasaux, de la pointe de l'épine nasale et du fond de l'orbite droite. La mandibule est également en parfait état de conservation et absolument complète à l'exception de plusieurs dents, comme d'ailleurs au niveau du maxillaire supérieur.

SEXE ET AGE

Son aspect gracile tient essentiellement à ses dimensions modérées et au relief adouci de ses empreintes d'insertion musculaire. Malgré le développement marqué des arcades sourcilières, la proéminence de l'inion, la présence des lignes courbes occipitales et des lignes temporales, le sexe féminin paraît indiscutable. Un tel diagnostic est pleinement confirmé par la verticalité du front au-dessus d'une glabelle modérée, la faible saillie des bosses frontales latérales, les arcades zygomatiques graciles, les apophyses mastoïdes assez peu développées et le menton triangulaire.

La suture sphéno-occipitale n'étant pas complètement oblitérée et les troisièmes molaires en cours d'éruption, on peut donc situer entre 16 et 18 ans l'âge de ce sujet au moment de sa mort. Il s'agit là d'un individu *juvenis* (H. Vallois 1960) dont la morphologie est cependant comparable à celle d'un adulte, comme le montrera par la suite l'étude anthropologique.

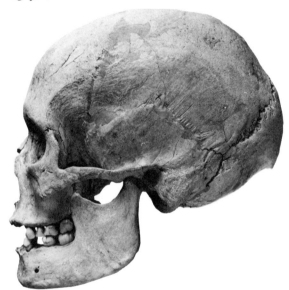

Figure 1. Le tête osseuse.

I. LE CRANE

A. CARACTERES GENERAUX

1. CAPACITE CRANIENNE

L'excellent état de conservation de la pièce a permis de déterminer directement la capacité endocrânienne par cubage au millet (1380 cm.^{3}) selon la technique de Broca. Des capacités calculées à partir des formules de Manouvrier (1520 cm.^{3}), ou de Pearson sur la base de la hauteur porio-bregmatique (1372 cm.^{3}), c'est la seconde qui se rapproche le plus de la valeur réelle. Ainsi l'insuffisance du coefficient d'épaisseur des os utilisé par Manouvrier pour les crânes fossiles se trouve une fois de plus vérifiée.

Bien que les mesures de cubage au millet soient généralement supérieures, selon Broca, à celles obtenues par cubage au plomb, on peut affirmer que la capacité du crâne de Pataud, située dans la catégorie aristencéphale définie par Sarasin, est assez considérable pour le sexe féminin. Une capacité relativement grande semble d'ailleurs de règle chez les femmes du Paléolithique supérieur comme l'attestent les chiffres du tableau II, à l'exception de l'adolescente du Mas d'Azil.

2. LONGUEUR ET LARGEUR CRANIENNES. INDICE CRANIEN

a. Longueur. Avec une longueur de 183 mm., le crâne de l'adolescente de l'Abri Pataud doit être considéré comme «très long» d'après la classification de Lebzelter et Saller. Une similitude frappante existe à cet

TABLEAU I
Mesures et indices du crâne cérébral de l'Abri Pataud [*]

Capacité mesurée au millet (en cm.^{3})	1380	
" calculée selon Manouvrier	1520	
" calculée selon Pearson	1372	
Epaisseur bosse frontale	4	
" bosse pariétale	6,8	
" au bregma	4,5	
" à l'obélion	6	
Longueur maximale (1)	183	
" glabelle-lambda (3)	174	
" glabelle-inion (2)	180	
" nasion-basion (5)	98	
" du trou occipital (7)	36,5	
Largeur maximale (8)	138	
" frontale minimale (9)	100	
" frontale maximale (10)	117	
" biauriculaire (11)	121	
" bimastoïdienne (13)	106	
" du trou occipital (16)	30,5	
Hauteur basion-bregma (17)	130	
" porion-bregma (20)	113,5	
" de la calotte (sur G1-I) (22 a)	95	
Périmètre horizontal (23)	515	
" transversal (24)	308	
" sagittal (25)	367	
Arc frontal (26)	125	
" pariétal (27)	120	
" occipital (28)	122	
Corde frontale (29)	111	
" pariétale (30)	107	
" occipitale (31)	97	
Angle du frontal (32$_{1a}$)	52°	
Angle de Schwalbe (32$_2$)	57°	
Indice crânien (8/1)	75,4	
" de hauteur-longueur au basion (17/1)	71,0	
" de hauteur-largeur au basion (17/8)	94,2	
" mixte de hauteur au basion (17/1+8/2)	81,0	
" de hauteur-longueur au porion (20/1)	62,0	
" de hauteur-largeur au porion (20/8)	82,2	
" de la calotte (22 a/2)	52,8	
" fronto-pariétal (9/8)	72,5	
" fronto-transversal (9/10)	85,5	
" frontal-sagittal (29/26)	88,8	
" pariétal-sagittal (30/27)	89,2	
" occipital-sagittal (31/28)	79,5	
" du trou occipital (16/7)	83,6	
" cranio-facial transverse (45/8)	95,6	

(*) Les chiffres entre parenthèses correspondent à la nomenclature de Martin. Les mensurations sont exprimées en millimètres à l'exception des capacités (en cm.^{3}) et des angles (en degrés).

TABLEAU II

Mesures et indices des crânes féminins du Paléolithique supérieur

	Abri Pataud	Cap-Blanc	Saint-Germain	Mas d'Azil	Duruthy	Laugerie Basse n° 2	Abri Lafaye	Obercassel ♀	Cro-Magnon ♀ n° 2
Capacité (en cm.³)	1380 (c)(*)	1434? (P)	1499 (M) 1354 (P)	1275 (c)	1140 (W)	–	1555?	1370?	–
Long. maximale	183	186	184	173	178	179	187	181	192
Larg. maximale	138	142	142?	132	138	134	134	128	138?
Haut. bas.-breg.	130	138?	124	120,5?	–	–	134	134	–
Haut. por.-breg.	113,5	115	108	103?	109,7	–	112	110	115
Larg. front. min.	100	99	98,5	90	86	97	94	93	97,5
Larg. front. max.	117	111?	115	–	104	117	112	112	120
Périm. horizontal	515	526?	524	489	–	510?	520	512	535
Ind. crânien	75,4	76,3?	77,1	76,3	77,5	74,9	71,6	71,0	71,9
Ind. h./L. (Bas.)	71,0	74,2	67,3	69,6	–	–	71,6	74,0	–
Ind. h./l. (Bas.)	94,2	97,1	87,3	91,2	–	–	100,0	104,7	–
Ind. h./L. (Por.)	62,0	61,8	58,6	59,5	61,6	–	59,9	60,8	59,9
Ind. h./l. (Por.)	82,2	81,0	76,0	78,0	79,5	–	83,6	85,9	83,3
Ind. frontal transv.	85,5	89,2	85,6	–	82,7	82,9	83,9	83,0	81,2
Ind. fronto-pariétal	72,5	69,7	69,3	68,2	62,3	72,4	70,2	72,7	70,6

(*) (c) capacité par cubage du crâne, (P) calculée avec la formule de Pearson, (M) de Manouvrier, (W) de Welcker.

endroit avec ceux de Saint-Germain-la-Rivière et d'Obercassel.

b. **La largeur** crânienne maximale présente une moins grande variabilité dans la série paléolithique et la dimension «moyenne» relevée sur le sujet de Pataud coïncide précisément avec celles des femmes de Cro-Magnon et de Duruthy; pour cette mesure, comme pour toutes les autres, le crâne du Mas d'Azil se caractérise par des dimensions réduites liées au jeune âge du sujet (environ 15 ans). On retiendra donc que l'adolescente de l'Abri Pataud, à âge sensiblement égal, présente des dimensions comparables à celles des femmes adultes du Paléolithique supérieur.

c. **L'indice crânien** horizontal (75,4) se situe à la limite inférieure de la mésocrânie. Or on sait que l'indice crânien, franchement dolichocrâne à l'époque aurignaco-périgordienne, évolue nettement vers la mésocrânie au cours du Paléolithique supérieur (Billy 1971). Par sa situation intermédiaire et sa position chronologique, le sujet de l'Abri Pataud peut être considéré comme un jalon de ce phénomène évolutif qui ne sera réalisé pleinement qu'au Magdalénien.

3. HAUTEURS CRANIENNES. INDICES DE HAUTEUR

a. **La hauteur basio-bregmatique** (130 mm.) se situe dans la catégorie «moyenne» de la classification de Lebzelter et Saller. Elle détermine des indices orthocrâne et métriocrâne définissant une voûte moyennement basse par rapport à ses deux dimensions horizontales, avec une tendance marquée vers la chamaecrânie. Le développement vertical du crâne de l'Abri Pataud est intermédiaire entre ceux observés sur l'homme de Cro-Magnon ou la femme de Saint-Germain-la-Rivière, à voûtes basses, et sur le sujet féminin de Cap-Blanc où la voûte est au contraire très élevée.

b. **La hauteur porio-bregmatique** mesure 113,5 mm.; elle semble relativement élevée en regard des dimensions des autres femmes paléolithiques, excepté celle de Cap-Blanc. Elle représente en effet les 87,3% de la hauteur basio-bregmatique, valeur plus élevée que la moyenne obtenue par S. de Félice (1965) sur un ensemble de 411 crânes modernes (85,4%). Une augmentation de ce rapport traduit en fait un aplatissement de la base du crâne, caractéristique des

Cro-Magniens (Billy 1970), plus particulièrement accusé sur le crâne éponyme où la hauteur au porion atteint 92,1% de celle mesurée au basion. Notons à ce sujet que seule la femme de Saint-Germain-la-Rivière présente un rapport comparable (87,1) à celui observé à Pataud, ainsi que celle de Předmost (86,8).

Les indices de hauteur au porion se situent dans les catégories «moyenne.» Néanmoins, l'indice de hauteur-longueur accuse une tendance marquée à l'hypsicrânie contrairement à son homologue au basion qui s'oriente franchement vers la chamae-crânie. En réalité, cette divergence ne fait que concrétiser l'aplatissement de la base du crâne, déjà mis en évidence par les dimensions absolues, qui se reproduit de façon absolument identique chez les hommes de Cro-Magnon. Ce sont en général les conformations orthocrâne et métriocrâne au porion qui prédominent chez les autres sujets du Paléolithi-que supérieur, à l'exception de la femme de Saint-Germain-la-Rivière.

B. NORMA VERTICALIS

Le contour du crâne, orienté suivant sa longueur maximale, présente une forme ovoïde à tendance pentagonoïde avec saillie très nette des bosses parié-tales situées en position avancée (cf. pl. I). Une telle conformation ovoïde paraît la plus fréquente chez les femmes magdaléniennes, celle de Laugerie exceptée. Le développement plus accentué des bosses pariétales confère cependant au crâne de Pataud une nette tendance au type pentagonoïde qui fut longtemps considéré à tort comme l'une des principales carac-téristiques des hommes de Cro-Magnon (Billy 1969). En vue supérieure selon le plan de Francfort (cf. fig. 2), débordent en avant l'extrémité des os nasaux et du maxillaire supérieur et, latéralement, les apophyses zygomatiques en entier; il y a phénozygie. En arrière, seul le bord supérieur de l'écaille occipitale est visible.

Dans l'ensemble, les indentations des sutures crâ-niennes sont assez simples. Bien qu'incomplètement visible, la coronale est presque rectiligne vers le bregma et à peine plus dentelée latéralement; la sagittale, un peu plus compliquée, décrit une large sinuosité dans sa partie pré-oblique, puis reprend sa direction primitive jusqu'au lambda. Enfin, la lamb-doïde, qui se complique dans sa partie astérique (nos 3 et 4 de l'échelle de Broca), présente deux os wormiens: l'un lambdatique de grandes dimensions (15 x 24 mm.) dans sa portion droite, et, l'autre, lambdoïdien de dimensions réduites à gauche.

Selon cette norma, le crâne présente une légère déformation déterminée par un développement plus

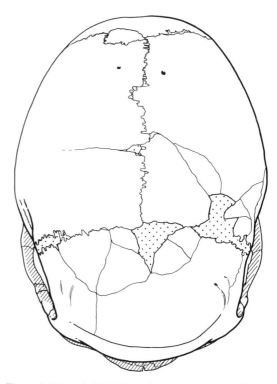

Figure 2. Crâne de l'Abri Pataud: norma verticalis, 1/2.G.N.

accentué de la bosse pariétale droite qui se trouve située plus en avant. Mais une telle asymétrie n'affec-tant pas le niveau frontal, ne peut être considérée comme une plagiocéphalie.

Le périmètre horizontal donne une idée des dimensions du crâne selon cette vue. Sa valeur est moyenne par comparaison à celles des femmes du Paléolithique supérieur (cf. tabl. II), tout en dépas-sant les moyennes actuelles.

1. LE FRONTAL

C'est en *norma verticalis* que le degré de développe-ment du frontal est le mieux apprécié, tant en valeur absolue que par rapport à la largeur crânienne.

a. Largeurs frontales. Le front est très large dans sa zone de rétrécissement maximal; sa largeur (100 mm.) dépasse notablement les moyennes observées sur les européens modernes et arrive en tête des valeurs comparatives du Paléolithique supérieur. Un tel développement, il est vrai, se retrouve chez les femmes de Cap-Blanc, de Saint-Germain, et de Cro-Magnon. Le front est par ailleurs moins développé dans sa partie postérieure. Cependant, la largeur

Planche I. Le crâne de l'Abri Pataud. 1. *norma verticalis;* 2. *norma lateralis.*

frontale maximale de la femme de Pataud (117 mm.), identique à celle de Laugerie, n'est dépassée que par celle de la femme de Cro-Magnon (cf. tabl. II).

b. Indices frontaux. L'indice frontal transverse qui compare ces deux largeurs est mésosème (85,5); l'écaille frontale est donc moyennement divergente. Notons à cet endroit la similitude existant entre le crâne de l'Abri Pataud et celui de Saint-Germain-la-Rivière; partout ailleurs, le front est plus divergent, tout particulièrement à Cro-Magnon et à Předmost (F. IV: 80,3).

L'indice fronto-pariétal qui rend compte du développement transversal du front par rapport au crâne est eurymétope (72,5). L'élargissement du frontal entre sa partie antérieure et la région des bosses pariétales est donc peu marqué. Une telle disposition se retrouve d'ailleurs sur tous les sujets du Paléolithique supérieur, sauf chez la femme de Duruthy.

2. LE PARIETAL

Les bosses pariétales sont moyennement développées, le renflement des parois latérales du crâne portant surtout sur le pariétal. L'écaille temporale fortement dilatée, ne le déborde vraiment que du côté gauche comme l'atteste la représentation du crâne en *norma verticalis* (cf. fig. 2).

On remarque la présence de deux trous pariétaux largement ouverts, le gauche étant le plus grand et le plus rapproché de la suture sagittale. Rappelons à ce sujet que l'absence des trous pariétaux est de loin le cas le plus fréquent au Paléolithique supérieur (Billy 1955).

C. NORMA LATERALIS

1. PROFIL DU CRANE CEREBRAL

La glabelle forme une saillie modérée, correspondant au type III de l'échelle de Broca modifiée par Martin, tandis que les arcades sourcilières sont plutôt fortes. Le front décrit une courbe régulière qui s'élève à peine obliquement dans sa partie antérieure, s'infléchit au niveau des bosses frontales, haut placées, et poursuit sa convexité jusqu'au bregma (cf. fig. 3 et pl. I). La voûte est alors sensiblement horizontale jusqu'au vertex, situé environ au premier quart des pariétaux, puis décrit en sens inverse une convexité régulière jusqu'au lambda. L'occipital forme un très léger chignon par un bombement notable de sa portion écailleuse jusqu'à l'inion. Au-delà, la courbe décrit une large concavité avec une dépression de la

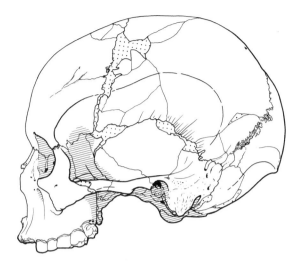

Figure 3. Crâne de l'Abri Pataud: norma lateralis, 40% G.N.

partie correspondant à la fosse cérébelleuse qui entraîne un aplatissement de la base du crâne, nettement visible sur le diagramme sagittal (fig. 4).

Cette voûte régulière et moyennement haute, à chignon occipital et aplatissement basilaire, n'est pas sans évoquer les caractéristiques essentielles des hommes de Cro-Magnon. Elle diffère au contraire de celles de l'homme de Chancelade, et des sujets d'Obercassel ou de Duruthy qui sont caractérisés par l'absence de chignon, une voûte plus haute et une base du crâne nettement plus élevée.

Le développement en hauteur du crâne cérébral proprement dit est évalué par la hauteur de la calotte au vertex sur le plan glabello-iniaque. Cette hauteur (95 mm.) indique une voûte relativement basse, aussi

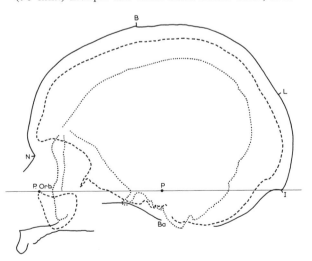

Figure 4. Profils sagittal et para-sagittaux selon Sarasin. Dessin au diagraphe, 40% G.N.

bien par rapport aux crânes d'Européens modernes que par rapport à ceux de Chancelade (107 mm.) ou des Magdaléniennes de l'Abri Lafaye (107 mm.) et de Saint-Germain-la-Rivière (105 mm.). Un tel aplatissement du crâne cérébral rappelle la conformation des crânes de Cro-Magnon où la hauteur de la calotte du sujet n°1 n'est que de 98 mm. L'indice de hauteur de la calotte, qui rapporte cette dimension à la longueur glabelle-inion, est par suite très bas, le chiffre obtenu à Pataud (52,8), se rapprochant de ceux trouvés chez l'homme n°1 de Cro-Magnon (49,0) et la plupart des individus de Předmost (F.X:54,4).

La longueur de la courbe sagittale totale est de 367 mm., valeur qui s'intègre parfaitement dans les limites de variation observées de nos jours. Toutefois, dans le contexte du Paléolithique supérieur, elle se situe parmi les valeurs les plus faibles rencontrées chez les femmes n°X de Předmost (364 mm.) et de Cap-Blanc (371 mm.). Par ailleurs, la part relative de chacun des os à la constitution de la voûte, se traduit par l'expression F > 0 > P qui résume les chiffres suivants:

Frontal	34,1%
Pariétal	32,7%
Occipital	33,2%

Ainsi, contrairement à la disposition de beaucoup la plus fréquente, la part de l'occipital est supérieure à celle du pariétal. Une telle disposition est particulièrement rare au Paléolithique supérieur et se retrouve seulement chez la femme n°X de Předmost. La participation du frontal est par ailleurs plus importante que celle du pariétal, comme c'est le cas pour les deux crânes masculins de Cro-Magnon, les hommes du Cavillon, d'Obercassel et de Předmost III, ainsi que pour les femmes de la Barma-Grande, du Mas d'Azil, de Duruthy, et de Předmost. La disposition inverse existant sur tous les autres crânes paléolithiques, il ne semble pas que la position plus ou moins avancée du bregma doive être retenue comme caractéristique.

a. Le frontal. Le front est relativement haut; les dimensions de l'arc frontal et de la corde qui le sous-tend sont élevées comme le laissait prévoir l'importance considérable de ce segment dans la composition de la courbe sagittale.

Le degré de courbure du frontal mesuré par l'indice fronto-sagittal (88,8) indique un front modérément bombé ou «orthométope.» Les valeurs très proches observées sur les autres crânes du Paléolithique supérieur rassemblées au tableau III montrent que le front était partout bien redressé. Sur les deux crânes masculins de Cro-Magnon, le degré de convexité du frontal est encore plus accusé comme le montrent les valeurs très faibles de l'indice (85,0).

L'obliquité du front, évaluée par l'angle bregmatique de Schwalbe (57°) ou par la pente de la corde nasio-bregma sur le plan de Francfort (52°), est très marquée; le front est droit, bien que sa verticalité soit en partie compensée par le développement de l'os en longueur. En regard des autres crânes paléolithiques (cf. tableau III), les chiffres obtenus à Pataud occupent une position intermédiaire.

b. Le pariétal. Compte tenu de l'architecture crânienne, les longueurs de l'arc pariétal, et de la corde qui le sous-tend, sont relativement faibles et comparables aux moyennes obtenues sur des séries modernes essentiellement brachycrânes. La brièveté du segment pariétal, déjà mise en évidence dans la constitution de la voûte crânienne, ressort également de l'examen du tableau comparatif III. Par compensation, sa convexité est plus accusée comme l'indique la valeur relativement plus faible de l'indice pariéto-sagittal.

En *norma lateralis*, mentionnons encore l'existence de lignes temporales supérieure et inférieure bien visibles sur tout leur trajet; ces dernières délimitent une fosse temporale assez accusée. La région ptérique présente une forte dépression transversale qui porte principalement sur la partie antéro-inférieure du pariétal et sur la grande aile sphénoïdale, laquelle est très fortement convexe. Notons enfin une disposition en H du ptérion.

c. Le temporal. La partie écailleuse du temporal est assez réduite et présente un fort bombement transversal; son bord supérieur suit un trajet très arqué, interrompu seulement dans sa partie postérieure par une incisure pariétale large mais peu profonde.

Plutôt gracile, l'arcade zygomatique possède un bord supérieur sinueux qui décrit une large convexité et un bord inférieur avec un tubercule post-glénoïdien assez développé. Dans le prolongement de l'arcade zygomatique, la crête sus-mastoïdienne forme une saillie en arc de cercle bien marquée qui s'étend jusqu'à la suture temporo-pariétale.

Le développement des apophyses mastoïdes paraît modéré. En effet, bien que la largeur et l'épaisseur soient notables, elles ont toutefois une hauteur faible: leurs extrémités n'atteignent pas le niveau des condyles lorsque le crâne repose sur un plan. Dans leur partie supérieure, elles présentent au-dessus d'une surface bombée et rugueuse, une large dépression transversale que surplombe la crête sus-mastoïdienne. En arrière de l'apophyse mastoïde, tout près de la suture occipito-mastoïdienne, s'ouvre l'orifice du canal mastoïdien. Enfin, la forme du trou auditif externe est quasi circulaire.

TABLEAU III

La voûte crânienne: comparaisons

	Abri Pataud	Cap-Blanc	Saint-Germain	Mas d'Azil	Duruthy	Abri Lafaye	Obercassel	Cro-Magnon 2
Arc frontal (26)	125	118	131	124?	123	124	124	132
– pariétal (27)	120	132?	140	116?	110	146	139	133
– occipital (28)	122	121	109	101	107	106	112	–
Corde frontale (29)	111	105	112	107	110	110	100	115
– pariétale (30)	107	121	?	109	102	128	124	122
– occipitale (31)	97	102	?	83	101	92	94	–
Angle du frontal (32 1a)	52°	61°	–	49°	–	54°	50,5°	49°
– de Schwalbe (32$_2$)	57°	56°	56°	56°	50°	61°	63°	–
Ind. fronto-sagittal	88,8	89,0	85,4	86,2?	89,4	88,7	80,6	87,1
– pariéto-sagittal	89,2	91,7	–	93,9	92,7	87,7	89,2	91,7
– occipito-sagittal	79,5	84,3	–	82,2	94,4	86,8	83,9	–

d. L'occipital. L'arc occipital semble relativement long (122 mm.) comparé soit aux moyennes d' Européens modernes d'architectures crâniennes différentes, soit aux autres crânes du Paléolithique supérieur (cf. tabl. III). En revanche, la corde occipitale présentant une longueur moyenne, il s'ensuit une convexité très accentuée (79,5) qui dépasse largement celle des autres Magdaléniennes et se rapproche de celle du sujet n° 1 de Cro-Magnon (79,0). Comme chez l'homme de Cro-Magnon, cette forte courbure dénote l'existence d'un véritable chignon occipital. Toutefois, la technique de mesure préconisée par Ducros (1967) pour en apprécier l'importance donne une profondeur de l'ensellure pariéto-occipitale de 0,5 mm., qui classe le crâne de Pataud dans la catégorie à chignon «esquissé.»

L'inion présente par ailleurs un développement très marqué atteignant le type 4 de l'échelle de Martin. Il forme une forte saillie en crochet dirigée vers le bas et située sensiblement sur le plan de Francfort; la bascule occipitale n'est donc pas complètement réalisée sur le crâne de l'Abri Pataud.

Le profil sous-iniaque est très fortement déprimé comme le montre la figure 4, une telle conformation se retrouve chez l'homme de Cro-Magnon et chez plusieurs sujets de Předmost dont la femme X tout particulièrement.

e. Le sphénoïde. La face temporale de la grande aile du sphénoïde est très fortement déprimée; elle détermine une véritable gouttière paraissant d'autant plus accusée que la saillie du malaire est considérable.

2. PROFIL DU CRANE FACIAL

En dessous d'une dépression nasale qui rappelle, en moins accentuée, celle de l'homme de Cro-Magnon et des Aurignaciens de Předmost, les os nasaux, légèrement concaves, font une forte saillie vers l'avant. Bien que son extrémité soit brisée, l'épine nasale forme une crête aiguë, non dédoublée, s'identifiant à la catégorie 2 de la classification de Martin.

L'avancée du massif facial, évaluée par l'indice gnathique de Flower (103,1) ou par l'angle facial de

TABLEAU IV

Prognathisme facial: comparaisons

	Abri Pataud	Cap-Blanc	Saint-Germain	Mas d'Azil	Abri Lafaye	Ober-cassel	Chan-celade	Cro-Magnon 1	Cro-Magnon 2
Ind. gnathique	103,1	99,0	97,2	94,5	90,3	89,5	92,0	102,0	–
Angle de Weisbach	69°	–	71°	–	–	–	74°	71°	–
Angle profil total	81°	89°	88°	88°	90°	84°	89°	88°	92°
Angle profil nasal	80°	85°	88°	–	–	87°	89°	95°	94°5
Angle profil alvéol.	77°	88°5	80°	92°	–	76°	87°	68°	83°

Weisbach (69°), se situe à la limite inférieure du prognathisme. La mesure directe des différents angles faciaux permet toutefois de préciser le niveau exact de cette projection faciale en avant: alors que les angles des profils total (81°) et nasal (80°) correspondent seulement au mésognathisme, l'angle du profil alvéolaire (77°) atteste l'existence d'un prognathisme très net. C'est donc essentiellement la composante sous-nasale du massif facial qui détermine le prognathisme facial.

De l'examen du tableau comparatif IV, il ressort que le profil facial est en général orthognathe au Magdalénien, à l'exception de la femme d'Obercassel qui présente, comme celle de Pataud, un prognathisme alvéolaire accentué. On retrouve cette même déclivité du maxillaire supérieur chez les sujets de Cro-Magnon dont les profils total et nasal sont aussi orthognathes.

La région alvéolaire est également haute, la fosse canine nette, limitée en avant par un léger relief au-dessus de la seconde prémolaire et, en arrière, par la racine du malaire. Ce dernier est large et fortement déjeté vers l'arrière, découvrant ainsi une grande partie de la cavité orbitaire (cf. fig. 3). Il présente encore une apophyse marginale sur son bord temporal, un tubercule maxillo-malaire, ainsi qu'une surface d'insertion massétérienne rugueuse et très marquée.

D. NORMA BASILARIS

1. CRANE CEREBRAL

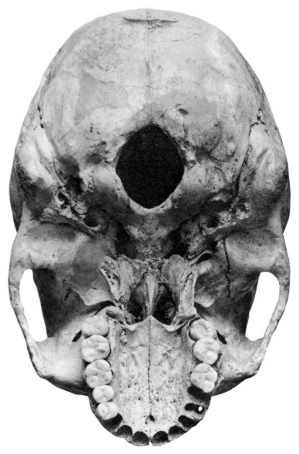

Figure 5. Crâne de l'Abri Pataud: norma basilaris.

Le trou occipital, de forme sensiblement losangique (cf. fig. 5), se situe dans la catégorie mésosème, avec un indice de 83,6. Son angle d'inclinaison par rapport au plan de Francfort est de -6°, ce qui implique une position peu inclinée vers l'avant du *foramen magnum.*

Les condyles occipitaux sont très arqués et saillants, en forme d'ellipse allongée sans aucun étranglement médian, avec des axes fortement divergeants vers l'arrière. Leur développement est tel que leur niveau dépasse quelque peu celui des apophyses mastoïdes.

La suture sphéno-occipitale est encore partiellement ouverte; sa synostose s'effectuant normalement entre 16 et 20 ans, on en conclut que le sujet n'avait guère plus de 16 ans, ce qui confirme nos précédentes observations (cf. p. 202). La face du basi-occipital est par ailleurs fortement convexe; de chaque côté, la crête transverse qui donne attache au grand droit antérieur forme une saillie très nette, alors que la fossette naviculaire est à peine visible.

En arrière du trou occipital, il apparaît sur l'écaille une crête occipitale externe très nette et seulement la *linea nuchae inferior* peu accusée qui se termine par un processus paracondylien.

Au niveau du temporal, l'apophyse mastoïde est épaisse avec une face externe très bombée recouverte de rugosités dues aux insertions musculaires. La rainure digastrique est large mais peu profonde. Par ailleurs, la cavité glénoïde est vaste et très marquée, allongée presque transversalement. La portion du tympanal, qui constitue sa paroi postérieure, se trouve assez réduite et reserrée entre l'apophyse post-glénoïde et la région pétro-mastoïdienne. L'angle pétro-tympanique, déterminé selon la technique établie par M.-C. Chamla (1956), est relativement fermé (153°); il se situe à la limite de la catégorie «très coudée» définie par l'auteur. Cette angulation prononcée doit être rapprochée de celle observée chez les hommes de Cro-Magnon (145°) ou d'Obercassel (140 et 145°); chez la femme d'Obercassel, au contraire, le tympanal se trouve presque dans l'axe pétreux (170°). En avant de la cavité glénoïde, le condyle temporal fait une saillie importante et le tubercule zygomatique antérieur, qui le limite extérieurement, est très apparent.

Au niveau du sphénoïde, les apophyses ptérygoïdes sont brisées. Les grandes ailes présentent une concavité très accentuée qui détermine une véritable gouttière; la crête sphéno-temporale séparant la fosse temporale de la fosse zygomatique est bien marquée.

En définitive, toute cette région inférieure du crâne cérébral présente un relief accidenté inhabituel pour un sujet féminin.

2. CRANE FACIAL

Vues en *norma basilaris*, les arcades zygomatiques sont très fortement projetées en dehors et décrivent avec le malaire un arc de faible rayon de courbure (cf. fig. 5). De profondeur modérée, la voûte palatine est moyennement large; son indice (81,1) la situe parmi les palais «mésostaphylins.» La suture palatine transverse suit un tracé dentelé de direction générale rectiligne (Stiéda).

Par comparaison avec l'ensemble magdalénien, le palais semble étroit (cf. tabl. VI); le rapprochement avec la femme d'Obercassel est là encore manifeste. A Cro-Magnon et à Předmost, la voûte palatine est au contraire beaucoup plus allongée. Malgré la présence de lésions pathologiques sur la face externe de l'arcade dentaire qui diminue la précision relative à la largeur maxillo-alvéolaire, celle-ci détermine un indice mésuranique (112,5). C'est dire que le maxillaire supérieur n'est que moyennement large. Enfin, le tracé de l'arcade dentaire est elliptique, la distance entre les troisièmes molaires étant légèrement inférieure à celle séparant les M_2.

E. NORMA OCCIPITALIS

Le contour crânien selon cette *norma* présente une forme classique dite «en maison» (cf. fig. 6 et pl. II). La réunion des pariétaux détermine en effet une légère carène puis, au-dessous de bosses pariétales, bien développées, les parois latérales du crâne sont renflées et convergent faiblement vers les mastoïdes. La largeur maximale du crâne se trouve placée sur le bord inférieur du pariétal, au voisinage de la suture squameuse.

Un tel profil crânien s'observe également chez les femmes du Mas d'Azil et de l'Abri Lafaye, chez plusieurs sujets de Předmost, chez les hommes de Cro-Magnon (n° 1) et de Veyrier. Mais il ne rappelle en rien le contour caréné et beaucoup plus haut observé à Chancelade. Il diffère aussi de la forme dite «en tente» rencontrée sur les têtes de Cap-Blanc et de Saint-Germain-la-Rivière dont les parois latérales divergent vers le bas.

A titre d'illustration, nous avons représenté sur la figure 7 les profils vertico-transversaux effectués, selon Sarasin, à trois niveaux crâniens différents. On voit que la voussure crânienne se reproduit à Pataud de façon presque identique sur les portions antérieure et postérieure du crâne. La comparaison avec les profils correspondants de l'homme de Chancelade et de la femme d'Obercassel, dont la ressemblance est bien connue, montre au contraire que la carène se situe chez ceux-ci au niveau du porion, puis s'estompe en avant et en arrière.

La valeur moyenne du périmètre transverse (308 mm.) traduit encore le développement modéré en hauteur et en largeur de la tête de Pataud. Située dans les limites de variabilité observées sur des séries actuelles de même architecture crânienne, cette valeur est néanmoins comparable à celles des Magdaléniennes de Cap-Blanc (308 mm.), de Saint-Germain (306 mm.), et de l'Abri Lafaye (310 mm.); mais elle diffère nettement de celle de Chancelade (326 mm.).

Selon cette *norma*, le relief musculaire de l'occipital est particulièrement visible: la ligne suprême paraît bien marquée et, en-dessous, la ligne courbe occipitale supérieure fait une saillie encore plus accentuée. Toute la région comprise entre ces lignes *nuchae suprema* et *superior* se soulève en un épais bourrelet saillant qui se détache du plan de l'os pour former un torus occipital transverse. Le *tuberculum linearum*, situé à la jonction des lignes suprêmes, est fusionné à la protubérance occipitale externe, formée par les

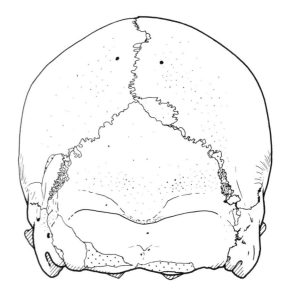

Figure 6. Crâne de l'Abri Pataud: norma occipitalis, 1/2 G.N.

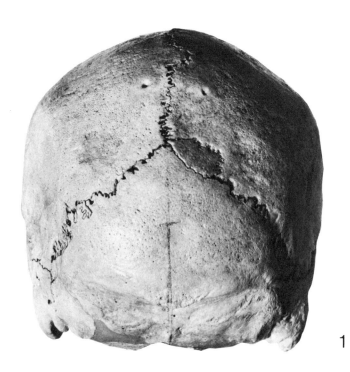

Planche II. Le crâne de l'Abri Pataud. 1. *norma occipitalis;* 2. *norma facialis.*

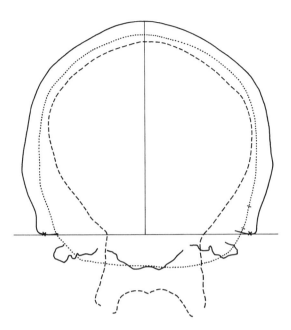

Figure 7. Profils vertico-transversaux selon Sarasin. Dessin au diagraphe, 1/2 G.N.

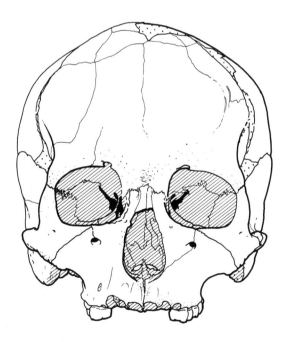

Figure 8. Crâne de l'Abri Pataud: norma facialis, 1/2 G.N.

lignes courbes supérieures; il constitue sagittalement une forte saillie «en crochet» recourbé vers le bas. Au-dessous du torus occipital, l'empreinte musculaire du grand complexus détermine une profonde dépression en forme de croissant. La ligne courbe occipitale supérieure, également très marquée, présente de fortes rugosités correspondant aux zones d'insertion du muscle occipital, du trapèze, et du sterno-cléido-mastoïdien; ces muscles devaient donc être puissants. En-dessous, la ligne courbe occipitale inférieure est visible mais peu développée; seule la crête occipitale externe est bien marquée.

Notons enfin, selon cette vue, le bombement des apophyses mastoïdes que surmonte une dépression transversale, puis la saillie marquée de la crête sus-mastoïdienne. A l'endroit des pariétaux, la présence d'os wormiens et de deux trous pariétaux a déjà été signalée.

F. NORMA FACIALIS

1. CRANE CEREBRAL

Son étude en *norma facialis* permet d'apprécier certains caractères du frontal non décrits jusque-là. On note ainsi l'existence d'une carène médiane nettement marquée (cf. fig. 8 et pl. II). A la fois large et haut, le front présente d'autre part un rétrécissement sus-orbitaire très prononcé; ses apophyses externes divergent fortement et leurs bords tranchants décrivent des concavités accentuées d'où partent les crêtes latérales du frontal qui sont très saillantes.

Les bosses frontales latérales sont proéminentes et très écartées. De chaque côté, on remarque la présence d'une gouttière vasculaire ramifiée, qui contournant la bosse frontale, court obliquement de bas en haut et de dedans en dehors. Livrant passage à des artérioles, de tels sillons osseux s'observent assez fréquemment sur des crânes de jeunes individus, comme c'est le cas sur l'adolescente du Mas d'Azil.

Le développement des arcades sourcilières est considérable. Constituées par les *arcus superciliaris* fusionnés dans la partie médiane avec la glabelle, elles décrivent une importante saillie en forme de V très ouvert qui s'étend jusqu'au milieu de l'orbite. Cette proéminence, de contour assez indécis, tombe directement sur le bord orbitaire supérieur qui offre une vaste échancrure à la limite supérieure de son angle interne. Si les Magdaléniennes de Cap-Blanc, de Saint-Germain, de Duruthy, et du Mas d'Azil présentent une formation sus-orbito-glabellaire extrêmement atténuée, il faut souligner néanmoins le fort développement des *arcus superciliaris* chez tous les

Cro-Magniens typiques de France et ceux de la série de Předmost. La présence d'une telle disposition, en dépit du sexe et de l'âge du sujet de l'Abri Pataud, doit être tenue par conséquent comme un caractère racial le rapprochant sans nul doute des Cro-Magniens.

En dessous, la suture naso-frontale est très dentelée et suit un tracé faiblement concave vers le haut.

2. CRANE FACIAL

a. Le massif facial. De hauteur moyenne (cf. tabl. V), le massif facial est «large» dans sa région zygomatique (132 mm.), selon la classification de Lebzelter et Saller adaptée au crâne sec; il détermine un indice facial total euryprosope de 81,8. Malgré la rareté des données comparatives pour cet indice, on peut en conclure que la femme de Pataud se situe, avec celles de Saint-Germain et de l'Abri Lafaye, en position intermédiaire entre les Aurignaciens des Eyzies ou de Předmost, dont les indices sont pour la plupart

TABLEAU V

Mesures et indices du crâne facial de l'Abri Pataud

Longueur basion-prosthion (40)	101
Largeur interorbitaire antérieure (43)	20,5
Largeur biorbitaire (44)	99
Largeur bizygomatique (45)	132
Largeur bijugale (45^1)	114
Largeur bimaxillaire maximale (46)	100
Hauteur faciale totale (47)	108
Hauteur faciale supérieure (48)	66
Hauteur faciale spino-alvéolaire (48^1)	17
Largeur orbitaire (51) G.	40,5
Largeur orbitaire (51) D.	41
Hauteur orbitaire (52) G.	31,5
Hauteur orbitaire (52) D.	31,5
Largeur du nez (54)	25
Hauteur du nez (55)	49
Longueur maxillo-alvéolaire (60)	56
Largeur maxillo-alvéolaire (61)	63
Longueur du palais (62)	45
Largeur du palais (63)	36,5
Indice facial total (47/45)	81,8
Indice facial supérieur (48/45)	50,0
Indice jugo-mandibulaire (66/45)	73,5
Indice orbitaire (52/51) G.	77,8
Indice orbitaire (52/51) D.	76,8
Indice nasal (54/55)	51,0
Indice palatin (63/62)	81,1
Indice gnathique (40/5)	103,1
Indice maxillo-alvéolaire (61/60)	112,5
Angle de Weisbach (72$_{(5)}$)	69°
Angle du profil facial total (72)	81°
Angle du profil nasal (73)	80°
Angle du profil alvéolaire (74)	77°

hypereuryprosopes, et les Magdaléniens de Chancelade ou d'Obercassel, franchement leptoprosopes (cf. tabl. VI).

Avec une hauteur supérieure de 66 mm., la face est dite «moyennement haute» et ne diffère pas de celles des autres femmes du Paléolithique supérieur (cf. tabl. VI). Couplée à une largeur considérable, elle détermine un indice facial supérieur de 50,0, qui correspond très exactement à la limite inférieure de la mésénie. Bien que mésène, la face de la femme de Pataud présente donc une tendance euryène très marquée.

Il a été montré récemment qu'il existe une augmentation sensible de la hauteur de la face au Paléolithique supérieur, alors que la largeur ne subit aucune fluctuation importante (Riquet 1970). Corrélativement, l'indice facial supérieur va donc augmenter tout au long du Paléolithique pour atteindre son maximum au Magdalénien. Or, les chiffres du tableau VI confirment cette analyse puisque les sujets euryènes se rencontrent précisément parmi les Cro-Magniens des Eyzies, les Grimaldiens, et la série morave de Předmost. Tous les Magdaléniens sont au contraire mésènes, à l'exception des sujets féminins du Mas d'Azil et de Saint-Germain-la-Rivière. La femme proto-magdalénienne de l'Abri Pataud présente donc un stade évolutif intermédiaire entre les deux groupes précités, situation qui correspond au mieux avec sa position chronologique.

Si la largeur bizygomatique n'excède pas, à Pataud, celles des autres sujets féminins (cf. tabl. VI), en revanche, les largeurs relatives à la face supérieure dépassent dans l'ensemble les rares valeurs comparatives trouvées dans la littérature. C'est ainsi que la largeur bi-orbitaire antérieure, mesurée d'un ecto-conchion à l'autre, est nettement plus élevée (99 mm.) que chez les femmes de Saint-Germain (93 mm.), d'Obercassel (94 mm.) et même que chez l'homme de Chancelade (97 mm.). Compte tenu de la différence sexuelle, elle se rapproche plutôt de la valeur observée chez l'homme n° 1 de Cro-Magnon (109 mm.). Malgré l'absence d'éléments de comparaison pour la largeur bijugale, il semble que la dimension obtenue à l'Abri Pataud (114 mm.) se tienne également dans les limites d'une différence sexuelle normale de celle du sujet 1 de Cro-Magnon (122 mm.). Enfin, les valeurs respectives obtenues en ce qui concerne la largeur bimaxillaire maximale (Pataud: 100 mm.; Saint-Germain: 93 mm.; Abri Lafaye: 96 mm.; Obercassel: 88 mm.; Chancelade: 97 mm. et Cro-Magnon n° 1: 105 mm.) parlent absolument dans le même sens. La face offre donc les caractères essentiels du type de Cro-Magnon; sa dilatation, qui intéresse principalement la partie supérieure, est essentiellement due au développement

TABLEAU VI

Le massif facial: comparaisons

	Abri Pataud	Cap-Blanc	Saint-Germain	Abri Lafaye	Předmost IV	Předmost X	Ober-cassel	Chan-celade	Cro-Magnon 1
Larg. bizygomatique	132	138 ?	134,5	132	136	141	124	140	142
Haut. faciale totale	108	?	110	112	105	110	112	127	106
Haut. faciale supérieure	66	75 ?	67	67	64	66	67	77	69
Ind. facial total	81,8	?	81,7	84,8	77,2	78,0	90,3	90,7	74,6
Ind. facial supérieur	50,0	54,3	49,8	50,7	47,1	46,8	54,0	54,2	48,6
Ind. orbitaire	77,3*	–	79,4	74,5*	71,0	65,8	71,4	78,4	58,8*
Ind. nasal	51,0	41,4	42,0	45,6	56,2	54,9	53,3	46,6 ?	47,1
Ind. palatin	81,1	–	90,9	94,8	–	–	81,0	80,0 ?	74,0

*Indice orbitaire moyen.

des pommettes, des apophyses orbitaires externes et des arcades zygomatiques, le maxillaire supérieur restant au contraire étroit.

L'existence d'une dilatation transverse de la partie supérieure de la face détermine la présence d'une fosse canine très marquée et une angulation très accusée de la face antérieure du maxillaire, le malaire réalisant le «type à flexion» tenu pour caractéristique des Prénéandertaliens et des hommes modernes (Sergi 1960).

L'association d'une telle face avec un crâne méso-crâne, à très forte tendance dolichocrâne, prouve qu'il existe, chez la femme de Pataud, une dysharmo-nie cranio-faciale qui peut être considérée sans nul doute comme un critère spécifiquement cro-magnoïde (Billy 1969).

b. **La région orbitaire.** Les orbites sont basses et larges, de forme rectangulaire et surbaissée caracté-ristique de la plupart des crânes du Paléolithique supérieur. La cavité orbitaire n'est pas très profonde mais large, avec un grand axe presque horizontal. Le bord supérieur, assez tranchant, décrit une légère concavité vers le haut dans sa partie externe, tandis que le bord inférieur est nettement rectiligne. Le côté externe ne présente pas de bord net, le malaire formant plutôt à cet endroit un épais bourrelet concave. Du côté interne, la crête lacrymale anté-rieure fait, en revanche, une saillie bien marquée.

D'un côté comme de l'autre, l'indice orbitaire est mésoconque, à forte tendance chamaeconque. Si l'on excepte les sujets franchement mésoconques de Saint-Germain, du Mas d'Azil (I. orb.: 80,2) et de Chance-lade, la chamaeconquie semble en fait de règle générale au Paléolithique supérieur. Une telle disposi-tion en effet, qui se manifeste à un degré extrême sur le sujet n°1 de Cro-Magnon, se retrouve néanmoins chez la femme n°2 (I. orb: 72,1), les trois sujets de la

Barma-Grande et l'homme du Cavillon, bien que Verneau ait utilisé l'ancienne technique au dacryon, et chez la plupart des sujets de Předmost (cf. tabl. VI). Ainsi donc, plus encore que sa tendance chamaeconque, la disposition caractéristique de l'orbite en forme de rectangle allongé transversale-ment rapproche la jeune femme de Pataud des véritables cro-magniens.

Une valeur relativement élevée de la largeur inter-orbitaire antérieure (20,5 mm.), mesurée à partir des points maxillo-frontaux, concrétise l'écartement con-sidérable des orbites qui paraissent par ailleurs légère-ment enfoncées.

La région sous-orbitaire est très déprimée, le *foramen infraorbitale*, largement ouvert et regardant en bas et en dedans, devait laisser passer un épais cordon vasculo-nerveux qui a laissé son empreinte sur l'os, au-dessous de l'orifice, dessinant une large gouttière verticale qui rejoint la fosse canine forte-ment excavée. L'angle antéro-interne du malaire est aigu et la suture maxillo-malaire présente un tracé très oblique en arrière.

Nous avons déjà mentionné la forte angulation du malaire avec la face antérieure du maxillaire, consécu-tive à un rétrécissement très prononcé de sa partie inférieure. Une telle disposition se retrouve plus ou moins prononcée sur la plupart des crânes du Paléoli-thique supérieur. Notons enfin, sur le bord postéro-inférieur du malaire, la présence d'un relief osseux tomenteux dans la région d'insertion du masséter.

c. **La région nasale.** Le nez débute par une suture naso-frontale très dentelée dont le tracé, sensiblement rectiligne, court au fond d'une dépression profonde due à la saillie des os nasaux et de la glabelle.

Bien que les os nasaux soient incomplets, ils permettent de préciser la forme de la pyramide nasale. Relativement étroite, celle-ci présente un fort rétrécissement non loin de sa racine, puis s'évase régulièrement avec une saillie prononcée nettement concave en *norma lateralis* (cf. fig. 3). Les os nasaux, qui sont très convexes transversalement, s'unissent sur la ligne médiane par une suture non synostosée en formant une ogive qui surplombe le plan de l'apophyse montante du maxillaire supérieur.

L'ouverture nasale est piriforme et l'aspect de son bord inférieur correspond au type I, ou type infantile, décrit par Martin et modifié par Hovorka. Ses dimensions déterminent un indice nasal de 51,0 qui coïncide exactement avec la limite inférieure de la chamaerhinie. Ainsi, avec une conformation nasale méso-chamaerhinienne, la femme de l'Abri Pataud présente une harmonie naso-faciale. Une telle disposition l'oppose aux Magdaléniennes de Cap-Blanc, de Saint-Germain-la-Rivière, et de l'Abri Lafaye, ainsi qu'à l'homme de Chancelade. En revanche, une comparaison avec les crânes de l'Aurignacien montre que, malgré une certaine variabilité, le sujet de Pataud se rapproche indéniablement des femmes IV et X de Předmost, III de Brno et de Grimaldi, du sujet de la grotte des Enfants et, à un degré moindre, des deux sujets de Cro-Magnon franchement mésorhiniens.

La région sous-nasale du maxillaire est assez haute chez la femme de Pataud, la hauteur spino-alvéolaire mesurant 17 mm., contre 15,5 mm. seulement chez la femme de Cro-Magnon et 19,5 mm. chez l'homme. Nous rappellerons à cet endroit sa forte proéminence vers l'avant et l'existence d'un net prognathisme alvéolaire. La fossette myrtiforme détermine en avant, au-dessus des racines des deux incisives centrales, une dépression bien marquée que délimite extérieurement la bosse canine qui fait une importante saillie.

II. LA MANDIBULE

La mandibule est presque complète; seul le condyle gauche présente à sa partie externe et postérieure une légère perte de substance et, en avant, le bord alvéolaire des incisives et des canines est quelque peu endommagé (cf. pl. III). N'ayant subi aucune déformation *post-mortem*, la pièce est parfaitement symétrique et ses condyles s'articulent normalement dans les cavités glénoïdes des temporaux.

A. ASPECT GENERAL

Son aspect plutôt robuste provient devantage de la conformation de sa branche montante, particulièrement large et basse, jointe à l'épaisseur considérable du corps, que de ses dimensions générales proprement dites (fig. 9). En effet, la longueur maximale de la mandibule (98 mm.) paraît relativement courte en comparaison de celles des femmes de Duruthy, de l'Abri Lafaye, et de Saint-Germain-la-Rivière. En revanche, la largeur bicondylienne est plutôt élevée, comparable en ce qui concerne les pièces féminines à celles d'Obercassel, de l'Abri Lafaye, et de Předmost. En fait, l'indice mandibulaire (84,8), qui rapporte la longueur maximale à la largeur bicondylienne, se situe à la limite supérieure de la brachygnathie, indiquant ainsi une mandibule large et courte. Une telle conformation se retrouve chez la plupart des Aurignaciens de Grimaldi si l'on en juge par les

TABLEAU VII

Mesures et indices de la mandibule

Longueur maximale (68)	98
Largeur bicondylienne (65)	115,5
Largeur bigoniaque (66)	97
Largeur bimentale (67)	43,5
Hauteur de la symphyse (69)	29
Hauteur du corps au trou mentonnier (69_3)	29
Hauteur de la branche montante (70)	60
Largeur de la branche montante (71)	42,5
Largeur du condyle	21
Hauteur du corps au niveau PM_2-M_1	30
Hauteur du corps au niveau M_1-M_2	29
Epaisseur réelle en PM_2-M_1	15
Epaisseur réelle en M_1-M_2	17,5
Epaisseur en projection au trou mentonnier	15
Epaisseur en projection en PM_2-M_1	17,5
Epaisseur en projection en M_1-M_2	20,5
Epaisseur du condyle	11
Angle goniaque (79)	107°
Angle symphysien (79_{1a})	90°
Angle mentonnier (Broca) ($79_{(1)}$)	82°
Indice mandibulaire (68/65)	84,8
Indice de largeur (66/65)	84,0
Indice de la branche montante (71/70)	70,8
Indice de robustesse au trou mentonnier	51,7
Indice de robustesse en PM_2-M_1	58,3
Indice de robustesse en M_1-M_2	70,7
Indice d'obliquité du corps mandibulaire	85,5
Indice condylien	52,4

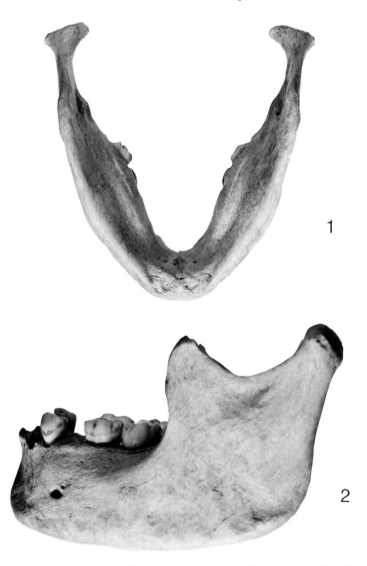

Planche III. La mandibule de l'Abri Pataud. 1. *norma inferior;* 2. *norma lateralis.*

distances angulo-symphysaires données par Verneau qui utilise une technique différente. Comme le montre l'examen du tableau VIII, tous les Magdaléniens sont au contraire dolichognathes, à l'exception de la femme de l'Abri Lafaye qui est mésognathe.

Le rapport relativement élevé des deux largeurs (84,0) traduit par ailleurs une tendance à la verticalité des branches montantes au-dessus du corps, ce qui contribue encore à accentuer l'impression de massivité de la pièce. Une telle disposition de la branche montante est extrêmement fréquente au

Magdalénien d'après les chiffres du tableau VIII; la femme X de Předmost présenterait toutefois, avec un indice de 75, une remarquable obliquité de la branche sur le corps mandibulaire.

La forme divergente du corps de la mandibule est classique; l'arcade dentaire, pointue dans sa partie antérieure, avec des branches latérales qui s'évasent fortement, détermine une conformation évoquant le tracé d'un V.

De hauteur moyenne, la branche horizontale est surtout caractérisée par une grande épaisseur à ses différents niveaux, notamment entre les deux

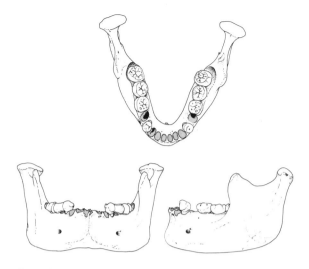

Figure 9. Mandibule de l'Abri Pataud. En haut: vue supérieure; en bas: vue faciale, à gauche; vue latérale, à droite, 35% G.N.

premières molaires, ce qui implique une robustesse particulièrement élevée à cet endroit (cf. tabl. VII). La hauteur du corps mandibulaire, qui décroît en général de l'avant vers l'arrière, varie très peu sur la pièce de Pataud, quel que soit le niveau; c'est dire que les bords supérieur et inférieur sont sensiblement parallèles. Le bord inférieur, très épais, décrit toutefois une large convexité centrée approximativement au-dessous de la partie distale de la seconde molaire. Sur un plan horizontal, la mandibule repose latéralement en un seul point de sorte que sa région antérieure, à partir de la seconde prémolaire, et toute

sa partie postérieure se trouvent soulevées, comme c'est le cas par exemple sur la mandibule magdalénienne d'Arlay (Ferembach 1954).

L'indice d'obliquité du corps mandibulaire, rapportant la somme des épaisseurs réelles à celle des épaisseurs en projection prises entre PM_2-M_1 et M_1-M_2 (Piquet 1956), indique un corps «moyennement oblique.»

La branche montante est extrêmement large par rapport à la hauteur; l'indice obtenu en rapportant sa largeur minimale à cette dernière (70,8) se situe parmi les valeurs les plus élevées observées au Paléolithique supérieur, lesquelles dépassent nettement celles des Européens modernes qui s'échelonnent de 47 à 50.

L'angle goniaque est par ailleurs mal défini, cette région présentant un bord de courbure régulière, sans aucune saillie angulaire (cf. fig. 9). Il est très fermé (107°) comme le laissait supposer une branche montante fort redressée sur le corps mandibulaire. Une telle valeur, identique à celle trouvée à l'Abri Lafaye, est excessivement faible par rapport à celles des hommes du Paléolithique supérieur qui oscillent de 118° à 130° et, a fortiori, par rapport aux Européens modernes. L'extrême largeur de la branche montante couplée à l'arrondi de l'angle goniaque confèrent à la mandibule de Pataud un caractère archaïque certain, les Néandertaliens ou Prénéandertaliens ayant précisément des angles du même ordre de grandeur (Mauer: 107°; La Ferrassie: 109° et La Chapelle-aux-Saints: 110°). De plus, les gonions ne présentent aucune rétroversion mais, au contraire, un rejet vers l'intérieur de leur partie verticale comme

TABLEAU VIII

La mandibule: comparaisons

	Abri Pataud	Saint-Germain	Duruthy	Abri Lafaye	Obercassel	Předmost IV	Abri Lachaud	Chancelade
Longueur maximale	98	114	100	101	–	111	88	113
Largeur bicondylienne	115,5	110	110	117	122	115	–	122
Largeur bigoniaque	97	95	–	100	104	102	78 ?	100
Hauteur symphysienne	29	–	–	34	30	–	27	> 30
Hauteur entre M_1-M_2	29	–	24	31	–	26	23,5	–
Epaisseur entre M_1-M_2	20,5	–	14,5	17,5	–	–	15	–
Hauteur de la branche montante	60	58	57	58	62	52	52	66
Largeur de la branche montante	42,5	34	35	36	37	37	31	41
Indice mandibulaire	84,8	103,6	90,9	86,3	–	96,5	–	92,6
Indice de largeur	84,0	86,4	–	85,5	85,2	88,7	–	82,0
Indice de la branche montante	70,8	58,6	64,9	62,1	59,7	71,1	59,6	62,1
Indice de robustesse en M_1-M_2	70,7	–	>60,4	56,5	–	–	–	–
Angle goniaque	107°	120°	–	107°	118°	122°	119°	118°
Angle symphysien	90°	–	–	86°	88°	–	–	–

sur les mandibules masculines de Předmost et de Cro-Magnon. Leur face externe porte la trace d'insertions musculaires vigoureuses.

Le bord postérieur de la branche montante décrit une faible concavité qui précède la projection vers l'arrière du condyle. Ce dernier est très massif et en forme d'ovoïde allongé, avec un grand axe, qui ne mesure pas moins de 21 mm., de direction oblique d'avant en arrière. Bien que la majeure partie du condyle fasse saillie à l'intérieur du plan de la branche montante, l'angle condylien externe présente néanmoins une forte proéminence en dehors.

L'apophyse coronoïde est large et basse; son sommet, à peine recourbé en arrière, n'atteint pas le plan du condyle comme c'est le cas le plus fréquent sur les mandibules du Paléolithique supérieur. Son bord antérieur décrit une nette concavité tournée vers l'arrière et cache en partie la troisième molaire, tandis que le bord postérieur est rectiligne et oblique. L'échancrure sigmoïde, excessivement large mais peu profonde, offre une conformation en harmonie avec celle de la branche montante, laquelle pourrait être la réplique de certaines mandibules néandertaloïdes.

B. FACE EXTERNE

1. REGION SYMPHYSIENNE

Vue latéralement, la symphyse présente une tendance marquée à la verticalité; la saillie mentonnière existe mais elle est peu prononcée. L'angle symphysien, délimité par le bord inférieur de la mandibule et la droite joignant l'infradentale au gnathion, atteint $90°$; mesuré au pogonion il n'est plus que de $82°$, comme l'illustre la coupe transversale de la figure 10.

Si l'on se réfère aux deux processus communément admis pour expliquer le développement du menton, recul du bord alvéolaire par rapport à la partie basilaire avec apparition de l'incurvation mandibulaire (*incurvatio mandibulae*), d'une part, et fusion des osselets avec formation du triangle mentionnier (*trigonum mentale*), d'autre part, il semble que le second processus soit seul pleinement réalisé sur la mandibule de Pataud.

L'éminence mentonnière se prolonge latéralement par un bourrelet jusqu'au voisinage de la seconde prémolaire; un tel épaississement de la portion antérieure de la mandibule lui confère un aspect encore plus massif. Au niveau du bord inférieur, l'échancrure sous-mentale est prononcée puis s'étire jusque sous la canine, caractère qui la rapproche des mandibules d'Obercassel. Signalons enfin, sur les bords latéraux du *trigonum mentale*, l'existence de deux trous mentonniers antérieurs symétriques.

2. LE CORPS

Les trous mentonniers sont très largement ouverts (5 et 6 mm.), dirigés vers le haut et vers l'arrière. Le gauche est dédoublé postérieurement mais le second trou est beaucoup plus petit (1 mm.). Ils se situent au niveau de la deuxième prémolaire (cf. fig. 9) dans la portion inférieure du corps mandibulaire, avec un bord supérieur placé exactement à mi-hauteur.

La crête oblique externe, ou *linea obliqua externa*, est bien marquée; elle débute au niveau de la première molaire. En arrière, elle surmonte une proéminence latérale très volumineuse puis se continue dans le bord antérieur de la branche montante. Le bord inférieur de la branche horizontale forme un épais bourrelet externe qui ne trouve d'équivalent que sur la mandibule n°3 de Cro-Magnon.

3. LA BRANCHE MONTANTE

Elle présente, dans sa partie supérieure, une fossette de forme triangulaire dont la base circonscrit l'échancrure sigmoïde et dont le sommet rejoint le tuberculum. Cette disposition, qui correspond au ventre et à la partie profonde du masséter, répond aux *fovea* et *crista musculi zygomaticomandibularis* étudiées chez les Primates par R. Cihàk et E. Vlček (1962). Sur la mandibule proto-magdalénienne de

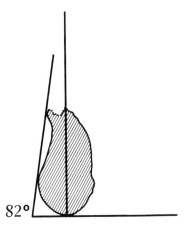

Figure 10. Coupe transversale de la mandibule au niveau de la symphyse. Dessin au diagraphe, G.N.

l'Abri Pataud, cette formation s'apparente au type B$_2$-C$_2$ défini par les auteurs, où ne subsistent que l'indice de la démarcation postérieure de la fossette et l'endroit de l'insertion du muscle, sous la forme du *tuberculum musculi zygomaticomandibularis*.

Cihàk et Vlček ont montré qu'il s'agit là d'un caractère évolutif ancien qui varie parallèlement au cours de l'ontogénèse et de la phylogénèse. La réduction de ce caractère s'observe en effet après la croissance et s'effectue des Néandertaliens, chez lesquels cette formation existe toujours (type B$_2$), jusqu'à l'homme moderne. Chez l'*Homo sapiens fossilis* la régression est amorcée, mais non complètement réalisée.

C. FACE INTERNE

1. LA REGION SYMPHYSIENNE

L'union des deux hémi-mandibules est marquée sur cette face par la présence d'un fin sillon.

À partir des alvéoles et sur un tiers de son parcours environ, la partie supérieure de la mandibule (*pars alveolaris*) décrit une faible pente vers l'arrière, déterminant ainsi un *planum alveolare*. Puis la face interne tombe à la verticale et s'incurve régulièrement en dessous des apophyses géni pour former le bord inférieur. Ce dernier constitue un bourrelet très épais non incurvé vers l'avant, contrairement à ce que l'on observe généralement chez les hommes modernes. Une telle conformation se trouve illustrée par la figure 10 qui représente la section transversale de la symphyse.

Les apophyses génioglosses se différencient en crêtes verticales parallèles surmontant une longue crête médiane intergéniohyoïdienne encadrée par les

Figure 11. Mandibule de l'Abri Pataud: vue interne.

deux fossettes d'insertion du muscle génien. Cette disposition des apophyses géni correspond au sous-type III-2 défini par Heim (1963). Il existe par ailleurs un trou génien et, à 5 mm. environ de part et d'autre des apophyses génioglosses, deux petits trous mentonniers.

Enfin, au niveau du bord inférieur, les insertions du muscle digastrique déterminent des fossettes courtes et larges. Contrairement à ce qui existe chez les hommes actuels, elles sont situées nettement sous le bord inférieur qui présente un élargissement notable et atteint à cet endroit plus de 15 mm. d'épaisseur. Le bord postérieur des empreintes digastriques est bien marqué et rejoint la partie antérieure de la crête mylo-hyoïdienne.

2. LE CORPS

En arrière d'une fosse sublinguale particulièrement profonde, la crête mylo-hyoïdienne détermine une forte saillie oblique qui disparaît au niveau de la troisième molaire; elle surplombe sur son parcours une fosse sous-maxillaire très excavée.

Le rebord alvéolaire est saillant et forme un *torus mandibularis* bilatéral qui débute sous la canine et se poursuit jusqu'au niveau proximal de la troisième molaire. On y remarque un série de bourrelets obliques de haut en bas et d'avant en arrière, séparés par des sillons plus étroits; le relief maximal se situe au niveau de la première molaire (cf. fig. 11). Ce torus mandibulaire correspond au type strié de Weidenreich.

Une telle formation a été signalée par H. Vallois sur la mandibule de Chancelade où elle est beaucoup plus accusée; mais un développement comparable se retrouve sur les mandibules masculines de Předmost, d'Obercassel, ainsi que sur celle d'Arlay. Le torus mandibulaire semble donc assez fréquent au Paléolithique supérieur bien qu'il n'ait été signalé jusque-là que sur des pièces masculines.

3. LA BRANCHE MONTANTE

Deux crêtes descendent du coroné. L'une forme le bord antérieur, mince et tranchant, qui se prolonge dans la ligne oblique externe; l'autre constitue la crête antéro-interne qui se poursuit par le bord alvéolaire et la ligne oblique interne. Ces deux crêtes délimitent sur la partie antérieure de la branche montante un espace triangulaire concave où s'inserre en partie le muscle temporal. Plus bas, le bord antéro-interne se dédouble avec formation des bords alvéolaires qui circonscrivent un diastème rétro-molaire. Une telle conformation rappelle celles observées à Předmost et à Cro-Magnon.

Toujours sur la face interne se trouve l'orifice du canal mandibulaire prolongé vers le haut et l'arrière par une large gouttière correspondant à l'empreinte des nerfs et vaisseaux qui y pénètrent. En avant de cet orifice, l'épine de Spix ou *lingula* mandibulaire, est seule marquée; il n'existe pas d'*antilingula*. En-dessous, le sillon mylo-hyoïdien est relativement court (17 mm.) mais très marqué comme le montre la figure 12. Toute la zone sous-jacente présente un relief excessivement tourmenté dû à l'empreinte du muscle ptérygoïdien interne; cette empreinte détermine de fortes stries parallèles formant de véritables crêtes au niveau de l'angle goniaque.

Enfin, la face antérieure du condyle est très excavée par la fossette d'insertion du muscle ptérygoïdien externe (*fovea pterygoïdea externa*).

En résumé, l'étude morphologique de la mandibule féminine de l'Abri Pataud a montré la survivance de certaines particularités anatomiques rappelant les formes néandertaliennes, ou considérées pour le moins comme archaïques.

Parmi celles-ci, nous retiendrons l'aspect massif de la pièce que lui confèrent la robustesse du corps mandibulaire puis celle de la branche montante (I = 70,8), particulièrement basse et large. De profil, la symphyse mentonnière est presque verticale; elle présente, du côté interne, un *planum alveolare* et un bord inférieur très épais, en forme de bourrelet saillant, sous lequel se situent les empreintes digas-

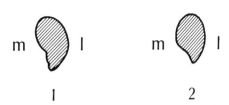

Figure 12. Coupes transversales de la côte droite n°1373; 1. à l'endroit de la plus grande hauteur; 2. à 3 cm distal de la tubérosité. Dessin au diagraphe, segment distal de la coupe, G.N.

triques. L'angle goniaque est par ailleurs très fermé (107°) rappelant la conformation de certaines pièces néandertaliennes. Il en est de même de la présence des *fovea* et *crista musculi zygomaticomandibularis* qui, nous l'avons vu, caractérisent les Néandertaliens.

Mais il existe aussi sur cette pièce plusieurs aspects morphologiques propres à l'*Homo sapiens*, parmi lesquels on peut citer le développement d'un *trigonum mentale* et d'une *incurvatio mandibulae* (peu prononcée il est vrai), le contour en V de l'arcade dentaire sans aplatissement bicanin, le parallélisme des bords supérieur et inférieur puis, enfin, l'absence de fosse génienne.

La mandibule de l'Abri Pataud semble donc correspondre à un stade évolutif intermédiaire entre Néandertaliens et Sapiens.

2. LE SQUELETTE POST-CRANIEN

I. LE TRONC

A. COLONNE VERTEBRALE

Il existe au total 12 vertèbres ou fragments de vertèbres, la plupart étant très endommagées. Une seule d'entre elles, un atlas non numéroté, fut recueilli lors de la première campagne de fouilles, à la limite des Trench I et II. Toutes les autres furent extraites en 1963 et proviennent de la Trench VII à 3 ou 4 mètres seulement du crâne. L'ensemble se répartit comme suit:

5 Vertèbres cervicales: atlas sans n°, n° 1397 B (axis), n° 1460 (C_3), n° 1366 (C_5) et n° 1380 (C_6).

5 Vertèbres dorsales: n° 1396 (D_3?), n° 1397 A (D_4?), n° 1400 (D_7?), n° 1406 (D_8?) et n° 1375 (D_{10}).

2 Vertèbres lombaires: n° 1382 (L_2), n° 1304 (L_3).

Dénombrement des individus et sexe. A l'exception de l'atlas, recueilli seul à environ 8 mètres du crâne, dont la patine et le volume l'écartent nettement des autres vertèbres, il paraît fort probable que les onze vertèbres trouvées assez près du crâne dans une aire de dispersion relativement réduite, de 1 mètre sur 0,5 m. de profondeur, appartiennent au même individu. Par comparaison aux vertèbres des hommes actuels, leurs faibles dimensions permettent de les attribuer sans aucun doute à un sujet féminin de constitution assez frêle, donc probablement à la jeune fille. L'atlas non inventorié est plus volumineux mais il est néanmoins impossible de préciser son appartenance sexuelle. Quoi qu'il en soit, l'existence d'au moins deux sujets adultes est acquise.

1. VERTEBRES CERVICALES

L'*atlas* est presque complet; seul manque un petit fragment de l'apophyse transverse gauche.

L'indice atloïdien (58,6) est relativement élevé par rapport à la moyenne (55,9) obtenue par G. Duparc (1942) sur les populations actuelles et, surtout, par rapport à la valeur (54,8) trouvée chez l'homme de Chancelade. Le développement de cette vertèbre dans le sens antéro-postérieur tend à rappeler celui de l'atlas de l'homme n° 1 de Cro-Magnon (I = 61,7), sans toutefois atteindre un degré aussi marqué.

TABLEAU IX

L'atlas

	Pataud	Chancelade (H.)	Cro-Magnon (H.)
Hauteur antérieure	11,5	14,5	—
Diam. ant.-post. maximal	42,5	46	50
Diam. transv. maximal	72,5	84 ?	81
Diam. ant.-post. canal rachidien	30,5	34	31
Diam. transv. max. canal rachidien	27	27	15
Indice atloïdien	58,6	54,8	61,7

Les dimensions de la pièce sont nettement inférieures à celles des sujets masculins du Paléolithique; il semble donc, malgré l'absence de données comparatives, que l'atlas de l'Abri Pataud devait appartenir à un second sujet féminin.

Les tubercules antérieur et postérieur sont peu développés; au contraire, ceux marquant l'insertion du ligament transverse de l'articulation atloïdo-odontoïdienne sont assez saillants. Sur la face interne de l'arc antérieur, la surface articulaire répondant à la facette de l'apophyse odontoïde de l'axis forme une concavité circulaire très profonde que limite un rebord rugueux. Enfin, les cavités glénoïdes sont elliptiques, de dimensions moyennes, et très concaves.

L'*axis.* Très incomplète, cette vertèbre est réduite à sa moitié droite sans l'apophyse transverse. De hauteur considérable comme le montrent les données du tableau X, l'apophyse odontoïde présente de plus une forme élancée; son corps surmontant un col étranglé se termine en pointe. La facette articulaire antérieure par ailleurs a la forme d'une ellipse allongée. La face inférieure du corps se prolonge vers le bas par un relief osseux très accusé.

TABLEAU X

L'axis

	Pataud (F)	Předmost (F)	Obercassel (F)	Chancelade (H)
Hauteur totale antérieure	38	35	36	39
Hauteur de l'apophyse odontoïde	16,5	18,5	16	13
Hauteur totale postérieure	33,5	30,3		−

Les autres vertèbres cervicales C_3, C_5 et C_6 sont également incomplètes; l'apophyse transverse manque aux deux premières et la troisième n'a pas de corps vertébral. Dans l'ensemble, elles présentent un corps assez bas de largeur considérable. Une telle conformation détermine un foramen vertébral en forme de triangle très aplati transversalement, particularité qui se trouve encore plus accentuée sur les vertèbres de Předmost. Par ailleurs, les quelques mesures relevées coïncident avec celles du sujet féminin IV de Předmost et de la femme d'Obercassel.

TABLEAU XI

Mensurations des autres vertèbres cervicales

	C_3 (1460)	C_5 (1366)	C_6 (1380)
Hauteur verticale antérieure	12,5	12,5	−
Hauteur verticale postérieure	13,0	12,5	−
Diamètre sagittal sup. du corps	13,5	13	−
Diamètre transverse sup. du corps	20	22	−
Diamètre sagittal du trou vertébral	12,3	11,7	−
Diamètre transversal du trou vertébral	21,5	24	23,2
Indice vertébral	104,0	100,0	−
Indice du foramen vertébral	57,2	48,7	−

Les indices vertébraux sont supérieurs à 100, même sur la 3ème cervicale, à l'inverse de la disposition existant chez les races actuelles où, pour cette vertèbre la hauteur postérieure est le plus souvent inférieure à la hauteur antérieure. Cette conformation a déjà été signalée au Paléolithique supérieur chez l'homme de Chancelade et la femme d'Obercassel. Enfin, l'apophyse épineuse de la C_6 n'est pas bifurquée comme cela a été signalé sur plusieurs vertèbres cervicales de Předmost.

2. VERTEBRES DORSALES

Toutes sont en très mauvais état, le corps vertébral n'étant jamais complet; une seule possède l'apophyse épineuse. Bien qu'aucune identification précise ne soit possible, leur articulation se fait néanmoins dans le sens décroissant des pièces 1397A, 1396, 1375, 1400, et 1406.

Leur faible volume laisse à penser qu'elles appartiennent à un individu très jeune et vraisemblablement à la première moitié du segment dorsal. De même, les dimensions du foramen vertébral sont petites, dans le sens transversal comme dans le sens sagittal, par comparaison à celles de séries modernes et de Předmost; la section du canal vertébral présente une tendance circulaire.

3. VERTEBRES LOMBAIRES

On ne dispose que de deux fragments de vertèbres L_2 et L_3, dont seul le premier permet de déterminer l'indice vertébral (cf. tabl. XII).

TABLEAU XII

Vertèbres lombaires

| | Pataud | | Chancelade | | Cap-Blanc | | |
	L_2	L_3	L_2	L_3	L_2	L_3	L_4
Hauteur antérieure	26	–	25,5	–	24	25,2	26,3
Hauteur postérieure	30	26,5	29	27	28	26,3	25
Diam. ant.-post. du foramen	14,2	13,5	–	–	–	–	–
Diam. transv. du foramen	20,7	20	–	–	–	–	–
Indice vertébral	115,4	–	113,7	–	116	104	95,2

Bien que le changement de sens de la courbure lombaire ne puisse être défini avec précision, l'indice vertébral relativement élevé de la L_2 permet de supposer que cette inflexion n'était pas située entre les seconde et troisième lombaires, comme c'est le cas de nos jours, mais à un niveau inférieur. Une telle disposition, absolument identique à celle observée sur le squelette de Chancelade, trouve sa confirmation à Cap-Blanc. La courbure lombaire aurait donc tendance à se faire légèrement plus bas. On sait par ailleurs (Vallois et Lazorthes 1942) que les hommes du Paléolithique, à l'exception des deux sujets de Předmost, ont des indices vertébraux plus élevés que ceux des Européens actuels; il existe chez eux un déplacement de la vertèbre où a lieu le changement de courbure. L'examen des vertèbres lombaires de la femme de Pataud tend encore à confirmer cette assertion.

B. THORAX

1. STERNUM

Un sternum incomplet, appartenant à un individu âgé de 20 à 25 ans, fut recueilli dans le complexe 22 de la Trench II, soit à 7 mètres environ du crâne de la jeune femme (pl. IV 3-4). Aussi paraît-il peu probable que ce sternum lui ait appartenu.

Il se compose du manubrium entier (*presternum*) et du corps (*corpus sterni* ou *mesosternum*) non soudés. Le corps est réduit aux deux segments supérieurs (sternèbres 2 et 3) et à un petit fragment du troisième (sternèbre 4); la suture entre les premiers segments étant encore visible. L'extrémité supérieure présente la facette articulaire du manubrium et l'extrémité inférieure est fracturée irrégulièrement au niveau de l'échancrure intercostale 4-5. Toutes les échancrures costales et intercostales apparaissent sur le bord gauche mais le droit est détérioré à partir de la seconde échancrure costale (tabl. XIII, p. 226).

Compte tenu du sexe, la longueur du manubrium est moyenne; mais sa largeur maximale, relativement plus grande, détermine un indice très supérieur à 100. La largeur à la base est faible, ce qui confère au manubrium une forme nettement triangulaire. La grande épaisseur de son bord supérieur détermine par rapport à la largeur un indice élevé si l'on s'en tient à la valeur moyenne (32,4) observée sur des Européens modernes (Anthony cité par Martin). Le bord supérieur est par ailleurs largement échancré dans sa partie médiane et présente latéralement de larges facettes claviculaires. Au-dessous de celles-ci, la première échancrure costale est très profonde. La face antérieure, enfin, est fortement convexe dans les deux sens.

En l'absence d'un *corpus sterni* complet, nous avons mesuré selon le procédé préconisé par H. Vallois (1965) les deux premiers segments C_1 et C_2 qui correspondent aux sternèbres 2 et 3. Nos mesures se situent légèrement en deça des valeurs moyennes obtenues par l'auteur sur une série de 38 sternums adultes français, d'âge et sexe non précisés. En revanche, la largeur du sternum de l'Abri Pataud paraît beaucoup plus étroite, ce qui entraîne un indice de longueur-largeur très inférieur. La longueur totale du corps peut être évaluée approximativement à 100 mm. en considérant, avec H. Vallois, que la longueur de C_1 et de C_2 représente les 53% de la longueur totale. L'indice de longueur-largeur correspondrait alors à 25,5 (tabl. XIV, p. 226).

On en conclut que le sternum de Pataud est à la fois allongé et relativement étroit par comparaison à ceux des hommes actuels. Sur la face antérieure, la ligne sternale correspondant à la soudure des deux premiers segments est apparente; elle est soulignée par une faible coudure des deux pièces. L'extrémité supérieure du corps légèrement endommagée sur le côté droit, présente une surface d'articulation avec le manubrium qui atteste l'existence d'une synchondrose comme c'est le cas général chez l'homme, et particulièrement sur les sternums étroits.

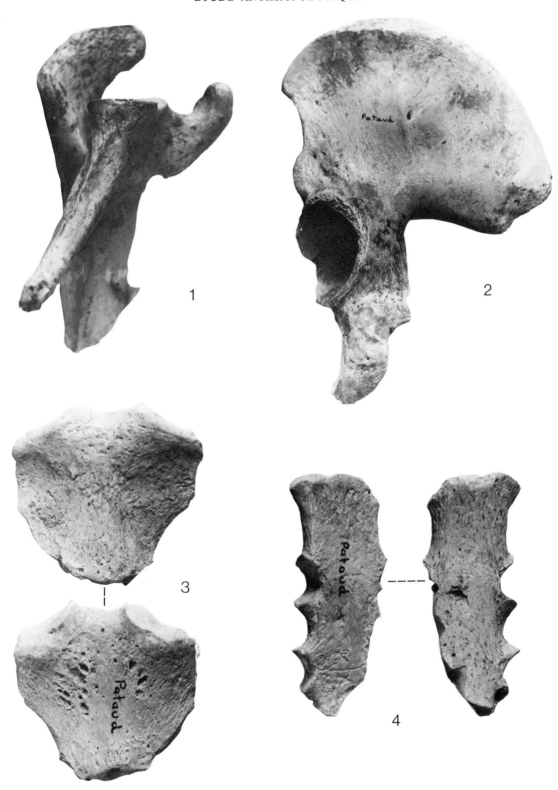

Planche IV. 1. omoplate droite, vue externe; 2. os coxal gauche, face externe; 3. sternum en haut: vue antérieure, en bas: vue postérieure; 4. sternum, corpus sterni, à gauche: vue antérieure, à droite: vue postérieure.

TABLEAU XIII

Mensurations du sternum

Longueur du manubrium (2)	44	
Largeur maximale du manubrium (4)	51	
Largeur minimale du manubrium (6)	34	
Epaisseur du manubrium (7)	11,5	
Indice d'épaisseur (7/6)	33,8	

	Pièce C_1	Pièce C_2
Longueur maximale	29	24
Longueur échancrure intercostale droite	14	?
Longueur échancrure intercostale gauche	17	11
Largeur minimale	21	?
Largeur supérieure maximale	25,5	?
Largeur inférieure maximale	25	?

TABLEAU XIV

Corpus sterni : comparaisons

	Pièce C_1		Pièce C_2	
	Pataud	38 Français	Pataud	38 Français
Longueur maximale	29	30,6 (24–37)	24	25,4 (18–31)
Largeur minimale	21	26,3 (19–33)	?	
Ind. de long./larg.	72,4	87,1 (54,2–132)	?	

Le bord latéral gauche du corps présente une série d'échancrures qui correspondent aux deuxième, troisième et quatrième côtes. Celles-ci sont très profondes et séparées par des échancrures intercostales dont la longueur diminue fortement vers le bas. On note une direction générale des bords nettement verticale, sans aucune divergence, comme c'est le cas chez les hommes modernes où le corps sternal s'élargit vers le bas. Enfin, seul le bord de la troisième échancrure costale se soulève en un léger processus costal.

Ainsi décrit, le sternum de la femme de l'Abri Pataud se range dans le type «primatoïde» défini par von Lubosch (1924) et explicité plus tard par Ashley (1956) en tenant compte du mode d'ossification du corps sternal. Il présente en effet toutes les caractéristiques de ce type primatoïde, phylogénétiquement primitif, retrouvé par H. Vallois sur quelques sternums néandertaloïdes: manubrium triangulaire et non soudé, corps allongé et étroit, comme l'atteste un indice très bas de 25,5, échancrures costales très profondes à processus costaux peu marqués, ligne sternale bien apparente entre C_1 et C_2, bords latéraux parallèles et largeur minimale de C_1 (21 mm.) nettement inférieure à la limite (28 mm.) définie par Ashley pour les sternums de type primatoïde. Un tel résultat méritait d'autant plus d'être souligné qu'il n'existe aucun autre élément de comparaison au Paléolithique supérieur.

2. COTES

Sur les 16 côtes ou fragments des côtes recueillis, 4 proviennent de la trench II, les autres se trouvant assez peu dispersées dans la trench VII.

Le premier lot, non numéroté, comporte une côte droite (5e ou 6e?), presque complète, trouvée dans le complexe 22. Cette côte est assez robuste, avec une forte tubérosité et une gouttière costale large et excavée. La face postérieure du col présente de fortes rugosités qui descendent jusqu'au bord inférieur. Sa hauteur (15,5 mm.) et son épaisseur (7 mm.) se rapprochent des mensurations rapportées pour les 5e et 6e côtes des hommes de Veyrier et d'Obercassel. Il est certes difficile d'en conclure pour autant à la présence d'un sujet masculin malgré la robustesse de cette côte.

Toujours dans le complexe 22 ont été recueillis, à peu de distance, un fragment de côte gauche, à gouttière costale large et excavée, et deux premières côtes à relief peu accusé qui, d'après leur courbure, semblent former la paire. Ces deux dernières pièces devaient plutôt appartenir à une femme.

Le second lot provenant de la Trench VII, à moins de 3 mètres du crâne, comporte:

5 fragments de segment moyen non identifiables, à gouttière costale à peine excavée (n°s 1312, 1367, 1379, 1405, et 1459).

4 extrémités postérieures droites correspondant aux pièces:

n° 1311: moitié de 11e côte, sans tubérosité mais gouttière costale visible.

n° 1365: segment postérieur avec forte tubérosité et col portant de nombreuses rugosités.

n° 1373: moitié postérieure.

n° 1384: moitié postérieure sans la tête avec une gouttière costale faiblement excavée.

3 extrémités spinales gauches avec les pièces:

n° 1377: segment postérieur avec tubérosité bien marquée.

n° 1511: moitié postérieure sans tête ni col.

n° 1514: moitié postérieure sans tête, dont le corps très aplati porte une gouttière haute mais peu profonde.

Tous ces os présentent une même gracilité et une forte courbure caractéristique d'un thorax étroit; ils correspondent très vraisemblablement au jeune sujet féminin dont le crâne fut recueilli à proximité. La hauteur maximale du corps, prise au niveau de son plus grand développement, varie de 14 à 17 mm., valeurs comparables à celles relevées sur la femme d'Obercassel qui constitue notre seul élément de comparaison. L'épaisseur mesurée à l'endroit de la hauteur maximale (de 8 à 9 mm.) est à peine moins élevée que chez la femme d'Obercassel (5 à 10 mm.) pour laquelle Bonnet établit un rapprochement avec les formes néandertaliennes. Quoi qu'il en soit, la forme de la section transversale de la côte paraît (cf. fig. 12) nettement plus arrondie que chez les hommes actuels.

II. LE MEMBRE SUPERIEUR

A. OMOPLATE

L'unique pièce recueillie provient du complexe 22. Il s'agit d'une omoplate droite à laquelle il manque le bord supérieur, ainsi que toute la région inféro-interne (pl. IV$_1$). Seules les dimensions de la cavité glénoïde, de l'acromion et de l'apophyse coracoïde ont été déterminées selon la technique définie par H. Vallois (1932).

TABLEAU XV

L'omoplate

Longueur de la cavité glénoïde	38
Largeur de la cavité glénoïde	27
Longueur de l'acromion	44
Largeur de l'acromion	28
Longueur de l'apophyse coracoïde	40
Largeur de l'apophyse coracoïde	15
Ind. glénoïdien de longueur-largeur	71,0
Ind. acromial	63,6

	Pataud	89 H.	77 F.
Longueur	38	37	32,5
Largeur	27	29,5	25,1

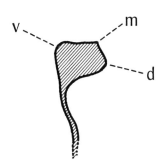

Figure 13. Coupe transversale du bord axillaire de l'omoplate n° 22, v: bord ventral; d: bord dorsal; m: crête médio-axillaire. Dessin au diagraphe, G.N.

La forme de la cavité glénoïde est piriforme avec une échancrure glénoïdienne marquée. Son indice indique une cavité comparable à celle de la femme d'Obercassel (70,3), un peu plus large que celle de Cap-Blanc (65,7). Comparées aux moyennes des Français rapportées par H. Vallois, ses dimensions se rapprochent des valeurs masculines comme le montrent les chiffres suivants:

Bien que la cavité glénoïde soit toujours plus longue et plus large du côté droit, il existe néanmoins une certaine présomption en faveur du sexe masculin. De plus, si l'on s'en réfère aux statistiques de H. Vallois, montrant l'existence d'une forte corrélation entre les hauteurs scapulaire et glénoïdienne, on trouve que la hauteur de cette omoplate devait être comprise entre 160 et 169,9 mm. Aussi approximative soit-elle, une telle évaluation correspond manifestement à une hauteur masculine d'après les moyennes obtenues par l'auteur sur 78 omoplates droites masculines (159,9) et 68 féminines (142,1).

L'épine est volumineuse; elle présente une direction oblique (angle axillo-spinal: 43°), sensiblement identique à celle des hommes modernes, qui correspond au type européen défini par H. Vallois (1932). Son bord dorsal possède un tubercule trapézien, très développé au niveau duquel l'épaisseur maximale atteint 12 mm.; cette valeur élevée se rapproche de la moyenne (12,9 mm.) obtenue sur 45 pièces masculines. En dehors du tubercule trapézien, le bord dorsal de l'épine décrit une large concavité vers le bas jusqu'à l'angle inférieur de l'acromion. Les dimensions de ce dernier, qui coïncident avec celles de l'homme III de Předmost, déterminent un indice légèrement plus élevé que celui des Français modernes (61,1); ainsi, l'acromion est large par rapport à sa longueur.

Vu la détérioration du bord supérieur de l'omoplate, on peut seulement affirmer la présence d'une échancrure coracoïdienne très profonde. Au-dessus, l'apophyse coracoïde est plutôt volumineuse et présente, à son extrémité interne, un petit tubercule correspondant à l'insertion du ligament coracoïdien.

Enfin, le bord axillaire correspond au type à deux gouttières parallèles dirigées vers l'extérieur et délimitant une crête médio-axillaire (cf. fig. 13). Une telle conformation semble très fréquente chez les hommes du Paléolithique supérieur; observée pour la première fois par Testut sur l'homme de Chancelade, elle se recontre en effet à Obercassel, chez les sujets III et X de Předmost, ou les Magdaléniens de Veyrier, de Cap-Blanc, et de Saint-Germain-la-Rivière.

B. CLAVICULE

On dispose de trois clavicules (pl. V) dont:
une clavicule droite, entière (n° 1513) provenant de la Trench VII, Square G;
une clavicule droite, recueillie dans le complexe 22, avec une extrémité sternale légèrement endommagée;
une clavicule gauche incomplète, provenant également du complexe 22, à laquelle il manque les extrémités.

TABLEAU XVI

La clavicule: mensurations

	1513 D.	22 D.	22 G.
Longueur maximale (1)	146	140	–
Diam. vert. au milieu (4)	10	10,5	–
Diam. horiz. au milieu (5)	10,5	11	–
Périmètre au milieu (6)	34	36,5	–
Larg. max. de l'extrémité ext. (Olivier)	20	19,5	–
Diam. horiz. de l'extrémité interne	21	22	–
Diam. vert. de l'extrémité interne	16,5	20	–
Ind. de robustesse (6/1)	23,3	26,1	–
Ind. diaphysaire (4/5)	95,2	95,4	–
Ind. de larg. ext. (diam. ext./1)(Olivier)	13,7	13,9	–
Ind. de volume interne (diam. horiz. + diam. vert. int./1) (Olivier)	25,7	30,0	–
Ind. de courbure interne	17,1	19,6	–
Ind. de courbure externe	19,9	22,5	–
Angle de déflexion (Matiegka)	-6°	-16,5°	-11,5°
Angle de courbure interne	156°	153°	–
Angle de courbure externe	142,5°	135°	–

L'aspect gracile et les dimensions de la première permettent de l'attribuer sans équivoque au sexe féminin. En ce qui concerne les deux os du complexe 22, la clavicule gauche paraît nettement moins robuste que la droite comme le montrent l'écart entre les dimensions transversales prises au milieu de l'os, d'une part, des insertions musculaires adoucies et le moindre développement du tubercule conoïdien d'autre part. De telles observations nous incitent à conclure à la présence de deux individus au moins dans le complexe 22.

Les longueurs maximales se situent dans la catégorie

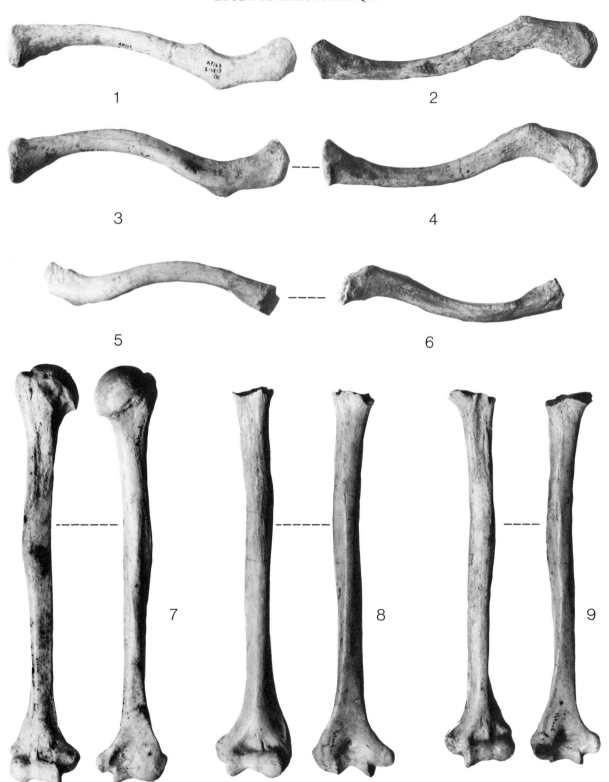

Planche V. 1. clavicule droite (n°1513), vue supérieure; 2. id, vue inférieure; 3. clavicule droite (n°22), vue supérieure; 4. id, vue inférieure; 5. clavicule gauche (n°22), vue supérieure; 6. id, vue inférieure; 7. humérus droit (n°22), vues antérieure et postérieure; 8. humérus gauche (n°22), vues antérieure et postérieure; 9. humérus gauche (n°1), vues antérieure et postérieure.

«longue» de la classification de Slowik citée par G. Olivier. Il ressort en fait du tableau comparatif XVII que les Paléolithiques avaient des clavicules en moyenne plus longues que celles des hommes actuels. Le périmètre au milieu de l'os est «moyen» sur les deux clavicules droites, et «grêle» sur la gauche d'après la classification proposée par G. Olivier (1951b).

La diaphyse présente par ailleurs une forme arrondie, à tendance quadrangulaire, que traduit une valeur très élevée de l'indice diaphysaire (95,3) par rapport à celle observée chez les Français actuels (88,0). Une telle conformation de la clavicule, à peine aplatie de haut en bas, est fréquente au Paléolithique supérieur (femmes de Předmost et d'Obercassel, sujet de Veyrier); elle va même jusqu'à s'inverser dans le sens d'un aplatissement dorso-ventral comme le montrent les chiffres du tableau XVII.

La largeur maximale de l'extrémité externe est faible, même en tenant compte du sexe. Cette dimension, rapportée à la longueur de l'os détermine des indices de largeur externe qui correspondent à des clavicules «étroites en-dehors» d'après la nomenclature de G. Olivier. Une telle particularité a été relevée également sur le squelette de Chancelade, la clavicule se caractérisant par une extrémité acromiale très étroite qui la différencie de celle des hommes actuels.

Cette gracilité relative des extrémités claviculaires au Paléolithique semble confirmée par l'examen de

TABLEAU XVII

La clavicule: comparaisons

	Pataud 1513 D.	22 D.	Saint-Germain	Cap-Blanc	Předmost F. IV		Obercassel F.	H.	Chancelade H.	Veyrier H.
Long. max.	146	140	145	131	156	–	156	162	148	150
Diam. vert. milieu	10	10,5	–	–	11,5	13	10	13	10	11
Diam. sagitt. milieu	10,5	11	–	–	13	12	11	12	10	12
Périm. au milieu	34	36,5	–	–	39	41	34	40	–	36
Ind. de robustesse	23,3	26,4	–	–	25,0	–	–	25,6?	–	24,0
Ind. diaphysaire	95,2	95,4	–	–	88,5	108,3	91	108,3	100,0	91,7

l'extrémité interne dont le volume est également faible. Ainsi les indices de volume interne trouvés à l'Abri Pataud (cf. tabl. XVI) sont très inférieurs à la moyenne (32,4) de Français (G. Olivier). Là encore, on note un rapprochement avec l'homme de Chancelade où nous avions relevé déjà un indice inférieur à ceux des hommes modernes. Signalons enfin que le grand axe de l'extrémité sternale est orienté horizontalement, comme il est de règle de nos jours.

Sur la face inférieure, la gouttière sous-clavière est à peine visible sur la pièce n° 1513, plus prononcée sur la 22 D. et nettement plus forte sur la 22 G. En dedans de la gouttière, vers l'extrémité sternale, l'empreinte du ligament costo-claviculaire est rugueuse et de forme ovalaire; elle est toujours bien marquée et présente même un contour saillant sur la clavicule 1513. En dehors, vers l'extrémité acromiale, on note un tubercule conoïde très développé (clavicule 22 D.) qui se prolonge par des rugosités dues à l'insertion des ligaments coraco-claviculaires. Seule la pièce n° 1513, en revanche, possède sur le bord antérieur un tubercule deltoïdien.

Le degré de courbure de la clavicule dans le sens horizontal a été apprécié selon la technique de Parsons. D'une part, la courbure interne décrit un arc assez ouvert intercepté par des angles de 156° (n° 1513) et 153° (n° 22 D.), qui sont plus élevés que ceux des hommes modernes (français: 151°2). La courbure externe, au contraire, est très accentuée, surtout sur la clavicule 22 D. (cf. tabl. XVI), dépassant de beaucoup toutes les valeurs citées par G. Olivier (français: 142°5). La somme de ces courbures traduit une sinuosité modérée pour la pièce 1513 mais très accusée pour la seconde clavicule. Notons à cet endroit que les courbures interne (147°) et externe (139°), trouvées sur la clavicule droite de l'homme de Chancelade, déterminaient une sinuosité globale encore plus accentuée. Les indices de courbure interne sont par ailleurs tout à fait comparables à ceux des sujets de Předmost qui varient de 17,5 (H. n° XIV) à 20,5 (F. n° IV). Malgré l'insuffisance des données, il semble donc que la clavicule des hommes du Paléolithique supérieur était en moyenne plus sinueuse que celle des hommes actuels.

La courbure dans le sens frontal, ou «*deflexio claviculae*» de Matiegka, a été évaluée en mesurant la déviation de la diaphyse par rapport à l'extrémité acromiale. Là encore les valeurs obtenues pour les deux clavicules de Pataud sont très différentes: la clavicule 1513 présente en effet une légère déflexion (-6°) alors que l'angle de la 22 D. (-16°5) indique une cassure très nette. Cette dernière pièce présente de plus une seconde courbure externe, concave vers le haut, et correspond au type III défini par G. Olivier (1956, p. 437). Une telle disposition, tenue par l'auteur comme caractère féminin, a cependant été retrouvée sur l'homme de Chancelade. Notons enfin que la *deflexio claviculae* de la clavicule 22 D. se place en marge des limites de variation observées sur les populations actuelles: Tchèques: -14° à +13°; Boschimans: -12° à +18° (Sauter et Danieli 1939; mais elle est comparable aux rares données du Paléolithique supérieur comme à Předmost: -20° (H. III) et -22° (F. VII) ou à Veyrier: -14°.

En résumé, les clavicules de l'Abri Pataud, qui correspondent à trois individus, se distinguent en premier lieu par leur longueur et leur gracilité. La diaphyse présente une section arrondie, à tendance quadrangulaire, tandis que les extrémités claviculaires se caractérisent par une extrême gracilité. De toute évidence, la clavicule 22 D. appartenait à un individu de constitution plus robuste, à musculature bien développée; elle se rapproche nettement des autres spécimens du Paléolithique supérieur.

C. HUMERUS

Sur les quatre humérus ou fragments d'humérus, un seul est entier; on dénombre en effet:

un humérus droit entier (n° 22 D.), (pl. V_7);

un humérus gauche incomplet, auquel il manque la tête (n° 22 G.), (pl. V_8);

un humérus gauche incomplet, sans la tête (n° 1 G.), (pl. V_9);

un fragment d'épiphyse inférieure d'humérus gauche (n° 1519).

Les deux premiers, trouvés dans le complexe 22 (Trench II) à très peu de distance l'un de l'autre, appartiennent manifestement au même individu; ils possèdent en effet une même longueur diaphysaire, le même volume, la même grosseur de la diaphyse et de l'épiphyse inférieure (cf. tabl. XVIII). Leurs dimensions relativement faibles les attribuent à un sujet féminin. Ces deux os présentent de nombreuses tâches brunâtres, de forme circulaire probablement dues à l'action du milieu.

L'humérus gauche n° 1, trouvé dans les éboulis de la zone A, entre les Trenches II et III, est plus robuste et possède des insertions musculaires plus marquées. Son épiphyse inférieure surtout montre un développement considérable qui semble le propre d'un sujet masculin.

L'extrémité inférieure gauche 1519, qui provient de la Trench VII, comprend la portion centrale articulaire ainsi que la majeure partie de l'épitrochlée et de l'épicondyle. Ses dimensions, plutôt faibles, l'apparentent aux humérus féminins.

Sur la base de ces données, on voit que les restes de Pataud comprennent au moins trois individus adultes dont deux femmes et peut-être un homme.

La longueur maximale dépasse les moyennes obtenues pour la plupart des races modernes (Hrdlička 1932 et Themido 1926), mais s'intègre dans les limites de variation observées au Paléolithique supérieur, comme le montre le tableau XIX. Le périmètre minimal situé au tiers inférieur de l'os paraît faible sur

TABLEAU XVIII

L'humérus

	22 D.	22 G.	1 G.	1519 G.
Long. maximale (1)	308	–	–	–
Larg. de l'épiphyse sup. (3)	47,5	–	–	–
Larg. de l'épiphyse inf. (4)	56	54	64	54,5
Diam. max. au milieu (5)	21	20,5	22	–
Diam. min. au milieu (6)	16,5	16,5	18,5	–
Périmètre minimal (7)	58	56	63	–
Diam. transv. max. tête (9)	40,5	–	–	–
Diam. sagitt. max. tête (10)	45,5	–	–	–
Angle d'inclinaison du col (17)	135°	–	–	–
Angle de torsion (18)	143°	–	–	–
Ind. de robustesse (7/1)	18,8	–	–	–
Ind. diaphysaire (6/5)	78,6	80,5	84,1	–
Ind. de la tête (9/10)	89,0			

les pièces du complexe 22, mais atteint, sur l'humérus n° 1 G., une valeur qui dépasse certains spécimens masculins, tels ceux de Veyrier (59 mm.) et d'Obercassel (62 mm.). Le seul indice de robustesse déterminé se range parmi les valeurs faibles des hommes modernes (Themido 1926). De plus, la femme du complexe 22 se caractérise par un bras relativement long et grêle par comparaison aux Magdaléniennes de Cap-Blanc et d'Obercassel.

Néanmoins, les diamètres extrêmes de la diaphyse en son milieu atteignent des valeurs identiques à celles des autres Magdaléniennes et de la femme de Cro-Magnon (cf. tabl. XIX). Malgré une certaine gracilité, cette femme de Pataud possédait donc un humérus aussi bien modelé que ses contemporaines. L'indice diaphysaire est partout eurybrachique, comme il est de règle au Paléolithique supérieur où, si l'on excepte la femme de Cap-Blanc pour laquelle l'indice fut évalué selon une technique différente, la platybrachie ne s'observe que sur un seul humérus de Chancelade, ou de Předmost, et sur le sujet 3 de Cro-Magnon.

Dans l'ensemble, les humérus de Pataud ont le corps sensiblement rectiligne et la coulisse bicipitale suit une direction verticale; son bord externe forme une grosse crête rugueuse qui se prolonge dans la branche interne du V deltoïdien. La branche externe, empreinte de l'insertion du deltoïde, forme un gros bourrelet que borde une dépression sous-deltoïdienne. Le développement en dehors de cette saillie est tel qu'il imprime une sorte de déviation angulaire de la diaphyse, ce qui dénote une musculature puissante particulièrement sur les humérus n° 22. A ce niveau, la diaphyse est franchement quadrangulaire comme le montrent les schémas des coupes transversales (cf. fig. 14).

La tête humérale est par ailleurs ovalaire, comme l'indique un indice assez bas. Les deux tubérosités sont bien développées et présentent des facettes d'insertion musculaire très marquées.

La largeur de l'épiphyse inférieure dépasse les valeurs données pour les hommes modernes (Themido), mais un tel développement semble général chez les Paléolithiques supérieurs compte tenu des chiffres du tableau XIX. L'extrémité inférieure présente d'autre part cet élargissement remarquable du bord interne replié sur lui-même qui correspond à la ptère sus-épicondylienne. Peu marquée sur les humérus 22, cette formation est particulièrement accentuée sur le n° 1 où elle confère à l'épiphyse inférieure une forme évasée, dite en «pavillon», caractéristique de certains types primitifs. La fosse olécrânienne est partout très profonde mais la cavité coronoïdienne n'est vraiment creusée que sur l'humérus masculin n° 1. Comme chez tous les hommes du Paléolithique supérieur il n'existe

TABLEAU XIX
L'humérus: comparaisons

	Abri Pataud				Cap-Blanc F.	Obercassel F.	Předmost (IV) F.	Chancelade H.	Veyrier H.
	22 D.	22 G.	1 G.	1519 G.	D.	D.	D.	D.	D.
Long. maximale (1)	308	—	—	—	309	276	324	302	312
Larg. épiph. sup. (3)	47,5	—	—	—	45,8	(45)	50	49	46
Larg. épiph. inf. (4)	56	54	64	54,5	(56)	(60)	62	62	62
Diam. max. au milieu (5)	21	20,5	22	—	22,2	—	22	25,5	21
Diam. min. au milieu (6)	16,5	16,5	18,5	—	16,1	—	16	18,5	17,5
Périm. minimal (7)	58	56	63	—	60	55	63	68	59
Diam. trans. max. tête (9)	40,5	—	—	—	39,7	(37)	42,5	—	39
Diam. sagitt. max. tête (10)	45,5	—	—	—	43,1	(44)	48	(47)	40
Angle de torsion (18)	143°	—	—	—	163°	(144°)	148°	160°	166°
Ind. de robustesse (7/1)	18,8	—	—	—	19,4	19,9	19,4	22,7	18,9
Ind. diaphysaire (6/5)	78,6	80,5	84,1	—	72,5	—	72,7	72,5	83,3
Ind. de la tête (9/10)	89,0	—	—	—	92,1	(84,1)	88,5	—	97,5

( ) Les chiffres entre parenthèses correspondent à des mensurations de l'humérus gauche.

pas de perforation olécrânienne, sauf pour la femme de Cap-Blanc.

La torsion de l'humérus (143°) paraît relativement faible en regard de celles observées sur certains humérus modernes (157°4, Themido). La valeur obtenue à Pataud se rapproche par ailleurs de celles des Magdaléniens d'Obercassel, de Saint-Germain-la-Rivière, ou de ceux de Předmost dont la valeur moyenne pour 6 humérus est de 144°8. Il semble toutefois qu'on doive attacher une importance limitée à ce caractère en raison de sa grande variabilité, du moins en ce qui concerne le Paléolithique supérieur.

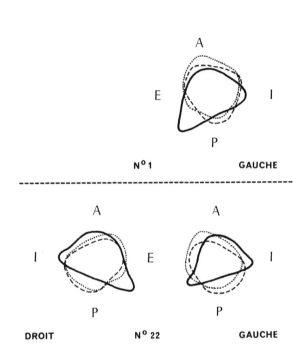

Figure 14. Coupes transversales des humérus. —— = 30 mm. au-dessus de l'épitrochlée. ------ = au milieu de la diaphyse. ······ = à 35 mm. au-dessus du milieu de la diaphyse. Dessin au diagraphe, segment distal de la coupe, 3/4 G.N.

En définitive, l'examen des humérus permet d'affirmer la présence de trois adultes à l'Abri Pataud; deux d'entre eux sont de sexe féminin, tandis que le troisième pourrait être masculin. On retiendra, d'une façon générale, le relief accusé des empreintes musculaires et, tout particulièrement, l'insertion deltoïdienne qui détermine une diaphyse quadrangulaire mais non aplatie. Il convient encore de souligner le fort développement des épiphyses, l'absence de perforation olécrânienne, la présence d'une ptère sus-épicondyllienne, ainsi que le faible degré de torsion de l'humérus.

D. ULNA (CUBITUS)

Les deux pièces recueillies (pl. VI) sont des ulna gauches; ils appartiennent de ce fait à des sujets différents. L'un, le n°7, qui provient de la Trench II (éboulis de la zone A), a été trouvé auprès de l'humérus gauche n°1 avec lequel il s'articule parfaitement; il appartient donc au même individu masculin.

TABLEAU XX

L'ulna

	n° 22 G.	n° 7 G.
Longueur maximale (1)	252	—
Longueur physiologique (2)	219	—
Périmètre minimal (3)	33	—
Largeur de l'olécrâne (6)	21	24
Hauteur de l'olécrâne (8)	18	21
Diam. antéro-postérieur (11)	13,5	14
Diam. transverse (12)	16	19,5
Diam. transverse supérieur (13)	17,5	20
Diam. antéro-post. supérieur (14)	23,5	25
Indice de robustesse (3/1)	13,1	—
Indice de robustesse (3/2)	15,1	—
Indice de haut. olécrâne (8/6)	85,7	87,5
Indice diaphysaire (11/12)	84,4	71,8
Indice de platôlénie (13/14)	74,5	80,0

L'autre (n°22) provient du complexe 22 et s'articule précisément avec l'humérus 22. Comme ce dernier il présente le même aspect gracile caractéristique d'un sujet féminin; ses indices de robustesse sont faibles (cf. tabl. XX) comparés à ceux des hommes modernes. Un tel caractère a déjà été signalé par Matiegka sur les Aurignaciens de Předmost où les indices de robustesse sont absolument identiques à ceux obtenus à l'Abri Pataud. Les cubitus féminins sont «particulièrement grêles» à Cro-Magnon, celui du sujet 3 présentant des indices extrêment bas. Cette gracilité se retrouve encore au Magdalénien chez les sujets de Saint-Germain-la-Rivière, de Veyrier, et, surtout, de Cap-Blanc. Seul l'homme de Chancelade possède des cubitus plus massifs (cf. tabl. XXI).

Sur les deux pièces, la courbure dans le sens sagittal affecte toute la moitié supérieure de l'os. Cette concavité très accusée vers l'avant, tenue par Broca comme caractéristique de la race de Cro-Magnon, semble spécifique des hommes du Paléolithique supérieur puisqu'elle existe à des degrés divers sur les cubitus de Předmost, de Veyrier, d'Obercassel, et de Chancelade, ainsi que sur les squelettes féminins de Cap-Blanc et de Saint-Germain. Latéralement, la diaphyse présente dans son tiers inférieur une seconde

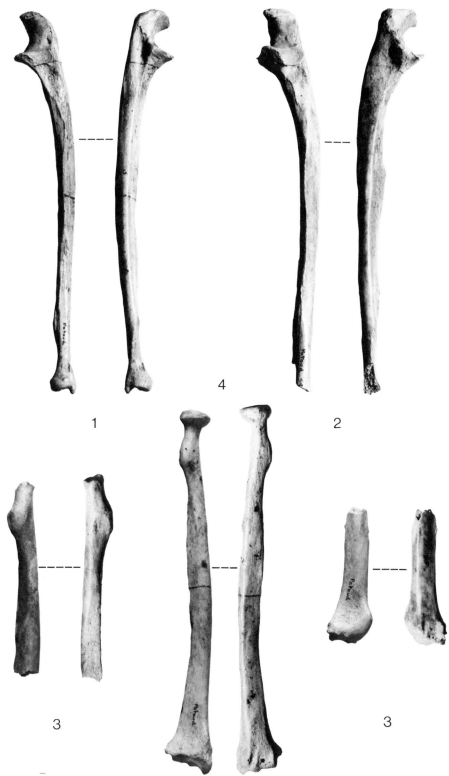

Planche VI. 1. ulna gauche (n° 22), faces externe et interne; 2. ulna gauche (n° 7), faces externe et interne; 3. radius gauche (n° 7), faces antérieure et postérieure; 4. radius gauche (n° 22), faces antérieure et postérieure.

TABLEAU XXI

L'ulna: comparaisons

	Cap-Blanc	Saint-Germain	Předmost F. IV	Ober-cassel F.	Veyrier H.	Cro-Magnon H. 3	Chan-celade H.
	G.	G.	G.		G.	D.	D.
Long. maximale	241 ?	242	275	–	274	294	257
Long. physiologique	216	–	238	–	244	263	222
Périm. minimal	29	32	36	–	34	39	38
Diam. ant.-postérieur	16,1	–	16	13	18	–	16
Diam. transverse	11,6	–	16	14	13	–	17,5
Diam. transv. sup.	18	18	–	17	18	21	24
Diam. ant.-post. sup.	24	21,5	–	23	25	26	28
Ind. de robustesse (3/1)	12,0	13,2	13,1	–	12,4	13,2	14,8
Ind. de robustesse (3/2)	13,4	–	15,1	–	13,9	14,8	17,1
Ind. diaphysaire	138,8	83,7	100,0	92,8	138,5	–	91,4
Ind. de platôlénie	75,0	–	–	73,9	72,0	79,6	85,7

courbure à concavité interne également très accentuée.

Au niveau de l'extrémité supérieure, l'olécrâne est volumineux avec un bord externe proéminent, tout particulièrement sur le cubitus n°7. Ses dimensions déterminent des indices élevés qui traduisent une forte hauteur par rapport à la largeur. Le bec de l'olécrâne se projette en avant, et sa partie supérieure déborde la surface articulaire en délimitant une véritable face supérieure à son sommet. L'apophyse coronoïde, également très proéminente, détermine avec l'avancée olécrânienne une grande cavité sigmoïde à concavité marquée. Les deux parties sont séparées par un sillon olécrâno-coronoïdien sur le cubitus n°1 qui réalise le schéma normal, ou type I de Manouvrier; le seconde ne présente en revanche aucune séparation et se rattache au type III. De plus, la petite cavité sigmoïde est vaste et concave, surtout sur l'ulna n°1. En dessous, l'empreinte du court supinateur détermine une dépression allongée et la crête qui la borde est très développée, avec un tubercule supinateur. La tubérosité du brachial antérieur fait une forte rugosité s'allongeant sous l'apophyse coronoïde. Notons encore, de chaque côté du bord postérieur, l'existence de larges dépressions imprimées par une musculature puissante.

La diaphyse présente une section nettement triangulaire (cf. fig. 15) avec une remarquable saillie de la crête interosseuse, comme l'attestent les valeurs très faibles des indices diaphysaires par comparaison aux données du Paléolithique (cf. tabl. XXI). A cet aplatissement diaphysaire antéro-postérieur correspond un aplatissement transversal au niveau de l'épiphyse supérieure. Le rapport des diamètres, mesurés juste au-dessous de la petite cavité sigmoïde, classe précisément le cubitus 22 en pleine platôlénie

et le n°7 à la limite inférieure de l'eurôlénie. Il s'agit là d'une caractéristique propre aux cubitus du Paléolithique supérieur car, si l'on excepte les squelettes de Chancelade et de Saint-Germain-la-Rivière, la platôlénie se rencontre chez les sujets de Cap-Blanc, d'Obercassel, et de Veyrier. A Cro-Magnon, cinq cubitus livrent un indice moyen de 81,7, témoin, selon Trouette (1955), d'un aplatissement épiphysaire antéro-postérieur corrélatif d'une crête supinatrice très marquée.

A l'extrémité inférieure, l'empreinte du carré pronateur forme un gros bourrelet saillant sur le bord

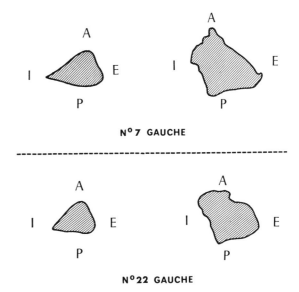

Figure 15. Coupes transversales des ulna; à gauche: coupe au milieu de la diaphyse; à droite: coupe au-dessous de la petite cavité sigmoïde. Dessin au diagraphe, segment distal de la coupe, 3/4 G.N.

antérieur. La tête présente une large facette articulaire en croissant et la gouttière qui la sépare de l'apophyse styloïde est particulièrement profonde.

Les ulna de l'Abri Pataud sont caractérisés en définitive par une gracilité certaine associée à des empreintes musculaires accusées. Nous rappellerons leur courbure sagittale très marquée, le fort développement de la crête interosseuse, la hauteur et la saillie de l'olécrâne, la profondeur de la grande cavité sigmoïde, la forme triangulaire de la diaphyse et la platôlénie. Ce sont là autant de caractères qui ne différencient pas les ulna de Pataud de ceux du Paléolithique supérieur.

E. RADIUS

Des trois pièces recueillies (pl. VI), on note:

un radius gauche entier provenant du complexe 22. Cet os présente des taches superficielles brunâtres, identiques à celles observées sur les humérus et cubitus 22 avec lesquels ils s'articulent; nous sommes donc en présence d'un squelette entier de bras gauche.

un radius gauche brisé (n°7), comprenant une moitié supérieure et le tiers inférieur, trouvé avec l'ulna 7 dans les éboulis de la zone A (Trench II). Les deux fragments recueillis à peu de distance appartiennent en effet au même os, comme l'attestent par ailleurs leur patine et leur robustesse identiques. Ce radius constitue, avec l'humérus 1 G. et l'ulna 7 G., un second squelette de bras gauche, mais de constitution bien plus robuste.

un radius droit réduit à trois fragments non susceptibles d'être étudiés et de provenance inconnue.

Comme les os qui lui correspondent, le radius 22 est caractérisé par un aspect général gracile. Sa longueur maximale élevée, dépassant certaines moyennes de séries modernes (Maïa Neto 1957, Martin-Saller 1959), couplée à un périmètre minimal très petit,

TABLEAU XXII

Le radius

	n°22 G.	n°7 G.
Longueur maximale (1)	232	—
Longueur physiologique (2)	216	—
Périmètre minimal (3)	35	43
Diam. transv. de la diaphyse (4)	15,5	17
Diam. sagittal de la diaphyse (5)	10,5	12
Angle collo-diaphysaire (7)	155°	—
Indice de robustesse (3/1)	15,1	—
Indice de robustesse (3/2)	16,2	—
Indice diaphysaire (5/4)	67,7	70,6

détermine un indice de robustesse relativement bas (cf. tabl. XXII).

C'est encore avec la femme de Cap-Blanc qu'il faut noter la plus grande similitude, celle de Saint-Germain se caractérisant par un avant-bras plus court et celle de Předmost par un segment plus long. De tous les squelettes du Paléolithique supérieur, c'est le radius de l'Abri Pataud qui atteint le maximum de gracilité, comme le montrent les chiffres du tableau XXIII.

Il présente une concavité interne de la diaphyse, moins accusée toutefois que chez certains hommes actuels. Modérément marquée sur les pièces de Cap-Blanc et d'Obercassel, cette concavité est remarquable chez la femme de Předmost et à Chancelade. L'aplatissement antéro-postérieur de la diaphyse, évalué juste au-dessus de la surface du rond pronateur, est bien marqué (cf. fig. 16) comme l'indiquent aussi des indices diaphysaires faibles, surtout pour le

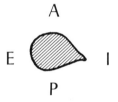

N°22 GAUCHE

Figure 16. Coupe transversale du radius n°22 au milieu de la diaphyse. Dessin au diagraphe, segment distal de la coupe, G.N.

radius 22 G. Cet aplatissement diaphysaire, plus prononcé que chez certains hommes actuels (74,0 Martin; 73,7 Mendes Corrêa) s'observe également sur les os de Cap-Blanc, de Chancelade, et des sujets masculins de Cro-Magnon où il atteint un degré extrême (cf. tabl. XXIII).

La crête interosseuse est tranchante bien que les faces antérieure et postérieure soient à peine excavées sur le radius 22. Sur le n°7 G. elles dénotent l'existence d'une musculature plus puissante.

La tête radiale est franchement circulaire mais pas très élevée (8,5 et 7 mm. respectivement dans ses parties interne et externe). En revanche, le col est haut, mince, et présente intérieurement une certaine obliquité vers le bas. L'angle collo-diaphysaire (165°) est beaucoup plus fermé que chez les Européens actuels (172°); une telle disposition semble assez fréquente au Paléolithique supérieur comme le montrent les données comparatives du tableau XXIII.

Au niveau de l'épiphyse inférieure, l'échancrure cubitale paraît large mais n'est vraiment concave que

TABLEAU XXIII

Le radius: comparaisons

| | Cap-Blanc | | Saint-Germain | Předmost IV | | Cro-Magnon | | | |
| | | | | | | F. n°2 | | H. | |
	D.	G.	D.	D.	G.	G.	D.	G.	D.
Longueur maximale (1)	231	229	222	253	252	–	–	–	–
Longueur physiologique (2)	217	217	–	237	239	–	–	–	–
Périmètre minimal (3)	39	38	37	41	39	40	43	41	–
Diam. transv. diaphyse (4)	15,3	15,6	14	15,5	15	16,5	18,5	17	16
Diam. sagittal diaphyse (5)	10,6	10,1	11	12	12	10	11	10	10,5
Angle collo-diaphysaire (7)	167°	164°	160°	166°	167°	–	–	–	–
Indice de robustesse (3/1)	16,9	16,6	16,6	16,2	15,5	–	–	–	–
Indice de robustesse (3/2)	18,0	17,5	–	17,3	16,3	–	–	–	–
Indice diaphysaire (5/4)	69,3	64,7	78,5	77,4	90,0	60,6	59,4	58,8	65,6

sur l'extrémité n°7 G. Le bord marginal de la face antérieure, qui forme un bourrelet saillant, circonscrit une surface d'insertion du carré pronateur fortement excavée.

En résumé, les principales caractéristiques des radius de l'Abri Pataud sont leur aspect gracile, leur aplatissement diaphysaire prononcé, l'obliquité du col par rapport à la diaphyse, et, enfin, leur courbure à concavité interne.

F. OS DE LA MAIN

Les différents ossements recueillis ont pu être attribués à quatre mains appartenant à trois individus adultes. Ils se répartissent comme suit:

TABLEAU XXIV

Inventaire des os des mains

| | | | Trench VII | | Trench II | |
			Droite	Gauche	Gauche	Gauche
CARPE	Scaphoïde (os naviculare)		–	2091	22	–
	Semi-lunaire (os lunatum)		1541	1510	22	–
	Pyramidal (os triquetrum)		1714	1716	22	–
	Pisiforme (os pisiforme)		1540	–	–	–
	Trapèze (os multangulum majus)		–	1385	22	–
	Trapézoïde (os multangulum minus)		–	–	22	–
	Grand os (os capitatum)		2086	2085	22	–
	Os crochu (os hamatum)		1832	1539	22	–
META-CARPE	1er Métacarpien (metacarpus)		1516	1538	22	–
	2e Métacarpien (metacarpus)		–	2081	22	–
	3e Métacarpien (metacarpus)		–	1521	22	–
	4e Métacarpien (metacarpus)		1404	–	22	–
	5e Métacarpien (metacarpus)		–	–	22	–
PHA-LANGE	1e Phalange (phalanx proximalis)	I	1520	–	–	–
	1e Phalange (phalanx proximalis)	II	1536	2077	22	–
	1e Phalange (phalanx proximalis)	III	1518	1530	22	5
	1e Phalange (phalanx proximalis)	IV	1532	–	22	–
	1e Phalange (phalanx proximalis)	V	1313	1711	22	–
	Phalangine (phalanx media)	II	1370	1712	22	13
	Phalangine (phalanx media)	III	1368	–	22	17
	Phalangine (phalanx media)	IV	1534	1402	22	–
	Phalangine (phalanx media)	V	1542	–	–	–
	Phalangette (phalanx distalis)	I	1829	–	–	–
	Phalangette (phalanx distalis)	II	2069	–	–	–
	Phalangette (phalanx distalis)	III	2095	–	–	–
	Phalangette (phalanx distalis)	IV	1537	–	–	–
	Phalangette (phalanx distalis)	V	1833	–	–	–

Deux de ces mains proviennent de la Trench VII, Square G, où les os étaient intimement mélangés et dispersés dans un espace assez réduit de 1 mètre sur 0,5 m. de profondeur environ. Leurs dimensions et leur patine identiques permettent d'affirmer sans équivoque leur appartenance à un même individu, une femme très probablement.

Une seconde main gauche, presque complète, fut trouvée dans le complexe 22, Trench II; elle constitue avec le squelette de bras gauche recueilli au même endroit le membre supérieur complet d'un autre individu féminin. On retrouve d'ailleurs sur les métacarpiens II à V les mêmes tâches brunâtres déjà signalées sur les os du bras et de l'avant-bras.

Les trois phalanges de main gauche portant les n°s 5,

13, et 17 sur l'inventaire furent recueillies parmi les éboulis de la zone A avec le squelette masculin de bras gauche. L'emplacement de leur découverte et leur robustesse par rapport aux autres pièces nous incitent à attribuer ces pièces à un homme.

1. LE CARPE

Les mensurations prises selon le procédé de Martin (1928) ont été comparées aux données de Sarasin (1931) sur des populations actuelles, dans la mesure des possibilités de concordance entre les deux techniques (cf. tabl. XXV).

Les dimensions des os du carpe de l'Abri Pataud présentent dans l'ensemble une grande similitude avec

TABLEAU XXV

Le carpe: comparaisons

| | Abri Pataud | | | Cap-Blanc | | Chancelade | Européens modernes (Sarasin) |
| | Trench VII | | Trench II | | | | |
	D.	G.	G.	D.	G.	G.	
Scaphoïde *(os naviculare)*		(2091)	(22)				
Long. max. (1)	–	23,5	24	22,0	21,5	27	28,0 (22,2-33,0)
Larg. max. (2a)	–	14,5	15	–	–	16	16,7
Haut. max. (3a)	–	11	11,5	–	–	14	–
Semi-lunaire *(os lunatum)*	(1541)	(1510)	(22)				
Long. max. (1)	16	16	16	16,5	15	20,5	18
Larg. max. (2)	13	12,5	12,5	–	–	14	13,4
Haut. max. (3)	18	18	17	–	–	19,5	18,3 (14,5-21,5)
Pyramidal *(os triquetrum)*	(1714)	(1716)	(22)				
Long. max. (1)	14	13	12,5	–	–	–	14,5
Larg. max. (2)	19	18	18,5	21,0	–	–	19,6 (16,5-23,5)
Haut. max. (3)	12	12	12	–	–	–	–
Trapèze *(os multangulum majus)*	–	(1385)	(22)				
Long. max. (1)	–	14,5	16,5	–	–	17	17,2
Larg. max. (2)	–	21,5	22,5	19,0	–	24	24,6 (20,2-28,5)
Haut. max. (3)	–	12,0	13,5	–	–	–	–
Larg. max. fac. art. Métacarpien I	–	13,5	13,5	–	–	–	15,9
Trapézoïde *(os multangulum minus)*			(22)				
Long. max. (1)	–	–	10	–	–	–	12,0 (9,0-15,0)
Larg. max. (2)	–	–	16	16,1	–	–	17,0
Haut. max. (3)	–	–	15,5	–	–	–	18,8
Grand os *(os capitatum)*	(2086)	(2085)	(22)				
Long. max. (1)	22	21,5	22,5	22,2	22,1	25	24,0 (20,0-28,0)
Larg. max. (2)	14	14	14	16,1	–	17	15,9
Haut. max. (3)	18	18	18	–	–	–	20,6
Os crochu *(os hamatum)*	(1832)	(1539)	(22)				
Long. max. (1)	20	20	20	–	–	28	21,7 (17,5-24,3)
Larg. max. (2)	14	14	13,5	–	–	16	16,3
Haut. max. (3)	21,5	21,5	20	–	–	24	24,1

celles obtenues par von Bonin sur la femme de Cap-Blanc. Toujours plus faibles que les valeurs moyennes de Sarasin portant sur des individus des deux sexes, elles indiquent une certaine gracilité du poignet féminin que l'examen du bras laissait déjà prévoir.

2. LE METACARPE

Il existe au total 10 métacarpiens dont un seul, incomplet, n'est pas mesurable. Leurs longueurs, sensiblement identiques à celles obtenues sur les autres squelettes féminins paléolithiques, et nettement inférieures à celles des hommes de Cro-Magnon et de Chancelade, confirment le diagnostic sexuel précédemment établi. Le tableau XXVI, tenant compte des données de Pfitzner relatives à des Européens modernes, montre par ailleurs qu'il n'existe aucune différence entre les dimensions de celles-ci et celles des femmes de Pataud.

De même, l'ordre décroissant de longueur des métacarpiens suit le schéma classique II, III, IV, V et I observé chez les hommes modernes. L'indice de longueur du carpe (37,5), rapportant la longueur du grand os à celle du troisième métacarpien, indique une main macrocarpe. Cet allongement du carpe par rapport au métacarpe est également le propre des Européens actuels d'après la valeur de l'indice (38,5) obtenue par Sarasin.

Le développement relatif des métacarpiens apporte

TABLEAU XXVI

Longueurs des métacarpiens: comparaisons

| | Abri Pataud | | | |
	Droits		Gauches	Gauches n° 22
Métacarpien I	(1516)	42	(1538) 42,5	43
Métacarpien II	-	-	(2081) 63,5	63,5
Métacarpien III	-	-	(1521) ?	60
Métacarpien IV	(1404)	54	-	52
Métacarpien V	-	-	-	48,5

| | Cap-Blanc | | Předmost IV | | Cro-Magnon | Chancelade | | Européennes modernes |
	D.	G.	D.	G.	G.	D.	G.	
Métacarpien I	-	41	47	-	-	44	44	41,4
Métacarpien II	-	63,5	-	62?	66,4	-	64	62,2
Métacarpien III	61	60	-	-	63,2	63	-	59,8
Métacarpien IV	-	·52,5	-	-	-	57	?	54,0
Métacarpien V	50	49	56	55	-	-	51	50,6

quelques précisions au sujet de l'architecture de la main. C'est ainsi que le pouce présente un allongement par rapport au médius, comme le montre la valeur élevée de l'indice (71,7) comparée à celle des Européens actuels (69,9). On sait que ce rapport est au contraire très bas chez les Néandertaliens (64,8 sur 3 sujets). Toujours par rapport au médius, le quatrième métacarpien serait plus court (86,7) que celui de l'Européen (89,9); il en est de même du cinquième dont l'indice 80,8 est faible en regard de celui des hommes modernes (83,7). On en conclut que, toutes proportions gardées, le métacarpe est caractérisé à Pataud par un allongement relatif du pouce et du troisième métacarpien.

En ce qui concerne le développement en largeur, l'indice rapportant la moyenne des largeurs de chacune des deux rangées d'os du carpe à la longueur du troisième doigt (42,5) situe cette main féminine du complexe 22 dans la catégorie métriocarpe, soit nettement moins large que celle des Européens actuels (45,9).

Signalons enfin l'articulation en selle du métacarpien I et, sur les autres, une nette courbure du corps telle qu'elle existe de nos jours. Les épiphyses, comme le corps des métacarpiens, sont plutôt grêles, mais présentent des insertions musculaires très nettes.

En résumé, les sujets féminins de l'Abri Pataud possèdent une main moyennement large à tendance allongée, mais peu différente de celle des Européens actuels.

3. LES PHALANGES.

Des 35 phalanges dénombrées, 11 furent recueillies dans le complexe 22 (Trench II), une (n° 13) dans la

Trench IV, trois (n°s 19, 20, et 21) dans la Trench VI et 19 dans le Square G de la Trench VII. Une phalange incomplète (n° 5) trouvée dans les éboulis de la zone A provient d'un locus non précise. Ces pièces se répartissent comme suit:

14 *phalanx proximalis*
12 *phalanx media*
9 *phalanx distalis.*

Les longueurs sont dans l'ensemble très proches de celles des femmes de Cap-Blanc et de Předmost IV et de l'homme de Chancelade qui se caractérise précisément par un raccourcissement relatif des phalanges (Billy 1969). A l'inverse, les quelques pièces trouvées à Cro-Magnon sont nettement plus longues (cf. tabl. XXVII).

Remarquons d'autre part que les dimensions ob-

TABLEAU XXVII

Phalanges

		Abri Pataud F.				Cap-Blanc F.		Předmost IV F.		Chancelade H.		Cro-Magnon H.	Européennes (Pfitzner)
		D.	G.	D.	22 G.	D.	G.	D.	G.	D.	G.	G.	G.
Phalanx proximalis	I	(1520) 27,5	—	—	—	—	—	32	31	—	30,5	41	27,7
	II	(1536) 37,5	(2077) 38	?	38	—	36	42	—	39,5	—	45,5	37,0
	III	(1518) 41	(1530) 41	?	41,5	42	39,5	46,5	—	41	—	43	41,2
	IV	(1532) 38,5	—	—	—	38,5	—	37,5	42,5	40	39	—	38,8
	V	(1313) 31	(1711) 30	—	30	—	28	30	—	32	31,5	—	30,6
Phalanx media	II	(1370) 23	(1712) 23	23,5	—	—	23	—	—	25	26	—	22,4
	III	(1368) 27	—	—	29	27,5	—	26,5	(30)	28	—	—	27,1
	IV	(1534) 26	(1402) 26	28	25,5	—	24,0	—	—	27	—	—	25,8
	V	(1542) 17,5	—	—	—	18	—	16	(17)	—	—	—	18,2
Phalanx distalis	I	(1829) 21	—	—	—	21	—	19	23	—	—	—	20,4
	II	(2069) 16	—	—	—	—	16	—	—	—	—	—	16,0
	III	(1537) 16,5	—	—	—	17	17,0	—	—	19	—	—	16,7
	IV	(2095) 17	—	—	—	17,5	17,8	—	—	—	—	—	17,5
	V	(1833) 15,5	—	—	—	16	14	—	—	17	—	—	15,7

servées à Pataud coïncident avec les moyennes d'Européennes actuelles (Pfitzner) rapportées par Martin. Corrélativement, l'ordre normal de décroissance des *phalanx proximalis* (III > IV > II > V > I), des *phalanx media* (III > IV > II > V), comme celui des *phalanx distalis* (I > IV > III > II > V) sont reproduits rigoureusement ici. Les longueurs des différents doigts présentent par ailleurs l'ordre normal de diminution observé de nos jours, soit: III, IV, II, V, et I. Il en est de même de la décroissance des longueurs des rayons qui suit le schéma III, II, IV, V, et I, caractéristique des populations actuelles.

Précisons encore que le rapport entre la longueur de la troisième phalange proximale et celle du métacarpien correspondant (69,2) est sensiblement identique à la moyenne obtenue par Sarasin pour des Européens modernes (69,4), ce qui implique des proportions absolument semblables des différents segments. La longueur totale de la main du complexe 22, après reconstruction, correspond à 175 mm., chiffre qui se situe dans les limites de variation $178,7 \pm 0,81$ ($\sigma = 8,1$) avancées par S. de Félice (1958) pour les françaises de 20 à 34 ans.

On en conclut que les sujets féminins de l'Abri Pataud avaient une main comparable à celle des autres femmes paléolithiques et actuelles; seules les dimensions absolues, qui sont sous une étroite dépendance sexuelle, peuvent les différencier.

TABLEAU XXVIII

Décroissance des doigts et des rayons

	DOIGTS			RAYONS	
	Droit	Gauche		Droit	Gauche
I	48,5	—	I	90,5	—
II	76,5	—	II	140,0	—
III	84,5	86	III	—	146
IV	81,5	81,5	IV	135,5	133,5
V	64	64	V	—	112,5

III. LE MEMBRE INFERIEUR

A. BASSIN

Un seul os coxal gauche (pl. IV$_2$) a été recueilli dans la Trench VI. Il comprend l'ilion en entier et la branche descendante de l'ischion avec sa tubérosité; la région du pubis manque. Deux autres fragments qui ne se prêtent guère à des mesures ont été recueillis. Ce sont, d'une part, une portion de crête iliaque gauche et, d'autre part, un pubis droit presque entier.

Tableau XXIX

L'os coxal

Hauteur maximale de l'os coxal	203
Hauteur de l'ilion	98
Hauteur de la grande échancrure sciatique	51
Hauteur de la cavité cotyloïde	52
Largeur de l'ilion	157
Largeur inférieure minimale de l'ilion (Genovès)	56
Largeur cotylo-sciatique (Sauter)	32
Largeur de la tubérosité ischiatique	22
Epaisseur maximale du tubercule moyen fessier	21
Indice de largeur coxale	77,3
Indice de largeur de l'ilion	160,2
Indice cotylo-sciatique	159,4
Angle de l'échancrure sciatique	65°

L'os coxal présente de petites dimensions par comparaison aux moyennes observées chez les Européens modernes. Celles-ci, ajoutées à plusieurs caractères de différenciation sexuelle, indiquent sans conteste une appartenance féminine.

L'indice de largeur coxale, rapportant la largeur de l'os à sa hauteur maximale (77,3), est comparable aux indices moyens obtenus par Genovès (1959) pour des séries d'Européennes modernes de Bruxelles et de Londres; il est nettement supérieur aux valeurs observées à Předmost qui sont toutefois relatives à des pièces masculines.

Les deux dimensions principales de l'aile iliaque déterminent un rapport relativement élevé (160,2) indiquant un ilion plutôt bas et large, comme il est de règle chez la femme.

La crête iliaque forme un bourrelet très prononcé, limité en avant par l'épine iliaque antéro-supérieure qui est bien développée. L'épaisseur du tubercule du moyen fessier dépasse nettement la moyenne (18,3 mm.) obtenue par Genovès sur des pièces féminines modernes. La fosse iliaque externe est fortement excavée dans sa partie moyenne et présente

un trou nourricier largement ouvert, juste en arrière de la saillie formée par la ligne demi-circulaire antérieure. Dans la partie antéro-externe de l'aile iliaque, la gouttière sus-cotyloïdienne, bien marquée, est criblée de trous vasculaires. Bien qu'incomplète, la cavité cotyloïde paraît petite; l'épine iliaque antéro-inférieure qui la surmonte forme une importante saillie mousse.

Sur le bord postérieur de l'os coxal, les saillies correspondant aux épines iliaques postéro-supérieure et antérieure sont très développées. En dessous, la grande échancrure sciatique décrit un angle très ouvert de 65°. Ses mesures, prises selon la technique de Sauter et Privat (1954) déterminent un indice cotylo-sciatique (159,4) supérieur à la moyenne obtenue sur des femmes modernes (152,7). La valeur très élevée de cet indice situe sans conteste l'os iliaque de l'Abri Pataud dans les limites du sexe féminin définies par Sauter et Privat.

Sur la face interne, la ligne innominée forme une saillie arrondie et mousse, au-dessus de laquelle la fosse iliaque interne fait une légère excavation et présente un vaste orifice nourricier dirigé obliquement vers le bas. En arrière, la tubérosité iliaque se traduit par une grosse protubérance qui surmonte une facette auriculaire relativement petite, dont le contour est bordé par un faible sillon preéauriculaire (*sulcus praeauricularis*). Une telle disposition rappelle en tous points celle observée sur les os de Předmost. Le bord antérieur de la branche supérieure de la facette auriculaire et celui de la grande échancrure sciatique correspondent par ailleurs à deux arcs qui se coupent conformément au schéma féminin de «l'arc composé» défini par Genovès.

Au-dessous d'une gouttière sous-cotyloïdienne très excavée, la tubérosité ischiatique forme une large saillie de 22 mm., présentant une surface boursouflée au relief tourmenté. Bien que moins épaisse que chez l'homme de Chancelade (33 mm.), cette formation n'en demeure pas moins volumineuse pour un individu féminin.

Le fragment pubien présente enfin une épine saillante, une surface angulaire large et mince, puis une facette articulaire très érodée, non susceptible de fournir quelque renseignement quant à l'âge du sujet.

C'est donc un os coxal gracile, particulièrement large et bas, qui caractérise le sujet de Pataud. Malgré la minceur de son aile iliaque et sa gracilité générale, cet os apparaît néanmoins parfaitement modelé. Il doit être attribué sans nul doute à un sujet féminin.

B. ROTULE (PATELLA)

Deux rotules, une droite (n°1376) et une gauche (n°1543), furent recueillies à faible distance l'une de l'autre dans la Trench VII (pl. VII₄). Leurs dimensions relativement faibles ainsi que leur patine identique permettent par ailleurs de les attribuer à un même individu, probablement féminin.

TABLEAU XXX

Les rotules

| | Abri Pataud | | Chancelade | | Předmost | | Cap-Blanc | | Européens modernes |
| | | | | | IV F. | XIV H. | | | |
	1376 D.	1543 G.	D.	G.			D.	G.	
Hauteur maximale (1)	42,5	41	44	45	40	40	39	39	43,7
Largeur maximale (2)	46	46,5	52	53	43	46	42,5?	41	44,7
Epaisseur maximale (3)	20	20	25	25	21	21	18,2	18,4	—
Ind. de larg.-haut. (2/1) Vallois	108,2	113,4	118,2	117,8	107,5	115	109,0	105,1	102,2

De hauteur légèrement plus faible que les moyennes obtenues par H. Vallois (1917) sur 85 Européens modernes, les rotules de Pataud sont en revanche beaucoup plus larges et déterminent corrélativement un indice rotulien plus élevé (cf. tabl. XXX). Leurs dimensions sont néanmoins très proches de celles des squelettes féminins de Cap-Blanc et de Předmost IV, mais nettement plus faibles que celles des hommes de Chancelade et de Předmost, plus volumineuses et surtout plus larges. Sans doute ne faut-il voir là qu'une différence sexuelle assez marquée.

Le bord supérieur est épais; il présente à l'angle supéro-externe une échancrure semi-lunaire réalisant le type *patella emarginata*, ou *vastus notch* des auteurs anglo-saxons (cf. pl. VII). Notons que cette particularité excessivement accusée chez l'homme de Chancelade, ne se rencontre ni sur le squelette de Cap-Blanc, ni sur ceux de Předmost.

La face antérieure est par ailleurs convexe, avec de nombreux orifices vasculaires et une série de stries verticales parallèles qui lui donnent un aspect fibroïde. Du côté postérieur, la facette articulaire externe est plus grande et beaucoup plus excavée que l'interne. Enfin, la base de la rotule, dont la surface est triangulaire, se trouve creusée dans sa portion antérieure par la facette d'insertion du quadriceps.

C. PERONE (FIBULA)

Parmi les trois fragments de diaphyse receuillis, on distingue:

Pièce n°8: moitié inférieure droite, sans épiphyse, provenant de la Trench II, Lens 3 (pl. VII₂),

Pièce n°16: tiers inférieur gauche également sans épiphyse (pl. VII₃), trouvé dans la Trench V (éboulis de la zone A),

Pièce n°18: très petit fragment de diaphyse non identifiable qui provient des éboulis de la zone A (Trench VI, Lens 1).

Ces restes appartiennent vraisemblablement à des individus différents comme le laissaient d'ailleurs prévoir les emplacements des découvertes; le fragment droit, beaucoup plus robuste, semblerait masculin, mais l'état trop fragmentaire des deux autres rend toute différenciation sexuelle illusoire.

Autant que l'on puisse en juger d'après le fragment droit, il apparaît que la direction générale de la diaphyse est sensiblement rectiligne. Sa section transversale est de forme triangulaire (cf. fig. 17), avec un bord antérieur aigü et une face antéro-externe très

FIBULA

Figure 17. Coupe transversale du péroné droit n°8 au milieu de la diaphyse. Dessin au diagraphe, segment distal de la coupe, G.N.

fortement excavée qui témoigne de muscles péroniers puissants. Cette cannelure, excessivement accentuée sur les péronés de Cro-Magnon, semble de règle générale au Paléolithique supérieur; elle se retrouve en effet chez les deux sujets d'Obercassel et tous ceux de

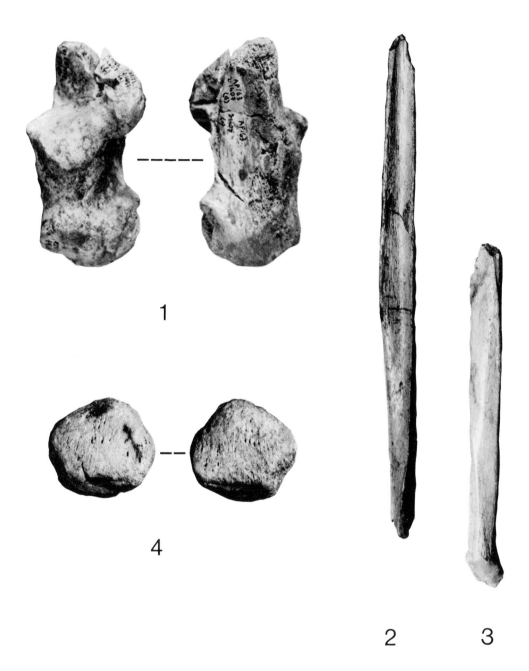

Planche VII. 1. astragale gauche (n° 1407), faces supérieure et inférieure; 2. péroné droit (n° 8), face antéro-externe; 3. péroné gauche (n° 16), face antéro-externe; 4. rotules, face antérieure.

Předmost, à Chancelade, à Cap-Blanc, ainsi qu'à Veyrier.

Les seules mensurations possibles ont permis de déterminer le degré d'aplatissement de la diaphyse sensiblement en son milieu. Il ressort du tableau XXXI que la diaphyse de Pataud se trouve moins aplatie que celles des autres squelettes du Paléolithique supérieur. En fait, le péroné est surtout caractérisé par une cannelure excessivement prononcée de sa face antéro-postérieure.

TABLEAU XXXI

Le péroné: mensurations et comparaisons

	Abri Pataud F.		Předmost				Obercassel F.	Veyrier H.	Cro-Magnon H.	
			F. IV		H. III					
	D.	?	D.	G.	D.	G.	G.	G.	D.	G.
Diam. max. au milieu (2)	17	15	16	15	19	21,5	16	15	18	19
Diam. min. au milieu (3)	13	10,5	11	13	14	14	11	9	10	13
Périmètre minimal (4)	37,5	-	34	-	34	35	42	36	33	-
Ind. diaphysaire (3/2)	76,5	70,0	68,7	86,7	73,7	65,1	68,8	60,0	55,5	68,4

D. OS DU PIED

On dénombre au total 32 os de pieds issus de la Trench VII, Square G, qui se répartissent comme indiqué dans le tableau XXXII.

Les os du pied droit se trouvaient disséminés sur une air de 75 cm. x 45 cm., sur 11 cm. de profondeur, et ceux du pied gauche dans une bande de terrain mesurant 50 x 55 x 14 cm. Il s'agit là en somme d'une dispersion assez faible.

TABLEAU XXXII

Inventaire des os des pieds

	Pied droit	Pied gauche
	Astragale (n° 1381)	Astragale (n° 1330)
	-	Calcanéum (n° 1407)
TARSE	Scaphoïde (n° 1408)	Scaphoïde (n° 1399)
	Cuboïde (n° 1331)	Cuboïde (n° 1512)
	1e cunéiforme (n° 1463)	-
	-	2e cunéiforme (n° 2090)
	3e cunéiforme (n° 1307)	3e cunéiforme (n° 1333)
	1e Métatarsien (n° 1309)	1e Métatarsien (n° 1326)
	2e Métatarsien (n° 1327)	2e Métatarsien (n° 1395)
METATARSE	3e Métatarsien (n° 1310)	3e Métatarsien (n° 1305)
	-	4e Métatarsien (n° 1332)
	5e Métatarsien (n° 1329)	5e Métatarsien (n° 1398)
	I (n° 1465)	I (n° 1403)
	II (n° 1386)	II (n° 1461)
1e PHALANGES	III (n° 1306)	III (n° 1387)
	IV (n° 1462)	IV (n° 1388)
	V (n° 1389)	V (n° 1467)
3e PHALANGES	I (n° 1466)	I (n° 1334)

1. LE TARSE.

a. Astragale *(talus).* Les deux astragales 1381 (d.) et 1330 (g.) sont entiers et en bon état. D'après leur volume général et leur morphologie, ils peuvent appartenir au même individu, probablement une femme.

Toutes les mesures sont très voisines des moyennes obtenues par Volkov (1905) sur des Européennes modernes, à l'exception de la longueur prise selon une technique différente (cf. tabl. XXXIII). En regard des autres pièces paléolithiques connues, les astragales de Pataud sont relativement courts et hauts, les

indices respectifs définis par rapport à la longueur se situant, comme ceux des femmes de Předmost et de Cro-Magnon, parmi les valeurs les plus élevées (cf. tabl. XXXIII). En revanche, partout la trochlée occupe les deux tiers environ de l'astragale. Ses dimensions sont quasi identiques sur tous les squelettes féminins comparés, et le rapport des largeurs trochléennes implique un rétrécissement moins marqué de la poulie sur l'astragale droit que sur le gauche. Une telle conformation caractérise également le sujet 1 de Cro-Magnon comme le montrent les indices de largeur de la trochlée. Enfin, la gouttière sagittale de

TABLEAU XXXIII

Astragale: mesures et comparaisons

	Abri Pataud 1381 (d)	1330 (g)	Cap-Blanc d.	g.	Předmost F.X. d.	g.	Cro-Magnon d. (F.?)	g. (H.?)	Européennes (Volkov)
Longeur (1)	49	49	50,6	50,1	52	52	49	55	–
Largeur (2)	41	40	41,0	41,2	44	43	42	44	–
Hauteur (3)	32	32	30,0	29,8	32	32	30,5	32,5	29,1
Long. de la trochlée (4)	32	32	33,0	31,2	33	34	34	37	31,2
Larg. de la trochlée (5)	28	27	28,1	28,3	28	28	–	–	–
Larg. post. de la trochlée (5₁)	24,5	22,5	–	–	22	23	24	27	23,2
Larg. ant. de la trochlée (5₂)	29	29	–	–	29	29	29	35	28,4
Long. max. de la tête (9)	31	31	32,6	33,0	36	35?	–	–	–
Larg. max. de la tête (10)	21	21	19,5	–	24	23	–	–	–
Long. fac. art. cal. post. (12)	32	31	29,1	29,0	–	–	33	36	32
Larg. max. fac. art. cal. post. (13)	20	19	20,0	20,8	–	–	20	23	22
Angle de déviation du col (16)	22°	23°	29°5	35°7	21°	23°	22°	24°	17°7
Angle de torsion de la tête (17)	30°	32°	–	21°2	–	–	–	–	37°
Ind. de larg.-long. (2/1)	83,7	81,6	81,0	82,2	84,6	82,7	85,7	80,0	–
Ind. de haut.-long. (3/1)	65,3	65,3	59,3	59,5	61,5	61,5	62,2	59,1	–
Ind. de long. de la trochlée (4/1)	65,3	65,3	65,2	62,3	63,5	65,5	69,4	67,3	–
Ind. de larg. de la trochlée (5₁/5₂)	84,5	77,6	–	–	75,9	79,3	82,7	77,1	81,7
Ind. de la tête (10/9)	67,7	67,7	59,8	–	66,7	65,7	–	–	–
Ind. de la fac. art. cal. post. (13/12)	62,5	61,3	68,7	71,7	–	–	60,6	63,9	68,7

la poulie est peu profonde et l'os *trigonum* peu développé.

En corrélation avec la forme générale de l'os, la tête de l'astragale est relativement plus courte chez la femme de Pataud, avec un indice un peu plus élevé; mais la facette articulaire calcanéenne postérieure est plus étroite comme chez les sujets de Cro-Magnon (cf. tabl. XXXIII).

Notons encore un angle de déviation du col plus ouvert que chez les femmes modernes mais comparable aux valeurs relevées sur les autres Paléolithiques. L'angle de torsion de la tête qui serait, selon Volkov, un critère de hauteur de la voûte plantaire est au contraire assez peu prononcé par rapport à celui observé de nos jours (37°). On en conclut que la femme de Pataud possédait une voûte plantaire peu marquée.

Enfin, sur chacun des os, la facette tibiale est très développée vers l'avant et l'intérieur où elle empiète légèrement sur le col astragalien formant ainsi une petite facette articulaire supplémentaire dite «d'accroupissement.»

b. **Calcanéum.** Il existe un seul calcanéum (1407: gauche), auquel manque la majeure partie de la portion antérieure qui correspond à la région de la grande apophyse. Il s'articule parfaitement avec l'astragale gauche 1330 et appartient vraisemblablement au même sujet féminin.

D'aspect général peu robuste, sa longueur s'intègre toutefois dans les limites de variation données par Volkov sur les Européennes, tandis que sa largeur est nettement plus faible comme le montre le tableau XXXIV.

Par rapport aux données du Paléolithique, la plus grande similitude s'observe avec les dimensions des calcanéum de Cap-Blanc. L'examen du tableau XXXIV montre par ailleurs que les dimensions du talon sont nettement plus faibles que chez les hommes modernes; on remarque au contraire que la longueur du talon rapportée à celle du calcanéum leur est très voisine. C'est donc un talon relativement long, bas et étroit qui caractérise cette femme de Pataud. Il présente néanmoins au niveau de l'insertion du tendon d'Achille un relief osseux tourmenté.

Sur la face supérieure, les facettes articulaires pour l'astragale sont à peine subdivisées, leur partage étant seul indiqué. En articulation, le canal osseux est dû essentiellement à l'existence d'une gouttière astragalienne bien excavée.

c. **Scaphoïde** *(os naviculare).* Les deux scaphoïdes 1408 (d.) et 1399 (g.) s'articulent respectivement avec les astragales féminins 1381 (d.) et 1330 (g.). Le gauche est légèrement plus volumineux avec une tubérosité plus développée et une surface articulaire pour le cuboïde plus marquée.

Si l'on s'en réfère au tableau comparatif XXXV, on voit que les dimensions se tiennent d'assez près; la facette articulaire postérieure présente partout une forme allongée à tendance ovoïde. Toutefois, le rapport des épaisseurs externe et interne est plus

TABLEAU XXXIV

Calcanéum: mesures et comparaisons

	Abri Pataud	Cap-Blanc		Předmost X		Européennes (Volkov)
	1407 (g.)	(d.)	(g.)	(d.)	(g.)	
Longueur maximale (1)	74	75,2	74,3	76	76	73,6
Longueur totale (1a)	72	68,8	69,2	73	72	–
Largeur médiane (2)	40	39,5	41,1	43	44	43,8
Larg. min. du corpus calcanei (3)	25	–	–	23	–	24,3
Hauteur du calcanéum (4)	33,5	36,0	35,9	39	38	36,5
Long. du corpus calcanei (5)	53,5	49,3	50,3	57	56	52,4
Larg. du sustentaculum tali (6)	15	–	–	15	17	–
Haut. du tuber calcanei (7)	41	40,0	39,0	43	41	43,2
Larg. du tuber calcanei (8)	28,5	28,0?	25,5?	31	–	32,3
Long. fac. art. post. (9)	28	26,5	27,0	29	28	–
Larg. fac. arc. post. (10)	22	22,0	22,1	21	22	–
Ind. de long./larg. (2/1)	54,0	52,5	55,3	56,6	57,9	59,5
Ind. de long./larg. (3/1)	33,8	–	–	30,3	–	33,0
Ind. de long. du corps (5/1)	72,4	65,6	67,7	75,0	73,7	71,2
Ind. du tuber calcanei (8/7)	69,5	70,0?	65,4?	72,1	–	74,8
Ind. de fac. art. post. (10/9)	78,6	83,0	81,9	72,4	78,6	–

TABLEAU XXXV

Scaphoïde: mesures et comparaisons

	Abri Pataud		Cap-Blanc		Předmost X	Européennes (Volkov)
	1408 (d.)	1399 (g.)	(d.)	(g.)	(d.)	
Largeur (1)	40	37	37,5	37,2	35	–
Hauteur (2)	30	28,8	23,1	25,0 ?	27	–
Long. max. fac. art. (3)	27	27	26,0	24,4 ?	24	24,0
Larg. max. fac. art. (4)	22	23	20,2	20,2	21	20,3
Epaisseur externe (7)	8	8	9,4	9,4	8	10,3
Epaisseur interne (8)	19	18	19,8	18,2	19	17,1
Ind. de haut./larg. (2/1)	75,0	77,9	61,6	67,2 ?	77,1	–
Ind. de la fac. art. (4/3)	81,5	85,3	77,7	82,8 ?	87,5	84,6
Ind. d'épaisseur (7/8)	42,1	44,5	47,5	51,6	42,1	60,2

faible que chez les Européennes modernes. Il s'ensuit une tubérosité interne du scaphoïde plus développée, ce qui dénote, au Paléolithique supérieur, un écartement beaucoup plus grand de la tête de l'astragale et, par là même, du premier métatarsien.

d. **Cuboïde**. Il existe deux cuboïdes entiers correspondant aux n°s 1331 (droit) et 1512 (gauche). L'articulation de ce dernier avec le calcanéum 1407 dont la facette cuboïdienne fait défaut ne peut être affirmée; en ce qui concerne le pied droit, il manque

TABLEAU XXXVI

Cuboïde: mesures et comparaisons

	Abri Pataud		Předmost X	Européennes (Volkov)
	1331 (d.)	1512 (g.)	(g.)	
Longueur de la face interne (1)	34,6	35	31	28,3
Longueur latérale (2)	17,5	17,5	21	16,5
Indice de longueur (2/1)	50,6	50,0	67,7	58,3

par ailleurs le calcanéum.

Les indices de longueur sont faibles par rapport à ceux de Předmost et des Européennes. Le tableau XXXVI montre qu'une telle conformation provient davantage d'un allongement de la face interne que d'un raccourcissement de la face externe, comme à Chancelade (51,2). Selon Volkov, cette disposition doit être tenue pour primitive.

Sur la face plantaire, la crête cuboïdienne détermine une forte saillie sur laquelle s'imprime la facette sésamoïdienne. La face d'articulation avec le calcanéum est très concave dans le sens vertical par suite d'un développement considérable de l'apophyse pyramidale.

e. Premier cunéiforme. Un seul os droit (n° 1463) s'articule avec le scaphoïde 1408 et appartient à une femme. Ses principales dimensions sont rassemblées au tableau XXXVII. La longueur inférieure dépasse la moyenne des Européennes; un tel allongement semble fréquent au Paléolithique supérieur, si l'on en juge par les mesures obtenues sur les hommes de Chancelade (28 mm.) et de Předmost (25 et 26 mm.).

f. Deuxiéme cunéiforme. Il paraît essentiellement caractérisé par un élargissement relatif comme en témoignent les valeurs élevées de l'indice de largeur-longueur des femmes de Pataud, de Předmost et de

l'homme de Chancelade (86,4) par rapport aux Européens actuels (cf. tabl. XXXVII).

g. Troisième cunéiforme. Les pièces n°s 1307 (d.) et 1333 (g.) s'articulent avec les scaphoïdes et cuboïdes correspondants et appartiennent au même pied féminin. Plus volumineux que ceux des hommes modernes, les troisièmes cunéiformes des femmes de Pataud et de Předmost présentent, comme le 2e cunéiforme, un élargissement relatif par rapport à celui des hommes modernes (cf. tabl. XXXVII).

2. LE METATARSE

Les 9 métatarsiens dénombrés ont déjà été identifiés au tableau XXXII mais 2 sont incomplets et n'ont pu être mesurés. Les longueurs ont été prises du centre de la surface articulaire proximale à l'endroit le plus saillant de l'extrémité distale.

Dans l'ensemble, les métatarsiens de Pataud, de Cap-Blanc, et de Předmost sont plus longs que ceux des femmes modernes. Un métatarse relativement allongé semble donc de règle au Paléolithique, comme nous l'avons démontré par ailleurs (Billy 1969). L'ordre décroissant des longueurs suit néanmoins le schéma classique II, III, IV, V, et I observé de nos jours.

D'autre part, les écarts entre les longueurs de deux

TABLEAU XXXVII

Cunéiformes: mesures et comparaisons

	Abri Pataud		Předmost X		Européennes (Volkov)
PREMIER CUNEIFORME					
	1463 (d.)		(g.)		
Longueur inférieure (1)	25		24		22,3
Longueur moyenne (2)	21,5		22		–
Longueur supérieure (3)	11,7		13		–
Hauteur proximale (6)	24		21		23,7
Hauteur distale (7)	30,5		29		–
DEUXIEME CUNEIFORME	2090 (g.)		(d.)		
Longueur supérieure (1)	16,2		16		16,6
Largeur au milieu (2)	15,5		15		14,7
Ind. de larg./long. (2/1)	95,7		93,7		89,0
TROISIEME CUNEIFORME	1307 (d.)	1333 (g.)	(d.)	(g.)	
Longueur supérieure (1)	23	23	25	24	21,4
Largeur au milieu (2)	15	15,2	16	16	13,5
Largeur distale (3)	13	12	14	14	–
Largeur proximale (4)	12,5	13	13	14	–
Ind. de larg./long. (2/1)	65,2	66,1	64,0	66,7	63,0

TABLEAU XXXVIII

Longueurs des métatarsiens

	Abri Pataud		Cap-Blanc		Předmost X		Européennes (Pfitzner)
	(d.)	(g.)	(d.)	(g.)	(d.)	(g.)	
I...	59	59	57	59	59,5	59	57,0
II..	–	68,5	71	–	–	–	68,7
III.	65,7	–	67	–	71	70,5	65,1
IV.	–	65	–	–	71	–	63,8
V..	60	60,5	–	–	67	68	59,9

Premier métatarsien

	Abri Pataud		Cap-Blanc		Européennes (Volkov)
	(d.)	(g.)	(d.)	(g.)	
Longueur du 1er métatarsien (1)	59	59	57	59	54,6
Largeur du corps (3)	11,8	11,5	13,0	12,6	12,8
Hauteur du corps (4)	12,3	12,5	12,5	12,2	12,8
Largeur de la base (6)	15	15	19	18,2	18,2
Hauteur de la base (7))	26,5	26,5	27	26,6	26,7
Largeur de la tête (8)	19,5	20,5	20,9	22,1	20,2
Hauteur de la tête (9)	20	21	22	22	–
Ind. de larg.-long. (3/1)	20,0	19,5	22,8	21,4	23,4
Ind. de haut.-long. (4/1)	20,8	21,2	21,9	20,7	23,4
Ind. de haut.-larg. (4/3)	104,2	108,8	96,2	96,8	100,0

métatarsiens consécutifs suivent exactement les variations observées chez les Européens et peuvent être considérés de ce fait comme normaux. Il existe donc une quasi certitude pour que les restes humains de Pataud appartiennent tous à la même femme.

En ce qui concerne les Paléolithiques, le sujet de Cap-Blanc possède un premier métatarsien nettement plus massif, chez lequel les dimensions transversales notamment sont toujours plus élevées. A l'inverse, les dimensions prises au milieu de l'os déterminent à Pataud un indice supérieur à 100, qui implique une section médiane du corps plus haute que large.

3. LES PHALANGES

Au total, il a été recueilli 13 phalanges dont 10 proximales et 2 distales.

Premières phalanges (*phalanx proximalis*). Elles semblent appartenir au même sujet et constituer la totalité des phalanges de deux mains féminines, à en juger par leur articulation avec les métatarsiens correspondants. Leurs dimensions sont données au tableau XXXIX.

Les longueurs, excepté celles du 5e orteil, sont toujours inférieures aux moyennes obtenues par Volkov sur des Européennes modernes; les largeurs sont au contraire plus élevées. L'ordre de décroissance des longueurs suit également le schéma classique: I, II, III, IV, et V.

Notons le manque d'éléments comparatifs pour le Paléolithique supérieur, abstraction faite des hommes de Cro-Magnon, de Chancelade et de Předmost dont les phalanges sont beaucoup plus longues et plus robustes. Seules les longueurs 26,3 (d.) et 26,0 (g.) et

TABLEAU XXXIX

Premières phalanges

Doigts	I		II		III		IV		V	
	1465	1403	1386	1461	1306	1387	1462	1388	1389	1467
	(d.)	(g.)	(d.)	(g.)	(d.)	(g.)	(d.)	(g.)	(d.)	(g.)
Longueur (1)	27,5	27,5	24,4	24,5	22	22,3	21,5	21,4	20,8	20,5
Largeur (2)	11,5	11,5	6	6	5,4	5,5	5,0	5,3	5,7	5,8
Indice (2/1)	41,8	41,8	24,6	24,5	24,5	24,7	23,2	24,8	27,4	28,3

largeurs 12,3 (d.) et 12,2 (g.) de la phalange du 1er orteil de la femme de Cap-Blanc peuvent leur être comparées bien qu'elles soient à la fois plus courtes et plus robustes. On en conclut que les phalanges de Pataud étaient relativement longues et graciles.

Troisièmes phalanges (*phalanx distalis*). Deux phalanges du 1er orteil ont été recueillies; les longueurs 22,6 mm. (1466 d.) et 22 mm. (1334 g.) sont absolument comparables à celle des femmes modernes (22,7) donnée par Volkov.

RECONSTITUTION DU PIED

Après reconstitution et montage du pied droit, le plus complet, sa longueur totale mesurée dans l'axe métatarsien II est de 232 mm.

IV. RECONSTITUTION DE LA STATURE ET PROPORTIONS DES MEMBRES

En l'absence d'os longs du membre inférieur, nous avons évalué la stature à partir des humérus, ulna, et radius du complexe 22. Comme nous l'avons déjà souligné, ces os appartiennent à un même individu de sexe féminin ne correspondant pas nécessairement au sujet dont subsiste la tête osseuse. Les résultats obtenus sur la base des méthodes de Manouvrier, Pearson, puis Trotter et Gleser sont consignés au tableau XL.

En prenant la moyenne des valeurs obtenues selon

TABLEAU XL

Stature du sujet féminin de l'Abri Pataud (en cm.)

	Manouvrier	Pearson	Trotter-Gleser
Humérus n° 22 d. (308 mm)	156,9	156,2	161,3
Ulna n° 22 g. (252 mm)	163,0	–	165,5
Radius n° 22 g. (232 mm)	161,0	158,7	165,0
Humérus + Radius		157,9	
Humérus et radius		156,5	
Moyennes:	160,3	157,3	163,9

les trois méthodes, on trouve une stature de 160,5 cm. Une telle stature, située dans la catégorie hypsisome ($\geqslant$ 160 cm.), est considérable puisqu'elle correspond à une taille masculine de 171 cm. environ si l'on tient compte de la différence sexuelle habituelle de 11 cm.

Autant que le permettent les rares estimations de la stature féminine au Paléolithique supérieur, il apparaît que la femme de l'Abri Pataud se situe en position intermédiaire entre les Aurignaciennes de Cro-Magnon et de Předmost d'une part, et les Magdaléniennes d'Obercassel, de Cap-Blanc, et de Saint-Germain d'autre part. Sa taille est équivalente pour le sexe masculin à celles des hommes 1 et 3 de Cro-Magnon. C'est donc à ces derniers que la femme de Pataud s'apparente en ce qui concerne la stature.

L'étude des proportions du corps est très limitée en l'absence du membre inférieur. L'indice claviculo-huméral, qui est un critère de largeur du thorax, est de 45,5, valeur du même ordre que celle donnée pour les Européens récents et qui correspond à une clavicule plutôt courte par rapport à l'humérus. L'indice huméro-radial (75,5) révèle par ailleurs la tendance au développement préférentiel de l'avant-bras constaté chez la plupart des populations du Paléolithique supérieur (Billy 1970).

TABLEAU XLI

Statures féminines au Paléolithique supérieur (Manouvrier)

Femme d'Obercassel	147,1 cm
Femme de Saint-Germain-la-Rivière	155,3 cm
Femme de Cap-Blanc	157,0 cm
Femme de Předmost X	162,5 cm
Femme de Předmost IV	165,0 cm
Femme de Cro-Magnon	166,0 cm

3. LES OSSEMENTS D'ENFANTS

Les ossements d'enfants recueillis dans la couche proto-magdalénienne sont très dispersés. On en retrouve dans les complexes 22 et 23, les Trenches III et IV, puis la Trench VII, Square G.

Les restes des complexes 22 et 23 étaient intimement mélangés; ils correspondent à deux enfants auxquels nous attribuons environ six mois à l'un et sept ans à l'autre. A ce dernier peuvent être rattachés, d'après leur texture et leur couleur identiques, les ossements des Trenches III et IV. On distingue enfin dans la Trench VII les restes squelettiques d'un nouveau-né.

I. L'ENFANT DE SIX MOIS

Un partie de son squelette reposait sur celui du membre supérieur gauche féminin entier du complexe 22. Il comporte un crâne complètement écrasé, 2 clavicules, 17 vertèbres ou corps vertébraux, et 19 côtes.

Crâne. Extrêmement détérioré, il se réduit à de nombreux fragments dont le plus important, un morceau de pariétal, mesure 65 mm. sur 45 mm. environ; son épaisseur au niveau de la bosse pariétale n'excède pas 1,5 mm. Nous avons pu identifier par ailleurs l'apophyse basilaire de l'occipital et deux fragments de temporal, le gauche étant très réduit et le droit constitué du rocher et de l'os tympanal. Ce dernier a la forme d'un anneau incomplet ouvert en haut et caractéristique des enfants du premier âge.

Clavicules. Les deux clavicules sont entières; leurs longueurs maximales correspondent à 51 et 52 mm. pour la droite et la gauche respectivement. On peut évaluer à six mois environ l'âge de cet enfant, compte tenu des résultats de Rambaud et Renault (1864) qui ont étudié l'évolution de la clavicule sur plus de 70 squelettes de foetus et de jeunes enfants.

Vertèbres. Les corps vertébraux, en forme d'éventail aux deux pointes latérales tronquées, ont leurs surfaces supérieures et inférieures boursouflées portant la trace de cartilages. Les pédicules encore séparés des corps vertébraux sont complètement ossifiés si l'on excepte le sommet de l'apophyse épineuse.

Côtes. Au nombre de 19, dont 11 droites et 8 gauches, elles sont pour la plupart dépourvues de leur extrémité postérieure. Des deux premières côtes, la droite est intacte et la gauche brisée au niveau de son extrémité sternale. La deuxième côte droite subsiste seule. Outre les onzième et douzième côtes droites, toutes les autres proviennent de la région thoracique moyenne. Du point de vue morphologique, on notera une gouttière costale toujours bien marquée malgré leur jeune âge; la tubérosité et la facette pour l'apophyse transverse vertébrale sont également bien visibles.

II. L'ENFANT DE SEPT ANS

Il est représenté par un frontal incomplet reconstitué à partir de 9 fragments (complexe 22), par une portion de temporal gauche et un malaire recueillis dans la Trench III. Le fragment de maxillaire supérieur de la Trench IV lui appartient aussi.

Frontal. Brisé obliquemment au-dessus de l'apophyse orbitaire externe gauche, il est privé de toute la partie correspondante de l'écaille. La forme générale de l'os n'offre rien de particulier par rapport aux enfants européens de même âge. La glabelle et les arcades sourcilières sont absentes, les bosses frontales latérales sont bien marquées, leur épaisseur étant de 2 mm. à droite et 2,5 mm. à gauche. Le bord orbitaire supérieur, qui porte une large échancrure dans sa partie interne, présente une forme sensiblement circulaire. La voûte orbitaire est bien incurvée, surtout dans sa partie externe qui correspond à la fosse lacrymale et détermine à ce niveau un bord supérieur extrêmement tranchant. Du côté interne, en revanche, la voûte orbitaire paraît basse et très aplatie. Dans la région sus-nasale, la suture médiane est encore apparente sur 1 cm. environ; les deux moitiés du frontal sont donc réunies et seule persiste la trace de leur séparation primitive, ce qui implique un âge approximatif de huit ans.

La largeur bimaxillaire maximale, prise par duplication est de 94 mm., valeur comparable à celles des enfants actuels d'âge équivalent, tandis que la largeur interorbitaire antérieure (22 mm.) leur est plutôt supérieure.

Temporal. C'est un temporal gauche incomplet (n°6) qui, d'après sa patine absolument identique, appartient au même sujet. Il est constitué par la partie postéro-inférieure de l'écaille, brisée à la racine de l'apophyse zygomatique, par une faible partie du rocher, et par le tympanal. La portion écailleuse est soudée à la base du rocher et forme avec elle la partie mastoïdienne; leur suture correspondant à la scissure pétro-squameuse postérieure est encore très visible. En avant, l'apophyse tubaire du tympanal est complètement formée et soudée à l'écaille par la scissure de Glaser, visible en son début. Ce degré de développement du temporal correspond sensiblement au stade définitif réalisé déjà chez un enfant de sept ans.

Malaire. C'est un malaire droit entier (n°11) dont le bord antéro-supérieur présente un angle bien marqué. Sur sa face externe, l'orifine antérieur du conduit malaire est largement ouvert et dédoublé.

Maxillaire supérieur (n°14). Il correspond à une portion de maxillaire supérieur droit avec 3 dents temporaires en place; une molaire isolée a pu également lui être rapportée. L'examen odontologique permet d'attribuer ce fragment à un enfant de six ans.

Après l'étude de trois éléments squelettiques différents, il paraît donc raisonnable d'estimer l'âge de cet enfant approximativement à sept ans.

III. LE SQUELETTE DE NOUVEAU-NE

Les fouilles de 1963 effectuées dans la Trench VII ont livré au total 16 fragments d'os d'enfant dispersés sur une aire mesurant environ 50 cm. de large sur 75 de long. Ces restes, qui sont tous numérotés, ont été identifiés comme suit:

n° 1371 ⎫
n° 1383 ⎬ fragments de côtes gauches.
n° 1533 ⎪
n° 1828 ⎭

n° 1515 ⎫
n° 1713 ⎬ fragments de côtes droites.

n° 1517 ⎫
n° 1531 ⎪
n° 1830 ⎬ fragments de côtes indéterminables.
n° 2092 ⎭

n° 1717 ⎫
n° 2093 ⎬ phalanges sans épiphyse.

n° 1372   épiphyse d'os long.

n° 1401   fragment de mandibule.

n° 1374   fémur droit incomplet.

n° 1409   tibia droit.

Seules les trois dernières pièces sont susceptibles d'apporter quelque précision quant à l'âge du sujet.

Fragment de mandibule. C'est une portion gauche de mandibule portant une seconde molaire temporaire que l'analyse odontologique permet d'attribuer à un foetus presque à terme ou à un nouveau-né d'un mois.

Fémur. En l'absence de l'extrémité supérieure, la longueur a été évaluée très approximativement à 87 mm. La stature de cet enfant correspond à 56,4 cm. d'après les abaques de Stewart établies pour la croissance du fémur. En appliquant d'autre part la formule de Balthazard et Dervieux (1921) relative au fémur, on trouve:

$$\text{Taille}_{cm} = \text{Diaphyse fémorale} \times 5,6 + 8 = 56,7 \text{ cm.}$$

Une telle valeur, qui recoupe la précédente, permet la détermination de l'âge foetal à partir de la formule:

$$\text{Age}_{(jours)} = \text{Taille}_{(cm)} \times 5,6 = 56,7 \times 5,6$$
$$= 317 \text{ jours.}$$

Il s'agit donc d'un nouveau-né de un mois environ, ce qui confirme les résultats de l'examen odontologique.

L'os n'offre qu'une très légère courbure dans le sens antéro-postérieur identique à celle des nouveaux-nés actuels. La ligne âpre est marquée mais peu saillante. L'indice pilastrique a une valeur de 100, avec des diamètres de 8 mm.; il n'y a pas de pilastre. Au niveau de l'extrémité supérieure, une grosse saillie de la diaphyse correspond à la base de la future région trochantérienne. Aucune platymérie ne s'observe à ce niveau, les diamètres antéro-postérieur et transverse étant respectivement de 10,5 et 11 mm., avec un indice de 95,4.

Tibia. Correspondant au côté droit, il a une longueur de 79 mm. La partie supérieure de la diaphyse est très légèrement incurvée en arrière, ébauche de la rétroversion que l'on trouve normalement chez tous les nouveaux-nés actuels. La crête antérieure de l'os est déja bien visible avec, en haut, le début de la saillie de la tubérosité antérieure. Au niveau du trou nourricier, le tibia est plus développé dans le sens antéro-postérieur que transverse, les diamètres respectifs 11 et 9 mm. déterminant un indice eurycnémique de 81,8.

La reconstitution de la stature à partir de la longueur de la diaphyse tibiale conduit, selon Baltha-zard et Dervieux, à une taille de 59,3 cm. qui correspond à un âge foetal de 332 jours. Compte tenu des deux évaluations précédentes, le nouveau-né de la Trench VII était donc âgé de un mois à un mois et demi.

4. LES RESTES HUMAINS NOAILLIENS

La couche archéologique noaillienne, sous-jacente au Périgordien VI et par conséquent plus ancienne, (27.000 ans B.P.) d'après la datation par le Carbone 14, n'a livré qu'un seul vestige humain recueilli dans la Trench III, Square D, Lens 5.

Ce reste fossile correspond à un fragment de diaphyse fémorale, aux extrémités brisées en biseau, mesurant 185 mm. dans sa plus grande longueur et qui constitue le tiers moyen d'un fémur droit (cf. pl. VIII). Le volume de cette diaphyse et surtout l'épaisseur considérable de l'os, qui atteint plus de 4 mm. en certains endroits, plaident en faveur du sexe masculin.

Etant donné l'état fragmentaire de la pièce, les deux diamètres (n°s 6 et 7) permettant de définir le développement du pilastre, ainsi que le périmètre (n° 8), n'ont été mesurés que très approximativement au milieu. Ces dimensions déterminent néanmoins un indice de 111,1 qui témoigne de l'existence d'un pilastre «moyen.» En fait, cet indice relativement bas n'exprime pas le degré de développement réel du pilastre, car la diaphyse est en même temps très large, avec une section transversale presque arrondie, comme le montre la figure 18. D'autre part, du côté externe, la branche fessière de la ligne âpre est de beaucoup la plus marquée et détermine une véritable arête faisant une saillie considérable, alors que la branche interne est nettement moins accusée.

Les quelques dimensions prises sur ce fémur noaillien s'intègrent parfaitement dans la série des hommes du Paléolithique supérieur connus (cf. tabl. XLII) bien qu'il soit moins vigoureux dans l'ensemble que ceux de l'homme n° 1 de Cro-Magnon.

TABLEAU XLII

Fémur: mesures et comparaisons

	Abri Pataud H.	Cro-Magnon 1		Předmost		Chancelade	Veyrier
				H. III	H. XIV		
	(d.)	(d.)	(g.)	(d.)	(d.)	(d.)	(d.)
Diam. ant.-post. (6)	30	40	37,5	30,8	26,4	30	29
Diam. transv. (7)	27	31	30	30	26,4	28	24
Périmètre (8)	89	114	107	92	80	91	81
Ind. pilastrique (6/7)	111,1	129,0	125,0	102,7	100,0	107,1	120,8

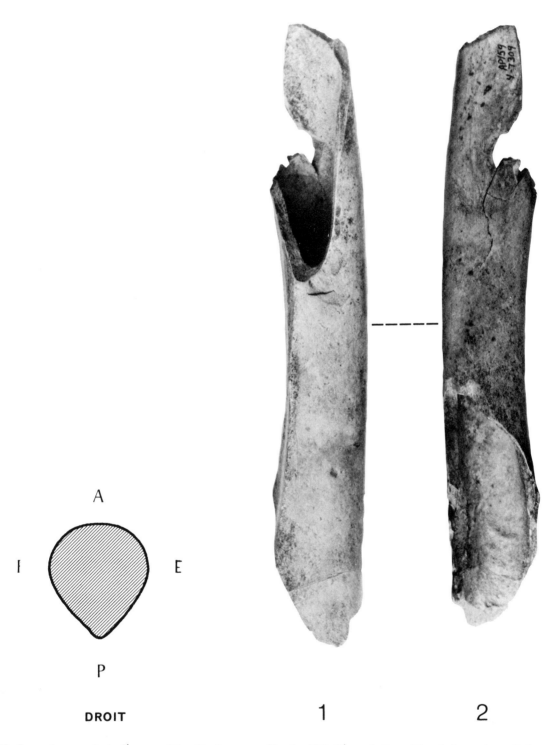

A

I   E

P

DROIT

1   **2**

Figure 18. Coupe transversale du fémur noaillien. Dessin au diagraphe. Segment distal de la coupe, G.N.

Planche VIII. Fémur droit noaillien. 1. face externe; 2. face interne.

RESUME ET CONCLUSIONS

Au cours de ce travail, nous avons analysé systématiquement les restes humains qui furent mis au jour à l'Abri Pataud en tenant compte de l'emplacement de chacune des pièces et en nous attachant à préciser, dans la mesure du possible, le sexe et l'âge. L'ensemble de nos résultats devrait ainsi permettre de dénombrer les sujets et de les localiser. C'est précisément à la discussion de ce problème que nous nous attacherons dans un premier temps. Puis nous envisagerons les caractéristiques anthropologiques essentielles de cette population proto-magdalénienne. Un dernier paragraphe sera consacré enfin à la discussion de leur position dans le contexte du Paléolithique supérieur.

I. DENOMBREMENT ET LOCALISATION DES SUJETS

En dehors du fémur masculin recueilli dans la couche noaillienne, tous les restes humains de l'Abri Pataud proviennent du niveau archéologique proto-magdalénien. Ils se trouvaient dispersés, nous l'avons déjà mentionné, sur une étendue de 10 à 12 mètres de long et de 3 à 4 mètres de large. Mais cette dispersion n'était pas homogène puisque, d'après le tableau XLIII qui résume la nature et l'emplacement des découvertes, ce sont les Trenches II et VII qui présentent, et de loin, la plus grande densité d'ossements.

Parmi ceux-ci, nous avons diagnostiqué sans conteste la présence de trois enfants dont un nouveau-né (Trench VII), un enfant en bas âge (Trench II), et un autre d'environ sept ans représenté par quelques fragments crâniens issus des Trenches III et IV.

TABLEAU XLIII

Emplacement des restes proto-magdaléniens et dénombrement des sujets

Nature	Trenches						
	VII	VI	V	IV	III	II	I
Tête		♀					
Vertèbres	♀					♀	
Sternum						♀	
Côtes	♀					♀	
Omoplates						♂	
Clavicules	♀					♂♀	
Humérus	♀					♂♀	
Cubitus						♂♀	
Radius						♂♀	
Mains	♀					♂♀	
Bassin		♀					
Rotules	♀						
Péronés		?	?			♂	
Pieds	♀						
Enfants	(1 mois)				(7 ans)	(6 mois)	

Le problème de la localisation des sujets «adultes» est autrement plus délicat. En effet, si la présence dans la Trench II d'un seul individu masculin ne prête pas à discussion, il existe deux jeunes femmes au moins comme l'atteste l'examen des vertèbres, des côtes, des clavicules et, surtout, des humérus et des os des mains. Dans chaque Trench II ou VII, aucun ossement n'est en double, ce qui permet de conclure à deux ensembles différents. Mais auquel des deux doit-on rattacher la tête osseuse recueillie à la limite des Trenches V et VI? Si l'on s'en tient au seul critère de l'éloignement, la logique voudrait qu'elle appartienne à la femme du Trench VII distante seulement de 3 mètres plutôt qu'à la femme du complexe 22 éloignée de 7 à 8 mètres. Mais on pourrait tout aussi bien admettre l'inverse dans l'hypothèse où la femme du Trench II aurait été décapitée. En effet, ne subsiste-t-il pas de cette femme un bras gauche entier et pratiquement rien d'autre, si ce n'est un sternum qui appartiendrait précisément à un sujet d'une vingtaine d'années? La tête osseuse ne proviendrait-elle pas non plus d'un troisième individu féminin? Ce sont là autant de questions que nous nous sommes posée jusqu'au jour où il fut prouvé que 4 dents isolées, retrouvées parmi les restes humains de la Trench VII, appartenaient à la tête osseuse. Ces dents étaient donc tombées *post-mortem* à l'emplacement de la Trench VII et il y avait eu dispersion bien plus tard.

En définitive, la population exhumée à l'Abri Pataud comprend les restes de 7 individus au moins d'après les résultats de l'étude ostéologique, dont un homme adulte noaillien représenté seulement par une diaphyse fémorale. Les 6 autres sujets du niveau proto-magdalénien se répartissent comme suit:

Trench II (complexe 22-23).
Une femme de 20 à 25 ans de grande stature (160,5 cm.) représentée par un bras gauche entier en bon état à côté de quelques vertèbres, côtes, et un sternum.

Un enfant de quelques mois dont les ossements sont intimement mélangés à ceux du sujet féminin. Selon toute vraisemblance, il s'agit là de la mère et de l'enfant. La sélectivité des ossements (bras gauche) laisserait penser à l'existence d'un rite funéraire si les restes ne se trouvaient en bordure de la fouille. Il se peut en effet, compte tenu de la dispersion, que tout le squelette féminin ne soit pas encore mis au jour.

Trench II (Éboulis de la zône A). Restes squelettiques d'un homme comprenant le membre supérieur gauche en assez mauvais état et une omoplate droite.

Trenches II, III, IV. Fragments crâniens dispersés d'un enfant d'environ 7 ans.

Trenches VI et VII.
Une jeune fille de 16 à 18 ans dont subsistent la tête osseuse en parfait état, des vertèbres, des côtes, un os coxal gauche, la plupart des os des mains et des pieds.

Un nouveau-né de un mois à un mois et demi maximum. Tout porte à croire qu'il s'agit, là encore, de la mère et de l'enfant morts des suites de l'accouchement.

II. CARACTERISTIQUES ANTHROPOLOGIQUES DE LA POPULATION PROTO-MAGDALENIENNE

L'analyse ostéologique a permis de définir les caractères fondamentaux de la population proto-magdalénienne qui vécut aux Eyzies il y a 20.000 ans. Il s'agit d'un groupe humain de stature élevée comme l'atteste une taille féminine de 160,5 cm.

L'aspect relativement gracile de la tête osseuse résulte surtout de dimensions générales modérées puisque son relief, sans être très accentué, est bien modelé pour un sujet féminin de 16 à 18 ans.

Le *crâne cérébral* est volumineux, aristencéphale, et faiblement mésocrâne. La voûte, très allongée et ovoïde en vue supérieure, est modérément large et haute (ortho-et métriocrâne), caractérisée au surplus par un aplatissement de la base, un développement accentué des bosses pariétales, et la présence d'un léger chignon occipital. A sa partie antérieure, la glabelle et les arcades sourcilières sont bien marquées; il en est de même des bosses frontales latérales. Le front, modérément bombé, mésosème, et eurymétope, est très haut; c'est le plus long des trois segments crâniens, le pariétal étant le plus court.
Excepté l'arcade zygomatique assez grêle, les autres reliefs sont plutôt saillants: lignes temporales très nettes, apophyse mastoïde courte mais épaisse, crête sus-mastoïdienne bien marquée qui se poursuit jusqu'à la suture temporo-pariétale, inion saillant, torus occipital transverse et profil sous-iniaque fortement déprimé.

Une dysharmonie cranio-faciale détermine par ailleurs une *face* euryprosope et presque euryène, caractérisée par un développement considérable des pommettes qui sont déjettées vers l'arrière. De hauteur moyenne, cette face présente une dilatation transverse, principalement dans sa région supérieure, la partie maxillo-alvéolaire n'étant que mésuranique.
Il s'ensuit une fosse canine profonde et une angulation très accusée de la partie antérieure du maxillaire.
Le massif facial dans son ensemble est mésognathe, alors que sa région sous-nasale présente un prognathisme très net. Les orbites sont mésoconques à tendance chamaeconque, en forme de rectangle très allongé transversalement. La région sus-orbitaire est fortement déprimée. Au-dessous d'une dépression nasale, les os nasaux, légèrement concaves, font une forte saillie vers l'avant. Une harmonie naso-faciale détermine en outre un nez méso-chamaerhinien tandis que le palais est mésostaphylin.

La *mandibule*, d'aspect massif, est brachygnathe. Le corps de l'os est caractérisé par une robustesse considérable, une obliquité modérée, un bord inférieur particulièrement épais et un *torus mandibularis*. La symphyse présente une tendance à la verticalité malgré la présence d'une éminence mentionnière d'ailleurs assez peu prononcée. Du côté interne, il existe un léger *planum alveolare*, des apophyses géni

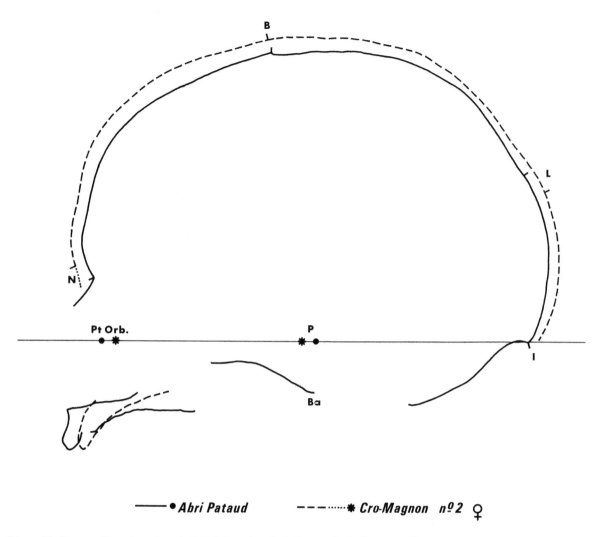

Figure 19. Superposition des crânes de l'Abri Pataud et de la femme de Cro-Magnon n°2 suivant le milieu de la distance point orbitaire-porion indiqués par les signes. ● Abri Pataud et * Cro-Magnon n°2. Dessin au diagraphe, 70% G.N.

différenciées en forme de crêtes et des empreintes digastriques en position inférieure. La branche montante est excessivement large, presque verticale et fort redressée sur le corps mandibulaire. Il s'ensuit une apophyse coronoïde large et basse, qui n'atteint pas le plan du condyle, et une échancrure sigmoïde très élargie et peu profonde.

Les os du *squelette post-crânien* sont en général relativement graciles. En ce qui concerne la colonne vertébrale, le changement de sens de la courbure lombaire se fait à un niveau inférieur à celui des hommes actuels. La clavicule longue et grêle, présente une section arrondie à tendance quadrangulaire; elle est aussi caractérisée par une gracilité relative de ses extrémités, une sinuosité très accentuée et une nette

deflexio claviculae. L'humérus possède un V deltoïdien prononcé qui détermine une diaphyse quadrangulaire mais eurybrachique; les épiphyses sont bien développées et, au niveau inférieur, il existe une ptère sus-épicondylienne mais pas de perforation olécrânienne. Pour l'ulna, on note une courbure marquée, le développement de la crête interosseuse, la forme triangulaire de la diaphyse, et la nette platôlénie. Le radius est gracile, avec une diaphyse présentant une forte concavité interne et un aplatissement prononcé; l'axe du col est très oblique. La main est moyennement large, à tendance allongée; malgré une gracilité relative du carpe, celui-ci est macrocarpe par rapport aux rayons digitaux.

Seul existe un os coxal gracile, typiquement féminin, constitué d'un ilion large et bas dont la crête

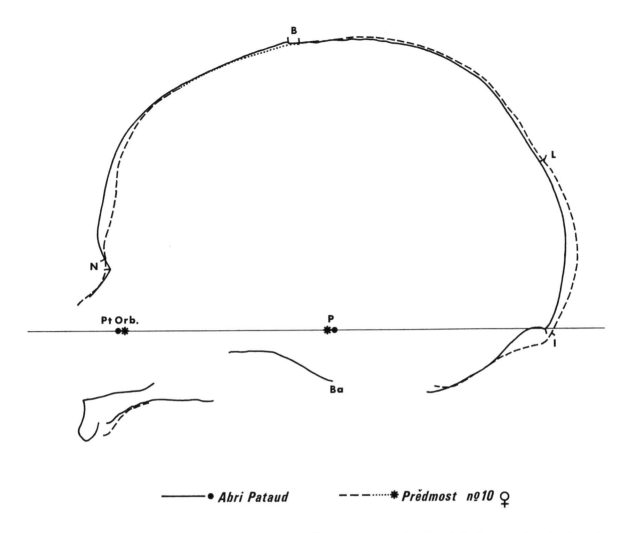

Figure 20. Superposition des crânes de l'Abri Pataud et de Předmost X suivant le milieu de la distance point orbitaire-porion indiqués par les signes. ● Abri Pataud et * Předmost X. Dessin au diagraphe, 70% G.N.

forme un épais bourrelet. La rotule très élargie est de type «*emarginata*» et le péroné caractérisé par une cannelure excessivement prononcée. Le pied comprend un astragale haut et court et un calcanéum étroit; il en découle un talon relativement long, mais bas et étroit, associé à un voûte plantaire assez peu marquée. L'écartement du premier métatarsien, et par là même du premier orteil, est plus prononcé que de nos jours.

III. POSITION ANTHROPOLOGIQUE

Les observations ostéologiques relevées sur les pièces de l'Abri Pataud ont été systématiquement comparées, en l'absence de documents synchrones, aux caractéristiques des Aurignaciens d'Europe occidentale, d'une part, et à celles des Magdaléniens du Périgord d'autre part.

L'examen minutieux de chacun des caractères anthropologiques a ainsi permis de déterminer la position relative des sujets de l'Abri Pataud. Toutefois, une majorité d'individus féminins relativement jeunes a orienté quelque peu nos apparentements vers d'autres sujets de même sexe, en ce qui concerne tout particulièrement les valeurs absolues des données métriques. En effet, des similitudes frappantes sont apparues tour à tour avec les femmes de Cap-Blanc, de Duruthy, d'Obercassel, et même de Saint-Germain-la-Rivière dont certaines forment une variété de la race de Cro-Magnon.

Or, il a été montré récemment (H. Vallois 1971) l'existence d'un groupe de «Cro-Magnoïdes magdaléniens» qui s'étendait en France de l'Ain au Landes, et du Proto-Magdalénien jusqu'à la fin du Magdalénien. «Remarquablement homogène» du point de vue anthropologique, ce groupe se caractériserait, selon l'auteur, «par une voûte crânienne basse, jamais carénée, mais parfois pourvue d'une ébauche de chignon occipital.» La face serait également basse, donc dysharmonique du crâne.

Une telle description, si elle englobe à coup sûr le crâne de l'Abri Pataud, nous paraît cependant ici trop restrictive. En effet, un analyse anthropologique rigoureuse a montré que le crâne de Pataud se place à la limite inférieure de la mésocrânie (75,4), entre la franche dolichocrânie des Aurignaco-périgordiens et la mésocrânie très engagée des Magdaléniens. Il en est de même des indices de hauteur où une tendance très accentuée à la chamaecrânie le situe en position intermédiaire. Rappelons encore cet aplatissement de la base du crâne, mis en évidence à Pataud, qui caractérise tous les véritables Cro-Magniens. En *norma lateralis*, la voûte régulièrement allongée, le développement considérable de la glabelle et des arcs sourciliers pour un jeune sujet féminin, le chignon occipital, l'inion très saillant, le torus occipital ne sont pas sans rappeler la conformation typiquement cro-magnienne. La participation plus importante du frontal que du pariétal à la constitution de la voûte, comme la faible hauteur de la calotte et son rapport à la longueur glabelle-inion, sont absolument comparables. De même, la présence sur ce crâne féminin de reliefs tels les lignes temporales, visibles sur tout leur trajet, et la crête sus-mastoïdienne très marquée sont autant de critères prouvant que le type de Cro-Magnon se reproduit ici sans aucune atténuation.

Au niveau du massif facial, nous mentionnerons surtout la dépression sus-nasale, la localisation du prognathisme à la partie alvéolaire, la dilatation de la face dans sa portion fronto-malaire le maxillaire supérieur restant étroit, la fosse canine marquée, et l'angulation du malaire. Enfin, les orbites en forme de rectangle allongé presque chamaeconques, la région sous-orbitaire très déprimée, la structure nasale méso-chamaerhinienne rapprochent indiscutablement ce crâne des Aurignaco-périgordiens bien plus que des Magdaléniens. La figure 19, qui superpose les profils

sagittaux des crânes féminins de Pataud et de Cro-Magnon 2, illustre d'ailleurs une telle ressemblance.

Les relations morphologiques avec le type de Cro-Magnon ne sont pas les seules mises en évidence au cours de ce travail. En effet, nous avons maintes fois relevé des similitudes frappantes, tant dimensionnelles que descriptives, avec la femme X de Předmost, similitudes qui sont d'ailleurs concrétisées par le tracé des contours crâniens de la figure 20. Or, on sait que ce groupe plus tardif d'hommes fossiles d'Europe centrale représente, du point de vue morphologique, «une population à larges variations englobant les types de Brno et de Cro-Magnon et aussi des types de transition» (Vlček 1970). A la lumière de récentes découvertes faites en Tchécoslavaquie, en Hongrie, en Yougoslavie, ou en Palestine, il paraît actuellement probable que certains Néandertaliens de transition représentent la base de la lignée conduisant aux *Sapiens* primitifs du type de Brno. En faveur également d'une phase néandertaloïde dans l'évolution humaine, thèse que partagent la plupart des anthropologistes soviétiques, se placent les conclusions de A. Thoma (1962) relatives à l'origine des mongoloïdes actuels. Sans aller aussi loin en ce qui concerne la France, où l'éventualité d'un ancêtre néandertaloïde est loin d'être prouvée, nous rappelerons néanmoins les nombreux caractères archaïques mis en évidence à Pataud et qui touchent surtout la mandibule.

C'est d'abord sa massivité extrême que lui confèrent un corps mandibulaire très robuste et une branche montante à la fois très redressée (angle goniaque: 107°) et excessivement large. Par ailleurs, le recul du bord alvéolaire par rapport à la partie basilaire est incomplètement réalisé, ce qui détermine une symphyse presque verticale (cf. fig. 10). Sur sa face interne, la mandibule présente un net *planum alveolare* suivi latéralement par un *torus transversalis superior*. La situation des empreintes digastriques sous le bord inférieur qui forme un bourrelet saillant et le dédoublement du trou mentonnier peuvent être également considérés comme des traits néandertaliens. Enfin, sur la face externe de la branche montante, en dessous de l'échancrure sigmoïde, l'existence des *fovea* et *crista musculi zygomaticomandibularis* est très nette, l'endroit de l'insertion du masseter subsistant sous forme d'un *tuberculum musculi zygomatico mandibularis* bien marqué.

Entre autres caractères paléanthropiens relevés à l'Abri Pataud, notons une forte largeur interorbitaire séparant des orbites très enfoncées, de même que la présence de bosses canines bien marquées. Au niveau du squelette post-crânien, nous avons déjà mentionné l'existence d'un sternum de type «primatoïde», type phylogénétiquement primitif et relativement fréquent chez les néandertaliens. Enfin, rappelons la forme trapue de l'astragale avec un col légèrement dévié en dehors comme chez l'homme de la Chapelle-aux-Saints.

Une telle coexistence de traits paléanthropiens aussi différents et qui font défaut à Cro-Magnon est pour le moins remarquable. Sans conclure pour autant à une origine néandertaloïde des restes proto-magdaléniens de l'Abri Pataud, nous nous devions cependant de souligner dans certains détails de leur structure anatomique la persistance en mosaïque de tels caractères paléanthropiens.

Juillet 1971

BIBLIOGRAPHIE

Ashley, G.T.
1956. «A Comparison of Human and Anthropoid Mesosterna,» *Amer. J. Phys. Anth.*, n.s., vol. 14, no. 3, pp. 449-465.

Balthazard, V., et Dervieux
1921. «Etudes anthropologiques sur le foetus humain,» *Annales de Médecine Légale, de Criminologie et de Police Scientifique*, t.1, pp. 37-42.

Billy, Ginette
1955. «Recherches sur les trous pariétaux,» *Bull. et Mém. Soc. Anth. Paris*, 10ᵉ sér., t. 6, pp. 147-158.

1969. «Le squelette post-crânien de l'Homme de Chancelade,» *L'Anthropologie*, t. 73, pp. 207-246.

1970. «Définition du type de Cro-Magnon *sensu stricto*,» in G. Camps, éd., 1970, pp.23-32.

1971a. «L'évolution humaine au Paléolithique supérieur,» Festschrift Gerhardt, *Homo*, Bd. 23, no.1-2, pp. 2-12; 1 fig., tables. Göttingen.

1971b. «Paléontologie humaine: Les restes humains proto-magdaléniens de l'Abri Pataud,» *C. R. Acad. Sc. Paris*, Sér D, t. 273, pp. 2482-2484.

Bonin, Gerhardt von
1935a. *The Magdalenian Skeleton from Cap-Blanc in the Field Museum of Natural History.* University of Illinois Bulletin, vol. 32, no. 34, 76 pp. 9 pls. Urbana.

1935b. «European Races of the Upper Palaeolithic,» *Human Biology*, vol. 7, no. 2, pp. 196-221.

Bonnet, Robert
1919. «Der diluviale Menschenfund von Obercassel bei Bonn,» M. Verworn, R. Bonnet, et G. Steinmann, Verlag von F. F. Bergmann, Wiesbaden. 193 pp., 28 pls.

Camps, G., éd.
1970. L'Homme de Cro-Magnon 1868-1968. Anthropologie et Archéologie, Centre de Recherches, Anth. Préh. Eth , Arts et Métiers Graphiques, Paris.

Chamla, Marie-Claude
1956. «La région pétro-tympanique chez les anthropoïdes et chez l'Homme,» *L'Anthropologie*, t. 60, pp. 236-267.

Cihák, Radomir, et Emmanuel Vlček
1962. «Crista et fovea musculi zygomaticomandibularis chez les primates,» *L'Anthropologie*, t. 66, no. 5-6, pp. 503-525.

Ducros, Albert
1967. «Evaluation et rapports de la planoccipitalie,» *Bull. et Mém. Soc. Anth. Paris*, 12ᵉ sér., t.1, pp. 359-366.

Duparc, Germaine
1942. «Contribution à l'étude anthropologique de la colonne vertébrale. Enquête portant sur 66 rachis de Boschimans, Hottentots et Griquas,» *Archives Suisses Anth. Gén.*, t. 10, pp. 139-272.

Felice, Suzanne de
1958. *Recherches sur l'anthropologie des Françaises.* Thèse d'Université, Faculté des Sciences, 295 pp. Masson, Paris.

1965. «Hauteur au basion et hauteur au porion, étude comparative,» *L'Anthropologie*, t. 69, no. 5-6, pp. 487-509.

Ferembach, Denise
1954. «Note sur une mandibule présumée de Magdalénien III,» *Bull. et Mém. Soc. Anth. Paris*, 10ᵉ sér., t. 5, pp. 25-34.

1957. «Les restes humains de l'Abri Lachaud,» *Bull. et Mém. Soc. Anth. Paris*, 10ᵉ sér., t. 8, pp. 61-80.

Genet-Varcin, Emilienne, et R. Arambourou
1965. «Nouvelle sépulture du Magdalénien final dans la grotte Duruthy à Sorde-l'Abbaye (Landes),» *Annales de Paléontologie,* t. 51, fasc. 1, pp. 129-150.

Genet-Varcin, Emilienne, et Marc Miquel
1967. «Contribution à l'étude du squelette magdalénien de l'Abri Lafaye, à Bruniquel (Tarn-et-Garonne),» *L'Anthropologie,* t. 71, no. 5-6, pp. 467-478.

Genovés, Santiago
1959. «L'estimation des différences sexuelles dans l'os coxal; différences métriques et différences morphologiques,» *Bull. et Mém. Soc. Anth. Paris,* 10e sér., t. 10, pp. 3-95.

Heim, Jean-Louis
1963. «Les apophyses géni, étude anthropologique,» *Bull. et Mém. Soc. Anth. Paris,* 9e sér., t. 4, pp. 585-658.

Hrdlička, Aleš
1932. «The Principal Dimensions, Absolute and Relative, of the Humerus in the White Race,» *Amer. J. Phys. Anth.,* vol. 16, pp. 431-450.

Lubosch, W. von
1924. «Weitere Mitteilungen über die Formverschiedenheiten am menschlichen Brustbein,» *Anatomischer Anzeiger,* t. 58, pp. 393-397.

Maia Neto, Maria A.
1957. «Estudo osteométrico do antebraço nos Portugueses. I – Radio,» *Contribuições para o Estudo da Antropologia Portuguesa,* t. 6, pp. 143-216.

Martin, Rudolf
1928. *Lehrbuch der Anthropologie in systematischer Darstellung.* 2e éd., 3 vols. Fischer, Jena.

Martin, Rudolf, et K. Saller
1959. *Lehrbuch der Anthropologie in systematischer Darstellung.* 3e éd., t. 2. Fischer, Jena.

Matiegka, J.
1934- *Homo Predmostensis; fosilní člověk z Předmostina*
1938. *Moravě;* I. «Les crânes,» Académie Tchèque des Sciences et des Arts, Prague, 1934, 145 pp. II. «Les autres parties du squelette,» 1938, 91 pp.

1937. «Deflexio Claviculae,» *Anthropologie,* t. 15, pp. 28-40. Prague.

Mendes Corrêa, A. A.
1923. Osteometria portuguesa. Esqueleto do braço e do antebraço. *Annaes da Acad. Polyt. do Porto,* t. 15, pp. 26-53.

Morant, G. M.
1930. *Studies of Palaeolithic Man;* IV. «A Biometric Study of the Upper Palaeolithic Skulls of Europe and their Relationships to Earlier and Later Types,» *Annals of Eugenics,* vol. IV, pp. 109-214. Cambridge University Press.

Movius, H. L., Jr., et Henri V. Vallois
1959. «Crâne proto-magdalénien et Vénus du Périgordien final trouvés dans l'Abri Pataud, Les Eyzies (Dordogne),» *L'Anthropologie,* t. 63, no. 3-4, pp. 213-232.

Olivier, Georges
1951a. «Techniques de mesures des courbures de la clavicule,» *C. R. Assoc. des Anatom.,* 38e, pp. 753-764, Nancy.

1951b. *Anthropologie de la clavicule;* III. «La Clavicule du Français,» *Bull. et Mém. Soc. Anth. Paris,* 10e sér., t. 2, pp. 121-157.

1956. *Anthropologie de la clavicule;* XIII. «Conclusions générales,» *Bull. et Mém. Soc. Anth. Paris,* 10e sér., t. 7, pp. 404-447.

Piquet, Marie-Madeleine
1956. «Etude sur la robustesse de la mandibule,» *Bull. et Mém. Soc. Anth. Paris,* 10e sér., t. 7, pp. 204-224.

Pittard, Eugène, et Marc R. Sauter
1945. «Un squelette magdalénien provenant de la station des Grenouilles (Veyrier, Haute-Savoie),» *Archives Suisses Anth. Gén.,* t.11, pp. 149-200.

Quatrefages, A. de, et Ernest T. Hamy
1882. *Crania Ethnica. Les crânes des races humaines.* 2 vols. J. B. Baillière, Paris.

Rambaud, A., et Ch. Renault
1864. *Origine et développement des os.* 1 vol. de texte et 1 atlas. F. Chamerot, Paris.

Riquet, Raymond
1970. «La race de Cro-Magnon: abus de langage ou réalité objective? » in G. Camps, éd., 1970, pp. 37-58.

Sarasin, Fritz
1931. «Die Variationen im Bau des Handskeletts verschiedener Menschenformen,» *Zeitschrift für Morphologie und Anthropologie,* t. 30, no. 1-2, pp. 252-326.

Sauter, Marc R., et J. Danieli
1939. «La clavicule des Boschimans, Hottentots et Griquas,» *Archives Suisses Anth. Gén.,* t. 8, pp. 321-335.

Sauter, Marc R., et F. Privat
1954- «Sur un nouveau procédé métrique de détermina-
1955. tion sexuelle du bassin osseux,» *Bull. Soc. Suisse Anth. Eth.,* 31e année, pp. 60-84.

Sergi, Sergio
1960. «Essai de radiographie du crâne néandertalien du Mont Circé,» *VIe Congrès International des Sciences Anthropologiques et Ethnologiques,* Paris, pp. 695-698.

Themido, Antonio Armando
1926. «Contribuições para o Estudo da Antropologia Portuguesa. VII: Sobre alguns caracteres sexuais dos humeros portugueses,» *Rivista da Universidade de Coimbra,* t. 10, pp. 103-173.

Thoma, Andor
1962. «Le déploiement évolutif de l'Homo sapiens,» *Anthropologia Hungarica,* t. 5, nos. 1-2. 179 pp., 6 pls.

1965. «La définition des néandertaliens et la position des Hommes fossiles de Palestine,» *L'Anthropologie,* t. 69, no. 5-6, pp. 519-534.

Trouette, Louis
1955. «La platôlénie: nature, signification et variations,» *Bull. et Mém. Soc. Anth. Paris,* 10e sér., t. 6, pp. 68-92.

Vallois, Henri V.
1919. «La valeur morphologique de la rotule chez les Mammifères,» *Bull. et Mém. Soc. Anth. Paris,* 6e sér., t. 8, pp. 1-31.

1929-
1946. «L'omoplate humaine. Etude anatomique et anthropologique,» *Bull. et Mém. Soc. Anth. Paris,* 7ᵉ sér., t. 7, pp. 129-158; t. 10, pp. 110-191; 8ᵉ sér., t. 3, 1932, pp. 3-153; 9ᵉ sér., t. 7, 1946, pp. 16-100.

1946. «Nouvelles recherches sur le squelette de Chancelade,» *L'Anthropologie,* t. 50, pp. 165-202, 10 figs.

1960. «Vital Statistics in Prehistoric Population as Determined from Archaeological Data,» in R. F. Heizer et S. F. Cook, eds., *The Application of Quantitative Methods in Archaeology.* Viking Fund Publications in Anthropology, no. 28, pp. 186-222.

1961. «Le crâne humain magdalénien du Mas d'Azil,» *L'Anthropologie,* t. 65, no. 1-2, pp. 21-45, 7 figs.

1965. «Le sternum néandertalien du Regourdou,» *Anthropologischer Anzeiger,* t. 29, pp. 273-289.

1971. «Le squelette paléolithique de Saint-Germain-la-Rivière et les Cro-Magnoïdes magdaléniens,» *C. R. Acad. Sci. Paris,* t. 272, sér. D, pp. 2677-2680.

1972. «Anthropologie,» *in* R. Blanchard, D. Peyrony, et H. V. Vallois, *Le gisement et le squelette de Saint-Germain-la-Rivière.* Mém. Inst. Pal. Hum., no. 34.

Vallois, Henri V., et Ginette Billy
1965. «Nouvelles recherches sur les Hommes fossiles de L'Abri de Cro-Magnon,» *L'Anthropologie,* t. 69, pp. 47-74 et 249-272, 15 figs.

Vallois, Henri V., et G. Lazorthes
1942. «Indices lombaires et indice lombaire total. Recherche sur la forme des vertèbres lombaires et disques correspondants,» *Bull. et Mém. Soc. Anth. Paris,* 9ᵉ sér., t. 3, pp. 117-131.

Verneau, René
1906. «Anthropologie,» in L. de Villeneuve, M. Boule, R. Verneau, et E. Cartailhac, *Les Grottes de Grimaldi,* t. II, fasc. I, 212 pp., 11 pls.; Monaco.

Vlček, Emmanuel
1970. «Relations morphologiques des types humains fossiles de Brno et de Cro-Magnon au Pléistocène supérieur d'Europe,» in G. Camps, éd., 1970, pp. 59-72.

Volkov, Th.
1905. «Variations squelettiques du pied chez les Primates et dans les races humaines,» Thèse d'Université, Faculté des Sciences de Paris, 266 pp. Laffray et Gendre, Beaugency.

XI

Présentation des Dents des Restes Humains de L'Abri Pataud

Pierre Legoux,

DOCTEUR EN CHIRURGIE DENTAIRE, PARIS

Les dents présentes sur les maxillaires, ou bien recueillies isolées, appartiennent à des fossiles divers et proviennent de niveaux différents.

A. LES RESTES PROTO-MAGDALENIENS

Ils consistent en:

1°. Une tête complète: crâne et mandibule, N°2, découverte sur la partie supérieure de la couche Proto-Magdalénienne (Niveau 2), dans le Carré F, sur la ligne des dix mètres, entre les Tranchées V et VI (voir la figure sur page 200). C'est *le premier sujet*.

Un lot de quatre dents, D5, D4, D7 ter surnuméraire, G2, provenant toutes du Carré G, Tranchée VII, situé à trois ou quatre mètres du crâne. La dent N°1715, D4, a été trouvée en surface du Niveau 2. Les N°2087, D5, 2088, G2, et 2089, D7 ter surnuméraire, proviennent des éboulis postérieurs du même niveau. Ces quatre dents peuvent être attribuées au premier sujet. Planches 1 et 2 (pp. 264 et 265).

2°. Une partie de mandibule droite, avec quatre dents: DIII, GV, dV, et gV. Trouvé dans la Lentille 2, cet ensemble constitue le *second sujet*. Planche 3 (p. 267).

3°. Une portion de maxillaire supérieur droit présentant DV et DIV évoluées et usées sur l'arcade, ainsi que D2 en désinclusion. Une D6 éparse lui est attribuée. Ce N° 14, provenant également de la Lentille 2, forme le *troisième sujet*. Planche 4 (p. 268).

4°. Deux incisives temporaires supérieures: DII et GI. Elles viennent encore toutes deux de la Lentille 2 et constituent le *quatrième sujet*. Planche 5 (p. 270).

5°. Un fragment gauche de mandibule infantile avec une dent isolée lui appartenant. Ce sont les N°1401 (a) et (b), trouvés dans le Carré G de la Tranchée VII, éboulis 1/2, à la surface du Niveau 2. Ils forment le *cinquième sujet*. Planche 6 (p. 271).

B. LES RESTES PERIGORDIENS

Dans cette catégorie, il faut distinguer:

(a) Les restes proprement Périgordiens

6°. Un fragment de molaire temporaire supérieure gauche: GV (?), N°6315. Elle a été découverte dans le Niveau 5, à la partie supérieure du Périgordien IV. C'est le *sixième sujet*. Planche 7 (p. 272).

7°. Une incisive temporaire centrale supérieure gauche: GI, N°10023. Elle est du même niveau que la précédente, mais appartient à la partie inférieure du Périgordien IV. C'est le *septième sujet*. Planche 7 (p. 272).

(b) Les restes Noailliens

8°. Une couronne de molaire temporaire inférieure gauche: gV. Elle provient du Niveau 4, Lentille 0-2, Tranchée III, Carré E. C'est le *huitième sujet*. Planche 8 (p. 273).

9°. Une molaire permanente inférieure droite: d6. Ce N°7523 est du même Niveau 4 que la précédente et aussi de la Lentille 0-2. C'est le *neuvième sujet*. Planche 9 (p. 274).

1. DESCRIPTION MORPHOLOGIQUE

PREMIER SUJET

ARCADE SUPERIEURE

Le crâne présente une arcade maxillaire supérieure en très bon état de conservation. Les dents encore en place sont: D876,G45678. Il faut ajouter au côté droit les deux prémolaires D54, ainsi que la dent conoïde surnuméraire D7 ter et à gauche la G2, retrouvées dans les dents éparses et qui appartiennent indiscutablement à ce sujet.

Toutes ces dents sont au niveau occlusal, sauf D8

qui est au stade d'éruption alvéolaire et ne devait même pas avoir atteint celui d'éruption gingivale. La rangée dentaire est assez régulière à gauche, sauf G8 qui est en malposition, sans contact occlusal avec son antagoniste malgré une évolution complète. A droite la rangée dentaire est irrégulière. Elle présente, outre la semi-inclusion de D8, deux surnuméraires dans la région vestibulaire de D7 qui est palatinée.

Les alvéoles vides ont un état osseux très net, mais quelques bords sont brisés ou émoussés, témoignant d'un processus de résorption infectieuse chronique. Planches 10 et 11 (pp. 278 et 279).

Les molaires supérieures

Les premières molaires sont très usées. Des ilots de dentine apparaissent à la place des sommets des cuspides mésiales. La disposition générale des reliefs et des sillons se présente comme celle des dents actuelles à quatre cuspides. On note toutefois une cuspidiole, marquée, non usée sur la crête marginale distale. Le tubercule de Carabelli est effacé mais devait, sur chacune des ces molaires, atteindre le niveau occlusal.

La disposition des cuspides des secondes molaires diffère de celle de nos jours. Celle de droite paraît encore avoir quatre cuspides principales, mais la marginale distale s'élève presque au volume d'une cinquième. Quant à la dent de gauche, elle possède nettement trois cuspides vestibulaires et une occlusale supplémentaire. Si la disposition des sillons ressemble encore un peu à celle des dents actuelles à droite, elle s'en écarte totalement à gauche. Sur ces deux dents, le tubercule de Carabelli est encore très marqué.

Les troisièmes molaires défient toute description raisonnée. Ce sont des complexes de cuspidioles disposés en un cirque au milieu duquel on a peine à distinguer la topographie originale. Elles possèdent aussi toutes deux des tubercules de Carabelli appréciables.

Les radiographies montrent des chambres pulpaires relativement petites quant au volume de chaque dent. En conséquence les faces occlusales sont extrêmement épaisses. Les racines au nombre de trois sont bien divergentes sur chaque première molaire, mais tendent ensuite à la convergence, au point qu'elles semblent fusionner sur la troisième molaire. Les canaux sont extrêmement fins.

Anomalies de droite. Autant en paléostomatologie que de nos jours, elles paraissent exceptionnelles.

1°. Une dent surnuméraire, conoïde, D7 bis, avec une racine naine, est accolée en oblique sur la face vestibulaire de la D7.

2°. Une seconde dent surnuméraire, D7 ter, également conoïde, mais avec une racine bien développée, s'applique sur l'ensemble D7, D7 bis, soufflant l'os vestibulaire.

Les pointes de leurs cuspides sont sensiblement au niveau occlusal. Cette disposition aura des répercussions pathologique importantes. Planche 10 (p. 278).

Les prémolaires supérieures

Elles sont d'aspect semblable à celui des prémolaires actuelles avec cependant quelques différences.

Elles ont deux cuspides et les vestibulaires sont assez usées, avec un sillon droit et des fossettes marginales nettes mais peu profondes. C'est la présence d'une cuspidiole supplémentaire mésiale qu'il faut signaler sur chacune, ce qui n'existe pas actuellement. Il faut noter aussi l'étroitesse des chambres pulpaires, situées plus dans la région cervicale que coronaire et la finesse des canaux radiculaires. Les comparaisons des dimensions seront également instructives. Planches 1, 2c et d, et 11 (pp. 264, 265, et 279).

L'incisive latérale supérieure gauche

Elle n'a aucune ressemblance avec une dent similaire contemporaine. Il fallait vraiment: 1°. qu'elle ait été trouvée avec les prémolaires du premier sujet: 2°. qu'elle s'adapte parfaitement à l'alvéole de G2 et non pas à celle d'une D1 ou d'une G1 pour la décrire comme une G2, car elle a tout à fait l'aspect d'une centrale et non pas celui d'une latérale. Planches 1 et 2 (pp. 264 et 265).

MANDIBULE

Son état de conservation est particulièrement bon. L'arcade dentaire et alvéolaire est très régulière sauf dans la région des d8, d7, et g8 qui sont en linguo-position, mais complètement évoluées. Sont présentes sur l'arcade: d8764 et g4678. Toutes les alvéoles vides ont un bon état osseux, mais comme au maxillaire supérieur, quelques bords sont brisés ou émoussés. Donc d5321 et g1235 sont perdues depuis la mort du sujet, comme les autres dents absentes de l'arcade supérieure. Planches 12 et 13 (pp. 280-283).

Les molaires inférieures

Les premières ont cinq cuspides principales et un réseau de sillons disposé comme de nos jours. Cependant, malgré une usure forte, différente d'ailleurs sur chacune, on distingue encore une cuspide supplémentaire sur chaque crête marginale

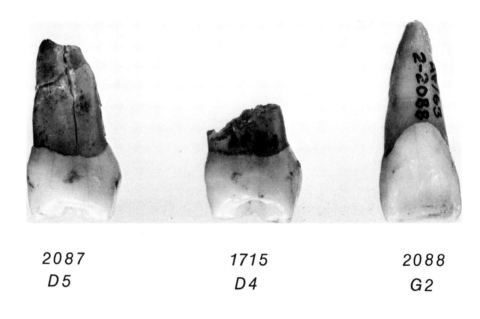

2087
D5

1715
D4

2088
G2

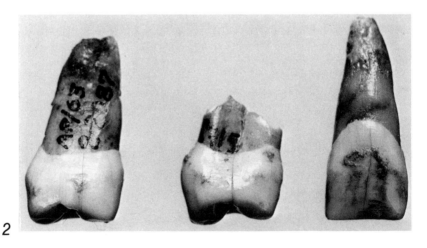

2

Planche 1. Proto-Magdalénien. Premier sujet, «La jeune femme.» Clichés R. Percheron, échelle: x 2,5 environ. 1. Face distale des prémolaires supérieures droites. Face vestibulaire de la latérale supérieure gauche. 2. Face mésiale des prémolaires supérieures droites. Face palatine de la latérale supérieure gauche. Dents permanentes éparses retrouvées dans la fouille et attribuées au premier sujet.

a

b

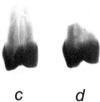

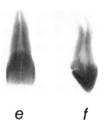

c   *d*   *e*   *f*

Planche 2. Proto-Magdalénien. Premier sujet, «La jeune femme.» Clichés R. Percheron, échelle: x 2,5 environ. Seconde dent surnuméraire D7 ter (n° 2089) attribuée au premier sujet: *a*. face distale; *b*. face palatine. Radiographies P. Legoux, échelle: x 1 environ. Faces distales: *c*. seconde prémolaire supérieure droite D5; *d*. première prémolaire supérieure droite D4. Faces vestibulaires: *e*. incisive latérale supérieure gauche G2; *f*. deuxième dent surnuméraire D7 ter.

distale. Pour étayer les commentaires sur la ciné-matique mandibulaire il est utile de noter qu'à droite, l'usure forme une vaste cupule qui n'atteint pas la dentine mais qui efface le côté vestibulaire de la crête marginale distale; que l'usure est plus accentuée, jusqu'à la dentine, sur la cuspide mésio-vestibulaire, moins marquée sur les cuspides mésio-linguale et vestibulo-centrale et pratiquement inexistante sur la disto-linguale. Par contre à gauche, les cinq cuspides sont plus ou moins usées et la crête marginale distale est effacée sur toute sa longueur. Les glissements n'étaient donc pas, à droite, identiques à ceux de gauche.

Les secondes molaires ont cinq cuspides principales et celle de droite a même deux cuspidioles supplé-mentaires. On trouve certes des secondes molaires inférieures à cinq cuspides chez les hommes actuels, mais il s'agit alors d'une variation, car de nos jours le type fondamental est à quatre cuspides. La disposi-tion des sillons n'est donc pas en croix mais répète celle de la première molaire. Ces dents ne sont pas usées. Leur relief est simplement adouci par une mastication qui n'a pas duré longtemps.

Comme les supérieures, les troisièmes molaires inférieures défient toute description. La gauche paraît conserver un schéma à cinq cuspides: trois vestibu-laires et deux linguales. Les trois vestibulaires sont dédoublées; des crêtes extrêmement marquées ornent les deux linguales et les cuspidioles supplémentaires apparaissent sur les crêtes marginales distale et mésiale et sur le bord lingual. Il existe de multiples sillons, trois fossettes principales et deux accessoires. Celle de droite est encore plus compliquée. Les trois cuspides vestibulaires sont diminuées au profit d'une très forte cuspide centrale, jaillissant comme un piton au beau milieu de la face occlusale. Rien ne rappelle la dent de sagesse actuelle et pourtant chez *l'Homo sapiens* c'est la dent dont la morphologie est la plus variable.

Les chambres pulpaires sont relativement petites et basses comme celles de l'arcade supérieure. L'épais-seur des faces occlusales est considérable. Les racines, bien divergentes sur les premières molaires, ont une tendance à la convergence sur la seconde; il semble en exister trois, deux mésiales et une distale, à la troisième. Les canaux sont toujours très fins.

Les prémolaires inférieures

Elles ont toutes deux une morphologie générale semblable à l'actuelle avec deux cuspides: une cuspide vestibulaire très importante haute et aiguë, l'usure a créé une cupule à son sommet; une linguale plus basse, adoucie par l'usure. Ce qui les différencie l'une

de l'autre c'est: 1°. l'existence d'un sillon courbe à convexité linguale, net, séparateur, entre les deux cuspides avec en corollaire, l'absence du pont d'émail, à gauche; 2°. l'absence de sillon, avec la présence d'un fort pont d'émail, bordé de deux fossettes marquées, à droite. Ces variations de disposition occlusale sont aussi observées de nos jours.

L'étroitesse des chambres pulpaires et la finesse des canaux persiste.

SECOND SUJET

Les molaires temporaires inférieures ont cinq cus-pides comme actuellement, mais de nombreux sillons secondaires et des amorces de cuspides supplémen-taires apparaissent. La molaire supérieure présente quatre cuspides principales, des cuspidioles éparses et des sillons tourmentés. La canine est un germe ayant seulement calcifié sa portion cuspidienne. Planche 3.

TROISIEME SUJET

La première molaire permanente supérieure droite a une disposition des cuspides semblable à celle de nos jours, mais elles sont toutes festonnées par des lobes et, comme il existe des sillons accessoires, l'aspect est beaucoup plus complexe que l'actuel. Elle a aussi une amorce de tubercule de Carabelli.

Les deux molaires temporaires se présentent comme leurs homologues contemporaines. Elle ne paraissent pas porter de cuspidioles supplémentaires, si toutefois celles-ci n'ont pas été effacées par l'usure.

Anomalie. La seconde prémolaire permanente droite, en évolution, est encore incluse, ce qui est normal étant donné le développement de l'individu. Ce qui ne l'est pas, c'est que sa face occlusale est tournée vers le sinus. Aucun doute que ce soit sa position réelle, du vivant de l'enfant, puisque la position de la racine vestibulo-distale de la DV et l'étroitesse du volume de son alvéole empêchent toute rotation *post mortem*. Ce qui est encore le plus étonnant, c'est que son degré de maturité semble être en parfaite harmonie avec le développement de la première prémolaire permanente, et que sa morphologie, avec toujours des cuspidioles supplémentaires, ne diffère pas des autres prémolaires des fossiles Proto-Magdaléniens. C'est une «anastro-phie.»

La première prémolaire et la canine permanente incluses, en évolution, sont déjà fortement calcifiées. La latérale permanente a une légère tendance à présenter une face palatine «en forme de pelle». Planche 4 (p. 268).

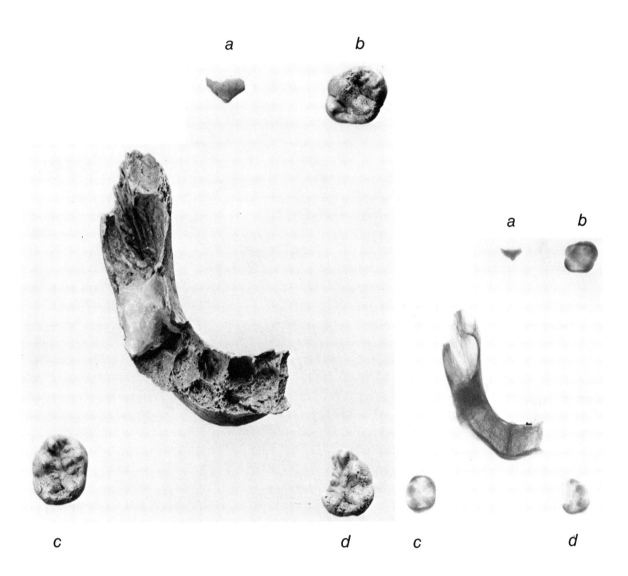

Planche 3. Proto-Magdalénien. Second sujet. Cliché R. Percheron, échelle: x 1,75 environ. Portion de mandibule infantile et quatre dents temporaires attribuées au même sujet; *a*. canine supérieure droite DIII; *b*. seconde molaire supérieure gauche GV; *c*. seconde molaire inférieure droite dV; *d*. seconde molaire inférieure gauche gV. Radiographie Drs. Rohr et Sarazin, échelle: x 1 environ.

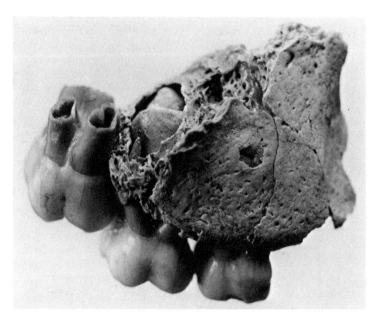

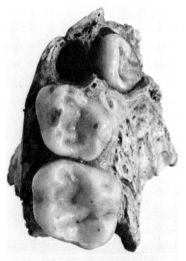

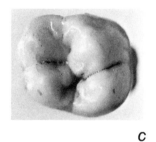

b

c

d

Planche 4. Proto-Magdalénien. Troisième sujet. Clichés R. Percheron, échelle: x 2,5 environ. Maxillaire supérieur droit–N° 14: *a*. aspect vestibulaire. La D6 est remise dans sa portion d'alvéole. Noter l'apex de la racine distale de la DV parfaitement appliqué contre la couronne de la D5, ce qui ne peut faire douter de son inversion naturelle; *b*. aspect occlusal; *c*. D6; *d*. radiographie Drs. Rohr et Sarazin, échelle: x 1 environ.

QUATRIEME SUJET

La latérale temporaire supérieure droite ressemble beaucoup à une dent actuelle, elle en a d'ailleurs l'aspect «en soc de charrue». Par contre, la centrale temporaire supérieure gauche, avec son talon palatin très développé, son bombé vestibulaire cervical très marqué et son peu de hauteur de face vestibulaire a plutôt la forme «en baril» des incisives temporaires néandertaliennes. L'usure et l'éclatement des angles donnent peut-être un aspect trompeur. Planche 5 (p. 270).

CINQUIEME SUJET

La portion de mandibule est moins bien conservée que celle du second sujet. On pourrait y reconnaître gII, III, et IV, mais ce n'est pas sûr. La seconde molaire temporaire inférieure gauche, se présente, en plus jeune encore, comme celle du second sujet. Planche 6 (p. 271).

SIXIEME SUJET

Il s'agit sans doute d'une seconde molaire tempo-raire supérieure gauche, mais ce fragment très usé est difficile à identifier avec exactitude. Planche 7 (p. 272).

SEPTIEME SUJET

Mieux conservée et plus jeune que celle du quatrième sujet, c'est une centrale temporaire supérieure gauche. L'aspect «en baril» est moins marqué. Planche 7 (p. 272).

HUITIEME SUJET

C'est encore une seconde molaire temporaire inférieure gauche très usée et en mauvais état de conservation mais apportant beaucoup de renseignements. Planche 8 (p. 273).

NEUVIEME SUJET

Seul témoignage de la présence d'un adulte âgé dans le gisement, c'est une première molaire permanente inférieure droite. Elle est tellement usée qu'il n'existe plus d'émail sur la face occlusale. Elle est en outre partiellement fracturée et fendue. Même dans cet état elle reste précieuse. Planche 9 (p. 274).

2. PATHOLOGIE

PREMIER SUJET

Quoique robuste et harmonieusement constituée, cette jeune femme présente des atteintes infectieuses graves provoquées par:

1°. Une usure importante et précoce des premières molaires.

Les témoignages en sont visibles dans la zone incisivo-canine des alvéoles déshabitées. Pour que les résorptions parcellaires aient atteint le degré observable, il faut qu'une parodontose se soit manifestée avant l'éruption des dents de douze ans et se soit amplifiée par la suite.

2°. Les dents surnuméraires supérieures droites.

Leur disposition concentrique crée naturellement des rétentions alimentaires, suivies de tassements, dont la fermentation continuellement entretenue, provoque une ostéite diffuse interstitielle qui détruit la racine vestibulo-distale de la première molaire. Ce douloureux processus purulent cause des troubles de la mastication qui s'installe à gauche, et favorise des dépôts de tartre abondants qui exacerbent la parodontose préexistante.

3°. Les évolutions ectopiques des troisièmes molaires.

Ces dents n'ont même pas été fonctionnelles. La supérieure droite est restée semi-incluse, en butée contre la seconde, créant ainsi un nouveau foyer d'ostéite. Les éruptions linguales des inférieures ont créé une péri-coronarite bi-latérale: la destruction importante des triangles rétro-molaires en est la preuve. Une stomatite odontiasique sévère se surajoute à la parodontose. On peut se demander comment la mastication était possible?

La mort paraît survenir au moment où la pathologie buccale atteint un degré de manifestations infectieuses, rares à réunir et dont nous avons cependant la preuve de la concomitance.

TROISIEME SUJET

La présence d'une prémolaire anastrophique est-elle à retenir? Si la position inversée ne paraît pas avoir créé de troubles pathologiques visibles, il faut cependant penser à un développement anormal de la lame dentaire, donc à une atteinte à un stade antérieur dans la formation de ce sujet.

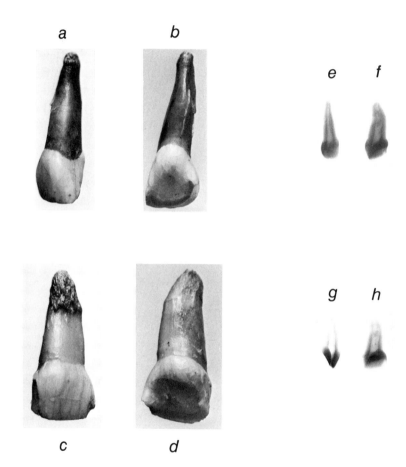

Planche 5. Proto-Magdalénien. Quatrième sujet, deux dents temporaires. Clichés R. Percheron, échelle: 2,5 environ, DII—incisive latérale supérieure droite: *a.* aspect mésio-vestibulaire; *b.* face palatine. GI—incisive centrale supérieure gauche: *c.* face vestibulaire; *d.* face palatine. Radiographie Drs. Rohr et Sarazin: *e.* DII, FV; *f.* GI, DP; radiographie P. Legoux: *g.* DII, FD; *h.* GI, FP; échelle: x 1 environ.

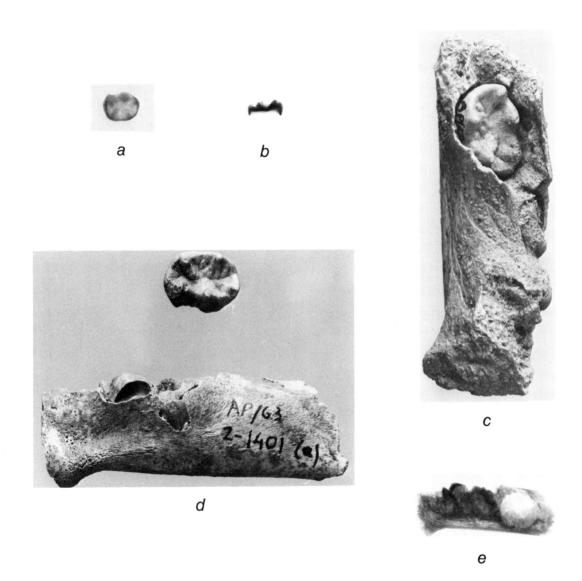

Planche 6. Proto-Magdalénien. Cinquième sujet, portion gauche de mandibule infantile N° 1401. Clichés R. Percheron, échelle: x 2 environ; radiographies P. Legoux, échelle: x 1 environ: *a.* radiographie occlusale de la seconde molaire temporaire inférieure gauche gV; *b.* radiographie vestibulaire de gV; *c.* aspect lingual de la mandibule avec la gV en place; *d.* aspect vestibulaire de la mandibule et face occlusale de la gV qui lui est attribuée; *e.* radiographie de la mandibule. Les infiltrations terreuses empêchent de distinguer les éléments.

Sixième sujet

a

b

Septième sujet

c

d

e

Planche 7. Périgordien. Sixième sujet, débris de molaire temporaire supérieure gauche GV (?) N°6315:*a*. face occlusale; *b*. face interne. Septième sujet, incisive centrale temporaire supérieure gauche GI N°10023 ; *c*. face vestibulaire; *d*. face palatine; *e*. radiographie de la face palatine. Clichés R. Percheron, échelle: x 2,5 environ; radiographie P. Legoux, échelle: x 1 environ.

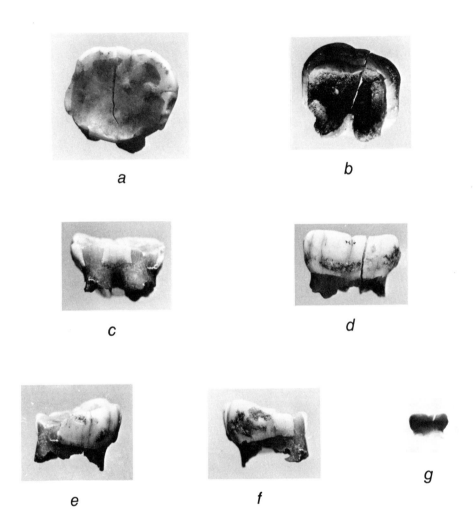

Planche 8. Noaillien. Huitième sujet, seconde molaire temporaire inférieure gauche gV: *a*. face occlusale; *b*. chambre pulpaire; *c*. face linguale; *d*. face vestibulaire; *e*. face mésiale; *f*. face distale; *g*. radiographie de la face vestibulaire. Clichés R. Percheron, échelle: x 2,5 environ; radiographie P. Legoux, échelle: x 1 environ.

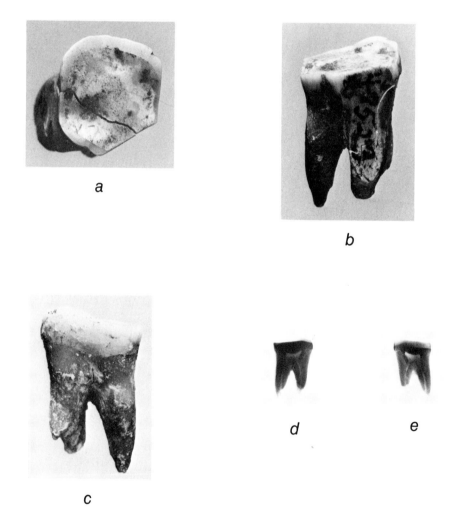

a

b

c

d   e

Planche 9. Noaillien. Neuvième sujet, N° 7523, première molaire permanente inférieure droite d6. Clichés R. Percheron, échelle: x 2,5 environ: *a*. face occlusale; *b*. face vestibulaire; *c*. face linguale. Radiographies P. Legoux, échelle: x 1 environ: *d*. face vestibulaire; *e*. face linguale.

NEUVIEME SUJET

On observe des altérations apicales, sous forme de concrétions irrégulières et même peut-être une lyse, aux apex des racines de cette dent. Seraient-elles la conséquence d'une nécrose pulpaire due à l'usure? On ne peut discriminer, faute de références à ce sujet, s'il s'agit d'une atteinte pathologique ou d'une altération *post mortem*.

Les autres fossiles ne paraissent pas présenter d'atteintes pathologiques au niveau dentaire.

3. PHYSIOLOGIE DE LA MASTICATION

PREMIER SUJET

Cette jeune femme a du présenter, dans sa courte existence, trois cinématiques mandibulaires.

1°. Avant même que les premières molaires permanentes aient atteint le niveau occlusal, une mastication très forte devait s'exercer sur les molaires temporaires. La preuve en est fournie par l'usure, prononcée donc précoce, de ces premières molaires puisque les secondes molaires sont à peine usées. Les prémolaires permanentes, dès leur apparition vers 9/10 ans, sont également vite usées puisque leurs cuspides vestibulaires ont des atteintes en cupules. Ce sujet a donc utilisé une première cinématique usant la partie postérieure de l'arcade dentaire, provoquant une surcharge, accompagnée de parodontose, et une usure précoce (G2) du groupe incisivo-canin.

2°. Des anomalies, localisées à droite, accompagnant l'éruption des secondes molaires, provoquent une mastication, hésitante de ce côté, mais plus affermie à gauche. Des mouvements de rotation s'installent (cupule margino-distale de d6). Les dents ne s'usent plus d'une façon régulière.

3°. L'évolution des dents de sagesse s'effectue d'une manière aberrante. Les inférieures sont totalement lingualées. La supérieure gauche pousse comme elle peut et la supérieure droite reste bloquée en sous-inclusion. Les douleurs provoquées par les mouvements de mastication reportent à nouveau, anormalement, les efforts sur le groupe incisivo-canin. Son ébranlement atteint alors un tel point que les chutes *post mortem* n'ont rien de surprenant.

Il faut donc retenir qu'à l'origine, une mastication d'aliments résistants et peut-être une certaine psychose d'anxiété, ont amené une usure rapide et importante des dents de six ans, qui déséquilibra l'orthognatisme évident de ce sujet. Des phénomènes infectieux veinnent augmenter ensuite ces troubles jusqu'à provoquer une véritable anarchie.

TROISIEME SUJET

Il ne reste que deux dents temporaires sur cette portion de maxillaire supérieur droit. Elles permettent de nous rendre compte que la mastication des aliments solides a été pratiquée de bonne heure. Les mouvements de latéralité devaient-être prononcés puisque l'usure des crêtes marginales est marquée dans le sens vestibulo-palatin, mais des mouvements de proglissement les accompagnaient puisque les cuspides palatines sont usées dans le sens disto-mésial. La cinématique mandibulaire aboutissait donc à des mouvements de rotation homogènes, puisque la régularité des usures prouve également que cet enfant devait avoir ses vingt dents temporaires en place avant son décès et que la chronologie de l'éruption s'est poursuivie à un rythme régulier, sinon, il existerait des facettes irrégulières d'usure, ce qui n'est pas. Son orthognathisme et son sevrage précoce paraissent évidents.

QUATRIEME SUJET

On peut noter une usure fonctionnelle très nette et très harmonieuse sur les bords libres de ces deux dents, la centrale gauche étant plus usée que la latérale droite. Des facettes d'abrasion existent du côté palatin. Les mouvements propres d'incision étaient donc aussi fréquents et prononcés que ceux de latéralité. Il existait sans doute une orthognatie très harmonieuse.

SIXIEME SUJET

Cette unique dent nous apprend qu'une première molaire inférieure permanente était présente sur l'arcade, car le degré d'usure ne peut provenir de la seule gV. L'usure étant orientée dans le sens vestibulo-palatin, une mastication très efficace s'est donc effectuée par de larges mouvements de latéralité.

SEPTIEME SUJET

L'usure très localisée fait surtout penser à des mouvements d'incision et de faible latéralité. Il est très probable que cet enfant n'avait pas encore ses molaires temporaires et se contentait seulement de mâchonner quelques aliments peu résistants.

HUITIEME SUJET

L'usure de la face occlusale dénote une mastication tout à fait régulière, très forte, menée jusqu'à ses dernières possibilités. Toutes les autres dents devaient donc avoir un même degré d'évolution et d'usure sur les deux arcades.

NEUVIEME SUJET

Ce sujet paraîtraît avoir employé pour mastiquer, deux mouvements principaux: $1°$. un de proglissement disto-mésial que démontrent les facettes d'usure distale et mésiale; $2°$. des mouvements de rotation prouvés par l'usure disto-vestibulaire. La mastication devait être beaucoup plus broyeuse que coupante.

On ne peut rien dire des second et cinquième sujets dont les dents ne sont pas parvenues au stade fonctionnel.

4. DETERMINATION DE L'AGE

PREMIER SUJET

L'usure est très nette sur toutes les dents qui évoluent entre six et douze ans. S'il y a concordance d'éruption entre les dents des Paléolithiques et celles des hommes actuels, ce sujet a au moins douze ans.

Le fait primordial à retenir est que l'usure des secondes molaires est très faible. Le décès est donc intervenu peu après que ces dents eurent été en contact occlusal. Or les troisièmes molaires ont évolué et leurs apex sont calcifiés. On pourrait donc estimer que l'âge de vingt ans est un minimum: mais les secondes molaires n'ont pas une usure correspondant à cet âge.

Il faut se rendre à l'évidence: la chronologie d'évolution de ce sujet est différente de la nôtre. Elle fut dans son ensemble plus précoce qu'est l'actuelle, surtout et sûrement en ce qui concerne les troisièmes molaires.

Cette jeune femme ne devait pas avoir beaucoup plus de *quatorze à quinze ans*, si ce n'est pas moins, car nous nous basons seulement sur des estimations.

SECOND SUJET

De nos jours, à la naissance, la couronne de la canine temporaire est calcifiée aux deux cinquièmes et celle des molaires temporaires se réalise environ six mois après. Or la canine et les molaires temporaires de ce sujet sont calcifiées environ aux deux tiers.

Si l'on admet d'une part, que la chronologie de calcification des dents des hommes fossiles est différente de la nôtre, ce qui paraît évident et d'autre part qu'elle est plus précoce, ce qui ne semble plus à prouver (Vallois 1937; Koski et Garn 1957; Legoux 1966), cet enfant ne devait avoir en réalité que *deux à quatre mois*, au maximum.

TROISIEME SUJET

Ici encore, il faut constater que l'évolution des dents est légèrement différente de la nôtre. La première molaire et les incisives permanentes apparaissent plus précocement. Pendant ce temps, les molaires temporaires restent bien plantées, mais étant donné le degré de calcification et d'évolution des prémolaires permanentes, elles ne tarderont pas à être remplacées rapidement. La canine viendra compléter l'arcade de bonne heure.

La dentition de ce fossile ne diffère pas essentiellement de la nôtre dans l'ordre de remplacement des dents, mais elle est plus précoce et c'est cet aspect qui peut tromper un observateur superficiel.

Cette portion de maxillaire, malgré sa robustesse n'a qu'un âge de *cinq ans* environ, mais plutôt moins que plus.

QUATRIEME SUJET

Il devait exister un très léger début de résorption des racines au moment du décès. Cet enfant devait donc avoir entre *trois ans et demi et quatre ans*. L'âge le plus précoce devant correspondre à la vérité.

CINQUIEME SUJET

La couronne de la gV n'est pas calcifiée à la moitié. Ce stade s'étendrait d'un âge foetal de huit à neuf mois à celui d'un ou deux mois après la naissance. En tenant compte des remarques précédentes, l'âge de l'enfant se situe entre les limites de *huit mois in utero* à *un mois après la naissance*.

SIXIEME SUJET

L'épaisseur occlusale émail/dentine est assez forte. Le volume de la chambre pulpaire est faible pour une dent temporaire. L'usure est marquée. Les racines sont résorbées jusqu'au collet.

L'âge de cet enfant doit très vraisemblablement s'établir aux *environ de neuf ans* ou un peu plus, mais il ne dépasse pas onze ans et il n'a certainement pas moins de huit ans.

SEPTIEME SUJET

La dent est peu usée et sa racine est incomplètement calcifiée. L'âge serait de nos jours de treize à quinze mois au maximum, mais en fonction de la précocité vraisemblable, celui de *dix à douze mois* paraît beaucoup plus logique.

HUITIEME SUJET

Cette seconde molaire temporaire est complètement usée et ses racines sont lysées jusqu'à l'extrême limite. De nos jours cet enfant aurait environ onze ans. Ce fossile peut donc avoir de *dix à onze ans*, sans pouvoir être plus précis.

NEUVIEME SUJET

La morphologie et la physiologie de la mastication démontrent indéniablement que cette dent est une molaire permanente très usée, qu'elle a calcifié ses apex et que sa chambre pulpaire est réduite. Son âge peut-être supposé mais non prouvé. Avec prudence, l'âge de *trente ans* au moins devait-être atteint mais tout âge supérieur pourrait lui être attribué si de nouvelles précisions ou des recoupements pouvaient être apportés.

COMMENTAIRES

DIMENSIONS GENERALES DES DENTS

Si l'on compare les dents de l'Abri Pataud à celles de fossiles d'ancienneté voisine découverts en France, on peut constater que toutes les dimensions de toutes les dents permanentes du premier sont plus grandes que celles des autres. Tableaux 10 et 11 (pp. 296 et 297).

Comparées à celles des fossiles plus anciens, Néandertaliens ou Aurignacien, toujours découverts en France, les dimensions de l'Abri Pataud leurs sont très voisines quand elles ne les dépassent pas dans certains cas. Tableaux 12 et 13 (pp. 297 et 298).

MORPHOLOGIE

Les séries molaires du maxillaire présentent des volumes dans l'ordre: M2>M1>M3 et à la mandibule: M1<M2<M3. Chez l'homme actuel, on note en général: M1>M2>M3, en haut comme en bas.

Le nombre des cuspides principales est de 4 sur M1, de 4 sur M2, de 4 + n sur M3, au maxillaire et de 5 sur M1, 5 sur M2, 5 + n sur M3 à la mandibule; de nos jours il est de 4, 4, 3 et 5, 4, 5. Il faut aussi noter qu'à la mandibule le rapport des diamètres est inversé: Ø VL > Ø MD.

Les molaires temporaires se présentent comme les dents actuelles mais les faces occlusales ont beaucoup de petits sillons secondaires et les dimensions sont toutes plus fortes.

Toutes les molaires permanentes ou temporaires portent des tubercules de Carabelli plus ou moins développés.

L'aspect général des prémolaires permanentes ressemble à l'actuel. Il faut toutefois signaler que les dimensions générales sont plus importantes, sauf le plus petit Ø MD qui est beaucoup plus étroit, et la présence, à l'encontre de maintenant, des cuspidioles sur les faces occlusales.

Les deux incisives latérales supérieures permanentes s'écartent assez nettement de la morphologie actuelle.

La canine temporaire, autant qu'on puisse en juger, est d'un aspect assez contemporain. Par contre les incisives temporaires «en baril» semblent présenter des caractères archaïques.

Il faut encore noter que toutes les chambres pulpaires sont relativement étroites et basses et que si la fusion pyramidale des racines n'existe pas, certains éléments semblent avoir une tendance au rapprochement.

PATHOLOGIE

Elle consiste, pour le premier sujet en des affections dont les causes sont diverses, s'imbriquent et se surajoutent les unes aux autres. Elle sont d'origines:

1. traumatiques/ c'est surtout évident pour le groupe incisivo-canin. Il est indéniable que la première molaire permanente fut la première des permanentes à apparaître sur l'arcade. Même si les molaires temporaires sont restées longtemps en fonction, même si les

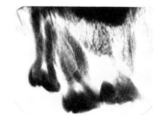

Planche 10. Proto-Magdalénien. Premier sujet, arcade supérieure: côté droit. Cliché R. Percheron, échelle: x 2,5 environ: aspect des trois molaires de la série habituelle et des deux surnuméraires D7 bis et D7 ter. Radiographie P. Legoux, échelle: x 1 environ: les chambres pulpaires peu développées sont cervicales. La racine disto-vestibulaire de D6 a fondu dans un vaste foyer infectieux.

Premier sujet

a

b

Planche 11. Proto-Magdalénien. Premier sujet, arcade supérieure: côté gauche; Cliché R. Percheron, échelle: x 2,5 environ: aspect des molaires et des prémolaires. Radiographies P. Legoux, échelle: x 1 environ: *a*. l'orientation de la radiographie donne un aspect pyramidal des racines de G8; *b*. une orientation différente dissocie les racines vestibulaires de G8.

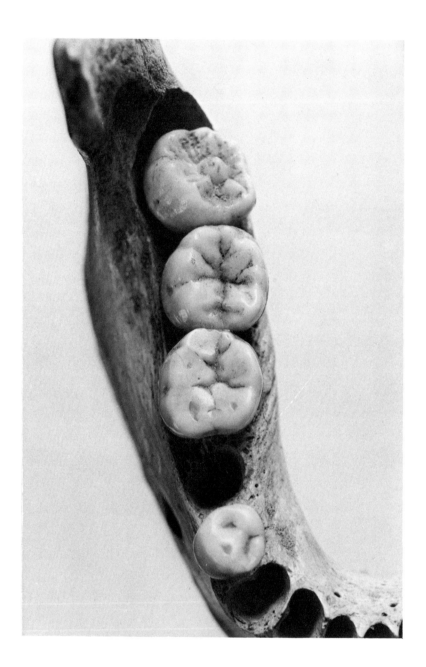

Planche 12a. Proto-Magdalénien. Premier sujet, mandibule: côté droit. Cliché R. Percheron, échelle: x 2,5 environ: aspect des molaires et de la prémolaire.

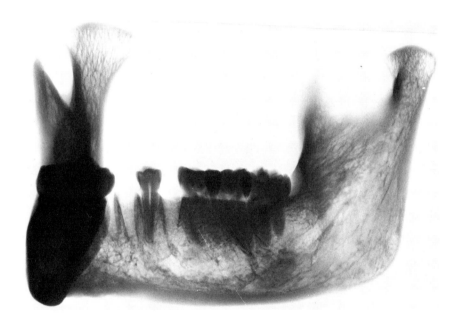

Planche 12b. Proto-Magdalénien. Premier sujet, mandibule: côté droit. Radiographie Drs.
Rohr et Sarazin, échelle: x 1 environ: radiographie défilée. Tous les apex de toutes les dents
sont fermés.

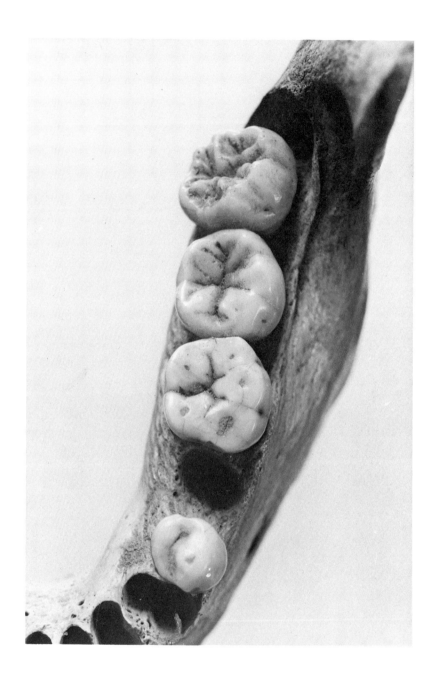

Planche 13a. Proto-Magdalénien. Premier sujet, mandibule: côté gauche. Cliché R. Percheron, échelle: x 2,5 environ: aspect des molaires et de la prémolaire.

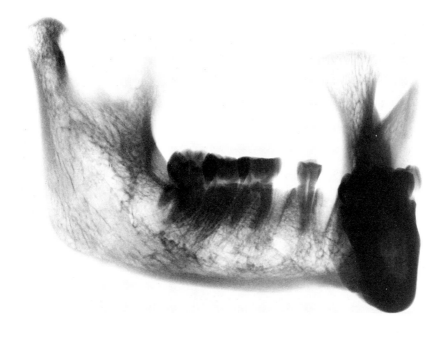

Planche 13b. Proto-Magdalénien. Premier sujet, mandibule: côté gauche. Radiographie Drs. Rohr et Sarazin, échelle: x 1 environ: radiographie défilée. Tous les apex sont également calcifiés.

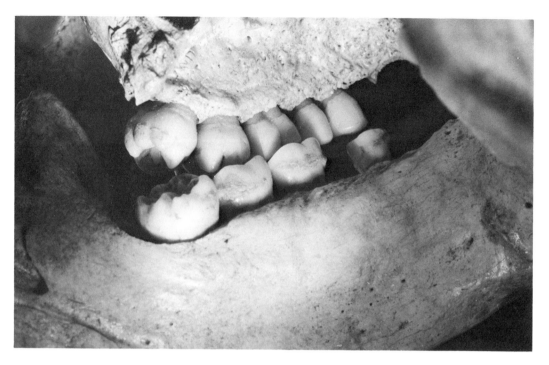

a

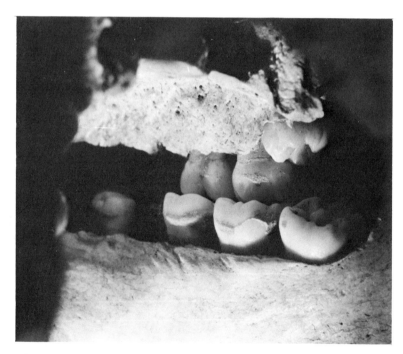

b

Planche 14. Proto-Magdalénien. Premier sujet, maxillaires en articulation, aspect lingual: *a.* côté gauche, *b.* côté droit. La malposition des troisièmes molaires est parfaitement mise en évidence à gauche, et encore plus flagrante à droite, côté des surnuméraires. Clichés R. Percheron, échelle: x 2,5 environ.

incisives temporaires ont été rapidement remplacées par les permanentes, ces dernières ont commencé à fonctionner trop tard. L'usure des groupes molaires mixtes préexistait. On ne peut pas invoquer non plus que l'apparition des secondes molaires permanentes ait ralenti le processus d'atteinte traumatique du groupe antérieur, car elles n'ont pas été longtemps fonctionnelles et l'âge de ce sujet est déjà assez jeune pour qu'on ne puisse raisonnablement pas encore rajeunir la date de la naissance de ces dents pour les faire apparaître à sept ans. Ce serait défier le bon sens dans les observations biologiques. L'atteinte parodontique du groupe antérieur, de cause traumatique par abaissement précoce de l'occlusion et surcharge fonctionnelle est donc démontré.

2. ontogéniques/ l'apparition des molaires surnuméraires provoque des troubles dans la mastication qui s'installe à gauche. Les dépôts de tartre, plus importants à droite qu'à gauche, augmentent la parodontose.

3. odontiasiques/ les évolutions vicieuses des troisièmes molaires créent une stomatite chronique, favorisée par la parodontose qu'elle exacerbe.

4. infectieuses/ l'apparition progressive de plusieurs foyers importants révolutionne encore les mouvements de mastication qui ne doivent plus s'effectuer que «du bout des dents».

5. réflexes/ la bruxomanie, renforcée par le faciès pathologique, s'exacerbe pendant les rémissions douloureuses, augmentent les surcharges aberrantes. Une déformation de l'articulation temporo-mandibulaire, si elle n'existe pas déjà, mais nous ne connaissons pas l'état des ménisques, n'aurait pas tardé à s'installer.

L'état pathologique buccal, au moment du décès, devait former un tableau difficilement descriptible et ses répercussions sur l'état général ne sont pas douteuses.

PHYSIOLOGIE

La pathologie provoque des troubles dans la cinématique mandibulaire, mais elle n'est pas la seule en cause. Il faut encore penser à:

1. **La diététique/** le premier sujet a profité d'un allaitement naturel, administré dans de bonnes conditions, puisqu'il n'existe aucune trace de déformation du massif antérieur de la face. Le sevrage a du être précoce et une cinématique plus broyante que coupante s'installe avant l'achèvement de la dentition

temporaire. L'incisive supérieure gauche, dont le bord libre est proportionnellement moins usé que la face occlusale de la première molaire, en est la preuve. Le bol alimentaire infantile devait être composé d'aliments résistants, à mâchonner longuement. L'orthognatie originelle s'en trouve précocement altérée.

2. **Le mode de vie** qui est à considérer sous un double aspect:

(a) Social. Le climat, assez froid et humide, nécessitait une protection corporelle. De nos jours, l'assouplissement final des peaux est, chez les Esquimaux, exécuté par les jeunes femmes, par mâchonnement prolongé. Rien ne s'oppose à ce que les Proto-Magdaléniens aient déjà appliqué la même méthode.

(b) Psychique. Des facteurs de tous ordres, inhérent à l'insécurité et à la brièveté de la vie, ne pouvaient qu'entretenir chez certains sujets un bruxisme permanent.

Les nécessités sociales et la précarité de la vie augmentent encore l'usure des dents.

ONTOGENIE

Les déterminations des âges dentaires ont mis en évidence que la calcification et la migration des dents diffèrent assez largement des processus actuels.

Il semblerait que l'arcade dentaire des enfants n'attend pas l'âge de trois ans pour être complète. La rapidité du remplacement des temporaires par les permanentes, comme en témoignent les élaborations précoces des alvéoles et des couronnes, était plus accélérée que de nos jours. De plus, l'achèvement de la calcification des racines permanentes s'effectue à un âge beaucoup plus jeune que maintenant: tous les apex sont calcifiés vers 14/15 ans chez le premier sujet. L'horloge de l'évolution dentaire Proto-Magdalénienne est en avance sur la nôtre.

La présence simultanée d'alvéoles d'incisives temporaires et permanentes, d'un degré d'élaboration très voisin, est une constatation inhabituelle. Bien des signes actuels tendraient à démontrer que la région antérieure de la face serait le siège de lentes transformations, encore inachevées de nos jours. La diversité, peu explicable des opinions contradictoires émises sur l'ordre d'éruption des incisives pourrait en être un témoignage. La seule observation des contemporains étant insuffisante, l'étude du développement de ces alvéoles chez les enfants fossiles fournirait sans doute des observations de valeur.

Les anomalies. L'anomalie supérieure droite du premier sujet: deux molaires surnuméraires, est très rare. Bolender (1964) rapporte un cas de deux molaires temporaires supérieures gauches et Brabant (1963) publie un crâne gaulois montrant la gémination d'une paramolaire avec une seconde molaire supérieure gauche permanente.

L'anomalie supérieure droite du troisième sujet, une seconde prémolaire supérieure droite permanente, en évolution inversée, est une anastrophie. C'est le premier cas signalé en paléostomatologie et le troisième dans la littérature odontologique occidentale.

COMPARAISONS

I. Les Proto-Magdaléniens entre-eux

Les molaires permanentes ont un aspect morphologique semblable. Par contre, l'aspect des incisives latérales présente des variations. Nous relevons à la fois une tendance à la forme «en pelle» et une similitude parfaite avec la morphologie d'une centrale néandertalienne.

Les molaires temporaires ne présentent pas de variations dans leur morphologie.

II. Les Périgordiens et les Noailliens entre eux

Aucune comparaison ne peut être faite par carence d'éléments homologues.

III. Les Proto-Magdaléniens par rapport aux Périgordiens et aux Noailliens

L'élément Noaillien est trop usé pour qu'on puisse être affirmatif. Il semblerait cependant que l'aspect morphologique n'ait pas varié dans les molaires permanentes.

Il ne semble pas y avoir non plus de variations dans les molaires temporaires supérieures. On observe la même morphologie de type archaïque. Les dispositions fondamentales paraissent semblables dans les molaires inférieures, seules les dimensions sont très différentes. Il faut se garder de conclure à une évolution des dimensions, car l'âge de ces fossiles, pour l'un la naissance, pour l'autre 10/11 ans, présente un trop grand écart.

Par contre, les incisives centrales temporaires gauches des Proto-Magdaléniens et des Périgordiens conservent, malgré les millénaires qui les séparent, le même aspect archaïque que l'on trouve déjà chez les Néandertaliens du Pech de l'Azé ou du Roc-Marsal.

IV. Le sujet n° 1, Proto-Magdalénien, par rapport à d'autres fossiles Magdaléniens

Les différences sont considérables. Toutes les dimensions de l'Abri Pataud sont plus fortes que celles des fossiles de comparaison: Abri Lachaud, Magdalénien ancien, Cap-Blanc, Magdalénien supérieur, Farincourt, Magdalénien final. De plus, au point de vue morphologique, l'archaïsme de l'Abri Pataud est mis en évidence.

Il est permis de prétendre:

1° Pour les molaires

(a) que la jeune femme de l'Abri Pataud présente non seulement des caractères archaïques, mais aussi un mélange très complexe, différant totalement et de l'aspect actuel et de l'aspect des autres Magdaléniens.

(b) que les trois autres fossiles de comparaison, malgré la différence de temps qui les sépare, présentent une ressemblance nette avec la morphologie des dents contemporaines.

2°. Pour les prémolaires

(a) que celles de l'Abri Pataud, tout en ayant des dimensions supérieures, ont une morphologie voisine des prémolaires actuelles.

b) que celles des trois autres fossiles, non seulement sont semblables à celles de l'*Homo sapiens*, mais annonceraient même une tendance à la réduction.

3°. Pour les incisives

que la morphologie et la taille de ces dents était déjà variable au Proto-Magdalénien et le sont encore actuellement.

V. Les dents temporaires des divers fossiles de l'Abri Pataud et celles d'autres fossiles Magdaléniens

Le regroupement des dents temporaires de cette période n'est pas encore ébauché. Leur étude est incomplète, car elles sont souvent seulement signalées. Quant aux références générales actuelles, elles sont encore fragmentaires. Une recherche ultérieure plus complète sera faite à ce sujet.

VI. Les dents permanentes de l'Abri Pataud comparées à celles de fossiles Néandertaliens et Aurignacien

De la comparaison des dimensions relevées dans les tableaux 12 et 13, il apparaît que le premier sujet de l'Abri Pataud s'inscrit dans les variations présentées par les fossiles de La Quina, du Moustier, Néandertaliens, et de Combe-Capelle, Aurignacien.

La morphologie présente également beaucoup de points communs. Cependant, il faut remarquer que sauf deux exceptions, dans les molaires inférieures de comparaison, tous les Ø MD sont plus grands que les

Ø VL. Or c'est l'inverse pour l'Abri Pataud, sauf une exception. Serait-ce un témoignage de variation dans les séries molaires?

Dans les séries des prémolaires, les dents de l'Abri Pataud sont plus petites et leur morphologie, plus semblable à la contemporaine, s'écarte franchement des dents néandertaliennes.

Quant à l'incisive G2 elle est nettement semblable à celles des fossiles plus anciens avec cependant encore une étonnante différence en diminution dans le Ø VL.

Pour fixer mathématiquement tous les éléments de comparaison entre les dents de l'Abri Pataud et celles des fossiles magdaléniens et antérieurs les tableaux 14, 15, 16, 17, et 18 donnent les mesures des modules, des valeurs de surface et des indices de la couronne. Les appréciations qui ont pu être faites sont ainsi traduites en chiffres, effaçant les approximations, pour traduire des réalités faciles à comparer avec les tableaux 6, 7, 8, et 9 (pp. 294-296).

VII. Comparaison générales entre le sujet N°1 de l'Abri Pataud, les fossiles Magdaléniens, les fossiles Aurignacien et Néandertaliens et une population d'âge franc de Coxyde (Belgique).

Pour qu'une comparaison soit valable entre les fossiles étudiés et l'Homme récent, il fallait disposer d'une publication sur une population assez nombreuse et pour laquelle les moyennes, les écarts types et les déviations standard aient été calculés. A partir de ces données, il devient possible de dresser des tableaux qui permettent d'estimer les différences entre les valeurs moyennes des caractères d'un individu et d'une population.

Une seule étude est présentée sous cette forme en Europe occidentale. C'est celle d'une population d'âge franc de Coxyde en Belgique (Twiesselmann et Brabant 1967). Elle servira donc de base à nos comparaisons.

Toutes les valeurs des σ ont été calculées pour tous les fossiles et sont exprimées dans les tableaux 19 à 27 (pp. 301-305). Elles permettent des constatations fort intéressantes:

1°. Ø MD – Maxillaire. Pour l'Abri Pataud, les molaires de droite (ne pas oublier que ce sont les plus contraintes par les dents surnuméraires) et les prémolaires s'inscrivent entre + 2 et + 3 σ, soit à la limite supérieure de variation. Par contre à gauche où elles se sont épanouies sans contrainte, la M1, la M2, et la G2, au delà de 3 σ, franchissent la limite de variation.

Le Cap-Blanc et Combe-Capelle varient entre + 2 σ et - 2,50 σ, le premier confirmant sa tendance vers une réduction dans la forme *Homo sapiens*, le second ses caractères de variabilité en plus ou en moins, mais à l'intérieur des variations possibles pour des dents présentant les caractères humains actuels.

Quant aux Néandertaliens, La Quina a des molaires dont les dimensions sont variables mais s'écartent peu des moyennes de Coxyde, alors que ses autres dents s'en écartent fortement; Le Moustier, sauf les canines qui sont à la limite de la variation supérieure, est totalement en dehors de la limite supérieure de + 3 σ.

2°. Ø VP – Maxillaire. Seules D7, D4, G4, G7 et G8 de l'Abri Pataud franchissent la limite de + 3 σ. Le reste est très voisin de la limite supérieure.

Le Cap-Blanc et Combe-Capelle varient très harmonieusement autour de la moyenne de Coxyde entre + 2,50 σ et - 1 σ.

Le Moustier et La Quina sortent pratiquement de la limite supérieure de + 3 σ.

3°. Ø MD – Mandibule. L'Abri Pataud voisine la limite supérieure avec cependant une chute pour la première molaire.

Le Cap-Blanc et Farincourt s'inscrivent dans les variations négatives de σ, les canines de ce dernier dépassent même la limite - 3 σ. L'Abri Lachaud reste régulièrement au dessus de la moyenne de Coxyde, sauf d2. Il est très voisin de l'Abri Pataud dans la série molaires.

Combe-Capelle varie fortement au dessus et en dessous de la moyenne. Le Moustier et La Quina voisinent ou dépassent fréquemment la limite + 3 σ.

4°. Ø VL – Mandibule. L'Abri Pataud s'inscrit ici nettement, avec les Néandertaliens, au dessus de la limite de + 3 σ, atteignant + 5 σ pour d8.

Les Magdaléniens s'harmonisent au dessus et au dessous de la moyenne de Coxyde et l'Abri Lachaud est ici très différent de l'Abri Pataud.

Combe-Capelle a un côté molaire droit qui dépasse + 3 σ sauf la d8, un groupe incisif de même valeur de variation que la moyenne de Coxyde et un côté molaire gauche dépassant à peine + 2 σ.

Ces tableaux étayent encore les appréciations que l'on pouvait faire sur les dents de l'Abri Pataud. Les chiffres prouvent nettement que les variations des dimensions des dents de ce fossile ont beaucoup plus de points communs avec celles des Néandertaliens qu'avec celles des Magdaléniens et s'écartent assez nettement des caractères actuels.

CONCLUSIONS

L'étude odontologique des fossiles de l'Abri Pataud met en évidence une masse de renseignements, souvent inhabituels et parfois contradictoires. Les lacunes dans les incisives et les canines permanentes, l'absence de séries dans les éléments temporaires, ne permettent pas une appréciation complète des caractéristiques relevées. En outre, on est forcé de constater que les renseignements sur les dents contemporaines ne sont pas toujours suffisants pour faire nettement ressortir les divergences. Enfin, les études sur les autres fossiles sont la plupart du temps trop succinctes pour qu'on puisse s'y référer sans qu'un doute subsiste.

Il n'en résulte pas moins qu'au point de vue morphologique on peut prétendre que le premier sujet de l'Abri Pataud s'écarte nettement, dans les séries molaires, et de l'homme actuel et des Magdaléniens qui le suivront. Les plus grandes dimensions, la disposition et le nombre des cuspides, l'inversion très nette à la mandibule du $\emptyset$ VL $>$ $\emptyset$ MD, sont des preuves évidentes d'un archaïsme que les tableaux de comparaisons font parfaitement voisiner avec les Néandertaliens. Par contre, l'aspect des prémolaires est, sauf encore les dimensions, beaucoup plus voisin de la morphologie actuelle. Quant à la seule incisive permanente, elle est de dimensions et de forme archaïque. Un mélange de caractères apparaît donc à cette époque.

La pathologie des sujets ne laisse pas également de surprendre. Les surnuméraires, l'ectopie des troisièmes molaires, l'anastrophie, autant d'affections qu'on retrouve çà et là et encore exceptionnellement, dans le cours des temps, mais pas ainsi groupées dans une population aussi réduite. Ou bien il s'agit d'un lot de malades, ce qu'aucun autre signe ne laisse supposer, ou bien ces anomalies sont des témoignages d'évolution.

La physiologie de la mastication prouve d'ailleurs que ces sujets présentent un orthognatisme naturel très net. Si leur alimentation ou leur mode de vie provoquaient une usure précoce des éléments dentaires, il semble que leur développement ait été vigoureux, leur sevrage précoce, enfin qu'aucun signe anormal puisse faire penser à des êtres déficients, sous-alimentés ou en dégénérescence.

Quoique l'ontogénèse actuelle ne soit pas encore suffisamment précisée, on peut cependant certifier que celle de ces individus était plus précoce et certainement plus accélérée. La plus belle preuve en est la calcification des apex des troisièmes molaires, alors que les secondes ne présentent pour ainsi dire pas de trace d'usure et que l'on sait que l'alimentation était coriace. Non seulement les éruptions devaient être plus précoces, mais les remplacements des temporaires par les permanentes devaient être accélérés.

Il ne fait pas de doute que l'ensemble des caractères du sujet N° 1 de l'Abri Pataud est fort différent de la moyenne des contemporains. Les tableaux de comparaison avec la population de Coxyde démontrent que les variations sont toutes situées vers la limite supérieure, quand elles ne la dépassent pas. A ce point du vue, il est très intéressant de constater que les Néandertaliens s'en écartent également fortement. Le fossile Aurignacien de comparaison présente lui de très grandes variations dans les deux sens, comme s'il était le témoignage de grands changements encore mal coordonnés. Il faut aussi constater que le fossile de l'Abri Lachaud est celui qui se rapproche le plus de l'Abri Pataud, sans voisiner autant les Néandertaliens, et qu'il diffère également nettement des autres Magdaléniens plus récents.

Toutes ces observations qui reposent sur des appréciations contrôlées par des tableaux de rapports, pourraient faire prétendre que vers la période Aurignacienne, des transformations apparaissent dans la morphologie dentaire du phylum humain. Les caractères archaïques des dents néandertaliennes demeurent encore mais en se modifiant. Certains s'effacent dans certaines séries dentaires seulement, les dimensions diminuent, mais pas pour tous les éléments ni dans tous les diamètres. Une évolution vers une morphologie dentaire simplifiée deviendrait plus nette vers le Proto-Magdalénien pour s'affirmer ensuite.

D'autres recoupements et des études comparatives plus poussées seront encore nécessaires, mais la découverte des restes humains de l'Abri Pataud sont d'une importance primordiale pour la compréhension de l'évolution de l'humanité. Si, comme tout semble le démontrer des individus de la période Proto-Magdalénienne présentent des caractères intermédiaires entre les Néandertaliens, les Magdaléniens et les hommes contemporains, ils sont le témoignage d'un sens d'évolution qui ne serait plus contestable.

Abri Pataud
PROTO-MAGDALENIEN
Mesures en mm

PREMIER SUJET
"La jeune femme"
MAXILLAIRE

Tableau 1

Dents	Plus grand ø V.P.	Plus grand ø M.D.	Plus petit ø V.P.	Plus petit ø M.D.	Haut. FV	Haut. FP	Haut. FM	Haut. FD	Face occlus. ø M.D.°°°	Face occlus. ø V.P.°°° M D
D 8	12,9	9,9	10,3°	6,2	7°	non mesur.	non mesur.	5,9	7,2	4,6 4,2
D 7	13	10,9	11	8	9	8,3	6,8	6,6	7,7	5,9 6,1
D 6	12,5	11	10,3	8,6	7,7	7,1	6,2	7,3	8,7	5,8 5,5
D 5	10,2	7,2	8	4,5	8,2*	7,7	5,4	5,5	5,5	5,5
D 4	10,5	7,3	8,3	4,3	8,5	7,2	5,5	4,8	5,3	5,2
D7 1ère surnum.	4,3	7	non mesur.	5,7	8,4	non mesur.	7,9	7,9	non mesur.	non mesur.
D7 2ème surnum.	7,8	6,5	7,1	5,3°°	9,1**	10,1	9,5	8,5	conoïde	conoïde
G 8	13	10,2	9	6,3	8,8	8	8	7,3	7	6,3 5,8
G 7	13,5	11,7	10,6	7,6	8,7	7,7	6,2	7,4	8,5	7,5 7,6
G 6	12,3	12	10,7	7,9	7,3	6,7	5,1	6,2	9	6,2 6
G 5	10,3	7,2	8,1	4,2	7,5	7	5,7	5,5	6	5,5
G 4	10,5	7,5	8,5	4,6	8,5	7	5,5	5,3	5,5	4,9
G 2	7	8,5	6,2	7	9,6***	10,5	6,4	6,7	7,6	1,6

° A titre indicatif, les faces vestibulaire et palatine n'étant pas entièrement dégagées.
°° Approximatif, car l'éclatement de la racine peut avoir gonflé légèrement le côté mésial.
°°° Lorsque la face occlusale est peu usée, le diamètre est pris au sommet des cuspides. Lorsqu'elle l'est, la mesure est faite au niveau des sommets usés des cuspides.
* Longueur de la racine (éclatée et brisée à l'apex): 11,7.
** Longueur de la racine (éclatée): 13,5 (environ).
*** Longueur de la racine: 11,9.

Tableau 2

PREMIER SUJET
"La jeune femme"
MANDIBULE

Abri Pataud
PROTO-MAGDALENIEN

Dents	Plus grand Ø V.L.	Plus grand Ø M.D.	Plus petit Ø V.L.	Plus petit Ø M.D.	Haut. FV	Haut. FL	Haut. FM	Haut. FD	Face occlus. Ø M.D. V	Face occlus. Ø M.D. L	Face occlus. Ø V.L. M	Face occlus. Ø V.L. D
d 8	12,9	12,5	10	10	8,8	7,3	6,4	5,4	9,4		6,5	7,3
d 7	12,2	11,7	8,1	9	8,6	7,7	6,1	8,1	10,1		6,1	6,4
d 6	11,9	11,7	7,7	8,8	7,7	7,2	5,5	6	9,7		6,9*	6,5*
d 4	8,7	7,7	6,6	4,7	8,2	5,8	5	5,2	6,6	3,5	4,3	
g 8	12,8	12,5	9,5	8,7	8,7	7,5	6,4	5,2	9,3		5,1	8,1
g 7	12,2	11,8	8,3	9,4	8	7,4	6,4	6,6	10,1		6,1	6
g 6	11,9	11,9	7,8	8,5	7	6,8	5,5	5,5	9,7		7,3*	7*
g 4	8,7	7,7	6,5	4,9	8,5	5,5	5,5	5,5	6,3	4,6	4,8	

*Les mesures sur ces faces usées sont très approximatives.

Abri Pataud
PROTO-MAGDALENIEN

Tableau 3

DEUXIEME SUJET
Quatre dents temporaires

Dents	Plus grand ∅ V.L.	Plus grand ∅ M.D.	Plus petit ∅ V.L.	Plus petit ∅ M.D.	Hauteur F.V. M	Hauteur F.V. D	Hauteur F.L. M	Hauteur F.L. D	Hauteur F.M.	Hauteur F.D.	Largeur entre cuspides M.	Largeur au centre	Largeur entre cuspides D.
d V	8,8	10,8	8,2	8,6	5,7	4,6	5,2	4,7	4,5	2,8	4,1	6	4,5
g V	8,3	10,1	non mesurable		5,2	4,1	non mesurable		4,5	non mesurable	4	non mesurable	
D III	3,3	6,4				4,2	2,9*		non mesurable				
G V	9,4	9,2	7,9	7	5	5	5,6	3,9	4,4	2,3	5,1	6,1	6,1

TROISIEME SUJET
Dents de la portion du maxillaire supérieur droit

Dents	Plus grand ∅ V.L.	Plus grand ∅ M.D.	Plus petit ∅ V.L.	Plus petit ∅ M.D.	Hauteur F.V. M	Hauteur F.V. D	Hauteur F.L. M	Hauteur F.L. D	Hauteur F.M.	Hauteur F.D.	Largeur entre cuspides M.	Largeur au centre	Largeur entre cuspides D.
D V	11,2	9,4	9,7	7,5	6,6	6,7	6,8	6,2	4,7	4,9	5,4	5,5	6,6
D IV	9,9	7,5	7	5,5	6,2	5	5,5	4,4	4	3,7	5,7	4,2	4,2
D 6	12,5	10,9	11	7	8	8,2	8,8	8,5	5,5	5,6	6,5	7 bord libre	6,1
D 2	6,7	6,6	non mesurable				9,7		non mesurable			2,2	

*Fracturée.

Tableau 4

Abri Pataud
PROTO-MAGDALENIEN

QUATRIEME SUJET
Deux incisives temporaires supérieures

Dents	Plus grand ⌀ V.P.	Plus grand ⌀ M.D.	Plus petit ⌀ V.P.	Plus petit ⌀ M.D.	Hauteur F.V.	Hauteur F.P.	Hauteur F.M.	Hauteur F.D.	Longueur racine	Longueur totale
D II	5,5	5,9	4,6	4,8	5,9	7,2	4,3	3	10,6	16,5
G I	5,7	7,3	4,4	5,6	5,5	7,1	5,5	5	10,2	15,7

CINQUIEME SUJET
Molaire temporaire inférieure

	Plus grand ⌀ V.P.	Plus grand ⌀ M.D.	Plus petit ⌀ V.P.	Plus petit ⌀ M.D.	Hauteur F.V.		Hauteur F.P.		Hauteur F.M.	Hauteur F.D.	Largeur entre cuspides M.	Largeur au centre	Largeur entre cuspides D.
					M	D	M	D					
g V	7,7	10	non mesur.	8,5	4,7	3,8	4,5	4,2	3,6	2,5	4	6	4,7

Tableau 5

Abri Pataud
PÉRIGORDIEN

Dents	Plus grand ⌀ V.P.	Plus grand ⌀ M.D.	Plus petit ⌀ V.P.	Plus petit ⌀ M.D.	Hauteur F.V.		Hauteur F.P.		Hauteur F.M.	Hauteur F.D.	Longueur racine F.V.	Longueur totale
					M	D	M	D				
SIXIEME SUJET — Un débris de molaire temporaire supérieure (?)												
G V(?)	10,3	7	10		5,8		4,9			3,8(?)		
SEPTIEME SUJET — Une incisive temporaire supérieure												
G I	5,4	7	4,6	5,1	6,6		7		5,8	5,1	9,2	15,8
HUITIEME SUJET — Une couronne de molaire temporaire inférieure (1)												
NOAILLIEN												
g V	9,6	10,4	6,8	8,3	4	3	4,7	4,8	3,5	3,6		
NEUVIEME SUJET — Une molaire permanente inférieure (1)												
NOAILLIEN												
d 6	11,7	11	9,9	10	Fracturée	2,2	3,8	3,4	3,3	2,5		

(1) Mesures approximatives.

Tableau 6

Abri Pataud
PROTO-MAGDALENIEN

PREMIER SUJET
"La jeune femme"

MODULE: $\dfrac{\text{Ø MD} + \text{Ø VL}}{2}$ VALEUR DE SURFACE: Ø MD x Ø VL INDICE DE LA COURONNE: $\dfrac{\text{Ø VL x 100}}{\text{Ø MD}}$

Dents	D 8	D 7	D 6	D 5	D 4	G 2	G 4	G 5	G 6	G 7	G 8
Module	11,40	11,95	11,75	8,70	8,90	7,75	9	8,75	12,15	12,60	11,60
Valeur de Surface	127,71	141,70	137,50	73,44	76,65	59,50	78,75	74,16	147,60	157,95	132,60
Indice de la Couronne	130,30	119,26	113,63	141,66	143,83	82,35	140	143,05	102,50	115,38	127,45

	d 8	d 7	d 6		d 4		g 4		g 6	g 7	g 8
Module	12,70	11,95	11,80		8,20		8,20		11,90	12	12,65
Valeur de Surface	161,25	142,74	139,23		66,99		66,99		141,61	143,96	160
Indice de la Couronne	103,20	104,27	101,70		112,98		112,98		100	103,38	102,40

Abri Pataud   **DEUXIEME SUJET**   Tableau 7

PROTO-MAGDALENIEN   Quatre dents temporaires

MODULE–VALEUR DE SURFACE–INDICE DE LA COURONNE

Dents	d V	g V	DIII	G V
Module	9,8	9,2	4,85	9,3
Valeur de Surface	95,04	83,83	21,72	86,48
Indice de la Couronne	81,48	82,17	51,56	102,17

TROISIEME SUJET

Dents de la portion de maxillaire supérieur droit

Dents	D V	D IV	D 6	D 2
Module	10,3	8,7	11,7	6,65
Valeur de Surface	105,28	74,25	136,25	44,22
Indice de la Couronne	119,14	132	114,67	101,51

Abri Pataud   **QUATRIEME SUJET**   Tableau 8
PROTO-MAGDALENIEN

MODULE–VALEUR DE SURFACE–INDICE DE LA COURONNE

Dents	D II	G I
Module	5,7	6,5
Valeur de Surface	32,45	41,61
Indice de la Couronne	93,22	78,08

CINQUIEME SUJET

Dent	g V
Module	8,85
Valeur de Surface	77
Indice de la Couronne	77

Abri Pataud **SEPTIEME SUJET** Tableau 9
PERIGORDIEN

MODULE–VALEUR DE SURFACE–INDICE DE LA COURONNE

Dent	G I
Module	6,20
Valeur de Surface	37,80
Indice de la Couronne	77,14

NOAILLIEN **HUITIEME SUJET**

Dent	g V
Module	10
Valeur de Surface	99,84
Indice de la Couronne	92,30

NOAILLIEN **NEUVIEME SUJET**

Dent	d 6
Module	11,35
Valeur de Surface	128,70
Indice de la Couronne	106,36

Abri Pataud Tableau 10

Comparaison des ∅ M.D. et ∅ V.P. des
dents de maxillaires magdaléniens

Dents	Cap-Blanc		Abri Pataud	
	∅ M.D.	∅ V.P.	∅ M.D.	∅ V.P.
D 8			9,90	12,90
D 7	9	11,20	10,90	13
D 6	9,60	11,40	11	12,50
D 5	6	9	7,20	10,20
D 4	6,30	9,20	7,30	10,50
D 3	7	8		
D 2	6,10	6,10		
D 1	7,20	7		
G 1	7	7		
G 2	6	6,20	8,50	7
G 3	7	8,10		
G 4	5,50	9,20	7,50	10,50
G 5	6	9,20	7,20	10,30
G 6	10	11,50	12	12,30
G 7	8,90	12	11,70	13,50
G 8			10,20	13

Abri Pataud   Tableau 11

Comparaison des ∅ M.D. et ∅ V.L. des dents de mandibules magdaléniennes

Dents	Farincourt		Abri Lachaud		Cap-Blanc		Abri Pataud	
	∅ M.D.	∅ V.L.	∅ M.D.	∅ V.L.	∅ M.D.	∅ V.L.	∅ M.D.	∅ V.L.
d 8			11,20	9,60			12,50	12,90
d 7	9,40	8,70	11,10	9,60	9,20	10,10	11,70	12,20
d 6	10	9,50	11	10,30	9,80	10,30	11,70	11,90
d 5	6,50	7,30	7	8	6	8,50		
d 4	6,60	7,20	7	7,80	5,80	7,60	7,70	8,70
d 3	5	7,30	7,20	8,20	5,80	7,30		
d 2	5,50	6,30	5,40	6,40	5	6,10		
d 1	4,40	5,60	5,30	6,30	4,10	5,10		
g 1	4,40	5,70	5,70	6,20	4	5,20		
g 2	5,20	6,40	6	7	5	6		
g 3	5,10	7,40	7,40	8,30	6	7,20		
g 4	6,50	7	7,40	7,90	6	7,60	7,70	8,70
g 5	6,50	7	7,50	8,10	6,20	8,10		
g 6	10,30	9,30	11,10	10,40	10,20	10,20	11,90	11,90
g 7	9,80	8,70	11,20	9,70	9,10	10,10	11,80	12,20
g 8	9,30	9,10	11,80	9,40			12,50	12,80

Abri Pataud   **MAXILLAIRE**   Tableau 12

Comparaison des ∅ M.D. et ∅ V.P. de l'ABRI PATAUD et de fossiles antérieurs

Dents	La Quina		Le Moustier		Combe-Capelle		Abri Pataud	
	∅ M.D.	∅ V.P.	∅ M.D.	∅ V.P.	∅ M.D.	∅ V.P.	∅ M.D.	∅ V.P.
D 8	9,50	14,50	11	12	8	11,50	9,90	12,90
D 7	10	14	11,50	13	10,50	12	10,90	13
D 6	10,50	12,50	12	12,50	10	12	11	12,50
D 5	8	10,60	8	11	6,50	9	7,20	10,20
D 4	8,30	11,20	8	10,50	6	9	7,30	10,50
D 3	9	10	9	10	7	9		
D 2			9	9	5	6		
D 1	9	8,50	12	8	9	6,80		
G 1			11,50	8	9	7,50		
G 2	8,50	9	8,50	9	6	6	8,50	7
G 3	8,50	10	9	10	8	9		
G 4	9	11	8	10,50	6	9	7,50	10,50
G 5	7,30	10,50	8	11	6	8,50	7,20	10,30
G 6	10,50	13	12	12,50	10,50	12	12	12,30
G 7	10	14	11,50	13	10,80	12	11,70	13,50
G 8	9,60	13,50	9	11	8,20	11	10,20	13

Abri Pataud   **MANDIBULE**   Tableau 13

Comparaison des ∅ M.D. et ∅ V.L. de l'ABRI PATAUD et de fossiles antérieurs

Dents	La Quina		Le Moustier		Combe-Capelle		Abri Pataud	
	∅ M.D.	∅ V.L.	∅ M.D.	∅ V.L.	∅ M.D.	∅ V.L.	∅ M.D.	∅ V.L.
d 8	11,50	13	13	11	10	10	12,50	12,90
d 7	12,50	12	12,50	11,60	12	11,50	11,70	12,20
d 6	12	11,50	12,50	11,80	12	12	11,70	11,90
d 5	8	10	8,20	10,50	7	9,50		
d 4	7,20	10	8	10	6	9	7,70	8,70
d 3			8,60	9,50	7	9		
d 2			6,60	7,80	5	6		
d 1			6	7,20	5	6		
g 1			6,90	7,50	5	6		
g 2			6,60	7,50	6	6,50		
g 3	8,50	9	8		8	8		
g 4	8,30	10	8	9,60	6	7	7,70	8,70
g 5	8,50	10	8,30	10,20	7	8		
g 6	12	11,50	12,40	11,50	12	11	11,90	11,90
g 7	12,30	12	12,50	11,60	11,50	11	11,80	12,20
g 8	11,50	12			11	11	12,50	12,80

Abri Pataud   **DENTS MAGDALENIENNES**   Tableau 14

MODULE–VALEUR DE SURFACE–INDICE DE LA COURONNE

MAXILLAIRE

Dents		D8	D 7	D 6	D 5	D 4	D 3	D 2	D 1
Cap-Blanc	Mod		10,10	10,50	7,50	7,75	7,50	6,10	7,10
	Sur		100,80	109,44	54	57,96	56	37,21	50,40
	Ind		124,44	118,75	150	146,03	114,28	100	97,22
		G 8	G 7	G 6	G 5	G 4	G 3	G 2	G 1
Cap-Blanc	Mod		10,45	10,75	7,60	7,35	7,55	6,10	7
	Sur		106,80	115	55,20	50,60	56,70	37,20	49
	Ind		134,83	115	153,33	167,27	115,71	103,33	100

Abri Pataud **DENTS MAGDALENIENNES** Tableau 15

MODULE–VALEUR DE SURFACE–INDICE DE LA COURONNE

MANDIBULE

COTE DROIT

Dents		d 8	d 7	d 6	d 5	d 4	d 3	d 2	d 1
Farin-Court	Mod		9,05	9,75	6,90	6,90	6,15	5,90	5
	Sur		81,78	95	47,45	47,52	36,50	34,65	24,64
	Ind		92,55	95	112,30	109,09	146	114,54	127,27
Abri Lachaud	Mod	10,40	10,35	10,65	7,50	7,40	7,70	5,90	5,80
	Sur	107,52	106,56	113,30	56	54,60	59,04	34,56	33,39
	Ind	85,71	86,48	93,63	114,28	111,42	113,88	118,51	118,86
Cap-Blanc	Mod		9,65	10,05	7,25	6,70	6,55	5,55	4,60
	Sur		92,92	100,94	51	44,08	42,34	30,50	20,91
	Ind		109,78	105,10	141,66	131,03	125,86	122	124,39

Abri Pataud **DENTS MAGDALENIENNES** Tableau 16

MODULE–VALEUR DE SURFACE–INDICE DE LA COURONNE

MANDIBULE

COTE GAUCHE

Dents		g 8	g 7	g 6	g 5	g 4	g 3	g 2	g 1
Farin-Court	Mod	9,20	9,25	9,80	6,75	6,75	6,25	5,80	5,05
	Sur	84,63	85,26	95,79	45,50	45,50	37,74	33,28	25,08
	Ind	97,84	88,77	90,29	107,69	107,69	145,09	123,07	129,54
Abri Lachaud	Mod	10,60	10,45	10,75	7,80	7,65	7,85	6,50	5,95
	Sur	110,92	108,64	115,44	60,75	58,46	61,42	42	35,34
	Ind	79,66	86,60	93,69	108	106,75	112,16	116,66	108,77
Cap-Blanc	Mod		9,60	10,20	7,15	6,80	6,60	5,50	4,60
	Sur		91,91	104,04	50,22	45,60	43,20	30	20,80
	Ind		110,98	100	130,64	126,66	120	120	130

Abri Pataud

FOSSILES ANTERIEURS

Tableau 17

MODULE–VALEUR DE SURFACE–INDICE DE LA COURONNE

MAXILLAIRE

		D 8	D 7	D 6	D 5	D 4	D 3	D 2	D 1
La Quina	Mod	12	12	11,50	9,30	9,75	9,50		8,75
	Sur	137,75	140	131,25	84,80	92,96	90		76,50
	Ind	152,63	140	119,04	132,50	134,93	111,11		94,44
Le Moustier	Mod	11,50	12,25	12,25	9,50	9,25	9,50	9	10
	Sur	132	149,50	150	88	84	90	81	96
	Ind	109,09	113,04	104,16	137,50	131,25	111,11	100	66,66
Combe-Capelle	Mod	9,75	11,25	11	7,75	7,50	8	5,50	7,90
	Sur.	92	126	120	58,50	54	63	30	61,20
	Ind	143,75	114,28	120	138,46	150	128,57	120	75,55

		G 8	G 7	G 6	G 5	G 4	G 3	G 2	G 1
La Quina	Mod	11,55	12	11,75	8,90	10	9,25	8,75	
	Sur	129,60	140	136,50	76,65	99	85	76,50	
	Ind	140,62	140	123,80	143,83	122,22	117,64	105,88	
Le Moustier	Mod	10	12,25	12,25	9,50	9,25	9,50	8,75	9,75
	Sur	99	149,50	150	88	84	90	76,50	92
	Ind	122,22	113,04	104,16	137,50	131,25	111,11	105,88	69,56
Combe-Capelle	Mod	9,60	11,40	11,25	7,25	7,50	8,50	6	8,25
	Sur	90,20	129,60	126	51	54	72	36	67,50
	Ind	134,14	111,11	114,28	141,66	150	112,50	100	83,33

Abri Pataud

FOSSILES ANTERIEURS

Tableau 18

MODULE–VALEUR DE SURFACE–INDICE DE LA COURONNE

MANDIBULE

		d 8	d 7	d 6	d 5	d 4	d 3	d 2	d 1
La Quina	Mod	12,25	12,25	11,75	9	8,60			
	Sur	149,50	150	138	80	72			
	Ind	113,04	96	95,83	125	138,88			
Le Moustier	Mod	12	12,05	12,15	9,35	9	9,05	7,20	6,60
	Sur	143	145	147,50	86,10	80	81,70	51,48	43,20
	Ind	84,61	92,80	94,40	128,04	125	110,46	118,18	120
Combe-Capelle	Mod	10	11,75	12	8 25	7,50	8	5,50	5,50
	Sur	100	138	144	66,50	54	63	30	30
	Ind	100	95,83	100	135,71	150	128,57	120	120

		g 8	g 7	g 6	g 5	g 4	g 3	g 2	g 1
La Quina	Mod	11,75	12,15	11,75	9,25	9,15	8,75		
	Sur	138	147,60	138	85	83	76,50		
	Ind	104,34	97,56	95,83	117,64	120,48	105,88		
Le Moustier	Mod		12,05	11,95	9,25	8,80		7,05	7,20
	Sur		145	142,60	84,66	76,80		49,50	51,75
	Ind		92,80	92,74	122,89	120		113,63	108,69
Combe-Capelle	Mod	11	11,25	11,50	7,50	6,50	8	6,25	5,50
	Sur	121	126,50	132	56	42	64	39	30
	Ind	100	95,65	91,66	114,28	116,66	100	108,33	120

Abri Pataud

Tableau 19

Ø MD – DENTS PERMANENTES – MAXILLAIRE

COTE DROIT

Valeur de $\sigma \rightarrow$ COXYDE

Dents	D 8		D 7		D 6		D 5		D 4		D 3		D 2		D 1	
	M Ø MD	SD	M Ø MD	SD	M Ø MD	SD	M Ø MD	SD	M Ø MD	SD	M Ø MD	SD	M Ø MD	SD	M Ø MD	SD
Coxyde	8,32	0,94	8,86	0,78	10,00	0,57	6,33	0,41	6,47	0,40	7,60	0,49	6,43	0,57	8,30	0,51
	Ø MD	σ	Ø MD	σ	Ø MD	σ	Ø MD	σ	Ø MD	σ	Ø MD	σ	Ø MD	σ	Ø MD	σ
Cap-Blanc			9,00	+0,17	9,60	-0,70	6,00	-0,80	6,30	-0,42	7,00	-1,22	6,10	-0,57	7,20	-2,15
Combe-Capelle	8,00	-0,34	10,50	+2,10	10,00	0	6,50	+0,41	6,00	-1,17	7,00	-1,22	5,00	-2,50	9,00	+1,37
Le Moustier	11,00	+2,85	11,50	+3,38	12,00	+3,50	8,00	+4,07	8,00	+3,82	9,00	+2,85	9,00	+4,50	12,00	+7,25
La Quina	9,50	+1,25	10,00	+1,46	10,50	+0,87	8,00	+4,07	8,30	+4,57	9,00	+2,85			9,00	+1,37
Abri Pataud	9,90	+1,68	10,90	+2,61	11,00	+1,75	7,20	+2,12	7,30	+2,07						

Abri Pataud

Tableau 20

Ø MD – DENTS PERMANENTES – MAXILLAIRE

COTE GAUCHE

Valeur de $\sigma \rightarrow$ COXYDE

Dents	G 8		G 7		G 6		G 5		G 4		G 3		G 2		G 1	
	M Ø MD	SD	M Ø MD	SD	M Ø MD	SD	M Ø MD	SD	M Ø MD	SD	M Ø MD	SD	M Ø MD	SD	M Ø MD	SD
Coxyde	8,32	0,94	8,86	0,78	10,00	0,57	6,63	0,41	6,47	0,40	7,60	0,49	6,43	0,57	8,30	0,51
	Ø MD	σ	Ø MD	σ	Ø MD	σ	Ø MD	σ	Ø MD	σ	Ø MD	σ	Ø MD	σ	Ø MD	σ
Cap-Blanc			8,90	+0,05	10,00	0	6,00	-1,53	5,50	-2,42	7,00	-1,22	6,00	-0,75	7,00	-2,54
Combe-Capelle	8,20	-0,13	10,80	+2,48	10,50	+0,87	6,00	-1,53	6,00	-1,18	8,00	+0,81	6,00	-0,75	9,00	+1,37
Le Moustier	9,00	+0,72	11,50	+3,38	12,00	+3,50	8,00	+3,34	8,00	+3,82	9,00	+2,85	8,50	+3,63	11,50	+6,27
La Quina	9,60	+1,36	10,00	+1,46	10,50	+0,87	7,30	+1,63	9,00	+6,32	8,50	+1,83	8,50	+3,63		
Abri Pataud	10,20	+2,00	11,70	+3,64	12,00	+3,50	7,20	+1,39	7,50	+2,57			8,50	+3,63		

Abri Pataud   Tableau 21

Ø VP – DENTS PERMANENTES – MAXILLAIRE
Valeur de σ → COXYDE

COTE DROIT

Dents	D 1 M Ø VP	SD	D 2 M Ø VP	SD	D 3 M Ø VP	SD	D 4 M Ø VP	SD	D 5 M Ø VP	SD	D 6 M Ø VP	SD	D 7 M Ø VP	SD	D 8 M Ø VP	SD
Coxyde	7,10	0,45	6,21	0,50	8,33	0,58	8,59	0,59	8,81	0,60	11,22	0,50	10,65	0,71	10,13	0,92
	Ø VP	σ	Ø VP	σ	Ø VP	σ	Ø VP	σ	Ø VP	σ	Ø VP	σ	Ø VP	σ	Ø VP	σ
Cap-Blanc	7,00	-0,22	6,10	-0,22	8,00	-0,56	9,20	+1,03	9,00	+0,31	11,40	+0,36	11,20	+0,77		
Combe-Capelle	6,80	-0,66	6,00	-0,42	9,00	+1,15	9,00	+0,69	9,00	+0,31	12,00	+1,56	12,00	+1,90	11,50	+1,49
Le Moustier	8,00	+2,00	9,00	+5,58	10,00	+2,87	10,50	+3,23	11,00	+3,65	12,50	+2,56	13,00	+3,30	12,00	+2,03
La Quina	8,50	+3,11			10,00	+2,87	11,20	+4,42	10,60	+2,98	12,50	+2,56	14,00	+4,71	14,50	+4,75
Abri Pataud							10,50	+3,23	10,20	+2,31	12,50	+2,56	13,00	+3,30	12,90	+3,01

Abri Pataud   Tableau 22

Ø VP – DENTS PERMANENTES – MAXILLAIRE
Valeur de σ → COXYDE

COTE GAUCHE

Dents	G 1 M Ø VP	SD	G 2 M Ø VP	SD	G 3 M Ø VP	SD	G 4 M Ø VP	SD	G 5 M Ø VP	SD	G 6 M Ø VP	SD	G 7 M Ø VP	SD	G 8 M Ø VP	SD
Coxyde	7,10	0,45	6,21	0,50	8,33	0,58	8,59	0,59	8,81	0,60	11,22	0,50	10,65	0,71	10,13	0,92
	Ø VP	σ	Ø VP	σ	Ø VP	σ	Ø VP	σ	Ø VP	σ	Ø VP	σ	Ø VP	σ	Ø VP	σ
Cap-Blanc	7,00	-0,22	6,20	-0,02	8,10	-0,39	9,20	+1,03	9,20	+0,65	11,50	+0,56	12,00	+1,90	11,00	+0,94
Combe-Capelle	7,50	+0,88	6,00	-0,42	9,00	+1,15	9,00	+0,69	8,50	-0,51	12,00	+1,56	12,00	+1,90	11,00	+0,94
Le Moustier	8,00	+2,00	9,00	+5,58	10,00	+2,87	10,50	+3,23	11,00	+3,65	12,50	+2,56	13,00	+3,30	13,50	+3,66
La Quina			9,00	+5,58	10,00	+2,87	11,00	+4,08	10,50	+2,81	13,00	+3,56	14,00	+4,72		
Abri Pataud			7,00	+1,58			10,50	+3,23	10,30	+2,48	12,30	+2,16	13,50	+4,01	13,00	+3,11

Abri Pataud

Tableau 23

ØMD – DENTS PERMANENTES – MANDIBULE
Valeur de σ → COXYDE
COTE DROIT

Dents	d 1 ØMD	d 1 SD/σ	d 2 ØMD	d 2 SD/σ	d 3 ØMD	d 3 SD/σ	d 4 ØMD	d 4 SD/σ	d 5 ØMD	d 5 SD/σ	d 6 ØMD	d 6 SD/σ	d 7 ØMD	d 7 SD/σ	d 8 ØMD	d 8 SD/σ
Coxyde	5,07	0,39	5,73	0,41	6,63	0,43	6,42	0,43	6,56	0,51	10,72	0,65	9,96	0,69	9,97	0,89
Farincourt	4,40	-1,71	5,50	-0,56	5,00	-3,79	6,60	+0,41	6,50	-0,12	10,00	-1,10	9,40	-0,81	9,30	-0,75
Abri Lachaud	5,30	+0,58	5,40	-0,80	7,20	+1,32	7,00	+1,34	7,00	+0,86	11,00	+0,43	11,10	+1,65	11,20	+1,38
Cap-Blanc	4,10	-2,48	5,00	-1,78	5,80	-1,93	5,80	-1,44	6,00	-1,09	9,80	-1,42	9,20	-1,10		
Combe-Capelle	5,00	-0,18	5,00	-1,78	7,00	+0,86	6,00	-0,97	7,00	+0,86	12,00	+1,96	12,00	+2,95	10,00	+0,03
Le Moustier	6,00	+2,38	6,60	+2,12	8,60	+4,58	8,00	+3,67	8,20	+3,21	12,50	+2,73	12,50	+3,68	13,00	+3,40
La Quina							7,20	+1,81	8,00	+2,82	12,00	+1,96	12,50	+3,68	11,50	+1,71
Abri Pataud							7,70	+2,97			11,70	+1,50	11,70	+2,52	12,50	+2,84

Abri Pataud

Tableau 24

ØMD – DENTS PERMANENTES – MANDIBULE
Valeur de σ → COXYDE
COTE GAUCHE

Dents	g 1 ØMD	g 1 SD/σ	g 2 ØMD	g 2 SD/σ	g 3 ØMD	g 3 SD/σ	g 4 ØMD	g 4 SD/σ	g 5 ØMD	g 5 SD/σ	g 6 ØMD	g 6 SD/σ	g 7 ØMD	g 7 SD/σ	g 8 ØMD	g 8 SD/σ
Coxyde	5,07	0,39	5,73	0,41	6,63	0,43	6,42	0,43	6,56	0,51	10,72	0,65	9,96	0,69	9,97	0,89
Farincourt	4,40	-1,71	5,20	-1,29	5,10	-3,55	6,50	-0,19	6,50	-0,12	10,30	-0,64	9,80	-0,23	9,30	-0,75
Abri Lachaud	5,70	+1,62	6,00	+0,65	7,40	+1,79	7,40	+2,27	7,50	+1,84	11,10	+0,58	11,20	+1,79	11,80	+2,05
Cap-Blanc	4,00	-2,74	5,00	-1,78	6,00	-1,46	6,00	-0,97	6,20	-0,70	10,20	-0,80	9,10	-1,25		
Combe-Capelle	5,00	-0,18	6,00	+0,65	8,00	+3,18	6,00	-0,97	7,00	+0,86	12,00	+1,96	11,50	+2,23	11,00	+1,15
Le Moustier	6,90	+4,69	6,00	+2,12	8,00	+3,18	8,00	+3,67	8,30	+3,41	12,40	+2,58	12,50	+3,68		
La Quina					8,50	+4,34	8,30	+4,37	8,50	+3,80	12,00	+1,96	12,30	+3,39	11,50	+1,71
Abri Pataud							7,70	+2,97			11,90	+1,82	11,80	+2,66	12,50	+2,84

Tableau 25

Abri Pataud

ØVL – DENTS PERMANENTES – MANDIBULE

Valeur de σ → COXYDE

COTE DROIT

Dents	d1 M ØVL	d1 SD/σ	d2 M ØVL	d2 SD/σ	d3 M ØVL	d3 SD/σ	d4 M ØVL	d4 SD/σ	d5 M ØVL	d5 SD/σ	d6 M ØVL	d6 SD/σ	d7 M ØVL	d7 SD/σ	d8 M ØVL	d8 SD/σ
Coxyde	5,96	0,38	6,26	0,39	7,77	0,52	7,32	0,45	7,86	0,59	10,28	0,49	9,72	0,55	9,46	0,68
Farincourt	5,60	-0,94	6,30	+0,10	7,30	-0,90	7,20	-0,26	7,30	-0,94	9,50	-1,59	8,70	-1,85		
Abri Lachaud	6,30	+0,89	6,40	+0,35	8,20	+0,82	7,80	+1,06	8,00	+0,23	10,30	+0,04	9,60	-0,21	9,60	+0,20
Cap-Blanc	5,10	-2,26	6,10	-0,41	7,30	-0,90	7,60	+0,62	8,50	+1,08	10,30	+0,04	10,10	+0,69		
Combe-Capelle	6,00	+0,11	6,00	-0,66	9,00	+2,36	9,00	+3,73	9,50	+2,77	12,00	+3,51	11,50	+3,23	10,00	+0,79
Le Moustier	7,20	+3,26	7,80	+3,94	9,50	+3,32	10,00	+5,95	10,50	+4,47	11,80	+3,10	11,60	+3,41	11,00	+2,26
La Quina							10,00	+5,95	10,00	+3,62	11,50	+2,48	12,00	+4,14	13,00	+5,20
Abri Pataud							8,70	+3,06			11,90	+3,30	12,20	+4,50	12,90	+5,05

Tableau 26

Abri Pataud

ØVL – DENTS PERMANENTES – MANDIBULE

Valeur de σ → COXYDE

COTE GAUCHE

Dents	g1 M ØVL	g1 SD/σ	g2 M ØVL	g2 SD/σ	g3 M ØVL	g3 SD/σ	g4 M ØVL	g4 SD/σ	g5 M ØVL	g5 SD/σ	g6 M ØVL	g6 SD/σ	g7 M ØVL	g7 SD/σ	g8 M ØVL	g8 SD/σ
Coxyde	5,96	0,38	6,26	0,39	7,77	0,52	7,32	0,45	7,86	0,59	10,28	0,49	9,72	0,55	9,46	0,68
Farincourt	5,70	-0,68	6,40	+0,35	7,40	-0,71	7,00	-0,71	7,00	-1,48	9,30	-2,00	8,70	-1,85	9,10	-0,52
Abri Lachaud	6,20	+0,63	7,00	+1,89	8,30	+1,02	7,90	+1,28	8,10	+0,41	10,40	+0,24	9,70	-0,04	9,40	-0,09
Cap-Blanc	5,20	-2,00	6,00	-0,66	7,20	-1,09	7,60	+0,62	8,10	+0,41	10,20	-0,16	10,10	+0,69		
Combe-Capelle	6,00	+0,11	6,50	+0,61	8,00	+0,44	7,00	-0,71	8,00	+0,24	11,00	+1,46	11,00	+2,32	11,00	+2,26
Le Moustier	7,50	+4,05	7,50	+3,17			9,60	+5,06	10,20	+4,03	11,50	+2,48	11,60	+3,41	11,60	+3,41
La Quina					9,00	+2,36	10,00	+5,95	10,00	++3,69	11,50	+2,48	12,00	+4,14	13,00	+5,20
Abri Pataud							8,70	+3,06			11,90	+3,30	12,30	+4,50	12,80	+4,91

Abri Pataud **DENTS PERMANENTES** Tableau 27

DES

3EME ET 9EME SUJETS

Valeur de σ → COXYDE

	D 6		D 2		d 6	
	M Ø MD	SD	M Ø MD	SD	M Ø MD	SD
Coxyde	10,00	0,57	6,43	0,57	10,72	0,65
Abri Pataud	Ø MD	σ	Ø MD	σ	Ø MD	σ
3ème Sujet	10,90	+1,57	6,60	+0,29		
9ème Sujet					11,00	+0,43
Coxyde	M Ø VP	SD	M Ø VP	SD	M Ø VL	SD
	11,22	0,50	6,21	0,50	10,28	0,49
Abri Pataud	Ø VP	σ	Ø VP	σ	Ø VL	σ
3ème Sujet	12,50	+2,56	6,70	+0,98		
9ème Sujet					11,70	+2,89

BIBLIOGRAPHIE

Bolender, Ch.
1964. «Les anomalies de nombre et d'éruption de la denture temporaire,» *L'Orthodontie Française*, vol. 35, t. 1, pp. 373-397.

Brabant, H.
1963. «Observations sur la denture humaine en France et en Belgique à l'époque Gallo-Romaine et au Moyen-Age,» *Bulletin du G.I.R.S.*, vol. 6, pp. 169-296.

Koski, K., and S.M. Garn
1957. «Tooth Eruption Sequence in Fossil and Modern Man,» *Amer. J. Phys. Anth.*, vol. 15, pp. 313-331 and 469-488.

Legoux, P.
1966. *Détermination de l'âge dentaire de fossiles de la lignée humaine.* Maloine S.A., Paris.

1971. *Etude odontologique des restes humains de l'Abri Pataud.* Thèse doctorat en sciences odontologiques. Paris.

1972. «Etude odontologique des restes humains périgordiens et proto-magdaléniens de l'Abri Pataud (Dordogne),» résumé, 1ère partie, *Bull. et Mém. Sté. Anthrop. de Paris*, t. 9, pp. 293-330.

1974. Idem, résumé, 2ème partie, *Bull. et Mém. Sté. Anthrop. de Paris*, t. 1, pp. 45-84.

Twiesselmann, F., et H. Brabant
1967. *Les dents et les maxillaires de la population d'âge Franc de Coxyde* (Belgique). G.I.R.S., Bruxelles.

Vallois, H.V.
1937. «Les hommes fossiles et les races anciennes,» *C.R. Acad. Sci. Paris*, t. 204, pp. 60-62.